The New Wealth of Cities
City Dynamics and the Fifth Wave

JOHN MONTGOMERY

ASHGATE

Published by
Ashgate Publishing Limited
Gower House
Croft Road
Aldershot
Hampshire GU11 3HR
England

Ashgate Publishing Company
Suite 420
101 Cherry Street
Burlington, VT 05401-4405
USA

Ashgate website: http://www.ashgate.com

British Library Cataloguing in Publication Data
Montgomery, John
    The new wealth of cities : city dynamics and the fifth wave
    1. City planning 2. Urban economics
    I. Title
    307.1'216

Library of Congress Control Number: 2006931600

ISBN: 978-0-7546-4789-8 (hardback)
ISBN: 978-0-7546-7415-3 (paperback)

Printed and bound in Great Britain by TJ International Ltd, Padstow, Cornwall.

THE NEW WEALTH OF CITIES

WITHDRAWN

Books are to be returned on or before
the last date below.

7 – DAY
LOAN

LIBREX–

Contents

List of Figures

List of Tables

Acknowledgements

Books of this nature cannot be written without the help of other books, or of other people. There is no research grant or academic department to thank for more material forms of support, but there is a list of good friends and others who have helped over the years.

At various times in my career I have been much influenced by the people I have worked with. Early influences included Bob Ross, Megan Munro, Phil McGhee, Cliff Hague and Patsy Healey. During my time at the Greater London Council in the early 1980s, I found myself a colleague of such leading thinkers as Robin Murray, Maureen Mackintosh, George Nicholson, Bob Colenutt, Drew Stevenson, Peter Newman, Iain Tuckett, Andy Thornley and my friend Michael Synnott. It was there that I was first introduced to economic sector studies in the form of the Greater London Industrial Strategy. Geoff Mulgan and Ken Worpole would introduce me to the cultural industries in around 1985. I went on to work with Robin Murray, Sarah Bissett-Johnson, Michael Ward and others on the South East England Economic Development Strategy. Nicky Brigginshaw was also a great influence at this time.

In 1986 I became friendly with Ken Worpole and first met Charles Landry with whom I worked closely from 1988 to 1991. Ken also introduced me to the phenomenal Franco Bianchini, and we collaborated on *City Centres, City Cultures* (1987) together. Other colleagues at Comedia I recall with admiration and affection are Liz Greenhalgh and Simon Blanchard.

I set up Urban Cultures Ltd in 1991, as a breakaway from Comedia (these things happen) with Tony Colman. Important collaborations during the early 1990s included working with Peter Luxton, Jean Horstman, John Lyall, Bruce McLean, Madeline Simms, Paul Owens, Janet Mein, Clive Bell, John Punter, Jo Burns, Phil Griffin, Andy Lovatt and Justin O'Connor. This was the time of our Temple Bar project, the Manchester Cultural Strategy, the *24 Hour City* conferences and designs for new public squares in London and Yorkshire; and also my membership of the London Arts and Urban Regeneration Group with Nicky Gavron, Julia Isherwood and Tony Cumberbirch amongst others.

By this time I was working in urban design. I was asked by a client, Tony Kemp of Blue Circle Properties, to design "a piece of city" at Ebbsfleet in Kent. We had been introduced by my old university friend Chris Hall. Fortunately for me, others working on this very large project included David Lock and the very special Will Cousins, and also the economist Bridget Rosewell and Jason Prior. Around about this time I met Jan Gehl for the first time. Much of the 1990s was spent working on area regeneration, cultural and creative industry quarters (Sheffield, Manchester,

Glasgow, Belfast and Dundee) and on master-planning. Colleagues and friends dating from this time include Paul Skelton, Matthew Conduit, Owen O'Carroll, Pauline de Silva, Mark Pennington, Kevin Murray, Mick Timpson, Janet Brenton and Doug Wheeler. There was a short stint at Reading University. I did manage to publish some refereed articles, and I have retained great respect for the late Michael Breheny, Doug Hart, Alan Rowley, Joe Doak and Prof Lyn Davies, as well as John Delafons

By the late 1990s I was working mostly on ways to manage and regulate the evening economy of cities, and embarked on a number of important collaborations with John Whyte and Chris Rawlinson, Alan Tallentire and Nick Williams. My article on café culture grew out of somewhat relaxed discussion with Paul Opacic, Bernie Kilmartin, Brian Pierce and Peter Colman in *Le Cochonnet* in Maida Vale. Other living examples of café society from 1990s London were Leo McGlaughlin, Maggie Opacic and Val Kitchen.

In 1998 I was invited to Australia by Peter Dungey and Barbara Meldrum to give the key-note address to the Urban Design Forum conference on night-time cities. Visiting Australia had a profound affect on me, and I was very pleased to be invited back to work on Adelaide's lighting plan with Wendy Bell and Phil Keane. I was invited to speak at the *City as a Stage* conference in Adelaide in 2000, with the likes of Jan Gehl, Charles Landry, Bea Campbell and Peter Sellers (then the Adelaide Festival director). That same year, I also spoke at the *City Edge 2* conference in Melbourne, forming a friendship with Rob Adams and his wife Rosie in the process. Jane Andrews, Susan Law, Steve Hamnett and Greg Mackie were also helpful and kind. Our good friends in Adelaide who encouraged me to write this book are Gray Hawk, Susanne Carmody, Alison Dunn, David Reid, Sally Turner and Alan Merchant, Phillip White, and Joe and Jessica Dames. Without their pushing me – and the vital help of Hamish Barrett, thanks to Sally's prompting – this book would never have been written.

Most of the hard graft on this book was undertaken during the Australian summers of 2004, 2005 and 2006, that is from the day after Boxing Day through to the end of February. During the rest of the year I work to earn fees, but as ever this has resulted in new inspiration and new friendships. In the past two years, since moving to northern New South Wales, I have had the good fortune to work with Ken Maher, Sara Lee, David Borger, Anita Brown, Malcolm Snow, Cathy Hunt, Sarah Starke, Ian James, Virginia Ross, Tanya Neville, Jon Lindsay, Barbara Heaton, Ed Duc, Deborah Mills, Graeme Burns, Tiffany Lee-Shoy, Pauline Peel, Scott O'Hara, Paul Graham, Sue Clarke, Jim Holdsworth and Gabrielle Castellan.

From a young age, I have been fascinated by the writings of Jane Jacobs, both on cities and economic development. Her work and that of Michael Porter, Robin Murray, Robert Beckman and Peter Totterdill has underpinned much of the economic theory referred to in this book. As well as Ken Worpole and Franco Bianchini, I have drawn heavily on the work of Raymond Williams and Matthew Arnold in my understanding of culture. Peter Hall's book *Cities in Civilisation* is simply one of the best books of its type ever written, and I have found it a reservoir of knowledge and ideas. One thing that surprised me was how much I enjoyed delving into urban, artistic and economic history. Reading the essays and reviews of Peter Ackroyd, for example, has been a delight. I learned a great deal by doing so, but would be the first to agree that there is a lot more to learn. I am very glad there are people like Camille Paglia and John Carroll arguing for a return to learning and artistic appreciation. The great writers in urban design have also shaped much of my own writing on built form, particularly Kevin Lynch, Gordon Cullen, Christopher Alexander and more recently Taner Oc, Matthew Carmona and colleagues. Richard Sennet's work has always fascinated, although I rarely share his conclusions.

Not having published a book of such complexity before, I have been surprised at the amount of work that goes into not only the writing but the editing, laying out, proofing and the various stages of publication itself. It has been made much easier and certainly more pleasant working with Valerie Rose and her colleagues at Ashgate, especially Jacqui Cornish and the splendid Neil Jordan. I have also been helped a great deal in the layout of the text and in the drawing of diagrams by Hamish Barrett, Rachael Playford and Alana Wilson.

At the writing end of the spectrum, I have been helped enormously by my wife Julia. She has read every draft of this book, helped select the illustrations and indeed some of the photos are hers. More than this, she talked me into writing the book in the first place and has always been able to provide good advice. She also has the kindest heart of anyone I know. Young Phoebe has helped in less tangible ways, simply by being here. Amongst my immediate family, I should also like to thank my parents John and Marion, and my grandmother, Jean Montgomery who always urged me to "stick in at the school". This I have always tried to do.

JRM
Heron Waters

Note

Every effort has been made to trace all the copyright holders but if any have been inadvertently overlooked, the author and publishers will be pleased to make the necessary arrangement at the first opportunity.

For Julia and Phoebe

Preface

AN EXPLANATION

This book argues that a new long period of wealth creation is just beginning. Throughout western history, there has been an interplay between dynamic economic growth and wealth creation – under a free market or capitalist economic system – and cultural life, applied creativity and innovation, city building, place-making the public realm, and the regulation of public morality. The crucial link is between technology, new work and the emergence of certain cities as economic and cultural leaders at particular points in time. This includes the coming new wave of wealth creation – the fifth wave – built on new technology and new industries that is just getting underway. This, in turn, has far-reaching implications for the development and organization of city economies, but also for the built form and spatial planning of cities and city regions in the western democracies and in other societies where market economies are coming into being.

There is a tide in the growth and decline of cities. For the past 500 years, cities have developed in periodic spurts of wealth creation, artistic development and physically. Cities that have come to prominence during these growth periods include Edinburgh, Manchester and Birmingham in the late 18th century, Glasgow, London and Paris in the early 19th century, Detroit, Pittsburgh, Birmingham and Stuttgart in the late 19th century, New York, LA and San Francisco in the mid 20th century, and most recently Seattle, Austin and Bangalore. The rise of these cities historically is closely linked to the very intellectual and technological developments which gave rise to the great industries of each age: cotton in Manchester, steel and railways and ships in Glasgow and Pittsburgh, automobiles in Detroit and Birmingham, aviation and household consumer goods in Los Angeles, Seattle and Tokyo, computers in southern California, and, since the mid 1970s, computer software, digital compression, mobile communications and bio-technology. In fact, a similar dynamic – between the economic development of specific industries and the rise to prominence of certain cities – can be traced back to the Florence of the 14th century (wool and clothing), and Amsterdam and London in the 17th century (commodities such as spices, tea, coffee). The "golden age" of most cities is associated with a particular episode of growth and wealth creation. This dynamic process has occurred four times since the late 18th century. It is as old as capitalism itself.

Long periods of economic growth are followed by periods of stagnation and low growth, as night follows day. This occurs because the goods and services associated with particular phases of growth become exhausted, in the sense that there are no longer profitable markets to be sold into. The outcome is that particular goods and services – cotton in the 18th century, steel and transport in the 19th, automobiles and electric goods in the early 20th, consumer electronics in the late 20th – reach the limits to market penetration. Because of this the level of sales fall, prices are cut, the rate of profit falls, share prices fall, businesses fail, jobs are lost and a cycle of decline sets in as aggregate levels of demand fall again.

The only way out of such down-turns or slumps is for a set of new products to be brought to the market, that is a range of goods and services for which no market previously existed. For this to happen, such goods and services need to be invented. This almost always involves the application of new technologies to either invent whole new products, or else to production processes to increase productivity or improve design. For, as advances in technologies are applied commercially, sales will increase, profit levels will rise, economic growth will follow and so too will wealth creation. The next wave of growth is then underway.

In this way, the capitalist or market economy follows a pattern of growth and contraction, similar to business cycles but over a much longer period. For each of these long waves of wealth creation, the crucial development – sometimes more so than the original invention – is its application by one or more creative entrepreneurs. Examples of these include Arkwright, Andrew Carnegie, Henry Ford, Boeing, and Sony, and their respective competitors. Markets for new products develop and produce a period of economic growth, an upwave, during which time the rate of profit rises with volumes of trade and the general level of wealth increases. The result is a profit cycle over a long period of some 55 years which operates alongside shorter cycles which variously extend over periods of 3, 9 and 25 years.

During these waves of economic development, cities themselves grow, that is to say they experience rapid population growth. This is usually accompanied by rising densities, surges in land values, pressures to expand into the surrounding countryside and a pattern of property booms. Very often, the pressures brought to bear result in calls for planned expansions of the city. This occurred in London and Paris in the 18th and 19th centuries, in Edinburgh in the 1770s, in the expansions of Barcelona, Amsterdam and Copenhagen, and in the planning of new American and Australian cities. It was also a feature of new town planning in the UK from the 1920s. Not all property booms are associated with primary wealth creation, and during the cycle other booms – associated with speculation and panic – will materialize. During all of this, those responsible for planning and managing the development of cities try to maintain a balance between the city as an engine of wealth creation and a domestic living environment. This tension runs throughout the history of city making. This is because it is in cities and city-regions that economic development occurs, that wealth is created, that new ideas and technologies are invented, tried and tested. Cities are also the places from which civilizations have grown, and where the arts, culture and creativity flourish. Reconciling these sometimes competing forces is a role that urban planners and designers have grappled with for centuries. This is a role that is no less important today – and into the future – if individual cities are to

TOP OF THE BOOM

Going Up

Rising interest rates	Falling demand
Rising real estate prices	Falling rates of profit
Rising share prices	Falling share prices
Increasing demand	Falling interest rates
New products and services	Rising real estate prices
New inventions	

Coming Down

DEPTH OF DEPRESSION

Figure 0.1   The Profit Cycle
Source: John Montgomery.

prosper and also become good places to live. For the fifth wave is just beginning, and with it will come a new great age of city building.

The preceding wave, the fourth wave, lasted roughly from 1948 to 2002, and was led by new technologies and the application of these to new goods and services. These were defence and then consumer electronics, aero-space, the modern medium of television and popular recorded music. The upswing gained momentum in the 1950s, through the 1960s and peaked in around 1974. During this time, moral restrictions were loosened as people with money to spend refused to be bound by the social conventions of a previous generation. However, low growth rates from the late 1960s, coupled with the failings of Keynesian economics, produced the phenomenon of "stagflation", followed by the stock market collapse of 1987 and a slump from then until the late 1990s. During this time, whole industries were lost from certain cities, established industries were forced to restructure, new marketing strategies were adopted and the time was ripe for new industries, based on new technologies, to appear. These would be a combination of pharmaceuticals (advances in science applied to human health), bio-technology and engineering (DNA, genetic modification), software, mobile communications and digital technologies. These are the industries of the fifth wave, and some of them at least are linked to new forms of artistic expression and entertainment, notably in the convergence of the computer industry, digital media and the internet.

But something else is also happening, a development from the new consumer-led economy of post-Fordism. More and more people – it seems – are buying one-off or original pieces of art or designed objects. This is a reaction to the "end of scarcity" – the fact that most people in the western democracies now have fridges, televisions, washing machines, hair-dryers, stereos and now home movie systems and personal computers and mobile telephones. Other than buying more of the same, and new models, the only way to express your identity through possessions is by having original works and limited editions, or luxury goods. Thus, as well as the leading industries referred to above, the fifth wave will see increased demand for art, design and bespoke objects. This in turn means that the more successful city economies will be those that have a good representation of the new economy and the creative arts.

Indeed, a similar long-wave pattern can be observed in the emergence of new art forms and movements, and these too are a reflection of "product life cycles" but also the search for the new and the struggle between the generations. For example, Impressionism was partly a reaction to the conservatism of the Academy, Cubism developed out of Impressionism, Abstract Expressionism was a response to Cubism and Expressionism, and Action Painting grew out of a quest to develop an art form beyond Cubism. Much the same process can be seen in the various movements in music (the Baroque, Classical, Romantic, Impressionist, a-tonal) and literature (the traditional novel, Romantic poetry, social realism, the modern novel, modern poetry). These artistic movements represent a paradigm shift, and are usually "sparked" by a beneficial combination of circumstances and events, including most especially artistic genius. These sparks almost always occur in cities, that it to say in the "creative milieux" of the time. The point is that paradigm shifts occur in the arts, and these relate to the long waves of capitalist economic development.

The relationship between artistic and scientific or technological innovation is therefore complex, and involves far more than a simple linear process where wealth creation produces new demands for art. In some cases, the new art form influences the production of goods and services, notably in the case of design and the Bauhaus. In others, changes in technologies produce whole new art forms, as in the film industry or sound recording. And, of course, as in Florence, rising levels of wealth do fuel demand for art. Yet this is not a one-to-one relationship. Indeed, very often innovations in technology and art occur simultaneously and often in the same cities. This was true of London in the early 19th century, Paris in the late 19th century, Los Angeles in the early part of the 20th century, Berlin in the 1920s, New York in the 1940s and 1950s, London in the 1960s.

Before proceeding further with this line of argument, it is important to explain what the fifth wave is not, or at least should not be confused with. The first of these is the "global economy" which, as a concept, describes the opening up of more markets to capitalist economic development. This really is no different to what has gone before, except in terms of scale and the speed with which goods and services can be transported. This has involved, in the past 15 years, for example, the signing of Free Trade Agreements between the USA and Mexico, between Australia and the USA and, shortly, between China and both the USA and Australia. Both China and India have opened up to capitalist economic development, and this is led by the cities. Russia is still struggling to come to terms with capitalism following the botched privatization of key industries; the South American countries are recovering from super-inflation. Only the corrupt regimes of Africa and fundamentalist Islamic countries are failing to engage in legitimate trade. Of course, the largest trade of all is in money – that is currencies on the foreign exchange. Telecommunication means that capital can be bought and sold in the blink of an eye, and moved from country to country. This can lead to a run on currencies where investors believe there is an over-valuation relative to the real value of a country's economic stock. This occurred in the "contagion" of the Far East economies in the late 1990s, and also in Mexico a few years earlier. The adoption of the Euro was in large part an attempt to limit currency trading, but is in danger of simply creating a cartel and a trading bloc frustrated by low growth. The fifth wave will certainly be greatly influenced by the "global economy", but its real importance lies in the development of new technologies, industries and forms of production in addition to expanded trade links.

Similarly, the fifth wave is not the end of industrialization, the so-called "post industrial society",[1] for the simple reason that goods will continue to be produced and consumed: food, clothing, shoes, cars, fridges, TVs, computers, stereos, prescribed drugs, jewellery, musical instruments, stationery, ... and the rest. What is true is that under "post-Fordism" the distribution of such goods tended to be organized by service industries (retailers especially), but without goods being produced there would be little to service. We cannot all live off pensions and insurance policies. So, under the fifth wave, goods will continue to be produced and services provided. All that will change is the geography of production with more industrialized goods being manufactured in lower-wage economies, while services will become more complex and sophisticated. New industries are already developing and the higher-value products will continue to be fragmented according to fashion, image and design-consciousness. In all of this, critics, advertisers and other arbiters of taste will play an increasingly important role.

Writing in 1992, the American political theorist Francis Fukuyama proclaimed the "End of History".[2] By this he meant the end of the Cold War, the collapse of Communism and the final triumph of capitalism and western democracy. This argument is flawed to the extent that Fukuyama overlooked the growing emergence of Islam as a world ideology. There will continue to be debates about the allocation of resources within capitalist economies and democratic societies. That said, there is little doubt that capitalism will continue to develop. And so, just as the Fifth Wave is not simply the "global economy" or the end of industrialization, it also does not represent the end of history or ideology. It is simply another phase of capitalist economic development: an emerging, new mode of capitalist production which will co-exist along-side earlier forms of industrialization, mass production and flexible specialization.

---

1   Bell, D., *The Coming of the Post-Industrial Society* (New York: 1973).
2   Fukuyama, F., *End of History and the Last Man* (New York: Free Press, 1992).

It is also the case that new forms of city planning and urban economic development have emerged during the past twenty years: since the mid 1980s in Britain, from the late 1970s in a handful of American cities, and in Western Europe largely since the early 1990s. These combine a return to the more traditional, that is to say pre-modernist, concerns of city building, with a paradigm shift in the practice of urban planning in the form of urban design. This reflects a much keener understanding of the importance of the layout, proportions and scale of urban places, but also of primary and secondary mixed use and relative density. At the same time, there has been a marked rise in our understanding of cultural development and its role in the design, economy and life of cities. This ranges from early attempts to use the arts as one means of urban regeneration, through notions of the public realm, public art and active streets, to the development of the industries of culture. In philosophical terms, we can see that this amounts to a rejection of modernism and its replacement with a more rounded view of cities and city-regions as places, built environments, cultural repositories and loci for dynamic forms of the new economy. This is what I mean by the term "city dynamics", which is referred to throughout this book: a set of interlocking processes of economic and cultural development, the evolution and design of the built form, city governance and the impact of technology on all of these. This raises the interesting question as to what such cities will be like, certainly in their economic and spatial organization, and as places to live, culturally and as built forms. In previous long-waves, particular types of city building and artistic movements have emerged alongside changes in the system of economic development. These include the mercantile city, the industrial city, the modernist city of mass production, and the de-centred and suburbanized city. These, in turn, have been associated with particular architectural styles and approaches to urban planning: the neo-classical city of the Enlightenment, the industrial Victorian city, modernism, garden cities and suburbia.

Another simple truth about cities is that they simultaneously trade and compete with each other. Manchester and Liverpool, Edinburgh and Glasgow, Barcelona and Madrid, Milan and Turin, Sydney and Melbourne, Rotterdam and Amsterdam, Chicago and New York. It is no accident that the keenest sporting rivalries are between competing cities within nations. With the growth of international trade, cities across continents and beyond now compete and trade with one another. Cities, then, must compete to survive, and they must also trade. If they do not, their economies will die and they will become dormitory towns, increasingly bland and uninteresting. This might not necessarily affect all people – retirees or middle-ranking public servants spring to mind – but in time the young and dynamic will move away. For urban history reveals that some cities have enjoyed at times explosive episodes of wealth creation and economic development, whilst others have not. Some were once places of great dynamism, and now they are not. In some cities, not only have whole industries been lost, but also the skills, crafts and entrepreneurship that went with them. Why does this happen, and can city planners do anything about it? Why are Manchester and Melbourne recovering from economic decline, while Liverpool and Adelaide are not? What lessons can be learned from the revival of certain old cities – Dublin, Barcelona, Copenhagen – over the past 20 years; and why is it that certain new cities grow faster than others? Is this explained by new technologies, new industries, new architecture, new urbanism, new creative and cultural forms – or, more than likely, some potently beneficial combination of these. Are cities and city planners passive observers in all of this, or can they make their own history? If someone made you the Mayor of some declining city or a new growth centre tomorrow, what would you do?

Only by understanding what cities are, how they work, what makes them grow, what makes them die, what makes them good or bad places in which to live – only by a deep felt understanding of these can we succeed in making cities better in the coming decades. It should be possible to manage and design old and new cities so that they are economically vital, culturally dynamic and also good urban places. While recognizing that cities are "organic structures" of great complexity, I believe that we now know how best to manage, design, develop and promote cities and city-regions. In some ways, this involves learning from the past, especially in the importance of commerce, culture and human-scale built forms. Yet we also have to understand new technologies, new products and initiatives, changing demographics, tastes and preferences, and contemporary concerns over environmental sustainability. For the first time in 100 years, we are sophisticated enough in our comprehension of cities to make them better. This is partly a return to pre-modernist concerns such as scale, city blocks, legibility and permeability – partly a reaction against the English empiricist town planning idiom, and partly a much clearer understanding of how commerce and trade underpin city life, and how wealth creators interact with culture.

So what will the city of the next 50 years be like? Will it be decentralized or more compact? High or low density? Low-rise or high-rise? Will it extend ever outwards into its surrounding region? Will it be a good place to live, have a successful career, bring up children, enjoy the arts and other trappings of civilization, be entertained? How will these cities be remembered in future? Will there be another golden age of city building, and if so where? These are the questions this book is seeking to answer. If you are a planner, an architect, an urban sociologist, an urban historian, urban designer or urban economist, then you will need to read this book. If you are simply one of the 85 per cent of the developed world who live in urban settlements – and who would like to see urban living made better – then this book should also interest you. If you are running a small business, are an actor or musician or artist – and you wonder why some cities are simply more creative and interesting than others – then this book is for you. For this is a book about the economy, culture and design of cities.

Very few books emerge word-perfect, fully-formed as a single piece. This is no exception. My observations and ideas have evolved over time as a student of cities, an occasional academic, but mostly as a consulting practitioner. I have learned a great deal from the places I have worked in; and also from my readings of the urban literature. In the early 1980s, I was trying to relate economic development (in the shape of the London Industrial Strategy) with strategic urban planning (the Greater London Development Plan). Later I was doing much the same at a broader spatial level for the South East of England, for example by studying the economic and social impacts of sectors such as tourism, defence electronics, furniture, financial services, pharmaceuticals and retailing. Many of these economic and social impacts were, of course, felt most keenly in cities and towns. I began to realize that orthodox views of industrial location were missing out on something important: that certain industries needed to be based in places where the quality of life is better, that is to say bigger houses, gardens, good schools, golf courses and the arts. Far from being "white noise" getting in the way of rational economic decision-making, these issues of everyday life were of central importance. For the first time, I realised that rather than opposing forces, the economic well-being of a city should run in tandem with the quality of life, each supporting the other. This led to a further realization – gleaned from U.S. examples such as Pittsburgh and Lexington – that the arts and culture generally can (should) be part and parcel of city and economic development. No culture, no city; and not much of an economy either. My conclusion at this time was that cities had to be understood in the round – as places of wealth and job creation, as sites for old and new culture, and as places offering stimulus and delight. And they also had to be designed.

The 1980s and 1990s were a period (dating from the 1970s in truth) of great economic change, restructuring and downsizing. The impact on most UK cities (Belfast, Glasgow, Newcastle, Birmingham, London, Liverpool, Sheffield, Manchester) was immense, and in many cases cataclysmic. Places which had "never had it so good" only 20 years earlier were now in a spiral of decline. This was true also of many of the great northern cities of the USA and, to varying degrees, to many European cities. We needed to regenerate and revitalize our cities and their economies, fast. It was perhaps appropriate that Britain should find itself having to cope with these issues and problems before most other countries. Here was the home of the industrial revolution and the first industrial cities, facing regional decline in core industries such as steel production, ship-building, heavy engineering, electrical engineering, motor vehicles and machine tools. In some cases, Britain was out-competed (cars, ships). In other sectors, new technologies rendered certain processes and even whole industries redundant (steel, print); and in others (docks, rail) labour disputes led effectively to closure and job loss. How was Liverpool to cope with the closure of the docks? How was Glasgow to earn its living without ship-building? What on earth could be done with London Docklands? These very issues were addressed by insightful approaches to local economic development, such as the *London Industrial Strategy* on which I worked in the early 1980s.

It is fair to say that the 1980s and the early 1990s were somewhat experimental in the new field of urban regeneration in Britain. Some very good examples of urban regeneration date from that time, but also many disasters where rather than solutions, more problems were grafted on to the old. But by the mid-1990s, we had learned that good "local" or city economies needed to be as diverse as possible, needed to export goods and services, needed networks of inter-trading businesses, needed to target their markets, needed to invest in technology, needed high rates of business formation, breakaways and business growth. We also knew from writers such as

Charles Handy that much future economic activity would be in the "knowledge industries", combining "information, intelligence and innovation". Amongst these knowledge industries were the cultural or creative industries – the arts, design, the music industry, film, television, publishing, computer games, contemporary craft – activities which to varying degrees combined ideas with material production; new images, texts and sounds with developing technologies. Rather than a subsidized "public good", the arts and culture were suddenly (or so it seemed) about wealth creation too.

So now in addition to being a key influence on industrial location (as a quality of life "good") the creative industries were all about economic development at the sharp end. But would they really create jobs in the cities of Manchester or Sheffield or Dublin as opposed to London, New York and Los Angeles? The answer, it turns out, is yes, although some cities are centres of production on a national and global scale; most of the others are not, but they can still generate work. So what are the conditions for growing a successful cultural or creative industries "cluster"? Again in the UK, in the late 1980s and early 1990s, we learned that the cultural industries prefer to be located in places with an urban edge: that is, a mix of old and new buildings, an active streetscape, mixed use, contemporary design, cafés and bars, nightclubs and what we came to refer to as "the evening economy". The trouble was, urban planning regulation and property investment attitudes made mixed use very difficult to achieve; whilst liquor licensing legislation in the UK effectively ruled out café culture. As a consequence, I spent much of the 1990s arguing for liberation of liquor licensing, the development of the evening economy, new mixed use in city centres, and improvements to city safety and amenity at night. This raised as many questions as it answered, notably the emerging conflict between new city apartment-dwellers and those looking for entertainment, live music, alcohol and general naughtiness. A potential solution to the problem of dull and lifeless cities at night would in turn become another set of problems.

Let us now imagine that as a new city manager: you know what economic sectors you want to grow and attract, you know you will need to increase business start-up and growth rates, you know the creative industries are important, so too the formal arts and the wider cultural *milieu,* and you know that mixed use is a good thing, an active evening economy brings added economic benefit, and the image of a city on the move is important to project – what then? Specifically, how do you create all of this activity in a physical form, that is within the built environment of the city- the buildings, streets, and spaces? Having mastered the dynamics of economic development, the knowledge economy, new technologies, cultural life, creativity and innovation, the task is then to design a city form which offers – in the words of the urban designer Kevin Lynch – the best "fit". In other words, do certain urban forms stimulate economic and cultural dynamism? And, by corollary, do certain building and development types stifle innovation? The answer to both questions, is again yes, and this means that it should be possible to design new environments, and refit older ones where necessary to achieve levels of business activity and cultural sophistication, as appropriate to the type of place in question.

From about 1993 my work in the UK and mainland Europe (Barcelona, Dublin, Prague, Copenhagen) turned towards urban design as a means of achieving a good "fit" for dynamic cities. Paradoxically, it is the built forms of the twentieth century – office blocks, modernist housing estates and projects, garden cities, most new towns, suburbs laid out on Radburn principles – that fail to provide a "good fit" for city economies in the twenty-first century. Oddly enough, we are returning to pre-modernist, "pre-industrial" built forms such as the apartment, the townhouse and the flatted factory, set around legible networks of more or less active streets and public spaces. We have also to deal with the car, of course, but that is mainly a management issue. The point is, by looking back to past models of city design, we now know how best to design cities in the future. This is no trifling point, as much of the world continues to urbanize at a rapid rate. It would be a great pity if the Chinese and the South Americans were to commit the very same modernist mistakes as did the U.S, UK and France in the 1930s–1970s, but on current trends that is precisely what is happening. It would also be a terrible shame if cities such as Dublin and Copenhagen and Barcelona were to become economic backwaters (again), or if the only thing Florence or Vienna have to offer is tourism. Are most U.S. cities destined to become lifeless dormitory towns? Can there be another Seattle? Will Edinburgh ever have another Enlightenment?

The answers to these questions cannot be known in advance, although some good guesses can be made. But who would have predicted the rise of Tokyo, or Seattle, Dublin as Europe's most fashionable city, or the death of Liverpool? Or even Bilbao as a cultural attraction? Decisions and choices we make today will alter the future. And like businesses, cities need to grow economically (if not always in size or population) to survive and prosper. My own view is that in dynamic cities technological innovation and artistic creativity occur simultaneously, each influencing the other more often indirectly than directly. This means that the question as to what comes first – wealth or art – is largely meaningless. The lesson of time is that cities which generate wealth are also creative artistically; cities of cultural innovation also grow economically. This is not to argue that the arts are an alternative to commerce, for that can never be the case. But cities that fail to innovate, to create, to reinvent cultural forms – such cities will stagnate. Without artistic creation and technological innovation, economic development will remain periodic and in some cases stuttering. Cities that fail to understand this crucial point will largely fail in the new economy of the coming fifth wave.

A NOTE ON STRUCTURE

This book is organized as follows. A general model of city development – *city dynamics* – is presented in the introductory chapter – *Theory*. This in part revolves around the interface of key themes: commerce and technology, culture and artistic creativity, time and public morality, place and the built form, and the notion of cultural quarters as dynamic creative milieu in the new economy. This is intended as a working theory of how cities work on a day-to-day basis, and over longer waves of growth and stagnation.

The main sections of the book are presented in five Parts, rather than more conventional chapters. Each Part is designed to be read on its own as well as being important to the overall argument of the book. In each of the main Parts, I set out a basic argument or proposition, and follow this up with small case studies of cities in history and currently. I then reflect on what this means for the coming period of city growth. It is likely that some readers will find more of interest in certain sections than others, so each Part can be read in full or in the sections that the reader finds most relevant. For example, Part I on *the economy* looks at the way cities generate wealth, before going on to consider the new economy, the knowledge economy and the creative industries. It does so with reference to the rise of London's creative industries since the 1980s. Readers who find tables of figures and a descriptive account of research findings somewhat dull can skip over the section on the rise of London's creative industries. Part II on *culture* deals with the role of the arts in urban regeneration but goes on to look at the arts and learning in cities that have enjoyed golden ages (London, Paris, New York, Edinburgh, Florence) culturally as well as economically. This Part also considers key artistic movements in relation to the long waves of capitalist economic development. In doing so, it acknowledges individual creative geniuses who sparked paradigm shifts in the arts, some of them also leading to new technologies, products and wealth creation. I make no apology for this: it has always seemed odd to me that the urban literature is replete with more detailed accounts of inventors, architects, economists and planners such as Ebenezer Howard or Patrick Abercrombie, but rarely gives much information on the lives of great artists. There would have been no Renaissance without Brunelleschi, no Enlightenment without Voltaire and Hume, no modernism without Cezanne, Klee, Kandinsky and the Bauhaus.

Part IV on *place* looks at the history of city building with examples of Nash's London, Edinburgh New Town, Barcelona's Eixample, Copenhagen, Amsterdam and Melbourne. It also provides a critique of modernism and placelessness, and concludes with a treatise on how to build new cities and city districts. Again, for those well-steeped in the theory and practice of urban design, the section on *making a city* may be skipped, but I hope that new readers to this exciting new paradigm of urban planning will find the framework provided of help and value. Part III looks at the city at night, the city in the temporal dimension and the related issues of *morality and regulation of "pleasures"*. It includes case studies on London, Manchester, Shanghai, Paris, New York and Berlin. It looks in particular at current measures to regulate licensed premises in the UK, Europe and America, arguing these are the latest instalment in an ongoing cycle of tightening and relaxing opening times of liquor outlets and entertainment venues through the ages. Part V looks more closely at the urban quarter as a concentrated, more intense version of the city economy and its relationship to place. It considers such places are creative poles, and looks in close detail at the urban qualities necessary for success. The case studies this time are Temple Bar in Dublin, Sheffield CIQ, Adelaide West End, Manchester MNQ,

Wood Green in North London, plus some historical material on Paris, SoHo and Pittsburgh. As with the previous Parts, Part V concludes with a discussion of the implications for the coming wave of city development. This Part, in fact, draws material from each of the four preceding Parts and as such makes renewed reference to concepts discussed earlier in the book. I have tried to be as ruthless as possible in cutting out any unnecessary duplication, but I apologize for any that remains.

In conclusion, my argument is that the world economy, from around mid 2004,[3] is certainly at the start of a long wave, probably delayed by the events and aftermath of 9/11. The upswing this time will last until around 2030. During the coming period the economy of cities will change as, indeed, will technology. Artistic creativity will also develop, and the moral regulation of time will alter too. As with earlier modes of capitalist production, these changes will make demands upon and change in turn the use of space in the city, and the organization of the built form. None of this is easy. But it's not impossible either. If you want to know what to do, to understand how good cities work, read on.

3　This is based on observations of sustained, if initially modest, growth in publicly quoted share values throughout 2004, and into 2005. See "Economic Focus: Down But Not Out", *The Economist*, 4 June 2005, p. 74.

Two Inter-locking Theories of City Development

1. DEATH OF THE CITY?

"We have saved the city as a cultural concept", wrote the Mayor of Barcelona, Pasqual Maragall, in 1992. He was speaking just after the Olympic Games of that year, hosted by Barcelona and widely acclaimed. This statement reflects obvious satisfaction with the event, the projection of Barcelona as an exciting and contemporary city on the world stage; but also a more fundamental truth about this city's Renaissance during the late 1980s. Following the death of General Franco in the 1970s, Barcelona began to emerge from decades of bureaucratic control and ideological suppression. Traditionally a creative and artistic people, the Catalans were now free to express their cultural identity. They did so in the visual and performing arts, in theatre and dance, in the revival of previously banned folk traditions, and through the design industries. The post-Franco generations grew up in a city that was increasingly contemporary, fashionable and convivial. New waves of investment in cafés, bars and restaurants took place and entrepreneurs began to open avant-garde nightclubs, so that by the late 1980s, Barcelona had a reputation as a city for stylish clubbers. During this time the State and City Governments turned their attentions to improving the city as a living environment, by supporting the refurbishment of residential blocks and by embarking on a programme to create 150 new public spaces across the city. The award of the Olympic Games provided the investment necessary to tackle strategic town planning issues, notably in the construction of the Olympic Village, the provision of new relief roads and the re-connection of the city to the sea. There is much more to Barcelona's story than this, of course – including Cerda's masterplan of the 1850s, Gaudi's architecture, Miro and Dali. But the point I want to make here is that what happened in Barcelona in the 1980s was significant not only for that city itself, but for declining and stagnant cities more generally.

The death of the city has been forecast with enthusiastic gloom at various points during the last 150 years. The best-known would be Lewis Mumford's 1938 classic *The Culture of Cities*[1] in which he predicted that the "Megalopolis" would eventually strangle itself. The city of the future, for Mumford, was the Necropolis: the city of the dead. Indeed the emergence of the discipline of town planning in the late nineteenth century – with the emphasis on garden cities, planned decentralization

---

1   Mumford, L., *The Culture of Cities* (New York: Harcourt, Brace, 1938).

and new towns – was a response to the unsanitary and disease-ridden industrial cities of that time, one which also, through slum clearance and central area redevelopment contributed to the decline of larger cities. The evils of large-scale redevelopment, modernist architecture, and planned decentralization were most elegantly exposed by Jane Jacobs in *The Death and Life of Great American Cities.*[2] Her work, and that of urban design theorists such as Kevin Lynch and Christopher Alexander, has only begun to bear fruit in a practical sense of real-world planning and development, since the mid-1990s.

The point is that most cities in the developed world had reached a hiatus by the mid-1980s, the early signs of which were evident from the 1970s. In the United States, great cities such as Detroit, Chicago, and Boston appeared to be in terminal decline, some of them consigned to the status of "rust-belt". This was the time of a collapse in manufacturing, high inflation and unemployment and the flight of the middle classes from cities. New York, for example, lost 500,000 manufacturing jobs in the 1960s and 1970s, leaving some 4000 acres of industrial land unused.[3] In the United Kingdom, urban policy was effectively reversed in the 1977 Urban White Paper, with the ending of the new towns programme, the identification of stressed "inner cities" and redirection of government funding into urban regeneration. By the early 1980s, the great northern cities of Manchester, Liverpool, Leeds and Newcastle were in apparent free-fall; Birmingham and the West Midlands too.

It is clear that this cumulative decline had many causes, the combinations of which are the subject matter of this book. To put it crudely, planned decentralization of industry and people produced an exodus of the better-off away from the cities. Technologies in personal transportation had helped along a process of sub-urbanization of newly affluent residential areas. Some industries prepared to move to new campus-style industrial estates and business parks. The development of the motorway network led to increased road freight and a new science of logistics. However, it is also true that many established "staple" industries were already in decline due to disruption to established trade routes (the end of Empire), misguided industrial mergers, nationalization, a loss of innovation and virulent trade unionism. Added to this was the fact that, from the early 1970s to the end of the twentieth century, the capitalist economies were in a protracted long-wave slump, as conceptualized by Kondratieff.[4] Whatever the causes, and however complex and self-reinforcing they were, the fact is that by the mid-1980s, the cities were evidently "in crisis".[5] It seemed at the time that Lewis Mumford had been right all along.

---

2   Jacobs, J., *The Death and Life of Great American Cities* (Harmondsworth: Penguin Books, 1965) (American Original 1961).

3   Perine, J., *Brownfield Redevelopment in Bushwick, Brooklyn, New York*, paper presented to the International Cities and Towns Conference, Yepoon, Queensland, Australia, June 2005.

4   Kondratieff, N. D., *The Long Wave Cycle* (New York: Richardson and Snyder, 1984).

5   Rees, G. and Lambert, J., *The Cities in Crisis* (London: Edward Arnold, 1985).

But something happened in the Barcelona of the 1980s to bring life and economic dynamism back to the city, hence Mayor Maragall's claim. To varying degrees other cities have followed suit: Manchester and Stuttgart, Rotterdam and Antwerp, Pittsburgh and Chicago, Melbourne and Glasgow. All have become centrally concerned with urban regeneration, urban revitalization, urban renaissance ... Not all of this, of course, has been problem free, and many mistakes have been made along the way. Yet it is true that perhaps for the first time since the early nineteenth century the prime concern of urban policymakers is to build cities which combine economic dynamism with cultural vitality, creative innovation and urban design.

Many of the skills and knowledge we require to do this comes from a reinterpretation of the past, particularly in the built form and the development of an entrepreneurial culture. Yet these must always be considered against the new modes of production, new technologies and changing demographic patterns. We must too be sophisticated in our understanding of the potentials and consequences of increased movements of trade generally. For whilst air travel allows people to visit other countries, and goods to reach overseas markets quickly, it also helps to spread infectious disease. Communications technologies might very well promote the establishment of call, billing and service centres in India, but might this be accompanied by job loss and downsizing in the United Kingdom and Australia?

Nevertheless, the view I have come to is that the current generations of urban professionals (planners, surveyors, engineers, architects, urban designers) have for the first time in a century the apparatus to make the cities better. The golden age of the baby boomer might well be marked by a legacy of good urban design and strong city economies, as much as by popular music and digital art. I hope to show in the rest of this book how we can make cities better. I do so by proposing two inter-locking explanatory theories: the long waves of city development and the ongoing process I have termed "city dynamics".

2. A GENERAL MODEL OF CITY DYNAMICS

The model I now wish to elaborate holds, I believe, for most of city development since the emergence of Florence during the Renaissance of the early fifteenth century. It applies to the growth of cities in the middle ages, during the Enlightenment, for the industrial, and the post-industrial city, and for the city of the foreseeable future. The model has had a lengthy gestation. It draws heavily on the works of other theorists, writers and thinkers: David Canter for the basic structure; Jane Jacobs on the economy of cities, Michael Porter on industry clusters, Charles Sabel and Robin Murray on flexible specialization; Kevin Lynch, Christopher Alexander, Jan Gehl and Peter Buchanan on built form; Ken Worpole, Franco Bianchini and Raymond Williams on culture; Charles Handy on the knowledge economy, Nick Garnham on the cultural industries; Adam Smith on governance. There are many others I have borrowed from here and there, and I hope I have remembered to acknowledge them in the appropriate place. In proposing the model that follows, the ways in which others' work has been combined is mine alone.

The basic proposition is that for all cities, across many time-frames, it is essential to retain in balance a creative and dynamic economy, an innovative cultural life and a "good fit" of the built form to activity. These conditions will be found in any study of successful cities at a given point in time. Some cities are successful

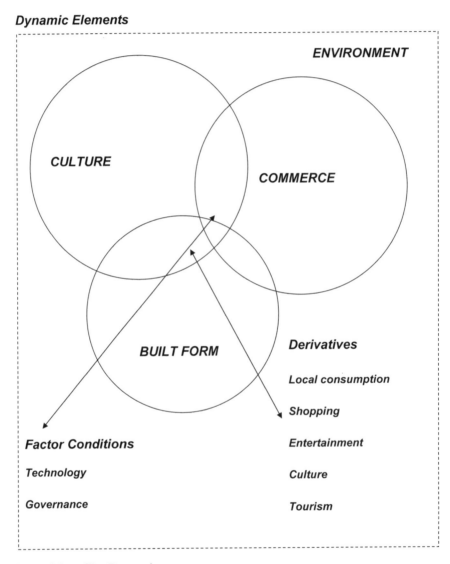

Figure 0.2   City Dynamics
Source: John Montgomery.

and flexible enough to adjust to changing economic conditions; others, historically, have not been. London enjoyed a golden age in the sixteenth century, another in the 1840s and one in the 1960s. Paris's golden age was in the late nineteenth century, Edinburgh's in the 1770s, Vienna for most of the nineteenth century, New York in the 1920s and 1950s, Los Angeles in the 1930s and 1990s. Some cities only manage episodes of rapid growth and cultural pre-eminence once in a lifetime. In the 1870s Buenos Aires and Adelaide were the two fastest growing cities of the time, but since then have stagnated and/or declined.

Each individual city, moreover, is created in an unique place, that is to say a particular environment with individual topographical and fertility characteristics. In most cases, some element of physical property – deep water for a sea port, a river, raw materials, particular soil characteristics – have given rise to the city's initial development. As time and technologies progress, this originally fundamental relationship will very often become less dominant. Yet the local landscape will always retain a set of cultural associations and remain part of the city identity. Thus San Francisco and Melbourne are no longer agriculturally-based market cities, yet their relationships with local topographical features and forms of agriculture remain strong.

Over time, the balance of commerce, culture and built form will change and adapt, particularly in relation to changes in patterns of trade. But two other "factor conditions" are at play: technology and governance. Each of these can and do impact on city economies, built types and form and cultural life generally. For example, a policy of increasing local taxation will usually lead to business closures, relocation and economic stagnation. Changes in technology can lead to new products, new production processes and changes in the skills base and the division of labour. Changes in the built form can also be brought about by governance (building height restrictions, the taxing of windows in Bath in the eighteenth century), as well as by technology in the form of new building techniques. Culture will also change with variations in regulation. One thinks here of the Theatre Acts in Victorian London or the Chicago speak-easies. Technology also affects culture in the means of producing and circulating images, texts and sounds – the rise of the cinema for example or broadcast radio and popular music, or sound recording. Jazz, photography and film were the art forms of the twentieth century; literature and fine art of the nineteenth century; classical music in the eighteenth century and theatre before that. In the twenty-first century it will be digital media and designed objects.

Cities, then, must have commerce to earn their living, cities would be dull uninteresting and lacking in innovation without culture; the built form should give identity to a city but also provide a good "fit" for its unique blend of activities. Changes in technology will alter the balance of commerce/culture/form almost continually, although to varying degrees. Governments can either help maintain this beneficial balance by policies on taxation and regulation – and by investment in key economic and social infrastructure – or by over-regulating, killing the goose that lays the egg. Meanwhile, cities will maintain a separate relationship with their local hinterland or environment, perhaps through economic transplants, the seeding of new industries (winemaking in South Australia for example) or simply in terms of meaningful natural features – the Sydney Harbour, the London green-belt, Edinburgh's crag and tail … And when all of these processes are operating in relative balance, local citizens will tend to have greater levels of income to spend on items of personal consumption: dresses and hats, cakes and hairdressing, nightclubs and restaurants. A city which offers all of these goods and services might then find itself a key destination for tourists and other visitors. To some degree, the new economic geography is linked to choices and preferences in personal consumption.

The cities which will achieve greatest growth and prosperity over the next fifty years will be those which are technologically advanced, have networks of inter-trading business clusters and offer urban lifestyles attractive to creative and artistic innovators. This is what the remainder of this book is about. This book will follow the logic of this "model" or "theory", with chapters on each element and process. Nevertheless, it is incumbent to explain this in a little fuller detail in this essentially introductory chapter. Before doing so, we must also consider why it is that particular cities grow at particular points in time, while others do not.

3. THE LONG WAVES OF CITY DEVELOPMENT

An important concept to introduce at this point is the long-wave cycle of capitalist development. This posits that capitalism is subject to a pattern of long business cycles or "waves" where falling rates of profit generally produce periodic crises or changes. The economist Nikolai Kondratieff argued that this was because the economic "exploitation" of existing technologies has been exhausted, so that growth can only come from a new generation of technologies.[6] Each cycle lasts for roughly 55–60 years, with peaks of economic growth at the mid-point:

> The upswing in the first long wave embraces the period from 1789 to 1814, i.e. 25 years; its decline begins in 1814 and ends in 1849, a period of 35 years. The cycle is therefore completed in 60 years. The rise in the second wave begins in 1847 and ends in 1873, lasting 24 years. The decline of the second wave begins in 1873 and ends in 1896, a period of 23 years. The length of the second wave is 47 years. The upward movement of the third wave begins in 1896 and ends in 1920, its duration 24 years. The decline of the wave, according to the data, begins in 1920.[7]

Kondratieff would not live to see the end of the third wave, the crash and Great Depression of the 1930s: he died in a Siberian concentration camp, found guilty of being a heretic and harbouring dangerous views on economic development. Using commodity prices, Kondratieff had been able to show that periods of strong growth occur every 45–55 years, separated by periods of sharp decline. Between 1814 and 1843, for example, prices fell by 59%. From 1843, economies were growing once more – prices jumped 33% between 1852 and 1854 alone. Prices levelled off and

---

6   Kondratieff, N., *op. cit.*

7   Ibid.

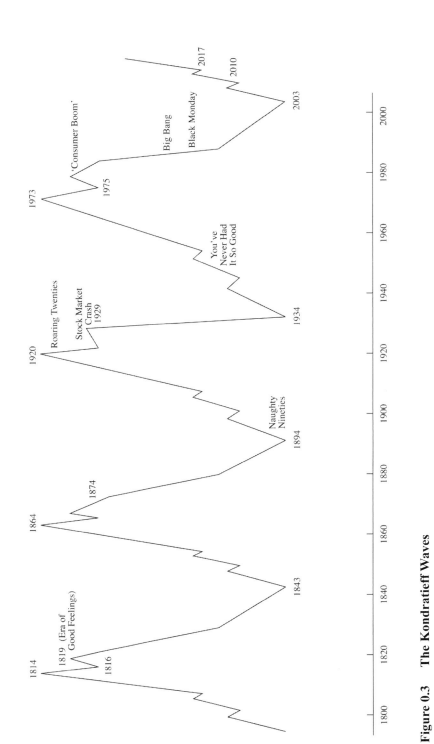

Figure 0.3 The Kondratieff Waves

Source: Adapted from Beckman (1983), by John Montgomery.

began to fall again from 1864, leading to a deep recession which only bottomed-out in 1894. By the late 1890s prices were increasing again, albeit slowly. By 1920, business was booming but prices peaked that very year. This was disguised for a while during the Roaring Twenties, but led finally to the "Great Crash" of 1929.

The Kondratieff waves have been the subject of much debate amongst economists and academics for over sixty years now. They continue to be referred to in works by other authors over the years, most notably by Robert Beckman[8] and in Peter Hall's *Cities in Civilisation.*[9] Beckman plots a fourth wave which he dates from 1946 to until 2000. Writing in 1983, he predicted the onset of a "secondary depression" from 1983/84, leading to a stock market collapse and followed by a deep trough which would bottom-out in the early mid 1990s.

The most serious work on long wave business cycles was carried out by Joseph Schumpeter at Harvard University in the 1930s.[10] Schumpeter identified three "Kondratieff cycles", each associated with the rise of new industries: from 1789 (the early industrial revolution), from the 1840s (the age of steam, steel, rail and ships) and from 1896 (electricity, motor cars and "Fordism"). Schumpeter argued that the important point is not the invention of a technology, but rather its applications to commerce, trade and production processes. He argued that economic growth is triggered by the emergence of new groups of entrepreneurs, prepared to take on new forms of work just as previous generations are tiring, dying or retiring! Moreover, Schumpeter argued, the new innovations would tend to be invented during periods of economic depression, would then generate new processes and products and the next upswing would happen.

Writing in 1939, Schumpeter would know that the next upswing – lasting roughly until 1974 – was about to happen. As it turned out, the technologies this time around were electronics, commercial aviation, consumer household goods, radio and sound-recording. These technologies would become exhausted, to varying degrees, by the 1970s and 1980s, at which point new technologies were being invented and/or applied. Thus the period 1975–2002 roughly equates with a Kondratieff depression, during which time the general rate of profit fell, older industries declined, unemployment rose and new technologies – in this case computers, digital media, pharmaceuticals – were invented and began to be applied commercially. If this is true, then it seems likely that the capitalist economy in the year 2005 is entering an upswing that will last for twenty-five to thirty years, that is until 2030 or thereabouts. Following this, the rate of profit will once again fall, and new technologies will need to be invented. It is possible that these will be in bio-technology (buy your health and a long life here!), but this is only a guess.

Schumpeter himself drew upon the work of two other economists, Kitchin and Juglar both of whom argued that market economies develop along the path of a

---

8   Beckman, R., *The Downwave* (London: Pan Books, 1983).

9   Hall, P., *Cities in Civilisation* (London: Weidenfeld & Nicolson, 1998).

10   Schumpeter, J., *Business Cycles* (New York: McGraw & Hill, 1939; Philadelphia: Porcupine Press, reprinted 1982).

business cycle. Juglar's cycle lasts nine years, and is based on the fluctuation in commodity prices. Economic growth and prosperity brings higher prices, exports become more difficult and foreign exchange moves out of the country. The end of the cycle is marked by the ending of price rises. Schumpeter discovered that Juglar's 1919 peak coincided with the longer Kondratieff wave peak at the end of a long period of prosperity; but at the following Juglar peak in 1928, the long wave was already in a downswing and this combination led to the collapse in stock markets and the global economy.

Juglar divided his cycle into three periods: prosperity, crisis and liquidation, which appear also to correspond with Kitchin's 40 month business cycle – that is to say growth and decline occurs within all three of Juglar's periods. Simon Kuznets[11] would later argue that the long waves last only for 22–25 years and are in fact based on variations in construction activity. The geographer Brian Berry,[12] writing in 1970, proposed that both economists were correct. In fact, argued Barry, the Kuznets waves operate within the longer Kondratieff cycle, so that each Kondratieff wave has two Kuznets booms in construction. Within these 20–25 year cycles, the shorter Juglar cycles sit at a ratio of three Juglars to a Kuznets, and therefore six Juglars to a Kondratieff. This led Beckman, writing in 1983, to conclude that the periods of "acute panic and danger" in the world economy occur where all three cycles are in downswing simultaneously. This occurred in 1974 and again in 1983. It also occurred in 1992 and 2001, by which time the global economy was approaching the start of a Kondratieff upswing. The next Juglar downswing will be at its depth in around 2010, but by that time the fifth Kondratieff wave will be well underway.

What does this mean for cities and their development? Each of the waves is associated with the rise of particular industries: cotton in the first wave, steel, rail and shipbuilding in the second, automobiles and electrical engineering in the third, civil aviation, plastics and pharmaceuticals in the fourth. For a variety of reasons, these new industries take hold initially in particular places, so that the early pioneering cities are very often those who succeed the most in economic development and wealth creation. Thus, the ascendant city of the first wave was Manchester, the second wave was powered by new industries in Glasgow and Pittsburgh, the third wave automobile industry was centred on Detroit, Birmingham and Stuttgart, the aviation of the fourth wave was centred on Los Angeles, Seattle and Bristol. Meanwhile, cities such as London, Paris, New York and Tokyo are able to adapt from one wave to the next, either because they contain their own clusters of new economic activity or because of their trade in stocks and shares. It is this phenomenon that gives rise to episodic periods of spectacular growth and city development. Less certain is whether those cities where primary new inventions are made always themselves prosper. This

---

11 Kuznets, S., *Schumpeter's Business Cycles, American Economic Review*, 30, 1940, 250–71.

12 Berry, B.J.L., *Long-Wave Rhythms in Economic Development and Political Behavior* (Baltimore: Johns Hopkins University Press, 1991).

seems not necessarily to be the case as the Edinburgh of the 1770s, the Paris of the 1880s or Berlin of the 1920s would imply. In these cases, the inventions were often taken up as successful new industries elsewhere.

It seems there is a distinction that can be made between primary invention and its secondary application. This is true of scientific and technological advances, but it also might apply to the development of artistic movements, and the relationship between these and wealth creation. In philosophical terms, this would be referred to as a "paradigm shift". This concept was proposed by Thomas Kuhn in 1962.[13] Kuhn argued that scientific progress does not proceed in a gradual upward curve, but rather in a series of creative leaps. For most of time, Kuhn argued, scientists are content to accept a particular set of accepted laws and norms – a "paradigm". But at particular points in time these particular paradigms are discovered to be limited in their explanatory power. New theories and laws are required – a new paradigm – so that scientific progress is marked by a series of "paradigm shifts". In physics for example, the key innovators who challenged and overturned previous orthodoxies would be Galileo, Copernicus, Newton and Einstein. In medical history the surgeons of eighteenth century Edinburgh, Dr John Snow, Madame Curie, and Alexander Fleming. In philosophy, Thomas Hobbes, John Locke, Rousseau, Voltaire, Hume, Jeremy Bentham, Kierkegaard, Marx, Sartre, even Foucault.

We might apply a similar logic to the arts as texts, images, sounds and movement. For example, the innovators in literature might be Austen and Scott, Balzac and Dickens, Conrad and Joyce, Eliot and Auden. In fine art those responsible for the beginnings of new paradigms might well include Constable and Turner who were painting in the early 19th century. Later an artist associated with the Impressionists, Paul Cezanne, would in fact spark a new fine art paradigm of Cubism and later Expressionism as in the works, for example, of artists such as Klee, Picasso, Kandinsky and Miro. The next break or paradigm shift would come in the 1940s, in New York. In music, paradigm shifts appear to have been occasioned by Bach (Baroque), Haydn and Mozart (Classical), late Beethoven and Schubert (Romantic), Debussy (Impressionist and modern), Schoenberg (a-tonal), Stravinsky (neo-classical) Charlie Parker and Dizzy Gillespie (modern jazz), Michael Nyman and Philip Glass (minimalism). On this logic the early applications of new paradigms would come from Schumann, Mendelssohn and Brahms, Ravel and Poulenc and Hindemith, Copland and Bernstein, Miles Davis and Dave Brubeck. This is something I wish to explore more fully in this book.

At this stage, however, we can conclude that bursts of wealth creation and city development occur in particular places at particular times because of the development of new technologies which give rise to new industries, new production processes and new art forms. This explains why most cities tend to develop in periodic spurts. It also explains why, if they allow their main industries to die, they also can decline as places of wealth creation. We shall explore this notion further, particularly in Part I.

---

13 Kuhn, T. S., *The Structure of Scientific Revolutions* (Chicago: University of Chicago Press, 1962).

4. CITY DYNAMICS

Commerce

Cities are first and foremost economic entities. This has probably always been the case, although many medieval cities were originally built as defensible spaces, seats of government or holy places. From as early as the tenth century, patterns of trade across Europe were emerging, which to a notable extent explains the locations and development of many of today's cities. The essential dynamic – trade – underpinned the development of mercantile capitalism in Europe over the period 1400–1750, more or less. Mercantile capitalism in turn transferred into early and then full industrial capitalism from the late-1700s onwards. By the 1930s industrial capitalism was already entering a long period of decline, so that the era of so-called "flexible specialization" can probably be dated from the 1950s. It seems likely that this relationship between cities and trade will last as long as capitalism itself.

In *Medieval Cities* the Belgian economic historian Henri Pirenne[14] argued that trade in raw materials (furs, fish, wool, tin, salt, leather) across northern and western Europe, sparked the development of settlements on rivers, on coast-lines and at cross-roads on the great trade routes. Jane Jacobs, in *The Economy of Cities*[15] argues that these elementary patterns of trade led to the growth of market towns and medieval cities. As trade grew, so too did spending in the local economy. New divisions of labour emerged, eventually to be formalized in the guilds of London and Paris, for example. Jacobs argues that without the strategic development of trade between Venice and the Far East, the economic and urban history of Europe would have been altogether different. As it is, traders and adventurers such as Marco Polo were able to bring new fabrics and spices (even noodles!) to Europe, in exchange for woollens and furs.

Jacobs proposed a model of city economic growth, which she refers to as "The Two Reciprocating Systems of City Growth". Her argument is that cities achieve growth primarily through a process of exporting goods and services in order to earn surpluses with which to purchase imports. As the economy develops, more and more exports generate greater surpluses, during which time the division of labour among local producers becomes more complex, and various supply chains develop. Over time a strong and or growing city economy will develop the skills and the capacity to replace or substitute imports and make these products locally. By this means, a city economy can then import other goods with its export surpluses and meantime the newly replaced imports may become another successful export product. The wealth that is created is then re-invested in productive capacity, raw materials or stock; and a good proportion of it will also be spent by local citizens on consumer goods and services. We will return to consider Jacob's work in more detail in Part I, but what we take from her analysis at this stage is the importance of adding new work to old

---

14　Pirenne, H., *Les Periodes de l'Histoire sociale du Capitalisme*, *Bulletin de l'Academie Royale Belgique*, 5, 1914, 258–99.

15　Jacobs, J., *The Economy of Cities* (London: Jonathon Cape, 1969).

work more or less continually, the diversification of the division of labour, and the ongoing dynamic of exporting, importing, import replacements, export multipliers, import multipliers and local consumer spending.

Jacobs wrote *The Economy of Cities* in 1969, and it was immediately controversial and not well received by economists. It was not until 1990 and the publication of Michael Porter's *The Competitive Advantage of Nations* that the model she devised gained widespread acceptability. Porter argues that competitive success tends to concentrate in particular industries and groups of inter-connected industries. A "cluster" is a grouping of industries linked together through customer, supplier and other relationships which enhance competitive advantage. These clusters are characterized by the presence of internationally competitive firms, which also continuously upgrade and innovate. The similarities with the Jacob's model are striking. Later, in Part 1 I shall apply Porter's model to the case of the creative industries.

One final point on *The Economy Of Cities* needs to be made at this juncture. In the appendix, Jacobs tantalizingly refers to "changing patterns of economic activities". She notes that in early developed economies goods and services are the product of systems of "craft production" organized by merchant and guilds. With the emergence of industrial capitalism, this mode of production is itself transplanted by mass production organized by manufacturing concerns. In the future, she suggested, economic activities would reflect a system of "differential productiveness" organized by suppliers of services. Jacobs quotes Dr Clarke Kerr who used the phrase "putting-out system" in 1964. The "putting-out mode of production" these days is referred to as "Post-Fordism" or "flexible specialization" as proposed in the work of economists such as Sabel[16] in the United States, and Robin Murray[17] in the United Kingdom. Flexible specialization tends to be characterized by a diverse chain of production, differentiated products, "life-style" placement, the application of high-end technology, craft skills and design, targeted marketing and "just-in-time-delivery". The example most often quoted is the fashion and clothing sector of the "Third Italy" where a complex range of small companies supply the design houses (Armani, Zegna, Versace) and large-scale marketer/retailers such as Benetton.

The importance of this line of argument for the future economy of cities is firstly that such clusters develop around a core of propulsive companies, often applying cutting-edge technology either to make new products or to improve production processes. Networks of supplier businesses and chains of production form, and these are less horizontally integrated than under industrial capitalism. This in itself encourages new business formation and thus feeds entrepreneurial activity, generated by a steady supply of individuals with the prerequisite skills and attributes. Such clusters or complexes or agglomerations are very often centres of great invention and innovation. Unless this dynamic is maintained, economic decline will set in.

---

16 Sabel, C., *Work and Politics* (Cambridge University Press, 1982).

17 Murray, R., *Benetton Britain, Marxism Today*, July, 1985.

This means that at the present time – the early years of the twenty-first century – city economies that are growing rapidly are most likely to be those with clusters of flexibly specialized industries – places such as Seattle or Austin, Texas or Silicon Valley; Bristol and the M11 Corridor in England; the Third Italy; Helsinki, Dublin and Barcelona. Such cities and city-regions will also have more established Fordist industries, such as aircraft production or car-making, yet their economies will no longer be dominated by these. Stagnating and declining cities by contrast will tend to have very few flexibly-specialized industry sectors, and will often be dominated by large branch-plant businesses (albeit with more localized supply chains) and a higher proportion of service businesses serving predominantly local consumer demand.

In a strange way, this is in part a return to the economic organization of cities of mercantile capitalism, based around exporting firms and business networks. It is as if industrial capitalism, rational planning, assembly-line production and decentralization of factories and plants were an aberration. If this is the case, then the implication is that cities need in future to be more flexible in their systems of economic organization, and in the adaptability of the built form. This point is of key importance when we consider urban or built form in more detail in Part IV. The conclusion at this stage, however, is that without a dynamic, innovation-oriented and flexibly-specialized economy, a city will stagnate, and decline. The roll call includes Glasgow, Liverpool, Sheffield, Detroit, Pittsburgh, Brooklyn…

Culture

Raymond Williams referred to culture as "one of the two or three most complicated words in the English language",[18] but went on to suggest three broad definitions. The first of these he defined as "a general process of intellectual, spiritual and aesthetic development". This might cover, for example, the cultural development of Western Europe and that found in the works of philosophers, artists and writers. This view, propound by theorists such as Matthew Arnold and F.R. Leavis, sees culture more or less as "the best that has been thought and said". In other words, the high arts[19] as a body of knowledge, with education being "the road to culture". Arnold was writing in 1867, and his work reflects the dominant politics of the time, particularly in his dismissal of working-class culture, and his categorization of society into three groups: Barbarians (aristocracy), Philistines (middle class) and Populace (working class). This train of thought later influenced F.R. Leavis who, writing in the 1930s, argued that "culture has always been in minority keeping".[20] This conception of culture was attacked as such by writers such as E.P. Thompson (on English working class culture) and those seeking to understand the rise of mass popular culture in the United States

---

18 Williams, R., *Keywords* (London: Fontana, 1983).

19 Arnold, M., *Culture and Anarchy* (Cambridge University Press).

20 F.R. Leavis, *Mass Civilisation and Minority Culture* (Cambridge University Press 1930), 3.

in the 1950s.[21] However, the study of great art remains a valid endeavour. Culture is, to a significant extent, made up of the historical body of knowledge produced by a civilization, and which in turn shapes that civilization.

Williams' second definition of culture is a "a particular way of life, whether of a people, a period or a group."[22] This is largely "anthropological" definition, allowing us to understand how different societies come to form specific ideas about themselves, language and customs, things such as local festivals, national holidays, regional cuisines, sports and religious practices. This definition encompasses later work on sub-cultures and multi-culturalism. Williams' third definition of culture is as "works and practices of intellectual and especially artistic activity", in other words the production or "signifying" of meaning. In this, Williams is close to the definitions employed by French Structuralists such as Levi-Strauss (the structure of myths), Saussure ("semiology" or the study of signs) or Barthes (signifying practices). This definition would include the high art forms of literature, poetry, music and fine art, but would also encompass popular forms such as pop music, soap operas and comics – in other words, "cultural texts".

For the purposes of this book, the author is content to rely on these three definitions provided by Williams, at least in terms of the development of civilizations and cities and the ways of living in cities. This is partly a reluctance to enter the intellectual cul-de-sac of Marxist cultural theory and the post-modernists. However, the Marxists are right to some extent, even if limited to the observation that artistic and cultural creation occurs within an economic and social framework at any given point of time. It matters a great deal whether the cities in which artists live and work are in decline or are growing, are using technology to create new work and wealth, or not. But by the same token, a society that is wealthy will not necessarily produce great art. Wealth, particularly the old forms of money, is not necessarily a guarantee of artistic and creative innovation, quite often the reverse. Yet a link between economic development and culture exists, just that it is impossible to "read-off" or predict.

One aspect of cultural development which is relatively straightforward to understand is the notion of the "culture industry", a term first coined by Max Horkheimer and Theodor Adorno in 1947.[23] These writers used the term to denote the products and processes of mass culture. However, they denounced the culture industry as homogenous, uniform and predictable, characterized by "structuralization, stereotype, conservatism, mendacity, manipulated consumer goods".[24] In this way, the "role" of the culture industry in "late capitalism" is to discourage "the masses"

---

21 See for example Bernard Rosenberg's *Mass Culture in America* or David Macdonald's *A Theory of Mass Culture*, both published in B. Rosenberg and D. Manning White (eds), *Mass Culture: The Popular Arts in America* (New York: Macmillan, 1957).

22 Williams, *op. cit.*, p. 90.

23 See *The Dialectic of Enlightenment* (New York: Herder and Herder, 1972).

24 Lowenthal, L., *Literature, Popular Culture and Society* (Palo Alto, CA: Pacific Books, 1961), p. 11.

from thinking beyond the confines of the present, akin to the "prole-feed" of Orwell's *1984*. For the Frankfurt School of Marxists, then, the culture industry is reactionary, obfuscatory, and an important part of the hegemonic dominance of late capitalism.

We need not detain ourselves much longer on Marxist cultural theory, yet it is important to acknowledge the origins of the term "culture industry", to which we shall return in Part I. In any event, the best we can hypothesize at this stage is that cities which are dynamic economically will also tend to be more interesting culturally. Over time this has been demonstrated in Venice and Florence, Paris and London, Vienna and Berlin; New York and San Francisco, and lately Dublin, Manchester, Melbourne and Barcelona. It does appear, in the age of the knowledge economy and "the culture industry" that creative places are now more likely to succeed economically. If this is so, then we can logically ask the question: What are the physical characteristics of cities (if any) that attract creative people?

Built Form

The physical built form of cities can be conceptualized as two interlocking planes. The first of these is the spatial structure of the city, that is to say the spatial distribution of activities and buildings across the area covered by the city. This covers such familiar types of place as the CBD, inner urban areas, outer residential areas, suburbs and event satellite settlements and new towns. This element was a traditional concern of town planners who, simultaneously, were attempting to reduce over-crowding in central areas, prevent urban sprawl and develop new towns. This is the structural level of city form.

The second element is what are we might term the micro-environment, the pattern of streets and buildings, the relationship between building heights and street widths, building edges and spaces, adaptable usage of the built stock, legibility and permeability and the public realm. This is the area of study of urban designers, who in recent years have been rediscovering the old skills of city building or place-making. This is the element of built form on which I shall concentrate in Part IV.

The spatial structure of cities has fascinated economists, planners and sociologists for some 150 years at least. The work of the Chicago School of urban theorists in the 1920s and 1930s was arguably the first attempt at a systematic theory of the city. In doing so, writers such as Robert Park and Louis Wirth drew substantially on earlier works by Georg Simmel, Charles Darwin, Emile Durkheim and Max Weber. The "urban sociology" of Park and his colleagues[25] argued that urban development and spatial structure were the outcomes of inter-acting processes of competition for space, dominance, succession and invasion. It was Burgess who went on to suggest that the city could be conceptualized ideally as five zones arranged in concentric circles: the central business district, the inner city zone of transition, the zone of working class housing, the zone of middle class housing and the urban/rural fringe

---

25 For a discussion of these writers, see P. Saunders, *Social Theory and the Urban Question* (London: Hutchison, 1981).

and outlying suburbs. That this conception can be described as empiricist is not in any doubt, yet it does tend to support the work of urban land economists such as William Alonso who, following on from David Ricardo, developed the theory of urban rent bidding.[26]

This, too, sees the outcome of the city as a series of concentric rings based on the rent levels different activities can afford to pay to occupy space. This is held to explain why higher-value activities occupy central zones, and lower-value activities tend to locate further from the centre – initially the market place. The exception is the "zone of transition" where there is an ongoing struggle between competing uses, and into which the CBD is threatening to expand (Broadgate and Spitalfields in London or Darling Harbour East in Sydney would be good contemporary examples).

The import of these types of theories is that, along with the traditional town planning concern to separate and decentralize land uses, they legitimized the importance of an order of rational zoning on the city. Thus, from the 1950s until the mid-1970s at least, city planning orthodoxy was the zone, the new town, separation of land uses and redevelopment informed by modernist design principles. As Jane Jacobs in her classic work *The Death and Life of Great American Cities* noted: "This is not the rebuilding of cities. This is the sacking of cities."[27] Jacobs argued that the imposition of zoning ordinances was destroying the very mixed use and transactions base that underpins city economies. As broad descriptive labels, phrases such as the CBD (Central Business District) and the "zone of transition" are helpful to some degree, but not if they are used as a rationale for destroying city diversity. So we were left with a situation where theoretical notions of city spatial structure were being imposed in such a way as to kill the mixture and life of cities. Thankfully, we no longer make such mistakes.

Jane Jacobs identified the essential conditions for "city diversity" which she defined as a complex mix of uses, shared use of streets and networks of inter-trading enterprises. These can be summarized as: the need for mixed primary uses; the need for small blocks; the need for aged buildings; and the need for density. In other words, a combination of relatively high densities, mixed uses, variety of building types, ages, condition and cost, and a permeable and legible streetscape. She argues that it is only in such environments that the creative patterns of trading which cause cities to develop can be sustained. This ran counter to the orthodoxy of the time, and is probably the first successful attempt to conceptualize the built form conditions which underpin city diversity, and therefore innovation and creativity. The importance of this insight cannot be over-stated, and we shall consider this and the urban design literature more fully in Part IV.

That mixed use is the new planning orthodoxy is by now evident, although as recently as the early 1990s, this could not be said. This acceptance by town planners, and adoption by developers and investors, happily coincided with demographic

---

26 Alonso, W., *Location and Land Use* (Harvard University Press, 1964).

27 Jacobs, J., *The Death and Life of Great American Cities* (New York: Random House, 1961), 14.

changes, changes in employment and the "lifestyle" generations, and not forgetting the falling demand for office accommodation, so that even prime spaces in city CBDs are becoming places of residence and more mixed. Paradoxically, this phenomenon is bringing added pressure to bear on lower value uses in so-called "zones of transition", with many activities being driven out by new wealthier residents. This trend was termed "gentrification" in London in the 1970s,[28] and is most tellingly described in Sharon Zukin's 1982 study of "loft living" in 1970s New York.[29]

Zukin explores the trend for former (usually light) manufacturing spaces to be converted to residential and cultural use, in cities such as London, Amsterdam, Boston and New York. She charts the decline of these areas for manufacturing purposes, the fall of rent levels and land values, and their colonization by artists who brought with them not only new spending, but also alternative lifestyles and urban frisson. She focuses on Manhattan, Greenwich Village, the Lower East Side and SoHo. In the end, she concludes, the artists created new landscapes within the city, and this attracted "real estate agents" and marketeers who began selling a "lifestyle" to urban professionals and "wanabees". This is by now a familiar enough scenario, and one that we will consider at length in later discussions of cultural quarters, in Part V. What is important at this point for our own argument, is that Zukin identified – although this apparently was not her main focus – what it was about the lofts which attracted the artists and "cultural producers" in the first place. She notes, for example that lofts, though constructed on a small scale offer large spaces. Each floor has between 2000 and 10 000 square feet of floorspace, with high ceilings supported by vaulted arches or columns. Lofts are spacious and can be used as artists studios, small galleries, workshops, design studios and apartments, often some combination of these. Zukin argues that lofts represent a "terrain of conflict" between the various social groups that compete for their use, including small manufacturers, artists, middle class tenants, real estate developers, potential tenants, the banks and the "patrician elite of cities".

Zukin's Marxist ideology for me spoils an otherwise engrossing account. For in a mixed use city, surely all manner of activities and users would compete for and cohabit in beneficial locations and spaces. The secret appeal of the lofts was their central locations – within the zone or zones of transition, allied with the in-built robustness and adaptability of the building types themselves. Allied to this, the areas in which lofts existed would have traditional street patterns providing space for shops, restaurants and galleries on ground floors. These are precisely the types of places to which artistic creators are attracted. So if we can build or redevelop city neighbourhoods and districts with similar physical characteristics, then we should be able to provide local environments which provide a good "fit" with certain types (not necessarily all) of economic and cultural creativity. This has been attempted most notably in Temple Bar in Dublin, and in Sheffield and Manchester.

---

28 Smith, N. and Williams, P. (eds) *Gentrifcation of the City* (Boston: Allen & Unwin, 1986).

29 Zukin, S., *Loft Living: Culture and Capital in Urban Change* (New Brunswick: Rutgers University Press, 1982; reprinted 1989).

This is not to argue that every district or neighbourhood in the city should be redeveloped for mixed use to higher densities. Nor does it imply that all uses can be mixed successfully everywhere, all of the time. There is, for example, a growing conflict in many cities – notably Leeds, Melbourne, Soho in London – between the burgeoning night-time economy and new apartment dwellers. This is a question we shall return to in Part III. The point to stress here is that not all areas of the city warrant "full-on" mixed use, but rather subtle gradients of these depending on the primary use of the area. For many areas should remain primarily residential neighbourhoods with varying levels of supporting services and (often) local civic centres. It would be a mistake to re-zone such areas for higher density mixed use.

Yet the simple truth remains that all cities must have mixed use, high density areas within which myriad small businesses can develop and prosper, and from which they can take on the world if need be. Without built environments of this type, creative enterprise will not prosper.

Technology

Cities throughout history have had to respond and adapt to changes in technology. In some cases, technology leads to changes in production processes, new products and entire new industries. In others, the impact is on cultural forms. And in others there is a direct impact on the spatial and physical organizations of the city itself. Some examples will hopefully demonstrate these points.

In his book *The Conscience of the Eye*, Richard Sennett[30] argues that the most devastating example of technological development changing city form was the invention of the cannon. Until this point, walled cities were largely defensible, notwithstanding siege weapons and other military devices, and indeed this was their primary purpose. The Scottish Wars of Independence in the late thirteenth century and early fourteenth centuries would be a case in point, as would the ongoing conflicts between the city-states of fifteenth century Italy. Up until the late fifteenth century, medieval towns and cities were highly centralized and densely populated, with new walls being added in concentric rings as population growth required. The advent of the cannon which could break city walls changed all this. The walls were no longer a guaranteed protection, warfare itself had to change with pitched battles of opposing ranks more or less the norm until the 1930s and the perfection of the warplane and motorized artillery. But back in the late fifteenth century we find that cities began to grow outside their walls (or in another location entirely), particularly where markets could be set up without the costs of paying taxes to be protected within the city walls. The cannon changed the city forever.

My next example is the clock. Properly measured time was a Roman invention, but the important change for our purposes was the invention of the medieval clock. Peter Hall[31] notes Lewis Mumford's argument that mechanical clocks were eagerly

30 Sennett, R., *The Conscience of the Eye* (London: Faber and Faber, 1990).
31 Hall, P., *op. cit.*, 1998.

adopted by the monasteries to overcome what Marc Bloch referred to as "a vast indifference to time" in feudal society. Thus Sennett wrote "the Benedictine monks began to give precise time meaning".[32] At first this was innocent enough – when to wake, when to eat, when to sleep – but later the mechanical clock would allow the payment of labour by the hour, a key feature of industrial capitalism. Eventually the clock would become critical to the economic (labour paid by time) and social (closing times) organization of the city. Changes to working hours would become an ongoing feature of labour struggles, while control over entertainment and liquor consumption could also be linked to the clock. Along the way, the clock and the regulation of the time would produce such delights as the rush hour. On the plus side, grand clocks located in public spaces within cities helped provide features around which people could gather, a relationship between time and space which was all but lost by the 1980s. Following the invention of the mechanical clock, city life would never be the same.

The most important technological impact of the eighteenth and nineteenth centuries was of course the industrial revolution. This is too large a matter to be considered in any detail here. Nevertheless, we should note that without Watt's steam engine (1788) there would be no mass production, no steel ships and no railway age. Without John Kay, James Hargreaves and Richard Arkwright there would be no spinning jenny, no rapid growth of the cotton industry in late-eighteenth century Lancashire, and no "Cottonopolis". Manchester and the Lancashire towns owed their growth and economic ascendancy of the next thirty years to such inventions. This generated the first rapid industrial urbanization of any city, in Manchester. Further rounds of new technologies created a new system of production, that is to say the factory system. The social consequences of higher rates of urbanization, densely packed workers housing, poor sanitation and outbreaks of disease have been well documented by Engels as well as others.[33] It was such conditions that ultimately would lead to the various sanitation, health, housing and early Town Planning Acts of the late nineteenth century in the United Kingdom. In this way, town planning as it exists today was initially a response to the sanitary, health and housing conditions of urbanized industrial England in the mid-1800s.

The next great technological invention was the railway. Peter Hall's 1988 work *Cities of Tomorrow*[34] demonstrates that London was the first great city to experience regional urban spread (if not yet sprawl). By the late nineteenth century new commuter railways and underground lines would allow people of modest incomes to escape the congestion of the central city. London spread along radial routes in all directions, to the new suburbs of Grange Hill or Stanmore, Dulwich and New Cross, Wembley and beyond (Figure 0.4).

---

32 Sennet, R., *op. cit.*, 1990.

33 Engels, F., *The Condition of the Working Class in England* (Oxford: Blackwell, 1958).

34 Hall, P., *Cities of Tomorrow* (Oxford: Blackwell, 1998).

**Figure 0.4   London Estate Agents Advertising Poster for Prickett & Ellis, by
                Dudley Hardy (1901)**

Source: The National Archives (C177/ folio 11), with permission.

The great stations of Easton, Waterloo, Kings Cross, Paddington, Victoria, Blackfriars, Charing Cross, Cannon Street and Liverpool Street were built from 1837 onwards. By 1877 London's railway network was complete. Thus the spatial structure of London was forever changed, and so too was the built form with the rise of terraced housing. Later, in the 1920s and 1930s, new suburbs would be opened up, notably to the north-west (Middlesex and "Metroland") – places such as Ruislip, Ickenham, Epsom and Finchley. These were the first outlying suburbs, entirely dependent on commuting, but nevertheless growing their own local parades of shops, schools and town halls. The infilling of spaces between railway stations would follow, given added impetus by the invention of the horseless omnibus, and later the private motor vehicle. What was clear by the 1930s was that transport technologies had transformed a city in less than 100 years from one which was relatively compact and where most people walked to work, to one where 2.5 million people commuted daily. London, and other cities which followed this model, would never be the same.

The next technological innovation I wish to consider is street lighting. Although medieval cities were lit by torches and lamps, usually from within dwellings, the great change came in 1685 with Edward Heming's contract to light up London,[35] using a system of oil lamps and reflectors. Improvements came with the use of gas from about 1807, and the first electric light in London appeared upon the Embankment in 1878. Paris by this stage "The City of Light" had gas street lighting throughout the city, and this was converted to electric lighting by the 1890s. This made it, technically at least, safer for people to walk the streets at night, so that the second half of the nineteenth century witnessed rapid growth in night-time entertainment in both cities. This is a theme – the evening economy – to which we shall return in Part III.

The next invention is important because it allowed the central areas of cities to be built to higher plot ratios. Paris, for example, was able to build to six and seven storeys as opposed to four or five. But the biggest impact was in the United States, in Chicago and New York. The innovation in question is the elevator, the first of which was presented by Elisha Otis to the Crystal Palace exhibition in New York in 1853. By the 1880s buildings over 200 feet high – skyscrapers – were appearing on the Manhattan skyline. These would rarely exceed ten storeys, however. Much higher building heights became possible with the invention of steel-frame building, then referred to as "Chicago construction", and curtain-wall construction. It was Chicago which led the way in the building of skyscrapers, but New York would soon catch up, driven in part by escalating land prices in Manhattan. Cities the world over, would never same again, both in their spatial structure and the built form.

The final technological example is communications technology. This is far too complex a subject to do justice to here, but my interest lies in how technology impacts on the organization of cities. That is in terms of their economies, cultural life and built form. Even this is a complicated subject as we are dealing with inventions and technologies as diverse as radio, sound recording, cinema, telephones, computers, information technology and the internet. Most of these came into prominence in

---

35 Ackroyd, Peter, *London: the Biography* (London: Chatto and Windus), chapter 48.

the mid to late twentieth century, although the telegraph was well established in the nineteenth century. Cinema, for example, developed from photography to become the first media-industry form of mass entertainment. This had an effect on the social life of cities (the opening of cinemas and closure of theatres), but its more important impact was cultural. In the process an entire industry was born in Los Angeles, and even although its heyday was 1910 to 1950 (when it began to be supplanted by television) it still exerts enormous cultural influence. Smaller centres of film production exist – notably around London, in France and India and Australia, but film is a truly global industry which totally transformed Los Angeles (along with the aerospace industry and the automobile). Meanwhile, radio was responsible for the rise of popular music from the 1920s onwards, the earlier innovators including Bing Crosby who was the first to use audio tape to broadcast his show across three different time zones. From 1948 radio stations in the United States were broadcasting pre-recorded music on vinyl long-playing records (LPs). Magnetic tape allowed the development of multi-track sound recording from about 1954. Barely two years later, Elvis Presley recorded "Heartbreak Hotel". Now, of course, the music itself had to already exist for the recordings to be made. Peter Hall argues convincingly that popular music was an amalgam of blues, jazz, Negro spirituals and Scottish and Irish country music which could only have developed in the southern United States.[36] That it should have occurred in Memphis was in large part due to Elvis himself, Sam Phillips and Sun Records, but also to early innovators such as Muddy Waters, Bo Diddly and Carl Perkins. Again, these technologies not only changed popular culture (and with it dance halls and diners in cities the world over) but they spawned a major industry which still exists today, although under attack from internet music sales.

The most widespread impact from technological development in the late twentieth century has undoubtedly been in computer technology, IT, communications and the convergence of these with entertainment industries (music CDs, internet, DVDs, digital art). The repercussions of these changes are still under debate, but two points are obvious. One is that new technologies have led to new production processes globally, but particular concentrations of activity in particular places. Examples include Silicon Valley, Seattle (Microsoft), Helsinki (mobile phones), Austin, Texas (computer technology), and now Banglalore. These centres of new technology were the fastest growing city economies of the late twentieth century, alongside older cities such as London, New York and Los Angeles. The more widespread impact is that these technologies underpin the growth of the knowledge economy, including the creative and cultural industries, and the global exchange of information and cultural products (images, texts, sounds). This has been accompanied by the "destruction of distance", and also time. For these technologies make it possible to send information and products electronically in a blink of time. It is possible to locate call centres across different time zones, providing customers with around-the-clock access. It is also possible to send a recording made in New Zealand to a record company in New York, or the text for a novel from the south of France to London. Digital technology and the internet make it

---

36 Hall, P., *op. cit.*, 1998.

possible to operate businesses and create new work across time and over continents. But note that it is not the technology in itself that generates product and new wealth but its application to processes of production. If this is true, we might be about to witness a flattening-out of locational advantages across the world allowing "almost infinite decentralization" from higher-cost/less efficient locations to lower-cost/more efficient ones. This would also produce conditions in which people could live and work outside of cities. In the process, as we have seen, cities can now compete globally so that routine clerical work and manufacturing jobs are lost from developed economies to India and China. Nowhere, it would seem, is safe.[37]

But whether this presages the death of the city, as long predicted, is another matter. Most of the activities that are already decentralizing are more routine forms of processing and forms of manufacturing which require controlled environments. But the "hi-touch" activities which require face-to-face human contact *need* cities to flourish. This is especially true of the creative industries, as we shall see, and it is these and similar activities which combine artistic an intellectual creativity and technological innovation. Such business activities will continue to agglomerate because of the importance of business networking, contracting-out and inter-trading. Only if they fail to innovate will cities such as London, New York, San Francisco and Paris lose out in the new economy; and indeed recent evidence suggests most Internet-related high-tech businesses prefer to locate in urban areas.[38] Businesses will need to locate where creative and artistic people can be found, a conclusion which turns orthodox locational analysis on its head.[39] For it is in cities that individuals find stimulation through attending exhibitions and concerts, trying out different restaurants, meeting friends for coffee, going to clubs – generally being part of a creative milieu. This is not to say that some of these elements cannot be found in country towns and villages, but simply not to the same scale, complexity or level of sophistication. People will always need the company of other people – friends and strangers – for large periods of their lives. The conclusion must be that centres of creativity, the arts and a sophisticated urban culture will be the places which will continue to hold economic advantages (provided businesses enjoy low taxation rates). This should not come as a great surprise since, dating from well before the industrial city, this relationship between commerce and culture has been central to the growth of city economies. Face to face contact will remain important both for production activities and for local consumption.

All of these technologies have altered the way we live, the way we make and sell things, and even where things are made and where we live. Other examples we could pursue further include the invention of refrigeration and especially air conditioning

---

37 Atkinson, R., *Technological Change and Cities, Cityscape: A Journal of Policy Development and Research*, 3, 1998, 129–171.

38 Gorman, S. P., "Where are the Web Factories: The Urban Bias of E-Business Location", *Tidschrift voor Economische en Sociale Geografie*, 93, 5, 2002.

39 Hall, P., M. Breheny, R. McQuaid, and D. Hart, *Western Sunrise: The Genesis and Growth of Britain's Major High Tech Corrector* (London: Allen & Unwin, 1987).

so that cities with what were previously considered difficult climates are now liveable. This includes places of high humidity in the South of USA (Atlanta) or Australia (Brisbane) or even parts of Europe (Barcelona, Milan), now perfectly comfortable living environments, and, because of this, good places for businesses to relocate to.

Environment

Since at least the 1980s – and before then in some variants – environmentalism and a growing concern to "green" the cities has gathered momentum.[40] This is a concern not only with the amount and quality of open space in the city, but includes important considerations such as recycling, alternative energy sources, energy conservation, green building design, air quality, water quality, waste disposal and recycling. These and other matters of environmental policy are grouped under the catch-all buzzword "sustainability". Policies and programmes to improve sustainability have a long pedigree in Germany, Scandinavia, the Netherlands, and Canada. The first regional "Green Plan" in the UK was prepared for the South East of England in 1985. A "Green Strategy" for London was prepared in 1991.[41] In 2003, Adelaide in Australia commenced its own "Green Plan".

This is rightly an issue for our age. Yet the point I wish to make here is that the relationship between cities and their local environment is at once unique, complex and has a long history. Cities under mercantile capitalism would tend to locate on rivers and on the coast, or else on established overland routes. Examples would include Baltic seaports of the Hanseatic League, Venice and Lisbon. The important thing was to be able to trade via the transport technologies of the time – sailing ships. Having a hinterland which produced tradeable goods – grains, wool, furs, spices, leather – would also be essential. Movement of goods within countries, between the ports and other centres of population, was achieved by internal waterways and canal systems.

Under industrial capitalism cities created above deposits of raw materials (coal, iron ore, lime) would grow rapidly – Sheffield, Newcastle, Stoke-on-Trent. By the time of "Fordism" cities would need to be close or connected to centres of steel production. Some of the successful ports also became centres for heavy engineering and shipbuilding, Glasgow being a case in point. In the USA, Pittsburgh became the centre of the steel industry, Detroit was "motor city" and Chicago was opening up the mid-West via the railways. The new cities in Australia were all planned as or very near to ports so that grains and wool could be exported from the hinterland. Later still, new industries would bring phenomenal growth to cities because of the climate; Southern California being the most notable example.

---

40 For an interesting discussion, see D. Gordon, *Greening the Cities: Ecologically Sound Approaches to Urban Space* (Montreal, 1990).

41 See L. Greenhalgh, *Greening the Cities in Town and Country*, A. Barnett and R. Scruton (eds) (London: Vintage, 1999).

During all of this there is a close relationship between the built environment (the city) and the natural environment. Thus, the local environment will have its own unique micro-climate and social conditions, making it possible to grow particular types of food, which in turn creates local cuisines. The local environment will have its own topographical features – mountains, coastlines, woods, lakes, rivers – which become significant makers of place. Inhabitants of cities come to form attachments to such features although city growth has always posed a threat to open land, agriculture and biodiversity.

There is, then, a tension running through the relationship between the built and natural environments. That environmental damage has been caused in the past is not in question. However, my own view is that most damage historically was caused under industrial capitalism in the form of mineral extraction, rapid urbanization and pollution of the air, land, and waterways. Under "post-Fordism" leading industries have become progressively cleaner. Under the fifth wave, the lead industries themselves – bio-science, computers, creative industries – require clean environments. This will be true of the developed world, but also in China and India as these economies grow. For it also seems to me that only wealthy economies can afford *not* to cut down the rainforests or cut industrial pollution; poorer economies cannot, unless they are themselves pre-industrial.[42] Rather, the biggest threats to western city and local environments in the coming thirty years will be population growth, sprawl and changes in household formation.

Perhaps the most difficult issue is the car, and the impact on air quality and global warming. My view is that these matters will – as they already are – be addressed by technological improvements, so that engines will become cleaner and may no longer be based on petrol and diesel. This will still leave the issue of traffic congestion to be addressed, but I see this as an urban management rather than an environmental issue *per se*. The basic point is this. All cities have a relationship with their environments, whether as sources of food, raw materials, water supply; or even as symbolic landscapes. This has always been the case. The trick for city managers is to retain a balance between the city, its built form, the wider environment and wealth creation.

Governance

The Scottish economist Adam Smith wrote in 1775: "Little else is requisite to carry a state to the highest degree of opulence from the lowest barbarianism but peace, easy taxes, and a tolerable administration of justice." This seems perfectly true, although during the 20th century the role of government would extend into areas such as health care, social work and welfare benefits. In any event, according to our model of city development, governance, good or bad, is a factor condition in the growth or otherwise of city economies. It must be stressed that governments do not create

---

42 For a discussion of how improvements in prosperity bring about improvements in environmental conditions, reductions in poverty and greater protection of natural habits see B. Lomborg *The Skeptical Environmentalist*, Cambridge University Press, 1998.

wealth and prosperity – this is the outcome of trade and commerce – but they can provide an environment in which trade and commerce can flourish, or not.

The first requirement is peace and justice administered under the rule of law. This is similar to the "social contract" of Thomas Hobbes[43] where the individual's rights to behave as he or she pleases is tempered by respect for law, in return for peace and stability. It was often to pay for protection and security that people were most prepared to pay taxes – to live within the city walls of the medieval city, for example. By contrast, when walled cities could no longer guarantee protection, markets grew up outside of the city walls, partly to avoid taxes, or else in completely new locations. In our own times, arguably the fastest growing of economies of the last fifteen years have been Dublin, Dubai, and Las Vegas, all of which – as well as other advantages – have relatively low taxation requirements for business. The same can be said of Singapore.[44] History is also cluttered with examples of cities that, once thriving, fell into decline through (usually a combination) of high taxes and restrictive work practices. Raymond Unwin blamed the relative economic backwardness of the Scottish burghs compared to the little cities of England and Continental Europe, on a rigid separation between the work of craftsmen and the work of trade.[45]

Of course what this analysis omits is the fact that since the 1880s the state has been drawn into building infrastructure (or in the case of the railways enabling land purchase) and the direct provision of social services. Historically this was to correct the spread of disease in London, Paris, Berlin, New York and Chicago, and also to provide homes for the urban poor. Hospital services and schools would follow so that by the 1930s Britain at least was well on the road to the Welfare State. The Beveridge Report of 1944 systematized state social welfare in the form of health insurance, pensions, unemployment benefits and social security – "cradle to grave socialism".

These measures undoubtedly addressed the issues of the time (from clean drinking water and a system of underground sewers in the 1880s to the 1947 Education Act), and also contributed to economic growth in the 1950s (through improved health, numeracy and literacy). But since the 1970s, it has become increasingly clear that such programmes cannot be paid for without taxation levels which are too high.[46] It seems likely that governments everywhere will need to move to models of health and pension provision based on investment and private insurance, but that is another story.

What does seem clear is that governments will have a choice on spending priorities in future, only if the problem of welfare dependency can be addressed. The choice, it seems to me, is between spending programmes which boost or underpin economic development and those which remain essentially social services. Thus, capital

---

43   This notion dates from Plato and Lucretius but its chief exponent was Hobbes who argued that the creation of the State in turn created mutual obligations between the State and the people.

44   Jones Lang Lasalle, *Rising Urban Stars* (World Winning Cities Program, 2003).

45   Unwin, R., *Studies in Economic History*, as quoted in Jacobs, J., *The Economy of Cities, op. cit.*, see pp. 12, 134, 156, 177, 184.

46   See "The Overload Thesis … "; Bacon, R. and Eltis, W., *Britain's Economic Problem: Too Few Producers* (London: Macmillan, 1976).

infrastructure works on roads, airports, and rail connections will remain important, as will investment in up-to-date communications technology. The other important spending areas will be in entrepreneurial skills and artistic and creative innovation. If this analysis is correct then good governance in the future will more or less revolve around the following: peace, law and order and stability; low business taxation; investment in necessary capital projects; investment in training and skills development; and education.

Property Booms

Peter Hall[47] has argued, that because of the Kuznets curve (the 25 year construction peak as proposed by Simon Kuznets, discussed earlier), each Kondratieff cycle has two booms in construction activity, one coming with the upswing and the other "just before the descent into depression: the 1900s and 1920s are obvious examples". These would correspond with the mid 1950s and the early 1970s during the fourth Kondratieff Wave. Hall argues that the property boom during an upswing is due to investment in new plant, property and transport infrastructure; while the second property boom is characterized by speculation in land and property as the rate of profit in the economy falls – investors switch from stocks and shares into land and property. This certainly would seem to explain what happened in the 1950s and early 1970s, but what of the booms of the 1930s, or more recently the late 1980s and *fin-de-siecle*? My own view is that, just as there are three Juglar cycles to a Kuznets (and therefore six to a Kondratieff), there are two property cycles to a Kuznets, and therefore four to a Kondratieff. This would mean, roughly speaking, there would be a property boom peak every thirteen to fifteen years. If true, we would expect to find property booms peaking in 1959, 1973, 1987, and 2002. Of these, we know that there were strong booms followed by property crashes in 1973 and 1987, the first owing to the end of the upswing and the second at a point where speculation in land and property became fevered following a stockmarket collapse. The major growth boom occurred during the 1950s (with transport infrastructure opening up new viable locations, and also rebuilding after the war), and its continuation into the 1960s was most likely simply a reflection of growing general prosperity. The boom of the late 1990s would appear to be a reaction to low returns in the stock market.

Thus, we can posit that there are four important property booms to every Kondratieff wave, as follows. First, the boom of the first quarter of the Kondratieff driven by new investment in transport technologies and construction, with the largest increases in value during the second seven years of the upswing – the 1900s and the late 1950s. This period of property development is an outcome of general economic growth. Second, the boom of the early part of the second quarter occurs where increases in general prosperity feed through into home ownership – the

47 Hall, P. *op. cit.* 1998, p. 616.

early 1920s, and the 1960s. This period marks the spread of wealth into new home ownership, and is often associated with over-development and urban spawl.

The boom of the end of the third quarter, that is the crisis point at which the rate of profit becomes negative and investment switches into speculative property trading – the late 1920s and the late 1980s. This is a speculative boom which inevitably crashes. Finally, the boom of the end of the downswing occurs when the rate of return on other investments is historically low – the late 1930s (interrupted by the War), the late 1990s and early 2000s. This boom makes up some of the losses of the preceding crash and reflects the fact that the downswing is beginning to bottom out. The boom at the beginning of the upwave may not be especially noticeable, at first, compared to the others, but is an important indication that the upswing is underway. I would expect this to become evident by 2010 as the fifth Kondratieff Wave takes hold.

5. OLD MONEY AND NEW WORK

City economies can only grow if there is general capital growth worldwide. If the world economy is depressed, then growth in particular city and city-regions is likely to be sporadic if it exists at all. Thus, in addition to maintaining a healthy balance between commerce, culture and form, successful cities will also need good timing. They need to be ready to take advantage of the upswings, to have the technology of the day available, and to encourage entrepreneurs to make the necessary commercial applications. They will also need to be able to distinguish between property booms which herald new wealth creation, and those which are more or less speculative.

Schumpeter wrote of the association of innovation with "the rise to leadership of New Men" – and women these days (Schumpeter was writing in 1939). If you are a young innovator, entrepreneur or businessperson, then the best time to be at your peak is as the long-wave cycle turns from depression to the start of an upswing. This is precisely the position the world economy is in now. This implies that people now in their teens, 20s and early 30s are the innovators and entrepreneurs of the next twenty-five years, plus those in middle age who do not suffer from hardening of their entrepreneurial arteries. By contrast, the best time to be an inventor is in the middle of a slump (most recently in the 1930s and the early 1980s), for it is at the bottom of each cycle that key inventions are made (or perhaps, more exactly, are ripe to be commercialized). Primary scientific and technological research will always hopefully, be ongoing. But we can posit that the crucial times in which new research is undertaken is during the second half of the downswing, that is during the fourth quarter of the Kondratieff Wave.

This notion of "New Men" is not too dissimilar to the concept of the "paradigm shift" as developed by Thomas Kuhn,[48] and discussed earlier. Paradigm shifts in science would include the work of Copernicus and Galileo, Newton and Einstein; the development of anatomy as a field of science; chemistry during the nineteenth century; the theory of evolution; the Enlightenment of late eighteenth century

---

48 Kuhn, T. S., *op. cit.*, 1962.

Edinburgh and Paris; the rise of modernism in the 1920s; the discovery of micro-biotics and DNA. In most of these cases, the established "order of things" – to borrow from Michel Foucault – was challenged and in some cases overthrown. Progress, it seems, depends on change, and change depends on progress.

The point is that individuals – Schumpeter's "New Men" – who want to succeed must be in the right place at the right time, and must also be open to new ideas and technologies. Much the same can be said of cities. In this sense, the past fifteen years have been critical in shaping the economic urban geography of the next fifty years, even although this is by no means self-evident. The next two to three years will be crucial. If your city hasn't made its move, it's almost too late to start.

For there is a final simple truth, first proposed by Jane Jacobs. In *The Economy of Cities*[49] she argues that the primary conflict is not between competing existing businesses, nor between labour and capital as economic classes as the Marxists would have us believe. Rather the important conflict is between "people whose interests are with already crystallized economic activities, and those whose interests are with the emergence of new economic activities". Where established interests predominate – as in the guilds of medieval London or the Scottish burghs – to the detriment of the new, then only economic stagnation can follow: Vienna, Glasgow, Manchester, Pittsburg, Adelaide, Birmingham and Chicago. Where new activities come to predominate, economic growth will result: Los Angeles, Tokyo, New York, Dublin, Austin, Seattle, 1990s Manchester, Barcelona. Only the larger cities, to date, seem to be diverse enough to move from one long wave cycle to the next: New York, London, Tokyo, Los Angeles, maybe Hong Kong. In circumstances were new growth is a possibility, the role of city and state governments is not to defend the old against the new, or simply to remain neutral, but it is to actively promote new forms of economic growth. Otherwise, as Jacobs notes[50] cities will lapse "into stagnation for the benefit of people who have already become powerful". Governments need to keep opportunities for economic and technological development open, not closed.

At the end of the day, there are only a handful of means by which city and urban regional economies can grow. One is the application of new technologies to existing production processes and services so as to create new work and new divisions of labour, as we have seen. More important than this even is the extension of new technologies to create new products and therefore economic sectors. The growth sectors of the fifth wave will be: biotechnology in relation to the human body; marine and crop biotechnology; environmental husbandry, including protecting habitats, waste recycling and the repair of polluted places, alternative forms of energy generation, notably solar power; and water management; digital and creative industries, linked to communications technologies and computer convergence; be-spoke objects – contemporary crafts, furniture, fine art, linked to fashion; cuisine and food.

Growth can also be secured through enlarged markets, and by increasing the stock of exports. Meanwhile the non-exporting local economy can also be stimulated

---

49 Jacobs, J., 1969, *op. cit*, 249.
50 Jacobs, J., 1969, *op. cit.*, 250.

through enlarging the pool of wage-earners, and thereby increasing demand locally. With the passage of time, city economic activities can be transplanted into new locations within the city region, opening up new locations to increases in prosperity and value. Finally, investing local capital in new ventures in other places, including competing centres of trade, also leads to growth.

All of this can only be achieved if new work is allowed to grow even if this is against the established interests of old money. This point, it seems to me, can be transferred to artistic and creative forms too. We might refer to this as traditional forms (say in theatre, dance or music concerts) versus new art and contemporary design; or to new architecture as opposed to post-modernism and replica heritage. If your city spends most of its time subsidizing old art and trying to replicate old architecture, then it is likely that your economy is dominated by old money and established interests. If your city embraces new art forms, new technology and new architecture, then the chances are it is succeeding in generating new work too. That is the way to go.

The New Economy and the Creative Industries

Part I argues that cities in the coming period must develop and/or maintain a dynamic and innovative economy, made up of exporting firms and producer networks, and using technology as a source of new work. The leading industries of the Fifth Wave will be part of a larger knowledge economy, and these will include the creative industries. This is demonstrated by reference to the phenomenal growth of London's creative economy since the 1980s.

1. THE ECONOMY OF CITIES

Cities have always been the great centres of innovation, both technological and cultural. It is in cities that risks are taken, problems raised, experiments tested, ideas generated; moreover, it is historically to cities that creative people gravitate, for employment, stimulus or the comfort of strangers. City economies, where they work well, are a complicated process of adding value, exporting products, services and expertise, import substitution and, above all, creating new work.[1]

The gloomy science of economics, in the modern sense, began with the publication of *The Wealth of Nations*, in three parts, by Adam Smith in the 1770s.[2] Smith argued that economics is the study of the production, distribution, exchange and consumption of goods and services under a system of markets for those goods and services. He argued that it was this process that led to wealth creation and improvements in prosperity. Smith saw that the more complex an economy's "division of labour", the more wealth would tend to be created. He supported his arguments by examining not only this new concept of the division of labour, but also the pricing of commodities, wages of labour, rent, the origins and uses of money, the accumulation of capital, interest and the division of stocks and shares. This has come to be known as micro-economics, concerned as it is with market conditions, supply and demand, commodity prices, wage rates, interest and rent. Businesses compete with each other to provide goods and services to satisfy consumer needs and aspirations, expressed as consumer

---

1   Urban Cultures Ltd, *Prospects and Planning Requirements for London's Creative Industries* (London Planning Advisory Committee, 1994), Preface.

2   Smith, A., *The Wealth of Nations* 1776, version published by Penguin Classics, London, 1986.

demand. This set of relationships underpins all forms of wealth creation, and is the most dynamic system of economic development in history.

Smith's model is still applied today, even although it tends to be considered within a framework that also contains macro-economics (the largely ill-informed quest for equilibrium in the economy by balancing unemployment against inflation) and monetary policy (the control of the money supply to prevent governments printing paper money of declining value). Even so, micro-economics undoubtedly helps in our understanding of competition, industry sectors, and the ups and downs of commodity prices. Where Smith was mistaken was to assume that the division of labour would of itself lead to greater wealth creation. As Jane Jacobs would point out, this is only the case if the labour so organized is producing "new work" that has a value in exchange.[3]

Jacobs proposed a model of city economic growth, which she refers to as "The Two Reciprocating Systems of City Growth".[4] Her argument is that cities achieve growth primarily through a process of exporting goods and services in order to earn surpluses with which to purchase imports. As the economy develops, more and more exports generate greater surpluses, during which time the division of labour amongst local producers becomes more complex. Various supply chains develop, so that networks of businesses provide inputs to the final export product. (An example in clothing might be the weaver, the button-maker, the stitcher, all supplying to a shirt exporting business). Some of the producer service businesses might themselves become exporters in their own right. The outcome should be a dynamic network of local businesses, a good proportion of which must export, others of which are producer input suppliers, and over time there will be a continual process of mergers, breakaways, new start-ups ... and failures too.

The next stage is very important, for over time a strong and/or growing city economy will develop the skills and the capacity to replace or substitute imports and make these products locally. Jacobs applies this model to the Japanese motorcycle industry in the 1920s, which grew from bicycle repair workshops which initially serviced and repaired imported English bicycles. It grew to include marques such as Honda, Suzuki and Yamaha. By this means, a city economy can then import other goods with its export surpluses and meantime the newly replaced imports may become another successful export product. Of course, during this time the city economy continues to export its existing goods and services, while the local division of labour becomes more diversified and complex. The wealth that is created is then re-invested in productive capacity, raw materials or stock; and a good proportion of this will also be spent by local citizens on consumer goods and services. The growth of local consumer spending in periods of rapid economic growth, will closely be followed by, and in turn will create, increasing demand for new products – chocolates and coffee, fashions and jewels.

---

3   Jacobs, J., *Cities and the Wealth of Nations* (New York: Random House, 1984).

4   Jacobs, J. *The Economy of Cities*, (London: Jonathan Cape, 1969).

Jacobs goes on to demonstrate how these processes inter-lock and go on to produce multiplier effects for both exports (more local producers and exporters) and import-replacement (to meet local demand initially but later as new exports). She uses the examples of sixteenth century London, Tokyo in the early twentieth century, and Pittsburgh and Chicago, to show that cities where these processes are self-generating and dynamic can enjoy periods of "explosive growth". Of course, they can also go into decline. Indeed, Jacobs notes that "... the processes have to be reinvented in cities which have become economically stagnant, for unless they are, nothing else can halt the city's decline".[5] It is just this sort of approach that is having to be followed in cities such as Leipzig, whose economy had virtually died under Communism.[6]

1990 saw the publication of Michael Porter's *The Competitive Advantage of Nations*.[7] Porter argues that competitive success tends to concentrate in particular industries and groups of inter-connected industries. For Porter, the determinants of competitive advantage are four-fold: business strategy, structure and rivalry so as to encourage innovation, investment and competition; "factor conditions" notably the presence of specialist skills, technology and infrastructure; related and supporting industries who supply specialist services and imports, and access to technology and innovation; and "demand conditions" in the form of sophisticated and demanding customers.

Porter argues that successful industries tend to co-locate in dynamic clusters. A "cluster" is a grouping of industries linked together through customer, supplier and other relationships which enhance competitive advantage. These clusters are characterized by the presence of internationally competitive firms, which also continuously upgrade and innovate. This is broadly consistent with the economic literature on industrial districts and the work on "agglomeration" by Marshall,[8] dating from the late 19th century. Marshall argued that there were competitive advantages to firms who "agglomerate", because of access to available skilled labour, shared technologies and inter-trading between firms (a form of Smith's division of labour). This happens at key locations within cities, but also – for certain activities – across wider city regions as mobility improves. It is these places – districts, cities and city regions – that are the engines of economic development. This relationship of exporting, inter-trading, wealth creation and the development of local economies was present in Europe from about the tenth century onwards, but is particularly evident under early mercantile capitalism, industrial capitalism and late capitalism.

---

5   Ibid., p. 198.

6   Gerkens, K., *Strategies and Tools for Shrinking Cities – the Example of Leipzig*, paper presented to the International Cities, Town Centres and Communities Conference, June 2005, Capricorn Coast, Queensland.

7   Porter, M. *The Competitive Advantage of Nations* (London: Collier Macmillan, 1990).

8   Marshall, A., *Principles of Economics* (London: Macmillan, 1920).

However, what this model does not address is why there should be periodic booms and slumps in the capitalist economy, and why particular cities benefit most under certain booms. For an explanation of why this happens, we must look to the long waves of capitalist economic development, as conceptualized by Kondratieff, whereby economic growth and wealth creation follow a pattern of 30 year growth cycles interspersed with 25 year slumps. Since the late 1780s, there have been four long waves.[9] The first of these began in England and France in the 1780s, following a period of deep depression made all the worse by the South Sea Bubble in England and the Mississippi Bubble in France. The depression was characterized by a collapse in raw material prices, especially wheat, and bottomed out in around 1783. By 1789, prices were beginning to rise again, surging from 1798, during which time Britain and France were at war. A further surge occurred in 1812 but within two years prices and economic activity had passed their peak. A sharp downturn occurred in 1815, followed by a short-lived period of "secondary prosperity", known at the time as the "Era of Good Feelings". By 1819, the economy was once again in recession, triggered by a collapse in wheat prices, and followed by a similar collapse in cotton a few years later. Land prices in the United States fell, and the long depression would last from the 1820s to the 1840s. Between 1814 and 1843, prices fell by 59%. The first wave had lasted 54 years.

The second wave kicked in from 1843, led by industrial production, and an upturn in exports and commodity prices. Between 1852 and 1854, consumer prices leapt by 33%. The peak came in 1864. In 1873, a series of financial panics in Germany signalled the onset of a deep depression. This would last until 1896, so that the second wave lasted 54 years. Prices began to recover in the late 1890s, and began to increase steadily until 1920 when the commodity market collapsed. This time the speculative bubble that burst was in Argentina. The recession lasted for two years and was followed by a period of secondary prosperity – the "Roaring Twenties" during which time fortunes were made on the stock market, fashions changed dramatically and liquor consumption increased. The crash came in 1929, followed by a severe depression which hit its lowest level in 1934. The recovery was led to a significant extent in rearming for war, but also from the emergence of new technologies and, later, consumer products. The third wave also lasted some 54 years.

The fourth wave was clearly underway by the mid 1950s. Britain was booming, as indeed were the United States, Germany and later Japan. This time around the growth industries were civil aviation, plastics, pharmaceuticals, household goods and consumer electronics. The upwave lasted throughout the 1960s and early 1970s, peaking in 1974. The short recession of 1973–75, was followed by the "consumer boom" of the mid 1970s, driven by rising house prices and the expansion of credit. The main secondary depression kicked in from the early 1980s, and was evidenced at the time by falling commodity and factory gate prices, falling oil prices and falling property prices. This much was evident when Beckman wrote *The Downwave*[10]

---

9   Beckman, R., *The Downwave* (London: Pan Books, 1983).
10 Ibid.

(published in 1983). Beckman went on to forecast the stock market collapse of 1987, the property boom of the late 1980s and the long recession throughout the 1990s. This was characterized by very low growth in the 1990s as the depression bottomed-out, a stagnant stock market and a switch of investment once more into property. The stock market only began to make real gains in 2004, signalling the start of the fifth wave. The fourth wave lasted from around 1949 to 2003, again a period of 54 years.

A pattern across the waves can be seen. Peaks in commodity prices occur ever 54 years – in 1920 and 1974, and in 1868 and 1814. These peaks are followed by a "corrective" recession which last for two years or so, in turn followed by a short recovery. There then follows a stock market collapse, as in 1929 and 1987, a fall in interest rates, a property boom and a deep depression which lasts some 15 years. That is, until the next upwave begins. This then certainly appears to explain the existence of periodic booms in economic development and wealth creation, as brought about by new technologies, production processes and consumer goods and services. Cities which came to have a golden age of prosperity are those who were positioned to take advantage of the new industries, either because of their existing status as entrepots, because a new technology was invented there, because a new generation of entrepreneurs were at hand or because a tradition of innovation and enterprise was maintained even during the preceding depression. Thus, Manchester and cotton, Glasgow and ship-building, Pittsburgh and steel, Detroit and automobiles, Bristol and Seattle and aerospace, Silicon Valley and semi-conductors, Tokyo and consumer electronics, Helsinki and mobile phones, Seattle and software. Some cities, however, lose their ascendant position as leaders in new industries, others are the products of short-lived booms which never again materialized. In the 1920s, Buenos Aires was the fastest growing city in the world, but this was built on speculative fever rather than real wealth creation.

As Jane Jacobs has pointed out, the cradle of the industrial revolution was not in fact Manchester at all, but Birmingham[11] with all its wonderfully inventive new entrepreneurs in the mid 18th century. It was in Birmingham that steam was first harnessed to industrial production, that the world's first iron bridge was built and that the great pottery industry of the Midlands would grow. This came about because of the inventiveness of people such as Erasmus Darwin and James Watt, Josiah Wedgewood, the preacher and chemist Joseph Priestley and the great entrepreneur Matthew Bolton and his "manufactory" at Soho, just outside of Birmingham. Others involved at the time included the Scots chemist James Kier and the clockmaker John Whitehurst. Known as the Lunar Society of Birmingham, because they met monthly on the Monday night nearest to the full moon (so they could ride home by the light of the moon), these were the amateur experimenters, inventors and entrepreneurs that shaped the modern world.[12] Many of them were either Scottish or had studied in Edinburgh and Glasgow in the preceding years. Between them

---

11 Jacobs, *op. cit.*, 1969.

12 Unglow, J., *The Lunar Men: The Friends Who made the Future* (London: Faber and Faber, 2002).

they would alter the course of geology and chemistry, experiment with electricity, develop the bone china and glass industries, build canals, develop steam power, experiment in mechanical engineering, develop the science of botany and even write on the *Construction of Roads and Carriages* (Richard Lovell Edgeworth, 1813). The last surviving member of the Lunar Society, Samuel Galton – merchant banker and experimenter in optics, colour and light, died in 1832, some 25–30 years after Darwin, Bolton and Priestley.

We have seen, then, that four different eras of capitalist economic development coincide with the Kondratieff long-waves of the capitalist business cycle. During these various eras of capitalist economic development, the way in which production itself was organized also varied. Thus early capitalism was based on craft production organized by guilds and the merchant class; early industrial capitalism produced the "Dark Satanic Mills" and a more rapid urbanization; industrial capitalism was based on factory production and was organized by industrial producers – the so-called Fordism; and late capitalism was and is characterized by flexible specialization, the putting-out mode of production and is largely organized by service producers. It also would appear that different forms of production can survive and be carried over into a later age when the dominant mode of production is changing. Thus the bespoke tailoring of Savile Row and the jewellery industry of Hatton Gardens, both in London, still operate as craft guilds, more or less. Likewise, the film industry of the 1920s to the 1950s was essentially a form of factory production organized by the studio system. Whereas Hollywood today is a hybrid of the studio system combined with a classic post-Fordist network of independent producers and sub-contracted specialists. Industries such as the car industry in Japan or Korea are post-Fordist to the extent that production models are differentiated, but remain largely Fordist in that production occurs along assembly lines. Modern computers were invented in the 1940s and 1950s, and would later revolutionize electronics and consumer household goods; yet their biggest impact is only now being witnessed in the age of digitization and the convergence of computer technology and all manner of service industries.

In the attached diagram (Fig. 1.1), I have plotted instances of primary, applied and derived technological advances. This reveals that the technologies that gave rise to the cotton industry were invented by Kay, Hargreaves and Arkwright in the mid 18th century: the boom which followed would last until 1810 or thereabouts. The technologies of steel pressing, steam engines, railways and steam-ships were invented in the early 19th century, prompting a boom that would last until the 1880s. Important inventions by Otto and Langen, Benz and Daimler, Edison, Alexander Graham Bell and Marconi would develop as the new industries of the 20th century. Innovations by Turing, Hewlett and Packhard, Jack Kilby at Texas Instruments[13] and

---

13 Jack Kilby invented the first monolithic integrated circuit, the micro-chip, in 1958. He shared the Nobel Prize for Physics in 2000 for his part in the development of the information age. Kilby's microchip has been compared in importance to the steam engine. Kilby went on to head teams that built the first military systems and computers using integrated circuits. He died in 2005.

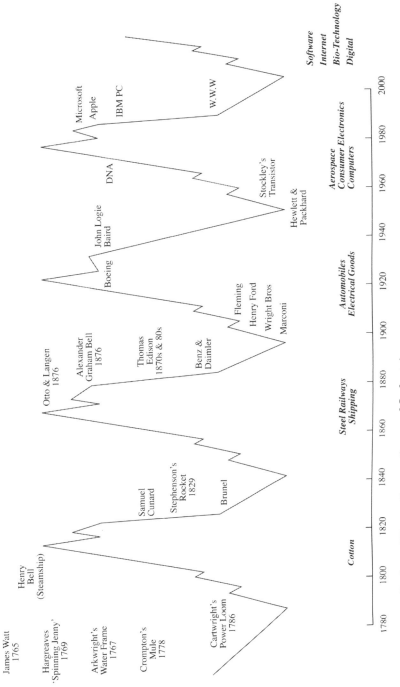

Figure 1.1 The Long Waves: Innovations and Industries

Source: John Montgomery.

Stockley would lead to the computer age, micro-chips and consumer electronics. New innovations in software in the 1970s would enable the development of personal computers, lap-tops and various communications devices, as well as the Internet. It is notable that most of the primary inventions occur at the end of a down-wave, that is to say as scientific and technological devices of the previous paradigm are over-exploited. So it seems likely that the origins of the next Kondratieff Wave (2004 to around 2060) are already in place. That these industries will emerge from IT, communications, digitization and forms of cultural creativity is in little doubt. They will also include bio-technology and environmental technologies. Many of these will continue to be organized on a post-Fordist model for several years at least; others will need to change more rapidly, that is, where the relationship between the producer and the consumer is closest. Of particular interest is the argument that culture and creativity should be seen as an economy. The creative industries is one of the key growth sectors of the fifth wave. As in previous waves, the impact of the knowledge and creative economies will be most keenly felt in the cities.

KNOWLEDGE ECONOMIES AND CREATIVE CITIES

Writing in 1990, Charles Handy observed that the organization of work was being re-structured, and with it everyday life.[14] He argued that economic organizations would become larger through a process of mergers and takeovers, but that they would also sub-contract increasing amounts of work to small and medium entrepreneurs, and to the "do it yourself economy". Handy argued that this was especially true for economic activities where computer technology was changing the nature of work itself, the "knowledge economy". This was characterized, according to Handy, by the "three 'I's": information, intelligence and innovation. Information is the very stuff of the knowledge age, intelligence refers to the skills required to make sense and use of that information, and innovation refers to technology and new means of doing things. Handy refers to this as "clever people doing clever things with clever machines". The Henley Centre[15] estimated, as long ago as 1988, that fifty per cent of all occupations in Britain require brain skills rather than manual skills. This is the so-called "knowledge economy" (Table 1.1).

Sustaining this level of "brain skill" requires an increase in the numbers of people entering higher education, so that education itself becomes a growth sector. Not all of these occupations are "post-industrial"; indeed, many of them still involve the making of goods (rather than the delivery of services), for example, films, books, computers and so on. The point is that these activities are becoming more not less important, and the blend of economics and technology they are in part driven by will continue to reorganize manufacturing as well as the service economy.

---

14 Handy, C., *The Age of Unreason* (London: Century Business, 1990).
15 The Henley Centre for Forecasting, Henley, Buckinghamshire, UK.

Table 1.1 Knowledge Economy Activities

Technology	Business	Public Sector	Cultural Industries
data processing	selling	teaching	creative arts
computer software	accountancy	office work	architecture
R & D	banking	public service	design
communications	real estate	administration	music
post &	law	psychiatry	the media
telecomms	management	psychology	films
	advertising	social work	theatre
	stockbroking	church	photography
	journalism	trade unions	book publishing
	conferences	government	printing
	consultancy	local government	Museums/galleries
			television

Source: The Henley Centre for Forecasting, adapted to include the cultural industries.

Allied to these changes, part cause and part effect, are the changes in technology which enable people to work and live in different ways. Since the late 1980s, the following have been most evident:

- e-mail, faxes, portable phones and lap-top computers, so that people can run businesses almost at any location; this means that businesses tend to employ fewer people than before, and that the problem of geography has to some extent been overcome by communications technologies which shorten time;
- advances in medical research so that people now live longer; in the process medical research has become big business, a knowledge industry in itself, spawning new fields, new ways of working and new companies outside of but working alongside the public health sector;
- tele-shopping and telecommuting; people can order deliveries via their e-mail, TV and the Cable system; rather than commute to work in a central office every day, they will work at home – the office bedroom, connected by fax, modem, phone and computer, or at a localized work centre which itself is wired up to other centres and perhaps a central office. For these people, the daily grind of the rush hour becomes a thing of the past.

Of course, these trends do not in a direct sense affect everyone in employment, but they do affect the core workers around whom companies will tend to organize their location strategies. This is a notable conclusion of an important study by Mike Breheny and colleagues on the pharmaceutical and hi-tech industries of southern England in the 1990s.[16] Breheny's research found that hi-tech, largely research and laboratory-based industries such as micro-electronics and pharmaceuticals in large part arranged their location decisions around the perceived lifestyle wants of key workers: that is to say clean air, access to open countryside, good schools, lower congestion, countryside hobbies and pursuits. For the first time – in the UK at least – it was clear that being able to attract key staff was a prime consideration in deciding where to build a new facility.

Before discussing the nature of the knowledge-based economy in more detail, it is useful to recall how traditional, high-volume industrial manufacturing evolved during most of the 20th century, and how it is currently changing. There are two key elements in this process – the way in which the production process has changed, and the growing influence of the consumer. On the production, supply side, the paradigm for industrial manufacturing was that developed by Henry Ford as part of the mass production of relatively low-cost cars in Detroit, called the Model A and the Model T. In doing so, Ford changed not only the mobility pattern of millions of Americans but also the structure of industrial production. His name has been used to describe this structure. "Fordism" refers to an industrial era based on the mass production of standardized products. This means that each task in the production process can be isolated, divided into its component parts and reproduced over and over. Initially, this was done by sub-dividing activities so that human labour could become as machine-like as possible, and time and motion principles were applied to "scientific management" of the workforce based on ideas developed by F.W. Taylor.

Industrial firms based on these principles grew to enormous size, employing thousands of people, and would later be known as "trans-national" – they produced and traded across the boundaries of a number of different countries. However, over time it became apparent on the production side that the workers became tired, bored, ill and continually needed to draw wages, however "scientifically" they were managed. As both a cost-cutting and production-enhancing consequence, highly automated techniques were devised to reduce the need for labour input, including robotics. In comparison with old craft-based traditions, in particular, with their emphasis on individual skill, the workforce became "deskilled", often doing little more than monitoring and making small adjustments to the machines working on the production line. This process is demonstrated satirically in Charlie Chaplin's film *Modern Times*. Although output increased dramatically, the production process became highly automated, and the economic control of the firm became increasingly bureaucratic, hierarchical and centralized at the company's head office. The sheer volume of this mass production system – exported throughout the world – was taken

---

16 Breheny, M., Hart, D. and Howells, J., *Health and Wealth: The Development of the Pharmaceutical Industry in the South East* (Stevenage: South East Economic Development Strategy, 1993). See also Hart, D., Breheny, M., Doak, J., Montgomery, J. and Strike, J., *Bright Green: an Industrial Strategy for Hertfordshire* (Hertfordshire County Council, 1994).

up by increased consumption through higher levels of disposable income. Eventually the majority of consumers in the more advanced economies acquired a substantial array of goods including cars, refrigerators, domestic appliances, and TVs.

A parallel set of forces was also at work which related to increasing consumer choice. Certainly during most of the first half of the 20th century consumption was as standardized as the early production lines, hence Ford's reputed famous quote about his Model T, that "you can have any colour you like, as long as it's black". The supply side emphasis during this period was on scale, standardization and assembly line production. Of course, this approach is still partly true of some industries. Increasingly though, even cars are not assembled in one place, and there are many variations on the model one can buy – and the colour one can order. Today, industrial goods are no longer a producers' market. For a number of reasons including technological change of the kind mentioned above, increased worldwide competition, and growing consumer sophistication, the demand-side of production matters now more than ever. Customers in the developed countries are less prepared to accept a single, standardized product. They are more choosey, and more conscious of both value and quality. In the latter part of the twentieth century things changed with regard to both the location and the nature of industrial production – and there is no conceivable reason to believe that this change will be reversed in the near future. Standardized mass production has given way to "customization" with great product variation and smaller production runs to cater for a wide variety of tastes and the consumption of different, and changing, types of lifestyle goods from jeans to cruise ships. This makes it difficult for producers and market researchers to guarantee sales success for any kind of produced goods over a protracted period of time. So goods and advertising campaigns must be constantly updated to attract the consumer, increasing numbers of whom are striving to be "different", or more simply, individual. Consumer choice and production innovation, in the widest sense of that term, are increasingly the key to industrial success.

There are a number of ways of achieving this success – all are based on the systematic application of knowledge. Computer-aided design and manufacture (CAD-CAM), for example, enables production to be less standardized and geared towards carefully researched "niches" in the consumer market; rather than, as in the past, the market as a whole. Many of the new industries – computers, pharmaceuticals, business services – are office and laboratory based as much, or more, than factory based, as in the past. Small, specialists batches of goods are produced for different market segments, and as a consequence flexible production systems, and firms with flexible workforces, have been created – which are far more adaptable and agile than their Fordist predecessors. They are also, as a general rule, smaller than their, often, lumbering forebears which until very recently were viewed as the very models of modern industrial production. In 1993, for example, IBM declared the biggest corporate loss in history and made thousands of people redundant worldwide. Large firms throughout the world are continually seeking to reduce their size – particularly in terms of full-time employees. If small is beautiful, then large is becoming unsightly.

But the introduction of flexible production systems is not solely a reflection of changes in consumption, it is also geared at increasing the efficiency of labour, lowering overheads, and through the application of new technology, achieving stronger control over stock levels and distribution. Firms constantly innovate to compete effectively, so that while the horizontal competition between firms is producing a concentration of ownership (fewer and larger corporations – although often with smaller workforces overall), the compulsion to innovate is weakening vertical coordination within companies. Firms and their products must be more flexible to achieve this innovation; quality must be maintained and improved and new forms of modular working employed. The new industries and new production techniques are therefore based on: niche marketing; careful design; the use of advanced technology both in production and as products; market segmentation; more flexible and decentralized forms of production and; perhaps above all, highly skilled, well paid and highly motivated core staff. Industrialists compete for the best graduates, and the increasing "ruralization" of industry – outside of, but often adjacent to, major urban areas – is often a reflection of the lifestyle preferences of key workers (the scientists, technicians, computer experts and accountants) rather than being based purely on cost-based corporation location analysis. This is true in the UK of the high-tech sector around Cambridge (silicon fen), for example, and the electronics sector in Berkshire along the M4 Corridor. It is not true, however, of all knowledge industries, as we shall see.

It is sometimes suggested that a knowledge-based economy is synonymous with the growth of the service sector and that we are entering a "post-industrial era". This assertion is not necessarily correct. Not all of the emerging occupations will be "post-industrial"; indeed, may of them still involve the making and modifying (or "customizing") of goods – including manufactured goods (in addition to the delivery of services). These goods include the production of information, for example, television programmes, books, reports on stocks and shares, and the making and distribution of music. These are the new industries of culture.

Thus, post-Fordism or "flexible specialization" is a move away from labour-intensive manufacturing. It represents a long-term shift within the process and organization of economic production, away from mass production and standardized products for mass consumption, to an era of "flexible specialization" and lifestyle or differentiated consumption. This is producing a new geography of production. Assembly lines are moved to countries where unit labour costs are lower. But the designers, technicians, market researchers and advertising agents are all based in countries with more direct links to markets. Many of them, moreover, are sub-contracted, so that the large producers, Benneton[17] for example, is in reality a purchaser-retailer-marketer buying goods from myriad small suppliers, and front-loading sales through the use of consultant image makers. Only those producers who come up with good designs at competitive costs, and as small batch "limited

---

17 Murray, R., *Benetton Britain, Marxism Today*, July 1985.

editions", are retained. Creativity needs to be applied, and new goods and services must emerge if new episodes of wealth creation are to occur.

3. THE CULTURAL OR CREATIVE INDUSTRIES

This is why the "cultural or creative industries" are so important. The "cultural industries" are those sectors of the economy which have a substantial artistic and creative input, and whose primary purpose is to transmit meaning in commodity form. Some are coherent economic sectors in themselves, for example the record or broadcasting industries. Others such as design, architecture and industrial design input into industrial and consumer goods, feeding into a range of economic sectors. The term "culture industry" was first coined by Max Horkheimer and Theodor Adorno in 1937.[18] These writers used the concept to denote the products and processes of mass culture. It was taken up again in the early 1980s, certainly in the UK, by Professor Nick Garnham[19] and then policy analysts at the Greater London Council,[20] as part of the London Industrial Strategy.

The now accepted definition of the term cultural industries takes account of the following: the performing arts, the music industry, broadcasting, the film, video and photographic industry, publishing, the crafts industry, design and fashion, and the visual arts. All of these industries combine cultural expression and creativity with material production, tradeable goods, and to greater or lesser extent, market-based consumption. Each of the above "sectors" has its own production chain, ranging from pre-production to production, to post-production and distribution, and to various forms of consumption. Each sector also has its own economic "profile" with varying degrees of economic concentration, stages of capital formation and small firm development. It is important for policy makers to understand trends, nationally, locally and internationally for each cultural sub-sector.

Many of the cultural industry sectors are dominated by a handful of major organizations, increasingly at the international as well as the national levels: TV companies and satellite operators, fashion empires, global advertising agencies, film production companies, the big five record companies, and so on. Yet this concentration of economic power is usually disguised, as markets and consumption are broken down from the old mass markets to increasing niche consumption, and with it the customization of product and consumption. Whilst large corporations require to make large investments in R&D, product development and financing creative work, there are increasing problems in ensuring flexibility and innovation and consequently a far greater use of sub-contracting and competitive profit centres. At the other end of the spectrum are the small, independently owned firms and organizations producing

---

18 *The Dialectic of Enlightenment* (New York: Herder and Herder, 1972).

19 *The State of the Art or the Art of the State? Strategies for the Cultural Industries in London*, Greater London Council, 1985. See also *Altered Images: Towards a Strategy for London's Cultural Industries*, Greater London Enterprise Board, 1986.

20 Including Geoff Mulgan, Phil Hardy, Simon Blanchard, Nick Garnham and Ken Worpole.

cultural product in competition and often collaborative competition, with each other and larger firms. By collaborative competition is meant joint-work, sub-contracting, shared R&D and the building up of industrial networks and business linkages. Employment in the cultural industries this covers a wide range of activities: from struggling young designers and artists to successful record producers and film makers; from desk top publishing operatives to people who staff auditoria and venues.

These then are the quintessential knowledge age industries: involved in the creation and communication of meaning and entertainment; hi-tech, and requiring a high skills base. They generate huge turnovers worldwide, they create and sustain popular cultural icons and they are shaped by and help to shape fashion, identity and sub-cultures. The products are CDs, DVDs, television programmes, books and magazines, videos, films, fashions, records and tapes. They require hardware (equipment, technology, studios) and software (creative people, image-makers, ideas). Creativity generates new ideas, new ways of working and new products. Potentially at least, the cultural industries add to the stock of work which makes up a city's economy.

However, as these industries become more closely integrated with each other – and as technologies converge – the boundaries between them blur. At the same time, many of the sub-sectors (and cross-sectors) are experiencing significant and often far-reaching restructuring brought about by changes in technology, organizational practices, shifts in consumer demand and niche markets, and by a restless cycle of attempted and successful mergers and take-overs. During the 1980s and 1990s most industry commentators agreed that the lead creative sectors were film, television, the music industry and publishing, and it is within these sectors that technology is converging most rapidly with the computer industry. However, at least from the mid 1990s, sub-sectors such as fashion, ceramics, jewellery, furniture design and the plastic arts have also seen growth led by increased consumer demand for distinctive products.

There is now a growing recognition of the economic significance of the what are now referred to as the creative industries.[21] The European Community White Paper "Jobs and Competitiveness" (1995) argued that creative and cultural industries were at that time one of only three industrial sectors with the potential for economic and employment growth across Europe. In 1998, the UK Department of Culture, Media and Sport officially categorized the creative industries by Standard Industrial Classification (SIC) Codes. Somewhere along the way a distinction was drawn between the creative as opposed to the cultural industries. The creative industries are now understood as those which have their origins in individual creativity, talent and skill, and which have potential for wealth creation through the generation and exploitation of ideas and intellectual work. The cultural industries include the creative industries but also extend to include the performing arts and building-based facilities such as art galleries, museums and concert halls. The main creative industry sub-sectors are now defined as shown overleaf:

---

21 One of the earliest "reflective" pieces on the cultural industries was by Colin Williams: "Cultural Industries and Local Revitalization", chapter 9 of his book *Consumer Services and Economic Development* (London: Routledge, 1997).

Table 1.2 Creative Industries – SIC92 Codes (UK)

Publishing of Books	Code 22.11
Publishing of Newspapers	22.12
Publishing of Journal and Periodicals	22.13
Publishing of Sound Recordings	22.14
Other Publishing	22.15
Reproduction of Sound Recording	22.31
Reproduction of Video Recording	22.32
Reproduction of Computer Media	22.33
Software Consultancy and Supply	72.20
Architectural and Engineering Activities	74.20
Printing of Newspapers	22.21
Printing Not Elsewhere Classified	22.22
Other Activities Related to Printing	22.25
Advertising (Marketing & Promotion & Graphic Design)	74.40
Photographic Activities	74.81
Other Business Activities Not Elsewhere Classified (Textile Design, Other Design, Exhibition & Conference Facilities & Organisation)	74.84
Technical and Vocational Secondary Education	80.22
Higher Education	80.30
Adult Education Not Elsewhere Classified	80.42
Motion Picture and Video Production	92.11
Motion Picture Projection	92.13
Radio and Television Activities	90.20
Artistic and Literary Creation and Interpretation (Dance, Other Design, Performance Sound & Lighting, Music Performance and Production,Theatrical Production and Support, Visual Arts& Sculpture, Combined Arts, Crafts, Writing,Arts Management)	92.31
Operation of Arts Facilities (Galleries & Other Arts Facilities, Theatres & Concert Halls)	92.34
Other Entertainment Activities Not Elsewhere Classified (Leisure & Entertainment)	92.32
Library & Archive Activity	92.51
Museum Activities & Historical Sites/Buildings	92.52

Source: Department of Culture, Media and Sports, UK Government, 2002.

It has to be acknowledged that this much fuller definition of the creative industries has been criticized from various quarters as over-inclusive. It goes some way beyond the early published accounts of the creative industries:[22] For example, the inclusion of printing has been made on the grounds that such activity is an important part of the supply chain in other industries such as graphic design; and that printing these days usually involves computerized design. The problem is that – at a stroke – people who were only a few years ago categorized as working in industrial processes are now "creatives". Similarly, Advertising is an integral part of TV and film especially, yet this category also includes local public relations agencies and people selling advertising space. It is clear, with the best will in the world, that not all of those who work in advertising are themselves creative.

Perhaps the largest area of contention is the inclusion of Secondary, Further and Higher Education. Although it is true that these sectors educate and train the new creative producers, it is mistaken to include more than a small proportion of their staff in any employment estimates. One would similarly take issue with the inclusion of Library, Archive and Museum Activities, preferring to see these as no doubt valued activities but of a different nature to primary creation. Likewise, the inclusion of such activities as nightclubs stretches credulity. To counter some of these arguments, the Department has stressed that organizations should be considered for inclusion where the role of creativity is considered to be "core" or "related" as opposed to "peripheral". Again, these distinctions are not always easy to make in practice, and are difficult to "estimate" from the raw data. The upshot is that there remains a degree of disagreement over the current official definition of the creative industries in the UK. One unfortunate side effect of this is that proponents of the creative industries as an economic generator are often charged with over-exaggerating the sector's real significance.[23]

To be sure, the statistics are eye-opening. A statistical bulletin issued by the UK Department of Culture, Media and Sport in July 2003[24] revealed that the creative industries accounted for 8.2 per cent of Gross Value Added with the UK economy in 2001 (Table 1.3). The creative industries as a whole grew by eight per cent per annum, an average between 1997 and 2001, compared to an average of 2.6 per cent for the whole economy over the same period. The most rapidly growing sectors in terms of value were radio and television (seventeen per cent per annum), advertising (fourteen per cent), and software (ten per cent) (Table 1.4). In 2001, exports by creative industries contributed £11.4 billion to the balance of trade, around 4.2 per cent of all goods and services exported (see Table 1.5). Exports for the creative industries grew at around fifteen per cent per annum over the period 1997–2001. This compares with a growth of four per cent per annum for all goods and services exported.

---

22 Urban Cultures Ltd, *op. cit.*, 1994.

23 Heartfield, J., *Great Expectations: The Creative Industries in the New Economy* (London: Design Agenda, 2000).

24 Department of Culture, Media and Sport (DCMS), *Creative Industries Economic Estimates*, Statistical Bulletin, July 2003.

Table 1.3 Contribution of Creative Industries to Gross Value Added (Gross Value Added, £ million)

	Advertising	Architecture	Video, film	Music, arts	Publishing	Software, games	Radio and TV	Art antiques	Designer fashion	Craft	Design	Total
1997	3,400	3,100	1,900	2,700	6,500	9,800	3,500	100	280	n/a	n/a	n/a
1998	3,500	3,200	1,800	2,900	7,300	13,200	3,700	100	270	400	n/a	n/a
1999	5,500	3,200	2,100	3,100	8,000	13,900	4,600	200	300	n/a	n/a	n/a
2000	6,100	3,500	2,100	3,200	8,400	14,800	5,900	200	310	n/a	6500	51,100
2001	6,400	3,700	2,200	3,200	8,900	16,000	7,300	200	320	n/a	6700	54,800
% GDP 1997	0.6	0.5	0.3	0.5	1.2	1.8	0.6	0.02	0.05	n/a	n/a	n/a
1998	0.6	0.5	0.3	0.5	1.2	2.2	0.6	0.02	0.05	0.07	n/a	n/a
1999	0.9	0.5	0.3	0.5	1.3	2.3	0.7	0.03	0.05	0.07	n/a	n/a
2000	0.9	0.5	0.3	0.5	1.3	2.3	0.9	0.03	0.05	0.07	1.0	7.9
2001	0.9	0.5	0.3	0.5	1.3	2.4	1.1	0.03	0.05	0.07	1.0	8.2

Source: DCMS based on Office for National Statistics Annual Business Inquiry.

Table 1.4 Contribution of Creative Industries to Gross Value Added (% growth)

	Advertising	Architecture	Video, film and photography	Music, visual and performing arts	Publishing	Software, computer games and electronic publishing	Radio and TV	Art and antiques	Designer fashion	Crafts	Design	Total
1997–1998	0	3	-9	4	8	30	3	7	-8	n/a	n/a	12
1998–1999	52	-5	13	4	7	3	30	8	7	n/a	n/a	10
1999–2000	9	7	2	2	2	4	26	7	2	n/a	n/a	7
2000–2001	3	4	0	-4	4	6	21	9	2	n/a	1	6
Average												
1997–2001	14	2	1	1	5	10	17	8	1	n/a	n/a	8

Table 1.5 Exports of Creative Industries

	Advertising	Architecture	Video, film and photography	Music, visual and performing arts	Publishing	Software, computer games and electronic publishing	Radio and TV	Art and antiques [1]	Designer fashion [2]	Crafts [3]	Design [4]	Total
1997	680	380	700	250	680	1400	500	n/a	n/a	n/a	n/a	n/a
1998	630	470	700	250	830	1700	600	n/a	350	40	n/a	n/a
1999	560	410	700	270	860	2300	700	1400	n/a	n/a	n/a	n/a
2000	710	420	900	300	950	2500	700	2000	n/a	n/a	1000	9500
2001	730	520	900	290	830	3900	900	1900	390	n/a	1000	11,400

Sources: DCMS based on Office for National Statistics Inquiries with the following exceptions:

1. *Antiques Trade Gazette* analysis of HM Customs and Excise data; 2. *Design Fashion Report 1998*, A study of the UK designer fashion sector, 2003 (both for DTI); 3. Creative Industry Mapping Document estimate (1998); 4. Overseas fee income to British Design Consultancies, Design Industry Valuation Surveys, British Design Initiative.

Table 1.6 Creative Employment

	Advertising	Architecture	Crafts	Design, design fashion	Film, video photogrphy	Music, arts	Publishing	Software, games,	Television & radio	Art/antiques trade	Total est. for creative employment in Great Britain
Employment in creative industry companies											
June 02	88,600	82,700	-	n/a	54,500	202,600	212,100	351,500	98,600	21,700	1,115,900
Employment I creative occupations in businesses outside the creative industries											
June 02	137,300	29,800	117,200	n/a	12,000	46,800	80,400	231,600	11,800	-	787,400
Total creative employment											
June 95	192,000	97,400	122,400	88,500	50,800	220,000	333,700	284,500	96,600	19,700	1,505,700
June 96	192,000	108,300	103,300	95,200	46,200	218,000	327,400	327,400	99,300	19,700	1,536,800
June 97	203,000	99,100	100,900	89,400	52,600	237,600	317,000	393,400	98,400	20,400	1,611,600
June 98	207,700	101,500	127,200	98,200	50,700	229,000	328,700	436,700	100,400	20,100	1,700,300
June 99	204,000	103,400	102,800	104,200	56,100	261,100	337,200	511,000	92,200	21,100	1,793,100
June 00	209,500	107,000	118,200	109,600	57,400	246,200	304,900	558,400	112,200	21,300	1,844,700
June 01	211,700	106,900	122,200	116,100	62,600	238,000	306,500	579,700	110,300	21,200	1,875,200
June 02	225,900	112,600	117,200	123,900	66,500	249,500	292,500	583,000	110,400	21,700	1,903,300
Annual growth											
1995–2002	2	2	-1	5	4	2	-2	11	2	1	3
1997–2002	2	3	3	7	5	1	-2	8	2	1	3
2001–2002	7	5	-4	7	6	5	-5	1	0	2	1

Source: Analysis of National Statistics Labour Force Survey.

Table 1.7 Numbers of VAT-based Businesses in the Creative Industries

	Advertising	Architecture	Art and Antiques	Designer Fashion	Video, film and photography	Music and the visual and performing arts	Publishing	Software, computer games, and electronic publishing	Radio and TV	Total
1996	10,600	3700	1400	1400	4100	33,100	7,200	48,100	2300	111,900
1997	10,400	3800	1500	1400	4800	32,600	7000	49,500	2300	113,300
1998	10,300	3900	1600	1300	5500	32,500	6800	52,600	2300	116,800
1999	10,000	4000	1700	1300	6000	32,200	6800	55,700	2700	120,400
2000	10,000	3800	1800	1300	6500	32,500	6700	56,700	3000	122,300
2001	10,100	3700	1800	1300	6800	32,600	6700	56,100	3400	122,500
2002	10,100	3100	1800	1300	7400	32,300	6700	55,800	3600	122,100

Source: Estimates based on Interdepartmental Business Register, Office for National Statistics.

As far as employment is concerned, some 1.9 million people are employed in creative employment (this includes self-employment), or 1.1 million in a narrower definition of "creative industry companies". This represents an annual growth rate of three per cent per annum since 1997, compared with one per cent for the United Kingdom's economy as a whole. The fastest-growing sectors were software, design and fashion, and film, video and photography (see Table 1.6). The numbers of companies trading in the creative industries was 122,000 companies, an increase of some 10,000 since 1997. The biggest sectors in terms of the number of VAT-based businesses was software (55,800) followed by music and the performing arts (32,300), although in the latter case the total number of companies has declined since 1996 (see Table 1.7). The lion's share of this creative industry activity is based in London, particularly for the company-based activity (the performing arts tend to have a more general geographic spread across the country). Nevertheless, important regional and city "clusters" have also grown. For example, Scottish Enterprise – the economic development agency for Scotland – estimates that the creative industries sector employs more than 100,000 people in Scotland and has an annual turnover of £5 billion. In Sheffield, meanwhile, some 7.2 per cent of people in employment work in the creative industries, exceeding the UK average of 4.2 per cent.

This official interest in the creative industries is not confined to the UK. Data published by the *Australian Bulletin of Statistics*, based on ANZSIC codes, and identifies seven creative industry sectors.

Film, television and entertainment software:
Film and video production;
services to film and video production (i.e. production services such as casting, set design, animation, special effects and post-production services such as editing); film and video distribution (leasing or wholesaling of motion pictures); motion picture exhibition (including film festivals); television services (production and broadcasting of television programs); and electronic games and entertainment software writing and publishing (interactive entertainment software used on personal computers, video game consoles, the internet and mobile devices).

Writing, publishing and print media:
writing;
book publishing and distribution;
newspaper and magazine printing, publishing and distribution; and other periodical and journal publishing and distribution.

Music composition and production:
music composition (bands, singer-songwriters);
music festival organizers;
record labels and producers; and
sound recording studios, lighting technicians and equipment suppliers.

Architecture, visual arts and design:
architects and landscape services;
urban design companies;
photographic studios; and
other industries with a creative design element, i.e.
interior design, fashion or furniture design.

Advertising, graphic design and marketing:
advertising services;
graphic designers/concept designers;
marketing firms; and
commercial art and display services.

Performing arts:
music and theatre productions;
creative arts;
services to the arts; and
performing arts venues.

Museums and libraries:
museums; and
libraries.

Source: Australian Bureau of Statistics

The data reveals that some 220,000 people in Australia work in the creative industries, with the majority of these (185,000) being in New South Wales (mainly Sydney), Victoria (mainly Melbourne) and Queensland (mainly Brisbane and an emerging film cluster on the Gold Coast) (Figure 1.2). As a proportion of all employment, the creative industries in Australia account for between two and three per cent, that is just over half of the levels achieved in the UK (Figure 1.3). However, in the Australian case over thirty-five per cent of all employment in the creative industries is accounted for by libraries and museums. This suggests that a "truer" estimate of employment in the creative industries is in the region of 150,000. Sydney is regarded as the most cutting edge of the Australian cities, with strong specialisms in film (Fox studios), visual art and the theatre.[25] Melbourne is the pre-eminent centre for design, fashion and music, and has recently seen the opening of a major film studio, Central City Studios, in the Docklands area,[26] although there are fears within the industry that Australia has over-developed the number of film studios. Meanwhile, Brisbane is in the process of developing a creative industries precinct as a joint venture with

---

25 *Sydney Morning Herald*, "The Beat Goes on", 7 September 2005, p. 11.

26 *The Australian Financial Review*, "Film Studio Hopes Slowly Fading to Black", 23 June 2005, p. 44.

Figure 1.2   Total Employment in the Creative Industries, Australia (2001)
Source: Australian Bureau of Statistics.

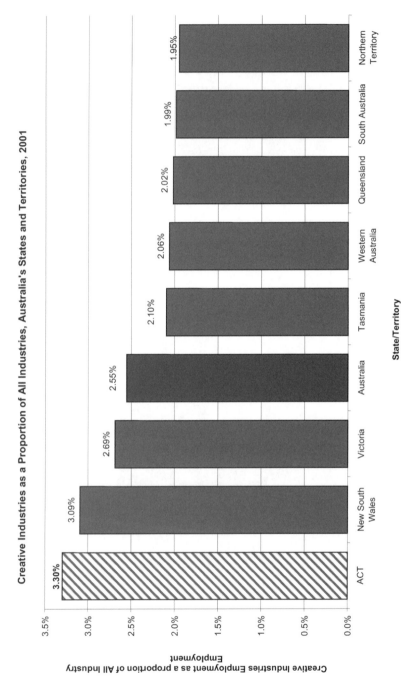

Creative Industries as a Proportion of All Industries, Australia's States and Territories, 2001

Figure 1.3   Creative Industries as a Proportion of All Industries, Australia (2001)

Source: Australian Bureau of Statistics.

Table 1.8   Market Size Industries of the Creative Economy (billions of US dollars, 1999)

	Global (dollars)	US (dollars)	US Share (percentages)
R&D (Research and Development)	545	243	44.6
Publishing	506	137	27.1
Software	489	325	66.5
TV and Radio	195	82	42.1
Design	140	50	35.7
Music	70	25	35.7
Film	57	17	29.8
Toys and Games	55	21	38.2
Advertising	45	20	44.4
Architecture	40	17	42.5
Performing Arts	40	7	17.5
Crafts	20	2	10.0
Video Games	17	5	29.4
Fashion	12	5	41.7
Art	9	4	44.4
TOTAL	2240	960	42.8

Source: J. Howkins, *The Creative Economy: How People Make Money from Ideas*, The Penguin Press, 2001, p. 116.

Queensland University of Technology. Perth, long-regarded as the least culturally interesting of Australia's State capital cities, is now branding itself as a creative city.[27]

At the global level, estimates suggest[28] that the "core creative industry sectors" generate a turnover of $2,240 billion dollars, with the USA accounting for over 40 per cent in 1999. John Howkins classifies the core creative industries as R&D,

---

27 *Sydney Morning Herald*, "Perth: A City on the Edge", 9 August 2005, Insight, p. 9.

28 Howkins, J., *The Creative Economy: How People Make Money from Ideas* (New York: Penguin, 2001), p. 116.

Publishing, Software, TV and radio, Design, Music, Film, Toys and Games, Advertising, Architecture, Performing Arts, Crafts, Video Games, Fashion and Art (see Table 1.8). Excluding R&D (research and development) , the total value of the creative industries in 1999, according to Howkins, was US$1,700 billion. Following this, Richard Florida[29] has estimated that over 2.5 million "bohemians" were employed in the creative industries in the USA in 1999; plus five million scientists and engineers working in R&D.

There is now evidence from around the world that the industries of creativity are amongst the fastest growing of all. Toronto, for example, one of North America's most diverse economies with specialisms in medical research and biotechnology, IT and New Media, financial and professional services, and design sectors, is in the midst of an unprecedented cultural renaissance. Toronto has the largest design workforce in Canada and the third largest design workforce in North America (after New York and Boston). There are 25,000 designers in Toronto working in six design disciplines – architecture, landscape architecture, graphic, interior, industrial and fashion design. The more than 170,000 people working in IT and New Media help make Toronto's cluster the 3rd largest in North America and a global hub for IT and new media development. Toronto is home to Canada's national broadcaster, CBC, and the nation's largest private broadcaster CTV; as well as a variety of specialty and multilingual television channels including HGTV, OMNI, and Telelatino. Toronto firms dominated the national sound recording industry in 2000–2001, despite having fewer sound recording firms than Montreal. Toronto is also the dominant film industry cluster. The technical expertise available within the sector's 25,000-strong workforce has been extensively used to create special effects, children's programming, speciality TV channels and programs and a capacity for translation and dubbing, propelling innovative approaches to film and television making. Toronto is also home to the Sheridan College and Canadian Film Centre. The Toronto International Film Festival, in its 30th year, is the largest publicly attended festival in the world.

Meanwhile, Berlin's creative economy represents 3.6% of Germany's GDP.[30] The media and related industries total 11,000 companies, employing over 130,000, the fourth most important employment sector in the city (after transport, biotech, and medicine). The largest sectors are advertising, publishing, film, software and multimedia. There are 7,000 firms in media and advertising, 800 publishers, 1,100 firms in the audio-visual industries, and some 1,400 firms, 20,000 professional musicians, 70 studios and 600 record labels. A number of creative clusters (media, music, *Silicon Allee)* are located in inner urban districts, with the exception of film/TV (studios, production) in the outer Berlin-Brandenberg area. An estimated 13,000 work in the cultural sector in Mitte which operates an advisory *Kulturburo* and workspace programme. Berlin has the highest concentration of national and

---

29 Florida, R., *The Rise of the Creative Class* (New York: Basic Books, 2002) p. 47.

30 Kratke, S., "City of talents? Berlin's Regional Economy, Socio-Spatial Fabric and Urban Governance", *International Journal of Urban and Regional Research*, 2004.

Figure 1.4   A Design Gallery Door, Barcelona
Source: Julia Montgomery.

international radio & TV broadcasters in Germany. There is a cluster of production/ post-production studios at *MediaCity* in Adlershof.

Finally, Barcelona is emerging as the most important creative industry centre in Spain.[31] Prior to and immediately following the Franco regime, major film and music recording industry activity moved to Madrid. From 1975 the Congress of Catalonian Culture was formed and autonomous provincial status granted. The Department of Culture and Media was formed in 1980, with devolution of much cultural governance from Madrid by 1986. Cultural facility development followed with the Modern Art Museum, the Centre for Contemporary Culture in Barcelona, the National Arts Museum of Catalonia, the National Archive, the History Museum, the Picasso Museum, and the reconstruction of Opera and Theatre houses. The highest concentration of creative industry activity is in the Eixample, Sarria de Gervas, Sant Marti/PobleNou and Ciutat Vella districts (Fig. 1.4).

Production-based publishing and printing is the largest sector, including newspaper/magazines, followed by TV & Radio, Film/Video and Music. Barcelona dominates in Publishing/Press and the region accounts for over 60% of

---

31 Marshall, T., *Transforming Barcelona* (London: Routledge, 2004).

the Spanish market. Planeta is one of the largest 10 publishing companies in the world and international firms also have interests. There is a strong design tradition and network, particularly in graphic design. The *Fomenta of Artes Decoratiovas* was founded in 1903 and a trade association formed in 1961. Architecture and Industrial Design account for some 3,000 firms. International Contemporary Art is also very important. There is an exhibition circuit, over 100 galleries, of which half are proprietor-owned. There are some 1,475 professional artists/firms registered as companies.

The data, though probably flawed, is irrefutable. The creative industries are now a major part of the global economy, particularly in the USA and the UK. Governments, city councils and economic development agencies have come to realize that these are engines of wealth creation, job growth and business formations. The question now being addressed is whether and by what means these valuable sectors can be encouraged to grow.

Creative Industry Production Chains

During the late 1980s, researchers at the UK consultancy Comedia[32] proposed that the creative economy should be conceptualized as a production chain, as described in Figure 1.5 below. This was based largely on the economic sector approach advocated by the London Industrial Strategy.[33] The sector approach advocates analysing and understanding the dynamics of the production process – the supply side – in order to evaluate how well locally based industries are performing. According to this view, the productivity of industries can be improved by interventions at the micro scale, in such matters as start-up capital, business planning, training, access to suitable property, marketing and the overall business or sector development strategy within the context of industry-wide trends and opportunities. The technique of the "production chain" is used to assess an industry's workings from production through to market demand, distribution and how the product is eventually consumed. In this way, it is possible to target local intervention to help local businesses develop and grow.

Thus for the cultural and creative industries, the production chain identifies the various stages a sound recording, film or other cultural product must go through before it is eventually consumed. In economic development terms, the production chain allows us to trace the actual process of production. In this way, it is possible to shape a particular form of intervention in order to overcome some blockage or obstacle to local economic development of the creative industries.

The problem may for example be providing opportunities for creative people to make a living in their home city rather than having to move to Sydney, London or

---

32 Comedia: Charles Landry, John Montgomery, Simon Blanchard, Ken Worpole, Franco Bianchini, Liz Greenhalgh. Comedia *The Position of Culture*, Appendix to the London World City Report (London: HMSO, 1991).

33 Greater London Council, *The London Industrial Strategy*, London 1985.

Beginnings	ideas, creativity, intellectual property, R&D
Production	ideas into products, places for production
Circulation	distribution, wholesale, marketing,
Delivery Media	retail, hardware, venues
Markets & Consumption	watching, ordering, interacting

Figure 1.5   The Creative Industries Production Chain
Source: Comedia 1989.

LA, or it could be that changes in the industry structure are spinning off new-start companies, led by talented individuals, but inexperienced entrepreneurs. There may be gaps in the local infrastructure which drive creative businesses into larger centres. The production chain allows us to see the whole of the sub-sector and to visualize where a locality, or indeed a particular business, fits.

Beginnings: Creativity, ideas and concepts, patents and rights, intellectual property and trademarks. Are there enough clever people, coming up with new ideas, sounds and images? Economic development considerations: education, training, and opportunities for shared R&D or inter-personal communication. How should policy makers set about fostering and attracting creative and innovative individuals and providing a stimulating environment?

Production: How to turn ideas and intellectual property into consumable product. This requires people, resources and productive capacities: impresarios, managers, producers, editors, engineers as well as suppliers and makers of equipment, film or photo labs, and studios. Is the right equipment available, are there imports that could be substituted, is there space (property) for businesses to grow in and through? Economic development measures may be required to assist in finding suitable property/space and access to technology, production finance and funding arrangements.

Circulation: How does the product reach the broadcaster, publisher or distributor? This is the realm of agents and agencies, distributors and wholesalers, TV stations, packagers and assemblers of product. This also includes the circulation of market intelligence through catalogues, directories, archives, stock inventories and so on which aid the sale and circulation of creative products. How do local companies reach their markets? Do enough of them export?

Delivery Media: These are channels/outlets/media through which products are consumed and enjoyed: cinemas for film; terrestrial TV (analogue and digital), cable or satellite; VCRs, DVDs. To break into this locally is very difficult, high-risk and costly, but not impossible. Some combination of local cable channels/slots and/or Regional Film Theatres or virtual galleries may be possible, as well as producing theatres, concert halls, and other venues, book shops, record stores, localized fashion outlets, galleries and open studios....

Consumption: This is the final, perhaps repeated, consumption of product, by the buyer. This is the prevail of marketing, advertising and publicity, pricing and market targeting. Key questions: which delivery mechanism? Who "owns" the consumer? These considerations drive the industry at the global and national scales (e.g. Fox versus ABC) but the large companies and commissioners are always on the lookout for new ideas, programmes and products. For other sub-sectors, the issue is reaching new consumers via industry fairs, the Sydney Affordable Art Fair, the Melbourne Design Show, London Fashion Week, The International Contemporary Glass Expo. Locally and regionally, market demand is likely to come from other businesses and the public through independent galleries and retail outlets. Cities can also attract buyers via general tourism, arts festivals but also specific creative industry conventions and fairs.

It is important to recognize that the production chain for each creative sub-sector varies considerably, and can operate at differing geographical scales. Film and Television tend to be dominated by Los Angeles, London in the UK, and Sydney in Australia – the difficulty lies in securing a broadcast commission or a distribution deal. Design can operate, via the Internet, at the local, regional, national and even international levels, and locally through showrooms, open studios and galleries ... The Performing Arts can be produced almost anywhere, but are consumed in actual (as opposed to virtual) places. The strength of a local visual arts scene might depend on a few organizations running galleries and studio spaces. Music recording, notwithstanding the importance of the Indies, is still more or less controlled by the Big Five recording labels – but without live music there would be no distinctive local music scene. In this way, it is important for any locality to understand precisely which sectors and elements of the creative industries it has to build upon.

Technology: Digitization of the Creative Industries

The key innovation driving technological development within the creative economy from the mid 1990s, has been digitization: a new way of transmitting information – through cable, by satellite or through the UHF frequency. Sound and pictures are processed electronically and converted into binary digits – the noughts and ones of computer language known as "bits". This bit code can then be transmitted and reconverted into sounds and pictures by appropriate receivers in radio and television sets, as well as between computers. Digitization – or digital compression – allows much more information to be sent using less power and less capacity, thus making possible many more channels, better quality sound and pictures and new services such as wide-screen television and advanced teletext services. The "digital revolution" has brought media production ever closer to three other major global industries: telecommunications, computers and electronics. The digitization of both sound and image enables ever more complex and precise manipulation of both these elements and the computer control of them. It also increases, to an enormous degree, the volume of information that can be stored (on Compact Discs or DVDs for example) or sent through conventional copper or more flexible fibre-optic cables.

Partly because of this, the main organizational and industry structure changes of the 1990s were mergers and takeovers amongst US, Japanese, European, British and Australian concerns. The 1993 deal between MAI and Time Warner to form the world's largest media company was a case in point. Media giants such as Sony, News Corporation, Time Warner and Disney continue to jostle for position. This has been referred to in the trade(s) as the "multi-media revolution", a by now familiar term in popular culture. It helps explain why it is that an Australian newspaper publisher, Rupert Murdoch, now owns several television stations and Twentieth Century Fox; why Sony now owns Columbia Pictures and TriStar.

Many claims are made as to the growth potential of the creative industries. Yet, with the exception of the larger organizations, the sectors themselves are volatile by nature and often in a state of flux. This means that new ideas and products can be produced and marketed, but energy levels are difficult to maintain without some longer term growth plan for the sector. Creative people come and go, and often the very best move away to make a living elsewhere. Apart from technological development, it is difficult to predict almost anything else with absolute certainty. Many variable factors come into play including: regulation, alliances, competition from other countries, consumer preferences and future patterns of demand. But this is no different from any other economic sector. Consider this: twenty years ago there were virtually no creative industry clusters in Sheffield, Manchester, Dublin, the East End of London or North Kensington. Now they are engines of growth.

Nevertheless, we can predict that a number of trends will have important implications for the industry, and especially its development in local economies. The first of these is content-driven markets. Though technology enhances and diversifies the means of production and distribution, the commercial expansion of the creative industries is both content and demand driven. It is not broadband itself which attracts the customer, but the information and entertainment those technologies can deliver. Content creation and production is therefore a key factor in the future development of the creative industries, up and to the point where levels of consumer demand can sustain viable delivery. This content will, with the exception of near-monopoly producers, be produced by creative people working in micro, small and medium enterprises (SMEs).

The future of SMEs will depend on their ability to react to market trends, to cater for niche markets and to create new markets. In other words their *modus operandi* will have to be one of flexible specialization. They will have to tackle the challenges of investment in new technology and skills development. It is possible that many small and micro businesses will shift between products and services in their attempts to remain ahead of the market. Others will fail. There is a need for a multi-skilled workforce in this which combines creative, technical and business skills. Young designers coming out of College will need to be business people as well as artists. As well as direct employment, creative business activities produce many knock-on effects of a direct and indirect nature, what economists refer to as "dynamic benefits". Direct effects include employment relating to specialist inputs/ support services such as prop buying, or scene building. The creative industries also produce "income multipliers" or derived consumption – jobs in restaurants, cafés, bars and retailing, and, of course, tourism.

The overall position is something of a double-edged sword. On the one hand, changes in technology produce more opportunities for micro and SMEs to thrive and innovate; on the other hand, the creative industries are highly competitive, with downward pressure on commissioning budgets and profit margins. This suggests that those cities or regions seeking to grow or expand their creative industry economy must not only know what they already have, but how this relates to the broader workings of the sector at the national and global levels. Moreover, it will be important to understand how the various sub-sectors within the creative industries – film, fashion, music, design – differ from each other in their industry structures, supply chains, markets and modes of production.

Film and Television

This sub sector consists of broadcasting (TV and radio), video production, film production, exhibition and distribution, and photography, including related activities such as photographic and cinematographic equipment and materials. While film and television, for example, are overlapping activities, they can be seen as distinct sub-sectors in their own right, with their own economic structure and differing prospects. Photography is also a distinct sub-sector, more closely connected to the print media and advertising than to the industries of the moving image.

Globally, according to John Howkin's figures for 1999 (Table 1.8), the Broadcasting industry (Television and Radio) was worth $157 billion US. In the UK, the sector was worth £7300 million in 2001. The UK industry achieved growth of 17 per cent from 1997 to 2001, and exported to the value of £900 million in 2001. The industry in the UK employs some 110,000 people, while the number of VAT-registered trading businesses (that is those with a minimum turnover of £150,000 annually) has jumped from 4100 in 1996 to 7400 in 2002.

Most of this phenomenal growth occurred in London at a time of restructuring across the industry.

Television production and broadcasting in the UK comes from two main sources: the public sector British Broadcasting Corporation and the commercial or independent industry. The BBC runs two national free-to-air television stations, a digital multiplex, the Teletex channel Ceefax and the World Service, an international operation which reaches 125 million people through radio and has a rapidly expanding satellite television network. The vast bulk of the BBC's national TV production and broadcasting work takes place in London.

In 1990s Britain, the single most important piece of recent legislation was the Broadcasting Act of 1990. This created a new competitive market-based environment by removing many of the public service responsibilities of ITV, changing its regulatory system, expanding commercial radio and making the re-issuing of ITV franchises the subject of a blind auction. This led broadcasting companies in the public and commercial sectors to cut costs, shed staff, and to move from using in-house to contracted production facilities. The upheaval and increasingly competitive market created by the Broadcasting Act also made commercial TV companies for a time less willing to invest in film production. The independent television industry consists of the terrestrial channels ITV (Channel Three), Channels 4 and 5, many satellite channels and a cable network. ITV and Channel 4 also operate digital channels. There are two ITV companies operating London franchises: Carlton and London Weekend Television. Channel 4 is based in London as well as the majority of satellite companies, the chief one of which is SKY, located in Isleworth.

Both the BBC and the independent sector underwent dramatic change in the wake of the 1990 Broadcasting Act of 1990. The BBC began a process of fundamental restructuring in order to adapt to the increasing commercialization of the industry as a whole and in preparation for the renewal of its Royal Charter in 1996. The single most important change was the introduction of Producer Choice in 1993 – a system which created an internal market within the BBC, whereby producers with their own budgets buy labour and resources from the various other departments in the organization – or from the private sector if they are cheaper. The ITV network was reshuffled in 1992 with the granting of new franchises based on a new bidding system. This saw four of the existing sixteen broadcasters lose their licenses. In London, Thames was replaced by Carlton, which itself was later taken over by Granada Television. Channel 4, in the meantime was gaining audience and was regularly up at 11 per cent of national viewing figures. Channel 5 was launched in 1997.

The independent production sector was already showing signs of being concentrated in fewer and fewer hands. A small number of London based independents (Hat Trick in comedy, Cheerleader in sport, Channel X in entertainment) dominated production across all broadcasters and markets. These stronger companies are usually based around one or several successful programmes, which are produced on a series basis and therefore guarantee a certain amount of stability. All of this pointed to a markedly different industry structure from that which pertained in the late 1980s. The large broadcasting companies would henceforth make fewer of their own programmes and would increasingly be in direct opposition with cable and satellite companies. As far as programme production goes, commissioning editors would become increasingly more powerful, with in-house producers (for the BBC and some ITV companies) competing against independent producers to have programmes commissioned.

Film production is a global industry, dominated by Hollywood but with significant (culturally if not always economically) centres in India, France, Italy and the UK. Howking (Table 1.8) estimates that the industry was worth $57 billion US in 1999, of which 30% was accounted for by Hollywood. In the UK, the industry (including pop videos and commercials) was worth £2200 million in 2001, representing a modest growth from 1997. However, this masks the fact that the industry endured a period of decline in the early to mid 1990s. Only twenty-six were films made in the UK in 1991, compared to 156 in France, 129 in Italy and sixty-three in Germany. This was largely because of the extremely low level of investment in the industry either by the government or private sources. According to the British Film Institute, investment fell from £39.2 million to £9.9 million between 1989 and 1992. The few films that did get made received over fifty per cent of their funding on average from overseas investors, both European and North American. The single largest British funder is Channel 4 which has commissioned many excellent films as part of the Film on Four series. BBC2 plays a similar role with Screen Two. The films, though produced for cinema release, are ultimately intended for TV broadcast and to be sold to TV satellite and cable companies around the world. Employment in the film industry is difficult to quantify, but the data (Table 1.6) indicates some 55–60,000 people working in the industry in 2002.

The vast bulk of film production in the UK takes place in and around London. This is because London is where most of the production companies, studios and facilities houses are based. The production companies and many facilities houses cluster in the West End, particularly around Soho, while production studios and distributors tend to be found outside central London or just outside London itself: for example Ealing Studios, Elstree Studios, Pinewood Studios and Shepperton Studios. These facilities were periodically under threat of closure during the 1980s and early 1990s. By the mid-1990s there was an upswing of activity with the emergence of a small and much-heralded group of young film-makers who seem determined to make exciting youth-oriented films cheaply, for a primarily British theatrical audience. This coincided with the availability of lottery funding for film production (from 1998) and this very possibly accounts – at least initially – for the rise in the sector's turnover from that time.

Video production became an increasingly important part of the audio-visual economy from the mid 1980s. It is now, in many ways, woven into the related activities of film and particularly television production. Advances in video technology, later DVD, mean that while it remains the cheapest audio-visual form, the quality of picture and sound are coming ever closer to those of film. There are four main areas of video production activity: broadcasting; corporate video (consisting of commercial companies who produce videos for other companies and organizations, notably for training marketing and information purposes); music video (the production of music videos – later DVDs – has become an integral part of the sales and marketing of recorded music product); and the community media sector. Video lends itself to many applications, not only corporate production, but also music composition (bands, singer-songwriters), broadcasting and screening but also in visual arts installations and interactive computer games.

The Music Industry

This refers mainly to the sound recording industry, that is the production of records, tapes, CDs music videos and DVDs, and also digitized "tunes" and downloads. As well as the musical artists themselves, there is a plethora of other types of individual and organization who contribute towards the production and distribution of musical products. Globally the industry was worth $70 billion US in 1999. In the UK, official statistics combine the recording and live music industries with other performing arts, so a precise value of the recording industry is difficult to ascertain. Nevertheless, some 200,000 people were directly employed in the sector in 2002, plus a further 50,000 in related activities. By the late 1990s the industry was worth over £3000 million to the UK economy. Growth in this sector remains sluggish, and the industry attributes this to digital piracy and free internet downloading. The industry has always both benefited and suffered from changes in technological formats.

Five transnationals or majors (EMI, Sony, Polydor, RCA and Warner Brothers) dominate the industry. Smaller independent companies only survive through entering into relationships of collaborative competition with the transnationals, with the majors using the "indies" as their A&R (artists and repertoire) arms. This practice has given rise to hybrid organizations known as "Mandies" (Major + indy) – smaller companies searching out new talent on behalf of the parent company (e.g. Virgin with Virgin Hut, RCA with Indolent Records). All five majors have a base in central London. As well as the recording companies (majors, nationals and "indies"), the recording industry includes:

- producers: most records are made under the supervision of an independent producer, who receives a fee and a percentage of sales;
- recording facilities and equipment hire: the larger record companies have their own studios; smaller record labels simply hire this type of equipment when necessary.
- music publishers – who are appointed by the artists to collect royalties from broadcast, performance and sales and to bring their compositions to the attention of other performers;
- retrieval or collecting societies (eg Performing Rights Society, Phonographic Performance Ltd, Video Performance Ltd) who collect royalties which arise from performance, recording, broadcast and sales copyrights;
- retail outlets – independents (such as Rough Trade and Honest John's, often found in "alternative" areas such as Portobello Road) and multiples such as

Our Price, Virgin and Tower Records, who prefer town centre locations;
* video production companies – who are playing an increasingly important part in the music industry, by creating the images which accompany the sound track.

There are also a large number of related activities including music journalism, photography, merchandizing and public relations consultants. The music industry, therefore, is extremely diverse and complex and very difficult to define for the purposes of estimated turnover and employment. Not only does it consists of a plethora of activities around the core element of the artists themselves, there is also a huge range of forms of music from classical to rock and pop, from traditional folk to avant-garde jazz to music associated with particular ethnic groups. It can also be difficult to make a distinction between music as a hobby or interest and music as a career. Many people who operate as musicians do not make a full-time living out of it.

The live music industry consists of solo artists, performing organizations, ensembles and the venues in which they perform. As well as the artists themselves, there are a large number of other individuals and organizations involved in the process of production, distribution and performance. These include: *Managers*, who handle all aspects of business, promotion and contracts; *Agents,* who book artists, receive bookings, and act as an intermediary between promoters and venues; *Promoters*, who hire venues and contract artists to appear; *Production Companies,* who specialize in the design and construction of performance sets (particularly important in the pop/rock side of the business); and *Sound and Lighting Engineers,* who are responsible for specific aspects of the live performance and might be part of the venue, hired by the group or freelance. As well as these, there are also a number of related activities such as: public relations and promotion (image consultants), PA and equipment manufacture and hire, trucking and catering and legal and financial services. Most of the live music industry operates on an exclusively commercial basis, particularly at the pop/rock part of the spectrum. Classical music, however, tends to be subsidized, both performers and venues. In terms of turnover (approximately 70 per cent), it is the recorded industry and the closely related broadcast medium which represent the heart of the industry.

The digitization of both sound and image enables ever more complex and precise manipulation of both these elements and the computer control of them. Two examples would be computer generated sound and computer-controlled lighting. Digital technology also enables the rapid transfer of data via optical telephone cables, through the Integrated Services Digital Network. This has led to the practice of inter-studio recording, sometimes connecting artists in different continents, with no adverse effect on the quality of the sound recording. Compact Discs (CDs) came to dominate the market for recorded products, with sales of records and tapes declining dramatically in the late 1980s. Other recording formats, such Digital Compact Disks and MiniDiscs, appeared on the market, but even these were rapidly overtaken by MP3 players and the internet. Whilst in the 1990s only the large transnationals could afford the investment necessary to keep up with this pace of product development, this is no longer true. Just about anyone can download music – often for free – from the internet. There is a great deal of concern in the industry about the impact of this particular new technology on music product and consumer sales.

The Design Industries

The design industries are difficult to define, spanning such a wide range of activities. Nevertheless, according to the design industry lead body, there were 66,000 people working in the different forms of design in the UK in 1991. This had increased to almost 90,000 by 1995, although much of this is probably accounted for by the inclusion – for the first time – of designer fashion in the statistics from 1999. Employment in the design industries in the UK rose from 88,000 in 1995 to 124,000 in 2002, an increase of 7% annually. Including designer fashion, the industry was worth £7000 million to the UK economy in 2001. Meanwhile, at the global level, Howkins estimates the value of the design industry as $140 billion US, and a further $12 billion for designer fashion.

Clearly since "image" (how something looks or comes across) is central to marketing and related activities like advertising, the existence of the design sector (excluding fashion and architecture) is closely tied to the amount spent on marketing. There are several different markets for design and the larger companies tend to specialize in one or two fields. The markets include: graphic design and commercial art; package design, product design, corporate design; interior, exhibition, display and retail; television, film and theatre design (sets). This of course covers a considerable range of skills and practices linking into other creative industries – music, film, publishing, photography – but also into very large industries such as construction, fashion and clothing. In these latter cases, it is not always easy to separate out design from production. Many architects, for example, use interior designers and artists. Similarly, not all the "design" in the clothing and fashion industry is undertaken by fashion designers. There is a great deal of copying and pattern cutting. Thus it is not always clear where clothing ends and becomes fashion, and where fashion is designer fashion.

The design industries then, are not one industry but several. People working in design usually have a visual arts training, specialist graphics training or fashion design. The link with formal education is crucial. London has many schools of design which are renowned the world over, and which produce highly talented and skilled designers: Goldsmiths College, Middlesex University Fashion School, the University of East London, the London Fashion Academy, St Martins, the various architecture schools to name but a few. Many graduates end up working abroad – in Paris or Milan or New York.

Growth in the sector in the 1980s rested largely on the rapid expansion of "chains" in the "High Street" – that is to say shop-fitting – and the extremely high level of corporate work stimulated by organizational change and company takeovers. Most of the larger scale designers occupy premises and locations which reflect their design ambitions, that is to say in prestigious city centre real estate. Small graphic design company start-ups by contrast require little other than access to a range of local markets, at least initially. Most of the design industry in the UK is based in London. The sub-sector numerically is largely dominated by small to medium sized companies and freelance individuals, though there are a number of large companies with a high profile at the heart of the industry. These "majors" tend to contract work out to the smaller companies viewing them as "quality suppliers". The larger companies, for example, Imagination or the Design House (in London), tend to specialize in corporate identity, packaging and retail identity (branding). They might typically employ forty to fifty people on a steady basis, plus a pool of ten or so freelancers. There was a great deal of merger and takeover activity in the late 1980s, and this helped fuel an increase in freelance work and the emergence of small companies. This emerging pattern was evident from the findings of the 1993 study of London's creative industries, to which we shall now turn.

4. THE RISE OF LONDON'S CREATIVE INDUSTRIES 1982–2002

By the early twenty-first century, it was estimated that the creative industries employed more than 525,000 people in Greater London,[34] and that the creative industries in London had a combined turnover of £21 billion. The growth in output for the period 1995–2000 was 8.5 per cent per year so that by the year 2000 the creative industries were the third largest economic sector in London. This remarkable growth apparently came as something of a surprise to government officials. Yet a major research project on the creative industries was commissioned by the London Planning Advisory Committee as long ago as 1993, published in 1994.[35] This was to establish the economic and employment prospects for, and planning requirements of, London's creative industries. The study was commissioned following publication of the London Labour Market (1992) report[36] which had suggested that the creative industries sector may have potential for growth in output (but not jobs) over the period 1991–2006.

The research methodology for the 1993 creative industries in London study was based on the sector approach, already tried and tested in Manchester.[37] An analysis

---

34 Greater London Authority, *Creativity: London's Core Businesses*, London 2002.

35 Urban Cultures Ltd, 1994, *op. cit.*

36 London Labour Market Study 1992, available from the London Planning Advisory Committee.

37 *Film, Video and Television: The Audio-visual Economy in the North-west*, December 1988, Comedia Consultancy, for the Independent Film Video and Photography Association, North West Arts, Manchester City Council, the British Film Institute, Channel 4 and Lancashire County Council. The study found that the sector in the North West was dominated by BBC North West and Granada Television, between them accounting for 80% of turnover and 50% of employment. However, the study also noted the emergence of independent producers,

of available official statistics on employment levels within the creative industries over the period 1981 to 1991 was undertaken. Estimates of the number of businesses working in London's creative industries were then drawn from various sources, mainly business directories. This was used to cross-check business numbers and also to compute likely employment levels. A series of interviews and discussions were held with a range of businesses and individuals who earned their living in the creative industries. These ranged from executives in large well established broadcasting companies and institutions to small start-up arts and design companies. The intention was to gain insights into the day-to-day workings of sub-sectors such as film, fashion, TV production and the music industry. Some of the report's findings were at the time surprising, to say the least.

According to the 1992 London Labour Market report, there were 190,000 people employed in the creative industries in London in 1991, but this was six per cent down on 1981 when the figure was 203,560. Future employment projections predicted a further fall in employment to 173,000 in 2006 – a decrease of 10 per cent from 1991. The 1993 London creative industries study found, however, that the number of job losses had been over-estimated in the official data, and that the levels of new small business start-ups and self-employment was under-estimated. Taking this into account, the 1993 study argued that there would be *an increase* in employment in the creative industries in London between 1991 and 2006. In the event, employment grew to over 500,000 by 2002, more than doubling the London Labour Market Study estimate.

Even by the mid 1990s, the creative industries accounted for just over 5 per cent of London's total employment. For most of the creative sectors – especially advertising, video and the music industry – there had been a growth of employment during the 1980s, but falling employment levels from the late 1980s until about 1995. Changes in employment levels were partly due to the impact of economic recession of 1988–1994, but also to industry restructuring, and the ongoing process of mergers and takeovers. All the creative industries sub-sectors experienced restructuring in the 1980s, with a move towards core-periphery models of employment. This was true even of the public sector (eg the BBC) which had to change to survive in the increasingly competitive media markets, but particularly to television companies, advertising and the music industry. The process of re-structuring led to job losses and to much greater flexibility within the labour market, with a large increase in freelancing, self-employment and contractual labour.

The census data for 1991 indicated that over 11,000 companies and organizations made-up the creative industries in London in the early 1990s, generating an estimated turnover of £7,440 million and export earnings of £2,656 million. By 1992, an estimated 15,300 businesses/organizations were engaged in London creative industries. This was largely made up of businesses trading in the audio-visual sector (3245), the music industry (2174) and design (3732) (Tables 1.9–1.11). The balance

---

corporate video and facilities houses, so that some 300 business were actively trading in the region at that time.

Table 1.9 Audio-visual Industries, London, 1992

Broadcasting Services	300
Cinemas	115
Film Producers and Directors	410
Film Processors	45
Photographers – Commercial and General	675
Photographic Processing and Printing	370
Photography Goods Mfr and W/sale	65
Photographic Libraries	110
TV, Film and Video Production Services	720
Video Services	310
Video and Film Distributors	125
Total	3245

Source: Urban Cultures Ltd, 1994.

covered the performing arts, the visual arts and publishing in the main. This was the strongest indication yet that the growth in the numbers of companies during the 1980s and early 1990s was accompanied by falling employment levels.

The study also found that the geographical spread of the creative industries varies from sub-sector to sub-sector. The inner west, particularly Westminster and Camden, was, and still is, the geographical heart of these industries. The chief example of this is Soho, where London's single largest concentration of film, video and television, music, advertising and design companies can be found. But there are many other London creative industry locations such as Camden (film and TV production), Fitzrovia (television production and fashion design), Clerkenwell (crafts) and North Kensington (film and video production and music recording). The chief design – particularly graphic design – cluster is alongside advertising and the other media industries in Soho and Fitzrovia and also in Covent Garden. Textile or fashion designers cluster in the rag trade area of Fitzrovia in and around Great Titchfield Street. There is also a cluster of more "alternative" designers around the Kings Road. This was the heart of the punk street fashion explosion of the 1970s. Other small clusters (more to do with graphic and product design) can be identified around London Bridge (SE1), around Hammersmith Bridge (W6) and around the Portobello Road area (W10). The evidence from those interviewed was that small firms are attracted by the interesting buildings and locations offered by the first two locations and by the "alternative" cultural milieu offered by the third. Many locate

Table 1.10   Recorded Music Industry, London 1992

Record Companies	397
Music Publishers	356
Recording Services	165
Recording Studios	153
Production Companies	178
Record Distributors	120
Pressers and Duplicating	50
Artist Management	355
Record and Cassette W/sale	170
Equipment Hire	70
Agents and Promoters	85
Venues	75
Total	2174

Source: Urban Cultures Ltd, 1994.

Table 1.11   The Design Industries, London, 1992

Design Consultants	785
Designers – Advertising and Graphics	1230
Product Designers	55
Textile Designers	77
Display Artists and Designers	30
Exhibition Designers	53
Architects	1400
Architectural Services	102
Total	3732

Source: Urban Cultures Ltd, 1994.

Figure 1.6   A Group of Workers from Cubitt & Co, constructing the new Marconi factory in Chelmsford, Essex (1912)

Source: The National Archives (C1/566), with permission.

in managed workspaces, for example the Barley Mow in Chiswick and any number of similar buildings in Covent Garden.

One of the most striking characteristics of the creative industries, then, is the tendency for similar or related activities to cluster in certain locations. They do so chiefly for the purpose of networking: they are fuelled by the exchange and movement of information, knowledge and ideas and inter-trading. A key feature of the creative industries is that they are not only "hi-tech" but also "hi-touch". This means that personal life-styles, the ability to mix work and play, the opportunities for personal contacts and networking in less formal surroundings – bars, cafés, restaurants, clubs – are of paramount importance for the creative industries. The 1993 London creative industries study argued for policies to recognize this trait and to take advantage of it to foster existing activity and attract new activity. This might be done, the report argued, by the designation of *cultural production districts*. This approach was followed through in 2004 when the London Development Agency announced the designation of ten creative industry clusters across the capital.[38] These include Soho, White City, North Kensington, Wood Green, New Cross, Hackney, Brentford, Spitalsfields, Whitechapel and Hammersmith and Ealing in West London.

However, there are also more "space-hungry" types of activity such as film production studios and tape and CD production and distribution facilities. Film studios in particular, most of which are located just outside London form a key part of the London film economy. This situation emerged historically as the studios needed grounds in which to build studios and sets. Also, West London was from the 1920s, and again from the 1950s, the UK's fastest growing industrial district. This occurred as new industries sought space to locate and expand: activities such as electrical engineering (Marconi – see Fig. 1.6), lighting (Lee), household appliances (Hoover), and food processing (Heinz) clustered in places such as Park Royal, Alperton and Wembley.

This produced a built form characterized by large factory buildings (many of them art deco), set in large grounds with easy road access and ample room for storage. Thus, if the UK film industry was to grow, then West London was the best place.

A more detailed study of the media industries in West London was commissioned in December 1995 by the West London Training and Enterprise Council.[39] This focused on the broadcast media and related industries in outer West London (the area administered by the London Boroughs of Ealing, Hillingdon, Hounslow and Richmond). This study found that the total number of companies trading in the creative industries in West London in 1995 was nearly 4,000. Of these, some 1500 (thirty-eight per cent) comprised of advertising agencies, marketing consultants and public relations consultants, while a further 660 (sixteen per cent) were advertising and graphic designers. The nature of the inter-relationship between such business and the broadcast media is complex and varied. A proportion of advertising and PR

---

38 Greater London Development Agency, 2002.

39 Urban Cultures Ltd *A Strategy for the Development of the Broadcast Media and Related Industries in West London*, unpublished consultancy report prepared for the West London Training and Enterprise Council, 1996.

companies will have only fairly tenuous links with film and television (and radio), but a great many tend to either commission product, work on TV and radio adverts or manage PR events involving media personalities including pop stars and disc jockeys. Excluding advertising and PR, there were just under 2000 companies who are more or less completely focused on producing films, videos and sound recordings, including TV, films and theatre designers.

Table 1.12   Film Television and Video Industries, West London 1995

Sixteen per cent	Film Producers and Directors	225
Fifty eight per cent	TV, Film and Video Production Companies	806
Seven per cent	Film and Video Distributors	99
Nine per cent	Video Services	130
Ten per cent	Audio-visual Services	133
TOTAL		1393

Source: Urban Cultures Ltd, 1996.

A total of 1393 companies in West London either made, distributed or broadcast films, TV programmes and videos (Table 1.12). In addition, there were seventeen listed TV, film and theatre designers and thirty-three listed news and photography agencies (who provide news reporters and reports), who spend a large proportion of their time in broadcast related activity.

The other large category was the music industry which amounted to 426 listed companies (Table 1.13). These, again, inter-relate with film and TV broadcasting in various ways, for example: providing sound tracks, permission for copyrighted material to be broadcast or used as backing. Thus, while the main focus of music publishing and recording remains CDs and other format sales, the industry also produces music videos and provided material for the broadcast and related visual media in various ways.

Table 1.13   The Music Industry, West London 1995

Music Publishers	70
Music Studios and Practice Rooms	33
Record Companies	174
Provided Sound Recording Services	149
TOTAL	**426**

Source: Urban Cultures Ltd, 1996.

The study found that sixty per cent of all media and related companies in West London had five or fewer employees (Table 1.14). A further twenty-one per cent had between 6 and 10 employees, and eight per cent have more than 10 but fewer than 20 employees. In this way, close on ninety per cent (3684) of all companies had fewer than 20 employees, and the bulk of these (eighty-one per cent, 3347 companies) had fewer than 10 employees.

Table 1.14   Audio-visual Industries by Company Size, West London 1995

Sixty-two per cent	have fewer than six employees	836
Twenty per cent	have between six and ten employees	283
Eight per cent	have between eleven and nineteen employees	111
Ten per cent	have between twenty and 100 employees; and only	144
One per cent	have more than 100 employees	19
TOTAL		**1393**

Source: Urban Cultures Ltd, 1996.

Of the medium sized companies (20–99 employees) the bulk were advertising agencies and public relations consultants, plus a handful of record companies and film distributors. Only 58 companies (less than two per cent) had more than 100 employees, and this included the BBC, the major recording companies and the larger advertising agencies. In this way, the large proportion of businesses active in the broadcast and related media industries in West London in 1995 were either micro (one to five employees) or small (six to ten employees) enterprises, with another much smaller layer of medium-sized enterprises and only a very few larger employers.

In hindsight, it is not surprising that West London should feature prominently as a location for the audio-visual industries, a media industrial district. What was not fully appreciated at the outset of the study was the degree of spatial organization and functional integration of the industry across such a large area. For it became clear that, in terms of geographical distribution, the industry could be broken down onto three locations (Fig. 1.8).

The first of these, *The Central Core* was centred on Soho, Covent Garden, Fitzrovia and latterly Victoria. It is here that the greatest mix of media business activities in London is found. This includes large numbers of micro and SME

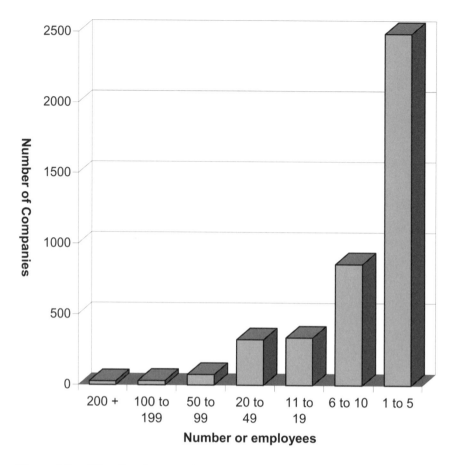

Figure 1.7   West London Media Companies by Size
Source: Urban Cultures Ltd.

companies in advertising and public relations and graphic design; most of the large
public relations and Advertising Agencies; large numbers of small and micro record
companies and music publishers, plus bigger players such as Faber, EMI, Warner
Chappell, MCA, A&M, BMG; the big film distributors (and Channel 4) and large
numbers of production companies and film makers; TV production companies, small
and some quite large; Facilities Houses, many in and around Soho; and various
support services, such as equipment and lighting, supplied to film crews. In this
way, Soho and environs remained the main focus of activity for the media/creative
industries in London and therefore the UK. Quite simply, there are places where
one must be – at least part of the time – to make it in the industry. This partly is a
reflection of the lifestyle preferences of people attracted into the media, and the fact

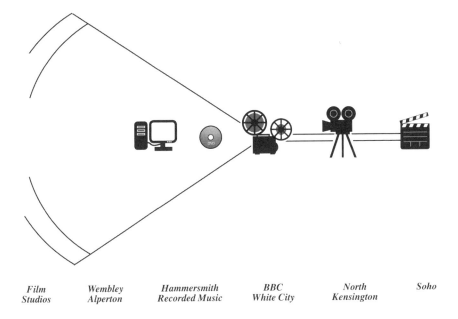

| *Film Studios* | *Wembley Alperton* | *Hammersmith Recorded Music* | *BBC White City* | *North Kensington* | *Soho* |

Figure 1.8   The West London Wedge
Source: Urban Cultures Ltd.

that so many deals are made and contracts worked in the bars, restaurants and clubs of West Central London.

The Inner West Arc is organized around the BBC at White City and Ealing. This area is largely characterized by a/v services, very often located on general industrial estates. There are also a few production companies located within easy reach of the BBC. This area contains many specialist companies in equipment hire, camera dollies, cranes, lighting, motion control, location facility vehicles, underwater equipment, even helicopter hire. In addition, Hammersmith is the major United Kingdom and European centre of recorded music, especially popular music. Hammersmith is home to four of the five major record labels, three big independent record companies, some recording studios and a whole public relations industry. There are also a number of small independent record companies and recording studios. The largest single concentration of activity in the sound recording sector is in Hillingdon and reflects the fact that the manufacturing and distribution divisions of EMI are based in Hayes, where the company was originally established in the 1920s. EMI might be seen as typical in this respect: it has a Head Office in W1, recording studios on the Abbey Road, but has its more "space hungry" functions outside central London or outside London itself. A further cluster of small music industry companies can be found in North Kensington. These originally formed around two successful nationals (now bought up by majors) which emerged in these locations in the 70s and 80s. These were Virgin (based behind the Harrow Road alongside the Grand Union Canal) and Chrysalis Records (based on Bramley Road close to Latimer Road underground station). It is still growing.

Finally, the *West London Wedge* extends more or less from the BBC at White City, westwards to the film studios along the West London Corridor. Throughout this area there exists a fairly even spread of advertising agencies, marketing and PR consultants and graphic designers, mostly micro-businesses and SMEs, also one or two larger businesses. Within the area, there are mini clusters of activity in Teddington, Twickenham and Ealing. In 1992, there were also four small studios within this area, one medium sized, twenty-three small record companies – mainly Chiswick and Ealing, but also Southall and Alperton. There were also companies specializing in sound mixing, editing and dubbing as inputs for TV and film production, this latter in an arc are from Wembley/Ealing/Shepperton. Film and TV production activity included A/V services such as lighting, show reels and titles; a few Film and TV designers based near Shepperton studios; eighty-eight micro-companies around Wembley, Twickenham, Richmond, Uxbridge, Chiswick and Ealing – mostly in TV, film and video distribution and services and video copying and distribution.

1990s London – A Conclusion

The creative industries contributed £21bn to London's GDP in 2000. Collectively, the total output of the creative industries was greater than any other industrial sector except business services, with creative industries output exceeding financial services, manufacturing, health & education, transport and retail.[40] The output of London's creative industries grew faster than all other industrial sectors in the city between 1995 and 2000, at a rate of 8.5% per year. Advertising, architecture, art & antiques, software & computer games, and film & photography all showed particularly strong growth rates, above the average rate for all of London's creative industries. In 2002, the creative industries workforce in London was 468,700, including those directly employed in creative industries sub-sectors, plus self-employed workers. An additional 182,000 people had creative jobs in London, but in sectors outside the creative industries (e.g. designers for car manufacturers, musicians in the education sector.) The creative industries is the third largest employment sector in London (after business services and health & education). Between 1995 and 2000, creative occupations were London's second biggest source of job growth, increasing by 111,000 and contributing roughly one in five new jobs. The annual rate of employment growth in the creative industries was 5%, nearly double London's overall rate. London dominates creative sector job growth in the UK. 40% of all new UK creative jobs generated between 1995 and 2000 were in London.

Thus the story of London's creative industries sector in the 1990s, and to the present day, reveals just how much economic activity there was and how important

---

40 Greater London Authority, *Creativity: London's Core Business*. London: GLA, 2002, p. 5.

the sector has become to the London and the UK economy. There was a lot going on. To an extent, the effect of recession was to mask the true extent of this activity, and the restructuring that was taking place. This is something of an irony as it was partly due to the recession – and changes to legislation – that these industries were restructuring in the first place. In any event, the analysis would seem to confirm that many of the creative industries were already moving to a core periphery employment model in the late 1980s.

The research from 1990s London reveals a somewhat more complex picture than a straightforward reading of the theories of post-Fordism would suggest. For one thing, it is clear that not all of the sub-sectors behave or are organized according to the "putting-out" mode of production. For example, the traditional points of cultural consumption (major galleries, concert halls, museums, libraries) continue to be organized more or less as "public goods" provided by the state. In this sense they remain more closely attuned to forms of state intervention which emerged under industrial capitalism in the nineteenth century. Those industries which were the primary focus of the research – broadcasting, music industry – are classic "cultural industries" in that they produce cultural goods (and entertainment) via technological media. It is clear, also, that these industries were organized along post-Fordist lines, and interestingly this dates from the very early 1980s, possibly before. The scenario was certainly one of sub-contracting, breakaways and start-ups, but this was accompanied by falling employment levels until 1996. Since 1996 these industries have achieved remarkable growth. By contrast, growth occurring in activities such as bespoke furniture, contemporary crafts, public art, digital art, design, fashion, visual arts generally and sculpture, has been more modest. These are not the "classic" cultural industries, but rather a set of artistic and craft skills dependent less on changes in technology than on the presence or absence of consumer demand.

5. THE CREATIVE INDUSTRIES AND THE FIFTH WAVE

The foregoing analysis suggests that there is not a single "creative industry" but three (at least) differing categories of activity: "traditional performing arts", creative industries and design. Again, this may not be especially surprising with the benefit of hindsight, and yet policy in the UK and elsewhere continues to combine all of these activities under the banner of "the creative industries". This, in turn, is not necessarily a problem provided those who intervene understand the differences between sectors. For it now seems to me that not only are the cultural or creative industries different in terms of product and distribution systems, they are also differently organized. Specifically, the high-profile, increasingly digitized, sectors of film, broadcasting and the music industry are the products of a more industrial form of capitalism, albeit restructured by post-Fordism. This means that these broadcast industries are based on technologies first invented in the late nineteenth century, industrialized in the first half of the twentieth century, and restructured from the 1970s onwards. The economic impact of digitization is only now being felt, since the late 1990s, but it is now certain that the broadcast media and music industries of the twenty–first century will be markedly different from those of the 1980s, the 1950s or the 1930s. Some of these industry sectors may be about to reach saturation point, certainly within the UK market. Future growth will depend on exports of films and programmes to networks around the world. It is more likely that new jobs and business generation will come through very small businesses innovating (new products, new cultural forms in the more fertile terrain of computer/communications, cultural convergence). All of this implies a distinction needs to be made between older forms of the cultural or creative industries, and the new.

This point is alluded to by Peter Hall's work *Cities in Civilisation*, notably the chapters on Los Angeles in the 1930s and Memphis in the 1950s.[41] Hall charts the "birth of modern pictures" from the late 1880s, with the invention of celluloid by Edison and George Eastman. From the late 1890s, it became possible to project images onto a screen. In other words, the technology that the film industry was based on developed during the period between the second and third Kondratieff cycles. The entrepreneurs who would develop commercial applications of this technology were (almost entirely) East European Jewish immigrants – William Fox, Adolph Zukor (founder of Paramount), Marcis Leow, Sam Goldwyn and Louis B Mayer (MGM) and Warner Brothers. Hall notes that the growth of the studio system dates from the early 1920s, so that by 1925 the industry had "reached maturity" and by the 1940s, the studio system had peaked. By the end of the 1950s, "the studio era had ended, and with it cinema's classical age".[42] The industrialized system of film production was fatally wounded by the introduction of newer technology (television), as well as law suits over the independence of actors and artists. Of course, the industry itself did not die, but it did restructure. The film studios still exist (largely as distributors and investors), but the industry is now characterized by independent producers, directors, actors and technicians brought together for individual productions. In other words, the industry structure moved towards flexible specialization or post-Fordism. This in fact is evident from the mid-60s when producers who might formerly have been regarded as mavericks were suddenly able to make in some cases experimental films: Peter Fonda, Robert Altman, Polanksi, John Cassavetes, Sam Peckinpah, Francis Ford Coppola.[43] The point is that the industry, though still with us, has had to restructure more than once. An industry invented in one era, grew as a form of mass production in another, and restructured to evolve and survive. It will change again as the impact of digitization grows.

Similarly, Hall's analysis of the growth of the music industry in Memphis (chapter 19) leads to some interesting conclusions, amongst them that the recording of popular music evolved from two earlier industries: music publishing and radio. The new technology of audio-tape made a more widespread recording of popular music possible from about 1954 onwards. Yet again the prerequisite new technologies had

---

41 Hall, P., *Cities in Civilisation* (London: Weidenfield and Nicholson, 1998).
42 Scholtz, T., *Hollywood: Filmmaking in the Studio Era* (New York: Pantheon, 1988).
43 Quinlan, T., *Quinlan's Film Directors* (London: B.T. Batsford Ltd, 1999).

been developed during a downwave and were later applied in an upswing. But the music business itself would later need to restructure from the 1970s, as seems to be confirmed in the London example discussed earlier. Much the same reasoning can be applied to television, itself a "new" industry in the 1950s, although first invented by Logie Baird in 1936. Television too was forced to restructure in the 1990s as we have seen, even to the extent where Britain's state-owned broadcaster, the BBC, has embraced "independent-producers" and contracting-out. What all of this implies is that the classic cultural industries have mutated from industrial forms of mass production to flexible specialization, and moreover did so in the second half of the fourth Kondratieff wave. If history teaches us anything here, then it is that it is unlikely that these self-same industries will survive in a recognizable form without further restructuring. This suggests that industries, like industrial products, have a "life cycle"[44] such that products must almost constantly improve due to a combination of changing customer tastes, technological advances and competitor activity.

For it also now appears that the studies of London's creative industries have stumbled on what might be a new or recently emerging trend. This is the growth of creative and business activity whereby a more one-to-one relationship exists between artists and designers and the public as consumers. These might well be mediated by physical points of sale – private galleries, shops, markets – but the essential difference is that consumers are tending increasingly to buy one-off, bespoke or specially-tailored items. This may, of course, be simply a logical extension of post-Fordism, but I suspect something else is happening, something which revolves around the "post-material effect", the rise of the ethical consumer, or the sovereign individual. It may be that we have reached a higher place on Maslow's "hierarchy of needs", whereby as individuals acquire enough material goods they move on to social prestige and then self-realization. En route the satisfaction levels of mass produced, and then differentiated, goods falls, so that consumers require original and individual products. If this is true then perhaps there will be an emerging new organization of production during the next thirty years, following on from those of previous waves.

Thus, it may well be that the emerging mode of production during the fifth Kondratieff wave will be towards what we shall term "individualized consumption" and "peer group purchasing" (communities of interest who collect certain art or objects, or who have hobbies and enthusiasms in common). Importantly, changes in style, fashion and taste will be mediated by what we might term "arbiters of taste", that is to say fashion, art and music critics writing in "lifestyle" magazines. This is already with us, and perhaps explains the cult of the C-list celebrity. Again, if true, this means that more artists and designers will make a living from direct commissions, exhibitions and gallery openings. The independent gallery/shop will be a more important point-of-sale in future. Artists and designers will increasingly be entrepreneurs too, and as such will need entrepreneurial skills. They will create

---

44 Boog Allen and Hamilton, *New Product Management for the 1980s*, quoted in H. Davidson, *Offensive Marketing* (London: Penguin Business Books, 1987 edition), p. 328.

Table 1.15 Long-wave Modes of Production Showing Typical Goods and Services

	Long Wave Cycle	Mode of Production	Organised by	Typical Goods and Services
1.	1781–1840	Late mercantile	Merchants and craft guilds	Clothing
2.	1840–1890	Early mass production	Industrialists	Rail, heavy engineering
3.	1890–1946	Mass production	Industrialists	Cars, electrical goods
4.	1946–2004	Flexible specialisation	Service providers	Computers, electronics, aviation, consumer, household goods
5.	2004–2060	Personalised consumption	Arbiters of taste	Design objects and art

Source: Derived from Jacobs 1969.

new work and sell it locally, nationally and globally. For the Internet and digital technologies (and air travel) will allow them to operate in markets beyond the places in which they themselves live. Many such businesses will be exporting firms, many will inter-trade locally and more will collaborate with other cultural entrepreneurs elsewhere. What is being described here is a new relationship between artistic and traditional craft skills, new design, new technology (of design and marketing as well as production) and new entrepreneurialism. The currency of such activities is ideas, skills and creativity. This is made possible by a new individualized relationship between the consumer and the producer.

The closest I can find to this "model" is the system of patronage and the emerging market for art on which the growth of the fifteenth century Italian city-states was based. Nothing less than "the birth of capitalism" was achieved by the steady accumulation of wealth – fortunes made in clothing, jewellery and furniture – the use of credit, new ways of organizing business (division of labour) and competition. Part of this new wealth was, in turn, spent on the arts and architecture, often by private patrons and most obviously by the church and the state. The artists, meanwhile, had emerged as a recognizable "class" from the development of craft skills, at the same time as a market for decorative arts came into being. By the 1450s, argues Hall, "private patronage began to transfer itself from the public sphere to the private patrician palace".[45] For the rich certainly, but also those of modest income, the "end of scarcity" led to greater spending on the arts. However, while there were a number of great individual artists during that time, most of those emerged from, were associated with, or collaborated with (often rival) workshops and, within these, groups of specialists. These developed, in large part, from the earlier guilds, set up to regulate quality and maintain skills and industry secrets. The key to all of this, argues Hall following Burke[46] was "conspicuous consumption", made possible by a "wide distribution of wealth". Crucially, production remained "small-scale and workshop based", and individual artists and their workshops became centres of innovation, enterprise and new work.

It is interesting to consider the similarities between Renaissance Florence and the present-day emerging economy for designed objects: "the end of scarcity", the hierarchy of needs, craft skills, workshops, patrons (or clients), individual commissions, new architecture and urban art, small-scale production. To this we can add new communications technologies. It is just possible that as well as the "knowledge economy", the classical creative industries, bio-technology and environmental products, the future will in part revolve around new patrons and new art. Which brings us back to culture, and in particular artistic creativity. We shall explore this theme in Part II.

6. DEVELOPING THE CREATIVE INDUSTRIES LOCALLY

To conclude, as shall be my practice for each of the major parts of this book, I offer a broad "what to do" guide, in this case for policy makers seeking to develop the creative industries locally. This advice is based on first-hand experience of doing precisely this in Manchester, Birmingham, East London, West London, North Kensington, Sheffield, Hull, Dublin, North London, Melbourne and West Sydney.

It is important to stress that the creative industries, though of the moment, are not a panacea nor are they a guarantee of employment and economic growth for all: other economic activity will continue to generate wealth and employment. But they are proper economic activity, a serious business, and competitive. Where they differ from most other economic activities – financial services, marine engineering, gas supply – is that they potentially at least combine cultural and economic development. They are simultaneously about production and value added as well as expression and creativity. Perhaps this is why so many young people are drawn to them. With some exceptions, they are also largely urban economic activities, that is to say they thrive in or around urban centres. People need the contact of other people to make soundings, generate ideas and make deals. Much of this happens in bars, restaurants and cafés.

45 Hall, *op. cit.*, 1998, p. 96.

46 Burke, P., *The Italian Renaissance: Culture and Society in Italy* (Cambridge University Press, 1987).

To some extent, the creative, cultural and media industries then are helping to find new roles for some previously declining urban areas. There will no doubt be a limit to how far the creative industries can expand. But we are some way from knowing what that limit will be. In the meantime, because of digitized technology the market for product will grow, and more than at any time previously it will be perfectly possible to generate, create and make cultural products from almost any part of a country. This is the lesson of recent intervention to develop local creative industry clusters in UK regional cities, as we shall see in the example of Sheffield in Part V.

The methods pursued have largely been based on the supply-side sector approach of the London Industrial Strategy of the early 1980s, and indeed on examples from other countries where particular economic sectors have achieved impressive and sustained growth. The most often referred to examples of this are the fashion, furniture, and ceramics industries of the Third Italy, the Emilia Romagna.[47] The Emilian government, from the late 1970s, played a central role in the growth of the region's economy. It has supplied a wide range of support and finance to the small and medium sized enterprises on which the economy is based. It encouraged export consortia, common service organizations, technology centres, data banks, sectoral market intelligence, computer-aided design systems, training programmes and craft colleges, the underwriting of financial cooperatives and the representation of regional interests at the national level.

The small firm industrial districts of Italy seem archaic to many, especially those who equate progress with size. The uncomfortable truth is that many – perhaps most – large firms no longer grow rapidly, particularly in employment terms. But Italy achieved an astonishing share of world exports for many industrial commodities during the 1970s and 1980s – men's suits, wooden chairs, knitwear, shoes, handbags, ceramic tiles. Most of these commodities are produced in the small firm industrial districts. Sassuolo, for example, is a world centre for ceramic tiles. Prato, near Florence, has 14,000 clothing firms which together produce twenty-five per cent of the world's mens suiting cloth. Carpi produces one quarter of Italy's exports of woollen clothing. These industry networks have strong collective public and private institutions – a largely invisible entrepreneurial infrastructure – which binds them together as if they were parts of a large concern. The social context in which this takes place is of great importance, with informal family and social networks often providing a solid and reliable framework for business transactions.

Throughout Italy, Regional Councils are empowered to develop policies to encourage the growth of small and medium sized enterprises – often, though by no means exclusively, the "artisan" firms who also enjoy legal exemption from labour and other welfare provisions. Emilia Romagna has seen a dramatic growth in the number of artisan firms over the past twenty years to the point where in employment terms they far outweigh the significance of larger enterprises. This growth has been supported by the development of a sophisticated "invisible" infrastructure, capable

---

47 I am grateful to my friend Peter Totterdill who informed me about the Emilia Romagna.

of delivering a near-comprehensive range of business services designed to lift the administrative burden on entrepreneurs, encourage innovation, and promote specific sectoral objectives. Examples include: book-keeping and auditing, legal services, industrial relations support and insurance; sector development programmes such as the "Centro Informazione Tessile ell" Emilia Romagna" (CITER); "Consorzio Carpi – Qualita" – a quality assurance scheme, joint marketing consortia, a clothing data centre, "Centro Dati Abbligliamento"; and credit consortia.

All of this is part of a broader strategy of assisting companies in the transition from mass market to higher value-added production. By these and other measures, coupled with the area's long-standing traditions of weaving, tailoring and entrepreneurship, the Third Italy has gone from strength to strength, even against a backdrop of sluggish economic growth in Italy. The example of the Third Italy is of more than passing interest, for many of the more innovative attempts to develop the cultural or creative industries in UK cities since the mid 1980s have pursued a broadly similar model. Not only was design seen as a source of value-added, but creativity more generally was seen as key to future economic development and wealth creation.

As with any sector development strategy, the actual forms which intervention can take are many and varied. I have set out the list of potential options in Table 1.16. The vertical axis of the table runs from less costly forms of intervention such as the production of directories, help in coalition building and various forms of marketing, to stronger forms of intervention such as the establishment of media agencies and fiscal policy shifts. The horizontal axis, meanwhile, moves from supply-side measures at one end to measures that are designed to stimulate demand at the other, for example trade fairs or even tax breaks.

The precise mix will vary from place to place, depending on local circumstances, the development stage already reached by the local creative industries, the culture of the place (whether it fosters and encourages creativity and cultural expression or not), and on the particular niche or profile which a local area can capture for itself. And so too, therefore, will the mix of measures that need to be taken and/or given priority change. For some places – cities or regions or even countries – the strategic thrust will be to market themselves as film locations; others will promote themselves as a production base (you can make anything here); yet others will deliberately encourage locally based creative people to write and make and record; and still others will seek to establish themselves as places not of production but of consumption – film houses, media galleries, museums of the moving image and so on.

The menu is not infinite, however, and it is likely to boil down to some combination of the initiatives and programmes summarized in Table 1.17. Essentially, the mix is likely to involve some combination of product development (new ideas and concepts and performances); business development (how to run and grow small businesses); market development (how to win contracts and network); skills development (training); area marketing as a business location and site for inward investment; and general profile-raising. Figure 1.7 is organized around eight strategic types of intervention, each of which contains a number of policy initiatives, projects and programmes. In total there

Table 1.16   Policy Options for the Cultural Sector

A. Supply side	B. Distribution and networks	C. Demand side
1. Directories, guides, explanatory leaflets, database/yearbooks, trade conferences/services	1. Coalition building, conferencing, agenda setting through public discussion	1. Promotion of cultural sector at local level and beyond (e.g. Year of Culture)
2. Small firm R and D support, business advice services	2. Joint public/private goalsetting and collaboration on objectives	2. Market research on existing and potential audiences
3. Niched business spaces or art form centres, managed workspaces and quarters/districts	3. Sector analysis and strategy development	3. Public/private purchasing
4. Project funding and initiation	4. Leveraged access for cultural operators via policy shifts, preferential vouchers systems or financial incentives	4. Festivals, trade fairs
5. Training and vocational education	5. Direct investment in purchase of network(s): Marketing consortia for the arts; TV station; Record distribution; Companies; Cable station	5. Media education initiatives and cultural policy research
6. Cultural agencies, commissions (e.g. film, public art, design)		6. Technology and facilities subsidies, pilot projects and flagship creation
7. Industrial policy (regional, national); subsidy/support for champions; joint network risk taking		7. Fiscal policy shifts (VAT rates, interest rates etc)

Source: Montgomery 1996, p. 166; derived from Simon Blanchard.

Table 1.17   An Ideal Type Media Industries Development Strategy

1. Product development
   Script Development Fund – to get more young writers started
   Programme Development Fund – risk funding of productions
   Programme and Film-making Competitions – to find new talent

2. Small business and enterprise development
   Business Advice and Information Bureau
   Fast Track Venture Capital Fund – for items of equipment

3. Training and skills development
   Pre-entry skills and awareness
   Customised media skills – short course programme
   Placement programs
   Training bursaries
   Industry briefing seminars

4. Property support
   Rent grants
   Managed workspaces – provision of
   Improvement and development grants

5. Product marketing and promotion
   Information agency and media desk
   Media directory
   Joint-marketing initiatives
   Conferences and trade fairs

6. Area marketing and promotion (raising the profile)
   Area branding
   Media campaign
   Film and TV festival
   Location bureau or film and television commission

7. Inward investment
   Media Club – to network in
   "Shop Window' or showcase project – gallery or film theatre

8. Creating a focus
   Urban vitality – café culture and the evening economy

Source: Montgomery 1996, p. 167.

**Figure 1.9 The Workstation,
Sheffield CIQ**

Source: John Montgomery.

are twenty-four such policies, programmes and projects in outline form.[48]

Perhaps the most important initiative is a business incubator or managed workspace of some kind (Fig. 1.9).

These have certainly proved successful in many UK cities, and are now being introduced in Australia. We shall return to this issue in Part V, a discussion of creative industry and cultural quarters.

At this juncture, we can conclude that there are a number of reasons why local authorities and agencies might consider it an important task to foster the creative industries. As far as the productive economy itself goes, the creative industries help to further diversify the local economic base, and in many cases it will be possible to build on an already developed or nascent creative industries economy. The aim should be to consolidate and further develop clusters of competitive activity, and in the process to create new forms of capital, new products and even new inventions and technologies. For local people, this raises the prospect of new jobs, employment opportunities in the creative industries and in spin-off activities. In the longer term, training schemes will help overcome blockages in the labour market, and provide access for local people wishing to undertake careers in the creative industries. This skills base must be maintained into the future if a creative economic cluster is to flourish. It will also be necessary to reduce any "brain-drain" of talented and skilled people to competitor areas and economies, although this can only be done by offering incentives and adopting city management policies which place a high premium on the arts, entertainment, style and the overall quality of life.

It is clearly important for contemporary cities to achieve a high development rate amongst entrepreneurs in the new industries, that is those that will power the fifth wave. As in the Third Italy, the role of public sector policy, is to foster initiative, innovation and risk-taking. This means not only encouraging economic development within the cultural or creative industries but, as we shall see, encouraging wider strategies for the city's public realm and seeing parts of the city as areas for cultural and small business experimentation. These are all vital to the development of a creative economy. Successful city and city-region economies are already being transformed

---

48 Montgomery, J., "Developing the Media Industries", *Local Economy*, Vol. 11, No. 2, August 1996, pp. 158–167.

by the technological innovation that is giving rise to the new economy. The question for any city is not whether it has the creative and technological resources, but also how these can be sustained and continually turned to its economic advantage. For here is the final point: creative people will only flock to or remain in cities that are worth the effort, or provide the opportunities.[49] Cities who do not do so will be left behind in the new economy.

---

49 Montgomery, J., "Beware the Creative Class: Creativity and Wealth Creation Revisited", *Local Economy*, Vol. 20, No. 4, November 2005, pp. 337–343.

Art and the City

Part II explores the relationship between artistic creativity, movements in the arts and city development. That is, the correlation between city growth, wealth creation, urban form, the arts and artistic genius. Why do certain cities develop golden ages of artistic creativity combined with great architecture and wealth creation? Why does this happen at particular points in time? What is the role of artistic genius? Does artistic creativity help engender wealth creation, or is it a passive recipient of new wealth, that is dependent on economic development in the first instance? Why is it that artists gravitate to particular cities at critical moments in time? It seems that there may be a link connecting cultural and artistic creativity, particularly the rise and fall of artistic movements – to the concept of the paradigm shift, and possibly to the long-wave cycle of the capitalist economic development. Let me say here that demonstrating this is no simple task, but shall be attempted by reference to the great movements in the arts, and by a set of case studies of particular cities: Florence, Amsterdam, Edinburgh, London, Paris, New York.

This raises the question of what cities might consider doing in relation to artistic creation, city development and wealth creation at the present time, over the next 10 years or so. Some lessons – good and bad – may be gleaned from recent attempts to use the arts as a means of urban regeneration. Is it true, for example, that those cities that have regenerated themselves economically have also revived themselves culturally? Does one lead the other, or are they simultaneously mutually reinforcing? Do cultural revitalization strategies work, and if so how? At a less theoretical level, if the creative class is crucial to city economic growth, then what should individual cities be doing to generate their own creative class? What should cities do to stimulate greater artistic creativity, and how might this support the creative industries (discussed in Part I) as an economic sector for the future?

This man's firm runs cafés and dance-halls in various London suburbs and provincial cities, so that you may say he makes his money out of the new frivolity of our age, which we so often hear condemned by people who do not happen to like cafés and dance-halls themselves and do not see why others should. He goes round visiting these places from time to time, had just inspected their Liverpool properties and now wanted to have a look at their big café in Manchester. He did not like Manchester. It seems that when his firm decided to open the café on Sunday evenings, they asked the Manchester City Fathers if they could provide their patrons with music, a little orchestra and a singer or two. The City Fathers said: 'No, we can't allow that sort of thing in Manchester.' So they asked if the café could have gramophone music. The Fathers promptly replied: "Certainly not, no gramophone in public on Sunday." Could they then install a loud speaker in the café, and thus entertain their patrons with the programmes that Sir John Reith himself passed for public consumption on the Sabbath? Again Manchester refused permission. So now, he informed me dryly, the café is open on Sunday evenings, and generally full, but nothing happens in the way of entertainment and his firm is saved the expense of providing it. The people are only too willing , on winter Sunday nights, to go in and stare at one another. It is a change from the streets or a back bed-sitting-room up the Oldham Road. There was a time when Manchester was known as the "home of living causes", but exactly what living causes are finding a home there now I do not know.

Still, when I was a boy, Manchester had the best newspaper and the best orchestra in the country, which is saying something: its citizens, who could read the Manchester Guardian in the morning and listen to the Hallé under Richter in the evening, were not badly off and could be said to be in touch with civilization. They had too, at that time, the best repertory theatre in the kingdom, and their own considerable school of dramatists and dramatic critics. It is perhaps significant that the critics were better than the dramatists. Manchester, I suspect, has always been more critical than creative; but that, let us admit, is much better than being neither.

To Lancashire. English Journey, J.B. Priestley
(London: Heinemann, 1994), p. 251

1. ARTISTIC CREATIVITY

The theory chapter of this book briefly reviewed some of the main concepts within cultural studies. This ranged from the "great art, great intellect" ethos of Leavis and Arnold,[1] through the "cultural industry" of the Frankfurt School, the French Structuralists,[2] the post-structuralists,[3] the post-modernists[4] and Raymond Williams. There is no real need to revisit this ground further, save only to make my position on post-modernism clear.

"Post-modernism" is a term used to describe the retreat from the certainties of modernism, particularly in architecture and fine art. Within literature, it developed from "post-structuralism". In all of its guises, but especially in cultural studies, post-modernism is a reaction to modernism which itself, once *avant*

---

1   For a useful introduction, see Storey, J., *An Introductory Guide to Cultural Theory and Popular Culture* (Hemel Hempstead: Harvester Wheatsheaf, 1993).

2   Saussure on semiology or life as the study of signs; Claude Levi-Strauss on structuralism; Roland Barthes on signs, denotation and conotation. All of these writers were structuralists.

3   Jacques Derrida on *difference* – meaning both to differ and to defer and deconstructivism or "hidden" meanings; Jaques Lacan on post-structuralist psychoanalysis; and Michel Foucault on discourse and the use of language in relation to power.

4   Lyotard, Baudillard, Jameson.

garde, had become accepted, mainstream and canonized. Although the term post-modernism dates back to the 1870s, its contemporary usage has developed from the 1960s, and the rejection of classicism and modernism. This was the time of generational rejection of former mores and values, the rise of pop music and popular culture. Beyond this simple observation, however, post-modernism itself then collapses into a series of contradictions. For example in the arts, pop art in the 1950s and 1960s was welcomed by some theorists as a celebration of diversity and affluence; while others lamented the decay of traditional values and forms.

Jean-Francois Lyotard published *The Post-modern Condition*[5] in 1979, and it was translated into English in 1984. Lyotard argues that post-modernism represents the collapse of all meta-narratives (by which he means universal truths or principles) and their replacement by a plurality of "voices from the margins" insisting on difference, cultural diversity and heterogeneity. Later post-modernists, notably Jean Baudrillard,[6] would go on to assert that phenomena, including art works, can be explained and interpreted in a number of different ways because there are no universal truths, nothing can be known, and so knowledge and truth are relative, subjective and dependent on the viewer's viewpoint and values. Interestingly, Lyotard himself lamented rather than celebrated post-modernity, dismissing it as an "anything goes culture", a culture of "slackening", to be replaced at some future date by a new modernism of taste and high art. More trenchant critics, such as Fredric Jameson,[7] would dismiss post-modernism as a "culture of pastiche" – the empty or meaningless copy, "a new kind of flatness or depthlessness", marked by an "essential triviality". Jameson was writing in a Marxist tradition, and sees post-modernism not as a break with capitalism but as a means of re-enforcing and re-intensifying it. In this, he was followed more or less by the urban geographer David Harvey.[8]

In this way, one can be a post-modernist who celebrates the collapse of certainty and the rise of "otherness"; or one can be a post-modernist who derides this simply as the next stage of capitalism, empty and trivial. Variations on these themes have been re-hashed and re-heated ever since, leading cultural historians such as Jim McGuigan to claim that the field of cultural studies is in the throes of a "paradigm crisis", a "crisis of qualitative judgement".[9] McGuigan calls for a return of the modernist intellectual and the Arnoldian view of culture as "the best that has been thought and said".

---

5   Lyotard, J-F., *The Post-modern Condition: A Report on Knowledge* (Manchester: Manchester University Press, 1984).

6   Baudrillard, J., *Simulations* (New York: Semiotext(e), 1983).

7   Jameson, F., "Post-modernism, or the cultural logic of late capitalism", *New Left Review*, 146, 1984.

8   Harvey, D., *The Condition of Post-Modernity: An Enquiry into the Origins of Cultural Change* (Oxford: Blackwell, 1989).

9   McGuigan, J., *Cultural Populism* (London: Routeledge, 1992).

For our purposes, the important point is that post-modernism rejects the notion of absolute rules, dominant styles or even recognized convention. Along the way, the concept of the artist as a creative genius is also dismissed. Shakespeare, Dante, Mozart, Michelangelo and the rest are belittled, in the odious phase of "dual-systems theory"[10] American feminists, as "dead white men". Dismissed too, are conventions such as "taste", art itself and, ironically, style. All of these, instead, have to be held up to the prism of class analysis or cultural diversity. From here, everything goes down hill rapidly: there can be no objective judgement of the value of art, indeed, the audience (the subjective) becomes more important than the artist (the objective). More important than the art itself is where it sits within the context of class relations, plus gender, race and sexuality. It is but a short step from this to arguing that art should always seek to highlight the concerns and issues of favoured "marginalized" groups. Essentially, post-modernism is both a legitimization of continuing an out-moded class warfare; and simultaneously rejoices in the splintering of society into more or less vocal, demanding and self-absorbed "communities".

The problem is that there is nothing left to value, set store by or believe in. In my view, post-modernism is mainly a form of leftist pseudo-intellectualism that has little practical value. It is, however, invasive and dangerous and has done much to undermine the core values, belief systems and codes of behaviour in countries such as England, Holland and Sweden. Its influence on cultural studies, art history and the humanities has been divisive. For one thing, it has taken the joy out of reading for it lacks and fails to comprehend humour, compassion, ethics, eroticism, wisdom and even artistic genius. The culprits in all of this are the French post-structuralists Foucault, Lacan and Derrida, the nihilists of the 1960s. In cultural studies, the result is that soap operas and sitcoms are accorded the same status as "texts" as the great masterpieces or even the films of Ingmar Bergman. The great architectural styles of the past are dismissed; for if we can get by with throwing up ornamented sheds, why bother? The lyrics of songs by the Spice Girls are pored over as if they were written by Dickens or Voltaire. *Big Brother* is considered as culturally relevant as *Henry V*. There is no joy in discovering art or celebrating genius;[11] indeed, recognizing genius is the last thing the idealogical left seems prepared to do.

This would not be so serious if cultural institutions and especially universities were maintaining the knowledge of and celebrating what is best in culture and art. The problem is that a sensible, joyful and often spiritually uplifting study of the arts has been replaced by politically correct "contextualization", stressing

---

10 The "Dual Systems Theory" is a combination of Marxist and radical feminism. It attests that women are oppressed by the twin systems of capitalism and patriarchy. By contrast, liberal feminism sees the problem deriving from male prejudice of women, as embodied in laws and certain customs or male-oriented ways of life.

11 Paglia, C., *Junk Bonds and Corporate Raiders: Academe in the Hour of the Wolf*, in Paglia, *Sex Art and American Culture* (London: Penguin, 1992).

"relevance" and "social inclusion". Sadly, in trying at all costs to avoid being seen to be "elitist" the study of the arts and culture has eschewed the very notion of genius; for if some people are geniuses, or even very talented, most of the rest of us are not – and that's not fair is it? The end result is that art itself becomes either ever more shallow and meaningless, or else will become further removed from the mainstream. By forcing parents to choose between politicized state school curricula and private education, it is no surprise that an increasing number choose the latter. Similarly with the arts: if the choice is between dumbing down and cultural relativism as opposed to more elitism, give me elitism any day. Meanwhile, the message to the masses is that they are just too stupid to appreciate art, the exact opposite of what was taught in state schools in the UK in the 1950s, 1960s and early 1970s. Back at the universities, a climate of wariness if not fear has been engendered, so that scholars must these days be careful not to offend the new politically correct orthodoxy. Try teaching art for its own sake at your peril, and never, ever mention the word genius.

> **Genius,** the special inborn faculty of any individual; consummate intellectual creative or other power, more exalted than talent; one so endowed.
>
> *Chambers Twentieth Century Dictionary*, Edinburgh

The above definition was the only one that could be found during researches for this book. It seems the very word has been expunged from the literature on cultural studies and the humanities. Yet, for the purposes of any historical study of cities, it is at least a possibility that the history of certain cities was changed forever, not only by periods of wealth creation, but also by artistic innovation, creativity and the genius of individuals. For example, would the Renaissance have occurred without Brunelleschi? Or would Paris have become the artistic centre of the world in the 19th century without Manet and Monet, Debussy and Ravel? Would Cubism have developed without Cezanne and Picasso? Would London look as it does today without John Nash? Would New York have become the centre for modern art without Peggy Guggenheim? At the very least, we should at least attempt to understand creative genius.

The problem is that there is not much in the literature that helps. It is one thing to recognize that geniuses have gifts that transcend mere talent, that art is capable of driving people to agonies and ecstasies, even that art can somehow define the human condition. But it is another thing to explain why this is so. If not simply a gift from God, then how can science explain creative genius. Freud and his followers were the first to subject art to "scientific" study, and Freud himself would conclude, more or less, that art is simply the making of socially acceptable symbols to express repression and desires. In other words, art is an expression of narcissistic neuroses; and by extension all artists are at least a little mad. Some have gone on to highlight a high correlation between artistic genius and Asperger's Syndrome (autism), so at least part of the answer will lie in the genetic makeup of the individual.[12] Examples

---

12 Fitzgerald, M., *The Genesis of Artistic Creativity: Asperger's Syndrome and the Arts* (London: Jessica Kingsley, 2005).

include Mozart, Beethoven, Andy Warhol, Yeats, Wittgenstein and Van Gogh, all of whom struggled to communicate in everyday social discourse. Of course, as in other people, artists will be subject to external influences, for example the home environment, the early introduction to an art form as in the case of Mozart, the opportunity to learn from other, often more mature, artists, a new experience such as Debussy hearing a gamelan (a Javanese percussion, woodwind and string orchestra), the rediscovery of techniques such as perspective, or some new insight from the world of science and engineering. In this way, it seems that artistic creativity is a process that emerges from the individual, working in a particular art form and in relation to his or her environment and other external influences, including mentors.[13]

Another observation we can make is that artistic (and scientific creation) tends to occur in short bursts,[14] often building on one's own earlier work or that of others. In this way, individual artists tend to have one concentrated period of intense creativity, and those who manage more than this – such as Picasso or Beethoven – will very often need to develop the art form further to achieve any further breakthroughs. Rather than simply arising out of what has gone before, such moments of creativity are a break with the past, a new beginning. This implies that the creative genius is able to change pre-existing patterns and logics, to make new art by not conforming. This might, these days, be referred to as a "step change" where the art form itself is altered radically.

In philosophical terms, this would be referred to as a "paradigm shift". This concept was proposed by Thomas Kuhn in 1962,[15] predominantly in relation to scientific knowledge. Kuhn argued that scientific progress does not proceed in a gradual upward curve, but rather in a series of creative leaps. For most of time, Kuhn argued, scientists are content to accept a particular set of accepted laws and norms – a "paradigm". But at particular points in time these particular paradigms are discovered to be limited in their explanatory power. New theories and laws are required – a new paradigm – so that scientific and artistic progress is marked by a series of "paradigm shifts". If this argument is true then we might apply a similar logic to the arts as texts, images, sounds and movement. Peter Hall notes[16] that Kuhn's theory of the paradigm shift was intended to apply to art as well as science. This, however, has rarely been followed through in the literature, possibly reflecting C.P. Snow's infamous "Two Cultures"[17] where he argues that a split between the arts and science has developed in society, education and intellectual life (although Snow was arguing in favour of science).

---

13 Gardner, H., *Art, Mind and Brain: A Cognitive Approach to Creativity* (New York: Basic Books, 1982).

14 Koestler, A., *The Act of Creation* (London: Hutchinson, 1964).

15 Kuhn, T., *The Structure of Scientific Revolutions* (University of Chicago Press, 1962).

16 Hall, P., *Cities in Civilization* (London,: Weidenfeld and Nicolson, 1998), Phoenix Giant Paperback edition, 1999, p. 16.

17 Snow, C.P., *The Two Cultures* (Cambridge University Press, 1964).

It would seem at face value true that the Impressionists or Bebop Jazz musicians fashioned a paradigm shift. Further, it seems likely that such new movements in art will be sparked by creative originators, although the precise "triggers" may vary considerably. For example, the innovators in literature might be Scott, Balzac, Conrad, Joyce and Eliot. In fine art those responsible for the beginnings of new paradigms would no doubt include Constable and Turner. Later an artist associated with the Impressionists, Paul Cezanne, would in fact spark a new fine art paradigm of Cubism and later Expressionism as in the works, for example, of artists such as Klee, Braque, Kandinsky and Miro. The next break or paradigm shift would come in the 1940s, in New York, with Pollock's "Action Painting". It is worth considering this notion further by exploring in more detail the recognized movements in the arts. Are bursts of "primary" creativity followed by subsequent forms of "applied" and/or derived creativity? Could it be that paradigm shifts in the arts happen at particular times because of other shifts in technology, philosophy and economic development? Does artistic creativity follow a wave pattern over time?

Within any such movements, it is likely that rivalries and competitiveness will have played a role, whether between contemporaries such as Matisse and Picasso or Shakespeare and Marlowe, or between individuals of successive generations, for example Pollock and Picasso or Raphael and Michelangelo. Edwards[18] explain changes within art forms in terms of "creative ideologies" and a "creative succession", and this ideological succession is brought about by clashes between the generations – the new supplants the old. A sporting metaphor might be seen in tennis, where each generation produces a great champion and one or more supreme contenders: Hoad and Gonzalez, Laver and Rosewall, Nastase and Conners, Borg and McEnroe and Lendl, Sampras and Agassi, Navratilova and Lloyd. New contenders herald the arrival of a new generation, for example John Newcombe, Boris Becker or Martina Hingis. In this way, part of the explanation for a paradigm shift comes from the almost irresistible urge to challenge and change what has gone before. In this way, for example, Expressionism can properly be seen as a reaction to Impressionism.[19]

Yet even this set of explanations for creative genius – the individual's genetic makeup, an element of madness, the art form itself, early influences, the individual's environment, the role of mentors, rivalries with contemporaries, the urge to break with the recent past – still fails to explain why it is that some changes are simply an evolution, while others are truly paradigm shifts. Finally, there is the question as to why such bursts of creativity should occur in particular places – normally cities – at certain points in time. This raises the issue of why certain cities are more likely to produce bursts of creativity, while others do not. Hippolyte Taine's[20] concept of the "creative milieu" is helpful here. Taine argues that where creative milieux exist,

18 Edwards, J.M.B., "Creativity: Social Aspects", in Sills, D.L., *International Encyclopedia of the Social Sciences*, 3, pp. 442–57 (New York: Macmillan, 1967).

19 Richard, L., *Expressionism* (Paris: S.P.A.D.E.M, 1978).

20 Hall, P., *op. cit.*, 1998.

these tend to be underpinned by "a general state of manners and mind", producing in turn a "moral temperature" which allows talent and artistic creativity to develop in particular places at particular times.[21] Taine asserts that artists and creative innovators always exist within human societies, and so the question becomes one of whether they are allowed or encouraged to pursue their art. Moreover, such people tend only to innovate, at least in their early years, where they have access to stimuli, opportunities to meet other people and freedom from censorship and heavy-handed regulation. This suggests that not only is creative genius itself essential to progress, but so too are the economic, cultural, moral and even built environments in which artists and inventors live. This may well provide the clue to why certain cities are or have been creative milieux, and others probably never will be.

2. ART MOVEMENTS AS PARADIGMS

In the following pages, I have devised a series of diagrams mapping instances of primary creativity, and later derivations and applications. These I have based on Kondratieff's theory of the long wave, and also on the diagrams in Robert Beckman's[22] book *The Downwave*. The first diagram plots the Kondratieff curves from 1785 to 1946, and then the fourth wave as proposed by Beckman (1946–2002), plus a projected fifth wave – 2004–2060. I have then applied this approach to the arts, namely music and literature (plus poetry and drama). The case of fine art will be considered separately in a series of city case studies.

Composition

If we take music as our main example, we can see that there are acknowledged movements in musical history.[23] The Baroque period in music dates from about 1600, and so pre-dates the first Kondratieff Wave and therefore early industrial capitalism (Fig. 2.1).

Nevertheless, it is important to understand that Baroque provided a setting for the development of Classical Music in the late 18th century. The term Baroque means `bizarre` and was originally applied to the ornate architecture of Germany and Austria during the 17th century. Musical development in the early 17th century saw an increase in harmonic complexity and an emphasis on contrast. In opera, interest was transferred from the recital to the aria, while in instrumental music there was the emergence of the sonata, the suite, the concerto grosso and basso conentuo. The important composers of the period were Bach, Handel, Vivaldi and Corelli, two Italians and two Germans. It was Handel (1685–1759) who, during a trip to Italy in 1706, would master the Italian style in chamber music and opera, taking it first to Hanover and later to London

---

21 Taine, H., *Philosephie de l'Art*, 1865, as translated by Peter Hall, 1998 *op. cit.*, pp. 15–16.

22 Beckman, R., *The Downwave* (London: Pan Books, 1983).

23 Taruskin, R., *The Oxford History of Western Music* (Oxford University Press, 2005).

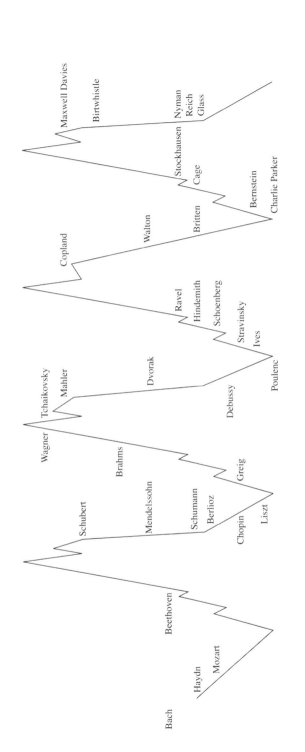

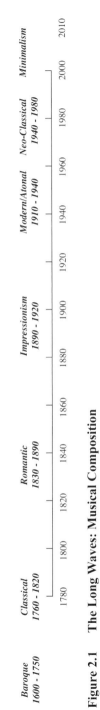

Figure 2.1   The Long Waves: Musical Composition
Source: John Montgomery.

where he lived the rest of his life as a naturalized Englishman. He continued to write opera and works such as the *Water Music* (1717), but is particularly associated with the development of dramatic oratorios such as *Judas Maccabeus* (1747) and *The Messiah*, first performed in Dublin in 1742.[24] Handel was important not only for his own compositions, but because he brought the Italian style to Germany and England, triggering what later would become Classical music.

Arguably the key figure in the development of western music at the time, however, was Johann Sebastian Bach (1685–1750). Bach was appointed organist at Mulhausen in 1708, and remained for nine years. During this time he wrote the two toccatas and fugues in D minor, the *Fantasia and Fugue in G* and many others.[25] He was appointed Kappelmeister at the court of Aunhalt-Cothen by Prince Leopold whose interest, importantly, lay not in religious works but instrumental composition. This fact in itself was important in the development of western music, as it allowed Bach to experiment with new musical forms. During his time at Cothen Bach would write several violin concertos, sonatas and suites, and the *Brandenburg Concertos*. In *The Well-Tempered Clavier* (1722), which profoundly influenced Mozart, Bach transformed the conventional structure of preludes and fugues. Bach left Cothen to take up the post of Cantor at St. Thomas's, Leipzig in 1723. He remained in Leipzig for the rest of his life, becoming court composer in 1729, and during this period he composed more than 250 Sonatas, the *St. Matthew Passion*, the *Mass in B Minor*, the *Christmas Oratorio*, the *Goldberg Variations*, and much more, including his final work, the unfinished *Art of Fugue*. During his life Bach's reputation as a composer was restricted to a narrow circle and his music was more generally regarded as old-fashioned. Comparatively few of his works were printed until a revival sparked by Mendelssohn's performance of the *St. Matthew Passion* in Berlin in 1829.

By the second half of 18th century a number of musicians were able to make a living from concertos, teaching and private commissions without needing to depend totally on patronage. At this time, music developed into the Classical era, the leading composers being Haydn (1732–1809), Mozart (1756–1791) and later Beethoven (1770–1827). The opening instrumental overtures or "sinfonies" of Baroque opera and oratorios developed into the symphony which came to have a four-movement form: an opening fast movement, a lyrical slow movement, a short fast movement and a fast finale. This was the form that Joseph Haydn[26] perfected in over 100 examples, together with another new musical genre, the string quartet. These works were ordered by the structural principal of "sonata form" in which an opening exposition, usually presenting two contrasting themes, is succeeded by a central "development" in which the themes are subjected to a variety of treatments. Then comes a "recapitulation" in which the opening themes are repeated, followed by a short "coda" to round off the movement. With its order and clarity of structure, this was the music of the Enlightenment.

---

24 Burrows, D., *Handel* (London: 1994).

25 Dawley, T., *Bach: His Life and Times* (London: 1985).

26 Butterworthy, N., *Haydn* (London: 1978).

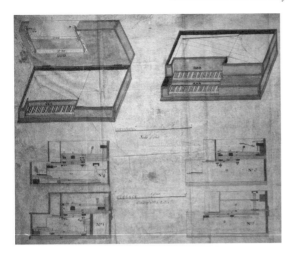

Figure 2.2   Design for a Keyboard (1792)
Source: The National Archives (c210/39), with permission.

Haydn's great Viennese contemporaries Mozart and Beethoven would develop the symphony and the string quartet. Mozart would also revolutionize the solo concerto, particularly the piano concerto as the 18th century harpsichord was overtaken by the more reliable and much more powerful pianoforte (Fig. 2.2).

Mozart would also develop the piano sonata and developed opera (following Gluck) in *Marriage of Figaro* and *Don Giovanni*. While Haydn prospered under the system of patronage, Mozart was often considered rebellious and radical,[27] and struggled to make a living as even his concertos were too complex for audiences of the day. The last 9 years of Mozart's life were an extraordinary out-pouring of masterpieces in almost every genre: *Figaro, Don Giovanni*, the string quintets in C and G minor, *Eine Kleine Nachtmusik*, the *Prague Symphony*, the last three symphonies, *Cosi fan Tutti*, the *Magic Flute*, the C minor piano concerto and the *Requiem*. Mozart combined elements of Italian, French, Austrian and German elements and, by doing so, transformed the course of the symphony, the piano concerto, the string quartet, the sonata and opera. Unable to earn a living, and suffering from ill-health in the last three years of his life, Mozart died a pauper in 1791.

Beethoven would act as a bridge between the Classical period, as in his early symphonies, sonatas and concertos, and the Romantic era. He would also be the first composer to succeed in making a living without the support of a patron. Beethoven was born in Bonn where his father was a tenor in the service of the Elector of Cologne.[28] He moved to Vienna in 1790 where he was taught by Haydn, Salieri and Johann Albrechtsberger. Beethoven's creative output is traditionally divided into three parts: his early period as a Classical composer, the middle period of heroic optimism and his late period during which time he composed the last string quartets, the *Mass in D* and the *Choral Symphony*. His middle period coincided with Napoleon's toppling of the *ancien regime* across most of Europe, and his music at this time reflects a new age of individualism and humanity's relationship with nature, a favourite theme of Romanticism. Beethoven was able to compose for much larger orchestras, following the invention of new instruments

---

27 Robbins Landen, H.C., *Mozart and Vienna* (London: 1991).
28 Marek, G.R., *Beethoven: Biography of a Genius* (London: 1969).

– for example the clarinet – and the improvement of existing woodwind and brass, so that his compositions achieved new heights of power, colour and tone. Beethoven is credited with emancipating music from the strictures of patronage, and of creating from inner spiritual necessity.

It is worth pausing as this juncture to reflect on the development of music up until Beethoven's death in 1827. The music of the Renaissance, largely based around the polyphonic song form of the "motet", had by 1600 developed into the Baroque era which would dominate European music until around 1750 and the death of Bach. From the late 1750s, Franz Joseph Haydn would develop the symphony and the string quartet of the Classical period. In this he would be followed by his brother Michael, Carl Webber, Mozart and the young Beethoven. Changes in technology – the invention of the piano-forte in the early 18th century, the clarinet and others, led to new forms such as the piano sonata and the piano, clarinet and horn concertos. By this time Vienna was the music capital of the world, a situation brought about by the long-standing promotion of music by the Austrian emperors. As the centre of the Austrian empire, Vienna attracted musicians from Italy, Bohemia, Germany, Hungary and Poland. As in art and architecture, Classical music was dominated by form and structure, as well as melody. As such it was a reaction against the ostentation and the period during which this break with the previous musical paradigm occurred was in the late 1750s through to Mozart's death in 1791, or Beethoven's early period. This coincides with the lead up to Kondratieff's first wave (1785 to 1840), during which time the industrial revolution was in its infancy and Edinburgh and Paris were the centres of the Enlightenment. In this way, the development of Classical music in Vienna corresponds with the end of the mercantile capitalism and its development into early industrial capitalism.

Vienna's primacy in the musical world would come to an end by 1830, following the death of Franz Schubert, aged only 31. Although some of his works were probably influenced by Beethoven, he was clearly influenced most by Mozart's melodic style and works for the voice, as well as Rossini's operatic overtures. Like Mozart, even when at its happiest, Schubert's music is affected by a deep sadness and romantic pathos.[29] He is particularly noted for his development of Lied – songs accompanied by piano. Schubert is regarded as an early example of Romanticism in music, whereby composers came to view music as an expression of their psyche, ideals and passion. A key notion is the belief in music's power to translate human experience and express higher order ideals. Describing emotions became more important than musical form. The early innovators were Beethoven himself and Schubert, being followed most notably by Robert Schumann, Mendelssohn and Brahms, Berlioz and later Bruckner and Wagner.

This paradigm – Romanticism – was also present in literature and poetry, and would last until the second half of the 19th century. It would evolve into various forms of nationalism in which composers began to use folk tunes to give their

---

29 McKay, E.N., *Schubert: A Biography* (London: 1996).

romantic music a national identity. This would include composers such as Greig (Norway 1843–1907), Dvorak (Czech, 1841–1904), Sibelius (Finland 1865–1957), Liszt (Hungary 1811–1886) and the Russian composers Borodin, Mussorgsky, Tchaikovsky and Rimsky-Korsokov. Romanticism, then, became the antithesis of Classicism just as Classicism had earlier broken away from the Baroque.

The next paradigm shift in music occurred in Paris, and was led by Faure, Satie, Debussy and Ravel. Usually referred to as Impressionists, French composers in the late 19th century began to experiment with a more fluid style and with tone variations. The term "Impressionism" derives from the art movement of the same name, and was applied to Debussy and his followers because they interpret their subjects (*La Mer, L'Apres Midi d'un Faune*) in a similarly impressionistic manner, conveying moods and emotions. This, however, should not be taken to mean that the music was vague or ill-defined for the sound was created by using new chord combinations (9ths, 11ths, 13ths), often ambiguous as to tonality. In fact, Debussy disliked the term Impressionism.

Debussy attended the Paris Conservatory from the age of ten (1873–1884), where he studied piano and composition and experimented in harmonic improvization. He became a devotee of Wagner and in 1888 and 1889 visited Bayreuth. He later came to the view that Wagner's music was "a beautiful sunset that was mistaken for a dawn", that is the end of Romanticism rather than a new musical movement. He was particularly influenced by a Javanese gamelan, performed at the Paris Exposition of 1889, but also his friendship with the Impressionist painters, fellow composer Eric Satie and writers and poets such as Mallarme and the "symbolists". He moved to an apartment in Montmartre in 1890, and spent much of the next 20 years writing. His opera *Pelleas et Melisande*, for example took ten years to complete.[30] Other important works include the *Suite Bergamasque* (1890) of which the third piece is "Clair de Lune", the *Suite Pour le Piano* (1894–1904) the *Fete Galentes* (1891 and 1904), the three orchestral nocturnes and *La Mer* (1905). His *Prelude de l'Apres Midi d'une Faune*, based on an erotic monologue by Mallarme was turned into a scandalous ballet by Nijinsky, performed in 1912 (Fig. 2.3).

Debussy was arguably the greatest and most important of 20th century composers both for his own music and in his inspiration of others, notably Boulez, Stravinsky and Bartok. In his use of block chords, modal harmonies and whole-tone scales, he was an innovator of the first degree. He was also the first composer to write for the then new saxophone.

Arnold Schoenberg, meanwhile, began to move away from a late Romantic style to experiment with atonality and free dissonance from 1907. He too became one of the most influential figures in the history of music. His twelve-note method – doclecaphony or serialism – was first used in his *Piano Suite Op 25* (1921–1923). He fled Germany in 1933, and set sail for USA in October that year, settling in Los Angeles and where he became a teacher at the University of Southern California. He was also a fine artist, and exhibited with Kandinsky and Der Blaue Reiter in the

---

30 Nichols, R., *Debussy* (London: 1973).

Figure 2.3   *Nijinsky as the Faun,*
               by L. Bakst (1912)

Vienna Seccession. Partly because of this, his music is associated with Expressionism in art, and can therefore by linked to the emergence of modernism as an intellectual force. He would later be joined in southern California by other European composers fleeing Germany and middle Europe, including Paul Hindemith, Kurt Weill, and Bartok, many of whom would write film music scores.

Composers who would follow Debussy and Schoenberg's interest in tonality included Maurice Ravel, who was influenced also by jazz, Bartok, Berg, Webbern, Stravinsky, Poulenc and Honegger, and Hindemith. This genre of modern classical music would extend, then, from the late 1880s until the 1940s. To some extent, it was mirrored in the development of modern jazz, notably the music of Charlie Parker and Dizzie Gillespie. This correlates with the third Kondratieff Wave of 1895 to 1948, and is contemporaneous with Modernism in architecture and Abstract Expressionism in art.

Igor Stravinsky is often hailed as the greatest composer of the 20th century, and it was he that would provide a bridge between modernism and neo-classical music. Diaghilev commissioned Stravinsky to compose music for his 1910 season in Paris of the *Ballets Russes*, and the resultant score, *The Firebird*, was a great success. This was followed by another commission for Diaghilev, *Petruchlia*, which was also another success, before the *Rites of Spring* was first performed in 1913, when it caused a riot among the outraged audience over scenes depicting the ritual sacrifice of a young virgin. Diaghilev's *Ballets Russes* were amongst the most extraordinary collaborations of the early 20th century. Not only were composers such as Stravinsky, Debussy (Fig. 2.4) and Poulenc involved, but so too were Picasso and Matisse, Prokofiev, Nijinsky and Fokine.

During the 1920s he composed the *Symphonies of Wind Instruments*, dedicated to Debussy's memory, the *Concerto for Piano and Wind*, the *Serenade in A* and the *Capruccio for Piano and Orchestra*. He continued to write ballet music, not only for Diaghilev, but also for Ida Rubenstein and the American choreographer

George Balanchine. Stravinsky became a naturalized French citizen in 1934, but found that most of his commissions were coming from the USA, and so he moved there in 1939, at least in part to make a fresh start following the deaths of his wife, mother and elder daughter. He took with him the *Symphony in C* for the Chicago Symphony Orchestra. In the coming years he would write *Scenes de Ballet* (1944) for a Broadway revue, the *Ebony Concerto* for the jazz clarinettist Woody Herman and the opera *The Rake's Progress* to a libretto by W.H. Auden and Chester Kallman. This marked the end of Stravinsky's second period of neo-classicism. His last 20 years produced many works inspired by sacred music. He died in New York in 1969[31] and was buried in the island cemetary of San Michele in Venice, near to Diaghilev, as he wished.

Stravinsky's second period

Figure 2.4   Claude Debussy with Igor Stravinsky (1910)
Source: Photographed by Eric Satie.

spanned the rise of neo-classical music, much of it linked with nationalism as in the works of Bartok, William Walton, Vaughn Williams, Aaron Copland, Charles Ives and Samuel Barber, and Janacek and Prokofiev, Manuel de Falla and Rodrigo. By this time, America had already grown its own tradition of modern music, led by the eccentric figure of Charles Ives (1874–1954). Ives was greatly influenced by his father, a town bandmaster, who experimented with acoustics, tonalities and tone clusters. The young Charles went on to study composition at Yale University in 1894. But after graduating he took up a career in insurance and, along with his partner Julian Myrich, became a millionaire. He had a heart attack in 1918, and during his year of convalescence embarked upon publishing his works, composed between 1904 and 1920. Many of these were inspired by American themes – landscapes, festivals or historical events – including *Central Park in the Dark* (1906), *Three Planes in New England* and the *Piano Sonata No 2 Concord*. Ives' innovative musical style would exert enormous influence on later American composers, notably Aaron Copland and

---

31 Griffiths, P., *Stravinsky* (London: 1992).

Leonard Bernstein. Copland in particular was keen to develop an American music combining the influences of Stravinsky and Les Six (Copland spent several years in Paris during the 1920s), with jazz and folk music. His best known works are the ballet *Billy The Kid* (1938), *Fanfare for the Common Man* (1942), *Rodeo* (1944) and the *Appalachian Spring* (1944), written for Martha Graham's dance company. After World War II, he also took up writing music for film, as indeed did Benjamin Britten and William Walton in England, Kurt Weill and Leonard Bernstein. Britten would turn his attention to opera and the Aldeburgh Festival, while Bernstein would write *On the Town* (1944) and *West Side Story* (1957). All of these composers had rediscovered tonality and developed distinctive styles with a wide appeal. Most of them, including Britten, were in the USA in the 1940s. In all of their work there is an accent on melody, neo-classicism and the influence of folk motifs. These then are the composers of the Fourth Kondratieff Wave, and although the term is not used in contemporary music, if any period in music evolution could be termed post-modern (in the sense of borrowing from many styles and influences) music composed from the 1940s onwards would appear to fit this description.

Contemporary music since the 1970s has seen a distancing from the music of the previous generation. This is exemplified by the "minimalist" group of American composers including Steve Reich, John Adams, Terry Riley and Philip Glass. This music is so-called because it applies a maximum repetition of minimum amount of material. John Adams is the most closely related to modern jazz, whilst Glass draws in Indian influences and Reich on African rthymns.

Literature

Much the same point can be made by plotting the serious movements in literature and poetry (Fig. 2.5).

The development of the modern novel is generally accredited to Sir Walter Scott. Scott was born in Edinburgh in 1771, son of a Writer to the Signet. He contracted polio as a young boy and was sent to his grandfather's farm in Tweedale to recuperate. This brought him into contact with the Borders, where many of his novels would be set, and he spent much time reading books by Fielding, Spenser, and German ballad poetry. His greatest influence was Thomas Percy's *Reliques Of English Poetry*, 1765. His first publication was a translation of ballads by Gottfried Burger in 1796, followed by Goethe's *Geotz van Berlichingen* in 1799. He began to write original ballads set in the Borders, and these were published by James Ballantyne of Kelso in a collected edition *Minstrelsy of the Scottish Borders*, in three volumes in 1802 and 1803. This work made him the most famous author of his day. In 1811 he bought land in Abbotsford, near Galashields, and set about building his country seat. He was declared bankrupt in 1826 following a misguided foray into publishing (with Ballantyne), and following this he publicly acknowledged his authorship of the Waverley novels. He had turned to writing novels from about 1813, as he believed his work as a poet was being eclipsed by that of Byron. As well as

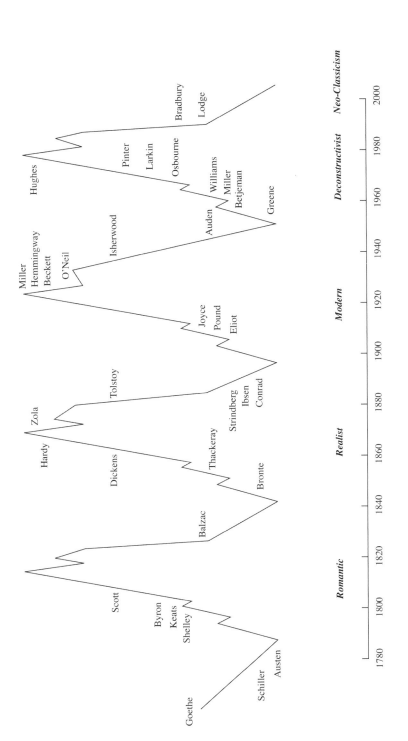

Figure 2.5   The Long Waves: Literature

Source: John Montgomery.

the three collections of *Waverley Novels* (including such works as *Guy Mannering* (1815) *Rob Roy* (1817) and the *Heart of Midlothian* (1818) *Ivanhoe* (1820), and *Quentin Durward* (1823). He also produced a large number of shorter works, four plays and some historical works, including "History of Scotland" (1829–1830).[32] Scott had a profound influence on 19th century literature, and was read and imitated by George Eliot, the Brontes and others. He is also credited, along with Keats, for the term "Romanticism" as applied to nineteenth century literature and poetry.

The next great movement in literature would begin in France in the mid 19th century, and is usually dated from Champfleury's manifesto *La Realisme* of 1857. Realism stressed "sincerity" as opposed to the "liberty" of the Romantics which it saw as idealized, exaggerated and melodramatic. Rather, realism would be based on accurate documentization, sociological insight, material facts and detail, with subjects drawn from everyday life. This reflected the interests of a more empirical and scientific age as well as a reaction to Romanticism. The leading creators of this new paradigm were Balzac and Stendahl (1788–1842), both of whom were writing in the 1830s, and later Flaubert. Stendahl's two masterpieces are *La Rouge et le Noir* (1830) and *La Chartreuse de Parme* (1839), both of which deal with political intrigue and psychological analysis. Stendahl was much admired by Honore de Balzac whose *Comedie Humaine* (1842–1853) was conceived as a complete picture of modern civilization. Among the masterpieces which make up this opus (91 works in all) are *Old Goriot* (1835) and *Illusions Perdues* (1837–1843). Balzac divided his Comedie into three catagories: *E'tudes de moeurs, E'tudes phiosophiques* and *E'tudes analytques*. He was particularly interested in the role of money in shaping personal and social relations, and in the effect of these on the individual. He is regarded as one of the greatest novelists, and his influence on later fiction was profound.[33]

Realism to a large extent was superseded by "Naturalism", again in France, from the late 1860s. As a movement, Naturalism referred to everyday human experience, and argued that human life is strictly subject to natural laws. Scrupulous care was taken to research everyday life, so that the novel was seen as social history. Emphasis was placed on the influence of economic position on behaviour. In Germany, the movement flourished from about 1885 until the 1890s, particularly in theatre and notably the works of Ibsen. The dominant figure was Emile Zola,[34] but also included Flaubert, and Edmond and Tules do Goncourt. Zola's first major novel, *Therese Raquin* (1867), is usually regarded as the beginnings of the movement, along with *Germinie Lacerteux* (1865) by the Goncourts. Between 1871 and 1873, Zola would produce a series of 20 novels, including *Nana* (1880), *Germinal* (1885) and *La Terre* (1887).

Meanwhile, in England the young Charles Dickens established his reputation as a novelist from the mid 1830s. He was born in Portsmouth in 1812 but spent most of

---

32 Lockhart, T.G., *Memoirs of the Life of Sir Walter Scott* (Edinburgh, 1839).

33 Robbs, G., *Balzac* (London: 1994).

34 Walker, P., *Zola* (London: 1985).

his childhood in Dartford where his father was a naval clerk. The family moved to London in 1821, but his father was imprisoned for debt in 1824. Young Charles was forced to work in a blacking factory at Hungerford Market, and this experience is credited with his recurring theme of poverty and social justice. He later worked as an office boy for a solicitor, and in 1828 became a free-lance reporter for the *Morning Chronicle*. In 1833 he published a sketch *Dinner at Poplar Walk* in the *Monthly Magazine* under the pen-name "Boz". He began to contribute sketches regularly and in 1836 the *Sketches of Boz* were published as a collection. He started writing the *Pickwick Papers* in March 1836, and began working on his first novel *Oliver Twist* in 1837,[35] initially published in monthly numbers. He went on to write *The Old Curiosity Shop* (1840), *Barnaby Rudge* (1841), *Martin Chuzzlewit* (1843–1844), *A Christmas Carol* (1843). He began to travel to America, Italy and Switzerland. In the 1850s he published *David Copperfield, Bleak House, Hard Times, Little Dorrit* and a *Tale of Two Cities*, followed by *Great Expectations* (1860–1861) and *Our Mutual Friend* (1864–1865). Separation from his wife Catherine in 1858, simply because he found her irritating, made him the subject of gossip, but he continued to give readings of his work in public. He toured America again in 1867–1868, and died suddenly in 1870. He was buried in Westminister Abbey. Dickens had captured the popular imagination as no other novelist had previously, and achieved great esteem during his life. His works remain highly regarded for their complexity, vivid portrayals of Victorian social life, his characters and concern with social deprivation and injustice.

By the 20th century poets such as T.S. Eliot, Ezra Pound and W.B. Yeats, and novelists such as Conrad and Joyce were writing in a new idiom which would later become known as modernism. These writers rejected the classic framework of narrative, description and rational exposition in favour of a "stream of consciousness", poetic imagery and myth. It was marked by continual experimentation – "the tradition of the new". The phrase "stream of consciousness" was originally coined by W. James in his early works on psychology (1890), to describe the flow of thoughts of the working mind. Modernists used this as a literary device to describe unspoken thoughts and feelings of their characters. The earliest examples in prose are considered to be Joseph Conrad's *Heart of Darkness* (1902) and *Nostromo* (1904), in which he explores each character's private version of reality, and the human tendency towards corruptability. Later examples would include Virginia Woolf and James Joyce.

> He walked frail, insignificant, shabby, miserable – and terrible in the simplicity of his idea calling madness and despair to the regeneration of the world. Nobody looked at him. He passed on unsuspected and deadly, like a pest in the street full of men.
>
> Joseph Conrad, *Under Western Eyes*, 1911

Joyce was born in Dublin in 1882 and studied at University College Dublin. As a young man he was greatly influenced by Ibsen, the German Naturalist Hauptmann and Yeats whom he would come to know well. Joyce fled the narrowness of Irish

---

35 Ackroyd, P., *Dickens* (London: 1990).

Catholicism, and went to Paris in 1902 where he wrote verse and discovered Dujardin's novel *Les Lauriers sout Coupes* (1888) which he later attributed as the source for his use of interior monologue. He returned to Dublin for his mother's death, then left with Nora Barnacle with whom he spent the rest of his life. They lived in Switzerland for several years, moved to Zurich in 1915 and settled finally in Paris after the First World War. His early works included *Dubliners* (1914) and *A Portrait of the Artist as a Young Man* (1914–1915), but securing publishing deals was difficult.[36] His masterpiece *Ulysses* was published in Paris in 1922 on his 40th birthday. It was hailed as a work of genius by Eliot, Hemmingway and Arnold Bennett. Together with his later work *Finnegan's Wake* (1939), *Ulysses* revolutionized the form and structure of the novel. His influence can be seen in the works of Virginia Woolf and Samuel Beckett, but also in later writers such as Saul Bellow, John Upcliffe and Anthony Burgess.[37]

Modernism would also develop in poetry, as in the works of T.S. Eliot and Ezra Pound. Modernist poetry's main characteristic is that it gives the appearance of dissonance and atomism. Some of its more extreme forms such as Dada-ism (a name meaning "hobby-horse, chosen at random from the dictionary), a movement founded in Zurich in 1916, were based on a rejection of all traditional values in art and literature, and of the role of the creative artist. Dada-ism found a home in the Paris of 1919, organized around Andre Breton's review *Litterature* until 1924, by which time the various groups had broken up to form, or join, other movements such Surealism, the Imagists (Pound, Doolittle) or the Vorticists (Pound, Wyndham Lewis).

The most important poet of the 20th century was T.S. Eliot who had been born in St. Louis, Missouri in 1888, the son of a successful businessman. He studied at Harvard and spent a year at the Sorbonne in Paris. He met Ezra Pound in 1914, and was encouraged by him to remain in England. In 1915 his poem *The Love Song of J. Alfred Prufrock* was published in *Poetry*. He taught briefly during the First World War, and in 1917 began to work for Lloyds Bank. His first volume of poetry *Prufrock and other Observations* (1917) was followed by *Poems* (1919), the latter hand-printed by Leonard and Virginia Woolf. These struck a new note in modern poetry. There followed *The Waste Land* (1922) and *The Hollow Men* (1925) which established Eliot's reputation as representing the disillusioned post-war generation. He left Lloyds in 1925 to become director of Faber and Faber where he built up the list of poets – Pound, Auden, Barber, Spender. He became a British subject in 1927, joined the Anglican Church and began to write poetry of a more spiritual nature. Around this time, Eliot described himself as "classicist in literature, royalist in politics and anglo-catholic in religion". His works at this time include *Ash Wednesday* (1930), and *The Journey of the Magi* (1927). He continued to write essays and literary criticism, and in the 1930s experimented with religious poetic drama. He received to Nobel Prize for literature in 1948. He died in 1965.[38]

---

36 Ellmann, R., *James Joyce* (London: 2nd edition 1982).
37 Bradbury, M. and McFarlane, J. (eds), *Modernism 1890–1930*, 1991.
38 Ackroyd, P., *T.S. Eliot* (London: 1984).

A cold coming we had of it,
Just the worst time of year
For a journey, and such a long journey:
The ways deep and the weather sharp,
The very dead of winter.

Journey of the Magi, T. S. Eliot

By the late 1920s and early 1930s, the "stream of consciousness" of modernist literature was already giving way to a new, simpler, narrative style. This is exemplified by the works of Ernest Hemmingway. Although Hemmingway had spent many years in Paris in the company of Pound, Joyce, F. Scott Fitzgerald, Gertrude Stein and others during the 1920s, it was following his return to USA that his more creative writing occurred. His best-known works include *A Farewell to Arms* (1929), *The Green Hills of Africa* (1935), *For Whom the Bell Tolls* (1940) and *The Old Man in the Sea* (1952), his last work. His style combined an economy of dialogue, narrative and characteristion. This would later influence the English writers Robert Graves, Graham Greene, George Orwell and others, although they would all approach the moral issues of the day in distinctive ways: Orwell was a socialist, Greene a Catholic, Graves a humanitarian. As in music, it is arguable that literature from the mid 1930s through the 1960s was following a neo-classical path, one which would morph into post-modernism.

By the 1930s, as with other art forms of the time, the centres of poetry and the novel were now London and New York. The most important dramatists of the time were living and working in New York. The most important of these was Eugene O'Neill who was in fact born in New York in 1888. As a young man, O'Neill had a varied career as a seaman, gold prospector, journalist and actor. He contracted tuberculosis in 1912, and spent six months in a sanatorium, during which time he began writing plays. He joined the Provincetown Players, an acting troupe, which performed several of his early one-act plays. His first critical success was *Beyond the Horizon* (1920), a naturalistic drama for which he was awarded the Pulitzer Prize. He became increasingly critical of materialistic values in the 1920s, and this was expressed most forcibly in *The Great God Brown* (1926) and *Marco Millions* (1927). He experimented with stream of consciousness in the 9-hour *Strange Interlude* for which he won the Pulitzer Prize in 1928. He wrote a trilogy based on the American civil war: *Mourning becomes Electra* (1931), *Ah! Wilderness* (1932) and *Days Without End* (1934), after which he retired from the stage for 12 years. He was awarded the Nobel Prize in 1936, and made a triumphant return in 1946 with *The Ice-man Cometh*. His late masterpiece *Long Day's Journey into Night* was first performed in 1956 after his death at the age of 65.

There ensued, from the mid 1940s, a golden age of American drama, driven by the creative genius of Tennessee Williams and Arthur Miller. Williams, in fact, was born in Mississippi and moved to New York in the late 1930s. He achieved acclaim with *A Glass Menagerie* in 1945, a painful family drama set in St. Louis, and for which he received the New York Drama Critics Circle Award. This was followed in 1948 by *A Streetcar Named Desire*, and *Cat on a Hot Tin Roof* in 1955, a Freudian family drama exploring alcoholism and homosexuality. Arthur Miller, meanwhile, was writing *Death of a Salesman* (1949), for which he won the Pulitzer Prize, and *The Crucible* (1953), an allegory of the McCarthy trials. Both writers would also produce film scripts, including for *The Misfits* (1960), and *Baby Doll* (1956). By 1960, to all intents, the golden age of modernist American theatre was over.

Poetry, meanwhile, had developed around a new movement of modernists from the late 1930s. The most influential figure in this was W.H. Auden. Auden's first volume of *Poems* (1930) was accepted for publication by T.S. Eliot at Faber and Faber, while Auden was still at Oxford. His contemporaries included Louis McNeice, Stephen Spender and Cecil Day-Lewis. For a time, this grouping was known as the "Pylon School" after the use of industrial imagery in their work. Auden quickly became recognized as the leading poet of his generation, publishing two more collections in 1932 and 1936, whilst also writing four plays for Rupert Doone's Group Theatre. He met Benjamin Britten in 1935 whilst working for the GPO film unit, and Britten went on to set several of his poems to music. That same year he visited Germany, marrying Thomas Mann's daughter Erika to provide her with a British passport with which to flee Nazi Germany. He collaborated with Spender (*Letters from Iceland*, 1936) before travelling with him to China and then to Germany with Christopher Isherwood. In 1939 he and Isherwood left England for America where he met Chester Kallman, a life-long friend and companion. Works produced during the early 1940s include *Another Time* (1940) and *The Double Man* (1941) which marked his rejection of socialism. His work became increasingly Christian in tone: *The Sea and the Mirror* (1944). In 1946 he became a US citizen and was appointed associate professor at Michigan University. He returned to England in 1956 as professor of poetry at Oxford. His major later works include *The Shield of Achilles* (1955). He also wrote several volumes of prose and literacy criticism, as well as the libretto for *The Rake's Progress* (1951). He died in Vienna in 1973. Auden is considered the most important poet of the 20th century, alongside Eliot, his work progressing from naturalism in his youth to a much more complex and wide-ranging material as he matured.[39] His influence can be seen in later poets such as Ted Hughes and Philip Larkin.

By the 1960s, literature was overtaken by the French structuralist school (Barthes, Todorov, Genette) which challenges the essentially humanist traditions of literature. This reached its logical conclusion in the work of the "deconstructivists" Jacques Lacan and Jacques Derrida who argued that all texts inevitably undermine their "determinate meaning". The end of the novel was declared, but this has turned out not to be the case. As often in the past, the best antidote to Marxist intellectual pretension has been English satire, and a return to the empirical traditions of literature. This can be seen in the works of Malcolm Bradbury, notably *The History Man* (1982), a satire on the morals of left-wing academics, and *To The Hermitage* (2000), a celebration of the Enlightenment, both of which manage to combine creative writing with humour and satire. Bradbury co-founded a creative writing course at the University of East Anglia, pupils having included Ian McEwan and Glen Paterson. His friend David

---

39 Carpenter, H., *W.H. Auden: A Biography* (London: 1981).

Lodge, has, as a literary critic, written widely on structuralism and modern writing, while stressing his own faith "in the future of realistic fiction". His own novels combine irony, a certain detachment, great humour and an underlying seriousness. Much the same combination of metaphysics, wit, satire and parody can be seen in the works of the playwrite Tom Stoppard.

What, if anything, has this revealed? For one thing it does seem clear that the development of western music can be divided into important periods or eras. The Baroque Music of Handel and Bach, the Classical Music of Haydn and Mozart, the singular genius of Beethoven, the Romantics such as Schumann and Brahms and ultimately Wagner, the early modern music of Debussy, Ravel, Schoenberg and Stravinsky, the new tonality of Copland, Britten, Walton and Bernstein, and the minimalism of Philip Glass. Jazz too can be divided into movements, from traditional to swing, bop, cool, fusion, free and retrospective. These movements seem to coincide with upswings during the Kondratieff Waves, so that Classicism is linked to early industrial capitalism, atonality with Modernism, and much of the music written from the 1940s with post-modernism. This also links, as we shall see, to movements in art – Impressionism, Pre-Raphaelites, Expressionism, Cubism, Action-Painting and Pop Art. Moreover, the primary innovators – Haydn and Mozart, late Beethoven, Debussy, Stravinsky – were all writing during a down wave, that is to say preceding the next long wave of economic growth and artistic creativity. In literature the corresponding movements or paradigms were Romanticism, Realism, Naturalism, Modernism, Deconstructivism and what might be termed a new classical realism.

One interesting question is whether and why such movements occurred in certain cities but not in others, and what this tells us about the relationship between cities as trading sites, urban places and generators of artistic creativity. We should at this point look to some historical examples in closer detail.

3. CITIES AND ARTISTIC CREATIVITY

Florence: Renaissance

Originally the strategic Roman garrison settlement of "Florentia", Florence in the Middle Ages developed a flourishing economy based on banking and commerce, and this in turn marked a period of growth, city-building and artistic development – the Renaissance. That this event – or process – changed the world forever, and that it was extraordinary, even miraculous, is universally accepted. That it was an artistic revolution derived in part from a rediscovery of ancient methods – classical antiquity – is also widely accepted. That this cradle of western civilization was the home of Dante, Machiavelli, Michelangelo, the Medici, Brunelleschi, Donatello and Ghiberti is an historic fact. The question, perhaps, is why it happened at all?

For, at the beginning of the fifteenth century – the *quattrocento* – Florence had suffered two outbreaks of plague within 50 years, and its economy had stagnated. In 1399, a religious movement developed in Lombardy, and began to travel southward to Rome, attracting followers and great interest on the way. The pilgrims reached Florence in August, bringing the normal life of the city to an abrupt halt. Unfortunately, the pilgrims – known as the Bianchi for their white linen penitent's robes – also brought the plague. The sickness spread rapidly, and 12,000 Florentines out of a population of 60,000 would die. This brought commerce to a halt, following as it did a period of heavy taxation to fund a drawn-out war with the Viscontis of Milan. A series of earlier banking collapses in the 1340s had already weakened the economy, while the Black Death of 1348 had previously cut the population from 80,000 to 30,000. The Renaissance which would follow (from about 1400 to 1430) was thus born of severe economic decline, the Plague, a growth in poverty and falling land prices.

The principal characters are familiar. As well as artists, they were craftsmen who had learned their trades in the guilds and workshops. Gitto, Brunelleschi and Leonardo were painters and sculptors, but also architects. Brunelleschi began as a goldsmith. Pisarello and Verrochio were also goldsmiths who became sculptors and painters. Raphael was a painter and architect, as was Michalangeo who was also, of course, a sculptor. Ghiberti was also a goldsmith who became a bronze-caster and sculptor, Donatello, his pupil, likewise. Because the artists themselves had served apprenticeships in the guilds and workshops, they had developed highly accomplished skills, so that they would emerge as a recognizable "class" at the same time that a market for decorative arts and architecture came into being. In a little over 30 years, they would change completely the history of art and architecture. Clearly, many of these artists were geniuses, but why were they all in Florence at the same time?

One explanation might be general wealth creation, although as we have seen the Florentine economy had stagnated at that time. Even so, Florence remained a wealthier and more advanced city than most. This is because the wealth creation that helped spark the Renaissance occurred not contemporaneously but up to fifty years earlier. According to Robert Lopez[40] nothing less than the birth of capitalism occurred not in the *quattrocento* but in the *trecento* (the fourteenth century). For at this time a steady accumulation of capital (money and goods) was accompanied by complex patterns of trade, the use of credit, complicated book-keeping, a growing division of labour and increased competition. This extended to the development of "modern" banking by merchant families such as the Bardi, Peruzzi and the Medici. The bulk of trade in the *trecento* was not in the fine arts at all, but rather in the crafts and, most importantly, the wool industry and export of finished cloth. The wool industry was in serious decline by 1400, however, and it never fully recovered. So if the Renaissance of 1400–1430 was built on wealth, it was wealth that had been accumulated over 50 years earlier. Peter Hall sees this as a "vulgar" explanation for the Renaissance, and yet it is not in the least surprising.

---

40 Lopez, R.S., *The Trade of Medieval Europe*, in Postan, M. and Rich, E.E. (eds), *The Cambridge Economic History of Europe, 2: Trade and Industry in the Middle Ages*, pp. 257–354 (Cambridge University Press, 1952), pp. 257–354.

A further explanation for the Renaissance is suggested by Paul Robert Walker,[41] who argues that a series of design competitions sparked a feud between Brunelleschi and Ghiberti, and it was this tension which sparked the Renaissance. Following on from Manetti's *The Life of Brunelleschi*,[42] Walker charts the story of the competition to design the doors for the north side of the Baptistry (the church of John the Baptist), a competition in the end that Ghiberti was to win. At the time, both Ghiberti and Brunelleschi were in their early twenties, and this seems consistent with the concept of "new men" of a generation bringing new innovations to bear, an "ideological succession".

The competition was announced in the winter of 1400/01, despite – or possibly because of – the fact that Florence had been ravaged by plague, was still at war with Milan and was suffering economic decline. Having lost the commission, Brunelleschi left Florence for Rome, accompanied by Donatello. The two men would undertake an astonishing survey of Rome, making drawings of a great many buildings, measuring street and block widths, examining the foundations of ancient monuments and estimating building heights. Scholars are divided as to whether this trip, as described by Manetti, ever took place. But in a sense it does not really matter one way or the other. For the fact remains that by 1417 Brunelleschi had also become an architect, and was therefore able to enter the competition to design and build the dome for the Cathedral, finally being appointed in late July 1420. Work was delayed in 1424 owing to a further outbreak of the plague and the resumption of hostilities with Milan. During that very year, Ghiberti's Baptistry doors were finally installed after over twenty years of work. The Dome was eventually completed in 1461.

Although the *Dome of Santa Maria del Fiore* is Brunelleschi's most famous work, an even greater contribution was the rediscovery of perspective in drawing and painting, taken up notably by Masaccio, as without this there would have been no Renaissance in art at that time. Brunelleschi went on to secure many private commissions to design buildings and make sculptures for the city fathers (the Signoria), wealthy bankers and merchants and the church. In the meantime, slowly at first but with increasing regularity, other artists were commissioned to execute public sculptures in the City. Of prime importance were Donatello's sculptures of David and St John the Evangelist, and the commissioning of statuary for the Orsanmichele church. Over a period of several years important works were commissioned from Brunelleschi, Donatello, Nanni and Ghiberti. These would form the centre-piece of a larger programme of public religious art. Sparked by these public commissions – both by the Signoria and the Church – the sheer amount of sculptures and paintings produced would later owe much to individual patronage, especially by the wealthy bankers and merchants. By the 1450s, Florence was enjoying an economic boom and at least part of this was spent on art and city building.

---

41 Walker, P.J., *The Feud that Sparked the Renaissance* (Perennial, 2003).

42 See Manetti, A., *The Life of Brunelleschi*, edited by Howard Saalman and translated by Catherine Enggass (Pennyslvania State University Press, 1970).

Brunelleschi died in 1446, Donatello in 1466 and Ghiberti in 1455, having prospered as had Florence itself under the rule of Giovanni di Bicci de Medici and his son Cosimo (who died in 1464). Later generations of artists would also prosper under the Medicis – notably Lorenzo the Magnificent – including Verrocchio, Leonardo, Boticelli, Lippi and ending with Michelangelo. Michelangelo would leave Florence for Bologna in 1492, and then for Rome in 1496. By this time, the Renaissance was all but ended.

In reviewing the detail on Florence it becomes clear – or at least a strong possibility – that the conditions for the Renaissance were indeed laid by the creation of wealth in the *trecento,* largely by the wool industry and trade. The creative "spark" for the Renaissance occurred in the early 1400s, that is during a period of serious economic stagnation. This involved not only the application of highly developed craft skills, but also the rediscovery of classical architecture and perspective. The individuals of the day – Brunelleschi, Ghiberti and Donatello – were of key significance. But so too were the church and city-state who commissioned new sculpture, decorative door panels and buildings. Eventually the taste for art would be taken up more widely, certainly by the merchants but also the middle classes, so that demand for art of itself would increase during a period of economic prosperity. In this way, the underpinning of the Renaissance was the wealth generated during a previous wave of prosperity, the "factor conditions" were the workshop system and the artists themselves, the enabling device was public patronage and the eventual boom was occasioned by a new cycle of wealth creators and demand for art. That is, in sequence: wealth creation, craft-skills, public commissions, new artistic creativity, greater consumption of the arts. It would seem that Paul Robert Walker is right in arguing that it was a feud – a competition – that sparked the Renaissance.

Amsterdam: New Wealth and Old Masters

You don't need an art critic to tell you the Dutch Old Masters of the 17th century were very, very good. The question that puzzles many is why such a small country should have experienced such an astonishing flowering of artistic creativity. The answer, of course, was trade. During the late 16th century, the Dutch East India Company, founded in 1609, was trading with the Far East, the Cape of Good Hope and Indonesia. Later, the West Indies Company would sail to West Africa and the Americas, creating colonies in Surinam, the Antilles and Nieuw Amsterdam (later New York). Amsterdam as a trading port had initially been part of the Hanseatic League, which it had joined in 1369. By 1650 Amsterdam had a fleet of around 15,000 vessels, about 60 per cent of the entire European fleet, and manned by some 50,000 sailors.[43] By the end of the 17th century, the city's population had grown to 200,000, from about 30,000 in 1578.

---

43 Jones, E., *Metropolis: The World's Great Cities* (Oxford: Oxford University Press, 1990), p. 55.

This pattern of trade created great wealth in Amsterdam, and also opportunities to manufacture using previously unavailable ingredients. For example the established wool industry developed into a thriving linen, and later silk, industry. Shipbuilding itself was a major industry, and oriental spices and crops gave rise to new forms of local consumption, in coffee, tea, spices and oils. Diamonds imported from South Africa gave rise to the gemstone industry which still exists today. In addition, new pigments were discovered by grinding various spices and exotic plants.

As wealth grew, the city attracted the finest craftsmen from all over Europe, and the wealthy merchants began to commission furniture, objects and art.[44] In comparison with other countries at the time, Holland, a Republic since 1588 when it broke away from Spanish rule, was considered a tolerant society. Although Calvinism was the official religion, Catholics were free to observe their religion (if not to hold public office). Jews were made more welcome than in other countries, and indeed many had come from Portugal, Poland and Germany. So free was Holland considered, that the French philosopher Rene Descartes moved there in 1631. A new class of wealthy bankers, manufacturers, shippers and merchants grew rapidly, and it was these people who would create the demand for a school of secular painting. This was Holland's Golden Age.[45] The arts flourished. By the mid 16th century, the Low Countries had more painters working in a greater variety of genres than many other countries combined.[46] Paintings would become the most common objects of art. The subject matter would range from portraits and genre scenes to landscapes and still life. Ways of seeing and ways of painting advanced, in part to keep pace with demand for new work.

The Dutch and Flemish traditions in painting had a pedigree dating back to the early fifteenth century. Indeed, at the same time as the Renaissance in Florence, the Netherlands was having a renaissance all of its own. The leading artists were van Eyck and van der Weyden, both noted for highly realistic scenes and great attention to detail. They were able to do this because they had perfected a technique of mixing ground up colours with oils to create oil paints, and because these dried more slowly than the previous, fast-drying egg-based (tempera) paints the artists were able build up layers of fine detail. Breugel would later, in the mid 16th century begin to paint landscapes and country peasants as he saw them, instead of the idealized style of the Italians. This gave rise to a tradition of humane non-religious art that continued in Holland and Flanders for 400 years.[47]

And it was from this tradition that artists such as Rembrandt, Vermeer, Hals, Maes, Jan Steen and Cuyp would emerge (Fig. 2.6).

---

44 Braudel, F., *Civilisation and Capitalism from the Fifteenth Century to the Eighteenth Century*, iii Perspective of the World (London), 1979.

45 Schama, S., *The Embarrassment of Riches: An Interpretation of Dutch Culture in the Golden Age* (New York, 1987).

46 Priem, R., *Dutch Masters* (Melbourne: National Gallery of Victoria, 2005), p. xxxi.

47 Bolton, R., *A Brief History of Painting* (London: Robinson, 2004) pp. 69–94.

Figure 2.6   The Old Masters
Source: John Montgomery.

Hals would become the most important portrait artist of his time, painting the merchant classes of his native Haarlem. He pioneered a fast and bold system of portraiture, and is famous for *The Laughing Cavalier*, and portaits of the Amsterdam brewer Nicolaes Hasselaer and his wife. His style fell out of fashion and he struggled to maintain a large family; he retired penniless on a small pension and died in Haarlem in 1666. Vermeer would also die in poverty, aged only 43. He was well-regarded as an artist during his life, but made his living as an innkeeper and art dealer. After his death in 1675, his work was largely ignored for 200 years, but is now revered for its simple domestic scenes, heavy with symbolism. Aelbert Cuyp is one of the most celebrated landscape artists in western art. He specialized in peaceful landscapes, bathed in early morning or late evening light. His work had a profound influence on Turner and Constable.

Rembrandt is acknowledged as the greatest Dutch Master. He virtually reinvented the media he worked in, bringing great technical artistry, a sense of drama and humanity to bear. His self-portraits are regarded as the first psychological studies in the history of art. Born in Leiden in 1606, he moved between his home city and Amsterdam before finally settling there in 1631, by which time he had already a high reputation as a portrait painter. In 1634 he married Saskia van Ulenburgh, a well-connected burgomaster's daughter, bought a big house and began to collect art and objects. Saskia features in many of his paintings from this time. Rembrandt prospered and reached the height of his popularity in 1642 with his most famous painting *The Night Watch*. Saskia died that same year, and Rembrandt's style began to turn more introspective to ever more penetrating portraits. By this time the fashion was for lighter and more colourful portraits then being produced by van Dyck and others. Demand for his work declined severely, and by 1757 he was forced to auction off his collection to avoid bankruptcy. He moved to a smaller house in a poor neighbourhood of Amsterdam, and had two children by his housekeeper Hendrickje Stoffels who would later set up a dealership with his son Titus. This enabled Rembrandt to continue working until his death in 1669.

The majority of Dutch artists of the Golden Age did not receive regular commissions from either public bodies or private citizens. Rather, painters were organized in guilds, established to afford some measure of financial security in hard times, and also to prevent artists from other cities competing locally. The Guilds had developed from the thirteenth century, and operated an extensive apprentice system that trained studio painters until they reached the level of "master". By and large, this meant that the artists were unable to sell their works outside of their local city, although there were exceptions in the case of Hals and Rembrandt during the peak of their fame. Artists were allowed to sell direct to individual members of the public visiting their studios, but exhibitions and auctions were organized by the guild. To get around this, many artists took to giving paintings to creditors, in exchange for settling debts with innkeepers and art dealers such as Hendrick van Uylenburgh. Some artists attempted to become dealers themselves, but most failed. So while there was indeed a great demand for art, making a living was not easy.

It was not only in the fine arts that the Northern Netherlands excelled. A tradition in majolica pottery had developed with the arrival of a number of Italian potters in the early 16th century. This would eventually lead to the creation of a major ceramics industry, as the local potters succeeded in responding to the threat from imported Chinese porcelain. By using new techniques and improved artistry and design, the potters were able to make their majolica thinner, the new product being branded as "Dutch Porcelain". The centres of this new industry were Delft and Haarlem, and during the period of the civil war in China (1644–1647) delftware filled the gap in the market brought about by the collapse in porcelain trade.

Fig. 2.7   Amsterdam: Urban Form
Source: John Montgomery.

City planning at the time reflected the fact that people would need to live and work in much the same space. The merchants built fine houses for themselves, set along canals and around squares, while many guildhalls, markets, exchanges and even warehouses occupied good locations. Amsterdam's urban character had not changed greatly since the 15th century, and the old city grew within the confines of the Singel canal (Fig. 2.7), which in turn had transformed from a system of ditch fortifications to an urban waterway. But the rapid growth of the Golden Age would necessitate a city expansion. In the 17th century, a large area to the west of the city, now known as Jordaan and Leyden, was laid out as a residential and workers district, with small factory buildings, tanneries, mills and dye works.[48]

By the middle of the 17th century, the economy of the Northern Netherlands was in decline, occasioned by the long slump in the European economy of that time. Competition from England and France had driven down cargo prices, and the Dutch were unable to compete with the now more innovative English shippers. The end came with the "Year of Disasters", 1672, when the Republic waged war on France, England and the bishops of Munster and Cologne. The Golden Age was over, and with it the extraordinary creativity of the Dutch Masters.

Edinburgh: Enlightenment

In 1763, the Lord Provost of Edinburgh, George Drummond, announced that an area to the north of the city would be developed as a splendid and magnificent city. This involved the small matter of draining the North Loch and building a

---

48 Kostof, S., *The City Assembled* (London: Thames and Hudson, 1992), p. 92.

causeway to connect the old city to the new. At the time, Edinburgh was built along a crag and tail (from an extinct volcano) linking the castle to the Royal Palace at Holyrood. The city itself (later known as the Old Town) was built on either side of the main road connecting the castle and the Palace, with steep streets and wynds (alleys) falling away on either side. The Old Town was developed to high densities with buildings, often set around courtyards, rising to fourteen storeys. There was no sanitation and livestock was also kept in the courtyards and on the streets. The city was known by two unappealing soubriquets: "auld reekie" for the smoke of thousands of coal fires; and "Gardy loo" for the practice of emptying chamber pots from windows into the street. During the early part of the 18th century, Edinburgh's population was some 30,000, but by the 1750s this had grown to over 60,000. Edinburgh was overcrowded, and disease was rife.

In 1766, Edinburgh Town Council launched a competition for the development of some hundred acres of land above the North Loch. It was to be developed as a "New Town", to "enlarge and improve" the city and provide public buildings. The only stipulation was that two churches would be provided and building heights restricted to three storeys plus basement, or forty-eight feet. The competition was won by a young mason, James Craig, previously largely unheard of. His plan was to lay the New Town out on a gridcross of three main east-west streets, with two large squares at either end, and a series of criss-crossing north-south streets.[49] Craig had gone so far as to name the principal east-west streets George Street (after King George III), Queen Street and Princes Street (after the two princes), with other streets named Hanover, Frederick, Drummond (after the Lord Provost), Rose and Thistle (the national flowers of England and Scotland). Craig even laid out the streets and avenues to the shape of a Union Jack. The point is that Edinburgh was a solidly Whig city, a supporter of the Hanovarians and actively sponsored the concept of a "United Britain". Craig had hit the nail on the head (Fig. 2.8).

Development followed at a surprisingly rapid pace. The first building was the Theatre Royal, completed in 1768, and in 1772 the North Bridge connecting the Old Town to the new was completed. Lots were sold to individuals, and these in large part were members of the new middle classes – bankers, master craftsmen, professionals (lawyers, surveyors), merchants, churchmen and university lecturers. Very few large residences were built for the aristocracy, although many of these had moved to the London court following the Act of Union in 1707. The cost of purchasing land and building a home (from sandstone) was some £2000, expensive but not beyond the means of the middle classes.

Amongst the merchants and craftsmen and bankers who moved in was the philosopher David Hume, who built a "small" townhouse on St Andrew Square. Hume believed the New Town to be the best example of urban planning to be found anywhere in the world. It offered comfort and space, views and vistas, wide streets and parklands, convenient shops and public houses and a pleasing symmetry of

---

49 Youngson, A.J., *The Making of Classical Edinburgh* (Edinburgh: 1966).

lay-out and proportion.[50] The New Town became increasingly popular, affluent and middle-class, leaving the Old Town to the working class and the poor, a situation which would remain more or less unchanged until the 1980s.

In the late 1780s, the Town Council announced their intention for a final (western) part of Craig's plan to be developed. This time, many of the street blocks would be designed by Robert Adam, son of the architect William Adam, tutored at Edinburgh University, "Architect of the King's Works", and by now famous for a number of buildings in southern England. Robert Adam and his brother James are largely credited with the re-discovery of classical proportions, a reaction to what they saw as the excesses and ponderousness of Palladian architecture. At one point the Adam brothers employed three thousand craftsmen in England and regularly contracted leading makers and artists such as Thomas Chippendale, Josiah Wedgewood and Matthew Boulton (the latter two from Birmingham).[51] They also had a notable workshop in Edinburgh and were friends with David Hume, James Boswell and Adam Smith. By 1792, Robert Adam was 66 years old, and although he would complete his design for Charlotte Square, he would die later that year. (He was buried not in Scotland but in Westminster Abbey.) Adam's simple neo-classical architecture would later influence architects such as Sir John Soane (London), Charles Cameron (architect to Catherine the Great), Charles Bulfinch (United States Capitol) and Thomas Jefferson.

It is interesting to reflect on two things at this point. Why was it that Edinburgh could be able at that time to build effectively a new city on such a scale? And how was it that this act of city building should coincide with the Enlightenment? The first question can be answered by the fact that, after the uncertainty of the 1715 and 1745 Jacobite rebellions (led by the self-proclaimed heirs to the Stuart kings), Scotland enjoyed a period of stability and economic growth as part of what was now Great Britain. From about the 1730s, the British economy had enjoyed a growth cycle, fuelled by trade with colonies in the Americas, India and Africa. It seems likely that the wealth that was necessary to pay £2000 to build a home in Edinburgh New Town in the 1780s, was generated at some point during the preceding thirty years. This is because the world economy in the 1770s and 1780s was in the grip of a deep recession. In other words, it was previously created wealth and credit that built Edinburgh New Town.

The second question, on the Scottish Enlightenment, requires a more lengthy answer. The acknowledged father of the Scottish Enlightenment was Henry Home, born in 1696, who would later take the title Lord Kames as a judge at the Court of Sessions. Home became a member of the Scottish bar and was friends with the poet Allan Ramsey (1685–1758). From 1757, Home became curator of the Advocates' Library which, with the help of Thomas Ruddimen, he built into one of the most extensive libraries in Britain, covering not only law but also philosophy, history

---

50 Herman, A., *The Scottish Enlightenment* (Fourth Estate, Levilon, 2001), chapters 7 and 8.

51 Fleming, J., *Robert Adam and His Circle* (Transatlantic Arts, 1978).

Figure 2.8   Edinburgh: Urban Form

Source: Edinburgh Map of 1830–31, General Post Office Directory.

and geography, anthropology and sociology. This library would provide the store of knowledge which gave rise to the Edinburgh Enlightenment.

Concluding from his everyday experience that the law is not simply a question of statutes and precedents, but that judgements are based on "experience and common life",[52] Home sought greater understanding of the principles governing human societies. Rejecting the notion of underlying laws of nature dictated by God, Home embarked upon his quest to understand the nature of man. Fitting his reading and writing in between his duties as an advocate, he enjoyed the arts and discussions with fellow intellectuals in the evenings – the beginnings of a tradition that would last 100 years. Regular attendees included John Millar, who would later become the University of Glasgow's first Professor of Civil Law, the young Adam Smith and James Boswell (advocate, writer and later biographer of Dr Johnson), and David Hume who was, in fact, a distant relative. Home's own publications, include *Essays on the Principles of Morality and Natural Religion* (1751) and *Historical Law Tracts* (1758). Home argued that the law exists to protect property, and that owning property (possessions) is itself "a principle of the law of nature".[53] Governments are formed and rules of society developed, argued Home, not to pursue some abstract notions of the "common good", but rather because individuals require a stable framework within which they can protect what is theirs. Moreover, without property, labour and industry are in vain. This argument would be taken up by David Hume in his doctrine of "enlightened self-interest", published in his *Essays Moral and Political* 1741 and 1742. Home himself, now Lord Kames, would conclude that the happiest societies can be found where the law, culture and "manners" match. In his later work, Kames would argue that societies evolve through four stages of development:[54] as hunter-gatherers; followed by the pastoral-nomadic stage; leading to the development of agriculture; and as wealth increases to the development of commercial society.

As societies progress through these stages of development, the law governing property, behaviour and transactions will become more complex and sophisticated. This argument would later be adopted and adapted by William Robertson who is credited with creating the modern study of history.[55] But the real importance of Kames' work was that, for the first time, the underlying cause of historical change was identified as changes in the organization of an economy, what Marx would later term the means of production. Moreover, the commercial stage – capitalism – represents the greatest break from the past, but also the greatest opportunity for progress.

By the 1760s, that is before the building of Edinburgh New Town, Edinburgh's reputation as a centre of intellectual and artistic life was matched only by London and Paris. Those attracted to Edinburgh included thinkers, scholars and artists such as Adam Smith, Benjamin Franklin, Robert Burns, the two Allan Ramseys (the

---

52 Herman, 2001, *op. cit.*, chapter 4.
53 Herman, 2001, *op. cit.*, p. 92.
54 Kames, Lord, *Historical Law Tracts* (Edinburgh: 1759).
55 Herman, 2001, *op. cit.*, p. 96.

father a poet, the son a portrait artist), William Robertson and Adam Ferguson. Numerous clubs and societies were set up, including the Oyster Club, the Miner Club, the Select Society and the Edinburgh Society for Encouraging Arts, Sciences, Manufacture and Agriculture in Scotland, founded in 1762. Many of these clubs met in taverns. The most important works to emerge from this period would be Hume's *Political Discourses* (1752), Smith's *Theory of Moral Sentiments* (1759) and *The Wealth of Nations* (1776) and Adam Ferguson's *Essay on the History of Civil Society* (1767). These ideas would resonate far beyond the borders of Scotland, to England certainly, but also to Germany (Hegel) across Europe and onto America, where many of them would be enshrined in the constitution, the rule of law, the market economy and concepts of civilization.

Other intellectuals would follow in Edinburgh, although by the early 19th century many were being attracted, as had Boswell and Robert Adam earlier, to London. Robert Burns arrived in Edinburgh in 1787, followed by the writer James MacPherson and Walter Scott. Other novelists would follow, among them Robert Louis Stevenson, Arthur Conan Doyle and James Barrie, but by the 1850s the Scottish Enlightenment was over. For a while at least, Scotland was the first modern society.

In reflecting on the Scottish Enlightenment one is struck forcibly by the power of ideas – reason – to understand, contemplate and improve society. What happened in Edinburgh in the second part of the 18th century, like Florence before, was nothing less than a paradigm shift in philosophy, economics, the study of society and the arts (mainly poetry and literature). At much the same time, Scottish engineers, scientists and physicians were changing forever the fields of industry, civil engineering, medicine and transport. This came about because Scotland had enjoyed a period of relative prosperity in the 1730s and 1740s, and because of the arrival of the age of reason. The key figure in all of this appears to be Lord Kames, not only for his own great works but in encouraging the likes of Hume, Smith and Ferguson. But interestingly, these thinkers and writers were at the height of their powers during a period of political uncertainty (the American wars) and economic stagnation (the 1760s and 1770s). It is as if the new thinkers of the time were trying to explain and avoid the failures of the preceding generation. In the process, they invented modern society. Scotland – and much of the western world and the colonies – would never be the same again.

London and Paris: A Tale of Two Cities

By the 1880s, Paris was the artistic capital of the world, certainly in the visual arts, painting and sculpture. This was the *belle epoche*, although it followed the travails of the Revolution, the Napoleonic Wars and the rather draconian re-design of Paris as a city by Baron Haussman during the 1860s and 1870s.[56] The paradigm shift that occurred in art at that time was Impressionism, the name taken from Monet's

---

56 See Hall, P., 1998, *op. cit.*, chapter 24.

Impression – Sunrise, painted in Le Havre in 1872. The genre was born of a technique of painting quickly *en plein air*, in order to capture moments of time represented by light and colour. Bright colours were applied in patches with brush strokes becoming more and more visible. The artists are perhaps the most well-known collection in history: Monet and Manet, Degas, Pissaro, Renoir, Sisley, and, later, Gaugin and Cezanne.[57]

Many commentators have argued that Impressionism was a reaction against the conservative conformism of the Academy, and to the bourgeois patrons of art.[58] However, an important observation is that from the 1850s there was a growing market in art[59] as wealth creation developed a growing middle class. From the late 1850s, young artists, independent of means and in thought, would meet at cafés since they were unwelcome in the Salon. In 1867, Manet declined to submit his work to the Salon, and with several other artists, planned an independent exhibition instead. Despite the onset of war in 1870, and the continuing opposition from the Academy and the Salon, the popularity of the Impressionists would grow, and with it sales of their work. This in turn would give rise to a new class of art critics and, importantly, dealers. By the early 1890s artists such as Pissaro, Monet and Renoir were making a substantial income.[60] The critics, meanwhile, would not only bring their art to a wider public, but would also help conceptualize what Impressionism was all about.

Although it would influence many other artistic movements, notably Cubism, Fauvism, Expressionism and Abstract Expressionism, Impressionism itself lasted only 30 years. Suerat, the pointillist, for example was painting in the early 1880s, while Cezanne was experimenting with the underlying forms of nature from 1886. The short life of Impressionism is often attributed to the invention of photography in the 1880s, so that light would be captured almost instantaneously; but it is just as likely that as a genre it had run its course.

In his chapter on the subject, Peter Hall asks the question why it was that Paris should have become the capital of art.[61] He points out that Paris had an established reputation as an artistic centre (dating at least from the mid 16th century when many artists had moved from Florence). This means that the skills and the training were in ready supply. Moreover, the Impressionists became popular at just the time that a burgeoning middle class could, for the first time, afford art. Paris itself also offered a highly developed intellectual life, café society and forms of entertainment that appealed to young Bohemians. The young artists not only had an orthodoxy to rebel against, they also had the capacity to meet each other regularly and pursue alternative lifestyles. From this analysis we can see how Impressionism developed,

---

57 Wechsler, H.J., *The Lives of Famous French Painters* (New York: Pocket Books, 1952).

58 Adams, S., *The Impressionists* (Philadelphia: Running Press, 1990).

59 Seigel, J.E., *The Bohemian Paris: Culture, Politics and the Boundaries of Bourgeois Life 1830–1930* (New York: Viking, 1986).

60 White, H.C. and White, C.A., *Canvases and Careers: Institutionalised Changes in the French Painting World* (New York: John Wiley, 1965).

61 Hall, P., *op. cit.*, chapter 6, 1998.

why it grew so rapidly and why it took root in Paris. It is still unclear, however, as to why it sparked into life in the first place. For this we need to turn the clock back a little further to London in the early 19th century.

Although Manchester and Birmingham were the first industrial cities, growing rapidly during the first Kondratieff Wave of the 1780s to the 1840s, London was the city which achieved even more spectacular growth and exerted greater influence than any other city of that time. This was the late Georgian period of English history, covering the reign of George III, the Regency Period (1811–1820) and the reign of George IV (1820–1830). By 1801, London's population was close to one million, and by 1851 this would rise to nearly 2.5 million. This astonishing growth is often referred to as the cause of the great rebuilding of London (railways, sewers, clean water, education, slum clearance, early town planning) which would occur from the 1840s.[62] Yet rarely in the urban literature is this period considered in its own right. Quite apart from its economic development, London's history at the time contained many notable events: the battles of Waterloo and Trafalgar, Pitt the Younger and the Duke of Wellington as Prime Ministers, the radicalism of William Cobbett; and the great city planning works of John Nash.

Despite the fact that architects such as Robert Adam and William Chambers were developing new, often large-scale, building projects in late 18th century London, the city as a whole grew more congested and chaotic. This would lead to John Nash's appointment to plan a grand scheme linking St James's Park in the south with Regent's Park in the north. With the creation of Regent Street itself, this was the earliest important exercise in new town planning. Nash drew up plans for Trafalgar Square, created Oxford Circus, and laid-out new terraces around the edges of Regent's Park. Nash himself was keen to create fine streets and squares to be occupied by "the Nobility and Gentry",[63] effectively a barrier or *cordon sanitaire* to separate them from the rest of society. The fact that Regent Street and Oxford Circus were built at all is due not only to Nash's genius but also to the property boom of the 1820s. However, the boom would collapse by 1830, and much of Nash's grand design would remain unbuilt. Regent Street itself would be extensively re-modelled in the 1920s and 1930s, while Nash's original colonnade was removed in the 1860s as concerns over public morality were raised: the columns were a handy place for prostitutes to ply their trade. Meanwhile, in other parts of London during the early 19th century such notable landmarks as the National Gallery, Carlton House Terrace, the British Museum, Marble Arch, Westminster Palace, the Law Courts, the Inner and Middle Temples, the screen and arch at Hyde Park Corner, the Royal College of Surgeons, London University ... were being built, often in a spirit of Triumphalism following the defeats of Napoleon at Trafalgar and Waterloo. Many theatres, hospitals, prisons and gentlemen's clubs were also completed at this time so that London "for the

---

62 Hall, P., *op. cit.*, chapter 23, 1998; Briggs, A. (1963) *Victorian Cities* (London: Odhams Press, 1963).

63 Ackroyd, P., *London: The Biography* (London: Chatto & Windus, 2000), p. 520.

first time ... became a public city".[64] By the 1830s, much of central London had been substantially re-built, the former close density replaced by fine buildings set along grand streets and squares. By 1834, London was regarded as the "leading capital of the world". The areas of London most frequented by tourists these days – Trafalgar Square, the Strand, Piccadilly Circus, Oxford Circus, Cambridge Circus and Bloomsbury were all laid out in the early nineteenth century. In this way, Nash's redesign of London's West End pre-dated Hausseman's re-design of Paris by almost 40 years.

In the arts this was the time of Romanticism and mythopoeia, and in London this was represented in the poetry, literature and painting of Keats, Shelly, Byron, William Blake, John Constable and Turner. Romanticism was, in the way of these things, a reaction against neo-classicism and rationalism, and it occurred across Western Europe (and Russia) at a time of social upheaval. Romanticism was more than a return to nature (the noble savage of Rousseau) but would also engender expressionism, nihilism and "the Pleasure Principle". Although it argues for "the primacy of the perceiver in the world he perceives", Romanticism would come to be associated with alienation, dejection and ennui.[65] Romanticism would dominate at least two, possibly three literary generations from the 1790s to the 1840s. As we have seen, in music, the Romantic movement belonged largely to the first half of the nineteenth century, and is particularly associated with the late works of Beethoven, Weber, Schubert, Schumann, Mendelssohn, Listz and later Wagner, as well as Berlioz. In literature, before the realism of Victor Hugo, Balzac, Zola and Flaubert (and also Dickens), romantic literature was led by Scott, Jane Austen and the Bronte sisters.

But, arguably, it was the poetry of Keats, Shelley and Byron that captured the imagination of the age. Percy Bysshe Shelley was born in Sussex in 1792, and was educated at Eton and University College, Oxford, from which he was expelled for contributing to a pamphlet *The Necessity of Atheism*. He lived variously in York, Dublin and Lynmouth in Devon, where he set up a commune, before moving to London in 1813. He eloped with the 16-year old Mary Wollstonecroft in 1814. With the exception of *Queen Mab* (1813) most of his early works were published during his stay in London, but he left England for Italy in 1818 and would live a further four years there until his early death in 1822.[66]

I see the waves upon the shore,
Like light dissolved in star-showers, thrown.

Percy Bysshe Shelley

John Keats was born in London, went to school in Enfield and became a medical student. He took up poetry after being introduced to the work of Shelley by his friend

---

64 Ibid., p. 522.

65 Abrams, M.M., *The Mirror and the Lamp: Romantic Theory and the Critical Tradition* (London and New York: 1953).

66 Cameron, K.N., *Shelley: The Golden Years* (London: 1974).

and neighbour Leigh Hunt.[67] He began to publish from 1816, culminating in the 1820 volume *Lamia and Other Poems* which was to become a landmark in English poetry. Keats was already seriously ill with consumption, and sailed for Italy in September 1820. He reached Rome, but died in 26 Piazza di Spagna, now known as the Keats-Shelley home.

Mortality
Weighs heavy on me like unwilling sleep

John Keats

Lord Byron was born in London of Scottish antecedents, educated in Aberdeen, Dulwich and at Harrow, before going up to Trinity College, Cambridge in 1805. His early published works were not well-received, and he set out on a grand tour of the Mediterranean (excluding France). On his return he published *Childe Harold's Pilgrimage*, followed by *Lara* in 1814 and the *Seige of Corinth* in 1816. He became the darling of London society, and lover of Lady Caroline Lamb. He was suspected of having an affair with his half-sister Augusta Leigh and was ostracized. He left England for the Continent, meeting up with Shelley in Switzerland, and then on to Rome and Venice. Some of his best work was produced from 1818–1824, when he also established a pro-revolutionary pamphlet with Leigh Hunt. In 1823 he joined the Greek insurgency against the Turks, but died of Marsh Fever at Missolonghi in 1824.[68]

Apart from the poets themselves, arguably the key figure in all of this was Leigh Hunt who introduced Keats to Romanticism, joined Byron in Venice, and would be at the last meeting of Shelley and Byron in 1822. Hunt was a poet and essayist in his own right, but crucially was also the editor of *The Examiner* from 1808 – 1821, a focus of liberal opinion which attracted leading "men of letters" including Thomas Moore, Byron and Charles Lamb. *The Examiner* introduced both Shelley and Keats to the public.

Aside from the fact that the great romantic poets all knew each other, were all in London at about the same time, were all linked with the upper tiers of society and published through many of the same organs – all of this is notable in itself; they also all left England for Italy at around the same time. Albeit for different reasons: Byron to escape scandal and ostracism, Keats in a sadly doomed attempt to regain his health, and Hunt to get over his time in prison (Hunt was imprisoned with his brother for two years for a libel on the Prince Regent). Only Hunt would return. However, there might also have been a common reason, probably to escape the narrowing morality of Regency England. For, in contrast to his behaviour as a young man, the Prince Regent, later George IV, would preside over a period of social reform and moral restriction which would continue for the rest of the 19th century. Why they should all choose Italy is no doubt connected to their classical education at the Grand Tour that Byron at least had already undertaken.

---

67 Motion, A., *Keats* (London: 1997).
68 Grosskurth, P., *Byron: The Flawed Angel* (London: 1997).

There is another possibility, that they were attracted to Venice by art, the painting of Canaletto, whose work was very popular in London at the end of the 18th century. Canaletto had in fact lived and worked in London from 1746–1756, before returning to this native Venice. This is, of course, conjecture and there may be no link between Canaletto's scenes of Venice and the fact that Shelley, Hunt and Byron would move there. What is clear is that Canaletto had a profound effect on a London contemporary of the Romantic poets, the artist J.M. Turner.[69] Turner was born in London in 1775, and was accepted into the Royal Academy aged only 14. Originally a water-colourist of great delicacy, Turner took up oil painting from 1796 and was much attracted by Titian and Poussin. He became increasingly preoccupied with shifting gradations of light on waves, skyscapes, shipwrecks, architecture and mountain ranges. He experimented in the use of vibrant colours, and developed a technique of combining watercolours and oils. He would visit Venice several times between 1819 and 1840, and there he completed a number of famous scenes of Venice, as well as "The Fighting Temeraire". Turner was a secretive man who, when not working, would spend much of his time in taverns. Turner's use of both watercolour and oil to depict light was a revolution in art, pre-dating Impressionism by over 20 years. Indeed, although the word "Impressionism" derives from Monet's painting of 1874, he and his fellow Impressionist Camille Pissarro had lived in London during 1870. They were greatly impressed by Turner's work, although in later life Pissarro would become more grudging.[70]

John Constable also exerted a powerful influence on the early Impressionists because of his brush-strokes, the layering of paint and the use of glazing for effects of light: "there is nothing ugly: for let the form of an object be what it may, – light, shade and perspective will always make it beautiful." His great love was landscape work, and particularly the effects of changing light and the movement of clouds. His most famous work, the *Haywain* (1821) was a great success in the Paris Salon of that year, and would have a powerful influence on Delacroix. Constable would go on to perfect two techniques: one his "sketches" which were finished works of immediate and fragmentary impressions; and his "pochades" which were rapid notes of impressions made on the spot. Arguably the first modern painting ever produced was Constable's *Rainstorm over the Sea*, painted between 1824–1828. While Turner was a master of light, Constable could convey the weather and air in fine detail, as he did in numerous pochades of clouds.

Thus, although art historians are divided on the issue, one version of events was that Impressionism's antecedents – as well as Corot and Delacroix – were Turner and Constable. As it turns out, Turner and Constable were contemporaries at the Royal Academy, and were born only a year apart. It is interesting, finally, to note that the Royal Academy was only established, by Royal Patronage, in 1768 (although it had its precursors). Unlike the Academy in France at that time (indeed, later), the Royal Academy for the first 100 years of its existence was keen to encourage innovation. Its first President was Sir Joshua Reynolds, the noted portrait painter

---

69 Herold, I., *Turner on Tour* (Munich: Prestel, 1997).
70 Pool, P., *Impressionism* (London: Thames & Hudson, 1967), p. 101.

and founder of the Literary Club in 1764 (fellow members included David Garrick, Oliver Goldsmith and Dr. Johnson). It seems then that in a city with a population of under one million people, many of the artistic and literary figures of the time knew each other, and occasionally collaborated. This notion which these days is called "networking" is one to which we shall return.

The point of this, admittedly brief, summary of the creative arts in London in the late 18th and early 19th centuries is not to argue that London pre-dated Paris (although it did), but rather that although Impressionism was a revolution in fine art, it was not quite as sudden as it may seem. It does, in addition, seem clear that cities at peace with each other and between whom there is trade, will also learn from each other.

As for Impressionism itself, the last great movement in art of the nineteenth century would carry over into the twentieth century. The forerunner of Cubism was Paul Cezanne, who although he exhibited at the first and third Impressionist exhibitions, lived in Provence, making occasional visits to Paris. Possibly because of this and his love of Provence, his work developed altogether differently from the other Impressionists. He began to construct his pictures not from light but from coloured planes and plastic form. He achieved limited public recognition in his last years, but by the turn of the century was revered as "the Sage" by many of the avant-garde. His work on the "structure" of nature can be most vividly seen in his paintings of Chateau Noir. It is fair to say that Cezanne's importance was largely unrecognized by his contemporaries. He died in 1906, by which time Cubism had been born. Cubism was as much a break from what had gone before as Impressionism was, perhaps more so. And while Cubism developed from Impressionism in the sense that Cezanne was both an Impressionist and an early Cubist, it is arguable that Impressionism owed more to Turner and Constable than Cubism ever would to Monet or Degas. Apart from Cezanne, the key figure in all of this was Pablo Picasso.

Picasso was born in Malaga, Andalusia, in 1881, the son of an art teacher, José Rinz Blasco and Maria Picasso y Lopez, whose maiden name he adopted. The family moved to Barcelona, and in 1895 the young Pablo entered the Academy there. He first visited Paris in 1900, and would alternate between the two cities until moving to Paris full-time in 1904 at the age of 24. Picasso was certainly attracted to Paris, not least because of the presence of other artists. He is known to have admired the Fauvists (Matisse, Dufy, Braque) and their colour, but his art did not directly follow their example. He was particularly in awe of Matisse, whom he referred to as "a magician".[71] In 1904, Picasso took a studio in the Bateau-Lavoir and became the centre of an avant-garde circle which included Max Jacob, Guillan Apollinaire, Andrew Salmon, Marie Laurencin and Gertrude Stein. He began to concentrate on the analysis and simplification of form, based on his studies of Cezanne and African sculpture. This culminated in the 1907 painting later named by Andre Salmon *Les Demoiselles d'Avignon*, which was seen as a revolt from Impressionism and the bright colours of Fauvism. The painting at the time was considered incomprehensible

---

71 Spurling, H., *Matisse: The Master* (London: Penguin, 2005).

to many artists – even Matisse and Derain (art critic and collector), let alone the public, and it was not publicly exhibited until 1937. It is now regarded as the most important single landmark in the development of modern art.[72] Picasso would go on to develop Cubism as the leading avant-garde movement, along with Braque and Gris. He would travel to Italy with Jean Cocteau, live in Spain for a time and return to Paris before retiring to the south of France. But by as early as the 1920s, Paris was no longer the greatest artistic city in the world,; the centre of gravity of modernism was already shifting to Berlin, and thence to New York.

New York: High Modernity

During the 1920s, a number of American writers would move, for a time at least, to Paris: Hemmingway, Ezra Pound, F. Scott Fitzgerald, later Henry Miller. But others too would visit Berlin, already a living experiment in Modernism, Expressionism and the "culture industry" in the shape of films and radio broadcasting. Berlin in the 1920s and the early 1930s was a place of great artistic innovation and sexual freedom. This was a golden age of the visual arts, architecture and design, and it was this that carried on the legacy of Cubism. Amongst the best-known of artists at that time was George Goosz – founder of the short-lived Neue Sachlichkeit movement and outspoken anti-capitalist – but the period is mostly noteworthy for the Bauhaus.

The Bauhaus was a school of architecture and the applied arts which became the centre of modern design in Germany, notable for establishing the relationship between design and industrial techniques.[73] The Bauhaus originated in 1919 by the fusion, under Walter Gropius, of the Weimar Academy of Fine Arts and the Weimar School of Arts and Crafts. The original staff, most of whom were connected with Expressionism, included Kandinksy and Klee, Feininger, the Hungarian architect and furniture designer Breuer and the typographer Herbert Bayer. Laslo Moholy-Nagy joined in 1923. The Bauhaus studios were avowedly left-wing, but became laboratories for prototype design and machine manufacture, so that many of the design products (especially furniture, textiles and lamps) were adapted for large-scale manufacture. The Nazis condemned the Bauhaus as "architectural socialism", and in 1925 the Bauhaus was relocated to a building in Dessau which Gropius himself had designed. There then followed a series of 14 books on design, edited by Gropius and Moholy-Nagy, so that by 1930 the Bauhaus had become the intellectual centre for architects and the applied arts across Europe. In 1928, Gropius left the Bauhaus to concentrate on his own architectural practice, succeeded as Director by Mies Van Der Rohe. Owing to opposition from the local Nazi party, the Bauhaus was forced to move to Berlin in 1932, but it survived less than a year after this date. Nevertheless, through the emigration of its staff and students after 1933, the Bauhaus ideas were widely disseminated. Gropius himself moved to England in 1934 where he designed several buildings in partnership with Maxwell Fry. He then took up

---

72 Coppelstone, T., *Modern Art* (New York: Exeter Books, 1985).
73 Whitford, F., *Bauhaus* (London: Thames & Hudson, 1984).

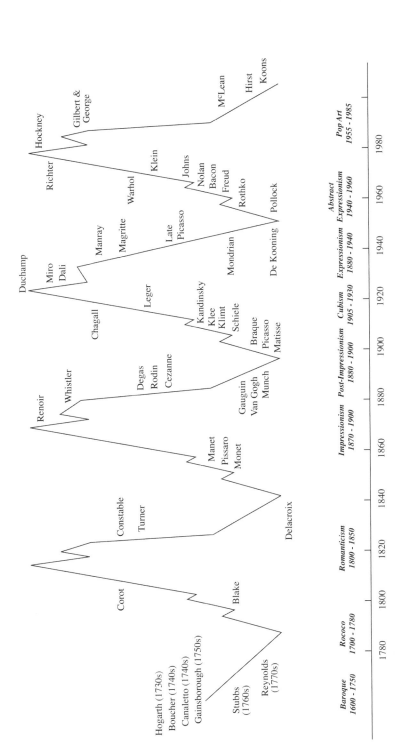

Figure 2.9   The Long Waves: Fine Art

Source: John Montgomery.

the post of Professor of Architecture at Harvard where he remained until 1952. He formed a partnership with Mariel Breuer from the Bauhaus days, and would later set up the Architects' Collaborative. He died in 1969. Moholy-Nagy moved initially to London, but in 1937 moved to Chicago where he founded the "New Bauhaus". Kandinsky moved to France in 1933, Klee remained in Berlin (where his work formed part of the Nazi's "Decadent Art" exhibition in 1937) and he would be dead by 1940. Mies van der Rohe became Director of Architecture at the Illinois Institute of Technology, Chicago, in 1938.

The Bauhaus architects and designers were not the only artists to flee Europe in the 1930s. Others who made the journey include Masson, Ernst, Tanguy, Matta, Miro, Dali, Grosz, Leger and Mondrian. All of these were Expressionists or modernists, or Surrealist.[74] Through contact with the artists, many Americans began moving towards Abstraction, and these included William De Kooning (himself a Dutch émigré), Pollock, Rothko and Robert Motherwell.[75] Some of these artists had studied under Hans Hofmann in New York in the 1930s. Collectively they became known as Abstract Expressionists from 1946. Pollock in particular was seeking a new form of art, and initially his work was a hybrid of Cubism, Expressionism and Surrealism. He began to take Surrealist theories of "automatism" to extremes such as dropping paint – industrial paint – onto huge canvasses laid flat on the ground. Pollock was regarded as a great innovator and his technique – which came to be known as "Action Painting" – was a paradigm shift away from the structure of Cubism. De Kooning, likewise, would experiment with a style of abstract black and white paintings. Rothko, Newman and Motherwell, by contrast, would develop a much less frenzied, more contemplative, style merging large rectangular bonds of colour, while Motherwell in particular would become well-known for collages. Most of these artists had known each other for a long time, since the 1930s when several of them had been involved in the Public Works of Art Project (a federal government initiative to provide employment for artists during the Depression). They would come to be known as the New York School,[76] and would regularly meet in The Club and the Cedar Tavern.

Thus, by the 1940s, New York following Paris and Berlin was the centre of modernism, certainly in art. Along the way, the city had acquired the Museum of Modern Art (MOMA) (1929), the Whitney (1930s) and the Guggenheim (1939), all of which featured the work of living artists. Peggy Guggenheim in particular was a strong supporter of the New York School, and was attracted to artists, briefly marrying Max Ernst. She lived in Paris during the 1920s and 1930s, attempted to set up a modern art gallery in London and later would buy and smuggle Expressionist Art out of Germany.[77] She set up the "Art of This Century" gallery in New York in

---

74 Richard, L., *Expressionism* (Paris: S.P.A.D.E.M, 1978).

75 Copplestone, *op. cit.*

76 Ashton, D., *The New York School* (New York: Viking 1972).

77 Dearborn, M.V., *Peggy Guggenheim: Mistress of Modernism* (London: Virago, 2005).

1942, exhibiting Pollock and Rothko.[78] Later in life, she would support the young Yoko Ono in Japan.

The Abstract Expressionism of the New York School would remain fashionable until the late 1950s, when a new paradigm – pop art – would emerge. Again, it is interesting to ponder why so many European artists would choose New York at that time, although more of the architects moved to Chicago. The answer is that New York already had a dynamic arts economy, as exemplified to some extent by the very existence of MOMA, the Whitney and the Guggenheim. By contrast, Chicago had an international reputation as a centre for architecture and urban studies. So the choice of New York is not such a surprise.

Visual art was not the only art form to flourish in New York in the 1940s. The other burst of creativity was in modern jazz. Compared to art there had been fewer "schools" and movements in music since the Romantic period. True, there were the Impressionists of the early twentieth century – Debussy and Ravel; and later Stravinsky and Schoenberg. But these did not amount to the panoply of movements found in visual art at the same time. This would begin to change with the development of jazz in general, but particularly modern jazz which is arguably the high point of modernism in music.

Modern jazz developed in New York in the 1940s. It was seen at the time – and still is – as a break with the "Swing" of the 1930s, the huge success of the big bands led by Glen Miller, Tommy Dorsey, Bennie Goodman and Artie Shaw. Swing in turn had evolved from the composition and arrangements of Duke Ellington during and after his residency at the Cotton Club in Harlem in the late 1920s and early 1930s. Prior to this, jazz had developed from the blues of the deep south, through ragtime and Dixieland (both centred on New Orleans) before establishing new variations in New York and Chicago. The "New Orleans in Chicago" movement was led by King Oliver, and it was in Chicago that the most famous New Orleans jazz recordings were made, as the phonograph technology became available after World War I. It was in Chicago that Louis Armstrong formed his Red Hot Five and Red Hot Seven, and where Jelly Roll Morton formed the Red Hot Peppers. Essentially a black music, centred on Chicago's South Side, it began to attract young white high school and college students who, in turn, began to develop what was known as "Chicago Style". This moved away from the overlapping of melodic lines, typical of New Orleans style, so that from this point the solo became increasingly important in jazz.[79] As a result, the saxophone would gain importance as a key instrument in jazz.

At the end of the 1920s, musicians playing the Chicago style moved to New York. This led to swing which was seen as a more "European" approach to the music. At much the same time, a second big band style – "riff" – developed in Kansas City, and this is thought to have derived from African "call-and-response" patterns. In both cities, soloists gained importance within the development of the big bands: Coleman

---

78 Gill, A., *Peggy Guggenheim: The Life of an Art Addict* (London: HarperCollins, 2001).

79 Berendt, J.E., *The Jazz Book* (London: Paladin 1964), Chapter 1.

Hawkins, Benny Goodman, Gene Krupa, Fats Waller, Johnny Hodges, Ray Eldridge ... Rex Stewart ... Swing was ascendant from about 1929 right through to the end of the 1940s.

Rather like the story of the Romantic poets or the Impressionists or the Renaissance artists, the new music – Bebop – was partly a reaction to what had gone before, the coming together in one place of like-minded artists and, amongst them, a general ennui with conventional society. The 1930s was also the time of the Great Depression. The conditions for a paradigm shift were in place, all that was required was a creative spark. This occurred not in New York but in Kansas City, where Charlie Parker was born in 1920. Although no-one in Parker's family was musical, he was playing baritone sax at the age of thirteen, largely self-taught. At seventeen, Parker joined Jay McShann's band, a typical Kansas City rift and blues orchestra. Although he admired the playing of Lester Young, Parker was already developing his curious style. He remained with Jay McShann until 1941 when, following a tour of the northern cities, he left the band at Detroit to return to New York. There he was a regular visitor to Minton's Club in Harlem, where the resident band consisted of Thelonious Monk, Charlie Christian, Nick Fenton and Kenny Clarke. It was also at Minton's that Parker would meet the trumpeter Dizzy Gillespie.

Dizzy Gillespie was born in South Carolina in 1917, into a musical family. Unlike Parker, he grew up in a stable and well-ordered family environment. Gillespie would study musical theory and harmony and by 1937 he was playing with the Teddy Hill Band. The band would tour Europe in the summer of that year where, along with the trombonist Dickie Wells, Gillespie attracted interest. In 1939, Gillespie joined Cab Calloway's orchestra, then coming to the end of its residency at the Cotton Club. From this time he began to solo for other bands, including Woody Herman's and Jimmy Dorsey's. In the early 1940s, he would work in the bands of Bonny Carter, Lucky Millinder, Earl Hines and Duke Ellington. On hearing Parker at Minton's, Gillespie was able, because of his musical training, to work out how Parker played.

Parker and Gillespie became inseparable, and for a while they played together in the Earl Hine's and Billy Eckstine bands. But in 1944 they co-led a combo which became "The Street of Bop" and went on to record together later that year. Later, the Charlie Parker quintet was formed, including Gillespie, but he would also tour with his own big bands. Gillespie would go on to experiment with new rhythms and drum patterns, and maintain his success well into the late 1950s. Parker, however, was a tortured genius and drug-dependant. By 1946 he had his first breakdown. Although he achieved some popular success in 1948–1950 with a recording made with a large string ensemble, he was never satisfied. He died in 1956, aged 35.

The accepted wisdom is that Parker provided the breakthrough and the raw genius, and that Gillespie was able to analyse and reassemble the music. This is probably unfair as Gillespie was also a noted innovator and brought much drive and energy. What Gillespie was able to demonstrate in notations was that Parker had found a way to use the higher intervals of chords as a melody line, blending these in with related changes. The flatted fifth became the most important interval of the new music, even although this would have seemed discordant to most ears at the time. The music seemed breathless and fragmented, and for many musicians it was simply too difficult.

Towards the end of his short life, Parker was asked whom he considered his most influential musicians. In order of importance, his answer was Brahms, Schoenberg, Duke Ellington, Hindemith and Stravinsky. Brahms possibly for his melodic qualities and emotion; Schoenberg, Stravinsky and Hindemith for their chromatic harmonies. It is arguable, at least, that the development of be-bop owed something to European post-Impressionist classical music, as applied by the creative genius that was Charlie Parker. But even before his death, jazz was again evolving. The 1950s would be the decade of "cool jazz" led by Miles Davis (who had played with Parker), John Lewis (who had played with Gillespie), Gerry Mulligan and Todd Cameron. However, Parker's influence continues to be heard today, not only in the playing of the current generation of saxophonists but because of a revival of Bop music since the late 1980s.

It is tempting to argue, in conclusion, that there was some very close relationship between the development of modern jazz and Abstract Impressionism in New York in the 1940s. Both, afterall, are modern idioms that can trace part of their roots from European music and art of 1904 to 1924. Both are concerned with underlying structure but also expressing emotions. Both occurred because the "new men" of the generation gravitated to New York. They did so because New York had already a knowledge store of modern art and the leading jazz musicians of the day. New York in this way was certainly a "creative milieu".

> I would not want to live anywhere else but New York. Here I feel right in the Twentieth Century. No other place, neither London nor Paris, gives that feeling of being 'contemporary'. If there is anything to compare to this New York sense of bubbling champagne, it would have been the Berlin of the Twenties. The same electrifying atmosphere I experienced in those Berlin years, I find in New York today.[80]

The Swinging Sixties

> Sexual intercourse began in 1963,
> between Lady Chatterley
> and the Beatles' first LP
> But that was too late for me.
>
> Philip Larkin

Just as the 20th century did not really begin until 1914, the Sixties did not commence in Britain until 1963, according to the poet Philip Larkin. For it was at that time that the moral codes of the earlier post-war generation began to be over-turned. This was exemplified by the *Lady Chattersley's Lover* obscenity case that freed publishing from censorship. Culturally, however, the Sixties were less of a radical

---

80 Lotte Lenya, quoted in *New York in Photographs* by Reinhart Wolf (Cologne: Taschen, 1985).

change from the 1950s than an evolution. We can see this in the rise of rock and roll, fashions, literature, theatre and in Pop Art. A simple listing of new works produced in the arts during the 1950s illustrates this point:

- *Theatre –*
  The Cocktail Party, T.S. Eliot, 1950
  The Consul, Carlo Menotti, 1950
  The Deep Blue Sea, Terence Rattigan, 1952
  The Crucible, Arthur Miller, 1953
  Camino Real, Tennessee Williams, 1953
  Cat on a Hot Tin Roof, Tennessee Williams, 1954
  Waiting for Godot, Samuel Beckett, 1955
  Look Back in Anger, John Osborne, 1956
  The Quare Fellow, Brendan Behan, 1956
  The Entertainer, John Osborne, 1957
  The Birthday Party, Harold Pinter, 1958
  Beckett, Jean Anouith, 1959

- *Literature –*
  The God that Failed, Arthur Koestler, 1950
  The Catcher in the Rye, J.D. Salinger, 1951
  The Cruel Sea, N. Montsarrat, 1951
  The Old Man and the Sea, Ernest Hemmingway, 1952
  Men at Arms, Evelyn Waugh, 1952
  Requiem for a Nun, William Faulkner, 1953
  Lord of the Flies, William Golding, 1954
  Under Milk Wood, Dylan Thomas, 1954
  The Quiet American, Graham Greene, 1955
  Lolita, Vladimir Nabukov, 1955
  The Organisation Man, W.H. Whyte, 1956
  Room at the Top, John Braine, 1957
  On the Road, Jack Kerouac, 1957
  The Sandcastle, Iris Murdoch, 1957
  The Habit of Loving, Dorris Lessing, 1957
  Dr. Zhivago, Boris Pasternak, 1958
  Advertisements for Myself, Norman Mailer, 1959

- *Film –*
  Sunset Boulevard, Billy Wilder (Dir), 1950
  A Streetcar Named Desire, E. Kazan, 1951
  The African Queen, John Huston, 1951
  From Here to Eternity, F. Zinnermann, 1953
  On the Waterfront, E. Kazan, 1954

Rebel Without a Cause, W. Ray, 1955
Richard III, L. Olivier, 1955
Baby Doll, E. Kazan, 1956
Gigi, V. Minelli, 1959
Room at the Top, J. Clayton, 1959

- *Music –*
  Billy Budd, Benjamin Britten, 1951
  The Rake's Progress, Igor Stravinsky, 1951
  Structures, Pierre Boulez, 1952
  Symphonia Antarctica, Vaughn Williams, 1952
  Tenth Symphony, Dimitri Shostakovitch, 1953
  Spring Symphony, Benjamin Britten, 1953
  Cello Concerto, William Walton, 1957
  Symphony No. 11, Shostakovich, 1958

- *Architecture –*
  Royal Festival Hall, London, Matthew & Morton, 1951
  Unite d'Habitation, Le Corbusier, 1952
  Roehampton Estates, London County Council, 1956
  Seagram Building, Mies van der Rohe and P. Johnson, 1958
  Pirelli Tower, Milan, Nervi and Ponti, 1958
  Guggenheim Museum, Frank Lloyd Wright, 1959

It was also during the 1950s, in the world of science and technology that the contraceptive pill was first manufactured (1952), the sound barrier was broken by the first time by a De Havilland 110 (1952), Crick and Watson discovered the structure of DNA, the first nuclear power station opened at Calder Hall (1956), radio telescopes were completed at Jodrell Bank and Cambridge (1957), and stereo sound recording was commercialized (1958).

In fine art, the most important shift was the development of Pop Art. The term "pop art" was coined by the English art critic Laurence Alloway for a movement which originated with meetings of the Independence Group in the winter of 1954–1955. As Alloway himself put it "the area of contact was mass produced urban culture". The Independence Group felt none of the dislike of commercial culture common amongst intellectuals, and not only accepted it as a fact of life, but embraced it enthusiastically. A characteristic of Pop Art would be that it rejected distinctions between good and bad taste. In New York, Pop Art was initially a reaction away from Abstract Expressionism, which more or less ended with Mark Rothko, mainly because its proponents brought back figural imagery. They were labelled Neo-Dadaists because they used commonplace subjects – comic strips, soup-tins, highway signs – in a similar fashion to Duchamp's "ready-mades" of 1915–1920. This can be seen in the work of Andy Warhol (soup cans) and Roy Lichtenstein (comic strips). Pop Art's most immediate inspiration, however, was

Jasper Johns' paintings of flags, targets and numbers and Robert Ragletuschenberg's collages, as for example in the work of Peter Blake (The First Real Target, 1961) and Richard Hamilton's "Just What Is It that makes today's homes so different, so appealing?" (1956). The major Pop Art sculptors were Claus Olderburg, whose subjects included ice cream cones and hamburgers, George Segal and Marisol Escobar.

In Britain the main figures were Richard Hamilton, (who taught at the Royal College of Art 1957–1966), Peter Blake, Eduardo Paolozzi and later David Hockney and Pauline Boty. Blake would go on to design album covers for the Beatles and other groups in the 1960s. Blake was a passionate collector of popular culture, and he used these in his work, as in his 1961 "Self-Portrait with Badges" which displays Converse sneakers, denim jeans, numerous badges, and an Elvis fanzine.[81] The popular arts of music and cinema provided several British Pop Artists with a recognizable set of images and an almost instant iconography. Blake himself painted the Beatles and Elvis Presley; Peter Phillips preferred Marilyn Monroe and Brigette Bardot; Pauline Boty produced her famous image of Christine Keeler, "Scandal", in 1963. Andy Warhol was doing much the same in New York, with series of works on Marilyn Monroe and Jackie Kennedy dating from 1962, as well as Elizabeth Taylor and Natalie Wood. Warhol too would move into the design of album covers with the Velvet Underground and then, in 1971, "Sticky Fingers" for The Rolling Stones. Meanwhile, bands like The Who appeared on stage wearing badges and Union Jacks in clear homage to Peter Blake's paintings. Pop Art, by this time, was strongly associated with hedonism, sexuality, the cult of the celebrity, the taking of instant pleasure. It was also very lucrative. It would, however, quickly become "Nostalgic", captivating brief moments in time that quickly would be gone.

By the late 1960s, Pop Art as a movement was already dissolving. By this time Warhol was something akin to a fashionable portrait artist, Lichtenstein was painting Monet-style haystacks and gold fish bowls as borrowed from Matisse. Tom Wesselmann's output largely consisted of female nudes and still lifes; Hockney became interested in exotic juxtapositions in his "Marriage of Styles" series. Just at the time it was fully assimilated into the canon of 20th century art, Pop Art as a new force was exhausted. Indeed, whether it can properly be described as a radical new departure is a moot point. For its early influences – such as comic heroes, Hollywood studio system celebrities, consumer goods – were in fact all products of an earlier time. And yet it was also an art for its own time, easily understandable on the surface yet also subversive and resonant of contemporary popular culture.

However, the main expression of this contemporary popular culture at the time was found not in art but in music. By the mid 1960s, London had overtaken New York as the centre of popular music. This occurred as the rock and roll of Bill Haley, Elvis Presley and Little Richard developed into the R&B of the

---

81 McCarthy, D., *Pop Art* (London: Tate Gallery Publishing, 2000).

Beatles and the blues-influenced music of The Rolling Stones and The Yardbirds, The Animals, Manfred Mann ... later The Who, The Kinks and Led Zepplin. The Beatles had formed by 1960 (with the exception of Ringo Starr) although John Lennon and Paul McCartney first met as they were growing up in Liverpool in 1957. Lennon, the early innovator and leader was influenced by the Beat generation of 1950s New York, and was interested in poetry and art as well as music.[82] The term "beat" was coined by the American novelist Jack Kerouac who is reported to have said "this is the beat generation" when referring to a generations of Americans that emerged from the late 1940s, but especially in the 1950s.[83] The word was a pun, referring to the weariness and defeat of the post-war generation, the "beatific", and those who followed the new music of rhythm and blues. Kerouac and his friends Allen Ginsberg, Neil Cassaday and Gregory Corso, helped shape the "generation" which was associated with a rejection of affluent society, indeed of all social values, in favour of oriental religions, drugs and free sexuality. The spiritual fathers of the Beats were Walt Whitman and Henry Miller, the followers Paul Goodman and Norman Mailer. Politically, the Beats found causes in civil rights and the anti-bomb movement, and were passionate in their hatred of injustice. In appearance they were distinguished by wearing black roll-neck sweaters and blue jeans. The beat generation is now viewed as somewhat immature and self-indulgent, although much the same can be said of the hippies in the late 1960s, and of much of Swinging London. In popular music, the bridge between the Beat generation and the 1960s was Bob Dylan, initially a folk music revivalist much influenced by Woody Guthrie and later Joan Baez. However, he was also inspired by the poetry of Dylan Thomas, and especially *From Under Milk Wood* (1954) and, following the Newport Folk Festival of 1963 began to write his own songs in earnest – the major breakthrough coming in 1965 with *Highway 61 Revisited*.

Back in Britain the new sound developed not in London but in Liverpool, home of Lennon and McCartney, Cilla Black, and Gerry and the Pacemakers. Pop music was not played on mainstream radio at that time, so people would tune in to Radio Luxembourg. The other source of inspiration was from records brought to Liverpool by sailors and crews of the great ocean liners which sailed between Liverpool and the New England ports at that time. However, the focus of Britain's pop music shifted in 1964 when the Beatles moved to London, initially to film *A Hard Day's Night* (1964). By this time Lennon and McCartney were writing their own songs. Other successful groups which formed in London in the early 1960s were The Rolling Stones (1962) and the Yardbirds (1961). Curiously, the films produced in London in the early 1960s lacked the edge of 1950s cinema, although by 1965 Michael Caine was starring in *The Ipcress File*, and later *Alfie*. Greater experimentation in film would come with the drug-fuelled psychedelic period of the late 1960s, marked by the later music of the Beatles and early Pink Floyd.

---

82 Norman, P., *Shout!* (London: 1981).
83 Kerouac, J., *On the Road* (Viking Press, 1957).

The main focus of popular culture remained music and fashion. In the world of fashion, the 1950s had not only favoured the New Look with its narrow waistlines and wide or pencil skirts, they had also introduced the A-line and the related trapeze line as developed by Yves Saint Laurent the then design director of Dior. These were "coats without a waist", narrow at the top and widening towards the bottom, and usually ending just above the knee.[84] These often had bold geographical or floral patterns in bright colours and were much shorter than the dresses of any previous period. These new dresses and coats were meant to appear gay and unconventional. By this time, of course, the first post-war generation had reached adulthood and, with growing prosperity in western economies, had the money to buy clothes that expressed their emergent identity and sexual liberation.

The young Mary Quant certainly found the style of the early 1950s too grown-up and boring. As early as 1955 she had opened her first boutique in Chelsea and, because she found it difficult to find the kind of clothes she was interested in, she began to make her own designs. She combined the tradition of English tailoring with what she observed on the streets of London. In 1963, some of her tunic dresses were shown in Vogue and within two years the miniskirt was born. Skirts grew shorter and shorter until they barely covered the bottom, and this was made possible by the invention of tights. Other designers of the time in London included Barbara Hulanicki who founded Biba, the first mail-order service for avant-garde fashion. Hairstyles too were changed, away from the back-combed styles of the 1950s, to the smooth, geometric short cuts of Vidal Sassoon, who was closely associated with Mary Quant.

Men's hairstyles on the other hand grew longer, beginning with the Beatles' mop-tops, which were controversial at the time. Within a few years this had evolved into the psychedelic look and then the long hair and beards of the hippies. Young men were also interested in fashion, from the look of Elvis, James Dean and Marlon Brando in the 1950s, and a curious home-grown style – the Teddy Boys. John Stephen opened his first male boutique in Carnaby Street (West Soho) in 1966, selling suits, shirts and ties in ever more adventurous cloths and materials. He used the boxer Billy Walker as a model to overcome any lingering doubts on whether it was masculine to wear brightly coloured clothing. Later, popular groups such as the Moody Blues and the Kinks would pose in crushed velvet trousers and frilly shirts. The moment is wittingly caracatured in the Kinks' *Dedicated Follower of Fashion*. (In passing, the Kinks were one of the very few groups of the time who used wit and satire in their songs, even though the post-modern sixties are held to be the time of irony and eclecticism.)

Odd though it at first may seem, the Swinging Sixties ended not in 1969 but in 1973 with the three-day week, the looming oil crisis and the peak of the fourth Kondrateiff Wave. By this time the Beatles had split (1970), R&B was being replaced by progressive rock and glam rock, and the centre of fashion was

---

84 Lehnert, G., *A History of Fashion in the 20ᵗʰ Century* (Cologne: Koremann, 2000).

shifting away from London to Milan and back to Paris, replaced for a time in the mid to late 1970s by punk. As a creative era, the Swinging Sixties had all but withered by 1969. It might even be tied to the embittered break-up of the Beatles' Apple Company, sadly a triumph of reality over idealism. It seems that, in the end, all you needed was not love at all. It also seems that the sixties did not begin in 1960, nor even in 1963 with "Please Please Me", but rather with the Pop Art of the 1950s, the politics and lifestyle of the Beat generation, the poetry of Dylan Thomas and the sudden arrival on the scene of the mesmerizing Elvis Presley. In turn, at least some of these "movements" can themselves be traced back to the Swing and blues of the 1940s, the Surrealists and even the poetry of T.S. Eliot and Walt Whitman and the novels of Henry Miller and D.H. Lawrence for their sexual explicitness. The Sixties were certainly a decade of hedonism, but we can now see that, like the 1920s before them, they were an ending rather than a new beginning.

Of course, some of the social developments of the Sixties still have ramifications for the present time and for the future. These include the relaxation of obscenity laws and censorship, female emancipation, the widespread acceptance of black cultural forms, especially in music and dance, a much more relaxed social attitude to sex and even, if we dare mention it, a falling birth rate caused not only by preventative birth control but also abortion-on-demand. This liberatarianism extends to a concern to see controls on all forms of public entertainment deregulated as far as is sensible – a sort of ethical reality. Included in this was the concern in the 1990s to relax liquor licensing in the UK in an effort to develop a more mixed and sophisticated "evening economy". We shall return to this issue in Part III.

4. THE ARTS AND URBAN REGENERATION

The Arts Come to Town

From the late 1980s, an increasing number of cities in Europe, North America and the UK turned their attention to using the arts and culture as new tools of urban revitalization. Central to this approach is the view that culture and cultural activities can be integrated into a widely based revitalization project. In the process, culture can help to provide the catalyst for physical and environmental renewal, attract spending and capital investment to an area, generate new economic activity and jobs and change or enhance an area's image. Cultural uses also adapt well to old buildings. The more recent examples of cultural regeneration date from the early 1980s in the USA, for example in Pittsburgh and Lexington, Mass.[85] This approach was proposed in the UK as long ago as 1987 by organizations such as the British American Arts Association[86]

---

85 Whitt, J.A., "Mozart and the Metropolis: the arts coalition and the urban growth machine", *Urban Affairs Quarterly*, Vol. 23, No. 1, 1987, pp. 15–36.

86 British American Arts Association, *The Arts and the Changing City* (London: 1989).

and the cultural consultancy Comedia.[87] Culturally-led urban development began to appear as a concept in the urban planning literature from the late 1980s.[88] Of course, culturally-led urban renewal programmes have had their critics. Ron Griffiths,[89] for example, argued that arts-based strategies of urban regeneration emerged in the 1980s, for three main reasons: the belief by city authorities that such strategies have the potential to generate spending and create jobs locally (both direct and indirect); the fact that arts-based strategies are "congruent with the consumption preferences of the culturally dominant and politically influential 'service class'"; and competition between cities, where each is keen to promote particular qualities and as good places to live – and as alternative business locations.

There is much truth in Griffiths' argument, and certainly the early examples such as the regeneration of downtown Pittsburgh in the 1980s (discussed in Part V) seem somehow clumsy and opportunistic. That in the early days those cites who were pursuing an arts-led recovery, or indeed any economic activity at all, were desperate is all too true, but then they can hardly be blamed for this. It is even tempting to agree with Griffiths who argues that there is no strong evidence that cultural investments "really do attract business and create jobs"; while the revenue costs (subsidy) required to run large venues might well be better spent on other social services – such as health or education. Griffiths also argues that it is not always clear who are the intended beneficiaries of cultural investment. A further criticism is that large-scale cultural investment tends to lead to a safe, uncritical and unchallenging cultural "context", especially where this is intended to attract visitors to the city. Griffiths' critique appears mainly to be about the distribution of benefits from such programmes – that is big business, developers and real estate owners over the artists and the urban poor.

This stance is also taken by Sharon Zukin in her 1995 book *The Cultures of Cities*. Zukin notes, however, that there are many different types of "cultural strategy": some focus on museums and other large cultural institutions, some preserve historic buildings for cultural uses; others support and promote the work of professional performance companies and orchestras; others link cultural institutions to local history. Zukin argues that not only is this dubious in terms of cultural "representation" but that "cultural strategies are often the worst-case scenario of economic development",[90] a sort of clutching at straws. She doubts, for example, that the emerging cultural strategies of cities in mid-1980s Britain are "realistic ... in the long term". More than this, cultural strategies "suggest the utter absence of new industrial strategies for growth". Not only this, but cultural strategies "scrutinize and homogenize history" in the interests of "civic order".

---

87 Bianchini, F., Montgomery, J., Fisher, M. and Worpole, K., *City Centres, City Cultures* (Manchester: Centre for Local Economic Development Strategies, 1988).

88 Montgomery, "The Art of City Planning", *Planning Practice and Research*, 5 (3) 1990.

89 Griffiths, R., "The Politics of Cultural Policy in Urban Renewal Strategies", *Policy and Politics*, 21 (1), 1993, pp. 39–46.

90 Zukin, S., *The Cultures of Cities* (Cambridge, Mass: Blackwell, 1995), p. 273.

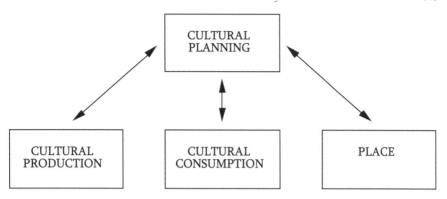

Figure 2.10   Cultural Planning as an Holistic Approach
Source: John Montgomery.

Such empty gestures for Zukin seem well-suited to (and help explain) ephemeral post-modern architecture. Zukin is writing from a Marxist perspective, and it shows. She goes much further than Griffiths but both writers doubt that cultural investment a) works; b) is necessarily a good thing; c) is progressive. It does rather seem that whether cultural investments succeed or not will depend on how they are shaped, what their objectives are and how they are brought into being. To suggest that all cultural investment urban renewal strategies will necessarily fail is somewhat deterministic to say the least.

To be fair Griffiths goes on to argue in favour of cultural strategies which promote and incorporate civic identity, everyday life, the public realm and public forms of social life. Quoting authors such as Franco Bianchini, Ken Worpole, Geoff Mulgan and myself, Griffiths argues that such an approach is preferable to the "narrow, explicitly anti-social, market rationality that gained ascendancy in the 80s". All of these authors adopted a "paradigm" of cultural planning as advocated by Franco Bianchini.[91] According to Bianchini, cultural planning is a "process of identifying, developing, managing and exploiting a city's cultural resources". As such, it involves monitoring and acting upon economic, cultural, social, environmental, political and symbolic trends and identities, cutting across the public and private sectors, different institutional concerns and different professional disciplines. Policies for cultural development should therefore relate to lifestyle, work and industry, leisure, sports, tourism, hobbies, political attitudes and moral values. Cultural planning includes three broad elements, and the linkages between them, as shown in the diagram. Essentially, this is an holistic approach to the development and management of cities, based on three interlinking concepts (Figure 2.10).

91 Bianchini, F., "Urban Cultural Policies in Western Europe", *Urban Networks in Europe*, undated.

By cultural industries is meant the production, distribution and transmission of cultural products (usually to mass audiences) namely books, records, films, videos, and TV programmes. These are economic sectors which can be analysed along a production chain as discussed in Part I. Arts and cultural policy refers, in the main, to the provision, production, performance and consumption of the arts and entertainment. Key issues here include the allocation of public subsidies, the questions of access and participation, audience development and marketing. Liveability and urban culture refers to the quality of life in city centres, the liveliness, vitality and animation of public life. These three categories are not mutually exclusive, they overlap. Indeed, the advantage of cultural planning is that it cuts across debates and disciplines, the way life does.

The cultural planning approach thus sees art as part of culture rather than vice versa. Nevertheless, it is still important to have a working definition of the arts, if they too are to be developed strategically. Such a definition might usefully be borrowed from *The Charter for the Arts in Scotland (1993)*, which is itself based upon Public Law 209 of the 89th United States Congress. This impressive definition reads as follows:

> The term 'the arts' includes, but is not limited to, music (instrumental and vocal), dance, mime, drama, folk art, creative writing, architecture and allied fields, painting, sculpture, photography, graphic and craft arts, industrial design, costume and fashion design, motion pictures, television, radio, tape and sound recording, the arts related to the presentation, performance, execution and exhibition of such major art forms, and the study and application of the arts to the human environment.[92]

This allows us to argue for the importance of innovation, creativity and excellence within and across particular art forms; whilst recognizing such questions as elite versus popular art/culture, minority ethnic cultures and sub-cultures, and the balance of development activity against building new venues. A definition of culture, however, takes us into deeper waters, including for example heritage and cultural tourism. The former relates in the main to historic and symbolic buildings and objects which contain special meaning for a local identity; while the latter introduces consideration of the "city offer", that is to say the various activities and environments which the city presents to visitors. Added to this Raymond Williams' argument that culture should be considered widely to include everyday activities such as eating and drinking, streetscapes and the very sense of place, and popular culture itself.

Accepting this argument means that city cultural strategies should address not only the performing and visual arts, but also the industries of culture, the seeds of creation and the culture of place. In turn this means that culture is not some separate, marginal and unconnected activity, but is rather a set of activities, processes and perspectives that can inform, and enrich the city in myriad ways. This implies seeing the city itself as a cultural resource. This approach is close

---

92 Scottish Arts Council, *A Charter for the Arts in Scotland*, Edinburgh, 1996.

to the one adopted in several European cities, enabling some of them to project themselves onto the European stage. One thinks here of Montpelier, Nimes, Grenoble, Barcelona, Cologne, Prato and, in the UK, Glasgow or Birmingham. The question then becomes one of profiling an individual city's cultural identity, its strengths and weaknesses, and opportunities to develop. Again, according to Bianchini, policy-makers can judge success or degree of development of a city's cultural life by assessing the following:

1. *The Cultural Economy*: The economic strength and significance of the pre-electronic media, such as the performing and visual arts and also in such contemporary "cultural industries" as film, video, broadcasting, photography electronic music, publishing, design and fashion.
2. *Risk and Innovation*: The emergence, development and management of local talent.
3. *Specialisms*: The presence of peculiar and specialized products and skills in particular forms of crafts, manufacturing and services (jewellery, ceramics, cuisine etc.)
4. *Urban Culture*: The vibrancy and attractiveness of the city encompassing as a physical and spiritual entity: diversity of shopping, cultural, leisure and entertainment facilities including clubs, bars and restaurants; the attractiveness, sense of place and legibility of the city's public spaces including urban landscapes, landmarks and amenities such as park systems and waterfronts; local traditions and events. This includes historical, artistic, architectural, archaeological and anthropological heritage.
5. *Image*: External and internal perceptions of the city which are constituted by the sum of cultural representations, media images and "conventional wisdom".[93]

In this way, the arts plans of the 1980s, and even the community arts development plans of the 1970s, have given way to more complex forms of urban cultural planning. In addition to important questions to do with the range of venues in a city or measures to increase audiences, cities are now having to consider the cultural or creative industries as economic sectors, the cultural "lifestyles" of urban places, the design of streets and spaces, and architecture. This is all the more important in a time when cities themselves must compete in the new creative and knowledge economies. This approach can be applied more or less to any liberal western city. Bearing these broad objectives in mind, a city can then fashion its own set of cultural policy measures, with the overall aim of developing the cultural economy, the arts more generally and feeding in to the development of the creative industries.

In deciding what to do about each of these policy areas, decision-makers will need to consult widely with artists, arts companies and organizations, creative entrepreneurs, venues, training and education providers, urban designers, local

---

93 Bianchini *op. cit.*, no date.

economic development agencies ... and more. This should hopefully allow for a broad agreement to emerge on the direction of the cultural strategy and its key measures, with the probable exception of the anti-capitalist left. Along the way, it might be necessary to polarize some issues and pose these as a set of strategic dilemmas to be resolved. One suggestion for framing these is set out in Table 2.1, itself developed from Bianchini's work in the early 1990s.

The reader will see that the sensible option in each case is to address both horns of the dilemma. Thus, cities must produce as well as consume arts, they must project a local identity but experiment in wider art movements; they should develop flagship venues where necessary but also support individual artists; they should embrace modernity as well as protecting traditions; they should direct new cultural investment to the suburbs as well as to the city centres; they should see art as both formative creativity and applied creativity, underpinning the industries of culture. None of this is trivial, nor is it easy. The thing to bear in mind is that the possible range of interventions will need to be directed not only to resolving historical or even current problems, but should also frame the future. As we shall now see, this approach was deliberately applied in Manchester in the early 1990s.

Manchester's Cultural Revival

One of the more successful city cultural strategies of the past fifteen years was that of Manchester, commissioned in 1991.[94] Manchester is located in the north of England, and jostles with Birmingham as England's second city. Its prosperity was built on the cotton and clothing industries, trading across the British Empire, notably with India, America and Australia (where, interestingly, bed-linen is still referred to as "Manchester"). Manchester itself became known as "Cotton-opolis", a status that was only made possible by advanced engineering projects such as the Manchester Ship Canal, extended to Liverpool sea port in 1766. Manchester became the world's first industrial city, triggered to a great degree by Richard Arkwright's patent of a steam-powered cotton manufacturing process, derived from earlier inventions such as Hargreaves' spinning jenny.[95] As well as the new production process, Manchester had access to imported raw materials and markets, plus plentiful local supplies of water and coal. This, plus the fact that Manchester had a repository of weaving skills following the settlement of Flemish weavers in the fourteenth century, led to cotton becoming the first industrial revolution.

The rapid expansion of industry led, during the nineteenth century, to rapid urbanization and conflicts would follow over both working conditions in the mills, and housing and public health: it was in Manchester that Engels would write *The Condition of Working Class in England.* Manchester developed a tradition of

---

94 Urban Cultures Ltd and ppartnerships, *Manchester First: A Cultural Strategy*, available Manchester City Council, Manchester 1992.

95 Hall *op. cit.* 1998, chapter 10.

trade unionism, the reform of working conditions and social welfare. It also has a strong self-help ethos, particularly in learning and the arts.[96] In the latter half of the nineteenth century, however, Manchester's economic growth slowed and began moving towards decline, largely as a result of competition and a failure to continue innovating. By the middle of the twentieth century the industries that had made Manchester great – cotton, engineering, machine engineering – were largely a thing of the past.

> Little is left of the world in which Manchester built its reputation. The great cotton Mills and warehouses have become converted entertainment venues, the terraced houses models for sets of Coronation Street. What is left, however, is the energy, the sheer spirit that made Manchester one of the great power-houses of the industrial age. And while that age is gone, Manchester is once again picking up steam.
>
> Nicholas Woodsworth, *Financial Times*

By the 1980s the city's economy was in serious decline, the professionals and middle classes were leaving, the city itself was relatively inert and uninteresting. The city fathers embarked upon a policy of attracting the financial services sector to the city, but this was an uphill task.[97] However, several interesting things *were* happening. Tony Wilson, an executive at Granada Television and music industry entrepreneur, established Factory Records, a recording label for what would become the Manchester Bands: the Happy Mondays, Joy Division, the Smiths. Wilson would also open the Hacienda nightclub and Dry Bar, a new generation urban bar. There was also the beginnings of regeneration in Castlefield led by local bookmaker Jim Ramsbottom and a team of young development professionals and architects. As well as the redevelopment itself, this would lead to the emergence of a network of design professionals and architects. The setting up of the Manchester Institute for Popular Culture (MIPC), with a brief to research popular culture, was also important. Amongst other things, an early contribution was a major study of "The Culture Industry", published in 1990.[98] There was also a timely recognition of the A/V industries (film, television, photography, video) as an important sector, in a study by Comedia in 1988.[99] All of these events were of crucial importance in what was to follow. The problem was that there was no bigger picture in place, no strategy for developing and

---

96 Kennedy, M., *Portrait of Manchester* (Manchester: Robert Hale, 1970).

97 Driver, P., *Manchester Pieces* (London: Picador, 1996), p. 14.

98 *The Culture Industry*, Manchester Institute for Popular Culture, Manchester 1990. Later re-published by Derek Wynne as *The Culture Industry: The Arts in Urban Regeneration* (Aldershot: Avebury, 1992).

99   *Film, Video and Television: The Audio-visual Economy in the North-west*, December 1988, Comedia Consultancy, for the Independent Film Video and Photography Association, North West Arts, Manchester City Council, the British Film Institute, Channel 4 and Lancashire County Council.

Table 2.1 Strategic Dilemmas in City Cultural Policy

Flagships and the Developmental Approach: In the climate of intense competition for prestige arts events and organizations, many cities have prioritized support for 'high' art forms both through the funding and the construction of new facilities. It is important to recognise that the cultural economy needs both high profile facilities (particularly where the city is attempting to boost its international profile) and a system of channels and feeders through which artistic talent can emerge and develop.
Local and International/Multinational: In cultural policy the local dimension is sometimes counterpoised with the international. The uniqueness of local products, practices and identities are the basis upon which international profiles can develop. Individual forms of expression often have a significance wider than the region in which they are made. A cynical approach to the production of work for a global market, devoid of roots, character or style is likely to be seen for what it is.
Consuming and Producing: Cultural policies should balance the objectives of stimulating cultural consumption – and the consumer service industries associated with it – and local cultural production. For a strong cultural economy must have both a strong demand side and a supply side of products. Each depends, to a degree, on the other.
Urban Regeneration and Problem of Property: An argument often put is that the new interest in arts and culture is simply a way of developers and property investors maximising their assets. In the longer term, as property prices and rents increase as the result of new interest generated in an area through cultural activities, the pressure on 'low value land uses' mounts to the stage where they are effectively driven out of an area. It should not be beyond the wit of policy makers to find the means to prevent or limit land use colonisation of this nature.
Life as well as Infrastructure: There is often a tendency to see cultural investment as being primarily about new capital projects or the upgrading of buildings. Networking, investment in 'soft' infrastructure such as marketing and promotion, and an opportunity for more and varied programmes and events and festivals can be extremely effective in raising a city's cultural profile to both residents and the outside world.
Nostalgia and Innovation: There is a danger that culture can become ossified – the city as a heritage park, with the emphasis exclusively on traditional art forms, pastiche and the conservation ethos. Living cultures should expect to grow, rather than looking ever backwards to some golden age or other. This means taking risks as well as playing safe, not only in programming and curation but also in architecture, urban design and public art, the visual flags of a successful city moving forwards.

Visitors and Residents: Policies chiefly aimed at attracting visitors, whether 'cultural tourists' or business tourists, and at making the city more attractive to residents are rarely consciously integrated. In my view, these two strands should be part of the same strategy. Spending generated by visitors can support facilities which the residents might not otherwise benefit from. Many cities should actively promote cultural tourism as a way of attracting more visitors and spending to the city.

City Centre and Periphery: Policies focusing almost exclusively on the city centre, predominantly aimed at tourists and higher income groups, can alienate from civic life those residents of deprived outer estates and inner city areas who may find the centre's cultural provision difficult to access – whether psychologically, physically or economically. These tensions are evident in many cities, but again are in principle reconcilable. Special consideration should be given to the city centre as this is where the visitor forms their first impression of a city. This does not mean that other areas are neglected – a core identity should be established, physically as well as in the network sense which allows for an interplay between the centre and its suburbs.

Art and Business: Policy-makers should recognise that cultural development extends beyond the confines of the subsidised arts, or indeed the voluntary and community sectors. The implication of this is that public money should – as in other industrial sectors – be used as pump-priming, leverage and seed capital to help art businesses set up, consolidate and expand. For a number of cultural industries, economic development has similar characteristics to other, perceived as more mainstream, sectors of the economy. By extension, this could mean that public funds might be used to part-finance risky ventures such as music festivals, conferences, even film productions.

sustaining creativity. The proof of this is that Factory Records would later go into liquidation, and even the Hacienda was closed.

In November 1991 Manchester City Council commissioned a major study of the arts and cultural policy of the city.[100] The main purpose of the study was to identify the strengths and weaknesses in the city's cultural economy. On the basis of this, the City Council asked the consultants to draw up a strategy aimed at maximizing the level and cost-effectiveness of investment in arts and culture; ensuring the accessibility of arts and culture to the city's inhabitants and users; and raising the profile of the city nationally and internationally. As can be seen, the original brief was for a fairly standard arts plan, with the additional goal of raising the city's profile. The consultants opted to challenge and develop this brief to include the cultural industries (production), the cultural economy (consumption and cultural tourism), café culture, the concept of the 24 Hour City, cultural quarters, the public realm, good urban design and architecture. The strategy took a year to develop, and was a big investment for Manchester at that time.

The strategy was entitled *"Manchester First"*, because it was the first urban cultural strategy of its type in England and Wales, but also because Manchester has always been a pioneering city in theatre, literature, invention and innovation. "What Manchester does today, London thinks tomorrow." The document sets a framework for much of Manchester's revitalization ever since. Other factors were certainly important – the Olympic Bid in 1992, City of Drama in 1994, the IRA bombing the Arndale Centre in 1996, *The 24 Hour City* initiative led by the MIPC and Urban Cultures, the redevelopment of the inner area of Moss-side. But the Cultural Strategy formed the basis of Manchester's City Pride Bid, several arts lottery projects, the relaxation of licensing laws, the explosion of café culture and the overall drive towards mixed use and the creation of distinctive quarters.

Manchester First provided the City Council and its partners with a strategic framework through which to pursue such investment, and through which to integrate culture into the broader infrastructure of the city: its economic base, its transport systems, its education, health care, housing and planning services. It was stressed that culture and the arts should be conceived of as a mixed economy and that, although the City Council must play an important strategic role, a large proportion of its recommendations and suggestions would be pursued by other public bodies, the private sector and voluntary sectors, and by artists and cultural businesses themselves. *Manchester First* showed that Manchester's cultural economy was the largest in the UK outside London, with impressive volumes of activity at every level from the grass-roots to the mainstream. Manchester's particular strengths lay in its popular music culture, a long tradition of theatre, an important portfolio of collections and galleries in the visual arts, as well as a large number of film, television and video companies. The city was also home to many fashion, design and graphic design companies. There were, however, a number of significant gaps or weaknesses in Manchester's cultural economy which merited serious attention. These ranged

---

100 Urban Cultures Ltd and ppartnerships, *Manchester First*, *op. cit.*, 1992.

Table 2.2 Strategic Urban Cultural Objectives

1. Developing the City's Cultural Heritage and Encouraging its Wider Use

This means supporting the city's basic cultural institutions, museums, theatres, galleries. But it should also be recognised that, important though they are, these are not the sole repositories of the city's culture. Equal attention should be paid to smaller institutions and organisations, both well established and recently formed, which embody the city's cultural life as much as the larger institutions.

2. Promoting Excellence, Creativity and Risk

This applies mainly to creators and artists. It is not only a question of new art and new art forms, but of new ways of interpreting and presenting existing art and new ways of establishing relationships between art, cultural expression and the citizens of the city. Creativity and risk can best be encouraged by promoting an atmosphere of freedom and open-mindedness through innovation and experiment.

3. Increasing Cultural Consumption

On the demand side, the objective should be to increase both the numbers and levels of arts audiences and cultural consumers. This involves the building up of new audiences for the arts – visitors as well as residents.

4. Promoting Wider Cultural Participation

The city is a workshop as well as a showcase. Participation can take place on many levels and for many reasons: artistic expression, learning new skills, as a hobby or as a means of beginning a career in the cultural industries. Culture is experienced actively as well as passively. There is opportunity to participate in the wider civic culture as well as in the cultural forms of a particular social or ethnic group.

5. Place and Culture

This involves promoting the city as a place, as a built form, to project a more up-beat, cosmopolitan and modern feel. It is in part a form of boosterism, aimed at attracting new investment to the city. But it is also about raising the cultural awareness of local citizens, and improving the layout and design of the city.

Source: *Manchester First: A Cultural Strategy for Manchester*, Urban Cultures Ltd and ppartnerships, 1992, two volumes, available from Manchester City Council.

from particular problems restricting the development of a particular cultural sector – for example dance or photography – to more general (though uneven) trends and tendencies such as the leakage of talent from the city in search of opportunity. The content of the strategy was organized around five strategic objectives, as summarized in Table 2.2.

We can expand a little on these. By *Developing the City's Cultural Heritage and Encouraging its Wider Use* was meant support for major cultural institutions such as galleries, theatres and orchestras. These organizations were the cornerstones of the city's cultural economy and play a crucial role in defining and developing the cultural heritage of the city for residents and visitors. In Manchester, the list of cultural cornerstones in 1991 included, amongst others: Cornerhouse, the Royal Exchange Theatre, the Hallé Orchestra, The Nia Centre (black arts), the Museum of Labour History, the Green Room, Library Theatre Company, City Art Gallery, Castlefield Gallery, Whitworth Gallery, Contact Theatre, Chinese View and The John Rylands Library. It was argued that City Council should recognize these organizations as a major resource and encourage them to develop new activities in line with the aims of the strategy. It was important that a close relationship be maintained between the Council and these cultural cornerstones.

In addition, a programme of cultural inward investment was recommended as the best way of addressing cultural weaknesses: in 1992 Manchester lacked its own opera and dance companies – serious shortcomings for a city of Manchester's size and aspirations. In this way, existing companies would be encouraged either to make Manchester their home base or to have a continuing special relationship with the city. This was not simply a question of prestige but of having these resources in the city. In both cases there was scope to attract middle-scale companies with a reputation for innovation. This was seen as complementing the European Centre for Advanced Opera Studies, then planned by the Royal Northern College of Music. Similarly, a dance studio base would fit well into plans to establish a national dance agency in Manchester and in association with the Northern Ballet School. There was also the need for a major new gallery showing contemporary visual art.

Developing the cultural heritage of a city not only involves maintaining current support and plugging gaps, but also investing in new infrastructure. The possibility of such investment was already being explored in Manchester in the form of a new concert hall and the proposed extension to the City Art Gallery. *Manchester First* made a number of other specific recommendations on this front. It identified the need for a new middle scale performance venue to bridge the gap in provision between the large theatres and small-scale spaces, and recommended the creation of a new kind of civic institution for the next century: an arts centre focussing on the "electronic arts" of sound and vision. This would act as a showcase for Manchester talent in the fields of music recording, film and video production, computer-based design and multi-media arts and provide a "shop window" onto the latest technological developments in these fields. The centre would have performance and exhibition space, but also give substantial space to cultural retailing, restaurant and bar facilities and the distribution of information.

Two other facilities were proposed, both dedicated to the fostering of the city's cultural heritage. The Manchester Heritage Centre was to be a centre for the study of the city. Situated in Castlefield, alongside many of the city's galleries and museums, the centre would collect and display historical material in all its forms from details of large building works like the Manchester Ship Canal to genealogical material on births deaths and marriages. The Manchester Centre for Architecture, modelled on the *Pavilion de l'Arsenal* in Paris, would be a mixture of a museum of the city's built heritage and a centre for discussion and public consultation on development plans and large cultural projects. It would play a large part in placing urban design and the public realm on the city's political and social agenda thus furthering another basic aim of the strategy: the enhancement of a sense of place and public culture. Between 1994 and 2002, Manchester developed the Nyrex Arena (1995), the Bridgewater Concert Hall (1996), the Lowry Centre[101] (2000), extended the City Gallery (2002), opened the Manchester Museum, rebuilt the Royal Exchange Theatre and developed "Urbis", a museum of cities.

The second strategic goal of *Promoting Excellence, Creativity and Risk* was intended to encourage myriad private endeavours to take place in the cultural sector, and to offer recognition and support where necessary so that these could realize their potential in the city. Stimulating this creativity and harnessing it for the good of the city became one of the central planks of the cultural strategy. The argument was that Manchester's central strength since the 1750s had been its capacity for creativity and innovation. The problem was, in the cultural sector, "cultural leakage", was resulting in loss of talent from the city – the tendency for cultural practitioners to move to other cities (most especially London) in search of opportunities denied them in Manchester. Cultural leakage was seen as the symptom of a much deeper problem which might be characterized as a lack of investment in, and support of, innovation and cultural enterprise. The City Council was urged to see itself in this context as a catalyst: by adapting some of its own resources, but more importantly working more closely with private initiatives. This role, in fact, was in keeping with changes in local government, where local authorities were changing from providers into enablers. One immediate task was to encourage more networking within the cultural sector by organizing seminars, by helping to produce printed information on active individuals and organizations and by developing an internet HOST network. Networking on an international level was seen as equally important to stimulating creativity and innovation.

Manchester First also recommended the establishment of a support and information service targeted at arts business to provide training, business advice, access to local and national networks, business appraisals and information on office and workshop accommodation. The proposed service included a Cultural Industries Venture Capital Fund which would provide soft loans to cultural enterprises. Another option was to establish an Arts Business Liaison Scheme to help arts businesses to raise loans from banks and other lending institutions. In the event, the Manchester Creative Industries Development Agency was established in 1998.

Working with appropriate partners, the City Council was recommended to develop a property strategy to help arts workers work and live in or near the city centre. This was done by using city owned property as a lever, by planning gain or by re-thinking planning guidelines, so that that arts activities are protected or, at least, so that there is a presumption against their loss. The Council needed to pay particular attention to the demand for artists studios, a new and extended lease for the Castlefield Gallery, and the future of the Craft Centre. This latter facility was later developed as managed

---

101   De Castella, T., "Salford's Cultural Catalyst", *Regeneration and Renewal*, 10 November 2000.

workshops with a retail outlet and a marketing and export function, with a larger mixed use redevelopment of Smithfield.

Property support for the arts is often easier to carry out in the context of cultural quarters – areas which have their own set of special policies aimed at stimulating cultural production and consumption. *Manchester First* recommended the creation of four cultural quarters:

- Building on its existing strengths, *Castlefield* was identified as Manchester's Museums Galleries and Attractions Quarter. This has now been achieved, including the addition of the Museum of Science and Industry.
- *Oxford Road* became Manchester's Theatreland and "stepping out strip", with a vibrant evening life. This area is now referred to as "Manchester's West End".
- *Oldham Street* was billed as Manchester's alternative nightlife and retail area, and has since been promoted as the Manchester Northern Quarter (see Part V).
- *Ancoats* was the natural location for Manchester's Cultural Production Quarter. This has been followed through in the context of a mixed used residential area closed to the city centre, "an urban village for the 21st century".

In the longer term, *Manchester First* recommended an investigation into the feasibility of creating a technopolis to exploit the link between cultural expression, education, research and technology. This was to be the equivalent of a science park, concentrating on innovative cultural production, with a range of seed bed companies in fields such as animation, film imaging, sound recording, industrial design, prototype manufacturing or new types of stage design. In many ways, this would build on Manchester's traditional strengths in education and technological innovation. This proposal is now being taken up (since 2003).

The third strategic goal was *Increasing Cultural Consumption*. The premise was that there was much potential to increase cultural consumption in Manchester, drawing on a catchment area that included Greater Manchester, the North West region and beyond. Research into attendance at Museums and Art Galleries in Manchester and national and regional surveys into cultural preferences and arts attendance indicated that the market share for the arts in Greater Manchester was just over 1 million – two fifths of the adult population – while the figure for the region as a whole was between 2.5 and 3 million. The city's cultural institutions had already recognized the importance of marketing their products in order to tap into this potential audience. Marketing of the city's arts facilities had been successfully conducted for several years by Arts About Manchester and this was developed further through an *integrated marketing approach* by the City Council and arts organizations. A place marketing strategy was also devised in cooperation with the Greater Manchester Visitor & Convention Bureau, Manchester Airport and North West Tourist Board and involving pubs, wine bars, restaurants and night clubs and supermarkets. This would later include a centralized ticket purchase scheme. Moreover, while *Manchester Evening News* and *City Life* contained comprehensive listings there was scope to increase the volume and visibility of arts information in the city. Noticeboards with details of facilities, attractions and events were erected on public buildings, in shopping centres and in bus and rail stations. A general directory in the form of a guide to facilities, activities and resources was produced as well as directories targeting niche markets such as a design guide. An arts, entertainment and leisure map was prepared in noticeboard form as a free publication, information points were established at the Town Hall, the City Art Gallery and other cultural institutions as well as in bus and rail stations.

The fourth strategic goal was to *Promote Wider Cultural Participation.* The strategy recognized that participation can take place on many levels and for many reasons, indeed that culture is experienced actively as well as passively. This meant providing opportunities for residents to participate in the wider civic culture of the city as well as in the cultural forms. Participation was an underlying theme of *Manchester First* and increasing participation was touched upon to one extent or another by all the other basic aims of the strategy. Developing the city's heritage, for example, was not only geared towards the larger institutions but also to smaller organizations around the city who worked closely with local communities, often well outside traditional cultural settings. For example, the important role played by the library service in providing access to culture and in promoting cultural development was emphasized. Similarly, the City Council was encouraged to acknowledge the crucial role played by the education service in promoting participation through the school system and through adult education. The role of Manchester-based organizations, in exploring the potential of the arts in the context of health care was also acknowledged.

The final strategic goal was *Enhancing Sense of Place and Public Culture.* This was aimed at improving external perceptions of the city, raising awareness of the city centre, its history and its potential. The whole question of the built form of the city, of its public spaces and how these are used by people, of urban culture and of Manchester as a place was of central importance in the cultural strategy. It was not a discrete consideration but one which affected cultural consumption, marketing, inward investment, civic pride and that intangible quality of excitement and expectation which embodies the inner spirit of a city. *Manchester First* advocated the establishment of a review body for the city centre, involving community representatives as well as representatives of the relevant professions and working to improve the aesthetic awareness of the built environment and put forward specific proposals for improvement. In this way, Manchester anticipated the UK Commission for the Built Environment by nearly ten years.

There was clearly a need to invest in new architecture and urban public spaces, as Manchester was failing to make the most of its cityscape. *Manchester First* urged the council to be as broad and imaginative as possible in the implementation of such schemes and suggests, for example, the inauguration of a *"Year of Public Space"*, where young architects and urban designers would be commissioned to re-model and create new public spaces in Manchester.

Table 2.3 Manchester's Cultural Strategy

1. Support for Key Cultural Institutions	Continue and review the financial, organisational and other support of the city's key cultural institutions in the light of overall strategic objectives.
2. Partnerships with Key Cultural Producers	Recognise, support and give status to key producing organisations and individuals in the cultural economy in the private as well as the public and voluntary sectors.
3. Encouraging Initiative and Innovation	Establish innovation funds to provide seed capital, production investment, bursaries, research grants to encourage and support the work of public, private or voluntary sector organisations and individuals.
4. Conferencing and Networking	Establish post of conference animateur and programmer. Promote Manchester as a venue for cultural conferences. Encourage networking through organisation of events and production of directories.
5. Investing in New Infrastructure	Continue to pursue plans for extension of the City Art Gallery. Support plans for new international visual arts facility in Castlefield. Undertake study into feasibility of a new middle scale performance venue. Undertake study into feasibility of new 'high-tech' arts centre focussing on sound and vision. Commission feasibility study into the establishment of a Manchester Heritage Centre. Establish a Manchester Centre for Architecture. Support with other partners the RNCM's initiative to create a European Centre for Advanced Opera Studies. Continue to support and advance the Pumphouse Development Project - the new visitor centre for the National Museum of Labour History.
6. New Agencies	Support proposals to establish a National Dance Agency in the city. Establish a Film Commission or Bureau for Manchester with the aim of boosting demand for Manchester companies.

7. Cultural Inward Investment	Explore the possibility of: Encouraging an established, middle-scale and innovative opera company to use the city as its home base. Attracting an established, small to middle scale dance company into the city. Increasing commercial publishing activity in the city.
8. International Links	Adopt a cultural foreign policy which aims to attract international visitors to the city and recognises the potential of using culture as a means of attracting inward investment. Adopt a strategic cultural twinning policy. Maintain the momentum and contacts already established through the Eurocities Network. Encourage other types of initiative such as touring, studio exchanges, residencies and co-productions.
9. Resourcing Other Services for Culture	Explore further the potential of the library service in the field of cultural development. Support cultural development initiatives in the education and health services.
10. Arts Business Investment and Advice	Establish a Manchester Cultural Industries Venture Capital Fund. Establish a cultural industries business advisory service.
11. Widening the Range of Cultural Products	Establish a prototype development fund for new cultural products. Explore means of branding Manchester products through signs, and the establishment of retail outlets in other cities. Commission a concept study into the creation of a cultural technopolis or cultural science park.
12. Property Support for Arts Production	Develop a strategy to help art workers work or live in or near the city centre which revolves around city-owned property, revising current planning guidelines as well as specific initiatives. Offer below market rents and dispose of property for less than market value to arts practitioners. Work with artists and craftspersons groups to develop low-cost workspace complexes.

13. Cultural Animation	Establish a comprehensive programme of cultural animation in square, parks, open spaces and in a range of other public venues aimed at bringing vitality to the public realm, particularly the city centre.
14. Investing in Architecture and Urban Spaces	Establish a review body for the city centre to raise awareness of city centre and put forward specific proposals. Inaugurate a 'Year of Public Space'.
15. Improving Street Life and Urban Culture in the City Centre	Encourage a 'culture' of people watching. Devise a series of lighting trails and promenading routes. Adopt temporary architectural lighting schemes. Encourage retailers to keep shop window lights on at night. Involve artists in the design of items of civic signage and street furniture. Review and develop a policy on city centre licensing. Encourage shops and cultural venues to stay open longer in the evenings to promote an evening economy in the city centre
16. Public Art	Develop a place-making programme of public art.
17. Art and Transport	Encourage the commissioning of permanent and temporary works of art and the programming of cultural events in appropriate contexts in the transport system.
18. Cultural Quarters	Formally designate the four following areas as cultural quarters: Castlefield, Oxford Road (Whitworth Street), Oldham Street, Ancoats. Establish a 'cultural trail' linking these areas to each other. Commission a study into the incorporation of cultural facilities into the Olympic-led developments in Manchester.

19. Culture and the Suburbs	Recognise and protect the productive inter-action between centre and suburbs in the city's arts and cultural development.
20. Marketing and Promotion and Audience Development	Increase the volume and visibility of arts information through such media as noticeboards and directories.
	Establish a series of information points at stations and cultural facilities in the city centre.
	Encourage greater integration in the marketing of city centre facilities.
	Establish a 'Manchester Card' Scheme.
	Develop a place marketing strategy based on culture in conjunction with NWTB.

Source: Urban Cultures Ltd and ppartnerships, 1992.

A comprehensive programme of cultural animation in the parks, squares and open spaces of the city was also recommended to bring more colour, activity and people to the city. Disused and under-used buildings, indoor shopping malls and places like churches and hotel halls could also be used for cultural events. A number of specific proposals were also put forward to improve Manchester's street-life and to make the city centre more user friendly, diverse and enticing. These revolved around considerations such as people watching, encouraging people to interact, directly and indirectly, in public space by providing, for example, informal outdoor seating and meeting areas, and ensuring that there are "transitional spaces" between shops, pubs, restaurants and the pavement/ street. The possibilities of lighting were explored from the point of view of safety and of aesthetic improvement, floodlighting buildings and creating linkages, of colour, shop-fronts and shop window lights, street furniture and signposting. A review of the Council's city centre licensing policies was also urged, with a presumption in favour of longer opening hours, more late-night licences and pavement seating. These were not small matters; the fortunes of a city centre often rest on considerations such as these. Manchester could not project itself as a European City without a city centre that is lively, colourful and inviting during the day and into the evening hours. In fact, this proposal led directly to the emergence of Manchester as the UK's first "24 Hour City", and the growth of café culture (as discussed in Part III). *Manchester First* also underlined the importance of the suburbs to Manchester's cultural economy. A summary of the strategy action plan is provided in Table 2.3.

This discussion of Manchester's cultural strategy and cultural revitalization suggests some possible wider lessons that may apply to or otherwise be helpful for other cities. For it appears that Manchester's example is characterized by a surprising mix of conditions, factors and triggers. First, Manchester endured a long period of economic decline culminating in a slump, but followed by a unique burst of creativity. The turnaround was only made possible by a strong city leadership operating within a clear and directed cultural policy. Reservoirs of creative talent based on traditional skills, cultural innovation and the presence of three major universities in the city were essential to the early growth of the creative economy, as was the emergence of a new breed of locally-based entrepreneurs. The availability of inexpensive property, brought about by suburbanization and dis-investment from the urban core, as the middle classes fled the city, allowed new businesses to co-locate in previously unfashionable areas. This in itself helped in the emergence of a network of local design professionals. The backdrop against which all of this occurred included a successful Manchester popular music scene in the 1980s, as well as a reputation for excellence in television production and a longer tradition of theatre and writing.

Clearly all of this could not be known and predicted in advance, contingent as much of it was on the right people being in the right place at the right time. The time at which Manchester's cultural revival began coincides with the final years (downswing) of the fourth Kondratieff wave. That is to say, 20 or so years of falling profitability had produced a stagnant, even mortified, economy. The depth of the slump occurred in the 1980s, with signs of recovery only becoming apparent by the mid-1990s. So the emergence of a "creative class" in Manchester in the late 1980s is probably in part a consequence of events of up to 30 years earlier (particularly in relation to popular music, fashion and arts education). For without the presence of such people in Manchester in the early 1990s, the cultural strategy could not have succeeded.

The immediately preceding age of cultural creativity was in the 1970s and 1980s, with the emergence of the Manchester Bands. This was in essence a fusion of popular music and fashion in Manchester in the 1980s. But the Manchester of the 1980s was also beginning to innovate in television production – the expertise to do so having been built up by Granada Television (where Tony Wilson started as a trainee[102]) and, to a lesser extent, BBC North West. Piccadilly Radio, one of the first commercial radio stations blended production with "Manchester Music" and advertising. Thus the convergence of popular music, fashion, film and television productions (and eventually digital art) was made possible. In addition, historical traditions of live music (the Halle Orchestra and the Northern Conservatorium) and theatre (a pool of actors, stage directors and technicians) and literature (scriptwriters) played their part, as did a steady supply of fine art students, photographers and commercial artists. These were the enabling factors and influences but the creative spark – or trigger – was Tony Wilson with Factory Records, the Hacienda, Dry Bar (Figure 3.4) and Granada Television.

5. CONCLUSION: ARTISTIC CREATIVITY AND THE LONG WAVES

In this Part II, I have argued that artistic movements correspond to Kuhn's concept of the paradigm shift in that new art genres are created as previous methods and assumptions are challenged. In this way, an original act of creation is followed by a "long-wave" of artistic creativity represented as movements and schools. Examples include nineteenth century poetry, Romantic Music, Modernism, modern jazz or Impressionism. Moreover, these instances of original creativity usually occur during down-waves in the economic cycle, with applied and derived forms of creativity – the new schools – following in the subsequent up-swing. In this, artistic creativity appears to follow a similar dynamic to achievements in scientific discovery and technology. However, artistic genius is also a biological gift or a result of genetic structure of an individual. It matters a great deal that Beethoven was Beethoven, Shakespeare was Shakespeare and Turner was Turner. That said, it is also true that great geniuses are influenced by what has gone before, as in the examples of Mozart and Bach or Auden and Eliot. This can either be because of mentoring (Debussy and Stravinsky) or a reaction against a past master

---

102   Tony Wilson was the founder of Factory Records, and also a TV producer at Granada. The film *24 Hour Party People* is about him. He discovered Joy Division, New Order and the Happy Mondays.

(Pollock and Picasso). Wider societal influences are also exerted, for example in Copland trying to capture the spirit of America or Gaugin's experimentation with colour in the South Sea Islands, or indeed in the rise of the Romantic movement. Technology also plays a role, for example in the invention of new pigments or new musical instruments.

One question is whether artistic creativity proceeds in advance of, alongside or lags behind wealth creation. In the earlier examples (Florence, Amsterdam) it would appear that wealth creation precedes artistic creativity (which can then be afforded), at least initially. The Dutch Masters were able to earn a living from painting (sometimes precariously) because of the wealth of merchant traders and their interest in portraiture and landscapes. Much the same relationship between wealth creation and art appears to have been present in the Renaissance, although in this case art itself would become part of the Florentine economy. In later examples it appears that wealth creation and artistic creativity feed and feed off each other, and in doing so both the economic and cultural characteristics of the next wave is shaped. For example, the Bauhaus, Cubism and the German film industry led to the establishment of important sectors of wealth creation in the USA from the 1940s. In this way, commercial applications of the arts and design have historically produced cycles of wealth creation. At some point in the past, artistic artefacts themselves became "products" and sources of wealth creation. This is undoubtedly true of Impressionism, for example, and certainly much of popular culture since the 1950s. It is certainly true of the new media and the creative industries.

It would seem, then, that it is too simplistic to argue that wealth creation precedes artistic development; rather that there is at work – certainly since the mid 19th century – a dual process where commerce and art are interwoven. This means, I propose, that in the most successful cities since the mid 19th century, commerce has not simply provided the wealth to pay for artistic creativity; nor does artistic spark directly create wealth-generation in a one-to-one sense. Rather each helps to create the other. This is very important because it means that the future of city economies is bound up in a combination of primary invention, applied innovation, artistic creativity and commercial applications. It seems too that most cities manage to achieve this combination at least once – otherwise they would not be cities, while others manage to repeat the process to varying degrees of success.

This also implies, again in broad terms, that certain phases of capitalism equate with key artistic movements: early industrialization with the Enlightenment and Classicism, the Industrial Age with Romanticism and Impressionism, industrial capitalism with modernism, and flexible specialization with post-modernity, structuralism and de-constructivism (Table 2.4).

Since the emergence of capitalism, the great centres of primary creativity have been Florence in the 15th century, Edinburgh in the 1770s, Vienna in the 18th and early 19th centuries, London in the early-nineteenth century, Paris in the 1880s and New York in the 1940s. However, it was not always these cities that benefited most from original creativity but those who were able to apply new ideas to commerce and new

Table 2.4 The Long Waves and Artistic Movements

	Music	**Fine Art**	**Literature**
Wave 1: Mercantile	Classical	landscapes	Romantic
Wave 2: Industrial	Romantic	Impressionism	Realist
Wave 3: Fordism	Modern	Cubism and Expressionism	Modern
Wave 4: Post-Fordism	Neo-classical	Pop Art	Deconstruction
Wave 5: New Economy	Minimalism	Brit Art	New Classicism

schools of art: Birmingham and Glasgow were strongly influenced by Edinburgh, Berlin was a forerunner of the entertainment industry in Los Angeles, London in the 1960s developed much from the art and popular music of New York in the 1940s and 1950s. This implies that cities to varying degrees learn from each other not only through trade in goods and services, but also in the currency of ideas and art.

It has to be admitted that much of the focus on the arts as a means of urban regeneration seemed not to articulate or understand this historic and ongoing relationship between technology, wealth creation, cities and the arts. Many of the early examples – Pittsburgh, Birmingham – certainly smacked a little of desperation, as critics at the time argued. Yet, with the emergence of the creative industries as a key component of the knowledge economy, released as it were by digitization and the convergence of communication technologies, we can now see that artistic creativity – original, derived and applied – will be central to the future economy of cities. The cities who understand this relationship will be best placed; those who fail to understand that cultural policy is more than just having a museum, a theatre and a gallery, or even a cultural precinct or quarter, will be left behind. Cultural quarters can certainly be exciting and innovative places, as we shall see in Part V. They can also be ghettos, dull and institutionalized.

The example of Manchester leads us to conclude that leadership and clear cultural policies are important, but that they will tend to reflect existing creative strengths. These in turn will partly derive from a local "creative milieu" which will tend to combine traditional art forms and skills with fairly recent technological developments, such as improvements in sound recording or television. The "trigger", however, will tend to be a creative or cultural entrepreneur such as a Tony Wilson. The irony is that Manchester's creative economy went on to grow without Factory Records, and indeed has now moved into new fields of art enabled by the internet, computerized design and digitization. In addition, Manchester's cultural strategy may well itself have been unique and innovative, a mini-paradigm shift in urban cultural planning. Cities could do worse than follow the approach adopted in Manchester, suitably adapted to and respectful of local circumstances.

One question all of this this raises is what might happen over the curve of the next up-swing, that is from 2004 to 2030. If the Kondratieff curves and Schumpeter's thesis are to be believed, then the clues for what might happen can be found in the period of the preceding down-swing; that is from about the mid-1980s (Black Monday was in October 1987). In Part I, I argued that the new industries are based on the internet and digitization, and also bio-technology and environmental sciences. Thus, the key inventions of the period were computer software, the internet, digital coding and decoding, DNA and energy saving, solar technology and water recycling plants. Applications of these will be the industries of the future. As far as the creative industries are concerned, I argued that media formats would remain (film, broadcasting, recorded music) but will continue to restructure along post-Fordist lines. By contrast, industries which rely on traditional skills married with new technology offer opportunities for growth where wealthier and more sophisticated customers are seeking "something different", especially things that one can wear or exhibit in one's home or office. That is to say the plastic arts, designed objects, architecture, interior design, contemporary crafts and fashion.

Some clues to how this might work can be gleaned from the fashion industry. These days, fashion is big business, a true global industry. It uses traditional skills, original creativity, is high profile, links to other creative industries (media, photography, music, film), is simultaneously mass produced, one-off and flexibly specialized, is connected both to high art and popular culture. It relies to a considerable extent on image-making, spawning a large phalanx of magazines, commercials and advertisements. Indeed, without the magazines, fashion would not reach as many consumers as it does. In this, the views of critics are paramount, not just in what sells but also in terms of what we all should be wearing. Seen in this way, fashion critics and commentators are a form of intermediary or "arbiter" of style, if not always taste. Which brings me to my final set of arguments in this Part II, the role of the cultural arbiters.

Writing in 1984, the French sociologist Pierre Bourdieu argues (from a Marxist perspective) that taste can only be understood in terms of class structure, and that the concern of the dominant class is to maintain its dominance over the dominated.[103] However, both "dominating" and "dominated" are fragmented by taste. This gives rise to a "class's habitus", that is to say its general outlook. This *habitus* includes clothes, furniture, artistic objects, leisure pursuits, food preferences, forms of eating,

---

103   Bourdieu, P., *Distinction: A Social Critique of the Judgment of Taste* (Cambridge, Mass: MIT Press, 1984).

carriage and the manner of speech. The basis of distinction between habiti is access to culture. People may be rich in economic assets and poor in cultural ones, and *vice versa*. This is reflected in their habitus.

This enables Bourdieu to argue that culture should be defined relatively, so the high art notion of the "charismatic aesthetic" (great art) is dismissed as being the aesthetic of the dominant class. Middle class people tend to aspire to the dominant aesthetic, although they are also more likely to experiment in ethnic fashions, arts forms and food. The working class are less likely to be rich in "cultural capital", and this is reflected in food choices, leisure interests, clothing and appearance. Bourdieu argues that the working class are concerned with being; whereas the middle class are concerned with "seeming". However, middle class people are also more likely to prefer "radical" art – Braque, Bach, Brecht, Mondrian, over Impressionism or Offenbach. Indeed, he goes on to propose that the middle class tend to take the game of culture too seriously – they do not know how to relax, for them it is a matter of life and death. This can lead to the phenomenon of "sacrificial consumption" where individuals and families within the middle class will give up certain items – cigarettes, alcohol, a new car – in order to secure "cultural capital" for themselves or their children. People who are rich in capital but poor in cultural capital (the nouveau riche), by contrast, may find it difficult to form artistic tastes – and this for Bourdieu is exemplified by not knowing how to be served in restaurants, and the inability to spend more in order to rise to a higher system of needs. The working class, on the other hand, are more likely to be set against "pretension" in culture, language or clothing: "not for the likes of us", "who does she think she is?" Bourdieu even suggests – writing in France, of course – that working class people predominantly drink beer, eat fatty foods and carbohydrates, while the middle class drink wine and eat more protein in smaller portions!

Bourdieu goes on to argue that "the new logic of the economy rejects the ascetic ethic of production and accumulation, based on abstinence, sobriety, deferred gratitude and calculation, in favour of a hedonistic morality of consumption, based on credit, spending and enjoyment."[104] The problem is that new art and fashions must continually be generated, so as to maintain distinction between fractions of these classes. Thus, as the working class came to favour Impressionism or Utrillo, the middle class will switch to Expressionism; with the aristocracy meanwhile maintaining their preference for Stubbs and portraiture.

Despite his claims to the contrary, Bourdieu's work can be seen to be reductionist in that it relates all cultural development back to class struggle. This aspect of his work is not especially helpful. Yet the central notion of taste, distinction and style is what intrigues me. Fashions, tastes and preference will continue to develop and change, but it also seems likely that the differentiation of people/classes into more varied and smaller *habiti* will continue. This means that for a good proportion of an advanced society, distinction and "individual" style will become increasingly important.

---

104 Ibid., p. 310.

Table 2.5 The Long Waves and Modes of Production

		Production Mode:	Organised by:
Wave 1	Early Capitalism	Craft and Industrial	Merchants
Wave 2	Industrial Revolution	Industrial	Industrialists
Wave 3	Fordism	Mass Production	Mass Producers
Wave 4	Post-Fordism	Flexible Specialisation	Suppliers of Services
Wave 5	New Economy	Personalised or Bespoke Consumption	Designer/Artist/Makers and Arbiters of Style

Source: Derived from Jane Jacobs, 1969, appendix.

People will achieve their individuality through purchasing limited editions, bespoke and one-off artefacts, art works and clothes. In doing so, they will be informed by their own store of cultural capital – but also, and especially amongst the *nouveau riche*, by arbiters of taste and style. This opens up the possibility for individuals and groups of artists and producers to have a more individualized relationship with clients. In this way, the new age of creativity will exhibit some of the same features of fifteenth century Florence.

The fifth wave will witness a new emergent mode of production just as the four previous waves have (Table 2.5).

As far as the various art forms are concerned, it is difficult to be overly-predictive, but I can offer some suggestions. Visual art will enjoy greater prominence and demand, although the ascendant genres are difficult to predict – probably a combination of organic abstraction, mixed media and landscapes, and also a return to portraiture. Performance art will continue to explore genetics and DNA. Literature and poetry are more-or-less exhausted as a cultural form – that is to say there is no new format in the offing. De-constructivism and post-modernism will be jettisoned in favour of a return to narrative and literary craft. New theatre and playwriting might re-emerge strongly in the coming period. Music is more difficult for I see little in the past twenty years that is remotely interesting, except for the minimalists. There may be a second age of modern jazz, mixed with minimalism and a further exploration of tonality. Interestingly, the best modern jazz these days hails not only from the USA, but also Canada, Sweden, Denmark, Finland, Australia and New Zealand.

This appears to be bringing us back to visual arts and contemporary design. Indeed, even popular music these days is presented as a piece of design in the form of the pop video, with attendant special effects and fashion. People will still, of course, read books, listen to music, go to concerts and the theatre, and see a film, but they will also be more selective in the purchase of art, objects, design; in what they wear and even in individual architecture. The products of this artistic age will be art works, furniture, jewellery, glass, sculpture, ceramics, fabrics, buildings, clothes and accessories.

Thus, it seems to me that the fifth wave will comprise some economic activities brought forward from earlier waves (industrial production in China, flexible specialization, the knowledge economy and the media industries). In addition, there will be more industrial production of objects, works and style, through bespoke making and small-batch production. However, the individuality that this portends will be underpinned by "arbiters of taste", in the form of curators, art critics, fashion editors and the local "cultural avant-garde". Some cities will simply be more fashionable than others. More than this, the more design-conscious and stylish the city, the greater its chances of being economically dynamic.

This leaves us with the question of what cities should be doing now to secure a share of the new wealth. Clearly they need to ensure access to new technologies, maintain traditional craft skills and develop new ones; attract, encourage and "grow" creative people and creative businesses; support or at least remove barriers to enterprise; maintain a creative milieu to help grow and retain "the creative class"; foster innovation and quality in cuisine and the night-time economy; encourage collaborations between artists, businesses and architects and indeed with local cultural institutions. In other words, become what a city ought to be – enterprising, creative, well-designed and ... interesting ... .

PART III: TIME

…and the Regulation of Public Morality

Part III explores the concept of time, and how changes in its measurement have led to greater control over the life and economy of cities. This is particularly true for the measurement of units of labour and therefore work and wages. Yet the regulation of time – opening hours – would also become a major struggle in the battle over public morality, decency and the accepted norms of public social behaviour. This struggle over the night-time character of cities, it turns out, dates back to the Norman Conquest, was a major issue in the periods before and after the English Civil War, and was brought into sharper relief by the invention of street lighting. Much of this was bound up in the development of public forms of entertainment, notably ale houses, gin palaces, cafés and coffee houses, the brown bars of Amsterdam, as well as the theatre, the music hall and later the cinema. At various times throughout British history periods of liberalization of liquor licensing and obscenity laws have been preceded and followed by a tightening of regulation. These things seem to happen in cycles.

Part III concentrates in some detail on the British experience of the *24-Hour City*, an attempt to develop, plan for and regulate the night-time city or "evening economy", believed at the time to be a new departure. By the late 1990s the evening economy and the management of night-time activity in cities had become an important policy area in the UK and Australian cities. Policy makers turned their eyes to other countries – France, Germany, Italy, the United States – to see how they organize their city night-time economies. It appears that even in the most liberal of cities, some element of strict control remains, as we shall see. This being the case, it is possible that England has deregulated its liquor licensing regime at the wrong time, and will shortly need to reintroduce stronger controls.

There once was a shy young man who left his country home, and moved to the city to be more free,

For in the city no one cared if you stayed out half the night. And people didn't notice every time you bought a new pair of pants. So he enjoyed a carefree life amongst the Broadway crowd, and attended shows they did not have in Minnesota. And the only thing that worried him was what if he got sick and fell down in the street, would anyone notice? He decided to find out, so he laid down in the gutter, and right away a woman came and knelt by his side. And it was Gladys, his old neighbour, who was in the city visiting her niece Denise. And she said to him, "Jim, I always knew that you were no good."

The Book of Guys, Garrison Keillor, Faber and Faber, 1993, pp. 6–7

ON TIME

Time: a dimension of reality characterized by flows of events and phenomena through an irreversible procession of moments. Also: a systemized demarcation of the passage of such moments into units of seconds, minutes, hours, days and years.

Night and Day: all the time, at all hours.

There was a time (or should that be an age) when you could walk down the streets of a city and always know what time it was. The Town Hall would have its clock, there might be another in the main public square and there were clocks outside the large department stores and in the railway stations. In New York, there is even Times Square. All you had to do was look up to tell what time it was. Quite often one would meet other people who would also be looking to see what time it was. Time helped to create public space in the city, or more precisely time would bring people into space and various forms of public social interaction would ensue. Only in the past twenty years has time, in this sense, disappeared from city streets. For we now have wrist watches to tell us the time, so in a way time has been "privatized". With mobile phones, fax machines, electronic organizers, lap-tops, wireless internet and the rest, time becomes fragmented. It might not actually matter what the time is where you are, but what the time is where your call or SMS Message will be received. So in the city today, not only has space been losing meaning, but so too has time.

It is not so long ago that absolute time was "invented" with the innovation of the mechanical clock. Time would tell you when to get up in the morning, when to catch the bus, when you had to "clock" in, how long you had for lunch, when you went home, when you had "tea" and when you went to bed. Instead of starting work around dawn, or finishing about dusk, time could be measured to the exact second. From about the mid 17th century onwards, city life itself became more and more organized by the clock. Indeed the industrial city itself was in part a product of time as factory shifts and labour wage rates were calculated by hours.

> Most city people are wedded to their jobs, and when you take these jobs away they soon become as empty and brittle as blown eggs. Work is for the idle. It gives a chaptered, tramline narrative to life; it empties suburbs and estates and provides the displaced, liberated residents with dramas structured by the clock.
>
> Jim Crace, *Arcadia*, Jonathan Cape, 1992, p. 188

The fear of being late or losing time seems ingrained within a city like London. This perhaps explains why everyone rushes about, trying to get things done in time. Commercial operations seem to be obsessively calculated and monitored to take the least possible time. Faxes and emails allow information to be sent, received and responded to in double-quick time – for if a message appears in an instant, it is clearly more deserving of your attention than a letter that arrived in the post the day before yesterday. Fast cars, fast trains, fast delivery, fast food. Time in London and other British cities must not be "wasted", and the same appears to be true in

Figure 3.1   Time and Space
Source: John Montgomery.

Australia. Getting home from work as quickly as possible seems to be the primary objective of the day. All these people must be rushing to do things that are very important. And yet we find that most will have their "tea", maybe mow the grass, have a beer and watch TV. Time slows down again. Time speeds up and slows down for each of us, at different times of the day and night.

But in the span of a human's life, the average speed of time gets quicker!

> Ticking away, the moments that make up the dull day,
> Fritter and waste the hours in an off-hand way.
> Kicking around on a piece of ground in your home town,
> Waiting for someone or something to show you the way.
> Tired of lying in the sunshine, staying home to watch the rain
> For you are young and life is long, and there is time to kill today
> And then one day you find ten years have gone behind you
> No-one told you when to run, you missed the starting gun.
> So you run and you run to catch up with the sun, but it's sinking
> Chasing around to come up behind you again
> The sun is the same in a relative way, but you're older
> Shorter of breath, and one day closer to death.
> Every year is getting shorter, never seem to find the time
> Plans that either come to naught, or half a page of scribbled lines.
> Hanging on in quiet desperation is the English way
> The time has gone, the song is over, thought I'd
> Something more to say.
>
>   Pink Floyd, *Time*, Pink Floyd Music Publishers Ltd, 1973

Or as older people often say, "the years go past so quickly ... I don't know where the time goes ...".

There are even places where time "has stood still", or so it seems. The Temple in London is not much different from 200 years ago; areas such as Spitalfields or Petticoat Lane seem to be doing pretty much the same things as they always have. Some city districts appear to be stuck in a time warp, a way of living in the past.

> The nature of time in London is mysterious. It seems not to be running continuously in one direction, but to fall backwards and retire ... Sometimes it moves steadily forward, before springing or leaping out, sometimes it slows down and on occasions, it drifts and stops altogether.[1]

The novelist Peter Ackroyd has argued that different periods in history have a different sense of time. In medieval times, time was measured by human memory – the time of the great flood, or the year of the plague. In the Middle Ages, time came to be measured by sacred rituals – morning matins, evening vespers, the ringing of the church bells. Later, time was measured by events such as Exchange time, when the merchants would meet to conduct business. By the eighteenth century, William

---

1   Ackroyd, P., *London: the Biography* (London: Chatto and Windus, 2000).

Blake would inveigh against "Watch Fiends", because London had become the centre of the mechanical measurement of time.[2] London was famous for its clocks. By this point, the life of the city was based on work, and work was measured in time. Time had become an aspect of industry. In the Victorian age, time had become a central fact of economic and social life – the keeping of appointments, the running of trains. But unlike previous generations the Victorians – great believers in progress and development – were largely uninterested in time past, history, what had gone before and even buildings left from previous times. They were only interested in what was about to happen rather than the past, with some exceptions such as William Morris, the Pre-Raphaelite Brotherhood or Ruskin.

This attitude would continue through the first half of the twentieth century, this time in the guise of modernism, slum clearance and new town planning. The past was forgotten as we looked forward to a New Jerusalem. As we shall see (Part IV) things did not go according to plan, and from the 1950s movements to protect and preserve reminders of the past would grow, led by people such as Ian Nairn, John Betjeman and Jane Jacobs. Arguably, measures to conserve the built environment themselves became so entrenched, in the 1970s and 1980s, that we began to forget about the future.

The lesson from all of this, argues Ackroyd, is that we cannot really understand the present without understanding the past, and we cannot look forward to the future unless we live in the here and now.

> Time present and time past
> Are both perhaps present in time future
> And time future contained in time past.
>   T.S. Eliot

It seems then that time is not absolute after all, but varies between individuals, across generations and even between different areas of the same city. It seems likely too, that time will vary between countries and cultures. How are we to make sense of this? Of course, our conception of time changed with the discovery of the speed of light and the theory of relativity. But surely this doesn't explain variations of time in a city? The physicist Stephen Hawking has argued that an "arrow of time" exists which distinguishes the past from the future, thus giving a direction to time. In fact, Hawking argues that there is not one but three arrows of time.[3] These are the "thermodynamic" arrow of time (based on the Second Law of Thermodynamics), which is the direction of time in which entropy (disorder) increases. Secondly there is the "psychological" arrow of time which Hawking says is the direction in which we "feel" time passes, so that we remember the past but cannot remember the future. Third is the "cosmological" arrow of time which refers to the direction of time in which the universe is expanding, rather than contracting, from the Big Bang onwards.

---

2   Ackroyd, P., "All the Time in the World", in *The Collection*, chapter 125 (London: Vintage, 2002).

3   Hawking, S., *A Brief History of Time* (London: Bantam Press, 1988).

Hawking goes on to show that the "psychological" and the "thermodynamic" arrows of time always point in the same direction, but that the "cosmological" can theoretically move in different directions ..., so that time travel itself is theoretically possible.

Thus our substantive sense of the direction of time, the psychological arrow, is determined within our brain by the thermodynamic order in which things happen, and entropy increases. So events and time occur in a sequence which is real, but which is also known to us. The trouble is none of us knows everything (which is just as well!) and our memories of time and events vary between individuals, groups, cultures, and also over the span of our individual lives. Maybe this is why time proceeds at 60 seconds per minute, 60 minutes per hour, 24 hours per day, 7 days a week, 365 days a year, 100 years a century ... but somehow seems to slow and quicken depending on where we are and what we are doing, and what we remember. So in this sense a certain individualized fragmentation of time exists, but only at the margins. Still, this means that the way you think about and spend your time will depend to some extent on who you are, what you do, your cultural background and your values. This is not to say that all time is relative (in Einstein's theory it is the position of the individual and not the speed of light that is relative), but it does mean that our internal subjective view of time can vary to a small degree. Small but not unimportant, for at issue is the question of the timing of activities and their playing out in space, in our case city space. This in turn means that the ordering of city activity by mechanical time is not necessarily an absolute. In Marxist terminology it can be "contested", again up to a point.

A recent concept is "time planning", a method of reorganizing the way uses and activities occur in time in cities. This approach is based on experiments in time planning in northern Italian cities from the early 1990s. This involves "changing hours to rationalize the efficiency and convenience of the times of opening of shops, schools, places of work and public services". Clara Greed associates time planning with the radical left and feminism, and most of what is suggested appears to be directed at working time and childcare. The overall stated aim is to reduce "functional inefficiency" in transportation (redistributing peak time flows), employment (working hours balanced against "caring") and domestic life (shopping, going to the Post Office). This conception is therefore not only about reducing wasted time but also about the more efficient use of space, a traditional concern of town planners.

The argument is that important but relatively small changes to opening times can change patterns of activity and movement. For example, moving the start of the school day forward from 8.00 a.m. to 9.00 a.m. makes it easier to take the children to school and get to work. (Although then we have the phenomenon of the "school run" which would appear to increase the "functional inefficiency" of transportation). Changes to working hours certainly lend greater flexibility to everyday life, as previously argued by Bianchini, et al.[4] This, it seems, is already happening in the

---

4   Bianchini, F., Montgomery, J., Fisher, M. and Worpole, K., *City Centres, City Cultures* (Manchester: Centre for Local Economic Development Strategies, 1988).

USA, Britain and Australia, if not in Italy. However, Greed points to the example of changes in car factory shift patterns leading to "reduced demand for and viability of public transport in the city, thus adding to private car use and competition".[5]

Other examples from Italy are more positive, notably changes in shop opening hours to start earlier and remain open longer (unless, you are a shop owner or assistant). Or being allowed to choose your day off, instead of always Saturday and Sunday. Meanwhile, local museums and galleries might remain open on Sundays and public holidays. Again these ideas were also proposed by Comedia and Bianchini et al in the 1980s.

Greed laments the "double-shift" of "work and home" duties for women, that "most people (especially women) spend much of their lives queuing, waiting and wasting time"; meanwhile "urban transportation and urban land use planning systems are still geared up to meet the needs of the now mythical full-time, car-borne and presumably "male" worker". I fear that Greed overstates her case as full-time workers, whilst reduced in numbers, are not "mythical" nor are people driving cars these days only or predominantly male. Perhaps the goals of "gender balance" and functional efficiency cut across one another, at least in transportation. Yet "time planning", it seems to me is undoubtedly a good idea, provided it is flexible and sensitive to the economic and cultural life of the city. This should not, in my view, be reduced to a concern with "functional efficiency" (the town planner's Holy Grail), nor is it necessarily an ideologically sound issue of gender. Greed concludes with a call for "temporal master plans" for British cities. But curiously, most of the possible measures she lists are spatial.

> We need to be planning for everyday life, encouraging short journeys, less land use zoning, mixed use districts, more emphasis on local distribution of shops, local facilities and communities, and childcare.[6]

This no doubt comes from the need for planners to plan, whereas what might really be at issue is adjustments to the time slots in which activities operate. Perhaps we should work out what a better distribution of activities over a day or week would look like, before launching into spatial planning simultaneously. This point is taken up by the urban designers Matthew Carmoda, Tim Heath, Taner Oc and Steve Tiesdell in their excellent book *Public Spaces Urban Spaces: The Dimensions of Urban Design*. In chapter 9,[7] they explore "the temporal dimension" of urban design. The authors argue that urban designers need to understand time for three key reasons: that environments are used by different and sometimes competing activities, differently, over different periods of time; that environments themselves change over time, some in subtle ways, others more dramatically; and that urban design projects and improvements to a city's environment are themselves "implemented" over time.

---

5   Greed, C., "Design and Designers Revisited", in *Introducing Urban Design*, Greed, C. and Roberts, M. (Harlow: Longman, 1998).

6   Ibid.

7   Carmoda, M., Heath, T., Oc, T. and Tiesdell, S., *Public Places: Urban Spaces* (London: Architectural Press, 2003).

Carmona, et al., remind us of something very important, that the way we measure time was originally based on the changing seasons (the progress of the earth's orbit around the sun, and the lunar orbit which gives rise to a break-down of a year into months). Hours in the day, moreover, were calculated from a division of 180° or 360° (the earth is round) by fifteen. This means that we know when it is morning or afternoon, and where the sun will be. We also know the seasons of the year and how the micro-climate changes, and with it patterns of public social life. Jan Gehl and Lars Gemzoe note that "summer Copenhagen"[8] and winter Copenhagen are different cities, in that patterns of movement, walking pace, time spent lingering alter dramatically. So too in terms of the general climate with hotter countries, such as Australia, needing to provide greater shade, but also explaining why it is also more difficult to walk longer distances in the heat. Nevertheless, we can see that most aspects of time measurement are derived from the natural rhythms of the earth itself, including night and day.

A more recent concept is that of the "24 hour city" initially proposed in Britain in Comedia's "Out of Hours" Study, 1991. Krietzman[9] would later argue that although an exaggeration (as most people would agree) the "24 Hour Society" is a useful shorthand for an emerging "different type of world". As a consequence the use of time is being variously scheduled and squeezed. In a 24-hour society – or city – patterns of use and activity become less regimented, more responsive to individual needs and preferences, and less predictable. Whether this all plays out happily for everyone is not certain. Some people will need to work "anti-social" or perhaps less convenient hours so that others can shop or go clubbing when they like (the example of the shop assistant needing to start work at 8.00 a.m. rather than 10.00 a.m.). While it is also not the case that all activities can be beneficially mixed everywhere, all of the time – the example here being the conflict between new city centre residents and noisy clubs, pubs and music venues. This leads us to consider an urban policy issue that would grow in importance in the UK and elsewhere during the 1990s, and it still a cause for concern today: the evening economy.

1. URBAN SOCIAL LIFE AND THE EVENING ECONOMY

> On successful city streets, people must appear at different times. This is time considered on a small scale, at different times throughout the day.
> Jane Jacobs, *The Death and Life of Great American Cities*, Vantage Books, 1961, p152.

> If people are out in the evening, going to the theatre, the cinema or filmhouse, the gym, the photography gallery, the jazz club or whatever, they will also use the restaurants, bars and cafés. This is what we mean when we refer to the evening economy.
> Comedia, *Out of Hours*, published by the Gulbenkian Foundation, 1991.

---

8   Gehl, J. and Gemzoe, L., *Public Spaces – Public Life* (Copenhagen: The Danish Architectural Press, 1996).

9   Krietzman, L., *The 24-Hour Society* (London: Profile Books, 1999).

Public Social Life

In Fitzrovia there is a special urban place. A little café, the Titchfield Café, nestles on the corner of Foley and Great Titchfield Streets, occupying a strategic point just off-centre on a small crossroads. This is the heart of London's wholesale fashion industry, the BBC is just round the corner and Oxford Street is in view. But strangely, unlike Soho which is almost a mirror image on the other side of Oxford Street, Fitzrovia is quiet, almost a backwater. It feels like a well-kept secret. The Titchfield Café has glass windows on two sides, and room for about 30 people. If the weather is fair, people sit outside, virtually doubling the number of covers. The café is a family-run concern, and the food is cheap and hearty, if not especially good. The proprietor is a bit of a character. He plays opera over a strange music system – the speakers are old-fashioned phonograph trumpets – always Maria Callas and Jussi Bjorling, never "The Three Tenors". Downstairs, someone has painted the walls of the lavatories with prehistoric cave drawings and Greek figures. Outside, the café has personalized the pavement area. There are boxes of shrubs, a bookcase, a birdcage hanging in a tree and even an old guitar. Fairy lights are strung across the windows, so that diners on summer evenings can sit in the warm glow of candles and the fairy lights. It is a surreal environment. This is a place that people like going to. They meet friends, make plans, read the newspapers, do some business, have a drink and a bite to eat. Every once in a while something special happens. One night people were there until after midnight listening to young actors reciting Shakespeare, a band played gipsy tunes and outside, on the pavement, there was a fire-eater. On another occasion, the author met Dennis Potter who was in for a light meal with his agent. We argued about religion, politics, and *The Singing Detective*.

So the Titchfield Café is a special place. Not only is it interesting in itself but it animates and gives vitality to the whole area immediately around the crossroads. Or at least it did. For the Titchfield Café has not been the same since 1991. It was at this time that two sets of regulations were enforced which have not only undermined the café's business, but have led in addition to a loss of the buzz that once characterized this little area. First it was the planners, who insisted that the plants and the funny little bits of furniture constituted an obstruction on the highway and so had to be removed. Then, someone – possibly one of the nearby licencees – complained that wine and beer were being served to people sitting out of doors at the pavement tables, and that this was not permitted under the Titchfield Café's liquor licence. So they had to take the plants down and then stop serving bottles of wine outside. Trade dropped dramatically. One of the few places in London where you could sit and watch the world go by, over a glass of wine or beer, was now no more. People stopped going.

Over the following few months and years, that is from about 1994, the author began to realize that this was not an uncommon occurrence. In Sheffield, during the Student Olympic Games, one could drink tea or soft drinks in the new Tudor Square outside the Lyceum Theatre, but not wine. The theatre had to submit an application for a pavement licence to the licensing magistrates four times before it was granted. In Brighton, English's Oyster Bar set up a petition in support of their application to serve wine with meals out in the little square on which the restaurant fronts. In Manchester, it transpired that there had been a policy during the 1980s to refuse all applications and renewals of liquor licences in the city centre. Things came to a head when a new hotel, developed by a respectable national chain, was refused a bar licence. In Bath, there are white lines painted on the pavement outside a popular wine bar: if you stand within these (about 6ft by 9 ft), you can consume alcohol; if you stray over the line, you are committing an offence. Council officials in Westminster unwittingly caused a furore by seeking to ban pavement cafés in Old Compton Street in 1993. And yet, there were those who had been arguing that one of the ways to generate greater diversity and activity in town and city centres was to encourage café culture and a more active street life. This essentially meant rediscovering public social life.

The concept of urban public social life is bound up with the equally important concept of the "urban public realm". Lyn Lofland[10] argues that the public realm can be distinguished from both "private" and "parochial" realms. The private realm is:

> ... characterized by ties of intimacy among primary group members who are located within households and personal networks [while the] parochial realm [is] characterized by a sense of commonality among acquaintances and neighbours who are involved in interpersonal networks that are located within communities.......

> Unlike small towns and villages, cities contain not only private realms (private households) and parochial realms (local neighbourhoods) but also public realms:... made up of the public places or spaces ... that tend to be inhabited ... by persons who are strangers to one another and who 'know' one another only in terms of occupational or non-personal identity categories.[11]

In this way, the public realm is a defining characteristic of city life in tandem with a diversity of uses and activities,[12] largely derived from relative intensity of people and transactions and the division of labour. Moreover, people who live in cities become increasingly more sophisticated and adept at handling the stimuli of city life, partly because they are able to separate the private self (located within the private and parochial realms) from the "public man"[13] the complex pattern of lifestyles and identities which people can adopt in cities. Thus, as Bianchini argues, "public social life" is "the interacting of socializing or sociability ... that occurs within the public realm".[14] Bianchini, however, goes on to widen the definition of the "public realm":

---

10 Lofland, L., "The Morality of Urban Public Life", *Places*, Fall, 1989.

11 Ibid., p. 19.

12 Jacobs, J., *The Death and Life of Great American Cities* (London: Jonathan Cape, 1961).

13 Sennett, R., *The Fall of Public Man* (London: Faber and Faber, 1977).

14 Bianchini, F., "The Crisis of Urban Public Life in Britain", *Planning Practice and Research*, Vol. 5, No. 3, Winter 1990, pp. 4–8.

... the realm of social relations going beyond one's own circle of family, professional and social relations ... the idea of the public realm is bound up with the ideas of discovery, of expanding one's mental horizons, of the unknown, of surprise, of experiment, of adventure.[15]

For Bianchini, then, the public realm is a much wider concept than the public spaces or places in the city, but refers rather to a distinctive set of social relations. The author is not entirely comfortable with this conflation of the public realm as space with public sociability, preferring to see these as certainly closely related but distinct concepts. The subtlety of life in the cities revolves around the capacity to switch between public and private roles within the spaces or realms within the city. Thus, when serfs fled the land to live in cities, they often used the phrase "city air makes free". By this they not only meant that they would enjoy freedom in a very real sense (from serfdom) but also that city life opens up the possibilities for economic achievement whilst simultaneously loosening the personal and family ties and jealousies that governed rural life. The attraction of the city is that it liberates individuals from deeply felt norms in the private self, and allows people to learn about themselves and others. But it is important to recognize that this is only possible because one can choose to be private (anonymous) in a public place, or public in a public place. This choice is made possible by the existence of the public realm. At one extreme, one might engage in public debate about the great issues of the time, celebrate democracy and be happy to be at one with the citizenry. At the other extreme, one might elect to follow some private desires to project an identity through one's public self – in seeking out sexual encounters, for example. For some writers, this polarity is seen to represent a clash of good and bad: the democratic public man versus the self-orientated private man where prime concern is personal gratification. This leads to a complete misunderstanding as to the role of the public realm in cities.

Richard Sennett's important work *The Fall Of Public Man*[16] is based on the hypothesis that economic development transforms community life, and encourages people to retreat into their private lives, avoiding inter-personal conflict and seeking out a purified identity (narcissism). This, in turn argues Sennett, encourages defensiveness, limits personal freedoms, isolates and insulates the individual and destroys concepts of sharing and the communal experience. These elements of social withdrawal create a new intensity within the family unit and "help to create the paradox whereby it is the diversity of the city that is seen as threatening the security of family life".[17] Thus, for Sennett, the issue is not the urban public realm – the spaces in the city – but rather the changes that have been wrought on "public social life" by the spread of narcissism. This leads Sennett to the rather depressing view that there is little possibility of changing or improving urban

---

15 Ibid.

16 Sennett, R., *op. cit.*

17 Punter, J., "The Privatization of the Public Realm", *Planning Practice and Research*, Vol. 5, No. 3, 1990, p. 9.

society by changing its public spaces. People no longer seem to be able to cope with the social and cultural diversity of the modern city, but choose to maintain their personal relationships within the "sealed communities" of physically and visibly segregated worlds, an analysis shared by Davis.[18] For Sennett, urban public spaces (the public realm) cannot bridge the gap between the private and the public social worlds, even though this is their primary role in the city.

Such an analysis is contradicted by several important urban design theorists, most persuasively by Jan Gehl's seminal work *Life Between Buildings*. Gehl argues that the public realm in cities has traditionally performed three roles: as places to meet other people socially, as market-places to transact in, and as channels of movement.[19] He goes on to argue that good public spaces are characterized by the presence of people staying or lingering when they have no pressing reason (or "necessary activity") to keep them there. Indeed, Gehl argues that the success of urban public space can be judged by whether or not people are engaged in "optional" and/or "social" activities, such as having a conversation, sitting or simply watching others. If Gehl's analysis is correct, then it ought to be possible to provide and design public spaces which allow for optional, social and stationary activities, even in an age of narcissism.

In Sennett's work, there is a strongly implied relation between the public realm and the specific character of public social life that one ought to find there: public places are sites for public meetings at which intellectual discourse takes place. This applies a norm which may or may not hold. Public spaces in the city perform many cultural, economic and social roles so that we cannot assume that there is only one "true" mode of public social life which should occur in public space. To be sure, there will be elements in the public realm which appeal to or represent "higher order values", for example sacred spaces or symbolic meeting places. But to confuse this with some idealized notion of public social life as "learned and democratic" is mistaken. The point about the public realm is that it provides space for public social life to take place in all its forms. Thus, those who expect street-life and café culture to signal a return to the idealized Greek polis will be disappointed.

> Today, the cinema and theatre have long since turned into the home video; the launderette and laundry into Ariston and Hotpoint; the library into Penguin and Pan; the concert hall into the compact disc. Even political meetings are now redundant when it is possible to see all one wants of candidates on the television, or join a political party by credit card.[20]

In the above quotation, the sociologist Laurie Taylor describes the impact of technological change and the ongoing process of economic development on public social life. He is arguing that new products, particularly media products,

---

18   Davis, M., *City of Quartz* (London: Vintage, 1990).
19   Gehl, J., *Life Between Buildings* (Copenhagen: Arkitekens Forlag, 1996).
20   Taylor, L., "Private View", *The Listener*, 24 November 1988.

have undermined public forms of entertainment and interaction, increasingly replacing them by privatized and "home" entertainment. People, it appears, would rather stay indoors than go out. During the early 1980s (1978–87), the Henley Centre for Forecasting identified a 40% increase in the volume of home-based leisure spending in Britain, accompanied by zero growth in out-of-home leisure. But it is now possible to see that this growth more or less corresponded with the emergence of new products onto the market at affordable prices. Later, still in the 1980s and throughout the 1990s, there was an upsurge in cinema attendance and the rise of the wine bar. There was also a dramatic growth in leisure spending on eating out, going to the theatre and attending education classes.

Nevertheless, the impact of technological advances during the early 1980s was to undermine, to a greater or lesser extent, public social life. This point was taken on board by the writers at Comedia[21] in their work on the public social life of towns and cities. Essentially, these writers argued that, rather than any deep-rooted cultural change, the collapse of public social life could be traced to technological change (product substitution), the suburbanization of cities, the problem of urban fear, the loss of diversity from city centres, the privatization of public space, the shoe-horning of life into a pattern dictated by the "nine to five", the out-moded regulation of public entertainment, and the overall loss of street life.

These writers would argue that the dilution of public social life is not therefore a necessary consequence of some deep-rooted cultural shift, the "fall of public man" towards a condition of narcissism, but rather the outcome of many years of technological, social and temporal change, some of it market led, some of it public policy led (slum clearance, city zoning) and some of it simply because of neglect or a failure to understand. Moreover the precise patterns of changing public social life have surely varied from culture to culture, not only in the sense employed by Sennett (Christian Judaism versus the Greek polis) but between, for example, European cultures. Thus, many commentators might argue that Denmark is more interesting than Sweden and so on. Within countries, some cities have more vibrant public social lives than others. Liverpool and Newcastle were always better than Manchester; Glasgow is miles better than Edinburgh; Leeds until about 1998 was much more lively than Sheffield. This means that the cultural influences on public social life exist at the "macro" level (e.g. Catholic versus Protestant, or Latin versus Norse). But they are also partly a reflection of micro-conditions, customs and traditions. It follows from this that change may be effected locally, and that one possible way to stimulate public social life is to encourage or enable new forms of activity to occur in the public realm. Which brings us back to pavement cafés, and the notion of the evening economy.

---

21 *Comedia Out of Hours: A Study of the Economic and Social Life of Town Centres*, The Gulbenkian Foundation, London, 1991.

The Evening Economy

From 1994 urban planning policy in the UK was changed, in the shape of Planning Policy Guidance Note 6 on the *Vitality and Viability of Town Centres*. This recommended that town centres should be protected from excessive "out-of-town competition" (shopping malls, leisure complexes) and that town centres should be revitalized by a range of integrated measures aimed at improving their attraction, safety and diversity. A key concept was the promotion of the "evening economy". It is clear that this conception of the evening economy was drawn from a Department of the Environment Research Study on "The Vitality and Viability of Town Centres", itself to a considerable extent based on *City Centres, City Cultures* and *Out of Hours*.[22] This more or less coincided with the holding of the "First National Conference on the Night-time Economy of Cities" held in Manchester in September 1993[23] at which the case for improved planning and regulation of the evening economy was made, in the broader context of more flexible, diverse and sophisticated city centres.

The argument was that, at the time, in most towns and cities there were an increasing number of businesses and activities that conducted their trade and offer their services – or would wish to do so – in the evening or night-time hours after 5 or 6pm. These included not just traditional places like public houses, bars, bingo halls, restaurants and discos, but also, shops, gyms, cinemas, music venues, art galleries, theatres and bowling alleys. Alongside these commercial activities, there were also a broad range of cultural and recreational activities such as evening classes, clubs and civic societies. Some of these take place in halls and other public facilities, others are private and entirely self-organized. These activities, it was argued, add up to an evening economy in many towns and cities; but also are examples of urban forms of public social life. However, by the late 1980s, the evening economy, where it existed in 1980s Britain, was largely defined – at least in the minds of people who make decisions about cities – by what it was not. A segment of time, micro-time, which repeated itself seven days a week, when the shops had closed and everyone had gone home. By and large it was empty time. And yet the possibilities of more activity around the clock were there. For the evening economy is really all about business, enterprise and transactions. People meet, they trade, buy and sell – a meal, a drink, a newspaper, a hotel room, a theatre performance; they also are stimulated by the possibility of meeting others, of seeing their friends, of enjoying the company of strangers. In this sense, the evening economy is really only about opening up the possibilities for transactions to take place in longer and more extended segments of time.

The degree to which all of these activities combine to constitute an evening economy is, of course, a function of critical mass and the level of economic maturity. This critical mass can also be dependent on the support structures that underpin

---

22 Comedia 1991 *op. cit.*; Bianchini et al., 1987 *op. cit.*

23 Montgomery, J., "The Evening Economy of Cities", *Town and Country Planning*, 63 (11), 1994.

the activities of the evening economy: transportation, lighting and policing. Early research indicated that the evening economy represented anything from 5 to 15 per cent of a local GDP.[24] Of course, the character of the evening economy varies from place to place, depending not just on size, but rather catchment area and the draw a place exerts, the nature of its appeal to different types of people and the extent to which the urban environment feels safe. The evening economy is predominantly a consumption-based economy. This consumption mostly revolves around entertainment, leisure and culture. So spending in the evening economy (or indeed activities which do not directly involve financial transactions) is closely related to lifestyles, to identity and to self-expression. This point is demonstrated in a city like Manchester where there are a range of different venues, each aimed at a different niche market defined by age-group and musical and leisure tastes. Even so, such places are just part of a wider spectrum of activity: the older couple who drink every Friday night at their "local" or go to the Bingo are also engaged in both consumption and cultural expression. As far as policy makers are concerned, the key point is to give equal consideration to the social and cultural impetus behind the evening economy as well as its economic core.

The facilities and services in UK towns and cities during the 1980s and early 1990s, however, largely continued to adhere to a time regime which was increasingly out of step with the lifestyles and time needs of modern town and city dwellers. Because of a large number of inter-related social and technological changes, the old 9 to 5 pattern of daily existence no longer formed the back-bone of daily life. Examples of some of these changes include the growing flexibility of labour in most economic sectors, particularly part-time work and self-employment; the growing incidence of new working patterns such as teleworking; the growing number and proportion of retired people; and the resulting increase in leisure time and, in some cases, disposable leisure spend. In turn people began to use their time in increasingly varied and flexible ways: the early morning swim, the night out in the middle of the afternoon, the breakfast meeting, the evening corporate hospitality event. It is like programming a video recorder to watch the late night film, *Bladerunner* or *Calamity Jane*, in the middle of the afternoon. People had more choice in how they organized time.

Meanwhile, the problem of dead town centres became apparent during the 1980s, and one the main reasons for not using town centres in the evening is fear over personal safety.

In many towns and cities, discussion about the centre in the evenings is now wholly contextualized by the language of law and order and of public security. 'Very dangerous', 'I wouldn't want to go there when the pubs close', 'I wouldn't let my wife go into the town centre on her own after the shops close'. How much of this anxiety has any basis in reality?

Comedia, *Out of Hours*, 1991.

---

24 Urban Cultures Ltd, *Developing the Evening Economy of Bristol City Centre*, unpublished consultancy report prepared for Bristol City Council, December 1994.

This anxiety arose for a number of or a combination of reasons: because particular social groups have come to dominate; because overall the centre was too empty of people to feel safe; because of isolated incidents which take on a representative dimension; or some potent combination of all three. In survey after survey, people expressed the view that it is no longer safe to go out in the evenings.[25] People were put off by the violence which is widely believed to occur in the evenings. A 1985 survey in London found that 56% of women felt "very unsafe" or "not very safe" walking at night; 22% never travelled after dark. In Southampton in 1987, 59% of women felt unsafe walking after dark, and over 90 locations were identified as being unsafe. Even in a small town like Wellingborough (1986), 59% felt they would be victims of violent street robbery, 54% feared they would be assaulted in the streets, and 60% of women feared sexual attack. The response to this rising public concern, in many places, has been to increase technological surveillance via the introduction of CCTV at key locations. However, in the early days most of these would be located in the main shopping streets where, often as not, few people go in the evenings.

Retailers began to express concern at the rise of crime committed against business premises.[26] Many had installed steel shopfront shutters to deter intruders. But this can have the effect of making the street outside, the urban environment, feel less safe because it restricts the scope for natural surveillance. It became clear that CCTV and intruder defence systems needed to be carefully designed so as not to detract from a street's natural surveillance system. Similarly, there were clear and proven connections between street lighting levels and incidence of crime. Research in the UK and the USA showed that improved and brighter lighting can reduce crime at night and makes people feel safer – particularly those groups such as old people and women who feel more vulnerable. Light on the streets comes not only from street lamps, but is also thrown out by shop windows and by the lights of venues such as pubs and restaurants. Cities and large towns should as a matter of priority undertake a comprehensive review of lighting.

Even so, with the best of wills, all the lighting in the world would not make places feel safer if they were dominated by particular social groups. This phenomenon, *the stylization of space* occurs where certain social or age groups dominating particular parts of a town or city during certain parts of the day. It often occurs in the early evening hours, when young people gather in groups to drink or simply to hang around; or in the small hours when the pubs and clubs close. In Newcastle, for example, large groups of young people (16 to 25) meet at the Monument, every Thursday, Friday, Saturday and Sunday nights. They are known locally as the "Friday Night Millionaires". People meet, eye-contact is exchanged, pairings and groupings are formed, and then they all go off around the pubs and clubs of the Bigg Market. In fact, this phenomenon has occurred across many of our cities. The problem with it, for anyone older than 30, is that it puts off other people from using the city centre.

---

25 Bianchini, 1990, *op. cit.*

26 Shopfront Security Campaign, *The Shopfront Security Report*, available from the British Retail Consortium, London, 1994.

The kind of behaviour associated with the "Friday Night Millionaires" is often loud, aggressive, sometimes violent and frightening. It impacts on the image of a place and radically decreases the diversity of people prepared to use the city or town centre in the evenings.

It is in the nature of evening economy activities for them to cluster. There is usually always an area or cluster of streets within a town or city which host the night time economy – the dock area in Bristol, Canal Street in Manchester, Lygon Street in Melbourne or Newhavn in Copenhagen. These activity nodes represent the grain of the evening economy, and where possible special policies and designations should be devised to consolidate such areas. This has to be balanced against consideration of other parts of the centre and the possibility that a single large agglomeration might drain trade away from other locations. It is also important that activities be allowed to spill into the streets or at least have some sort of interaction with the wider *public realm*. This means that ground floors should always, or as far as is possible, have active uses and active frontages. This is not just a question of seating, but of what might be called "transitional space": places to eat, drink or simply to sit which offer an opportunity to inter-act with the street, to be part of the street social dynamic even if only as a passive observer. Such transitional spaces contribute to the "buzz" and sense of activity and they also help to provide natural surveillance in the evening hours by adding to the number of eyes watching the street.

From all of this, it was argued that city decision makers should consider it an important task to foster and develop the evening economy. Local businesses might be encouraged to invest in new and improved premises and facilities. This would raise standards and also create more jobs. Local spending in the evening economy would increase by visitors and local people. The city itself might develop a stronger image, cultural status and identity. In addition, the aim would be to help revitalise social and public life and reclaim the urban public realm, and, in doing so, reduce the problem of urban fear. That was the theory.

Born to Binge?

More than ten years on from the original "manifesto" on the evening economy, many UK cities now have booming night time economies, and even a respectable café culture. This is certainly true of London and Manchester and Bristol, but no less the case for Sheffield, Nottingham and Newcastle. Newcastle, indeed, is an interesting example. Newcastle-Upon-Tyne is a city of only 200 000 in North East England which, nevertheless, is possibly the most lively night-time city in the UK. In truth, Newcastle acts as a regional night-time destination, serving the wider conurbation, including such places as Wallsend, North Tyneside and Gateshead. The city grew famous as a coal-exporting port, and in the nineteenth century became an important centre for steel, ship-building and engineering. These industries entered a long period of decline post-World War Two. Newcastle has had to find new economic activity to survive, and so since the late 1970s, has been in a process of diversifying the local economy. As well as marine engineering, the city also now has significant employment in car production (in truth, just 10 miles to the south in Sunderland), some financial services, call-centres of various kinds plus retailing and a sizeable night-time economy. Instrumental in all of this was the work of development agencies such as the Tyneside Urban Development Corporation who regenerated the old Quayside during the 1980s, now one of the two main evening economy locations (the other being the Bigg Market). This area retains a healthy mixed use character during the day-time, has markets every Sunday and is also a residential neighbourhood. The locals – Geordies – have always had a reputation as people who enjoy a good night out; in the past 10 years or so this has become something of a parody (though still true) and the city now styles itself as "Party Toon".[27] However, the city also offers a laid-back café culture, an attractive waterfront setting (with seven bridges spanning the Tyne), a good range of restaurants and a more than respectable range of cultural venues, including the Baltic Mill gallery of modern art and the Sage concert hall, both over the river in Gateshead. Newcastle has become an attractive location for professionals and businesses relocating from London.[28]

There has, however, been an increase in reports of drunkenness over the past seven or eight years, notably around the Bigg Market and related in particular to "happy hour" alcohol price wars when cheap and lethal drinks are made available, especially alco-pops and packaged "cocktails". That said, in Newcastle people continue to "go out" at night even as they become older, so the Quayside now tends to attract people in their thirties and forties as opposed to the Bigg Market which appeals only to the 19–25 year olds. Even so, there is growing concern that the night-time economy in Newcastle has become too much of a good thing.[29]

This situation is mirrored in other UK cities, even Manchester. Leeds, for example, is the self-styled first UK 24 Hour City, although the concept was "borrowed" from Manchester in 1993. The policy aim now is to bring people of all ages into the city centre by relaxing licensing restrictions, improving lighting and pedestrian access, promoting a range of entertainment and more city centre residential accommodation, in a drive to maximize the economic potential of the evening economy, generate jobs and promote Leeds as a European-style city and as a place to invest. In 1991 there were 63 pubs and cafés in Leeds city centre, by 2000 this had risen to 158. During the same period the numbers of restaurants and clubs also increased. As late as 2001, city officials were not concerned over "saturation"[30] levels. But this has changed with high-profile outbreaks of drunkenness and disorder since 2000. There have also

---

27 Chatterton, P. and Hollands, R., *Urban Nightscapes, Youth Cultures, Pleasure Spaces and Corporate Power* (London: Routledge, 2003).

28 Demos, *Northern Soul: Culture, Creativity and Quality of Place in Newcastle and Gateshead* (London: RICS Books, 2003).

29 *The Evening Economy and the Urban Renaissance*. HC 396–1. Twelfth Report of the House of Commons ODPM: Housing, Planning, Local Government and the Regions Committee. HMSO, July 2003.

30 Defined somewhat imprecisely, but taken to mean an over-supply or concentration of licensed premises.

been growing complaints on noise by new apartment-dwelling city centre residents. Some local councillors have called for the closure of the city's new landmark public space – Millennium Square – following repeated drunken "riots". The police have also expressed some concern over the number of late-night entertainment uses, and the fact that policing resources have not increased in line with the increases in the numbers of people using the city centre at night.

Meanwhile Glasgow, Scotland's largest city (population 612,000), has enjoyed a high profile cultural rejuvenation since the mid 1980s. This has been accompanied by a growth in evening and night-time economy activities, especially in the city centre and the west end. Concentrations of entertainment uses are found in the Merchant City (bars and clubs), Sauchiehall Street (pubs, bars and restaurants), Argyll Street (clubs and pubs), Blythwood Hill (upmarket restaurants) and others. In the city centre as a whole there are some 60 pubs and bars and 70 restaurants. Unlike in England the Scottish Planning system makes a distinction between Class 3 uses (cafés and restaurants) and *sui generis* uses including hot-food takeaways and pubs. This allows greater influence through the planning system over the character of licensed premises. There is also a general limit of *sui generis* uses up to 20% of a street frontage, that is to say only one frontage in five will be allowed to operate as a bar, café or restaurant. Late night uses in designated mixed use areas are not permitted to open beyond 1am where residents would be affected. The exception is Merchant City where premises may be allowed to open later, and in this case a "buyer beware" principle applies.

From this example, it would appear that distinctions between entertainment uses may offer the way forward in regulating the evening economy, that is to say using planning controls as well or instead of liquor licensing. This would mean that licensed premises would no longer be considered in isolation, but would increasingly be considered for positive and negative impacts on town and city centres. Local Planning Authorities would in future be under a duty to balance the needs of a successful evening economy against concerns for residential amenity, noise pollution, crime and public disorder. It does seem that a new era of control may be in the offing. The only trouble is, no-one seems to have told Her Majesty's Government.

From June 2004 responsibility for liquor licensing passed from local magistrates to local councils, taking full effect from January 2005. This is seen by the Government as a further step in the liberalization of the UK's drink laws, and it is hoped that it will make the management of the evening and night-time economies easier. Overall, liberalization is intended to help stimulate café society, a more sophisticated and urbane cityscape at night, and contribute to the so-called "urban renaissance".[31] But some commentators are now arguing that thus far the deregulation of the evening economy has led not to greater sophistication, but rather to binge-drinking, anti-social behaviour, and the tyranny of the yob. The question is whether these are matters that can be dealt with by better management of the city at night, or are they a symptom of English cultural identity and, as such, much more difficult to deal with?

---

31 The Reform of Licensing, Home Office White paper, HMSO, 2001.

As we have seen, in the UK the "24-hour city" concept was developed in the late 1980s at Comedia. It was either Ken Worpole or Franco Bianchini who suggested the term, and it was put forward in *City Centres, City Cultures*.[32] It seemed a great idea, and, speaking personally, I certainly had visions of elegant café society, with British people strolling about civilized streets as the Italians do – pullover draped over the shoulders, an attractive woman on one's arm. At that time, it is worth re-stressing, town and city centres in the UK were effectively dead at night, and there was not much choice of restaurants or café-bars, even in London. In places like Manchester, Sheffield, or Leeds the choices and level of sophistication were poor indeed. It was clear that mixed use and a wider understanding of culture (to include design, café culture, street life) were going to be important in revitalizing cities and urban areas. But even as the first 24-hour city conference was held in Manchester in 1993, it was becoming evident that, for most of the time, 18 hours is about enough. In Dublin especially, where the policy was to bring people back to live in the city centre (Temple Bar at that time had only 30 residents), it was clear that there would be a conflict between new residents and noise and rowdy behaviour associated with certain late-night activities, notably clubs and music bars. By the time of subsequent 24-hour city conferences in Cardiff (1994) and Sheffield (1996), the term was being used as a banner heading (signalling diversity, good urban design, and place-making), but always stressing the need for people to sleep! – and the need for all of this to be carefully planned and managed. At that time the UK economy was out of recession, but no-one seemed to believe it. So a lot of new investment in bars and restaurants occurred just at the time that licensing regimes across the country were being relaxed. In some ways this was all very positive – Sheffield is certainly an interesting place at night now; so too is Newcastle.

But there has also been a rise in alcohol consumption among the young (girls especially), and problems such as rowdy behaviour, violent incidents, and public urination. By the time of the final 24-hour city conference in London in 1998, the focus was on management approaches, the need for tighter planning policies, and urban design approaches to the city at night. Soho was in fact the main case study, led by Mr Matthew Bennett, a local resident and businessman. It now seems that the opening up of land use polices in the early 1990s was good, but these were often badly implemented at the local level. It is as though the evening economy was some sort of magic wand that would solve the problems of town centres – but of course this proved not to be the case. Local planners were not far-sighted enough in determining how much late-night activity should be allowed, and where it should be located.

By the close of the 1990s it became clear that the modern equivalent of "bad neighbour uses" is the night-club or the bar/pub playing loud music late at night. In most cities (Hull and Doncaster spring to mind) they actually have loudspeakers mounted on external walls blasting music out into the street. There are whole streets in some places which smell of urine throughout the day, and indeed there are fears that the day-time economy of such streets is being undermined by too much late-

---

32 Bianchini, et al., *op. cit.*, 1987.

night activity. Consequently, much work in this area will in future be to do with better management, better planning, and drawing up conditions to reduce noise and disturbance. This will mean controlling uses and opening times, and also making a proactive policy decision about where the late-night activities should be allowed. There are also all sorts of conditions to be attached on sound control, pavement tables and chairs, and so on. This is an approach to the night-time city that most UK towns and cities[33] will now need to adopt. Some tough decisions may need to be made – for example, closing down or relocating noisy bars and clubs. New definitions on what constitutes a bar (as opposed to a café or restaurant) or a restaurant (as opposed to a take-away) are required, as are changes to entertainment licences and noise control.

It is only fair to admit that these issues are also being raised in Australia, with calls in city media for zero tolerance of public drunkenness. Australians certainly like to drink and have fun, and in recent years there has not been quite the same aggression or atavism one finds in England. They know, too, how to put on a bit of style and how to dine on the streets at night. However, there is a growing problem of young people of both sexes ("hoons" in the local vernacular) cruising around in their cars, revving their engines, racing around suburban and city centre streets and burning their tyres. There has also been a marked increase in alcohol-related violence, vandalism and anti-social behaviour, particularly in Brisbane, Perth and Newcastle. Foul language is the least of it, although very off-putting for other, especially older people. Although the night-time environment of most Australian cities is nowhere near as coarse and uncomfortable or threatening as in the UK, a trend does appear to be becoming established towards more and more serious night-time disorder.

That said, the problem is nowhere near as engrained as it apparently is in England. This raises the question of whether, in some way, the English may temperamentally and culturally be incapable of the sort of sophisticated, civilized, evening economies envisaged back in 1987! It might be that a minority spoil it for everyone else (as in, say, football fans smashing up cafés in Belgium), but this does seem to have been going on for a long time. Could it be that there is something deeply engrained in the psyche of the English that causes them to drink too much and then behave aggressively? The only hope is that they will grow out of it, but the historical evidence, as we shall see, is not encouraging.[34]

The criminologist Phil Hadfield argues that the origins of the most recent phase of alcohol-related disorder in English cities can be traced to a period during the mid-1990s, from which time there was a rapid development of new pubs and bars.[35] He recounts the story of a councillor on Newcastle's licensing committee telling him that, "During the 1990s we had a hut in the town hall and if you wanted a licence you just put your ticket in and we stamped it." According to Hadfield, the over-concentration

---

33 Urban Cultures Ltd, *A Strategy to Tackle All Night Disorder (STAND)*, unpublished consultancy report prepared for Colchester Borough Council and Colchester Safer Cities, October 2003.

34 Burke, T., *English Nightlife* (London: Batsford, 1941).

35 Hadfield, P., "Invited to Binge?", *Town and Country Planning*, 73 (7) 2004.

of licensed premises in urban centres has had, a deleterious cumulative impact on town and city centres. He points out that the mono-cultural alcohol-based functions of the new night-time economy have tended to attract into areas of the city people who live elsewhere. Informal social control is that much more difficult where people are not known within a local community. Moreover, the presence of large numbers of intoxicated people, all of a similar social background, has largely nullified the self-policing of natural surveillance. Development of the evening and night-time economies, meanwhile, has not been matched by adequate support structures such as street lighting and transport. Against this backdrop, increased competition among licensed premises located within tightly packed "drinking circuits" gave rise to alcohol price wars, happy hours and an upsurge in early evening drunkenness. Large crowds of 18–25 year olds are thereby attracted to urban centres week in, week out, and this has had the effect of further intensifying the "stylization of space". Older people are put off more than ever, and problems of policing have also increased markedly.

There is, for example, growing concern being expressed by senior Police Officers across the country over problems associated with alcohol consumption in city and town centres at night.[36] These include concerns over public disorder, anti-social behaviour, rowdy behaviour, violent incidents, public urination and lewd behaviour. Moreover, it is apparent in some places at least that groups of intoxicated young women are these days behaving quite as badly as their male counterparts.

Opinion is not universal on how best to tackle these problems and their causes, as with crime and the causes of crime more generally. A moot point is whether English people are in some way more prone to anti-social and criminal behaviour when alcohol is consumed, or whether a more liberal and relaxed approach to liquor licensing will lead in the end to people behaving more responsibly. The jury, it has to be said, is still out on this issue and in certain cities and towns the increase in licensed premises and alcohol consumption has not to date been accompanied by improvements in behaviour. Rather than becoming more continental in their attitudes to drinking, the English appear to be regressing.

Residents groups and associations across the country are increasingly concerned about high concentrations of late night activity – and the attendant problems of noise, misbehaviour, public disorder and crime – in close proximity to residential areas. Many of these groups do not oppose flexible hours *per se*, but rather that this must be accompanied by better systems to deal with problems. The potential conflict within UK towns and cities between residents and late-night evening economy activities is likely to become more rather than less apparent. On the one hand, it an be argued that new residents moving into the city centre do so in part because of the attractions of the evening economy and, as it were, know what they are buying into. Yet even so, the levels of complaints from even new residents in their 20s and 30s appears to be on the increase. In many city and town centres moreover there are long-established residential communities whose tenure predates the recent growth of the evening

---

36 Morris, H., "Obstacles remain to continental culture", *Planning*, 8 Aug. 2003, p. 11.

economy. In any event, it would appear that the aspiration of encouraging more city centre living will need to face up to the potential conflict with any aspiration to develop a more vibrant evening economy.

Whether these measures will succeed in producing the more civilized and sophisticated evening economy in UK cities and towns remains to be seen. In the meantime, we might learn from other places and older times.

2. CITIES OF THE NIGHT

Morality is the herd instinct of the individual.
Frederich Nietzsche

London Entertained

The history of entertainment in central London dates back many hundreds of years. From the late 18th century, there is a narrative which can by summarized as follows: the rise of the gin palaces in the late 18th and early 19th centuries; the London pub which dates from the 1850s; the music halls and theatres of the 1880s and 1890s; the rise of West End cinema in the 1920s and 1930s; the growth of night clubs and casinos in the 1950s; the takeover by the sex industry in the 1960s and 1970s; and the development of super-pubs alongside an emerging restaurant economy from the late 1980s. Prior to the 1800s, there were the coffee houses. Much of London's entertainment economy, historically, has been concentrated in Soho.

Soho – "Soho" or "So-hoe", after the call of the huntsmen who often rode here – developed as an urban district from 1623, and began to thrive in the 1670s when Gerrard Street, Old Compton Street, Greek Street and Frith Street were developed. The area just to the east, around St. Martin's Lane, was already inhabited by artists and craftsmen, so that from an early time Soho became a centre for art studios and art schools, as well as taverns and coffee houses. In 1688, the Hugenauts were expelled from France and a large population settled in the then new district of Soho. The area transferred rapidly with the opening of shops, cafés and restaurants on the ground floor, and Soho became known as "a sort of petty France". Over the decades Soho would become the first port of call for new immigrants including Greeks, Italians, central European Jews and the Chinese. Soho has remained a draw for artists, bohemians and intellectuals. It also is the centre of London's sex industry.

By the end of the 18th century, Soho was notorious for courtesans, a noted example being Mrs. Cornely's who ran a house on the south side of Soho Square. Later establishments would include the night-houses of Kate Hamilton and Sally Sutherland in the 1860s. Street prostitution was also prevalent and by the 1950s the authorities became concerned to remove working girls from the streets. The prostitutes moved instead to walk-up rooms and attics in the same area. By this time, many of the old theatres had become strip-clubs, so that by 1982 there were some 185 premises in Soho used as part of the sex industry. Attempts to "clean up" Soho since that time have focused on the licensing of sex shops and clubs.

Nevertheless, Soho remains the centre of a flourishing trade in prostitution. It has also become a centre of "gay" pubs, clubs and "singles" bars, so that sexual encounters are a large part of the area's allure and excitement, whether paid for or not. Alongside all of this, Soho has a reputation as a media industries quarter while a wave of new investment in pubs, clubs and restaurants has grown since the mid – 1990s.

In *The Fall of Public Man*[37] Richard Sennett discusses the role of theatre (the gathering of audiences) in a city, and the fact that city life itself can be likened to drama – the symbols and meanings of clothing, speech and the gesture. Performing was one of the keys to urban life, with audiences and players interacting and the signals of public social life continually being learned and relearned. Sennett argues that the "urban institution" which connected the stage and the "system of speech" to the street was the coffee-house. The coffee-houses of the early eighteenth century were the new places for strangers to gather, along with the public houses, the pleasure gardens and the first restaurants. Sennett acknowledges that the coffee-house is a "a romanticized and over-idealized institution: merry, civilized talk, bonhomie and close friendship over a cup of coffee".[38] But he goes on to point out that the coffee-houses were the "prime information centres ... at this time". It was here that the newspapers were read, that tracts and leaflets were published, that insurance was invented, that all manner of business was transacted. Coffee-houses, by their nature, were places where speech was encouraged, and where people experienced sociability in them "without revealing too much about their own feelings, personal history or station. The art of conversation was a convention ... [which] ... permitted strangers to interact without having to probe into personal circumstances".[39] The coffee-houses declined as coffee was eclipsed by tea.

The important point here is that the coffee-houses were places of social interaction and public social life where the codes and rules of conversation were practised, upheld and developed. In fact, the coffee-houses were not necessarily unique in this respect. For one thing there were the summer pleasure gardens and the promenades where people would gather to observe and be observed by strangers. The building of new parks and promenades as places away from the danger of the street, where it was easy and safe to promenade, began in earnest in the 1830s. By the mid-eighteenth century walking and riding in the park in London had become a daily experience; indeed the English were renowned for their passion for the promenade. Unlike the coffee-house where one was drawn into conversation , the promenade occasioned contacts that lasted only a moment, a greeting, a wave of the hand, the tipping of hats to ladies. In this way, what we now think of as street life in part is derived from the market-place and in part from the promenade in the park.

---

37 Sennet, R., 1977, *op. cit.*

38 Ibid., p. 81.

39 Ibid., p. 82.

In London's case, however, by the late nineteenth century, all the pleasure gardens had gone, having more or less been replaced by the theatres and music halls and the gin palaces. The first of these were built from around the 1830s, and they were characterized not only by the provision of indoor entertainment but also by their lavish décor which contrasted with the squalor in which the majority of people lived. There were an estimated 17,000 gin-homes in London in the 1740s and 1750s. Often located in basement cellars or converted ground-floor workshops, these multiplied alongside the traditional ale-houses in poorer areas of the city. This was the time of "Hogarth's England"; when gin was held responsible for the deaths of many thousands of men, women and children. The novelist Henry Fielding, amongst others, observed that the drunkenness caused by "this Poison called Gin" would "destroy a great part of the inferior people".[40] Distilling was highly profitable, and taxation rates low. In 1751, some gin shops were forcibly closed, taxes were increased and the distilleries were subject to greater regulation. Each year, around 25,000 people were arrested for drunkenness in the streets. One outcome of the reduction in the number of gin houses, was that a proportion of those that remained evolved into gin palaces of the early 19th century. These were much larger establishments with plate-glass windows and decorative cornices.

The gin palaces were in fact the forerunners of the large London pubs. Duty of spirits had been reduced in 1825, with the free trade movement, and the official figures on the consumption of alcohol began to rise dramatically. This triggered a moral panic about gin-drinking, and in 1832 the *Beer Act* was passed, designed to encourage drinkers to switch from gin to ale, allowing anyone to set up an alehouse on the pavement for a small licence fee. Unlike the old coaching inns which were really stopping points – they had courtyards for carriages, stabling for horses, rooms for people, and they served food – the new alehouses were simply parlours for drinking in. The gin palaces adapted to this new development, so that the new pubs (from the 1860s) were built larger, redesigned with mirrors, had central rather than long bars and segregated rooms. In effect, the London pub was a new hybrid combining the gin palace with the ale house (Fig. 3.2).

The growth in the number of public houses was rapid. Weightman[41] notes that by the end of the nineteenth century "there were 48 drinking places in a one-mile stretch (along the Whitechapel Road); along the Strand there were 46 in less than a mile". Competition between publicans was naturally fierce, and singalongs and other entertainments were put on to attract customers. As the breweries became more powerful, they began to buy out and lend to publicans, so that many pubs became tied houses.

The theatre in London, meanwhile, had been the subject of strict regulation, a circumstance that led ultimately to the rise of the music hall. The first London theatres had developed in Shakespeare's day, around Whitechapel and in North

---

40 Quoted in Ackroyd, P., *op. cit.* 2000, p. 352.
41 Weightman, G., *Bright Lights, Big City* (London: Collins and Brown, 1992).

Figure 3.2   The King's Head, London
Source: John Montgomery.

Southwark, just outside the city walls. A hundred years later many of the theatres and playhouses were pulled down by Cromwell's Puritans, the actors being branded as vagabonds. Following the Restoration, theatres were once more permitted but subject to a strict regulatory system of Patents restricting performances to "legitimate theatre", and banning music. New licences were granted at infrequent intervals, so that by the mid-eighteenth century:

> ... there was a tremendous suppressed demand for drama in London, but whenever an actor or speculator ... tried to build a new theatre, the Patents objected and called in the Law, which was always upheld.[42]

For over a hundred years, from the late eighteenth century, there followed a procession of new theatres opening up, putting on plays, being closed by the authorities and their owners arrested and fined. To get around the Patents, all number of ingenious tricks were attempted, including "giving" away free tickets (free performances were exempt from the Patents) with purchased items of clothing. Eventually in 1843, the

---

42 Ibid., p. 21.

Theatre Regulation Act abolished the Patent monopoly, so that all manner of theatres could now apply for a Lord Chamberlain's licence.

However, few new theatres were founded in the period following the 1843 Act, but the music halls, or variety theatres as they were later called, arose "at an astonishing pace"[43] becoming the dominant places for popular entertainment. From the 1850s the music halls became increasingly refined and reputable, distinguishing themselves from the more bawdy proceedings in the saloon theatres and public houses. Women were allowed to watch the entertainment, often from upper galleries, provided they were prepared to give their name and address as a protection against prostitution. A typical music hall of the time (1860s) is described in F. E. Richie's *The Night Side of London*:

> A well-lighted entrance attached to a public house indicates that we have reached our destination. We proceed up a few stairs along a passage lined with handsome engravings, to a bar, where we pay sixpence if we take a seat in the body of the hall, and sixpence if we ascend into the gallery. We make our way leisurely along the floor of the hall, which is well lighted, and capable of holding 1500 people. A balcony extends round the room in the form of a horse-shoe. At the opposite end to that at which we enter is the platform, on which are placed a grand piano and a harmonium on which the performers play in the intervals when the previous singers have left the stage. The chairman sits just beneath them. It is dull work to him, but there he must sit drinking and smoking cigars from seven to twelve o'clock. The room is crowded, and almost every gentlemen has a pipe or cigar in his mouth. Evidently the majority present are respectable mechanics or small tradesmen with their wives and daughters and sweethearts. Now and then you see a midshipman, or a few fast clerks and warehousemen. Everyone is smoking and everyone has a glass before him; but the class that come here are economical and chiefly confine themselves to pipes and porter.[44]

In his compelling account of the history of public entertainment in London, Gavin Weightman describes the "battle over the Empire Theatre, Leicester Square" as combining all the ingredients of the moral struggle of the Victorian period and after: "sex, drink, prostitutes, popular taste and the profits of showbusiness".[45] The Empire had opened as a theatre in 1884 but had become a variety hall by 1887 and had something of a reputation as a gathering place by the 1890s. Weightman quotes an 1890 description from *Harper's*:

> You pass through wide, airy corridors and down stairs, to find yourself in a magnificent theatre, and the stall to which you are shown is wide and luxuriously fitted. Smoking is universal, and a large proportion of the audience promenade the outer circles, or stand in groups before the long refreshment bars, which are a prominent feature on every tier. Most of the men are in evening dress, and in the boxes are some ladies, also in evening costume, many of them belonging to what is called good society. The women in other

---

43 Ibid., p. 29.
44 Ibid., pp. 33–34.
45 Ibid.

parts of the house are generally pretty obvious members of a class which, so long as it behaves itself with propriety in the building, it would, whatever fanatics may say to the contrary, be neither desirable nor possible to exclude. The most noticeable characteristic of the audience is perhaps the very slight attention it pays to whatever is going on upon the stage.[46]

Moralists became deeply concerned at the prospect of men about town were drinking in the music hall, being stimulated by the girls on stage and solicited by prostitutes who patrolled the bars. Sex, often as not, was practised on the premises. In 1894, following complaints from two American gentlemen who were solicited in the promenade, a leading campaigner against vice, Mrs Ormiston Chant, led a campaign to close the Empire. She complained in particular of the lewd dancing and the use of flesh-coloured tights and bodices to "simulate nudity". Mrs Chant appeared before the Entertainments Committee of the London County Council to oppose the Empire's application for the renewal of its licence. The LCC was widely seen as being run by "Progressives", but they were social reformers of the "most humourless and puritanical kind"[47] who were "especially strict" in their administration of music and dancing licences. This was to become a recurrent theme in the licensing of British public social life.

The Empire was a fashionable and popular place, and was supported by the public, West End society and in the Press. The upshot was that the LCC decided to renew the Empire's licence but on the condition that a screen was put up between the promenade and the back row of seating, and that the sale of drink was banned from the auditorium. The Empire's manager, of course, complained that this would greatly reduce his profits and the shareholders' dividends, and that it was unfair if other establishments were not forced to do likewise. However, despite this threat to close the Empire in October 1894, it re-opened in November with the temporary screen in place. The scenes that followed are described in the *Pall Mall Gazette* of 5 November:

> The bar at the back had been shut off from the promenade by means of a screen of woodwork covered with canvas … gradually the crowd began to attack the screen. Well-dressed men – some of the almost middle-aged – kicked at it from within, burst the canvas, but hardly affecting the woodwork. The attendants – most of whom might have played the giant in the country show – watched in helpless and amused inactivity. Finally, there was an attack on the canvas, which was torn away in strips, and passed through the crowd, every one endeavouring to secure a scrap of it as a souvenir. Mr. Hitchens, the manager, attempted argumentative remonstrance, but was carried away by half a dozen enthusiasts. Then the woodwork of the screen was demolished by vigorous kicks from both sides. The crowd had already cheered itself hoarse, and now began to go out into London, brandishing fragments of the screen.[48]

---

46 *Harper's New Monthly Magazine* (1890), quoted in Weightman, *op. cit.* 1992, p. 78.
47 Weightman, *op. cit.*, p. 82.
48 *Pall Mall Gazette*, 5 November, 1894, quoted in Weightman, *op. cit.*, 1992, p. 84.

Figure 3.3 *The Gay Parisienne*, **Duke of York's Theatre (1896)**
Source: The National Archives (I/126/folio 372), with permission.

From the mid-1890s onwards, newly opened variety theatres (Fig. 3.3) were unable to get licences to sell drink in the auditorium, and a great many of the smaller halls – when their licences were refused renewal – closed. A few temperance music halls were established (for example the Victoria Theatre, later the Old Vic) but these failed because "they lacked the income from alcoholic drink … and tended to have a pious and unattractive atmosphere".[49] The Working Men's Clubs and Institute Union or CIU was formed in 1862 to provide alcohol-free uplifting entertainment for the masses, although eventually alcoholic drink was permitted. Eventually, many of the working men's clubs in Soho became the private drinking clubs and strip joints of the 1950s.

By the late 1880s, the West End was firmly established as London's theatre-land. Shaftsbury Avenue was opened in 1888, and quickly became the city's main theatrical street with a boom in theatre building that lasted until 1910. New customers were drawn from the suburbs, easily accessible by train and underground. During this time, the music halls began to be replaced by cinemas. The first West End cinema, the New Egyptian Hall in Piccadilly, opened in 1907. By 1912 there were 500 cinemas in London. The development of sound recording led to "the talkies", and from the late 1920s there was a new boom in cinema development. In 1928, the old Empire in Leicester Square was converted to a cinema with seating for 3000 people. By the late 1950s, cinema was on the threshold of a decline which would eventually see several cinemas converted to night-clubs and strip-clubs. Meanwhile, the area in and around Dean Street, and Old Compton Street in Soho became a centre for the new coffee bars of the mid 1950s. These attracted actors, intellectuals and students, and the early pioneers of British pop music.

By the 1930s, public entertainment in London had become more respectable and less dependent on strong drink. Not only was the notion of what a theatre ought to be shaped during the struggles over drink, sex and prostitutes, but moral control through licensing – of public house, entertainment venues, opening hours and drinking-up time – had been extended to cover many aspects of public social life. Thus, the tightening of liquor licensing, which is often attributed to wartime measures (ensuring that munitions workers were fit to work), was in fact in train from the 1860s and especially the 1890s with the control of public entertainment and the social reforming zeal of modern local government. The contrast between Victorian moral control and what had gone before in the late eighteenth century is marked.[50]

The purpose of describing, however briefly, the way in which theatres, music halls, gin palaces and public houses evolved, is to point to the ever-present tension between popular entertainment and respectability, the forces of market and cultural demand versus regulation, the conflict between entertainment and prudery. For it is in this ongoing struggle that we find the root of Britain's liquor and entertainment licensing laws of the twentieth century. In turn, this means that the impoverished

---

49 Ibid., p. 97.

50 Burke, T., Thomas Burke's *English Nightlife: From Norman Conquest to Present Blackout*, 1941 (Ayer, 1972).

public social life of UK cities which became evident in the 1980s, was at least in part a consequence of decades of earlier moral regulation and control of liquor licensing. For fear and moral panic over the behaviour of crowds and people in public places has been a recurring theme in the attitudes of city fathers and mothers.

> Night-life ... night-club ... night-bird. There is something about the word Night, as about the word Paris, that sends through some Englishmen a shiver of misgiving, and through another type a current of undue delight. The latter never get over the excitement of Sitting Up Late. The others see any happening after midnight – even a game of snakes-and ladders – as something verging on the unholy; as though Satan were never abroad in sunlight. A club they can tolerate. Call it a night-club, and they see it as the ante-room to Hell. This attitude towards entertainment after dark is held by most officials. Whenever they hear of some new development of night-life, they get a prickling of the thumbs, and give the impression that they would be happier if the universe had so contrived its system as to give the whole globe perpetual day. They always want to have their eye on us; always are ordering their subordinates to find out what baby is doing and tell him he mustn't. This impeding of the Englishman's night-life goes back to our earliest times, and has persisted ever since. In my own youth, a firm of billiards-table makers used to recommend its wares to respectable fathers, under the legend: Keep Your Boys At Home. But all through the centuries boys have refused to stay at home. So, when authority found it could not keep them there, it set about making things as difficult as possible for them, by devising budgets and laws and by-laws.[51]

Shanghai: The Whore of the East

In the 1920s and the 1930s, Shanghai came to prominence as the most decadent city on earth. Although other cities were noted for a relaxation of social mores (Paris), sexually explicit forms of entertainment (Berlin), organized crime (Chicago), jazz (New York) and prostitution, Shanghai managed to combine all of these. It was once said that if God allowed Shanghai to stand he owed Sodom and Gomorrah an apology. The city was known as the "Paris of Asia", but also the "Whore of the East".

Shanghai had been ruled by the British ever since the Opium Wars of the mid 1880s, and was a trading port, exporting teas and silks and importing opium. The city's growth had been fuelled by trade, and from rural immigration. From the 1890s the inner city areas were divided up to include the "French Concession" and the International Settlement. The French Concession was laid out as a series of large villas, apartment blocks, hotels, shops and cafés and was regarded as the most cosmopolitan part of a cosmopolitan city. It was home to around 30,000 foreigners and 1 million Chinese. Many of the foreigners – British, French, American, German, Japanese – referred to themselves as "Shanghai-landers". Some of them were there to run businesses along the Bund; others were travellers, adventurers and hedonists.[52] "French town", as it

---

51 Ibid., p. v.

52 Dong, S., *Shanghai: The Rise and Fall of a Decadent City* (New York: Harper Collins, 2001).

was called, was also home to numerous brothels, casinos and opium dens. At this time, there were 100,000 prostitutes in a population of 3 million.

Very little effort was made to clamp-down on activities that in most other cities of the time were considered criminal. This is largely because the brothels, protection rackets and opium dens were run by organized crime – the Green Gang – themselves controlled by high-ranking police officials.[53] Gang leaders such as Pock-Mark Wong and Big Ears Du effectively ran the city, or at least its darker side. By the late 1920s, Shanghai was a rich city and indeed accounted for one-third of China's GNP. This wealth was generated by the spending of foreigners – in brothels, bars, opium dens and casinos – but the everyday work of the city was as a trading port. The dock labour was Chinese, as were most of the manual occupations. Wealthy foreigners and rich Chinese employed a whole class of servants and bodyguards. Influxes of new overseas migrants were common as Shanghai operated no passport control. In 1921, 20,000 White Russians fled the October Revolution and settled in Shanghai; many of the men would find work as bodyguards, the women as dancers and prostitutes.

The city also became a focal point for leftist agitators, and in 1921 the Communist Party of China was established there. Following many skirmishes, a serious uprising in 1927 was brutally suppressed by the Green Gang and the army.[54] This led the young Mao to conclude that revolution in China would only succeed if launched from the rural areas. The city returned to normal. By this time – the late 1920s – the economy was so strong and so dependent on "entertainment" of various kinds, that it was effectively immune from the Great Depression. Instead of economic collapse, Shanghai entered into a period of property boom, and at this time skyscrapers (a concept imported from Chicago) and luxurious hotels such as the Café Hotel were built, many of them by the Jewish Iraqi tycoon Sir Victor Sassoon. At this time, Shanghai developed a thriving film industry and for a time the city was known as the Hollywood of China. More night-clubs developed, and cabaret jazz became popular. Meanwhile, opium dens and brothels continued to ply a "healthy" trade. Western intellectuals and writers also visited the city, many of them deciding to stay on, attracted by the personal freedoms and free love, although much of it wasn't free at all. By 1930, one in 130 people in Shanghai were prostitutes, compared to one in 430 in Chicago, one in 480 in Paris and one in 580 in Berlin.[55] Venereal disease was endemic.

The Sino-Chinese War broke out in 1937 and the Chinese parts of the city were heavily bombed and then occupied by the Japanese. Brutal executions of the Chinese became common-place and the Shanghai-landers realized it was time to leave. Shanghai's golden age was over. It would not return after the Second World War either, because of the Communist revolution, and the fact that Mao associated the city not only with "western" influence but also the failed uprising of 1927.

---

53 Wakeman, F., *Policing Shanghai* (Berkeley: University of California Press, 1997).
54 Sargeant, H., *Shanghai: Collision Point of Cultures* (New York: Crown, 1990).
55 Dong, *op. cit.*, 2001, p. 45.

Shanghai in fact would be, more or less, ignored by Communist Party officials for fifty years. Even during the 1980s, when economic reforms led Shenzhen and Fujian to flourish, Shanghai remained in economic limbo. By 2000, Shanghai was emerging economically as a growing city once more. Whether it reverts to its former role as the earth's naughtiest city remains to be seen.

Berlin

The Berlin of the Weimar Republic, that is from 1918 to 1933, was synonymous with experimentation in the arts, political extremism and a general loosening of public morality. Following its defeat in World War 1, Germany was on the brink of collapse. There was rioting in the streets and shortages of food. On November 9th, 1919 the Social Democratic leader Phillip Scheidemann declared a republic in Berlin, following the flight of Kaiser William to the Netherlands. At the Treaty of Versailles, however, France insisted on a harsh peace settlement and very large reparation payments. Germany was forced to accept these terms by an Allied blockade. The first President, Friedrich Eebert, was faced with a deteriorating political situation, and was forced to put down revolts by the left, the new Communist Party of Karl Liebknecht and Rosa Luxemburg, and the right – the Freikorps, led by Wolfgang Kapp. With support from the trades unions, the new republic survived two attempted coups.

The new leaders drew up a constitution in Weimer, a small town in Thuringia which is seen as the home of the German Enlightenment and is associated with Goethe, Schiller and Hegel. Economic collapse was fended off by the American Dawes Plan which reduced the level of war reparations, and despite futher episodes of political instability such as the Beer Hall Putsch of 1923, the Weimer Republic enjoyed a period of relative calm. During the 1920s and early 1930s, the Weimer would give its name to a period of intense cultural creativity.

German art was able, more or less, to pick up where it had left off before the war, with important Expressionist artists such as Klee and Kandinsky having survived (unlike Schiele and Klimt). Max Ernst started a Dadaist group in Cologne, and other movements such as "New Objectivity" and "Social Realism" would follow. In literature, the 1920s was the time of Hermann Hesse and Thomas Mann. Bertolt Brecht presented human-kind in gotesque absurdities of drama and poems. Kurt Weill was writing the *Three-Penny Opera* (with Brecht), the leading composer of the day was Paul Hindemith, and interest in jazz grew. The German film industry would enjoy its heyday, with works by Fritz Lang and Josef von Sternberg, and the emergence of Marlene Dietrich. Many of these genres would fuse into collaborations between musicians, artists, writers and film makers in a way previouisly unheard of, largely because of electrical sound recording and film. The "culture industry" was born.

Berlin would also see the rise of cabaret, a naughty and often explicit floor show combining music, dance and theatre. It was also a city of "free love", as described in the novels of Christopher Isherwood,[56] who lived in Berlin from 1929 (having followed Auden there) until May 1933 when he fled to Prague, fearful of arrest. Isherwood was partly attracted to Berlin by its reputation for sexual promiscuity and tolerance of homosexuality. By the 1920s Berlin had a large sex industry. Prostitution was widespread – even before this time, at the turn of the century, there were an estimated 50,000 prostitutes in Berlin. The birth rate fell by almost two-thirds (to 11.5 per thousand) between 1914 and 1922. In 1931 there were 1 million abortions in Berlin, exceeding the number of live births. Peter Hall refers to this as "Values in Disintegration".[57] The city combined free love, easy philosophies, cheap jazz, vulgar cabarets and any number of cultural excesses.

The upshot was that many German conservatives came to view Berlin, perhaps cities in general, as a breeding ground for degenerate sexuality and promiscuity. A backlash grew, focused on German mythology, the German spirit and social order.[58] This would prove to be fertile ground for the National Socialist German Workers Party led by Adolf Hitler. The Nazis would combine a highly centralized and bureaucratic brand of state socialism with the emasculation (and eventual murder) of "foreigners". They would also attack modern art as "degenerate". Berlin, then, fell pray to the excessive social control and cruelty of National Socialism; but it is also probable that, by being too tolerant, the Weimar Republic carried the seeds of its own destruction.

3. THE PROBLEM OF REGULATION: CASE STUDIES

Perhaps the biggest question facing contemporary policy makers is whether they properly understand the extent to which people in general can behave appropriately in the absence of moral regulation? How best to get the right balance between more relaxed liquor licensing and decent forms of public social life? This issue has been exercising the minds of policy makers in London and other UK cities, and they have looked to overseas examples, in cities such as Amsterdam, Utrecht, Berlin, Paris, New York, Copenhagen, Dublin and Lisbon for examples of better practice. Let us consider some notably "liberal" cities (see Appendix A for more detail).

Amsterdam

Amsterdam is a medium-sized European city of around 720,000 inhabitants, in a region with a population of 2 million. Its port is the fifth largest in Western Europe, its airport fifth. From 1966 government policy was to divert demand for more space to satellite towns, a policy known as "controlled decentralization". This proved so successful that the new satellite towns began to drain economic activity and

---

56 See *Mr Norris Changes Trains*, and *Goodbye to Berlin*.
57 Hall, P., *Cities in Civilisation* (London: Weidenfield and Nicholson, 1998), p. 270.
58 Gay, P., *Weimer Culture* (New York: Harper and Row, 1968).

residents away from Holland's major cities. Between 1965 and 1985, the population of Amsterdam fell from 865,000 to 645,000. At the same time, incoming commuting rose from below 80,000 to 145,000 trips. To counter these "unsustainable" trends,[59] Amsterdam city embarked on a "compact city" zoning plan in 1985. This aimed to limit distances between home and work, improve public transport, use space efficiently by building "connected properties" in high densities, maintain and create varied residential environments, and reduce the fragmentation of rural areas. Policy for the city centre was – and still is – to retain a mix of uses as well as its residential function.

The city is built on a network of concentric canals – the canal web. It is also known for its personal freedom, liberal drug laws and tolerance, dating from the 1960s, although this now appears to be under threat from Islamic fundamentalists and culturally motivated violence. The city itself has two main parts: the medieval core, bordered by the Kloveniersburgwal and Singel canals, and the more recent 17th century areas surrounding the core. Concentrations of city centre evening activities are found in in the Leidesplein, on the Singel canal just south of Jordaan, and the Rembrandtplein within the old city core. The Leidesplein is now the city's prime evening economy area, and is particularly liked by young people.

Licensed premises in Amsterdam include "brown cafés" (pubs), grand cafés, smoking coffee shops (cannabis) and coffee shops. Most bars and cafés in the city centre are able to stay open until 4 or 5 am at weekends, 11pm to 1am at other times. Planning policy, at its simplest is to agglomerate cafés and bars in two designated "zones of concentration", the Rembrandtplein and the Leidesplein. There is however, no policy to increase their numbers. Outside these zones, no new bars or restaurants are permitted. The policy aim overall is to maintain the balance of uses, but increasing the amount of non-entertainment uses in the central areas. Controls are exercised by the Department of Inner City Government, via licences for liquor, food and entertainment. There are 30 types of licence with detailed differentiation between them on opening hours and other arrangements. This includes shops open at night. Within the zones of concentration no further hot food takeaways, bars or restaurants are allowed, although some limited changes between types is permitted. Licences for new discos are not permitted anywhere, capacity having been determined by the numbers of existing outlets and safe fire egress. Regular checks are made on all licensed premises, both planned and unannounced. Precise categories of land use are employed to distinguish between night-time economy outlets. The categories are:

- I Fast food
- II Night clubs/discos
- III Grand cafés and bars ;
- IV Restaurants, cafés and bars serving food.

---

59 Oskam, A.W., *A Tale of Two Cities – Amsterdam*, paper to The European City – *Sustaining Urban Quality Conference*, Copenhagen, 24–28 April 1995.

A special category exists for cafés which are part of theatres, museums and hotels.

The issue of noise pollution is being taken very seriously, and decibel levels are specified in all licences. Decibel limiters may be fitted to sound equipment. Complaints from the public are investigated by enforcement offices and the police. Refuse collection is undertaken by the City Council at fixed hours in the early morning. Trams and metros run until about midnight when night buses take over. Night buses run hourly during the week and half-hourly at weekends on nine routes. Additional police are deployed in "stress area" at closing times. Extra surveillance is undertaken between 10pm and 7am, including police checks for weapons. On weekends, mobile plastic *pissoirs* are provided at night to reduce urination in the streets.

The authorities are highly concerned about saturation levels and the impact of the night-time economy on residential amenity, believing that this has contributed to a more recent exodus of the middle classes from the city centre. (It probably has, but so too drug dealing and multi-cultural violence). This has resulted in restrictions being imposed on both the locations and numbers of licensed premises. No further increase in entertainment uses will be allowed. It seems that Dutch liberalism has reached its limits, following the liberalization of the 1960s and 1970s.

Berlin

Berlin is a city of 3.4 million people. The centre of 19th century Prussian culture and military might, Berlin became one of the most innovative and *avant garde* cities in Europe in the 1920s, for a short time at least. The city centre, by and large, is made up of Prenzlauer Berg and Mitte in the east and Charlottenburg and Kreuzberg in the west. Mitte has become the fastest growing centre since Unification in 1989. The two main concentrations of evening economy activity, similarly, are Charlottenburg and Mitte. Mitte historically had been a largely residential area with retail uses at street level and crafts and small industries in rear courtyards. At the beginning of the 20th century Mitte was predominantly occupied by the city's then Jewish population. The area is now the centre of Berlin's bar and café culture.

Berlin's drinking culture traditionally has been one of discreet, tucked-away drinking establishments. These days, this includes small cafés, small bars which become clubs at night, temporary illegal bars and larger fashionable bars. The Mitte area now has 7–800 licensed premises; the area's population is 320,000. Planning policy for central Berlin is to develop all centres for mixed use, a polycentric urban structure based on residential neighbourhoods with a mixed-use character at key nodes. Policy towards the night-time economy is therefore aimed at concentrating entertainment uses on the main streets, subject to them not causing a nuisance. The City's Economic Development Department controls licensing. Licensed premises include bars, pubs, cafés, restaurants, clubs and fast-food outlets. There are no distinctions between types of licensed premises, although the playing of live music requires a special licence. Applications are dealt with on their merits. Fixed closing times are between 5am and 6am. The city authorities have recently concluded that cafés, pubs and restaurants have reached "saturation level".

The City Council and the local municipal police enforce strict policies on noise, the aim being to minimize disturbance to residents. Noise restrictions are set for each licensed premise individually. Higher fines for non-compliance are imposed during prescribed "quiet periods" which vary according to the type of entertainment cluster: 8pm to 10pm, 6am to 7am, 10pm to 6am, and all day on Sundays and bank holidays. Complaints must be dealt with by the Police within 14 days, and fines ranging from £200–£30,000 can be levied. Landlords and staff are responsible for music levels, and for noisy customers on the street outside their premises. Music is generally forbidden in outside spaces such as beer gardens and pavement tables and chairs.

S-Bahn, trams and the Metro end at midnight, when the night bus service commences. Advertising campaigns promote the frequency and safety of public transport at night. However, with its polycentric structure, Berlin offers enough choice for many people elect to remain in their local centre, certainly on week days. Public toilets are provided and maintained by the private sector, and financed by advertising revenue. It seems that in Berlin, you can still do what you like, as long as you don't make noise!

Paris

Paris is a city of 2.2 million, although it serves a much wider metropolitan region of 10 million. It retains its reputation as the *bijou extraordinaire*, the most beautiful city in the world, combining culture, style and elegance. The city is organized as a series of 20 *arrondissements*. In central Paris (Intra-Muros – within the walls), the Rive Droite (Right Bank) is north of the Seine, while the Rive Gauche (Left bank) is south of the river. Although the centre of the city tends to be busier, each arrondissement within the walls is a mixed-use neighbourhood, and as such has its own mix of café and other evening activities.

The eastern parts of central Paris have revived over the past ten or so years, including the Marais and The Bastille. The Marais (the marsh) for example, was originally laid out in the 17th century as a fashionable area for the nobility, fell into decline and was renovated from the 1960s onwards. It is now one of the city's most fashionable areas. Likewise, the Bastille area has developed as the largest concentration of evening entertainment in Paris in recent years. The area combines cafés, restaurants, clubs and galleries, cultural centres and a mixed resident population. The area is also much visited by tourists, and contains many low-priced hotels and hostels. The Bastille is part of the Fauborg St-Antoine arrondissement which has its own area-specific regulatory plan. This supports mixed-use, but there are no specific polices on this, nor any system of use classes No specific planning policies are pursued, other than maintaining a balance between residential and non-residential uses. The plan does contain plot ratios which set maxima building heights and density. Incentives are provided to preserve courtyards and allow their active use.

Policy on licensed premises is set down on The Code de la Sante Publique (Public Health Code). Each arrondissement has a quota of how many licensed premises can be in operation. No extra premises above this number are permitted. In recent years demand for licenses has far outstripped these quotas, so some horse-trading has occurred between arrondissements to move unused licences to other parts of the city. In addition, licensed venues cannot be within 75 metres of each other, nor within 100 metres of a school, religious institution or retirement home. These quotas are periodically challenged (or circumnavigated) with the interests of tourism and economic development offered as reasons for relaxation. Day-to day regulation and enforcement is carried out by the Prefecture de Police. All venues selling alcohol must close by 2am, and all customers must have left the premises. Venues are allowed to open again at 4am. Special dispensations can be granted to remain open between 2am and 4am, subject to noise levels, previous complaints and record of responsible management. Such matters are monitored by the Police as part of the general liquor licensing regime. Licensed premises can be closed down if complaints from the public are upheld, but this is rare. The issue of noise is dealt with at the city level. Action consists of a Paris-wide campaign of leaflets on noise reduction, and a grant programme to improve sound insulation in the residential stock. Night transport is well-organized in Paris. The Metro runs until 0:50 hours, night buses run from 01:30am until 05:30am and taxis are readily available.

Because of France's laissez-faire planning system, regulation of the evening economy is via the issuing and monitoring of liquor licences, up to pre-determined limits. There is growing evidence of licences being traded to get around these limits, and a concern that the system is restricting tourist-related business growth. It is a moot point whether the system of controls will continue to prove effective in the near future.

New York

New York city has a population of 7 million. The self-proclaimed "city that never sleeps" is arguably the most diverse and mixed city on earth. Previously known as New Amsterdam – it was founded by Henry Hudson on behalf of the Dutch East India Company – in the 1970s it developed a reputation as the "new Rome", a centre of culture, commerce and world-wide influence.

The most lively areas of night-time activity in New York City are also residential neighbourhoods, notably Greenwich Village, SoHo (South of Houston Street), NoHo and Little Italy, all of which are in Manhattan Borough. Manhattan is the oldest part of New York. North Manhattan is laid out on a regular street grid, with avenues running north-south and streets running east-west. Lower Manhattan has a more haphazard, organic street pattern (perhaps following ancient Indian trails), and it is here that SoHo, the Lower East Side, Chinatown and Little Italy are found. Just to the north of Houston Street (NoHo) are East Village and Greenwich Village. Midtown, which includes Broadway, lies between Lower and Upper Manahattan.

Planning policies are prepared by the Department of City Planning and administered by the City Planning Commission, an appointed city-wide body. Local consultation and deliberation is effectively maintained by local Community Boards. Applications for development approval are judged against the city's *Zoning Laws*. These are effectively a set of ordinances governing such matters as land uses, building heights and street set-backs. The land use zones are of three basic types: residential, commercial (offices and shops) and manufacturing. These are sub-divided into categories, according in the main to density and intensity of use. Restaurants and bars are included in Retail Use 6. The Local Community Board for Greenwich Village, for example, does not wish to see any further increase in bars and restaurants generally, but is less opposed to "white-clothed" restaurants. This is difficult to enforce as there is no difference in use class between bars, restaurants or shops within Retail Use 6. Liquor licensing is controlled by the State Liquor Authority, and no new alcohol licences are granted for premises within 500 ft of each other. Types of licence are varied, and include: Liquor Licences with closing times defined as 4am to 8am Mondays to Saturdays and 4am to mid-day on Sundays; Food Establishment Permits from the Department of Health.; Cabaret Licences for dancing; Place of Assembly Permits (fire and safety) for venues with a capacity over 75.

In addition, sidewalk Café Licences may be issued by the Department of Consumer Affair's on the payment of "security fees" of around $40,000. Sidewalk cafés are allowed to remain open until midnight Monday to Thursday, until 1am Friday and Saturday, and midnight on Sundays. Licencees are held strictly accountable for the maintenance of good order, for the conduct of their patrons and for noise. Holders of a Cabaret Licence are under a duty to ensure customers do not cause excessive noise or litter, or behave in a manner that would disturb the peace or compromise public safety. They must also have indoor waiting areas, and not employ door staff with a criminal record during the previous 5 years. All businesses are prohibited from operating sound systems for advertising purposes outside of their buildings. For residential areas levels of noise from a commercial establishment must not exceed 45 dB inside the dwelling. Sidewalks in front of any building in New York are the required to be maintained by the owner. This includes sweeping and cleaning of gutters. Businesses are also required to keep backyards, courtyards, alleyways and air shafts clean at all times. Refuse disposal is organized by commercial establishments themselves, usually by contracting licensed private operators. Evening transport is not a problem in New York as the New York subway operates 24 hours a day. Taxis are also plentiful.

Although it once had a reputation as a dangerous city, with high levels of street crime, New York is now considered a much safer city than London. Since 1994 there has been a dramatic decrease in reported crimes in New York City. This is due to the success of former Mayor Giuliani's policy of zero tolerance towards crime and anti-social behaviour. Perhaps more importantly, New York has 1 police officer for every 161 citizens. This compares, for example with 1 per 290 people in London. In 2000 the numbers of reported crimes in New York City was 288,000, compared to 1,052,000 for London. It would appear that the major crackdown on crime has been beneficial. The "City That Never Sleeps" is more regulated than it appears, not in land-use planning but in the various licence types required and their enforcement. As with some of the other cities we have considered, New York may well have to re-visit its zoning laws if sufficient distinction is to be made between activities such as "white cloth" restaurants, bars, takeaways and shops.

Melbourne

With a population of 3.3 million people, Melbourne is Australia's second largest city. Arguably less well-known outside Australia than its rival Sydney, Melbourne is nevertheless the most sophisticated and urbane of cities. Founded in 1835 by free settlers, the city experienced rapid growth during the gold rush of the 1850s. By 1861 the city's population had grown to 126,000 from around 70,000 ten years previously. The city teemed with life, not all of it, apparently, savoury. An English visitor in the 1870s referred to Melbourne as being in the grip of a "hairystocracy", bearded long-haired men galloping horses through the streets, getting drunk and brawling.[60] Prostitutes "paraded openly" in the Bourke Street bars and theatres[61]. The Chinese migrants, attracted by the prospect of discovering gold, brought opium dens. In the years that followed, the brothels and bordellos were moved out of the central city, and strict controls on the sale of liquor were introduced, in common with the rest of Australia. Somehow, by the 1950s, "Marvellous Melbourne" had become somewhat dull. During the filming of "On the Beach" in 1959, Ava Gardner remarked the Melbourne was a great place to film the end of the world. Tim Flannery recalls becoming so disillusioned by the "increasingly sterile environment" that he left the city of his birth for Sydney.[62] During this time, cinema fled to the suburbs and the high arts moved south of the Yarra to a new "arts precinct" not dissimilar to the South Bank in London.

In the 1990s, a major campaign – Postcode 3000 – was launched with the aim of reintroducing a residential population within the CBD. The aim to achieve a residential population of 3,000 people, although ambitious at the time, has comfortably been surpassed as city centre living has returned to Melbourne and other Australian cities.[63] This owes much to Federal government financial incentives to encourage investor development of housing. At the same time, Melbourne has

---

60 Flannery, T. (ed), *The Birth of Melbourne* (Melbourne: Text Publishing, 2002).

61 Lewis, M., *Melbourne: The City's History and Development* (City of Melbourne, 1995), p. 43.

62 Flannery, T., *The Birth of Melbourne* (Melbourne: Test Publishing, 2002) p. 22.

63 Adams, R., "Melbourne: Back from the Edge", in Charlesworth, E. (ed). *City Edge: Case Studies in Contemporary Urbanism* (London: Architectural Press, 2005), chapter 3.

pursued a policy of the CBD becoming a 24 hour city. This has involved a marked relaxation of liquor licensing restrictions and a reduction in the costs of applying for a licence. The result is that many small bars, cafés and restaurants have opened. These have sprung up all over the CBD, and include Arthur's on Corporation Lane, Bambu on Flinders Lane, Ding Dong Lounge on Market Lane, Double O in Sniders Lane, the Gin Palace, the Hairy Canary, the Purple Emerald, the Loop in Meyers Place, Misty Place on Hosier Lane, the Croft Institute, the Loft, Tony Starr's Kitten Club, and not forgetting Bennetts Lane Jazz Club. In addition, there are many good modern restaurants sprinkled throughout the lanes and along adjoining main streets, for example Becco, Mo Mo, Shoya, Yak, Movida, Felt and Café Segovia. Almost all of these establishments are patronized by in-the-know Melbournites, and some of them are so off the beaten track as to be difficult to find. They are rarely more than a short stroll from Melbourne's most fashionable boutiques, clustered around Crossley Street, Little Collins Street, Flinders Lane and Albert Coates Lane.

By 2004 there were an estimated 3000 people living in central Melbourne, including the CBD and areas such as the Southbank and docklands. A growing concern has been complaints by residents over noise associated with the evening economy and late-night activities. This culminated in a report to the Planning, Development and Services Committee of the Melbourne City Council in December 2002, on the noise impact of entertainment premises on nearby residences. This has prompted Melbourne City Council to establish a Project Team on the Management of Noise in the Capital City Zone, as of August 2003. The work of the Noise Management Team is in its infancy. Officers stress that the aim is not to move away from mixed use in the City Centre, but to deal with specific instances of noise through sound reduction measures.

Manchester

Greater Manchester has a population of around 875,000, but is a regional centre for some 3–4 million in Greater Manchester, Lancashire and Cheshire. The city itself numbers around 450,000. The development of the city's cultural and evening economies has been the policy of Manchester City Council since 1992, following the adoption of the city cultural strategy *Manchester First* (as discussed in Part II). Manchester, the first industrial city, has seen the collapse of traditional textile industries, and has sought to re-create itself as a financial centre and, latterly, a cultural city. During the 1980s, the emergence of café culture, lifestyle bars and clubs was gradual. The local broadcasting celebrity and entrepreneur, Tony Wilson, established the Hacienda and Dry Bar as new culture clubs, though not strictly speaking pavement cafés. Wilson was influenced by a trip to Barcelona where he observed the connections between style, fashion, music and the street life of the city with the emergence of up-market cafés, dance bars and designer bars. The Barcelona bar, Nick Havanna, which was designed in 1986, is believed to have inspired Manchester's Dry Bar. But at the same time during the 1980s – Manchester's police

Figure 3.4   Dry Bar, Manchester
Source: John Montgomery.

chief had an active policy to close down licensed premises in the city centre. With his departure in the late 1980s, Manchester's licensing regime began to relax a little. Dry Bar (Fig. 3.4) was opened in 1989, and a new generation of café-bars was heralded by the opening of Mantos on Canal Street in 1991.

Around this time, Manchester City Council commissioned an "arts and cultural" strategy for the city. The original brief, though somewhat narrowly focused on the performing and visual arts, was extended to included matters such as urban culture, the public realm, street life and café culture. The report contains longish sections on "Investing in Architecture and Urban Spaces" and "Improving Street Life and Urban Culture". The consultants argued that much of Manchester's public life went on behind closed doors, that "there is little life on the streets, the public spaces are obviously under-used ... Neither is there much sense of fun, humour or sophistication ... there is a closing down rather than an opening up of city life".[64] The consultants advised that the city should encourage café culture, its evening economy, re-create

---

64 Urban Cultures Ltd and ppartnerships, *Manchester First: An Arts and Cultural Plan for Manchester*, available from Manchester City Council, 1992, pp. 28–32.

its public realm and develop a policy on city centre licensing, the presumption being "in favour of longer opening hours, more late-night licences and pavement seating". This advice was followed up by a high-level round-table discussion by key opinion formers and leaders in the city, hosted by Manchester City Council. Overnight, almost, opponents to café culture melted away to be replaced by a shared enthusiasm for European Street Life.

Top of the Table: Café Society is Urged to Back Outdoor Style
Café society in Manchester is being urged to try a taste of the great outdoors ... all in the cause of being good Europeans of course ... Councillor Spencer, Chairman of its planning Committee ... is urging more café and bar owners to set up open-air tables. Several have already set up street cafés ... But the town hall is keen to promote the European influence in Manchester with even more permanent tables.
Manchester Evening News, June 1992

This announcement was followed up by the Leader of the Council personally writing to all existing licence holders in the city centre, encouraging them to apply for pavement licences and late night extensions. The licensing magistrates were taken on a tour of the city at night, personally conducted by Councillor Pat Karney, Chairman of the Leisure Services Committee. From late 1992 onwards, the softening of attitudes towards licensing, which was already in train, gathered momentum.

There are now over 500 licensed premises in Manchester city centre, an effective doubling since 1992. During this time the resident population of Manchester has also doubled to around 12,000. Between 100,000 and 150,000 people regularly visit Manchester City Centre on Fridays and Saturdays. Particular concentrations of evening economy activity are found in Peter Street, Castlefield, Canal Street (gay), China Town, Oldham Street (Northern Quarter – see Part V) and the Whitworth Street Corridor. The impact of entertainment venues on residential amenity is considered to be an issue for Manchester City Council, but policy makers believe that these have not yet reached saturation point. Overall planning policy for the city centre is to encourage the development of distinctive areas of mixed use. Policy therefore seeks to encourage both A3 land uses (pubs, cafés, restaurants) and new residences in mixed-use areas.

Under the Use Classes Order, A3 uses include restaurants, bars, cafés, clubs and hot-food takeaways. There is concern across the UK, not only in Manchester, that these categories are too broad in that planning permission for a restaurant or a café can easily "convert" to a fast food outlet or a pub, without any need for further approval. The City Council operates a very strict policy on Entertainments Licensing, licences needing to be renewed every 3–6 months. Breach of conditions – on matters such as the training of door staff, the closure of windows and doors after 11pm, the prohibition of external loud speakers, acoustic double glazing, double door sound vestibules – may lead to licences being withdrawn. Liquor Licensing has been the responsibility of the City Council from January 2005.

Manchester has adopted many innovative policy measures to reduce noise and disturbance. These are administered through conditions attached to new licences, renewals and planning consents. Measures imposed include acoustic glazing, acoustically treated ventilation, acoustic insulation, acoustic lobbies at entrances, sound limiters on amplification equipment, prohibition of external playing of amplified music, restrictions on the hours of operation of outdoor drinking areas, establishment of maximum noise levels, restrictions on hours of opening in sensitive locations, acoustic insulation of new residential units and separate entrances for apartment blocks above licensed premises. Outdoor café seating is encouraged but is only permitted outside licensed premises up to 11pm, 10:30pm on Sundays. Meanwhile, street cleansing times have been rescheduled to occur in early morning, to minimize disruption during trading hours but also when people are asleep. Manchester's tram system runs until around mid-night, at which time night bus services commence. Super-toilets have been installed in Stevensons Square and Piccadilly Gardens

Manchester has adopted a policy of high-profile policing and targeted action on crime "hot-spots". This is backed by referral schemes for alcohol abuse, awards for well-managed premises, leaflet campaigns on safe drinking, advice and assistance for licensed premises. There has also been a clampdown on problem licensed premises through policing and licensing controls.

Manchester's growth-oriented policy on the evening economy is credited, at least in part, with turning what was a somewhat drab and dark city around in the space of ten years. Manchester's aim over the past 12 years has been to encourage a more relaxed and civilized drinking culture, and café society. The "24 Hour City Concept" is still supported but a new emphasis is on making the city centre more family-friendly, including in the early evenings. In this way, the policy is being somewhat temporized as more residents move into the city centre, and in an effort to attract a wider range of clientele. Manchester is a good example of coordinated policies on planning, policing and liquor licensing. Even so, in 2002 there have been renewed calls from local MPs for greater action to reduce drunkenness and violence.

4. FUTURE FORMS OF REGULATION IN THE UK?

For much of the twentieth century there was no national or regional guidance on licensing policy in the UK. Rather, in England and Wales, control over the granting of liquor licenses was exercised by the Licensing Justices, through the Local Magistrates Courts. Licences cover operating conditions, typically opening hours, capacity, fire and safety precautions and control of noise. Liquor licenses were divided into various categories: on-licences, off-licences and restaurant licences. On-licences permit drinking of intoxicating liquor in the premises and have basic permitted hours of 11:00 to 23:00 Monday to Saturday, and 12:00 to 22:30 Sundays. Off-licences permit the sale or supply of alcohol, but no consumption on the premises. Restaurant licences permit the sale or supply of intoxicating liquor only to persons taking substantial meals. Supper Hour Certificates were available for extensions until 01.00 provided food would be served on the premises. Special Hours Certificates for the sale of alcohol until 02:00, could be granted provided a Public Entertainment

Licence (PEL) had been obtained from the Local Authority. Public Entertainment Licences (PELs) were administered by local authorities. The law required annual or occasional licences for public indoor music, dancing or similar entertainment, although pub and restaurant entertainment by up to two live musicians was exempt. (This exemption, granted under Section 182 of the Licensing Act 1964, somewhat paradoxically means that a violin trio would need a licence, but a state of the art sound system might not). Under the Licensing Act 1964, a restaurant wishing to provide a bar had to have a full justices' on-licence. For restaurants selling alcohol only with table meals, there was a special form of licence called a restaurant licence, a restaurant and residential licence (for hotels) or a Part IV licence. Restaurant licences were subject to different criteria from licences for premises whose main function was to sell alcohol.

The main planning legislation in relation to the entertainment industry, the evening economy and licensed premises was the Town and Country Planning (Use Classes) Order 1987 (UCO). The relevant use classes were:

A1. Shops. Including use for the sale of sandwiches or other cold food for consumption off the premises, as well as coffee shops;

A3. Food and Drink. Use for the sale of food or drink consumption in the premises or of hot food for consumption off the premises. This Use Class includes pubs, bars, restaurants, cafés and hot-food takeaways;

D2. Assembly and Leisure. Use a cinema, concert hall, bingo hall, casino, dance hall or sports recreation facilities.

This complicated system came under pressure for reform in the 1990s. By 1999, the Government had identified a series of measures, with the aim of modernizing and integrating the liquor, entertainment, theatre and cinema licences in England and Wales. These proposals were set out in the Licensing White Paper: *Time for Reform: Proposals for the Modernisation of Our Licensing Laws*, published in June 2000. The proposals were intended to provide greater freedom and flexibility for the hospitality and leisure industry. This would offer consumers greater freedom of choice, and in the process boost and diversify the night-time economy of many towns and cities. These broader freedoms, however, would be carefully balanced by tougher powers for the Police, the courts and licensing authorities. The new law would introduce a single integrated scheme for licensed premises to sell alcohol, provide public entertainment or provide refreshments at night. Responsibility for all licensing would be vested in local authorities. The standard permitted hours regime would be replaced by flexible opening hours for licensed premises, with the potential for up to 24-hour opening, seven days a week, subject to the impact on local residents. Premises licences would incorporate operating conditions, for example capacity, opening hours, noise control, egress, public safety and measures to prevent crime and disorder. There would be tough new powers for the Police to deal instantly with violent and disorderly behaviour by closing premises.

Not all interests were happy with these proposals. The Portman Group, an alliance of crime prevention professionals and organizations opposed to alcohol abuse, expressed strong reservations over the government's proposals. The Group publishes regular updates of its *Keeping The Peace Report*,[65] first produced in 1993. This includes regular briefings and updates on the law pertaining to alcohol consumption and public disorder. Topics, for example, include local partnerships to reduce alcohol-related disorder; bylaws prohibiting alcohol consumption in designated places; Pubwatch and Clubwatch schemes; curfews; door-staff registration schemes; training for licencees; designing-out violence; closed-circuit TV; and exclusion Orders. Perhaps the key concern is whether greater licensing flexibility will help reduce alcohol-related public disorder. For example, the British Entertainment and Discotheque Association (BEDA) challenges the assertion that flexible hours will minimize public disorder. Based on research in Scotland, BEDA contends that more flexible licensing hours will increase competition, making alcohol more affordable, thus increasing consumption and the incidence of alcohol-related violence.

The Use Classes Order is also under review. As far as licensed premises are concerned, further distinctions within the Food and Drink (A3) Class have been mooted. The National Planning Forum Working Party on the Use Classes Order has proposed the introduction of three separate subdivisions of the A3 Use Class:

A3(i)   Premises for the sale of food for consumption on the premises;

A3(ii)   Premises for the sale of hot food for consumption off the premises;

A3(iii)   Public houses, wine bars and other establishments for the consumption of drink on the premises.

This would enable local planning authorities – as in Scotland – to distinguish, in the granting of planning permission, between hot-food takeaways and restaurants, between café-bars and restaurants, and might also clarify the ambiguity between sandwich shops and cafés. As far as licensed premises are concerned, a proposal which has been raised by a number of local authorities is the A3(iii) Class might further distinguish between types of licensed premises, that is to say public houses, café bars, wine bars and restaurants.

In 2002 the City of Sunderland commissioned a detailed Policy Statement on Licensed Premises at a time when new investment in Sunderland's City Centre evening economy was growing, and when applications for new licenses and planning permissions were also on the increase. This is presented here as an example of how the future regulation of the night-time city in England might develop.

---

65 Portman Group, *The Keeping-The-Peace Report (A Guide to the Prevention of Alcohol-related Disorder)*, London, 2000.

Sunderland City Council had earlier commissioned a comprehensive study of *Sunderland's City Centre Evening Economy*, in 1999,[66] and which reported in August 2000. This report concluded that Sunderland's Evening Economy, despite recent new investment, was relatively underdeveloped and too narrowly focused on the 18–25 age-group. In particular, there was a lack of diversity, with pubs and clubs dominating but too few restaurants, bistros and café-bars. There was no central focus for the evening economy in Sunderland, but rather activity was concentrated in four separate clusters which ring The Bridges Shopping Centre. The City's major cultural institutions – City Library and Art Gallery, Museum and Winter Gardens, and the Empire Theatre – played too small a role in the evening economy. Finally, problems experienced in the city centre at night include noise, some anti-social behaviour and disturbance to city centre residents.

However, with its large catchment area, strong student base, lively pub and club scene, and the overall attractiveness and compactness of the city centre, and good transport infrastructure (including the Metro), Sunderland was well placed to sustain new investment in the city centre evening economy. The *Sunderland City Centre Evening Economy Study* proposed a set of objectives for developing and managing the evening economy in Sunderland. These would help broaden the appeal of the City Centre Evening Economy and attract a wider range of users and visitors to the City Centre at night, allowing Sunderland to compete more effectively with Newcastle to retain a greater proportion of monies spent on evening leisure and entertainment in the city. This would be achieved by building on the strengths of the existing evening economy locations or "clusters" within Sunderland City Centre in such a way as to improve the quality, diversity and choice of the Sunderland evening economy "offer". These themes were taken up in a more detailed policy on city centre licensed premises.

The overall aim of the *Statement on Licensed Premises*[67] was to manage and develop licensed premises and the wider evening economy in Sunderland city centre in order that it should contribute positively to the city centre's overall attractiveness, vitality and viability. This was not a question of simply allowing the evening economy to grow solely according to market principles, but to set a direction for growth which would improve quality, choice and diversity; minimize problems associated with the city centre at night; differentiate between different parts of the city centre; and maintain a balance between the evening economy and the day-time use of the city centre. The central premise of the Policy Statement was that this could best be achieved by having a coordinated policy on land use planning, liquor licensing, entertainments' licensing – and taking into account issues of policing and safety – in relation to licensed premises in the city centre.

---

66 Urban Cultures Ltd and Colin Buchanan and Partners, *Sunderland Evening Economy Study*, unpublished consultancy report prepared for Sunderland City Council, 2000.

67 Urban Cultures Ltd, *Sunderland Statement on Licensed Premises*, unpublished consultancy report prepared for Sunderland City Council, 2002.

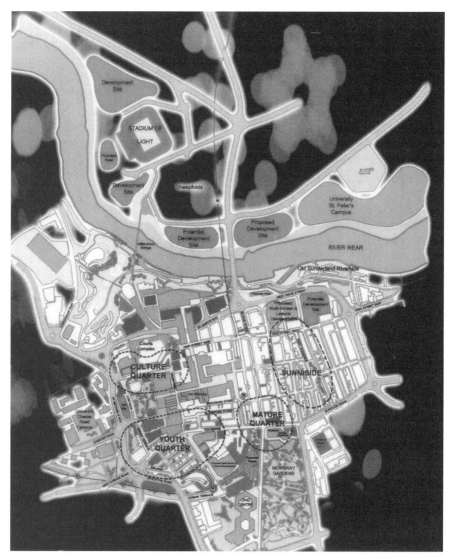

Figure 3.5   Sunderland: Evening Economy Quarters
Source: by kind permission of the City of Sunderland.

In this way, the new general policy for licensed premises in Sunderland City Centre is:

> General land use policy for the City Centre in relation to the evening economy is to encourage competition and new investment in evening economy uses; but to do so within an agreed framework including upper limits on the numbers and sizes of licensed premises.

Policy is directed towards improving quality, diversity and choice in the evening economy, in such a way as to contribute positively to the overall balance of land uses within the City Centre. It is an important land use policy objective for the City Centre as a whole to balance day-time and evening uses, so as to avoid streets and areas becoming deadened at certain times. Conditions attached to planning permissions will govern matters such as opening and closing times, noise reduction and improvements to the overall environment of the City Centre at night. Policy will control the location and operation of licensed premises adjacent to residential developments within the City Centre. Land use planning policy for Sunderland City Centre is to differentiate sub-areas within the City Centre in the interests of promoting greater distinctiveness and identity. This applies both to the day-time use of the City Centre and the evening economy. Four such areas have been identified in relation to the evening economy: the Theatre Quarter, the Cultural Quarter, the Night Life Quarter and Sunniside.[68]

Rather than blanket policies for the management of the evening economy across Sunderland City Centre, these sub-area designations are intended to strengthen the individual identities of important places within Sunderland. It was intended that, by identifying the character of each area or place during the evening as well as the day, the regulation and management of the evening economy would vary from place to place. Within the City Centre Evening Economy Policy Area, four defined zones were identified within which varying policy regimes for licensed premises would apply (Fig. 3.5).

The Theatre Quarter is bounded by the Inner Ring Road (St Michael's Way) to the North and East, Chester Road to the South and The Bridges Shopping Centre to the East. This area includes the Empire Theatre, and there has been recent and new investment in bars, one or two restaurants and a new hotel. The area is an established part of the City Centre evening economy, but it is in this area that most complaints from residents over late-night behaviour are generated. Policy is for the Theatre Quarter to evolve over time to become a distinctive part of Sunderland's evening economy and as a stronger place in its own right. This involves encouraging licensed premises that complement the Empire Theatre – that is to say restaurants, wine bars and cafés – so that the area becomes identified with theatre-going and more relaxed eating and drinking. Late-night bars, music pubs and clubs will not be encouraged in this location, and existing venues of this type will be encouraged to adapt or relocate.

The Culture Quarter is bounded by Station Street and the railway line to the west, Mowbray Park to the south, Athenaeum Street to the North and Frederick Street/Toward Road to the east. The defined area designation is derived in large part from the presence of the Museum, Winter Gardens, Art Gallery and Library, all located within a short walk of each other. In addition to their day-time roles, some of these important venues remain open on at least some evenings, and they have been identified as playing a potentially important role in developing greater diversity within Sunderland's City Centre Evening Economy. There is also the possibility that a new

---

68 Ibid.

live music venue might be developed in this area. Policy is for the Culture Quarter to develop a distinctive identity derived in large part from the inter-relationship between cultural uses and activities in the area and appropriate evening economy uses. This involves encouraging licensed premises that complement the Library and Gallery, and Museum and Winter Gardens, and thereby appeal to a wide range of age groups, including families. The policy presumption is in favour of outlets selling food as well as drinks, so that people attending concerts or gallery openings might also dine out. A limited number of venues providing live music will be permitted. It is envisaged that all age groups would feel comfortable within this area, older people as well as families with young children. Licensed premises uses which would normally be permitted include restaurants, wine bars, and café-bars offering hot meals. Uses which normally would not be permitted include night clubs, late night bars, disco bars and any additional full-on licensed premises. Licensed premises in this area would normally be expected to occupy up to 50 sq m at the ground floor or basement level. This is consistent with maintaining the existing urban grain of street frontages, doorways and windows. It is also important to prevent over-large licensed premises from dominating their immediate local environments.

Sunniside is bounded by Frederick and John Street to the West, Borough Road to the South, Villiers Street to the east and High Street West to the north. Sunniside as a distinguishable urban neighbourhood dates from the 1790s. A substantial part of the area was master planned during the later Georgian period, and much evidence of this is clearly visible today along John Street, Fredrick Street, Foyle Street and Fawcett Street. The area was a thriving business location and contained a significant residential community, along with a variety of public services and community buildings. A number of local landmark buildings of historic or architectural merit remain, including churches, the museum, the Elephant Tea Rooms and the Athenaeum Buildings. Sunniside has adapted and evolved over many decades, since the late eighteenth century. Undoubtedly, the area has experienced a difficult period over the past ten years as activity levels and investment have dropped. Although these changes were driven by competition from new business locations, there have also been changes in investor and occupier demand. The upshot is that there is now some loss of confidence and uncertainty over the future of Sunniside, which the area regeneration strategy seeks to address. The *Sunniside Area Regeneration Strategy*[69] proposes that Sunniside should become a "dynamic and distinctive mixed use quarter within Sunderland City Centre". In particular, the area should be: a recognized business location primarily for small businesses in the professions, media and creative activities; aniche retail area, with an emphasis on design, fashion, art, antiques and lifestyle products; a lively and varied restaurant and café quarter; and a desirable, centrally located living area offering a mix of apartments on upper floors, town houses and lofts. Policy for licensed premises in Sunniside is to support the area's regeneration as a mixed-use office, residential and retail area, including

---

69 Urban Cultures Ltd and David Lock Associates, *Sunniside Area Regeneration Strategy*, unpublished consultancy report prepared for Sunderland City Council, 2001.

a limited number of restaurants and wine bars to underpin a distinctive but modest local evening economy. The evening economy is but one part of the area regeneration of Sunniside, and must be balanced against other uses, particularly residential. Accordingly, strict control will be maintained over the location, types, numbers and sizes of licensed premises across Sunniside.

The Night Life Quarter is bounded by Stockton Road to the west, Cowan Terrace and the Civic Centre to the south, Waterloo Place and the railway line to the east, and The Bridges Shopping Centre to the north. It is centred on Park Lane and Holmeside, with significant clusterings of evening economy uses at Mary Street, Green Terrace and Albion Place Within this defined area, there are currently some 20 licensed premise, of varying types, including restaurants, café-bars, public houses, modern and themed bars and night clubs. Permitted developments still to be implemented include a public house/restaurant/club complex at the Galen building on Green Terrace, whilst development sites in the area include the former ABC Cinema. There are also around a dozen fast-food takeaways within this area. This means that the area already contains the largest concentration of evening economy activities in Sunderland. As well as its role within the City Centre evening economy, the area is an important route connecting the transport interchange and Civic Centre to The Bridges and the City Centre as a whole. Streets such as Derwent Street, Olive Street and Vine Place are important secondary shopping streets, offering a range of outlets not available elsewhere within Sunderland – art supplies, a doll's house shop and others. This area has benefited from significant improvements to street lighting, pedestrianization (of Park Lane) and the development of the bus station and metro station. There is also an established taxi-rank. There are very few residents living within this area. Northumbria Police advise that, in terms of public disorder and anti-social behaviour, the configuration of streets in the is area, the street-widths, lighting and the existing transport infrastructure make this area relatively easy to police. Policy is that this area should be better managed and regulated to become a more successful night-time environment. However, this should be balanced against its day-time economy and sense of place. Broadly speaking, this implies that shopping and having tea or coffee are the important activities by day (as well as walking about), but that more clubs and bars might be encouraged at night. Policy for licensed premises in the Night Life Quarter is designed to allow a higher concentration of evening economy uses and especially late-night activities within a manageable area. This will assist in the ongoing management of evening economy activity and associated social behaviour, with regard in particular to policing, transport and street lighting. By concentrating late-night activity in this area, residential amenity in other parts of the city centre will be protected. Within the Night Life Quarter there will be no restrictions on the types of licensed premises permitted, up to an agreed saturation level, and subject to conditions on noise and other environmental considerations. Of all the Sub-area regimes for regulating licensed premises, that for the Night Life Quarter is the least tightly drawn. All form of licensed premises will be permitted in this area, subject to capacity restrictions. These apply to individual buildings and the egress thereof, but also to the concept of "saturation" – that is to say the ability

Figure 3.6   Strategy to Tackle All Night Disorder (STAND)
Source: by kind permission of Colchester Town Partnership.

of the area as a whole to cope with large numbers of people at night. There would be no size restrictions on licensed premises within this defined area, although most premises would be unlikely to exceed 100 sq m at the ground floor level.

In this way, Sunderland's policy of differential licensing applies between these areas, so that licensed premises of varying types will be permitted and will operate to different trading times. This is intended to support the emerging distinctive identity of places within the city centre, and to assist in the management of the evening economy as a whole. For this to succeed, a clear delineation of types of licensed premises is being applied, so that there will in future be a real distinction between public houses, bars, café bars and bistros, wine bars and restaurants.

Sunderland's policy regime regarding the evening economy, liquor licensing and the problems associated with alcohol consumption in the city at night is probably the most sophisticated in the UK currently. Other examples include the *Strategy to Tackle All Night Disorder (STAND)* a Home Office funded pilot study of Colchester in Essex.[70] This study recommends much stronger enforcement of the law of public nuisance, indecency and disturbance – a low tolerance approach to anti-social and violent behaviour – backed by policies to grow a more diverse evening economy, voluntary agreements between licensed premises over such matters as low-priced drink promotions, exclusion orders and door-staff, as well as measures to improve the city centre's lighting and general environment at night (Fig. 3.6). Taken as a whole, and although the precise mix applied will of course vary from place to place, policy on licensed premises, the evening and night-time economies and public disorder may very well evolve to reflect the policies and measures adopted in Sunderland and Colchester.

5. TIME, MORALITY AND THE LONG WAVE

In this Part III I have argued that considerations of micro-time, how it is managed, how it relates to various public forms of entertainment and their regulation, and how activities occur in city space-time, all of these are important considerations in the cities of the past and those in the coming period. This essentially boils down to the questions of how and whether cities should seek to control or direct "entertainment activities", the evening economy, the city of the night. It can be argued that a city's night-time offer is part of its competitive advantage, or otherwise. This has led policy-makers in the UK to press for a de-regulation of night-life, and especially liquor licensing, in an effort to achieve a more cosmopolitan evening economy and public forms of social life.

However, as we have seen, it is important to distinguish between the urban public realm as places and spaces where public social life is possible, as opposed to the process and character of public social life itself. They are connected and each influences the other, but they are not the same thing. If this is true, then it may be

---

70 Urban Culture Ltd, *A Strategy to Tackle All Night Disorder*, unpublished consultancy report prepared for Colchester Borough Council, 2003.

possible to stimulate public social life by re-creating the urban public realm. But the extent to which this occurs will depend on the existence and removal of controls and other influences on how, in specific places and times, public social life occurs. The danger is, of course, that freeing up the possibilities for less restricted public social life in the urban public realm leads not to democratic gatherings and high intellectual discourse, but to the exercise of the pleasures of the body: sex, drink and prostitution. If "city air" makes us free to sit around and talk philosophy, it also makes us free to enjoy individual pleasures. This is the inherent attraction for some, and danger for others, of café culture and the more active public social life it represents.

Much the same point is made by Oosterman in his investigation of café culture in Dutch cities, who argues that, by seeing public space and the events which occur within it as contributing to "social organization, the fulfilment of societal needs",[71] planners and urban designers and urban sociologists ignore the perspective of the everyday user. Oosterman argues that, far from being in public space to participate in a wider, perceived by urban professionals as laudable, social activity of "citizenship", individuals congregate in public places to indulge personal and private interests. He notes that a trebling of cafés and bars in Utrecht during the late 1980s and early 1990s brought an upsurge in complaints over the blocking of streets, noise and dirt. Apart from drinking, relaxing and enjoying the sunshine, people enjoy a number of activities which derive from the public character of the setting: watching the world go by, being "entertained by street life", bumping into people one knows, showing off, seeing and being seen, meeting strangers, flirting and perhaps (though not always) a sexual encounter. The "best" cafés were those where the street life around them is heterogeneous, but that each café can be distinguished by special characteristics such as the age and consumption patterns and lifestyles of its clientele. These observations led Oosterman to conclude that

> it is not the meeting of strangers that is important, but the spectacle provided by them. Cultural and personal differences are neither left at home nor bridged [in public spaces] ... On the contrary, some public spaces, like the streets where one strolls past the cafés, are used to show personality, to show differences in culture, style, behaviour and taste.[72]

The secret to public social life in cities is, therefore, not so much to be public in public but private in public. Or both. On the plus side, the café culture phenomenon can be seen to bring several benefits to city life. Pavement cafés are places to meet people. They are also relatively relaxed, and there is more choice over what to eat or drink, and less expectation that alcohol will be consumed. Perhaps for this reason, pavement cafés tend to be more elegant and sophisticated than pubs, and usually less rowdy. This means that cafés are an important extension of choice in city life. It is noticeable that women seem to be more comfortable on their own or meeting other women in café-bars as opposed to pubs. Pavement cafés are places where, because

---

71 Oosterman, J., "Welcome to the Pleasure Dome: Play and Entertainment in Urban Public Space", *Built Environment*, 18 (2) 1992.

72 Ibid., p. 162.

of greater interaction with the street and improved visibility, one can sit and watch the world go by. This is surely one of the delights of urban life, and one which was almost lost to English cities. The simple fact is that cafés attract people who want to see and be seen by other people, even if all this means is strolling up and down the street. By performing this function, pavement cafés help to increase the natural surveillance of streets, simply because more people are around and watching over the streets and public spaces. This means that streets with pavement cafés tend to feel safer and are more likely to be used by a wider cross-section of people than streets with no cafés and no natural surveillance. Not only are cafés less likely to be dominated by rowdies and "lager louts", their presence might help to overcome the dominance of English pub culture, so that over time a greater mix of people of much more varied age-groups are to be found throughout the day and in the evening.

Research has also shown that for certain economic sectors-media, advertising, fashion, the performing arts-cafés and restaurants and bars are places where a great deal of business is transacted. If city policy makers wish to stimulate the economic development of these creative sectors, then the people who work in them and make things happen must have places to meet. Otherwise, creative people will vote with their feet. Of course, it is not just media types and pop stars who meet in cafés, but people from all walks of life including key opinion formers and decision makers in most cities. Cafés and bars and restaurants have arguably become sites for the all-important networking so necessary to transactional life in the post-Fordist, flexible, core-periphery economy. Increasingly, cafés and restaurants are places where business gets done (see Part I). Finally, and perhaps most important, in the modern city where many of the old functions of urban public space have been removed – doing business at the Corn Exchange, finding out what the latest news is, checking the time on the town clock – café culture and its attendant people-watching is one of the few urban activities remaining which require streets and public spaces. This means that café culture is perhaps one of the few antidotes to the fully privatized public realm, the sealed-off communities and fortress mentality that so many commentators fear.

The hope is that if people are allowed to exercise greater choice, they will also exercise responsibility. Sadly, this does not seem to be working, and it seems likely that regulation of the night-life of cities, in the UK at least, will need to become more rather than less sophisticated. In part, this reflects a recurring struggle over the night-time in English towns and cities – or more precisely between participants in night-life and officialdom. At various points in time, new laws and by-laws have been introduced in efforts to control or restrict night-time activities, because of attendant problems of drunkenness and rowdyism.

Robert Beckman[73] argues that cultural characteristics and values reflect consumer mentality, especially in the final stages of an upswing. He argues that the West rejected previous forms of authority in the late eighteenth century (the American and French revolutions), and in the late mid-nineteenth century (atheism versus the Church). The 1920s witnessed a surge in personal freedom with the development of

---

73 Beckman, R., *Downwave* (London: Pan Books, 1983).

Table 3.1 Night-life in English Cities, 1660–2004

Dates	Period	'Entertainment' Policy Shift
Late 17th century and Early 1700s	Queen Anne	The Royal Proclamation on Immorality 1698. Society for the Reform of Manners Gentlemen's clubs appear but must close by 10pm. Bath amusement facilities close at 11.00 pm. Campaign against 'obscenity in the theatres'.
1715–1730s	Early Georgian	Cheap gin available from 1720s. ''Tis noise and nonsense are their dear delight, and stupid pleasures drown the drunken night.' Hogarth's England, gaming houses, bagnios. Adultery becomes fashionable, as does upper class homosexuality. Bear-baiting, wife-selling and drinking amongst the working classes.
1740s to 1760s	George III	The rise of Methodism. Period of social reform of prisons, hospitals (Guy's), rise of Freemasonary.
1760s–1830s	Regency	Mrs Cornelly's first night-club opens in Soho Square 1762. Private theatricals: Music clubs, song and drama clubs, literary clubs. Rise of the gin palaces, song and supper houses (entertainment provided to encourage eating and drinking), increase in prostitution. 'Poses Plastique.' Abolition of duty on spirits in 1825; theatres open until midnight; casinos open from 1820. Growing interest in sado-masochism.
1840–1880s	Victorian	1832 Beer Acts introduced to cut alcohol consumption. Women allowed in restaurants. Food and drink not allowed in theatres. Rise of the Temperance Movement. 'Age of the theatre', rise of the music halls; dinner commonly eaten at 5.00 pm; Savoy Theatre opens; The Strand as a night-time promenade. Meals have fewer courses, emergence of winter gardens.
1890s and 1900s	Edwardian	Naughty nineties. 'What the Butler Saw'; night-club tableaux; dance halls; 'short skirts'; homosexual sub-culture; rising alcohol consumption. Bars stay open until 00.30 am.
1914 to 1918	First World War	Black-out measures restrict lighting, dinner hour now 8.30 pm. Restaurants have meatless days. Pub opening hours reduced: 6.30 pm to 9.30 pm.
1920s and early 1930s	Inter-war	Installation of electric lights widespread. Palais De Danse; Cabaret dance halls; Swing; Cinema; Supper and Dance Clubs; Popular Jazz; Women wearing more make-up.
1950s and 1970s	Baby boom	Post-war drabness later replaced by rock and roll; the 'teenager'. The return of fashion; R&B; pop music; Swinging London. Growth of night clubs; also strip clubs (e.g. Soho). Pub opening hours 5.00 pm to 10.00 pm. Closed on Sundays.
1970s–1980s	Thatcher/Major	Sunday opening allowed. Pubs open 11.00 am to 11.00 pm. Period of loss of licensed premises in many cities. Relaxation of licensing hours in 1992. Multiplex cinemas, chain restaurants and nightclubs. contraction of banking accompanied by development of super pubs, out-of-town leisure complexes, fast-food restaurants.
1990s	Blair	Increase in licensed premises allowed from mid 1990s. Licensing White Paper 2001; Licensing Act 2003; Provisions take full effect from January 2005.

Source: John Montgomery, based on Thomas Burke 1941. Also Thomson 1993.

the self (Freudian psychology) and syncopation (jazz). The late 1950s gave rise to rock and roll and "the teenager", followed in the 1960s by the "permissive society". Beckman argues that "fashion, music, literature, theatre and dance all fall under the influence of the upwave.[74] He notes particularly the "action-music and action-dances" of the 1950s (jive); 1920s (Charleston); and 1860s (waltz). Beckman also proposes that women's fashions are closely linked to upwaves and downwaves, particularly in relation to hemlines, necklines, and whether backs are covered or bare. Fashions such as low-cut bodices and accentuated *derrieres* were evident in the fifteenth century, in Elizabethan England and at the time of the Reformation (1660). In between times, necklines were higher and hemlines lower. In the most recent upswing we can see the rise of hemlines in the 1950s, the miniskirt in the 1960s, hot pants, glam and punk rock. By the time the downswing had produced evident economic crisis – the early 1980s – fashions were more formal once again. In the early years of the 21st century women are once again revealing more – this time the lower backs, abdomens and hips, as well as legs and breasts.

Beckman's argument linking fashion and wave cycles is really a discussion of public morality. For it can be argued that when women's fashions are more revealing, public morality is also less constrained by social mores. If this is true, then we should find some correlation between upswings and downswings, and such matters as changes to liquor licensing, prostitution and late night activities. Using Thomas Burke's history of the *English City at Night*, I have been able to plot changes in key aspects of legislation covering public morality, in relation to the long waves of economic activity (Table 3.1). The results are, at first sight, surprisingly, and there appears to be no correlation whatsoever between upswings and downswings and laws on public morality. That is until I realized that legislation would most likely *follow* a period of liberalization to which calls for improved public morality could respond. In this way, throughout English history clamp-downs on city night-life have tended to follow a period of relative relaxation, which normally occurs during the second part of an up-wave. For example, entertainment activities were subject to moral control under Cromwell, while the late 1600s were a reaction to the "excesses" of Charles II's reign (in England at least).

The reigns of William and Mary and Queen Anne were periods of more strict regulation. This was marked by closing times being imposed on taverns and restaurants, the rise of the coffee-houses and gardens for the relatively harmless pursuit of promenading. Theatre performances started at 6.00 p.m. Similarly, in the mid-1750s, the excesses of the previous age were declared as "noise and nonsense", and Beau Nash declared that all entertainment in Bath should finish by 11.00 p.m. The late eighteenth century brought concerns over public morality, "bare-knuckle fights", the opening of gaming houses. This was the age of the Prince Regent (later George IV) – the song dinner – with the Prince himself being a notable hedonist, dividing his time between London and spa-towns such as Brighton.

---

74 Ibid., p. 42.

During the early nineteenth century, by contrast, women's fashions were modest, and there was the rise of the Gentlemen's Club in Piccadilly and Pall Mall. No women were permitted in the clubs, and they were closed by 10.00 p.m. The next upswing began around 1840, and this was accompanied by the rise of the London pub alongside the gin palaces, the opening of the casinos, theatres remaining open until midnight and the advent of "Haymarket Actresses" or "Piccadilly Whores". Visitors to London would comment on the extent of public drunkenness: Verlaine (1873) remarked that Londoners were "noisy as ducks and eternally drunk"; Dostoevsky (1862) that "everyone is in a hurry to drink himself into insensibility".[75] The 1870s also saw the rise of temperance societies while "respectable" tradespeople and the middle classes preferred the music hall to theatre. The Temperance Movement gained influence during the late 19th century. Later, the 1890s witnessed the rise of the Savoy Theatre, the Café Royal, later pub and restaurant opening times, supper and dance clubs. This all came to an end with the imposition of restrictive pub opening times as part of the 1914–1919 war effort. It seems that the 1920s were the end of the upswing (as fashions and music indicate) yet were also a time when public morality refused to accept controls over dress, dancing and drinking.

In Britain (and Australia) the restrictions on opening hours were largely maintained during the 1940s and the 1950s. Pubs were not allowed to open on Sundays, so that men would often walk into the next Parish so they could drink as *bona fide* travellers. Even in the 1960s and 1970s pub opening times were set at 5.00 p.m. to 10.00 p.m. In Australia, the infamous "six o'clock swill" (the pubs were open for an hour each day!) remained in force until the late 1970s. Liquor licensing was however liberalized in the USA during this time, and to some extent in England in the early 1990s. It seems that for the last upswing the moralists managed to retain control over licensed premises, if very little else!

It would also seem that for Britain at least there is a relationship between the long waves and legislation designed to control public morality. Typically, it seems bursts of "excess" are followed by the emergence of more modesty in dress, less "boisterous" forms of behaviour and restrictions on the opening hours of entertainment activities. It seems, then, that the current relaxation of liquor licensing in England is following a pattern going back centuries. The periods of less controlled public morality occur during an upswing: the 1790s, 1870s, 1920s, 1960s (see Table 3.2). Legislative attempts to influence public morality occur at end of such a period, that is to say with the onset of the downswing: the 1830s, 1890s, 1930s and 1980s.

Oliver Thomson argues[76] that human history displays an oscillation between the virtues of self-restraint and family virtues, against "hedonistic self-gratification and abandonment of discipline". He muses that these swings may be due to the reaction of one generation against its predecessor at its simplest, but perhaps also a "... tendency to move towards extremes... to the point where a reverse swing becomes inevitable". He also argues – and this seems compelling – that the periods of strictest

---

75 Ackroyd, P., *London: The Biography*, 2000, p. 354.
76 Thomson, O., *A History of Sin* (Edinburgh: Cannongate Press, 1993).

Table 3.2 Long-wave Modes of Production Showing the Regulation of Entertainment and Public Morality

	Long Wave Cycle	Mode of Production	Entertainment Types	Regulation
1.	1781–1840	Late mercantile, late Georgian and Regency	Rakes, gambling dens and night clubs, gin palaces Prostitution, casinos, public houses, song and supper houses, Pose Plastique	Removal of duty on spirits 1825, followed by Beer Acts 1832. By the late 1830s a new morality was in place.
2.	1840–1890	Early mass production, Victorian	Theatre, music halls, Savoy Theatre, Café Royale	Rise of the Temperance Movement. Gradual increase in range of entertainment types. Naughty nineties.
3.	1890–1946	Mass production, World Wars,	Supper and dance clubs, cinema, jazz, cabaret, electric media	War Munitions Act 1916. Jazz age, 1920s, modern dress emerges, alcohol consumption rises. New morality emerges in 1930s.
4.	1946–2004	Flexible specialisation; rise of consumer goods	Popular music and fashion, liberalisation of society	*Lady Chatterley's Lover* Trial, sexual revolution, Abortion Act 1967, Licensing White Paper 2001.
5.	2004–2060	Personalised consumption	Cult of hedonism?	Anti-social Behaviour Orders and calls for National Identity Cards. A new morality?

control tended to be accompanied by everyday suffering or "man-made misery". To this we might add a fall in creativity. By contrast, much great art occurred during the Renaissance, the Restoration, during the Naughty Nineties and in the jazz age.

Even so, as Thomson argues, the end point of such periods of hedonism tend to be "... characterized by an aimless and never-quite-satisfied search for personal pleasure". Eventually, people become bored and cynical, as was the case of the Romantics in the mid 19th century. One response to this is towards self-restraint and greater virtue or even the return of manners; the other is further transgressions.

Perhaps the only sensible approach is to seek less extremes in morality, neither too self-indulgent nor too puritanical, a sort of moral "third way". The problem is that the waves in public morality appear to be linked to waves in material production and wealth creation, as Beckman has argued. This is probably why a period of liberalization is usually always followed by a marked, as opposed to a gradual, tightening of moral regulation. The immediate next few years may well be characterized by a further loosening of moral values amongst the majority (junk food, cheap television, alcoholic binges, foul language, public entertainments close to obscenity) while a minority will argue for restraint, decency and manners, at least in public. Meanwhile, the new left puritans will continue in attempts to ban smoking and drinking.

The likelihood is that during the coming up-wave it will be difficult to maintain what are perceived to be old moral values. This means that we have many years more of "falling standards" of behaviour, public "indecency", women behaving as badly as men, displays of body parts and a general coursening of public life. This may already be seen in Russia and China, as well as the western democracies. For it does appear that the liberalization being proposed in Britain is a hangover from an earlier time. It should have happened in the 1970s and 1980s. This might explain why relatively innocuous-seeming measures such as extending pub opening times are being accompanied by unexpectedly worrisome problems of anti-social behaviour.

O tempora, O mores.

The Art of Place-making and Urban Design

One of the great paradoxes of city development over the past 100 years or so, is that those urban professionals – planners, surveyors, architects – who have set out to "save" the cities have often achieved the opposite. From before the fifteenth century cities had developed – with local cultural and vernacular variations – along traditional patterns of human scale, street grids, building lines and public spaces. This would change from the 1890s onwards, as I intend to demonstrate in Part IV. The format for this section of the book is broadly similar to the earlier sections. We begin with a review of the history of town planning, suburbanization and city development in the twentieth century, considering along the way the rapid house-building of the 1890s, 1920s, 1930s, 1950s, early 1970s and the late 1990s. We shall learn how cities changed during this time, at least partly in line with new theories of town planning and modernism allied to new building and transport technologies.

The relatively new field of urban design is a paradigm shift in the way we think of the design and layout of cities, usually in the interests of improvements in vitality, economic performance or environmental condition – or some combination of all three. I then will demonstrate how urban design principles can be applied to the making and remaking of urban environments. One particular theme will be explored in detail: the importance of designing public spaces for public social interaction – the public realm. A further question surrounds the character and the built form of successful cities in the coming 50 years or so, that is during the coming long wave of economic and cultural development. The cities of the future will need to balance tradition and modernity, sense of place and image, economic dynamism and quality of life.

A NEW KIND OF MENTAL MAP?

The map of Lima, pinned down with thumbtacks, covered part of the wall. It now had more coloured patches, a number of strange symbols drawn in red pencil, and different initials labelling each district of the city. I asked him what these marks and letters stood for. He nodded, with one of his little mechanical smiles that always bore traces of a sense of self-satisfaction and a sort of kindly condescension. Settling back in his chair, he delivered himself of one of his perorations: 'I work from life; my writings are firmly rooted in reality, as the grapevine is rooted in the vinestock. That's why I need this. I want to know whether that world there is or is not as I have represented it." He was pointing to the map, and I leaned closer to see if I could figure out what he was trying to get across to me. The initials were hermetic; as far as I could tell, they referred to no recognizable institution or person. The only thing that was quite clear was that he had singled out the altogether dissimilar districts of Mirafores and San Isidro, La Victoria and El Callao, by drawing red circles around them. I told him I didn't understand at all, and asked him to explain.

'It's very simple,' he replied impatiently, in the tone of a parish priest. 'What is most important is the truth, which is always art, as lies, on the other hand, never are, or only very rarely. I need to know if Lima is really the way I have shown it on the map. Do the two capital A's, for example, fit Isidro? Is it in fact a district where one finds Ancient Ancestry, Affluent Aristocracy?'

He stressed the initial A's of these words with an intonation meant to suggest that 'It is only the blind who cannot see the bright light of day.' He had classified the districts of Lima according to their social status. But the curious thing was the type of descriptive adjectives he had used, the nature of his nomenclature. In certain cases he had hit the nail squarely on the head, and in others his labels were completely arbitrary. I granted, for instance, that the initials MCLPH (Middle Class Liberal Professions Housewives) fitted the Jesus Maria section of Lima, but cautioned him that it was rather unfair to sum up the districts of La Victoria and El Porvenir under the dreadful label BFHH (Bums Fairies Hoodlums Hetaerae), and extremely questionable to reduce El Callao to SFS (Sailors Fishermen Sambos) or El Cercado and El Augustino to FDFWFI (Female Domestics Factory Workers Farmhands Indians).

'It's not a scientific classification but an artistic one,' he informed me ... . 'It's not all the people who live in each district, but only the flashiest, the most immediately noticeable, those who give each section of the city its particular flavour and colour. If a person is a gynaecologist, he should live in that part of town where he belongs, and the same goes for a police sergeant.'

Extract from *Aunt Julia and the Script Writer*, by Mario Vargos Llosa,
Faber and Faber, 1982, pp. 48 and 49

1. STORIES, STONES AND MEMORIES

The city, however, does not tell its past, but contains it like the lines of a hand, written in the corners of the streets, the gratings of the windows, the banisters of the steps, the antennae of the lightning rods, the poles of the flags, every segment marked in turn with scratches, indentations, scrolls.

Italo Calvino[1]

In a MORI survey of "Attitudes Towards Heritage" commissioned by English Heritage in the summer of 2000 respondents were asked to define what they understood by the terms "heritage" and "the historic environment". Although initial perceptions of heritage were low, when prompted most people (over 50% in each case) agreed that the historic environment is made up of:

---

1   Calvino, I., *Invisible Cities* (London: Vintage, 1997).

Historic Buildings and Palaces	74%
Ancient Monuments	69%
Historic Gardens and Parks	66%
Local History	57%
Battlefields	56%
Industrial Archaeology	55%
Conservation of Buildings and Monuments	51%
History	51%
Art Galleries and Museums	50%
Archaeology	50%

A sizeable minority of people also agreed that the following are part of the historic environment:

National Parks	46%
Towns and Villages	45%
Canals and Rivers	44%
Landscapes	42%

This would suggest that people attach importance to places – towns, villages, landscapes – as a whole, as well as to particular historical features within them. Most people would agree that all of the above should be protected from demolition or redevelopment.

But in some cases, history itself is contested, and so too is the meaning attached to events and places. For some, the great ancestral homes symbolize class divisions in English society (and so too might the churches and cathedrals). Others simply do not value places as having historical relevance to them at all. For some, Trafalgar Square commemorates Nelson's defeat of the French navy, but for others its importance is as a gathering place for political rallies and demonstrations. These differing views of history are part subjective and part objective, but no less keenly held for that. There is no simple way out of this conundrum, no complete consensus on what the past is: historical dates and reported events? the documented past? the remembered past? the mythical past?[2] Does it matter whether Robin Hood or King Arthur really existed, if we all take some meaning from their reputed adventures? Is the Battle of Britain, or Gallipoli, only important to those who were there? Even so, it should be possible to reach agreement on the fundamentally important elements of the past, allowing scope for differing views of what particular events mean to us as individuals and groups within society. This implies the need for a baseline conception of the history we hold in importance. The present – and the future – are history in the making. But the importance of the past is that it tells us why we exist. The historic environment is the most visible connection to the past.

---

2   Grant, R., *History, Tradition and Modernity*, in Barnett, A. and Scruton, R. (eds), *Town and Country* (London: Vintage, 1999).

What are those blue remembered hills,
What spires, what farms are those?

That is the land of lost content,
I see it shining plain,
The happy highways where I went
And cannot come again.

A.E. Housman

Landscapes play an important role in both shaping and sustaining cultural values within societies.[3] The Housman quote is important not only because the hills are remembered, but because the poet is identifying with a place he remembers. If not who he has become, at least they help define who he was and where he came from. This occurs for all cultures including, for example, the Aborigine tribes of Australia whose history is represented and encompassed by Songlines across the land.[4] The upshot is that people identify with landscapes as representing their society and belonging to themselves and society. In England's case, most people carry with them mental images of landscapes which sum up Englishness: the White Cliffs of Dover, the Lakes, the Yorkshire Dales, the Vale of White Horse, Exmoor, Salisbury Plain, the Peak District. This is overlain with mental maps of landscapes closer to where people live – and especially for urban dwellers who might visit the countryside infrequently: the Fens, the North Downs, Warwickshire, Cheshire, the Malvern Hills, Shropshire. Within the cities themselves, people tend to have strong views on the importance of retaining parklands and places such as Hampstead Heath or Primrose Hill.

None of this is perhaps too surprising, yet the depth of feeling or affinity with the remembered landscapes of England is strongly held, particularly amongst urban dwellers. Or at least those urban dwellers – the majority it appears – who aspire to live in the country. For it is also true that the English tend to hold a romanticized view of the country as some kind of arcadian idyll, and this is reflected in much of the art, literature and poetry of the nineteenth century. The countryside is not at all like this any more, if it ever was. W. G. Hoskins'[5] classic text shows how, from earliest times, the English landscape has been created by human activity and cultivation, and so very little of what we see today is "natural". As with the cities, and with the past itself, the landscapes we hold dear are a combination of myth and reality. The romanticized conception of the rural contains within it a large element of nostalgia – the "land of lost content" in Housman's words. There is a sense, a culture perhaps, of loss and regret for what once was, or is imagined to have been. This is perhaps best summed up by Laurie Lee in Cider With Rosie:[6]

---

3   Cosgrove, D. and Daniels, S. (eds), *The Iconography of Landscape* (Cambridge: 1993).

4   Chatwin, B., *The Songlines* (London: Jonathan Cape, 1987).

5   Hoskins, W.G., *The Making of the English Landscape*, revised edition with notes by Christopher Taylor (London: 1988).

6   Lee, L., *Cider With Rosie* (London: 1959).

The last days of my childhood were also the last days of the village...I belonged to that generation which saw, by chance, the end of a thousand years' life. .. Time squared itself, and the village shrank, and distances crept nearer.

Lee describes how life in a village in the Slad Valley in the Cotswolds was altered by changes in technology, and particularly growing ownership of the motor car. Growing freedom of mobility meant that the villagers could shop further afield, and make day-trips to nearby cities; and, of course, more people could visit the village to see for themselves authentic English rural life. The irony is that, as more people visited, less of what they came to see remained authentic. Distance and travelling time had been altered, and so too had rural life.

This concern has arguably grown over recent years. Writing in 1972 – a special commission for the government inquiry into the "Human Habitat" – Philip Larkin mourned the loss of English identity:

And that will be England
                    gone,
The shadows, the meadows
                    the lanes,
The guildhalls, the carved
                    choirs.
There'll be books; it will
                    linger on
In galleries; but all that
                    remains
For us will be concrete and
                    tyres.

The changes we see in the relationship between town and country, in the rise of city-region economies, in increased travel, in global trading and in the pressures these bring to bear on landscapes, natural environments and the historic environment – all of these are likely to increase yet further. In any event, most people will tend to agree that the past matters, and that those monuments and buildings and streets and landscapes which represent important elements of the past should be protected. This includes not only recognizable features in the urban and rural landscapes – such as Salisbury Cathedral or Windsor Palace or Hadrian's Wall – but also the places where people live. Local streets and neighbourhoods and centres, and important local reference points: the town hall, the old theatre, the manor house, a group of buildings on the High Street, examples of vernacular architecture, favourite meeting places. This latter point implies an appreciation and understanding of local distinctiveness – the unique qualities of places and their distinctive cultures – which goes some way beyond individual buildings of even historical or architectural importance. Individual places have their own distinct sense of place or *genus loci*. It is these too that we are responsible for in the here and now. The West Indian novellist Mike

Philip[7] describes his first impressions of London, arriving in 1956. He goes on to argue that London is his city, that he feels a sense of ownership over the place in which he lives. He describes some of the activities – street markets, carnivals, shopping areas – which for him define London. Philips goes on to say that in London the buildings, streets, the monuments, the solid things are actually ephemeral, although they are always there because it is in the nature of the city that they should decay and die and be rebuilt again. All these he sees as merely the framework within which the real business of the city takes place. But he then goes on to write fondly of Notting Hill, the Harrow Road, Little Venice, the "perfect curve of Regent Street" and others, revealing that Alexandra Palace has been his secret place of over 30 years. "Give me time and I'll find another. The city is full of such places." What this reveals is that, although activity gives London its identity, so too do the places in which that activity occurs. We must therefore expect cities and other places to change, for new buildings to be built and new locations to be grafted on to the existing, for new cultures to make their own contribution. Indeed, unless there is new development, new designs, innovation and creativity, our cities and towns will become duller and inert. And if this happens, our culture will cease to grow. The important thing, then, is to achieve a balance between looking after and respecting what has gone before, and in allowing possibilities and opportunities for future growth and creation. This is an argument for sustainability, that is to say we have a duty to succeeding generations to both protect the important elements of our past, and to leave behind us places which succeed and where creativity can continue to flourish. To do so, we must understand what it is about particular streets and buildings, parishes and areas, landscapes and monuments that people value. Such an approach, combining urban archaeology and place character, is now referred to by English Heritage as "characterization".[8]

2. LOSING THE PLACE

> Come, friendly bombs, and fall on Slough
> It isn't fit for humans now.
>
> Sir John Betjeman

In the UK, there have been measures to protect elements of the historic environment for over 150 years. However, the legislation which enshrines (sic) much of current-day practice in conservation is the Civic Amenities Act of 1967. A response to comprehensive redevelopment of UK town and city centres, this legislation introduced such concepts and policy instruments as conservation areas, categories

---

7   Philips, M., "London: Time Machine", in *Whose Cities?* Fisher, M. and Owen, U. (eds) (London: Penguin, 1991).

8   English Heritage, *Conservation Bulletin: Characterisation*, Issue 47, Winter 2004–2005.

of listed buildings, the Civic Trust and statutory instruments dealing with the external treatment of buildings. The truth is that the 1967 legislation, as so often is the case, was a response to changes in the development of town and country over the previous 30–40 years, and to the success of people like Nairn and Betjeman in highlighting the loss of historical buildings and townscapes. There were five major concerns at that time: slum clearance and their replacement with high-rise housing; the redevelopment of central areas of cities and towns, again following the principles of high modernism; planning for greater use of the motor car, including traffic/pedestrian separation; urban sprawl into the countryside and the consequent connecting of settlements to each other; and the emergence of a new breed of apparently soul-less new towns and planned housing estates, occasioning a growing placelessness. Not much has changed …

For example, urban sprawl and ribbon development had been evident from the late 1920s, initially in those parts of the Home Counties made up Metroland – the growth and joining up of rail commuter villages and suburbs. By the early 1950s, urban sprawl had become a more obvious problem, but by now settlements were spreading not along railwaylines but roads. The early conservationist Iain Nairn launched his famous "Outrage" issue of the Architectural Review, in which he coined the term "Subtopia ... the annihilation of the site, the steamrollering of all individuality of place to one uniform and mediocre pattern....the world of universal low-density mess".[9] He feared that, unless checked, subtopia would cover the English landscape in a "desert of wire, concrete roads, cosy plots and bungalows". John Betjeman's essay on Middlesex warned that Middlesex as a place was being destroyed, and that "all the Home Counties will suffer the same fate".

> And over these mild home county acres
> Soon there will be the estate
> agent, coal merchant
> Post Office, shops and rows of
> Neat dwellings,
> All within easy reach of charming countryside.
> Bucks, Herts and Middlessex
> Yielded to Metroland
>
> John Betjeman

Modernism in architecture, meanwhile, was a heady mix of belief in technological progress, the role of the avant-garde, social progressivism through design, a design aesthetic based on simple lines, and social engineering through architecture. Allied to the twin post-war concerns (and electoral fighting grounds) to demolish slums and redevelop the centres of cities (Comprehensive Area Redevelopment), Modernism offered governments and developers the scope to build high and in greater volumes. Modernism also represented a complete break with the traditional city streetscape or morphology, as indeed was its primary purpose:

---

9   Nairn, I., *Counter Attack Against Subtopia* (London: Architectural Press, 1957).

Plans are the rational and lyrical monuments erected in the midst of contingencies. The contingencies are the environment, regions, races, cultures, typographies, climate. There are, besides, the resources brought by modern technology. These are universal.

Le Corbusier, La Ville Radieuse (1934)

The characteristics of individual places, climates and societies were dismissed by the stroke of a pen as mere contingencies. The aim must be to bring order to the city by separating uses from each other, to build to higher densities, to remove external streets and replace them with streets in the sky, and to build roads to accommodate the motor car. The results can be seen in every major city in the UK: the loss of permeability, the destruction of scale, damage to the micro-climate, the death of streets. This has led to large-scale urban transformations around the world, and across many different cultures.

But in the 1960s, Modernism and redevelopment held sway. Many of the planning controversies of the time make interesting reading, amongst them proposals to demolish and rebuild Piccadilly and drive a road through Covent Garden. It was during the early post-war period that the Euston Arch was demolished, that Tolmers Square was flattened, that whole neighbourhoods were raised to the ground to be replaced by "Streets in the Sky". The case of Covent Garden was important for many reasons, not least of which was that this historic and lively part of London was saved from the bulldozers by the actions of Civic Trusts, community groups and individual businesses and residents in the area. People were standing up for their place, as they have done since in other cities and in other parts of London including the interesting example of Coin Street.[10] Of course, Covent Garden and areas like it have gentrified, and so too have residential suburbs and neighbourhoods where traditional street patterns and building types were left intact. For some this is an indictment, but for others "gentrification" is the consequence of people and areas self-improving. The point is, simply, that people in general tend to prefer a variety of more traditional townscapes and patterns to simplistic and destructive modernism. In passing, a problem arises in that for many, modernism is synonymous with any and all modern design. It is important to draw a distinction between modernism as an all-embracing ideology, and modern design as a design aesthetic.

Still, at least we had nice new towns, spanking new estates on the edge of Glasgow and quaintly-named "urban additions" to places like Swindon. If not high-rise, then perhaps the New Jerusalem would be the garden city. Sadly, it seems that instead of understanding and nurturing cities, the garden city and the wider rational planning approach produces places devoid of culture and vitality. There is very little there, there.

There are several reasons for this. The first is that town planners have most often tended to view cities as problems to be solved. Indeed, planners have rarely felt comfortable with cities. The planned dispersal of cities and the tight control

---

10 Tuckett, I., *There is a Better Way*, in Montgomery, J. and Thornley, A. (eds), *Radical Planning Initiatives for the 1990s* (Aldershot: Gower, 1990).

over small-scale and one-off building in the countryside, has produced acres of suburbia rather than urban space. New towns are essentially suburbs in scale, form and activity. The urban designer Ali Madanipour[11] refers to this as "an anti-urban paradigm", made up as it is of suburbanism and planned "anti-urbanism". Second, such places were built to densities that were too low. This is because density was confused with overcrowding. True, cities can and do produce overcrowding, but this is not necessarily the same as density. Without a sufficient density of residents and varied activities, city neighbourhoods become empty of life and interest. Density – up to reasonably high levels – is good for a city. Third, the town planners of the post-war period believed that by separating out activities you achieve efficiency, that is by land use separation and zoning. Yet, by and large, zoning has been a disaster for cities, as well as for the new towns. This is often accompanied by great tracts of city land being taken up by grass verges, and roads and footpaths, creating left-over space. In turn, this affects the spatial layout of cities and towns. Instead of following established build-to lines, which shape streets, we allow buildings to be centred on plots, surrounded by parking spaces and unnecessary landscaping. Instead of streets and back courtyards, the city form becomes a series of isolated blobs.

The essential problem is the desire to pre-form places to a spatial and functional hierarchy, rather than allow them to grow organically. This route leads to centres and sub-centres failing to interconnect – because they were never intended to overlap in the first place. Successful areas in good cities nearly always overlap, and they have an identifiable, but soft edge, allowing for crossover and inter-mixing. The same is seldom true of new towns and dormitory estates. Perhaps part of the problem stems from the fact that the early town planning movement was steeped in the reforming zeal of Methodism which sought to control the behaviour of the individual and society at large. Consequently, planned towns of the twentieth century are notorious for having very few pubs. Until quite recently, it appears, people in new towns were not supposed to enjoy themselves. These ordered, tidy and neat attitudes continued to shore up much of planning practice, at least into the 1980s.

Of course, our environment is continually adapting to change. We can see this all around us, as places take on new identities and roles within city, regional and national economies. Interestingly, it is very often the oldest city districts and neighbourhoods which attract new entrepreneurs, investors and residents. This is as true of the Jewellery Quarter in Birmingham, Smithfield or Castlefield in Manchester or Grainger Town in Newcastle, as it is in Soho, Shoreditch or Fitzrovia in London or Surrey Hills in Sydney. People who live and work in such places tend to value the scale and proportion of old townscapes, and the fact that these districts are comfortable to walk around and easy to understand. Yet they also want comfortable accommodation and modern design, and why not since new buildings can also sit within a readable townscape.

---

11 Madanipour, A., *Design of Urban Space* (Chichester: John Wiley and Sons, 1996), p. 196.

New residents and communities shape the places they settle in, so that places are continually becoming more or less interesting, the local shops change and so too does the everyday way of life. If this is true then it will become all the more important to balance the desire for wealth creation and social improvement, against the need to protect where we live. Individuals, as we have seen, attach great importance to their local environment. But they also value places which they might only have seen on television or in a magazine, or which they visit infrequently, or which they have only read or heard about. This might be because of some unique geological formation, or a much-loved view, or a country house, or a cathedral, a palace, an ancient monument, or simply a place that we like or think we might like. For although history can be contested – what actually happened – the past belongs to us all. This is not an argument for ossified or frozen tradition, but rather a recognition that the past connects us to ourselves and to the future.

Still Sidmouth

> Broad crescents basking in the summer sun,
> A sense of sea and holidays begun,
> Leisure to live and breathe and smell and look,
> Unfold for me this seaside history book.
> I like to stand upon the Esplanade and look,
> Across to where some earthquake moved,
> millions of years ago,
> Those cliffs of red, bay beyond bay
> From sandstone head to head.
>
> Sir John Betjeman

So the built environment does matter; at least part of what gives a sense of place lies in the built form. There is now a burgeoning urban design literature on the physical properties that help create good urban environments. The important point is that it is perfectly possible to sustain and manage and even create urban environments which are not alienating or which give rise to urban fear. Above all, the built environment must be flexible enough to accommodate new activities and uses. This is because uses within individual buildings tend not to last as long as the buildings themselves. In turn, streets and streets patterns very often last much longer than individual buildings. This explains why there is an almost constant and recurring pressure to find new uses for old buildings. This sometimes brings into conflict the proposed new activity for the building with efforts to protect what is unique – historically or architecturally – about it. Yet at the end of the day, it is always important for buildings to find new uses. As the late architect and critic Iain Nairn put it "To re-use a palace as a town's post-office is better than turning it into a museum". Sadly, these days, it is the post-offices that are closing.

The attack on modernism and puritan notions of town planning in the UK was led by critics such as Gordon Cullen, Iain Nairn and the Advocate planners of the 1960s.

Much the same was happening in America too. In his enjoyable and perceptive book *The Geography of Nowhere* James Kunstler denounces most of the "development" of urban American since the 1930s as "depressing, brutal, ugly, unhealthy and spiritually degrading".[12] He asks why this should be?

Kunstler blames five interlocking processes for the decline of American urban places. The first of these was the "explosion" of suburbia from the late eighteenth century, occasioned initially by the growth of new railway suburbs such as Llewelyn Park in New York State and Riverside near Chicago. This was compounded by the layout of American suburbs on a landscape design approach based on the same Arcadian principles underpinning Andrew Jackson Downing and Frederick Law Olmsted's designs of Central Park. The spread of car ownership which followed, brought with it an infilling of the spaces between the railway suburbs and led to greater urban sprawl. This is similar to what happened in London, and was particularly marked in Chicago which is built on a flat plain – suburbs spread in all directions except north.

The rise of "Modernism" according to Kunstler is responsible for:

> ... cities ruined by corporate giganticism and abstract renewal schemes, public buildings and public spaces unworthy of human affections, vast sprawling suburbs that lack any sense of community ... a slavish obeisance to the needs of automobiles and their dependent industries at the expense of human needs, and a gathering ecological calamity ... .[13]

This led, in turn, to the construction of roads and freeways to accommodate the car, most famously in the case of Robert Moses in New York, but across the country as a whole. Later, the the adoption of Radburn principles would govern the width and layout of streets (roads) in new suburbs. To cap it all, zoning laws separated land uses from each other, and encouraged the spread of parking lots between buildings so that streets were replaced by shopping malls and parking. We can now see that for many places this signalled the death of the street.

Probably in the interests of fairness, Kunstler goes on to criticize the City Beautiful movement and other Town Planning Movements. In 1893, Chicago hosted the Columbian Exposition, a world's fair that also marked the 400th anniversary of Columbus' landing. It was an opportunity to celebrate America's manufacturing industries and also to display examples of various architectural styles of the 19th century. The site for the Expo was laid out by Daniel Burnham as a series of man-made lagoons along the shore of Lake Michigan.[14] The architecture of the individual buildings was "high classical", a style that would become known as the Beaux Arts, after the École des Beaux Arts in Paris where many American architects of the day had studied. In fact, the style – a sort of rational, orderly symmetrical, elegant classicism

---

12 Kunstler, J., *The Geography of Nowhere: The Rise and Decline of America's Man-Made Landscape* (New York: Touchstone, 1994), p. 10.

13 Ibid., pp. 59–60.

14 For an interesting exposition of the Chicago World's Fair, see Larson, E., *The Devil in the White City* (London: Bantam Books, 2004).

– owes much to Robert Adam, Christopher Wren, Indigo Jones, and John Nash. This new classicism was taken up in the US by Charles McKim and his partners Mead and White, and became the ascendant architectural style during the 1890s and later, even referred to as the "American Renaissance". This would lead to the layout and design of the "White City" in Chicago, by Daniel Burnham, as a "city beautiful",[15] and later the Canberra masterplan of Walter Burley Griffin.[16]

However, an alternative architecture was also presented at the Columbian Exposition, the early Modernism of Louis Sullivan who, with his partner Dankmer Alder, had begun to design new "office buildings". Sullivan perfected the architectural use of structural steel, the elevator and the curtain-wall to build the first skyscrapers in Chicago. Sullivan's catch-phrase "Form follows Function" sums up an architecture that favoured clean lines and minimum decoration, an architecture where the individual building was paramount. This would become the ascendant American and "international" style after the Second World War especially when the rebuilding of cities was being undertaken almost in every country. In the USA, the key figures would become Mies van der Rohe, Walter Gropius and Lazlo Maholy-Nagy, all of the Bauhaus, who settled in Chicago in the 1940s. Mies' famous phrase "Less is More" would later be attacked as "empty and hollow" by Lewis Munford.[17] Even Frank Lloyd Wright, these days remembered for his Prairie Houses and the Guggenheim Museum in New York, would build towers such as Price Tower in Bartlesville, Oklahoma, the Johnson Wax Building in Racino, Wisconsin or the monolithic Marion County Civic Center in San Rafael, California. Charles Jencks refers to this as a "collapse into formalism".[18]

Kunstler's explanation for the decline of America's cities as built places is broadly similar to Jane Jacob's famous critique in *The Death and Life of Great American Cities*[19] Jacobs argued that a combination of modernism and the early town planning associated with the Garden Cities Movement – that is, Ebenezer Howard, Sir Raymond Unwin, Robert Park – had ruined whole city districts, indeed whole cities. In truth, it can be argued that, since the Enlightenment, the city and its structures have been seen as the domain of reason. All we need to do is find the right transportation system, the most logical pattern of new development, the right balance between industrial and office areas and residential estates, ways of keeping vehicles and pedestrians apart, the right amount of green space.... This was especially true under modernism in the early 20th century, as we have see, but in truth it dates back to early Victorian times when government bodies and private philanthropists began to commission numerous surveys and plans in London, Manchester and Birmingham. The leading figures were people like Charles Booth,

---

15 Ibid.

16 Pegrum, R., *The Bush Capital* (Sydney Hale and Iremonger, 1983).

17 Mumford, L., *The Highway and the City* (London: Secker & Warking, 1964), p. 156.

18 Jencks, C., *Modern Movements in Architecture*, Second Edition (London: Penguin Books, 1985), chapter 3.

19 Jacobs, J., *The Death and Life of Great American Cities* (New York: Vintage, 1961).

and later the early town planners Sir Patrick Geddes, Lewis Mumford and Sir Patrick Abercrombie.

Seen in this way, the English garden cities movement was part of a reforming tradition rather than a complete break with the past. Whereas Geddes, the Chicago School and others believed that cities could be made more rational by redevelopment, Ebenezer Howard and Raymond Unwin gave up on the city entirely: the way to solve "urban" problems was to build new, hybrid settlements combining the best features of the town (employment, entertainment) and the country (clean air, access to landscapes). Each garden city, according to Howard[20] should be built to accommodate 30,000 people, cover an area of 1000 acres, and be surrounded by a rural area of 5000 acres. Howard founded the Garden City Association in 1899, and began preparations for the building of Letchworth and Welwyn Garden City, both of them in Hertfordshire some 40 miles north of London. To be fair, both of these towns have matured well and, although a little dull, are popular places of residence, especially for young families and retirees.

The problem was that some of the ideas associated with the garden cities began to be applied to the cities themselves. Thus, land uses were zoned and separated, neighbourhoods were planned to stand apart from each other rather than overlap, employment areas were to be located well away from residences, residential streets became cul-de-sacs or "estates", streets were turned into roads for the efficient movement of traffic, high rise blocks were set in acres of leftover space, traditional build-to lines were ignored – and the result would be the death of cities.[21]

Jacobs' work has become a bible for anti-modernists the world over, because not only did she critique modernism and the garden city movement, she also analysed the features of city life and form that succeed in producing or supporting dynamic economies and stimulating urban environments. She did so by understanding the human need for diversity of activities along city streets, human scale, permeability and a sense of discovery. Her analysis was based not on grand theories of class conflict but on observation of everyday life and individual behaviour. She was the first writer on cities to do so, but others would follow. Jonathan Raban's excellent book *Soft City* offered an alternative to the harsh world of civil engineering and rational planning, simply by telling the story of the city from the perspective of an individual observer.[22] Here was the world of early 1970s London, the street fashions and the foreign emporia, the restaurants and take-aways, the homeless, the poetry and the politics, the messiness and the fascination of places. A similarly evocative work is Patrick Wright's voyage of discovery through Hackney in London's East End.[23]

Critics such as Sharon Zukin or David Harvey, and other Marxist academics, have argued that Jacobs work, in not understanding class oppression, is naïve and

20 Howard, E., *A Peaceful Path to Real Reform* (London: Swan Sonnenschein, 1898).
21 Jacobs, J., *The Death and Life of Great American Cities* (New York: Vintage, 1961).
22 Raban, J., *Soft City* (London: Hamish Hamilton, 1974).
23 Wright, P., *A Journey Through The Ruins* (London: Flamingo, 1992).

liberal. Areas that have been saved from redevelopment – Greenwich Village, Covent Garden, Primrose Hill, Islington – are dismissed as having gentrified, although the irony is that it is in just such places that the urban left choose to live. It is probably true that Jacobs overstated the benefits of natural surveillance as an antidote to crime of itself, although writing in the late 1950s, she would not have foreseen the rise in gun crime or drug dealing.

There has also, of late, been a reappraisal of Jacobs' view that traditional town planning (the garden city variant thereof) was just as damaging as Modernism. Emily Talen and Cliff Ellis have recently argued that:

> ... it is time to reconsider the uncritical rejection of traditions that dominated the period from 1940–2000, and chart a new course.[24]

By "traditions", Talen and Ellis refer to the older, pre-modernist approaches to town planning as exemplified by the layout of cities in the 19th century. For Talen and Ellis, this involves a rejection of the "one size fits all" urban planning of the twentieth century, and a return to the classical:

> principles of city planning that allow cities to be collective works of art unfolding through time.[25]

This involves, amongst other things, a return to planning education based on the careful study of great cities; beauty in design; a rejection of zoning and its replacement by regulations based on "place-typologies"; and an understanding that slow, incremental growth produces a "fractal" quality of great cities. This is certainly compelling reasoning. It does seem, however, that this line of argument is more applicable to the master planners who laid out the great new cities (or new city districts) of the mid-nineteenth century, rather than to the reforming town planners. Examples of this would include the layout of Manhattan in the early 1800s, (the blocks were set at 3 chains or 198 feet deep), James Thompson's layout for Chicago, or the more interesting grid for San Francisco designed by Jaspar O'Farrell in 1845.[26]

Kunstler's own response to the decline of American cities is to call for a combination of a re-connected public realm, "Traditional Neighbourhood Development", the redesign of suburbs as "pedestrian pockets" (that is to say of a walkable scale), and the creation of activity nodes.[27] This Kunstler refers to as a "culture of place-making" akin to the "New Urbanism" of Andres Duany, Elizabeth

---

24 Talen, E. and Ellis, C., "Cities of Art: Exploring the Possibility of an Aesthetic Dimension in Planning", *Planning Theory and Practice*, Vol. 5, No. 1, pp. 11–32, March 2004, p. 23.

25 Ibid., p. 28.

26 Linklater, A., *Measuring America* (London: Harper Collins, 2003), Chapter 14.

27 Kunstler, *op. cit.*

Plater-Zyberk and Peter Calthorpe.[28] The problem is, as Ali Mandapouri has pointed out,[29] that new urbanism is largely based on the garden cites and new towns of 20th century Britain, with the exception that rather than modern the architecture itself is traditional, not to say post-modern. This appears to be the dilemma at the heart of new urbanism – is it modern or post-modern? Is it traditional city planning or garden city planning? For if it is limited in its application to small, new-build settlements such as Seaside in Florida, then can it be usefully applied to the cities? This point is alluded to by Philip Langdon, amongst others, in his book *A Better Place to Live*[30] in which he argues for the remaking of suburbs and older urban neighbourhoods. Most of the examples of good places he refers to, however, are suburban.

Here then is the conundrum. Is the best form of urban planning a return to the principles of garden cities up to and including their most recent manifestation as gated-communities? Perhaps for suburban areas it is. Yet, we remain with the question of how the older districts and areas of cities should be planned if they are to remain urban in character rather than becoming suburban. A series of case studies may help focus on principles of city design. From this, it should be possible to derive, in the abstract, how one might build a whole new city from scratch. For if we know how to do this, we should also know how to refit existing urban areas, inner suburbs, city districts and outer suburbs too.

3. CITY DESIGN

Barcelona: A Tradition of City Building

Although Barcelona was brought to the world's attention as a dynamic, contemporary city during the Olympic Games of 1992, the Catalan tradition of city building spans many centuries. From the 1980s, ambitious programmes of work were undertaken to establish quality public spaces and innovative architecture. These are rightly celebrated by the Catalans themselves, by architects and urban planners and by people who visit this fine city. There is perhaps no other city in the world where so much has been achieved in urban design and in improving the public realm. Though a radical approach, the public space policy of Barcelona over the past twenty years can nevertheless be seen as the latest instalment in its urban development.

As the art historian Robert Hughes has pointed out, Barcelona is really three cities.[31] On the perimeter lie the industrial suburbs of the 1950s, 60s and 70s, as depressing a muddle of roads, factories and apartment blocks as can be found anywhere. Inside this lies the nineteenth century grid of the Eixample (Enlargement),

---

28 Calthorpe, P., "The Region", in Katz, P. (ed.), *The New Urbanism* (New York: McGraw Hill, 1994).

29 Mandapouri, *op. cit.*, p. 213.

30 Langdon, P., *A Better Place to Live* (Amhurst: University of Massachussetts Press, 1994).

31 Hughes, R., *Barcelona* (London: Harvill, 1992), p. 3.

laid out by the engineer Ildefons Cerdà i Simyer, built between 1859 and 1910. Inside this is found the Old City or Gothic Quarter. The early city – Barcino – dates back to Roman times, the first century BC, when a port and Roman city grew up serving a region which had earlier assumed great strategic importance during the Second Punic War with Carthage. Extensive remains of Roman Barcelona can still be seen in the Gothic Quarter, including remnants of the defensive walls, six feet thick, which enclosed a 25 acre area. Following the collapse of Roman Spain, Catalunya was subject to various waves of invasion from Vandals, Suevians, Alani and Visigoths. Eventually the Visigoths would become rulers of Catalunya, and most of Spain, eventually moving their seat of power to Toledo. As invaders at the time went, the Visigoths were relatively benign and, according to Hughes the process of cultural change was "one of absorbing and merging".[32] However, this came to an abrupt end in 712 when the Saracens invaded southern Spain. By 719, the Islamic empire extended from Portugal to the borders of China, with Damascus as its capital. Attempts to invade France were repelled by Charlemagne in the 770s, and by 801 the Franks under Charlemagne's son, Louis the Pious, had driven the Saracens out of Catalunya. Although the Moors would continue to re-invade parts of Catalunya, over the next 200 odd years Catalunya began to grow in wealth and influence, culminating in the union with the neighbouring kingdom of Aragon after 1134. This would establish Aragon and Catalunya as a strong power bloc in the Mediterranean, and in the process Barcelona became a great sea power. This situation would remain broadly the case through the following centuries of trade across the Mediterranean, wars with the Moors and outbreaks of the plague.

Barcelona prospered, and its population grew. By the early thirteenth century, new city walls were under construction. These would take 100 years to complete, enclosing an area twenty times the size of the original Roman city, and this would become known as the Barri Gotic or Gothic Quarter. Although little from before the thirteenth century remains, Barcelona's Gothic Quarter contains the largest concentration of thirteenth to fifteenth century buildings in Europe, including churches, town houses, government buildings and the Cathedral. Barcelona would continue, with ups and downs, to create wealth for the next five hundred years, during which time it would also resist the Hapsburg Empire and be invaded by the Bourbons (in 1714). The Bourbons, in the guise of Felipe V, set about building a system of walls – muralles – which were reviled by the Catalans and would create many future urban problems.

A city plan, published in 1740 by the architect Francesc Renart i Closas, shows a new street connecting the Port of Barcelonetta to the northern edge of the city, running along the western edge of the Old City. The street follows the route of a former stream, and indeed the name rambla in Arabic means "riverbed". Built as an access road, the Ramblas would preserve the boundary of the medieval city despite being widened in the early nineteenth century. Along its route many fine palaces would be built in the 18th century. However, as the city's population continued to

---

32 Ibid., p. 72.

grow, urban densities increased to the point of severe over-crowding by the 1790s. Any plan to extend the city, however, would need to wait another seventy years during the power struggle between the Carlists (Madrid) and the Catalans, an emnity that exists to this day.

By the mid 1850s, Catalunya as a whole had a population of 1.67 million people. Of these, 189,000 lived in Barcelona.[33] At this time, based on industry, Barcelona accounted for over 25% of Spain's gross national product. The industries were iron and steel, and a rapidly expanding cotton industry (the fourth largest in the world). Catalan entrepreneurs had visited England and returned with designs for spinning jennies and machine looms. By 1861, there were almost 10,000 such looms in Catalunya.[34] Following a period of agitation for social reform, although not without the brutal suppression of a labour up-rising, the Bourbon walls were allowed to be removed over a period of some ten years, and by 1865 they had all but gone. Today, although sections of both the Roman wall and the medieval wall remain intact, nothing exists of the Bourbon wall. By 1865, the removal of the walls meant that at least Barcelona could expand.

Fig. 4.1 Barcelona: Urban Form
Source: John Montgomery.

The plan prepared by the socialist engineer Ildefons Cerdà follows a similar logic to Haussmann's redevelopment of Paris, except that Cerdà was building on agricultural land as opposed to demolishing the old city. Cerdà's plan won the competition, organized by the Adjantament of Barcelona in 1859, despite the fact that his plan made barely any acknowledgement of the Old City. There was, moreover, a rival plan prepared by the City's own municipal architect, Antoni Rovira i Trias. Rovira's design extended from the areas of the Ramblas into a new ceremonial square, and from here it radiated out into five segments divided by avenues. The outer edges were defined by a canal and a railway.

By contrast, Cerdà's plan was an unrelieved grid, the only exception being three great avenues criss-crossing the grid at 45° angles. The name of one of these – the Diagonala – gives the idea (Fig. 4.1). The City Council selected Rovira's plan but within eight months this decision was reversed on dictat from Madrid. This caused considerable resentment at the time, and still rankles even today, Cerdà's plan being criticized roundly as being monstrous, lacking in grace, "a disaster of gigantic proportions" and generally lacking in understanding of the realities of everyday urban life.

---

33 Ibid., p. 254.
34 Ibid., p. 255.

Cerdà's layout consisted of 550 city blocks converging on an area of nine square kilometres. This would be broken down into units of 100 blocks (ten by ten), each designed as a city district with its own shopping area. Two-thirds of each block would be left open as parks, so that the built foot-print of a block would be some 5,000 square metres. Every block would be 113.3 metres square, so that three blocks would equal exactly 400 metres. Corners would be set back at 45°, not for any aesthetic purpose but simply to allow turning space for public transport vehicles. Building heights would be limited to 57 feet. In the event, many and varied "relaxations" of the plan meant that building heights were increased to 65 feet but, more importantly, infill of the courtyards and parks was allowed. The Eixample as built was a more dense urban environment than Cerdà would have wished, yet this was probably an improvement on what might have been. Too much open space in a city can leave streets and blocks a series of disconnected islands. That said, the slow, disjointed progress of actually building the Eixample undermined any prospect of architectural unity, while the sanitation systems – which Cerdà had designed to reduce outbreaks of disease – were as bad as anything found in the Old Town. And as the city population was growing so rapidly, the Eixample was overcrowded almost from the outset. In stark contrast to Edinburgh's New Town, the Eixample brought as many problems as it solved.

Meanwhile, life and politics in Barcelona reverted to a familiar litany of uprisings against the Bourbons, disputes between Carlists and Catalan nationalists, left and right, an outbreak of phylloxera which wiped out the vineyards in the 1870s, followed by the deep recession of the 1880s. During all of this, the hated Bourbon Citadel was pulled down, leaving an enormous vacant site of some 270 acres. Once more a competition was held, this time to design a new park. The winning submission, led by Josep Fontseré i Mestres included a young Antoni Gaudi. Today it is known for the Cascade, a large-scale sculptural fountain, and for the zoo which occupies the park's southern half. In 1888 it would be the site of Barcelona's Expo.

Having built not one but two cities, a large park and some monumental art, the Catalans spent much of the next forty years erecting sundry statues and monuments, building many grand homes and palaces in the Art Noveau style (known in Barcelona as Modernisme), plus the odd park and even a cathedral – the Sagrada Familia. Architects busy during this time included Domenech, Gaudi and Josep Puig i Cadafalch.[35] Artists such as Santiago Rusinyol and Ramon Casas were also living and working in the city, as was the young Picasso. In the midst of their work, Casas and Rusinyol found time to open a "beer cellar" in 1896 as a centre for the Modernisme movement. Critics suggested that no-one but possibly four cats would turn up at the opening, so they named it "The Black Cats".

The last vestiges of Modernisme and the life of Barcelona would grind to a halt with the onset of the Civil War in 1936. The Catalans were pro-Republic and – as they had during the War of the Spanish Succession – ended up on the losing side.

---

35 For more detail on the work of these architects see Ignasi de Solà-Marales, *Fin De Siecle Architecture in Barcelona* (Barcelona: Gustavo Gili, 1992).

General Franco banned the public use of Catalan in teaching, publishing, the press and in government. Moreover, Barcelona's economy would remain depressed, with a modest upswing in the 1960s during which time many ill-considered industrial estates were built on the edges of the city and even along the waterfront. When General Franco died in 1975 without an heir apparent (his chosen successor having been blown up in 1973), the streets of Barcelona danced for joy.

Since that time, governments of both left and right have laid great stress on re-discovering Catalan cultural identity. In particular, the socialist mayor of Barcelona in 1982, Pasqual Maragall, set about a radical plan to re-make the physical form of the city. The city planning strategy would be to reverse the old zoning policies and move towards mixes of uses across the city. As well as the centre, the city's neighbourhoods and districts would be revitalized by the design and construction of a set of urban spaces throughout the city. One of the first projects was to recover the Ramblas as a strolling street, while cars were removed from the Avinguda de Gaudi. The city began to repair plazas in the Old City and to design neighbourhood and pocket parks in the Eixample. The award of the 1992 Olympic Games (in 1986) meant that Barcelona would have the opportunity to refurbish sports arenas in Montjuic, build an Olympic Village, address its traffic problems by constructing two relief roads, and re-connect the city to the sea. In doing so, Maragall's aim was not only to "recreate" the urban landscape, but also to "stimulate and direct the energy of the marketplace".[36]

In this way, planning policy was changed from the orthodox long-term, single-use zoning of areas towards a more active approach to place making.[37] It was considered essential that each neighbourhood of the city should have its own "living room", and each district – of which there are ten – a park, so that citizens could engage in everyday activities of public social life, which for so long had been constrained by Franco. In the peripheral areas, the stated goal was "to put a face on the faceless" estates of the 1960s and 1970s. Art and sculpture would play an important role, and was seen as integral to the design of each space. Many of the designs, such as the Parc de l'Espanya Industriel and Parc de l'Estació del Nord incorporate features that children can play on.

Whilst the spaces created or re-configured in the Old City tended to be under-stated in their design treatment – most of these are "stone rooms" designed to set off the old buildings, but also to act as meeting places (Fig. 4.2) – those in the Eixample feature much greater experimentation and are contemporary in layout, materials, public art and furniture.

There is no set menu of materials or lighting, but each space was designed individually in close discussions with local residents. Although expensive, this means that one does not find the same light fitting, bench or litter bin everywhere

---

36 Quoted in Gehl, J. and Gemzoe, L., *New City Spaces* (Copenhagen: Danish Architectural Press), p. 29.

37 Busquets, J., "Barcelona Revisitied: Transforming the City Within the City", in Charlesworth (ed.), *City Edge: Case Studies in Contemporary Urbansism* (London: Architectural Press, 2005).

Figure 4.2   Placa del Pi, Barcelona
Source: Julia Montgomery.

across the city. Spaces in the Old City which did not previously exist were created
by demolishing dilapidated buildings, Placa de la Mercè or Fosser de les Moreres
for example. Existing spaces such as Placa Reial or the Placa del Sol were also
renovated. Several squares were created by removing the dominance of road traffic.
Other types of space included play areas, large recreational parks, pocket parks and
"oases" – for example, Parc de Jaun Miro or Parc del Clot. Promenades have been
re-designed as walking routes, with places to sit provided. In their review of "New
City Spaces", the urban designers Jan Gehl and Lars Gemzoe have concluded that
Barcelona is:

> ... an undisputed leading laboratory in the design of city spaces in terms of imagination,
> variation and volume of solutions. In no other city is it possible to see such a large number
> of innovative designs for public space ... after this discipline had all but disappeared under
> the influence of modernism.[38]

Praise indeed.

---

38 Gehl and Gemzoe, *op. cit.*, 2000, p. 29.

Portland, Oregon: An Alternative Model for U.S. Cities

Portland is a city of almost 500,000 people, making it larger than Pittsburgh. It is the capital of the State of Oregon in America's north-west, a few hundred miles south of the Canadian border. The city straddles the two banks of the Willamette River, the valley running between two mountain ranges. The area was originally settled by retired trappers from the nearby fur-trading port of Fort Vancouver. The city was named on the flip of a coin: it could have been called Boston. It would grow to become the prime shipping centre for much of the North West seaboard, and enjoyed a ship building boom in the mid 20th century.

The River Willamette divides the city into east and west sides, while the main east-west thoroughfare Burnside Street proceeds in a north-south demarcation, so that the city is organized into four recognizable quadrants. The North-East and South-East quadrants are a mix of late 19th century housing – neighbourhoods such as Alberta Street or Hawthorne – with commercial centres. The city centre – Downtown – is in the South-West quadrant, while the historic Old Town is in the North-West.

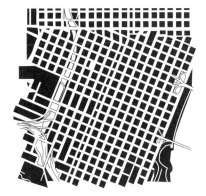

Fig. 4.3   Portland: Urban Form
Source: John Montgomery.

The climate in Oregon is notedly mild, and the Willamette Valley is known for agriculture produce including soft fruits and orchards. This might help explain the strong attachment Portlanders feel towards the environment. The port and shipping areas have moved further down-river, and these days the economy is more mixed. The high-tech firm Intel has its headquarters in Portland, as does the sportswear manufacturer Nike. Portland is generally considered the most liveable city in United States. This happy situation has arisen because of a beneficial combination of circumstances and events. To begin with, Portland is a well-laid out city with a much tighter urban grid than is the norm in America (Fig. 4.3).

City blocks in Portland are only 200 feet long, about a quarter of those in Seattle for example. This means that the city is compact, has a legible and human scale streetscape, more routes for pedestrians and a high proportion of street frontages from which to trade. Building heights in the city centre have been limited to twenty storeys since the 1970s, so there are only half-a-dozen tall buildings above this level. This allows more air and light into the city, shade cast by skyscrapers is not an issue and the micro-climate is not subject to excessive wind caused by tall buildings. In turn, this means that city life at the street level is pleasant, and there are many places to stroll or sit in comfort.

Of course, this situation might not exist today were it not for the fact that during the 1970s Portland eschewed – with one exception – the redevelopment of the CBD that was then fashionable across America. Local people, many of them early environmentalists, rejected "big footprint development", favouring instead an approach based on improving the existing city and its streets.[39] This led planning officials to revise the zoning code to prioritize active street frontscapes, build-to lines and a consistent scale of elevations. Tax incentives were introduced to encourage developers to build apartment buildings in the Downtown, with active uses on the ground floor. This led to an increase in people living in the city centre without the need for skyscrapers. A similar approach was extended to the inner suburbs, allowing the development of town houses as well as single-family homes.

This meant that the city would become a place much more oriented to people simply walking about, and so the issue of traffic needed to be addressed. As early as 1973, Portland introduced a new "Arterial Streets Classification Policy", which shifted the emphasis from road traffic capacity and peak flows to streets as shared spaces in the city. Pavements were widened, traffic levels managed and seating areas provided. New plans for the city centre were drawn up, emphasizing public transport and improved pedestrian spaces. In the 1980s two new tram lines were introduced. Bus and tram travel was made free in the city centre, and the provision of parking spaces limited to the level which could be accommodated within the existing built fabric. This removed the temptation to demolish buildings to make way for car parks. A four-lane expressway was uprooted to provide a new waterfront park, connecting the city to the river. At least one multi-storey car park was demolished to make way for a re-design of the city's main square, Pioneer Courthouse Square. Money to build the square – 150 million US dollars – was raised by a group of citizens from corporate and private sponsors. This new space added to two notable public spaces designed by Lawrence Hallprin, and sparked off a programme of space-making. The "Central City Plan Fundamental Design Guidelines" were prepared in 1990, and set the criteria for the design of quality city spaces. These were intended to promote Portland's identity, improve and extend the pedestrian environment and contribute to the overall city-scape (the relationship between spaces and buildings). Detailed guidelines cover such matters as ease of access, sunlight, safety, comfort, public art, scale and relationship to surrounding buildings.[40] All of this is set within a strategic framework of the "Urban Growth Boundary" which was established, also in 1973, to prevent urban sprawl, protect agricultural land and, by developing a more compact city, make public transport more viable.

The result is a city that confounds our sadly all-too-often realized expectations of American cities. To be fair, other cities in North America have set about the task of improving the built form, and also wider metroplolitan or spatial planning. Vancouver has produced its own "Livable Region Strategic Plan", Pasadena has revived its Old Town, San Francisco has developed a contemporary arts precinct

---

39 Kunstler, J.H., *op. cit.*, 1994, p. 201.
40 Gehl and Gemzoe, *op. cit.*, 2000, pp. 60–65.

at Yerba Gardens, and there are now many examples of mixed use development, including affordable housing.

Portland is alive day and night because people live there, this creates a larger market for businesses such as eating places, cafés and grocery stores to prosper. Mixed use, the control of traffic, the re-design of streets, public transport and new city spaces have combined to make Portland a very agreeable city. All of this has been achieved by conscious, clever planning.

As Kunstler puts it:[41]

> A vibrant downtown, the sidewalks full of purposeful-looking citizens, clean, well-cared for buildings, electric trolleys, shopfronts with nice things on display, water fountains that work, cops on bikes, greenery everywhere ... Could this be America?

Marvellous Melbourne

The focal point of Melbourne's city form, and for much of its cultural identity (along with the cultural institutions clustered on the South Bank), is the CBD. The CBD is one mile by one and a half miles, and is laid out on a regular grid.

The grid was designed by the surveyor Robert Hoddle,[42] who laid the city out as a series of one-and-a-half chain (33 yards) streets, dissected by half-chain (11 yards) lanes, on the north bank of the River Yarra. Hoddle's large blocks are some 220 yards long (or 200 metres), and this meant that little space was left for urban squares. A degree of smaller-grained permeability is provided by the lanes and the covered arcades.

The modern history of Melbourne began in 1835 when John Batman led a group of free settlers from Tasmania, looking for land. Melbourne provided a sheltered bay for shipping, a navigable river connecting to the interior, and a flat terrain. Tim Flannery argues that the local Aborigines were badly treated by Batman and his colleagues, their land being "purchased" and sold off in lots by as early as 1837.[43] According to Flannery, Hoddle's plan was drawn up remote in an office in Sydney, and was simply a grid "plonked" down "in an afternoon" so that

> ... the city would start life at odds with the topography.[44]

The truth of this is debatable, although the practice of drawing up city plans according an already prescribed grid was not unusual. The plans for Fremantle, for example, were drawn up not in Sydney but in London. A year later, Colonel Light would also lay out Adelaide in grid formation, while Hoddle himself would later design the grid

---

41 Kunstler, *op. cit.*, 1994, p. 200.

42 Lewis, M., *Melbourne: The City's History and Development* (Melbourne City Council, 1995), p. 12.

43 Flannery, T., *The Birth of Melbourne* (Melbourne: Text Publishing, 2002), p. 10.

44 Ibid.

for Brisbane. There are even claims that, occasionally, the office in London would send the wrong plans to the wrong continent, so that some of the early buildings in Port Adelaide, for example, have a somewhat Latin American flavour. Even if Melbourne's grid may not have been designed with enough respect for the local terrain, it has stood the test of time. It is robust. Nevertheless, in the city's early days there were many unfortunate incidences of flooding, while public sanitation was a distant 60 years' prospect.

At this early stage, Melbourne's economy was built on trade in agricultural produce, transported to port down the river Yarra and via a canal system. In return, Melbourne developed industries which serviced the rural hinterland: sawmilling, metal foundries, tanneries. By 1839, Melbourne had seventy-seven warehouses, thirteen merchants and agents and eight auctioneers, plus a market, shops, offices and tradesmen, and three banks.[45] By 1841, the population of Melbourne (Port Phillip District – named after Governor Phillip) had increased to 20,000. Unfortunately, the depression of the 1840s was just around the corner.

New wealth creation resumed in 1852 when gold was discovered at Ballarat, triggering a wave of city growth. In 1850, at the time of Victoria's formation as a state separate from New South Wales, Melbourne's population was 77,000. By 1861 this had grown to 126,000.[46] Wealth created by the gold rush even attracted large number of entertainers, some of them of the highest quality; the Theatre Royal opened in 1856, and a new breed of entertainment entrepreneurs began to emerge. By the 1920s, the impresario George Tallis would have built up the world's largest entertainment business, not in London or New York but in Melbourne.[47] A Public Library and the University were added in 1853, and the Victorian Society of Fine Arts was established in 1856.

By 1859, Collins Street was being compared favourably with London's Regent Street. The suburbs of Fitzroy, North Melbourne and Carlton were developed. During all of this, the city itself was developed in a more or less orderly fashion according to Hoddle's grid. This was a period of great city building, and many public buildings were completed. But the boom – confined as it was to gold – collapsed by 1859.

By the up-wave of the 1870s, Melbourne was a thriving port with an envied city form – "Marvellous Melbourne". High-rise buildings – a new innovation from Chicago – began to appear in the 1880s. A Chinatown developed around Little Bourke Street. A clearing out of the brothels in Stalen Street was ordered, so that a red light area developed in nearby Fitzroy instead. The economy continued to grow by a process of exporting primary products, importing capital and investing in new city development as well as the food, clothing and leather goods industries, these latter both for local consumption and export. This was a classic export-import-import substitution model as discussed earlier in Part I. Delicacies such as China tea and sugar were imported, giving rise to the tea-rooms of polite society. Specialist shops

---

45 Lewis, *op. cit.*, 1995, p. 22.
46 Ibid., p. 60.
47 Tallis, M. and Tallis, J., *The Silent Showmen* (Adelaide: Wakefield Press, 1999).

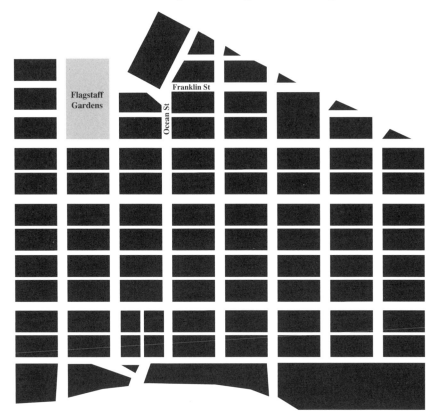

Figure 4.4 Melbourne: Urban Form
Source: John Montgomery.

opened in the Arcades. By the 1880s, rising land values in the city had encouraged manufacturing industries to relocate to the South Bank. Australian Rules Football, cricket and racing were established as spectator sports.

By the 1890s, the economy was in recession again. Flannery[48] blames this on "corrupt business practices, over-capitalization in the railways and "irresponsible" land speculations". There may be truth in this, but the 1890s were in fact the end of the second Kondratieff Wave – the slump was experienced in cities across the world. By 1901 Melbourne had been proclaimed the seat of government for the new Australian nation, at least until 1927 when the Parliament moved to Canberra. Melbourne's population had grown to half-a-million. The city's economic profile did not change markedly at this time, but steady growth was achieved. New planning controls were introduced, and a programme of slum clearance was embarked upon. Zoning was introduced in an effort to reduce

48 Flannery, *op. cit.*, 2002, p. 17.

Figure 4.5   **Melbourne CBD**
Source: John Montgomery

traffic congestion, and minimum residential plot sizes were set at a quarter acre. Meanwhile, all manner of public works were progressed, including sewage works, electrical lighting and the tramways. Spencer Street power station was completed by 1920. Many interesting examples of late colonial, American Romanesque and Art Noveau buildings survive from this time. More Arcades were built. Life in Melbourne continued, interrupted only by the catastrophe of Gallipoli. Until, that is, the Great Depression or, to put it another way, the end of the third Kondratieff Wave, followed by Word War II.

The world began to visit Melbourne in the 1950s, especially to attend the XVIth Olympiad held in the city in 1956. Melbourne had survived the Depression and World War II. The city centre became increasingly dominated by retailing and offices (11 million square feet of offices by 1953) accommodating the city's financial sector and professionals. A new telephone exchange was constructed, and modernist office blocks – for example the ICI building on Albert Street – began to dot the skyline. However, as in other cities at that time, people began to leave the city to live in the suburbs, so that by 1953 only 4,000 people lived in "The Golden Mile". This should come as no surprise, since policy for much of the twentieth century had encouraged industry and housing to de-centre.

The 1950s were followed by an "urban spurt"[49] in the 1960s and early 1970s, during which time waves of migrants were attracted to Melbourne (from the Greeks and the £10 Poms to the Vietnamese Boat People). In the 1970s, out-of-town retail malls began to appear around the Metropolitan Area. Industry, too, had decanted to the suburbs, and the clothing sector was about to enter a serious decline. By 1981, planning policy changed from suburbanization to increase densities in the inner suburbs. By this time the post-war boom of the fourth Kondratieff Wave was over. Sadly, office block developments in the 1960s and 1970s were allowed to break the building line along many of Melbourne's finest streets, in return for "plazas". By the 1980s, not only was the economy in bad shape, but the city planners had lost the plot.

In 1985, a reversal of policy towards the city centre for much of the 20th century was heralded with the setting up of a new Urban Design Branch within the City Council, led by the urban designer Rob Adams. The document *Grids and Greenery*, published in 1987,[50] set out a new guiding philosophy for the future development of Melbourne, identifying four key elements of urban form and character: the Yarra River and the parklands,[51] the traditional street network, that is the grid; the city's tram system; and the special characteristics of individual quarters within the city.

Strengthening the city's streets and the public realm became the key objectives of planning policy. Pavements were widened, trees were planted, traffic reduced in selected streets – notably Swanston Street, and new paving composed of bluestone

---

49 Lewis, *op. cit.*, 1995, chapter 7.

50 Melbourne City Council, *Grids and Greenery* (Melbourne: 1987).

51 Whitehead, G., *Civilising the City: A History of Melbourne's Public Gardens* (Melbourne: State Library of Victoria, 1997).

became the standard across the city. Active ground floor frontages were encouraged and a new lighting plan for the city centre prepared.

Meanwhile, the South Bank was redeveloped as a locale for the city's major cultural institutions, hotels, apartments, up-market shopping, a casino and restaurants. An elegant promenade now extends from the casino to St Kilda Road. There is also a new pedestrian bridge linking South Bank to Flinders Street railway station. To the west a large area of former docklands has been redeveloped, under the auspices of the Melbourne Docklands Development Corporation, for residential apartments generally in mixed use configurations with active uses on the ground floors, plus a major sporting venue, Telstra Dome, and architectural bridges spanning Spencer Street railway station to connect back to the city.[52] In part to address the lack of urban squares in Melbourne, design competitions were held for two major squares, City Square and Federation Square, while a new riverside park has also been established adjacent to Federation Square. Federation Square itself opened in 2001 and was immediately controversial, mainly for the architectural form of the surrounding buildings and for the choice of materials – a red stone from Australia's interior. The square contains galleries plus restaurants and a large outdoor performance area. It has proved extremely successful with visitors and young people (Fig. 4.6).

In 1998, the City Council produced a set of case studies on progress made in revitalizing the city centre.[53] The results were impressive, but since that time much more has been accomplished. Although the property boom of 1999–2004 is now history, the economy of Melbourne seems strong. Following the recession of the 1990s, the end of the fourth Kondratieff Wave, Melbourne's economy has diversified. As well as a strong financial sector, the fashion and clothing industry is strong again, so too the design industries. During the most recent wave of Melbourne's growth, more and more of the back lanes have become sites and locations for new economic activity. This is particularly noticeable in Flinders Lane east of William Street where former office, factory and warehouse buildings now house an impressive mix of boutique hotels, independent retail outlets, small galleries, design studios, cafés, bars and restaurants. Upper floors are given over to apartments, lofts, offices and studios. Perhaps more than any other place in Melbourne, this area is a centre of small to medium scale creative enterprise in design, fashion and the arts. (Other lively shopping and café districts are found in St Kilda, Lygon Street and Chapel Street, but these do not contain a similar concentration of small and medium creative businesses). The process of revitalization of the lanes has begun to spread, so that interesting new venues and clusters of activity continue to appear, for example in Market Lane or Albert Coates Lane or Melbourne Place or Crossley Street or Driver Lane. Many of the back lanes and arcades have been refurbished and re-lit,

52 Dovery, K., *Fluid City: Transforming Melbourne's Urban Waterfront* (Sydney: University of New South Wales Press, 2005).

53 City of Melbourne, *Grids and Greenery: Case Studies* (Melbourne: 1998).

Figure 4.6   Federation Square, Melbourne
Source: John Montgomery.

and an innovative installation art programme introduced into these lanes. The programme for 2004 included two projected works, a statue of Hoddle set in a refuse collection area and "Walking on Air", an installation using bubbles to change part of the flooring in one of the lanes. A deliberate policy of promoting international events in the city has been pursued including Formula I motor racing, Test cricket, rugby internationals, the annual arts festival, the comedy festival, Melbourne Fashion Week, the Australian Open Tennis Championship, a film festival, golf tournaments and major music concerts. Melbourne is now firmly on the international map, and it has a built environment most cities would be proud of. Welcome back, Marvellous Melbourne.

Copenhagen

Fig. 4.7 Copenhagen: Urban Form
Source: John Montgomery.

Copenhagen is the largest city in Scandinavia with a population of 1.7 million. It is also one of the most urbane, sophisticated and interesting cities in northern Europe. Its origins were as a fishing village which grew from around 1100 to become a successful trading port as part of the Hanseatic League. The name Copenhagen means "Merchant's Harbour". The city grew within a series of walls, some of which would later become city parks (Tivoli Gardens is one such). A series of fires in the 18th century destroyed most of the buildings up to that date, but the city was rebuilt largely to the original medieval street pattern.[54] From that time the city was rebuilt to a maximum of five storeys, with the buildings themselves tending to occupy the narrow plots of the old city (Fig. 4.7). This has resulted in a set of street frontages of much interest and activity.

Denmark's golden age was in the early 17th century at which time cities flourished as the economy grew. However, during the 18th and early 19th centuries, a series of ill-judged military campaigns, including the Thirty Years War with Sweden, undermined the economy. In 1864, Denmark was forced to cede the Schleswig and Holstein regions to Germany. According to Jane Jacobs,[55] Copenhagen was a poor and stagnant city by the early nineteenth century, and Denmark one of Europe's poorest countries. By this time, Denmark had lost most of the trade in agricultural produce to England and Holland, and there were no new streams of exports to compensate. Then, during the second quarter of the 19th century the rapid growth

---

54 Gehl, J. and Gemzoe, L., *New City Spaces* (Copenhagen: Danish Architectural Press, 2000), pp. 52–59.

55 Jacobs, J., *The Economy of Cities* (New York: Vintage, 1969), pp. 170–171.

of London led to greater demand for food and Danish produce was in demand once more. From this time, Copenhagen would grow and diversify its economy, and is still a strong exporter of goods today. This includes an acknowledged excellence in electronics (radio, television) which developed during the 1920s, pottery and crystal, jewellery, furniture and the design industries generally. This, of course, extends to the architecture of Arne Jacobsen, Fisher, Knud Muek and others; and to experimentation in urban regeneration and urban design, for example at Islands Brygge or the new urban village at Bolby.

Copenhagen's other advantage is that, despite its northerly latitude, the climate is comparatively mild owing to the prevailing westerly winds. The city form, and in particular the absence of very tall buildings also means that the micro-climate has not been harmed by the wind tunnel effect which affects many cities – for example, Chicago or Auckland. This, together with its compact layout means that Copenhagen is a good city for walking, even in the winter. There is also a city-centre resident population of over 7,000 people and a daily student population of 14,000.

From 1962, the City Council embarked upon a major but gradual policy of reclaiming the city's public realm. It was considered essential to address the dominance that traffic and parking were exerting on the life of the city and also its urban form. The city's built form developed in three distinct phases. The medieval city was set within a system of defensive walls dating from 1167, and extended in the 17th century. Districts outside the capital city walls were built on the canals at Christianshavn (from 1620) and at Frederiksstad from 1750. But the city's real expansion would come after the ramparts had been demolished from 1854.

By the early 20th century, Copenhagen's economy was more industrialized and the city was attracting migrants from the rural areas. By the 1930s, the city had spread in a semi-circle radius of 10 km from the old City centre. With increasing use of railways, buses and automobiles, Copenhagen's planners began to worry over urban sprawl, as indeed were city planners across Europe at that time. A Copenhagen Regional Planning Committee was set up in 1945, and commissioned a plan from a team of young planners led by Peter Bredsdorff, later the first professor in town planning at the Architect School of the Royal Academy of Fine Arts.[56] Under the "Finger Plan", the boundaries to future urban development were drawn (Fig. 4.8).

Urban renewal would reduce densities in the inner city areas, with new development being directed to well-planned suburbs along radial rail-lines. This was presented in the shape of a human hand – "The Open Hand" – showing the existing urban area as the palm of the hand, and the new extensions as fingers. The plans authors intended that population growth could be contained within this structure up until the year 2000. In the event, extensions to two of the western fingers were already becoming necessary in the 1960s, although delays in the planning process would put work back until the early 1970s. Regional planning

---

56 *The Finger Plan*, Skitseforslag til Engsplan and Storkobenhavn, 1947.

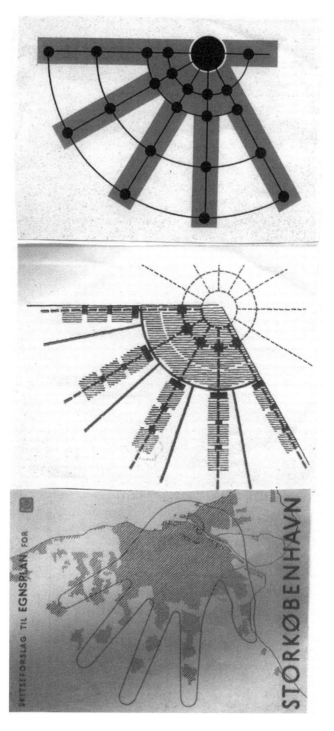

Figure 4.8   "The Finger Plan" Skitseforslag til Engsplan and Storkøbenhavn (1947)

was made mandatory in 1974, although by this time the post-war development cycle had already peaked. During the next 15 years the birth rate would fall and policy would shift towards increasing densities in established urban areas. The Finger Plan itself was updated in 1989 to include identified high-accessibility nodal points to channel growth to places well-served by public transport. The Greater Copenhagen Council which prepared the new plan was abolished at the end of 1989. Nevertheless, the shift towards urban renewal was accelerated, and today conservation, renewal and new construction are seen as equally important elements in urban strategy, so that the urban structure of Copenhagen is largely maintained.

Ever a pragmatic people, the Danes see the role of urban policy as balancing the need for wealth creation, welfare, the rural environment, city form and the quality of urban life.[57] This they see as a sensible approach to sustainability. A key objective in this has, since the early 1960s, been efforts to limit car traffic and parking. Formal pedestrianization – a model borrowed from the rebuilding of post-war German cities – was introduced in 1962 when the Strøget was converted initially as an experiment. The measure was controversial at the time with fears being raised over the impact on trade. The experiment was, however, deemed a great success and more pedestrianization of streets and squares followed. Gradually, a network of pedestrianized streets and routes emerged, so that by 2000 the areas of car-free streets and squares had grown to 100,000 square metres.[58] During this same period car parking in the city centre has been reduced by 2-3% annually, and a network of bicycle routes provided. This has allowed the renovation of a series of public spaces: Strøget, Radhus Pladsen, Gammel Torv, Hojbro Plads, Kongens Nyrtov and Amaliehaven. Most of these are new places for public social life, including the restaurants and bars of Nyhavn, itself once given over to surface level car-parking. Smaller streets have not been pedestrianized completely, but are now pedestrian-priority streets which cars can access at very low speed, and parking is either removed or limited to one side of the street. All of this has helped generate a remarkable upsurge in public usage of the city's streets and squares, and Copenhagen has grown a vibrant café culture (Figure 4.9).

In 1995 there were 126 outdoor cafés in Copenhagen old city centre, providing 5,000 seats which were not there in 1965.[59] This gradual transformation of the city centre from a car culture to a pedestrian culture has, in the words of Gehl and Gemzoe "made possible a gradual development of city life and city culture".[60]

---

57 Christensen, D., *A Tale of Two Cities – Copenhagen*, Paper presented to the conference: *The European City – Sustaining Urban Quality*, Copenhagen, 24–28 April, 1995.

58 Gehl and Gemzoe, *op. cit.*, 2000, p. 55.

59 Gehl, J. and Gemzoe, L., *Public Spaces – Public Life* (Copenhagen: The Danish Architectural Press, 1996).

60 Gehl and Gemzoe, *op. cit.*, 2000, p. 59.

Figure 4.9   Café Culture, Copenhagen
Source: John Montgomery.

Lyon

Lyon, with a population of 450,000, is France's second-largest conurbation, the urban region as a whole containing almost two million people. It is a prosperous city which today is known for its museums and cultural life and its cuisine, particularly the bouchons. Lyon was founded over 2,000 years ago by the Romans. The city is centred on the Presqu'île, a peninsular enframed by the Rhône and Saône Rivers. For several hundred years Lyon was the capital of a region extending from the Rhône to the Alps, and at one point the most powerful city in France. It has since been eclipsed by the growth of Paris.

Lyon's initial wealth was generated during the 16th century when it was a centre for trade with Germany, Alsace, the Italian port city of Genoa and the South of France. Lyon became a part of the Renaissance, experienced an influx of Italian bankers and was a centre for the silk industry. The latter would remain strong through the 17th and 18th centuries, and in the 19th century Lyon developed strong industries in metallurgy, chemicals and banking. As well as larger businesses, Lyon also grew a dynamic small and medium-sized cluster of industrial firms. However, several of the larger companies would move their headquarters to Paris, and in the 1970s there was a decentralization of people and businesses into the surrounding area. Even so, by the mid 1990s, Lyon had emerged from the economic recession with its economy relatively intact.

At the height of Lyon's economic restructuring (during the mid 1980s) a new policy was proposed by the Mayor such that Lyon should project itself as an international city as were Montpellier, Rennes and Lille at the time. The city embarked upon an ambitious programme of infrastructure works, including expansion of the underground system, a new exhibition centre, renovation of Les Halles Tony Garnier (named after the cosmetics innovator) and a new railway station. Measures to attract incoming businesses were also pursued, including the development of the Gerland Science Park and a new office location around the railway station.

Against this backdrop a strategic plan "Lyon 2010" was developed in the late 1980s, with the objective of promoting Lyon's status as a European city distinct from Paris. Key initiatives included the attraction of major arts exhibitions, a new opera house, and the redesign of important public spaces in the city. This was seen as a new type of urban planning, with the development of an integrated transport corridor, a more compact urban form, improvements to the suburbs as well as the centre and stronger environmental policies.

The new public space policy, as part of this wider strategy, was conceived as a response to traffic congestion and the attendant deterioration in the public realm. Three plans were formulated: a green plan, to improve the city's public spaces; a blue plan, to improve the connection of the city to the rivers; and a lighting plan to establish overall treatments for artistic and functional lighting of the built form, important buildings and landmarks, notably bridges. A particularly important aspect of Lyon's public space policy has been the replacement of on-street parking with large subterranean car parks, located beneath the re-designed public squares. This in itself has been an ambitious programme, and the car parks have become architectural and artistic icons in their own right. Great care has been taken to make the car park entrances and exits unobtrusive so that they do not detract from the street-scape.

The public space policy is managed by a project group, *Group de Pilotage Espaces Public*, which is made up of a cross-section of key interests in the city, and which oversees the work of a technical design group. Projects commence in a distinctly unorthodox fashion when a writer or poet is invited to interpret the spirit of the site and decide its essential characteristics. Only following this, and after public involvement in the design process, is the project passed on to designers. The designs themselves are contracted-out to private sector firms of architects, urban designers and landscape architects. A fixed palette of colours, finishes and street furniture is adhered to, giving an overall Lyon identity, but in such a way that each designed space retains an uniqueness. The many impressive squares re-created and re-designed in Lyon include the Place des Terreaux, with its fountains, water jets, lighting and distinctive planting; the Place de la Bourse; the Place Atonin Poncet, the Place de la Republique and the Place Charles Herna (Figure 4.10).

Figure 4.10   Lighting of the Public Realm, Lyons
Source: Phil Keane, with kind permission.

4. URBAN DESIGN

The studies of Barcelona, Portland, Melbourne, Lyon and Copenhagen were originally intended to give prominence to good examples of new city building over the past 20 years or so, primarily in relation to reclaiming and recreating the public realm. That these five cities have done so is not in any doubt, but a larger question has been raised almost inadvertently. If there is to be a new era of city building in the near future, how should this be approached? What lessons can be learned from successful city building in the past, including the recent past? If we wished to build a new city, how would this be different to planning a new town? What would we need to do to avoid suburbia or the sort of soul-less development that characterizes so many city centre redevelopments?

The European Commission "Green Paper on the Urban Environment"[61] was something of a landmark publication, representing a break with orthodox town planning in favour of a "holistic" approach to urban planning, development and management. In addition to strategies for sustainable and economic development, the Green Paper stressed the importance of generating and protecting the sense of place. The significance of this is that it presages a move away from zoning and land-use separation, the old tenets of town and country planning as practised for most of the 20th century.

It is a relatively simple task to think of a successful place, to go there and know that this is a good place. We all have our favourites. But it is much more difficult to know why a place is successful, and importantly, whether and how this success can be generated by setting the right conditions. As a former Secretary of State for the Environment once mused, what is it that "makes some places a pleasure to be in and others irredeemably dreary?"[62] This debate has been ongoing amongst urban designers for at least 30 years now and is one that we will revisit briefly. It is an important debate for it allows us to understand *why* places are successful rather simply than observing or appreciating that this is so. Nevertheless, it is not unreasonable to draw up a checklist of "urban success indicators", as Barry Sherman[63] has done (see Table 4.1). What Sherman has provided is a list of qualities or characteristics of successful urban places. He tells us what to look for but not why it is there. For in addition to the "surface appearance" which such indicators represent, we must understand that good urban places have a structure and an underlying dynamic of activity. Unless this is properly understood, it is more likely that rather than a successful urban place, what will be produced is an artefact, the ersatz city which, "even though it may appear exotic and picturesque, is superficial and has an effect only on the first-time visitor".[64] This is why it is so important to conceptualize fully what is meant by "place".

---

61 European Commission, *Green Paper on the Urban Environment* (Brussels: 1990).

62 Mr John Gummer, Secretary of State for the Environment, speech to the Civic Trust, 30th March, 1995.

63 Sherman, B., *Cities Fit to Live In* (London: Channel 4 Books, 1988).

64 Walter Benjamin, quoted in Davis, M. (1990) *City of Quartz* (London: Vintage 1990).

Table 4.1 Indicators of Successful Urban Places

1. Planning will be invisible and the results will look natural, as though they happened of their own accord;
2. There will be interesting and stimulating shapes;
3. The 'familiarity' of streets and street life will be celebrated;
4. There will be secret places which once discovered grow on you, making you look deeper to find more;
5. There will be surprises, to keep citizens awake, provide topics of conversation, prevent ennui;
6. Experiment will be encouraged, and there will be exciting things to do;
7. There will be areas and opportunities for informal, casual meetings to take place, including warm and friendly bars and pubs;
8. Food and drink will be a treat, and people will be able to purchase and consume it at varying prices and degrees of leisure;
9. There will be a variety of comfortable places to sit and wait – a city worth living in has to be a city worth sitting in;
10. There will be a good balance between the needs to prevent loneliness and to preserve anonymity and privacy;
11. Changing seasons will not draw attention away from the sterner pursuits of daily life but rather will be an integral part of a continually changing city, and celebrated as such;
12. The senses will be heightened: affection/friendliness/hospitality; a sense of belonging; historical and cultural continuity; a sense of fun/humour; opportunities for gossip; open-mindedness; vitality; fantasy; flamboyance; colour; beauty/aesthetic stimulus.

Source: Adapted from Sherman, 1988.

Over the years, there has been a split of sorts amongst urban designers over what constitutes urban quality or the sense of place. There are those such as Cullen[65] who place greatest emphasis on physicality – design styles, ornamentation and featuring, the way buildings open out into spaces, gateways, vistas, landmarks and the like. This is the rational objective classical view of urban design. Others such as Alexander[66] or Lynch stress the psychology of place, bound up in the notion of "mental maps" which people use as internal guides to urban places. In doing so, they rely on their senses to tell them whether a place *feels* safe, comfortable, vibrant, quiet or threatening. This is the romantic subjective view of urban design.

If we were to combine these approaches we would see that urban quality must be considered in much wider terms than the physical attributes of buildings, spaces and street patterns. To be sure, there are many physical elements which, if combined properly (with each other and with the psychology of place) produce urban quality: architectural form, scale, landmarks, vistas, meeting places, open space, greening and so on. Yet the notion of urban quality is clearly more importantly bound up in the social, psychological and cultural dimensions of place.

---

65 Cullen, G., *Townscape* (London: Architectural Press, 1961).

66 Alexander, C., *A Timeless Way of Building* (New York: Oxford University Press, 1979).

Few theorists have managed to bridge this divide, and most remain either predominantly physical determinists or subjective mental mappers. Initially something of a voice from the wilderness, Jane Jacobs[67] was the first to explore urban quality from the premise that *activity* both produces and mirrors quality in the built environment. She identifies four essential determinants which govern or set the conditions for activity: a mixture of primary use, intensity, permeability of the urban form and a mixture of building types, ages, sizes and conditions. Jacobs and others such as Gehl[68] and Cook[69] argue that successful urban places are based predominantly on street life, and the various ways in which activity occurs in and through buildings and spaces. This appreciation led Peter Buchanan to comment that:

> Urban design is essentially about place-making, where places are not just a specific space, but all the activities and events which made it possible".[70]

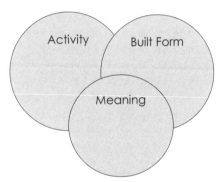

Fig. 4.11 A Visual Metaphor for the Nature of Places, by David Canter

Source: Canter, D. (1977), *The Psychology of Place*, London, Architectural Press.

Thus, we can now see that successful urban places must combine quality in three essential elements: physical space, the sensory experience and activity. Theorists such as Relph,[71] Canter[72] and others (and most recently reinterpreted by Punter[73]) show the components of a sense of place and the relationship (in abstract terms) between them.

Canter's metaphor (Figure 4.11) combines the urban design perspectives of those concerned with mental maps and "imageability", with those who consider the physical attributes of place, and with those who stress the essential importance of activity or what has also been referred to as "natural

---

67 Jacobs, J., *The Death and Life of Great American Cities* (London: Vintage Books, 1961).

68 Gehl, J., "A Changing Street Life in a Changing Society", *Places*, Fall 1989, pp. 8–17.

69 Cook, R., *Zoning for Downtown Urban Design* (New York: Lexington Books, 1980).

70 Buchanan, P., "What City? A Plea for Place in the Public Realm", *Architectural Review*, 1101, November 1988, pp. 31–41.

71 Relph (1976) *op. cit.*

72 Canter, D., *The Psychology of Place* (London: Architectural Press, 1977).

73 Punter, J., "Participation in the Design of Urban Space", *Landscape Design*, 200, 1991, pp. 24–27.

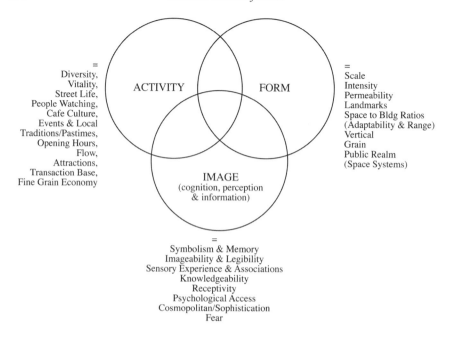

=
Diversity,
Vitality,
Street Life,
People Watching,
Cafe Culture,
Events & Local
Traditions/Pastimes,
Opening Hours,
Flow,
Attractions,
Transaction Base,
Fine Grain Economy

ACTIVITY   FORM

IMAGE
(cognition, perception
& information)

=
Scale
Intensity
Permeability
Landmarks
Space to Bldg Ratios
(Adaptability & Range)
Vertical
Grain
Public Realm
(Space Systems)

=
Symbolism & Memory
Imageability & Legibility
Sensory Experience & Associations
Knowledgeability
Receptivity
Psychological Access
Cosmopolitan/Sophistication
Fear

Figure 4.12   Policy Directions to Foster an Urban Sense of Place
Source: John Montgomery, *Making a City* (1997).

animation"[74] or the "city transaction base".[75] This has been most succinctly put by David Engericht[76] who argues (perhaps over-stressing the point a little) that cities were "invented":

> ....to facilitate exchange of information, friendship, material goods, culture, knowledge, insight, skills and also the exchange of emotional, psychological and spiritual support."

The important point is this: without a transaction base cities and urban places become progressively more lifeless, dull and inert – that is to say more suburban. Without activity, there can be no urbanity.

Figure 4.12 is a composite derived model, combining all the elements of good place discussed so far. We can use this to identify more precisely the cocktail of elements (or qualities or characteristics) that produce good places. We can consider these in turn.

---

74 Montgomery, J., "Animation: A Plea for Activity in Urban Places", *Urban Design Quarterly*, 53, January 1995, pp. 15–17.

75 Montgomery, J., "The Story of Temple Bar: Creating Dublin's Cultural Quarter", *Planning Practice & Research*, Vol. 10, No. 2, 1995, pp. 135–172.

76 Engericht, D., *Towards an Eco-City* (Sydney: Envirobook, 1992).

Activity

Activity is very much the product of two separate but related concepts: vitality and diversity. Vitality is what distinguishes successful urban areas from the others. It refers to the numbers of people in and around the street (pedestrian flows) across different times of the day and night, the uptake of facilities, the number of cultural events and celebrations over the year, the presence of an active street life, and generally the extent to which a place feels alive or lively. Indeed, successful places appear to have their own pulse or rhythm, a life force or *elan vital*. But this can never be taken for granted, as there are now many examples of previously lively places which have become dull and inert. Certainly, it is possible to generate more vitality, at least for particular slots of time, by programming events and activities to occur in the streets, buildings and spaces – what the French term *animation culturel*. However, in the long-term urban vitality can only be achieved where there is a complex diversity of primary land uses and (largely economic) activity.

The simple truth is that combinations of mixtures of activities, not separate uses, are the key to successful urban places. This mixture requires a wide diversity of ingredients, which in turn is dependent on there being sufficient levels of demand to sustain wide-ranging economic activity. City or urban populations, living in relatively close proximity, are large enough to support this economic activity, including such things as coffee houses and cafés, foreign grocery stores, delicatessens, cake shops, cinemas and galleries, pubs and clubs. It is possible to find all of these things in combinations of the large and small, the ordinary and the strange. This means that the key to sustaining diversity lies in there being, within easy travelling distance, relatively large numbers of people with different tastes and proclivities. In other words, a relatively high population density. With rising car ownership and more fluid travel patterns, it is nowadays more likely than it once was that quite small places (towns and even suburbs) can attract enough people to support diversity. But, on balance, the tendency is for larger, more dense settlements to be the ones which can maintain diversity.

Whilst vitality can be gauged by measuring pedestrian flows and movements, the uptake of facilities and the existence or otherwise of "things to do", the term "diversity" ranges across a far wider set of indices:[77]

- the extent of variety in primary land uses, including residential;
- the proportions of locally-owned or more generally independent businesses, particularly shops;
- patterns in opening hours, including the existence of evening and night-time activity;
- the presence and size of street markets, and types of specialism;
- the availability of cinemas, theatres, wine bars, cafés, pubs, restaurants and

---

77 Derived from Jacobs *op. cit.*, 1961, and Comedia *Out of Hours: The Economic and Cultural Life of Towns* (London: Gulbenkian Foundation, 1992).

other cultural and meeting places offering service of different kinds at varying prices and degrees of quality;

- the availability of spaces, including gardens, squares and corners to enable people-watching and other activities such as cultural animation programmes;
- patterns of mixed land ownership so that self-improvement and small-scale investment in property is possible;
- the availability of differing unit sizes of property at varying degrees of cost, so that small businesses can gain a foothold and not be driven out of business by sudden rises in rent and/or property taxes;
- the degree of innovation and confidence in new architecture, so that where possible there should be a variety of building types, styles and design;
- the presence of an active street life and active street frontages.

As a rule, the most lively and interesting urban areas tend to be places of complex variety, with a large representation of small-scale business activity which trades not only with "consumers" but with other businesses. The successful city economy will be as complex and intricate as possible with myriad networks of firms – and, crucially, a high proportion of small and medium enterprises (SMEs) inter-trading and sub-contracting. This is what is meant by "growing a fine grain city economy".[78] The key to successful urban places, therefore, is the transaction base, and this must be as complex as possible. Not all transactions take a monetary form, and not all are economic. Urban areas and cities must also provide space for social and cultural transaction. But without a transaction base of economic activity at many different levels and layers, it will not be possible to create a good urban place.

Image

Every place has both an identity and an image, but these are not the same. Whilst "identity" is an objective thing (what a place is actually like), image is a combination of this identity with how a place is perceived. To individuals, the image of a place is therefore their set of feelings and impressions about that place.[79] These feelings come from a filtering of information received and collected about the place. This filtering is partly based on individuals' values, beliefs and ideas, but also on wider cultural (whether received or otherwise) values, beliefs and ideas. This means that images of place are created from amalgamations of cognition (comprehension or understanding) and perceptions, as well as individual, group and cultural "personality" constructs or meaning. Thus, the Royal Circus at Bath has an identity (its physical form and setting) which can be comprehended, an image (how it is perceived which depends on the filtering

---

78 Jacobs, J., *op. cit.*, 1969.

79 Spencer, C. and Dixon, J., "Mapping the Development of Feelings About the City", *Transactions of the Institute of British Geographers*, 8, 1993, pp. 373–383.

of information received through the senses), and a meaning which, in this case, represents enlightenment, civilization and "good manners" architecture. Other places have altogether different identities, images and meaning, and quite often hold out different images and meanings to different people – Soho is one such example. And, of course, in no small part, image and meaning derive from the activity one finds there, and the built form.

An individual's knowledge of a city is, according to Lynch,[80] a function of the imageability of the urban environment: that is, the extent to which the components of the environment make a strong impression on the individual. In turn, imageability is influenced by a city's legibility: the degree to which the different elements of the city (defined as paths, edges, districts, nodes and landmarks) are organized into a coherent and recognizable pattern. By gathering information about these elements, the individual creates both an image of the city, and also a frame of reference. There is now a considerable body of literature dealing with the process of obtaining the spatial knowledge of these elements. One point of disagreement is whether it is paths and districts which serve as early learning frameworks[81] or whether primary nodes and reference points (landmarks) are the main building blocks in constructing an image of place.[82] It seems likely, however, that paths are more dominant for new residents (finding your way around on an everyday basis) while long-term residents produce more complex mental maps containing both paths and landmarks (environmental cues). Visitors to new places, by contrast, tend to use landmarks as anchor-points in constructing route knowledge.

It is also clear that most people acquire knowledge of a place by a piecemeal "bottom-up" process which is itself dependent on direct experience. Bits and pieces of knowledge are absorbed and then integrated through the individual's perceptual filters. This results in both an understanding of the city (its form and legibility) and an image of the city. And, again, these perceptual filters are partly individual values and ideas, and partly derived from wider cultural processes and identities.

Now, it is perfectly possible for a proportion of these wider cultural processes, values and identities to have emerged over time from associations of events and places. For example, "this is where Guy Fawkes was captured", "this pub is where Thomas Paine wrote "The Rights of Man"", "this is where I first met your mother, under the town clock .....". So places come to represent memory, meaning and association for individuals, groups and societies. Sometimes it is clear from the buildings themselves what sort of meaning is being conveyed, for example Whitehall could only be a seat of government. Sometimes it is an event

80 Lynch, K., *The Image of the City* (Cambridge Mass: MIT Press, 1961).

81 Appleyard, D., "Styles and Methods of Structuring a City", *Environment & Behaviour*, 2, 1970, pp. 100–116.

82 Golledge, R., "Learning About Urban Environments", in Carlstein, Parkes and Thrift (eds), *Timing Space and Spacing Time* (London: Edward Arnold, 1977).

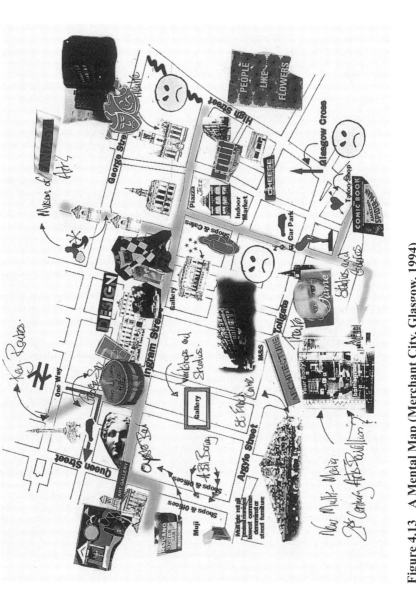

Figure 4.13   A Mental Map (Merchant City, Glasgow, 1994)
Source: John Montgomery.

(the Peterloo massacre, for example, or the George Square riots); and other times not from buildings or events or even landmarks, statues or place names, but simply space. This means that in addition to its contribution to a city's transaction base and its legibility, space (as well as buildings) can take on symbolic meaning. This explains the strong feeling which is often aroused when a public space is threatened with development, why civic spaces until recently were always considered an essential element in a city's identity, and why when asked to draw a mental map of their city (Fig. 4.13), so many people start with a public square or garden. It follows, then, that the spaces in the city, their sequences and proportions and the way they inter-connect are of cultural importance in the life of cities.

Before finishing this section there are three more concepts which we need briefly to allude to: psychological access, receptivity and knowledgeability. Over time, successful places come to represent a sense of identity for their users (in the sense of identifying *with* a place). And this often results in a sense of belonging to a place, of feeling involved and taking an interest or perhaps even an active part in its affairs. This we term psychological access, and places which achieve this are much more likely to be respected and looked after. This sense of local ownership, however, must also allow for tolerance of strangers, so that successful places engender respect for the place and its people, but also for those who visit. This we term receptivity. Finally, places which work well usually have all manner of invisible and informal networks and associations which, in themselves, are indicators of involvement: flower arranging, jam-making, judo, sports, clubs, keep fit, life drawing and painting. Information on these activities, local events and traditions are passed on by word of mouth, posters in shop windows, on notice boards and by leaflets. All of this can be supported and projected to wider audiences by more formalized marketing drives. The key point, however, is to encourage associational activity and to generate greater knowledgeability about what goes on in a place.

Form

In his later work Lynch[83] wrote of the *qualities* which urban design should seek to achieve, and so create a sense of place, while Alexander[30] writes of the "quality without a name", which he defines in terms of the recurring and interlocking patterns of events (and, no doubt, meaning) in buildings, spaces and places. Lynch offers five basic dimensions of city performance – vitality, sense, fit, access and control. For Lynch, a vital city is one which successfully fulfils the needs of its inhabitants within a safe environment – in other words, a good city allows maximum scope for activity. A sensible city is organized so that its residents can perceive and understand the city's form and functions – in other words, its legibility. An accessible city allows people of all ages and backgrounds to gain the activities, resources, services and

---

83 Lynch, K., *A Theory of Good City Form* (Cambridge Mass: MIT Press, 1981).

information that they need. And a city with good control is arranged so that citizens have a say in the management of the spaces in which they work and reside. To varying degrees, we have covered most of this ground in our preceding discussions of activity and image. The question, now, is how activity and image inter-relate with form to generate a sense of place. Or to put it more precisely – can city form be so designed as to stimulate activity, a positive image and therefore a strong sense of place?

Lynch's fifth criterion "fit" seeks to demonstrate how this might be achieved. A city with good fit provides the buildings, spaces and networks required for its residents to pursue their projects successfully. Now, in a very real sense, this "fit" will be governed by the type of place and the range and intensity of activity desired. That said, we can build up a picture of the fit necessary to achieve a successful urban as opposed to suburban place. Such a good urban place would be characterized by complexity, myriad patterns of movement (especially pedestrians), diversity of primary uses, a fine-grain economy, an active street life, variety in opening hours, the presence of people attractors, legibility, imageability and knowledgeability

The Public Realm

Perhaps the most important aspect of urban form is a town or city's public realm, simply defined as the network of spaces and corners where the public are free to go, to meet and gather, and simply to watch one another. It is therefore as important to think through the design of the public realm – its sequences, proportions and dimensions – as it is for city blocks and individual buildings. The public realm in towns and cities performs a number of "functions": as an integral part of the built form or townscape; as neutral territory where everyone has a right to gather; as a place where historical events occurred, and where collective memory resides; and as places where public forms of social life can occur.

Sadly, both the amount and quality of public space in many UK – and especially American – towns and cities has been diminishing in recent years, although there are now a few good examples of the public realm being reclaimed, recreated or created anew. Space within towns and cities has been lost for many reasons, the most important of which we can summarize. The first of these is that the meaning and purpose of public space was largely ignored or misunderstood during the post-war experiment with "functional cities" referred to earlier. The upshot has been that many streets have become roads, and many places are just too spaced out to have any real interest or meaning. Second, the fact that we have continued to build larger buildings with larger footprints on larger plots of land. This means that the permeability of an area is reduced as the number of intersections within the city form is reduced. Very often, such large buildings bring a deadening effect to a street because they have very few doors and windows which people can come and go from, and quite often the activity itself – an office block or even a bank or building society – contributes comparatively little to activity on the street.

The most visible culprit in the loss of public space has been the "mall-ization" or "privatization" of the public realm whereby streets and spaces which were once public have been roofed-over to form indoor shopping malls and atria. Such spaces are effectively no-go areas outside of standard shopping hours, and they are no longer places where the public has a right (as opposed to being permitted) to gather. A fourth reason for the decline of the public realm in British towns and cities is that, in many places it has been left to its own devices, whether as a consequence of spending cuts, neglect or simply a lack of appreciation. There are many high streets, parks and public spaces around the country which look neglected and uncared for. Fifth, there is the phenomenon of the badly and over-designed space. This often occurs because the space is viewed simply as a physical (as opposed to a psychological) entity, where the design itself is over-regimented, or perhaps "off-the-peg", and where those designing the space have not properly understood its scale, proportion, micro-climate and orientation. The net effect of all of this is that the amount of public space in our towns and cities has been declining, and so too has the diversity of use to which space can be put. The outcome is that there are fewer public spaces, fewer reasons for visiting or using them, and fewer people around.

The Danish architect and urban designer Jan Gehl,[84] as discussed briefly in Part III, has argued convincingly that the public realm in towns and cities performs three important functions in the everyday lives of townsfolk and citizens. He refers to these as the three Ms: Markets, Meetings and Movement. He argues that one of the great losses to urban living in many towns and cities has been the re-siting, removal or indoor siting of street Markets which, as places of exchange have been a focal point for all manner of social and economic transactions in urban history. Very often, as in Northampton say, the market square is the town's most important public space.

Gehl argues that Movement should be considered more widely than the flow of road traffic or even mode and grade separation, a fixation which damaged so many towns and cities. Although he is in favour of pedestrianization and the removal of cars from important public spaces, Gehl also sees that the resultant spaces must have activity along their edges, otherwise they will hold little appeal. He links his definition of Movement to other established urban design concepts such as legibility (whether an urban environment is simple to understand and in which people can orientate themselves) and permeability (the degree to which it is easy to move around an urban area).

By Meetings, Gehl is referring to all the human things which people do when they meet or watch each other in public places. He refers to these as optional, necessary and social activities.

- Necessary Activities: where participation is required (going to work, waiting for the bus, buying groceries).
- Optional Activities: where participation is voluntary (walking, standing, sitting).

---

84 Gehl, J., *Creating a Human Quality in the City*, unpublished paper (1995).

Figure 4.14   The Public Realm, Prague
Source: John Montgomery.

- Social Activities: where others are present in public space (watching, talking, hearing, meeting, touching, exchange).

The key to public social life is that, where they feel comfortable, are safe and have some time to spend, people rapidly switch from performing necessary activities (the things they have to do), to optional activities (things they enjoy doing) (Fig. 4.14).

Before long, in most if not necessarily all cases, people engage in social activities, even if this is only saying good morning, asking the time or borrowing a newspaper. This social activity can itself develop through varying degrees of contact, ranging from the polite greeting, to meeting your future partner for the first time, to renewing and maintaining established friendships, and even as a way of understanding the world – for example watching men digging a hole in the ground! People can be stimulated by their environment in many ways: by its design, the colours and textures used, perhaps by events and small gatherings, even by public art. The upshot is that in a good public space, necessary activities quickly take second place to optional activities, from which varying degrees of social activity can emerge, and in the end good places create their own dynamic of watching, being watched and meeting. Social activities in public space can then occur at varying degrees of intimacy: at a modest level as acknowledging other people in public space; as a starting point for contacts at other levels; as a means of maintaining established contacts; as a source of information; as a source of inspiration; and as a stimulating experience

This implies, it turn, that not all public spaces should share exactly the same characteristics. In his important work *The City Assembled*, Spiro Kostof[85] shows that urban spaces come in many shapes and sizes, and perform many functions, often simultaneously. He goes on to categorize a number of space types, not all of which need concern us here. The essential point to understand is that spaces in cities and towns are not uniform, either in their scale, shape, proportion or in terms of the activity they accommodate. Rather like appreciating that rooms in houses have different roles and varying degrees of flexibility as to the use they can be put, it is important that we recognize that "outdoor rooms" ought also to have differing characteristics. Not all spaces should be kept for Sunday best, not all spaces should be large and very formal civic spaces. We can also have a few parlours and waiting rooms, outdoor concert halls and galleries. The important thing is that the relationship between scale and activity is understood, so that spaces can be designed and managed appropriately. Above all, spaces should be designed to achieve high degrees of visibility within the spaces themselves and to and from the surrounding buildings.

Thus, any good public realm will consist of or contain: formal meeting spaces – the town square; quiet corners for reflection; outdoor rooms to meet friends and acquaintances; streets and edges for watching passers by; spaces where temporary events and exhibitions can be mounted; street markets; transitional spaces linking the indoor private realm to the outdoor public realm; meeting points and landmarks; historical and environmental references. Streets and public spaces therefore have the capacity to bring together people who do not know each other in a less intimate, social sense, including strangers. Such places allow people to be in contact with each other, but simultaneously for individuals to remain private if they wish and to respect other people's privacy. The public realm is a subtle balance of essential privacy and varying degrees of public and private contact.

City Making

By seeing the above discussion as a set of informing principles, it is possible to derive a "fit" for a good urban place, as Lynch argued. But, paradoxically, this fit cannot be too precise, for it must allow flexibility for the city to grow organically. (If a city does not grow organically it is merely a planned as opposed to a living thing). This also means that cities must never be wholly predictable, too "safe" or sanitized. Rather than excessive visual order and certainty, places that work well also allow for a degree of uncertainty, disorder and chaos. Order and disorder, then, rather than being opposites are part of one equation. The point about a good

---

85 Kostof, S., *The City Assembled* (London: Thames & Hudson, 1992).

urban place is that it should be expected to develop a life of its own. In order for this to happen, the physical form needs to be built up along the lines presented below.

Condition 1: Development Intensity

The essential condition for achieving urbanity is to generate enough diversity – the mixture of uses and activities – to be self-sustaining. This diversity must be sufficiently complex to stimulate public contact, transactions and street life. In order for this to occur, a city district must have a sufficiently dense concentration of people using it for a range of reasons, including residence. It is being concentrated which produces urbanity and convenience. Therefore, relatively high densities are essential. There is no simple arithmetic answer to optimum city density, as this varies depending on the characteristics of place and the mix of activities. Densities can be too low where they fail to generate vitality, and too high where they produce standardized buildings, regimented layouts and large development footprints. Thus, density in itself will not necessarily produce urbanity: density is a necessary rather than a sufficient condition for urbanity. Importantly, this can be achieved without over-standardization of buildings, and should always be accompanied by high representations of small scale businesses and enterprises.

This necessitates a building form of relatively high density and plot coverage, counter-balanced by the correct amount of open space. This should not be too cramped or mean in its level of provision – people need parks and city squares. But neither should high density be accompanied by large tracts of empty space (the Le Corbusier model), or streets and roads that are too wide. All of this implies a built form which averages around 5-6 storeys, but which includes some higher buildings and some lower ones too.

For residential neighbourhoods, both inner and outer suburbs, the presumption should be in favour of "mixed use urban districts": shops, restaurants and cafés, offices and studios being provided, usually in local parades, as well residential streets. Within any new city, therefore, there would need to be areas of high development intensity, but there should also be a wide range in style and density of residential neighbourhoods, ranging from low-rise low density to medium-rise higher density and high intensity mixed urban districts closer to the core areas. There should also be a mix of architectural styles. Each neighbourhood would have a clearly delineated edge and separate identities.

Condition 2: Mixed Use

Living urban areas must serve more than one primary purpose, preferably more than two. These primary purposes, and the "secondary" activities they attract, ensure the presence of people on the streets and in the spaces and buildings across different times of the day. People will use the place for a variety of different reasons, and also be able to use many facilities in common. Places that fail in urban vitality, such as the City of London, do so not because of a lack of people but because of insufficient mixture of primary uses at street level. Unlike Soho or Covent Garden, people go there for one reason only – to work in offices.

There are two types of mixed use diversity. Primary uses bring people to specific places and therefore act as "people attractors" – offices, residences, some shops and many (but not all) places of education, recreation and entertainment. Sometimes the primary use which attracts people is somewhat modest – a small family café, a shoe shop, a popular restaurant. However, no matter how successful the primary use, city diversity is only achieved where primary uses are combined. Secondary diversity refers to the enterprises and services which grow in response to primary uses, to serve the people the primary uses attract. If these secondary activities spread to provide a variety of consumer needs or tastes throughout the day, all sorts of uniquely urban specialized shops and services can survive. This process builds on itself, becoming increasingly intricate and mixed. For mixed use to operate successfully, three further conditions must be met: people must use the same streets and spaces, people must use at least some of the same facilities, and activity must not be concentrated into a particular time of the day.

It has recently become fashionable to speak of and plan for mixed use. But often what are described as mixed use developments fail because in reality they are not really mixed at all. A development site which has offices in one part, a drive-in restaurant in another and a retail warehouse on yet another might well be described as mixed use, but in the absence of self generating secondary diversity, shared facilities and streets, the mixture is one of oil and water. Thus it is important for mixture to occur not only within a city block or on a development site but also within building blocks both horizontally and vertically. This is fundamentally important for commercial areas but also in mixed residential neighbourhoods.

Areas of high development density can be planned to accommodate and stimulate mixed use and self-generating secondary diversity. Vertical zoning could be applied to ensure the presence of active uses on ground floors. Where possible, residential units, shops and even offices would be accommodated within city blocks and within building blocks. Space would be provided not only for primary uses, but also for secondary activities such as pavement cafés, galleries, specialist grocery stores and places of entertainment. A number of key "people attractors" would need to be strategically placed, not only in core areas, but also those residential neighbourhoods which are of medium density.

Condition 3: Fine Grain

The larger an urban place, the greater will tend to be both the number and proportion of small businesses. Large businesses have greater self-sufficiency, are able to maintain within themselves most of the skills and equipment they need, can warehouse or deliver for themselves and sell to a broad (not locationally specific) market. They need not be in cities, and often it is advantageous or deemed advantageous for them to relocate to green field sites or business parks. By contrast, small firms must draw on many and varied supplies and skills outside themselves, they often (but not always) serve narrow or place-specific markets. With some exceptions, such small firms cannot exist without city diversity, which they themselves do much to stimulate. For such enterprises (and for many larger ones) employees and executives need to be in close, face-to-face contact with clients, customers and suppliers, or feel able to pop out for a sandwich or a swim at lunch-time, or meet for drinks in the evening. This is not to say that all city enterprises are small, for cities accommodate both the supermarket and the delicatessen. It is to say that wherever lively and popular urban areas are found, the range of small businesses will outnumber the large. A lively city scene is lively largely by virtue of the collection of small elements and in particular its commercial diversity. The difference between urban areas that are dull and those that are vital can be traced to the presence or lack of small enterprises. Thus, any successful urban place must not only accommodate large enterprises (which employ large numbers of people and impact on the wider local economy), but must also allow space for small enterprises to grow. This means that an urban district should ideally mingle building accommodation that varies in age, condition, size and cost of occupation. This mingling must also be close-grained. Within mixed city blocks, smaller units of varying sizes would be provided, often on first and second floors (offices) but also on top floors (design studios) and ground floor frontages where the enterprise (a private gallery for example) attracts customers or browsers from the street.

Condition 4: Adaptability

As we have seen, successful urban areas accommodate complex patterns of diversity, mixture and economic grain. Places which continue to succeed despite changes in economic conditions, technology and culture, do so because their built form is itself mixed and/or highly adaptable. City streets tend, for example, to succeed over larger timescales than single-purpose office buildings that are susceptible to changes in demand (down-sizing of labour forces), technology (computer and cable ducting) and expectation (air conditioning, intimacy as opposed to open plan). This is because, as a general rule, the life of streets and urban areas is longer than the life of individual buildings, while the life of buildings is longer than the life of their original function. By extension, the successful urban area offers in-built adaptability rather than in-built obsolescence. There are a variety of building forms which offer much adaptability, and most of them tend to be buildings on several floors with a mixture of room sizes on each floor. Interestingly, whilst loft-living represents the adapting of old warehouse and light industrial accommodation for residential use, there are now many examples of residential accommodation being adapted as offices or studios, even galleries and cafés. Such forms, for example mansion blocks and town houses, are not only adaptable in the types of activity they can accommodate, but also the levels of intensity of activity.

Condition 5: Human Scale

Scale is a combination of the ratio of building height to street width, relative distance, permeability and the sense of grandeur, intimacy or space. As such it is closely related to intensity, for more intense places have higher buildings. Most of Soho and Mayfair, almost all of Amsterdam and much of ancient Rome fits into one square mile, while only part of San Francisco's downtown fits into such an area. Paris, on the other hand, has not one central area but a variety of connected *quartiers* and *arrondisement*, most of which adopt a similar scale and development intensity.

There are no hard and fast rules concerning the relationship between building heights and street widths, other than to say that higher buildings tend to require wider streets, and more generous allowances for natural light and ventilation. But even here, more intricate and complex places very often have high buildings but only very narrow streets and alleyways (Bairro Alto in Lisbon for example). The important consideration is whether one wishes to generate street life, and therefore whether the overall "shape"[86] of the street allows for this to happen. A related point is that most successful urban places operate at several scales, but importantly are more rather than less intricate, are capable of being walked in under 10 minutes, and have a large number of intersections. By and large, successful urban districts covering an area of one square mile will tend to have well over 250 intersections, sometimes more (Amsterdam has nearly 600, Toulouse has 330, Mayfair 420).[87] Deliberately planned or spaced-out places, by contrast, have fewer intersections – Washington DC has 155 within a square mile, and Brasilia only 92.

A corollary of the number of intersections is the number of building blocks (see Condition 6) within a given area. For the more intersections there are, the more building blocks there will tend to be. Many urban planners in the past advocated fewer and larger blocks and fewer streets and intersections in order to rid the city of overcrowding and achieve greater spatial efficiency. The problem is that by doing so, urbanity is destroyed. Alan Jacobs[88] points out that Boston's downtown area in 1895 had over 600 intersections and 400 blocks, but today has less than 400 intersections and fewer than 250 blocks. So Boston has become a less intricate and complex place. City blocks and land parcels have become larger, as have the "footprints" of individual buildings. And as this scale gets

---

86 Nairn, I., *Nairn's London*, Revisited by Peter Gasson (London: Penguin, 1988), p. 128.

87 Jacobs, A., *Great Streets* (Cambridge, Mass: MIT Press, 1994).

88 Ibid.

larger, not only intersections but also whole streets are either lost or become self-isolating. Of course, it is possible to have too much intimacy, too many intersections and therefore confusion. But this tends to occur only when both the number of intersections and blocks exceeds 700 per square mile. It is also possible to have many intersections and blocks but few public spaces – as in Bologna for example, and this does not help in generating street life. Thus, in order to achieve a pedestrian or walkable scale, more rather than fewer intersections are necessary as indeed is greater intensity and building height.

Condition 6: City Blocks and Permeability

The most beneficial combination of building heights, street widths (range of), intersections and blocks is likely to fall in the range of 250 intersections and 250 blocks per square mile. This scale would of course be lower in residential neighbourhoods, although those which are mixed and of medium density would be of a more intricate scale than more traditional suburban layouts. Two points can be made. The first is that most (not necessarily all) city blocks must be short, thus providing more streets to walk down and more opportunities to turn corners. This can also be achieved where the street pattern includes alleys, ginnels and courtyards. All of these serve to increase the permeability of an area, and therefore its potential "footfall", and in turn increases the number of economically viable points for trading (providing there are units to trade from). Psychologically, people are less inclined to walk down long unbroken streets with little activity or a mono-functional identity, so that such streets become self-isolating and stagnant. Long city blocks (see Diagram A) not only hinder permeability therefore, they also thwart the possibilities of small enterprise development. And as more streets become inactive, the reasons for keeping them in existence become fewer... "we might as well assemble a bigger plot because nothing happens around here".

By contrast, city districts which have more shorter blocks (see Diagram B) tend also to generate more street life, and even more streets where, for example, back alleyways and courtyards are opened up to active use. To be successful, then, city districts would be comprised of as many blocks as possible, and these should only rarely exceed 300 × 300 feet (90 metres).

Second, the blocks themselves must be just that: blocks rather than building plots. That is to say the building line must, leaving a sufficient pavement width, be set up right against the street and ideally build around a central courtyard. One of the failures of modern urban planning has been the insistence of situating simple building blocks in the middle of a plot (see diagram D) as opposed to being fully centred on the plot (see diagram C). By doing so, more land is used up and less activity is made possible. This is the reverse of what should happen: the building should help define the space rather than simply being set in it.

All of this means that for a new city, city blocks should ideally not exceed 300 × 300 feet. Buildings would not tend to be set back from the street or positioned

A.

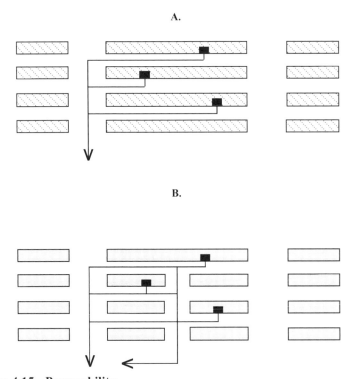

B.

Figure 4.15 Permeability
Source: derived from Jane Jacobs by John Montgomery.

C.   D.

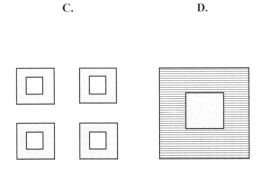

Figure 4.16 Plots and Building Lines
Source: derived from Michael Synnott by John Montgomery.

centrally within a plot but rather around central courtyards. This is especially true of the core areas, but again would apply to the more intricate mixed residential neighbourhoods. In these places more variety of layout can be accommodated, but the accent would still be on achieving a permeable grain.

Condition 7: Streets: Contact, Visibility and Horizontal Grain

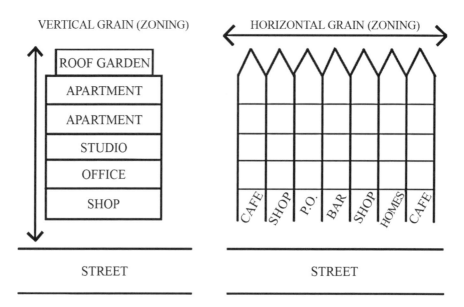

Figure 4.17   Vertical and Horizontal Grain
Source: John Montgomery.

Good urban places are judged by their street life. For it is in streets – as multi-purpose spaces – that all the ingredients of city life are combined: public contact, public social life, people-watching, promenading, transacting, natural surveillance and culture. Streets bring together people who do not know each other in an intimate, private social sense, including strangers. The street is a subtle balance of essential privacy and varying degrees of public and private contact. Streets also provide a high degree of natural surveillance where the presence of other people generates more "eyes on the street"[89] and therefore more self-policing. But for this to happen, streets need to be active, to accommodate and generate diversity and must be permeable. They must also engender a sense of belonging, a familiarity and the respect of users. There will also be a clear demarcation of public and

---

89 Jacobs, J., *op. cit.*, 1961, chapters 2 and 3.

private spaces, places to promenade and shelter from the wind. Good streets have well-defined edges and a quality of transparency or visibility at their edges (where the private and public realms meet). Thus, the design of a good street is perfectly possible provided that it is first and foremost considered as a street and not a road. For this to happen, there must be a good horizontal grain of active frontages along a street. Thus, in any block of 10 shop units, there might be two food stores, a video store, an off-licence, a patisserie, a café-bar, a gallery and restaurant, a pharmacy and a betting shop.

Thus, in contrast to many recent examples of new city building (for example EuraLille or La Defense) active city districts should be designed around a network of streets as opposed to roads. To stimulate more activity and natural surveillance, an element of horizontal zoning of street frontages would be applied so that there will be a procession of active frontages every 20–30 feet. Pavements will be wide enough to accommodate sidewalk cafés but not too wide so as to make the street itself over-spaced, i.e. about 10–12 feet.

Condition 8: Public Realm

Streets and spaces are undoubtedly the most important elements in a city's public realm. In fact, the public realm in a city performs many functions, not only as meeting places but also in helping to define the built environment, providing spaces for local traditions and customs such as festivals and carnivals, and representing meaning and identity. It is therefore as important to think through the design of the public realm – its sequences, proportions and dimensions – as it is for city blocks and individual buildings. Successful cities are in part shaped by the relationship of built form to space, and the range, variety and characteristics of the spaces made available: outdoor rooms, civic spaces, promenading routes, night-strips, quiet gardens, little corners to rest awhile, favourite meeting places. This is not simply a question of quantity or setting space standards (so many acres to population bands), but a rather more complex understanding of the attributes of spaces, their delineations, psychology and symbolism. In many cities around the world, until quite recently, not much thought has gone into the public realm, nor much of an appreciation of it or the fact that it is being lost to development schemes and private shopping malls.[90] Consideration of the valuable role played by the public realm ought to be a key development principle in city making.

Thus, in designing a city's built form around city blocks and streets, other elements of a public realm or space system would be built into the city form, including squares, meeting places and promenading routes. Attention would also need to be paid to the safety of such places by promoting natural as well as organized surveillance, by managing their upkeep properly and by installing lighting systems of a high standard.

---

90 Davis, M., *City of Quartz* (London: Vintage Books, 1990), chapter 4.

Condition 9: Movement

One of the major urban issues of our times is undoubtedly transport. There has been an at times charged debate over the pros and cons of traffic calming, public transport and road building. There is certainly a danger of congested roads and traffic choking the cities. But there is also perhaps a danger of policy swinging too heavily against cars. For no matter how good your public transport system is, there will always be a need to make some journeys by car – for businesses purposes, for going out at night, doing the weekly food shop or making a cross town or otherwise lateral trip.

That said, for peak rush hours in particular, much can be done to reduce trips by car: by traffic management, by investing in reliable and frequent public transport alternatives, and by establishing networks of bicycle lanes. Experience from elsewhere, notably Copenhagen, suggests that systems of integrated transport "nodes" bring many benefits in car trip reduction – particularly along rail and rapid transit routes. Simply by locating major employment areas next to such transport nodes, it is possible to achieve a reduction in trips made by car.

Even so, there will remain a requirement for people to travel by car. All of this means that car travel must be accommodated within cities but not allowed to dominate or impose. In this way, the more intensive "core" areas would tend to place more restrictions on car access and parking, while cars will always be an important feature of life in new residential areas. Routes whose primary purpose is to connect the city with other places sub-regionally and regionally will be of an altogether different type than those that permeate the built form. Perhaps the most difficult issues to address are not the commuters, but rather the school run and people driving their cars for leisure trips.

In addition, it is likely that some creative measures would need to be employed to provide off-street parking for residents and other users, particularly in core areas. This might include underground car parks, as in Lyon, car parks contained within city blocks but wrapped around by more active uses, automated car silos, and town houses with integrated garages.

Condition 10: Green Space and Water Space

Public green space and water areas are important to city life for many reasons, for example providing a range of informal and formal playgrounds, fields and gardens for varying degrees of passive and active pursuits; to promote exercise and healthier living; in filtering the noise, light and air of the city; and by framing development sites, providing views and landscape image. Again, Lyon is a good example. To these we can add parks and open areas which are people attractors in their own right, whether as botanic or Italian gardens or as amusement or pleasure parks such as Tivoli Gardens where one can stroll about, have lunch or dinner and watch concerts and other performances. Parks can also be used for fairs, fireworks displays, concerts and other cultural events.

Condition 11: Landmarks, Visual Stimulation and Attention to Detail

> At every instant, there is more than the eye can see, more than the ear can hear, a setting or a view waiting to be explored. Nothing is experienced by itself, but always in relation to its surroundings and sequences of events leading up to it, the memory of past experiences.[91]

Landmarks, meeting places and smaller scale signatures have always played an important role in the life and design of cities. In laying out modern Rome, Pope Sixtus was careful to situate a number of obelisks, designed to help pilgrims orientate themselves, to make the city more legible and to fore-shorten distances by placing objects on the vanishing point.[92] More recently, public art has become important for the way it contributes to a greater sense of place by upgrading the quality of the built environment, creating meeting places and talking points, coming to represent important points of reference and its capacity to animate public space. There are also now many examples of public art being used to reflect the aspirations and experiences of the local citizenry, a form of community expression, and there are even examples of such work discouraging vandalism.

As well as the more obvious elements such as sculpture and murals, it is important to consider decorative features such as reliefs, street furniture (everything from benches to streetlamps to signposts), even the design of public space itself. This can even be extended to provide orientation and direction to the people using an entire city or city district. In Phoenix, Arizona, for example, the public art programme has been designed to operate within "five spatial urban design systems": water, parks and open spaces, vehicular systems, pedestrian systems and landmark systems. One of the chief aims is "to create for the people of Phoenix a spatial structure of places, landmarks and experiences, evoking a strong sense of history and orientation". Such approaches have also been adopted in Temple Bar (Dublin) and La Defense in Paris where along the Grand Axis alone there are some 30 works of art, 70 fountains, manicured gardens, paved courts, cafés and street markets.

Of course, if the city itself is badly designed or lacking in activity, no amount of public art will make all that much of a difference. And indeed, many landmarks, reference points and meeting places needn't be overly arty at all. The place to meet in Lisbon is the San Salvatore Escalator (a functional piece of 19th century engineering), whereas the reference points in Liverpool are the two cathedrals and the Liver Building. That said, the possibilities for introducing exciting and innovative pieces and installations are many. And where this extends to the fine detail of reliefs and street furniture the opportunity is one of moving beyond the municipal over-design of the public realm that, sadly, has been a characteristic of city design in recent times. New city developments ought to incorporate a wide ranging programme of public art and land-marking, in its water, open space, vehicular and pedestrian systems, so designed as to underpin the legibility of the city overall and to provide individual

---

91 Lynch, K., *op. cit.*, 1961.

92 Sennet, R., *The Conscience of the Eye: The Design and Social Life of Cities* (London: Faber & Faber, 1990).

features and points of interest. This could extend to the design of street furniture and other detailing, to the creation of public spaces themselves, and even to lighting features and holograms.

Condition 12: Architectural Style as Image

City building and city design are not questions of architectural style, that is to say the design and appearance of individual buildings. Rather, the essential task is to design the form of the city in such a way as to achieve city diversity, activity and urbanity. That said, the question of architectural style is not unimportant for this also conveys meaning, shapes identity and creates image. This prompts a further question: if a place is to be a city in form, what message should its style convey? This is not an idle point. The options lie along a spectrum of neo-Georgian, fake Victorian, high modernism, post-modernism and replica vernacular. Certainly, good cities have always been places that personify or at least display strong elements of culture, technology, engineering innovation, civilization and cosmopolitanism. Cities should not be allowed to become non-places of transatlantic mono-cultural "international" architecture. But it is important to distinguish between modernism (an ideological project as well as an architectural movement) and modernity. The latter is simply about using design skills and materials to fashion objects which function well and are in themselves beautiful. A Georg Jensen watch, a Philippe Starck chair, the lines on a Pininfarina car. Not all cars look like 1930s Bentleys, beautiful though these are. So why need all buildings look like the Acropolis? Perhaps I am labouring the point. Put simply, cities should be places that are diverse, cosmopolitan and cultured, and this should include modern architecture.

5. PLACES IN THE FIFTH WAVE

In Part IV we have considered the built form of cities and how this can either support or hinder economic development, wealth creation and artistic creativity. We have explored the concept of "place" and shown that people tend to become attached to cities, districts, neighbourhoods, streets and individual buildings, parks and landmarks. This is because the places we inhabit, inhabit us. We have seen that "place" is a compound of three interlocking elements: activity, meaning and form. The playing out of these in a particular space gives cities their identity and image. The balance of activity, meaning and form changes over time, but very often the built form – "the stones" – remains and may be adapted to new economic and cultural conditions. That is, if cities are not comprehensively redeveloped as was the case under modernism. We have also seen that cities that allow inappropriate forms of development damage their sense of place, and with it the very built forms that support mixture and diversity in economic and cultural life. To help address this problem, we have even gone so far as to prepare a "guide" to city building.

Table 4.2 Summary Principles for Achieving Urbanity

A:	**Activity**
Principle 1:	Generating Pedestrian Flows and Vitality
Principle 2:	Seeding People Attractors
Principle 3:	Achieving a Diversity of Primary Uses
Principle 4:	Developing a Density of Population
Principle 5:	Varying Opening Hours and Stimulating the Evening Economy
Principle 6:	Promoting Street Life and People-Watching
Principle 7:	Growing a Fine-Grain Economy
B:	**Image**
Principle 8:	Legibility
Principle 9:	Imageability
Principle 10:	Symbolism and Memory
Principle 11:	Psychological Access
Principle 12:	Receptivity
Principle 13:	Knowledgeability
C:	**Form**
Principle 14:	Achieving Development Intensity
Principle 15:	Zoning for Mixed Use
Principle 16:	Building for a Fine Grain
Principle 17:	Adaptability of the Built Stock
Principle 18:	Scale
Principle 19:	City Blocks and Permeability
Principle 20:	Streets: Contact, Visibility and Horizontal Grain
Principle 21:	The Public Realm
Principle 22:	Movement
Principle 23:	Green Space and Water Space
Principle 24:	Landmarks, Visual Stimulation and Attention to Detail
Principle 25:	Architectural Style as Image

It is clear from the preceding analysis that, historically, city form has adapted itself to dominant system of economic productions of the time. This argument has been taken up by the urban academic Janet Abu-Lughod[93] who argues that five distinct cycles of urban development have been evident in the USA (and elsewhere). These are the era of mercantile capitalism which she dates from 1607 to 1820, early industrialization and canal building from the 1820s until the 1870s, high industrialization and the mass international migration of the period 1880 to the mid 1920s, the period from the 1930s to the early 1970s, and the current period

---

93 Abu-Lughod, J., *New York, Chicago, Los Angeles: America's Global Cities* (Minneapolis: University of Minnesota Press, 1999).

of restructuring. New York became a world city during the second cycle, Chicago during the third and Los Angeles the fourth.

Thus, it can be argued that city form largely adapts to the dominant systems of economic production of the time. This is most evident for the industrial cities of the 19th century – mills, back-to-back row housing, high densities, close proximity of home to work place. However, during the second part of the 19th century city form was also beginning to change by measures designed to improve health, sanitation and living conditions. But because of the lag effect between social reforms being agitated for, enacted and then brought into effect, the impact of these on city form very often only becomes evident a generation later. Thus, the early housing and town planning acts in Britain of the late 19th century only really became "concrete" following the First World War.

The Fordist city became a hybrid of modernism, reforming town planning and the suburbanization which, originally facilitated by the growth of railways, exploded out in all directions with the rise of car ownership. During this period cities became "more efficient", work was separated from home, land use zoning was the order of the day and the boundaries of cities grew and grew. As we have seen, it was during this period that cities sprawled and that land uses – previously mixed – became separated from each other. This period also saw the rise – literally – of the Central Business District (zones must have names) and the skyscraper. This much is evident from consideration of Chicago and Detroit, indeed London and Paris, but it was also prevalent in Melbourne which, as we have seen, was losing mixed use diversity from the city centre as early as the 1930s. In some cases, the attendant sprawl was carefully, if not always imaginatively, planned as is the case of Cerdà's plan for the Eixample, but most often the sprawl was largely unplanned. Attempts to address this sprawl would lead to the adoption of a "green belt" policy in the UK, and also to Copenhagen's "Finger Plan", amongst others.

The reason that modernism was so damaging to the fabric of cities is that it sought not to repair or re-build but rather totally to redevelop cities. Slums were cleared, market squares were torn up, streets were obliterated, to be replaced by tall buildings which often ignored completely the pre-existing street system and surrounding buildings and areas. As if reformist zeal was not bad enough, modernism brought with it the "heroic architect", the cult of the individual as an artist, the search for celebrity through new architectural forms, the ego, the "Fountainhead".[94] In the process, traditional elements such as the street or square or built-to line were rejected, or simply ignored, and well-intentioned civil engineers began to develop schemes for improving traffic flows (free-ways, urban motorways, roundabouts, wider roads) and to segregate pedestrians and cars. This would later help produce the conditions for enclosed shopping malls surrounded by car parking. The point about modernism is that it produced a fragmentation of the built environment, an unravelling of the sense of place, large areas of the city given over to heroic buildings, themselves often lost in left-over space. In Britain – as indeed in France and Sweden – this

---

94 Rann, A., *The Fountainhead* (London: Cassell & Co Ltd, 1947).

was made all the worse by a political drive to clear slums and build new high-rise housing schemes in the inner and outer areas of cities.

By the 1960s it was clear that the modernist city was no longer in vogue. People concerned about redevelopment proposals organized to lobby for conservation and rehabilitation of older buildings and neighbourhoods. This gave rise to the Civic Trust in the UK, and brought the New York city engineer Robert Moses to heel. Meanwhile, as capitalism entered its "post-Fordist" phase, new office buildings remained a necessity, but so too would business parks and shopping malls be developed. The "post-industrial" city continued to decentralize but in ever bigger chunks. To disguise this process – and to distance themselves from reviled modernism – architects began to decorate "boxes" in all manner of styles, giving rise to post-modernism. This essentially nihilistic and opportunistic response was mirrored in cultural movements of the time which promoted narcissism, relativism and personal freedom without responsibility. In a sense, this was the worst of all worlds: the high-rise monofunctional CBD, the loss of traditional street forms, continuing urban sprawl, the advent of "big-box" retailing, the suburbanization of even small towns and the loss of more and more countryside. No longer growing up, the cities were growing out.

From the early 1990s, that is the end of the Fourth Kondratieff Wave, resistance to almost any form of development was widespread amongst probably a majority of people in the western democracies. Bad mannered modernism was out, retail sheds were abhorred, shopping malls were no longer to be permitted, the sprawl and swallowing up of previously free-standing places was no longer acceptable. In continental Europe – Amsterdam, Copenhagen, Freiburg, Lyon – medium-sized cities reversed their policies of planned decentralization in an effort to "re-centre" the cities. Traditional city forms were once again favoured, the "compact city" idea was born. This concern to re-centre cities was also adopted in the UK in many of the urban regeneration projects of the 1980s and 1990s. In USA, cities such as Portland and Philadelphia were the exceptions rather than the rule, but even so by the early 1990s "new urbanism" was born. In Australia, urban policies began to favour place-making but large malls and residential sub-divisions continued to be developed. This is now changing, and in common with the UK, Europe and North America, Australian cities are once again being planned as cities, mixed use is considered essential in most settings, places are designed to be places, urban design is ascendant – a new paradigm in urban planning. To some degree, this reflects the changing demands of people for more stimulating environments, and a blurring of the boundary between the workplace and home. Also, car travel has proved not to be so efficient after-all as, if everyone else has the same idea, congestion follows. It is also the case, as we argued in Part I, that key workers in the knowledge and creative industries are drawn to places that are more mixed and offer a greater diversity of activities. We can see that the "post-industrial" service economy is still present – but then so too are outcrops of the industrial economy. In addition, the economy is tending to be driven by flows of capital certainly (that is the globalization of money exchange) but also the new products and/or processes of the digital age. This is being accompanied by rising living standards generally, and greater personal wealth. In turn this wealth is used to express one's "identity" (remember we are still narcissistic) so that demand for designed goods, crafted objects and art is increasing. This "new economy" does not yet have a name, but it should not be confused with either "globalization" which is simply an extension of markets and trade; or "post-industrialization" because goods as well as services are produced, and indeed many of the new technologies allow new goods to be invented or old products distributed in a different way. The "new economy", rather, is a hybrid containing within it elements of tradition and modernity, goods as well as services, industrialized forms of production as well as flexible specialization, the designed and the crafted, the real and the virtual. That said, the higher value products and services seem likely to be wrapped up in image and life-style.

At times, and quite independent of "the economic base", cities have changed their form in response to philosophical and artistic ideas, and in response to political reforms. On this, the history of social reforms is well-documented including the introduction of education, public sanitation and housing reforms in London during the late 19th century, or indeed of any major city at that time.[95] We have also seen that pressures for political reform led to the re-design of Barcelona in the 19th century, and again since 1979. Portland, too, is an example of local political movements resisting large-scale development proposals. So if place matters, so too does local policy and decision-making. More than this, cities such as Portland, Dublin or Copenhagen owe much of their economic success to the fact that they offer attractive environments, they have a good built form.

This brings us to the question of what the city form of the future will be. I intend to address this issue more fully in the conclusion to this book. Here, following from the above argument, it is my view that just as the beginnings of the new economy were evident from the late 1970s, so too are the basic building blocks of future city form. In truth, the form of cities will not change a great deal, and limits to urban growth will increasingly be the norm. Pressures for new development will be accommodated within existing city boundaries by a process of regeneration and some intensification of densities. At the same time, a modest number of new settlements will be built and more people will move to market towns, the sea-side and the country. Growth will occur in different types of place. This is true of Europe, the UK and North America. Countries like Australia will continue to develop its urban centres as the population is added to by immigration, while many older people will retire to "sea-change" or the countryside. City populations will grow, although this will be disproportionate in that ethnic minorities will continue to reproduce more quickly than indigenous Caucasians. With the best will in the world, this will produce a further migration of middle-class people away from the cities, as we are now seeing in London, Amsterdam and Vienna, not to mention Detroit. Lamentable though this may seem, it is already happening. Notwithstanding – and taking into account the possible distribution of populations between cities, towns and countryside – some

---

95 Hall, P., *Cities of Tomorrow* (Oxford: Blackwell, 1988).

observations on the characteristics of successful cities in the coming 50 years can be made. As in previous Parts, it is helpful to consider these as a series of polarities:

- Innovation v Creative Stagnation
- Dynamic Growth v Sluggish Growth
- Tradition v Modernity
- Distinctiveness v Homeogenity
- Centralization v Suburbanization

Many academics are, perhaps belatedly, turning their attention to the future of cities. For example, in April 2004 a major international Symposium, funded by the Leverhulme Trust, was held at the London School of Economics. Many of the writers seem to be in two minds whether there is a resurgence of cities at all. Ian Gordon, for example, concludes that urban resurgence is "an idea ... with some empirical as well as theoretical support, but remains in urgent need of evidence.[96] Beauregard,[97] meanwhile, researched 50 US cities during the second half of the 20th century. He found that only 12 of these (less than a quarter) showed signs of resurgence, that is to say a period of economic and population growth following a period of decline. Roughly the same proportion of cities had experienced decline without any form of recovery. The remaining 50 per cent all achieved growth throughout the period, although mostly this was steady rather than propulsive, and all of these cities were in the sunbelt of the South and southern California. This is not especially surprising. What the academics seem to be missing is the fact that the second half of the 20th century was the time of the Fourth Kondratieff Wave and that, moreover, two decades of growth (the 50s and 60s) were followed by stagnation (the 70s) and then two decades of decline. Within this overall scenario it is likely that some cities would grow with the development of new technologies and industries (Seattle, San Francisco, LA, Austin), others would achieve growth from the relocations of firms and people, either from the declining cities or from the cold northern climates (Miami, Atlanta), while others would grow because of their inherent attractiveness. It would seem that of the latter category, growth was achieved by local governments seizing the opportunities that became available to them.

The most interesting recent contribution by an academic is by Eric Heikkila,[98] Professor of Planning at the University of Southern California. Heikkila sets out to demonstrate that cities are shaped by four forces: markets, culture, geography and history. He argues that cultural values and purposes stand "in opposition to those of markets"; while geography and history are, somewhat fancifully, represented as

---

96 Gordon, I., "The Resurgent City: What, Where, How and For Whom", *Planning Theory and Practice*, 5, 3, September 2004, pp. 371–379.

97 Beauregard, R., *The Resilience of US Cities: Decline and Resurgence in the 20th Century*, Paper presented to the Leverhulme International Symposium *The Resurgent City*, London School of Economics, April 2004.

98 Heikkila, E.J., "What is the Nature of the 21st Century City?", *Planning Theory and Practice*, 5, No. 3, September 2004, pp. 379–387.

"being" and "becoming". Heikkila further argues that these forces are themselves shaped by "an even more fundamental dichotomy" between modernity and tradition. This allows Heikkila to construct "a simple taxonomy of cities" in which market values compete with cultural values; temporal identity ("becoming") is juxtaposed with spatial identity ("being"); and modernity operates in opposition to tradition. This in turn allows Heikkila to propose that there are four fundamental types of city:

- *The Traditional City*, where cultural values dominate and "where identity is strongly rooted in place", the examples he gives are Jerusalem and Rome.
- *The Modern City*, where market values dominate and where identity is temporal, that is to say subject to change. Examples include Shenzhen, "an instant city" and Phoenix.
- *The Bazaar City*, where market values dominate but these are also rooted in a sense of place, that is cities like Hong Kong and New York.
- *The Transformational City*, where cultural values dominate but in a context of placelessness, the example being Los Angeles.

Interesting although Heikkila's schema is, it is flawed for the simple reason that, as I have argued throughout this book, commerce (markets) and culture are not binary opposites but in fact feed and reinforce each other. Thus, the Renaissance was both a cultural movement and an explosion in wealth creation; so too was the Enlightenment, the Victorian industrial age and even modernism. To juxtapose culture against markets is a serious error, as pointed out by the British town planner Andy Farrell.[99] The more useful of Heikkila's observations is his focus on the qualities of place and the tension between tradition and modernity. As Gabriele Pasqui[100] points out in his account of Milan's fashion industry, the Milan urban region is " ... a mix of tradition and modernity, culture and market, geography and history". Milan's competitive advantage, he argues, is limited to a set of "intangible assets". These are: "knowledge, technologies, culture, networks, lifestyle and widespread social practices". In other words, commerce, culture, place and time.

In concluding this Part IV I should like to introduce my own schema for the city of the 21st century, derived in part from Heikkila. This is based simply on a juxtaposition of high levels of economic growth and wealth creation as opposed to stagnation or low growth on the one hand; and the tension between tradition and modernity on the other. By tradition, I mean established cultural forms, built forms and social customs; while modernity is a search for new art, architecture, fashions and social practices. Thus, following Heikkila, my own taxonomy (Fig. 4.18) also produces four broad city types:

---

99 Farrall, A., "The Nature of the City, its Resurgence and Planners", *Planning, Theory and Practice*, 5, 3, September 2004, pp. 389–392.

100 Pasqui, G., "The Perspective of the Infinite City", *Planning, Theory and Practice*, 5, 3, September 2004, pp. 381–389.

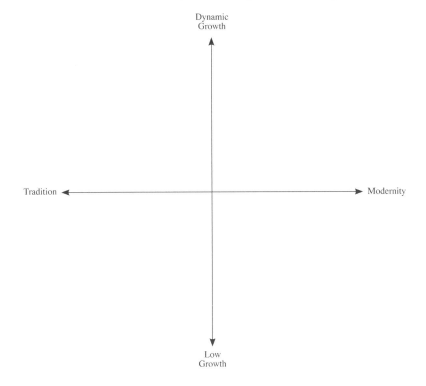

Figure 4.18   A Taxonomy for the Traditional-Modern City
Source: John Montgomery.

- *High Growth Modern*: the combination of a dynamic economy with modern cultural forms.
- *High Growth Traditional*: the combination of a dynamic economy with traditional cultural forms.
- *Low Growth Modern*: the combination of low growth modernity and placelessness.
- *Low Growth Traditional*: the combination of low growth with old cultural forms.

We shall consider this in a little more detail in the conclusion to this book. The important point is whether or not economic growth is present, and in what ways this inter-plays with the culture and form of a city. It is likely that in real life, most cities will combine some elements of high and low growth, tradition and modernity, place and placelessness, certainly across city regions such as Milan or Greater London or Southern California. The cities that have most to fear are those with low levels of new wealth creation and either a placeless form or identity or too much emphasis on the past. In all of this, much will depend upon existing levels of artistic creativity, investment in technology and R&D, a city's cultural life, its place identity and the quality of its environment. Much too will, as it did in Barcelona, Portland and Melbourne, depend on leadership. Urban environments such as those described above are already coming into existence. Several of these, as we shall explore in Part V, have developed since the late 1980s as self-styled cultural quarters.

PART V: CREATIVE MILIEUX

Quarters and Clusters

So far in this book, I have argued that cities and their economies are inextricably interlinked; indeed without new work, a diverse division of labour, networks of exporting and producer services and technological innovation, cities become stagnant and may even die. To innovate, cities must be creative, in the development and application of new technologies, in bringing new goods and services to the market, and in wider cultural and artistic development. The cultural life of the city is therefore not an add-on but a key point of difference, a specialism. For culture is the means by which cities express identity, character, uniqueness, make positive statements about themselves, who they are, what they do and where they are going. It also, increasingly, is one of the ways they make their living.

Part V reviews the concept of the creative milieu, that is as concentrated places within cities and city regions – quarters or industrial districts or clusters – where economic development of the creative industries, the arts and the everyday urban cultural economy of cities are concentrated to achieve inter-trading, agglomeration economies and city diversity. All of these concepts have been discussed in Parts I–IV of this book.

It is necessary to conceptualize the term cultural quarter, discussing in broad terms what is meant by this now almost-orthodox terminology. This will draw on the urban literature, especially on theories of city growth, economic development and urban design. From this we can derive an idealized typology of what makes for a "good" cultural quarter, presented as a series of necessary conditions and success factors. This is applied and evaluated in more detail by considering five case study examples drawn from the United Kingdom, Ireland and Australia. We also consider to what extent the leading dynamic cities of the fifth wave will need to contain cultural and especially creative industry quarters.

1. CREATIVE MILIEUX

Recent contributions in the dusty field of local economic development have stressed the key importance of creativity to city planning and wealth generation. Examples include Charles Landry's *The Creative City*, and Richard Florida's *The Creative Class*. Charles Landry argues that whether places and cities with these characteristics generate new ideas and processes is dependent on the existence or otherwise of "creative triggers", that is events, moments and influences that cause creative advances to occur at that point in time. These triggers include such things as scarcity (a need to be met), obsolescence, new discoveries, luck (the chance discovery), opportunities (for example, commissions), entrepreneurship (an example might be Matthew Boulton in 18th century Birmingham), competitive pressures (rivalries between individual artists, the race to register patents), debate, learning from others, changes in city leadership ... .[1] This is arguably the closest anyone has come to defining the "creative spark", and yet at its simplest it involves the right people being in the right place, at the right time, with a body of knowledge and skills to draw upon, access to new technologies, a bit of healthy rivalry and the means of communicating with markets. In modern societies, the key figures in all of this, it seems to me, are the visionary political leaders and the artists, inventors and entrepreneurs, the former creating the conditions for the latter to invest and prosper.

Richard Florida reaches a broadly similar conclusion in *The Rise of the Creative Class* (2002),[2] his work on the role of creativity in economic development. In chapter 14, he presents the "3 Ts of economic development", namely "Technology, Talent and Tolerance". His basic argument is that growth is "powered" by creative people (Talent) who prefer places that are diverse and open to new ideas (Tolerant). Concentrations of "Cultural Capital" wedded to new products and processes (Technology) lead to "business formation, job generation and economic growth". Florida has much less to say, however, about what triggers creativity and episodes of spectacular wealth creation in particular places at particular points in time. Instead he argues that cities and places where the creative economy will grow can be spotted in advance, and that all cities have the wherewithal to become centres of the creative economy.

Florida proposes four unorthodox indices from which one can read-off whether a city is part of the creative economy or not. The first of these is The Melting Pot index, or mixes of ethnic groups, which he argues is indicative of high levels of technologically-based industry in the United States. By this he means that high-tech industries cluster in cities with highly multi-ethnic populations. Second is the Gay Index which proposes that homosexuals as a group are more inclined to be tolerant of others, have higher disposable incomes and enjoy the cultural benefits of city living. The cities in which they choose to live, in turn, will tend to be more tolerant or liberal and therefore more appealing to artists and inventors. This supports the Bohemian Index, measuring the numbers of creative people in a city: "writers, designers, musicians, actors, directors, painters and sculptors, photographers and dancers." The final index, Good Lifestyles, refers to places of long-established artistic pedigree, and the good life of cuisine and entertainment. In other words, creative entrepreneurs tend to be attracted to cities where it is possible to enjoy the arts, entertainment and good food.

Florida has gone on to test these indices empirically both in the United States and the United Kingdom. His findings are interesting in that Manchester emerges as Britain's most creative city, well ahead of London. This in itself is surprising for

1   Landry, C., *The Creative City* (London: Earthscan Publications, 2000).
2   Florida, R., *The Rise of the Creative Class* (New York: Basic Books, 2002).

London is the dominant centre for the creative industries in the UK, with 2 in 5 of all employment in London being in the sector. Manchester is certainly an innovative and creative city, as the author knows first hand having devised that city's cultural strategy in 1991,[3] but it is mistaken to believe that it out-guns London. Meanwhile, Florida concludes that Leicester is the second most creative city in the UK. This is simply untrue, and points to serious flaws in Florida's conceptualization. More recently, in Australia, Florida[4] ranks Sydney, as a "second-tier" city, above Melbourne (a "third tier" city), even although Melbourne has the more developed creative industries economy, certainly in fashion, architecture, music, contemporary art and design. Along-side Sydney, Florida ranks Moscow, which is struggling to have a legitimate economy at all, and Brussels, possibly the last place one would look for creativity. Frankfurt is elevated to the status of "second-tier" city, even although it is primarily a finance centre. Barcelona is considered a poor performer, Dublin is not mentioned at all, and neither, in his new rankings, is Manchester. Shanghai makes the list, but only as a third-tier city, that is behind Beijing. There is no mention of Helsinki, home of Nokia, nor the Indian cities of Mumbai, home of Bollywood, and Bangalore, one of the fastest growing centres of software design. Something, here, is amiss.

There certainly appears to be a confusion in the direction of causality in Florida's indices: are multi-ethnic societies of themselves more creative, or is it simply that employment and wealth creating opportunities attract all sorts of people to a dynamic economy; do homosexuals *cause* city economies to be more creative of themselves, or are they attracted to places that are lively and interesting, not all of which might be especially innovative in terms of economic development? Amsterdam is a renowned liberal city, but is it any more creative and innovative than, say, Dublin and Barcelona where moral codes are more conservative? Is Melbourne any less creative than Sydney or Brisbane simply because its business people are more conservatively and generally better dressed? Is Lyon any more creative than Glasgow just because the food is better?

As regards the Melting Pot Index, we might consider that waves of migration occur because there are jobs to go to in the new industries, especially, historically, in mills or along production lines. If jobs in established occupations and professions are difficult to come by, many immigrants are more or less compelled to set up in family-owned business. Whether such businesses are really innovative or creative cannot be taken as read, for many will simply be in small retailing and restaurants, or driving taxis. This can be seen in all of the Australian cities currently. Are all we really saying is that creative people like eating ethnic food and being driven around in taxis? Meanwhile, back in the USA the cities of Detroit and New Orleans have the largest non-white populations of any American cities, but both are bereft economically.

---

3   Urban Cultures Ltd and ppartnerships, *Manchester First: An Arts and Cultural Strategy* (Manchester City Council, 2 volumes, 1992).

4   Florida, R., "Smart Move, Sydney", *The Sydney Morning Herald*, April 23–24, 2005, Spectrum, pp. 23–24.

Similarly, for the Gay Index we might read people in general who prefer the choices and stimulus offered by cities. There is much evidence to suggest that young couples are putting off having children so they can enjoy careers and urban lifestyles, while older people are also returning to cities once their families have left home. The question is therefore really about people looking for an urban lifestyle and greater sophistication in the arts and entertainment. This is something that attracts older people too, and even the boring old married couples.

The Bohemian Index we can take as read, although these days a relatively small proportion of creative entrepreneurs, designers and media professionals – neatly turned out in their black suits – tend to think of themselves as "bohemian". What about engineers, scientists and technologists, many of whom, moreover, appear to prefer working on campuses and living in small towns or in the country? For Lifestyles we could read the diverse artistic, creative and entertainment activities that cities have historically provided. Indeed, this very point was made as long ago as 1994 in relation to London's creative industries.[5] It would appear that Florida has devised is a set of indices which simply mirror or correlate more fundamental truths about creative milieux or dynamic cities. Perhaps the most serious shortcoming is that Florida fails to relate the emergence of leading cities in the creative economy to pre-established traditions of wealth creation and innovation, and possibly this explains the surprise omission of Helsinki. In addition, there is the issue of beneficial tax rates on businesses – as in Singapore, Las Vegas or Dubai, for example – and the all-important question of whether or not the local business environment or culture encourages enterprise. For example, why is it that Dublin is highly creative and economically dynamic – a creative milieu – but Edinburgh is not?

Early conceptions of "creative milieux" were developed by the Swedish urban historians Gunnar Törnqvist and Ake Andersson. Gunter Törnqvist developed his own concept of the creative milieu in 1978, arguing that there were four key features:[6] information (which must be exchanged and inter-traded); knowledge (bodies of work and data-bases); competence in certain activities; and creativity, which combines the other three features to create new products, ideas and processes. In this way, creative places have a set of characteristics that, in most cases, take a long time to evolve and develop. It takes time to build up libraries, archives, data-bases and traditional skills. Such places come to have a recognized set of creative specialisms, and these in turn act as a magnet to attract further generations of creative people. This is what happens in London and New York, but also Milan and Helsinki. Artists in particular, are attracted to places with a diversity of trades and businesses, and a strong element of chaos and the chance encounter. This is a role that cities have always performed, but some of them are better at it than others.

---

5   Urban Cultures Ltd, *Prospects and Planning Requirements of London's Creative Industries* (London Planning Advisory Committee, 1994).

6   Törnqvist, G., "Creativity and the Renewal of Regional Life", in Buttimer, A. (ed.), *Creativity and Context* (Lund Studies in Geography, B. Human Geography, No. 50, 1983).

Ake Andersson[7] argues that creative milieux are cities which have developed almost subliminal abilities to produce new work in art, technology and science. Such places tend to be culturally diverse (in terms of tastes and preferences, rather necessarily than ethnic variety), rich in knowledge, have a store of skills and competencies, and are well-connected through communications infrastructure. They will also tend to be relatively compact places, with variations and innovations coming from diverse small-scale elements in close proximity. In this way, creative milieux build up a capacity to learn, innovate, apply pre-existing skills and develop new ones. For Anderssen, creative milieux are predicated on six essential conditions. The first of these is a sound financial base, so that capital is available to develop new products and services, but regulation and taxation must be light. This side of the equation is often overlooked in the works of Florida and Landry. There must, as a pre-requisite be an existing base of original knowledge and competence, but incentives to encourage experimentation and the exploration and exploitation of new opportunities will also be necessary. Good communications and infrastructure are important to transport goods and services to export markets, but also to enable inter-trading and the development of myriad producer service relationships. Uncertainty over the future direction of scientific and technological progress is also helpful, paradoxically, as this encourages trial and error. Finally, creative people welcome the stimulus of the arts, entertainment and even opportunities to transgress. This latter point, and the idea of "tolerance" was first advocated by Taine in the 1890s, as we saw in Part II.

Such creative milieux, then, will be centres for the production and use of knowledge, and repositories of methods, skills and disciplines. To this must be added technology, both as a set of new goods and services, and as a means of communication. It is then necessary to create a working environment that encourages talent, welcomes initiative, promotes experimentation and encourages both formal and applied creativity. These latter attributes especially, suggest that it is quite likely that creative milieux, particularly in the artistic fields, will tend to agglomerate around places – usually cities – which are themselves interesting in terms of their cultural life, entertainment, street life, urban form and architecture. As Landry puts it

> ..a milieu is a physical setting where a critical mass of entrepreneurs, intellectuals, social activists, artists, power-brokers or students operate in an open-ended, cosmopolitan context and where face to face interaction creates new ideas, artefacts, products, services and institutions, and as a consequence contributes to economic success.[8]

This means that creative milieux are comprised of clusters of industries, networks of firms and individuals, social relations and cultural life; and that they tend to occur in geographical space. It is to this question – the role of place in developing creative

---

7   Andersson, A., "Creativity and Regional Development", *Papers of the Regional Science Association*, 56, 1985.

8   Landry, *op. cit.*, 2000, p. 133.

milieux – that we now turn. In doing so, we shall discover that very often a whole city is not of itself a creative milieu, but rather one or more parts of it. The sorts of places that achieve this are these days referred to as cultural quarters and creative industry clusters.

2. CULTURAL QUARTERS

Most great cities have identifiable quarters to which artists and cultural entrepreneurs are attracted, whether it's Soho in London, New York's Lower East Side, or the Left Bank in Paris. Such places have a long history, and appear to have happened by accident or at least in the general development of a city over time.[9]

The urban quarter is a city-within-a-city . . . it contains the qualities and features of the whole. The urban quarter provides for all the periodic local (daily and weekly) urban functions within a limited piece of land dimensioned on the comfort of a walking citizen, not exceeding 33 hectares in surface and 10,000 inhabitants. Urban functions are zoned block-wise, plot-wise or floor-wise. An urban quarter must have a centre and a well-defined, readable limit.[10]

Within any contemporary city, it is almost certain that places of concentrated cultural activity will be found. However, these come in many guises. It can be posited that urban districts with a strong cultural focus fall into four categories:[11]

- museum cultural districts (for example South Kensington in London, Adelaide's North Terrace);
- institutional cultural districts – a cross-over of the above with major performing arts institutions (London South Bank, Melbourne South Bank);
- metropolitan cultural districts – where cultural venues in the main are part of a dynamic urban mix (Temple Bar, SoHo), and these include smaller and medium-sized elements;
- industrial cultural districts – centres of production both for the plastic arts and the creative and design industries (Sheffield CIQ, London's "cultural clusters").

The first two of these are oriented towards art as a good thing, an expression of civilization and of cultural consumption. The third is more closely related to urban-place making and mixed-use city diversity (a combination of urbanism and arts-led urban regeneration). The fourth is directly linked to the notion of the new economy

---

9   Montgomery, J., "Cultural Quarters as Urban Regeneration: Conceptualizing Cultural Quarters", *Planning Practice and Research*, 18, 4, November 2003.

10   Krier, L., *Charter of the European City*, paper presented to the conference, *The European City – Sustaining Urban Quality*, Copenhagen, 24–28 April, 1995.

11   Santagata, W., "Cultural Districts, Property Rights and Sustainable Economic Growth", *International Journal of Urban and Regional Research*, 26 (1), 2002, 9–23.

and mixed media, to new forms of cultural production and new work. In what follows, I propose to focus primarily on industrial cultural districts and metropolitan cultural districts, as these are the new dynamic cultural quarters or "creative miliuex" within cities. By contrast the older, more institutionalized cultural quarters are usually places to reflect on previous generations of artistic creativity, and very often these are badly integrated with the rest of the city. Rather than urban places, they are very often cultural ghettos.

The more recent meaning of the term cultural quarter dates from the early 1980s in the USA, for example in the cases of Boston Midtown Cultural District where ten small and medium sized theatres and eight non-profit galleries were planned within a mixed-use regeneration area.[12] Around the same time, the late 1980s, similar designations were being made in other US cities, notably Dallas and Washington D.C. These broadly followed an approach first attempted in the US in Pittsburgh in the late 1970s, as we shall discuss later. Cultural Quarters were proposed in the UK as long ago as 1987 by organizations such as the cultural consultancy Comedia[13] and also the British American Arts Association. As we also saw in Part II, culturally-led urban development began to appear as a concept in the urban planning literature from the late 1980s. So too did the concept of the creative industries quarter. The early UK examples are the Sheffield Cultural Industries Quarter, dating from the mid 1980s, and the Manchester Northern Quarter from 1993. The most frequently referred to example is Temple Bar in Dublin which dates as an idea from the late 1980s and as an example of applied culturally-led urban regeneration from 1990/1. What is new about the development of cultural quarters since the 1980s is that they have been (and are being) used as a deliberate model for urban regeneration of declining inner urban areas, and more recently in city economic development. This begs the question of what such places are like physically, how are they designed and laid out within urban space, are there shared characteristics not only as industry clusters or social networks, but also as places?

It is possible, *a priori*, to identify a set of necessary conditions and success factors in establishing cultural quarters, in large part by deriving these from the various urban literatures. Following from Canter's[14] *Metaphor for Place*, as we saw in Part IV, one can posit that all successful urban places are comprised of three sets of elements:

- Activity   economic, cultural, social
- Form   the relationship between buildings and spaces
- Meaning   sense of place, historical and cultural

Within this framework, it is possible to build-up a set of indicators that can be used to assess the relative success of cultural quarters. Thus, under the heading *Activity*, in

---

12 Horstmann, J.J., Mayne, D. and Schuster, J.M.D., *Arts and the Changing City: Case Studies* (London: British American Arts Association, 1988).

13 Bianchini, F., Montgomery, J., Fisher, M. and Worpole, K., *City Centres, City Cultures* (Manchester: Centre for Local Economic Development Strategies, 1988).

14 Canter, D., *The Psychology of Place* (London: Architectural Press, 1977).

good cultural quarters – as in good urban places generally – one should expect to find a diversity of primary and secondary uses, as discussed in Part IV. This includes such elements as locally-owned businesses, particularly shops; patterns in opening hours, including the existence of evening and night-time activity; the presence and size of street markets, and types of specialism; the presence of cinemas, theatres, wine bars, cafés, pubs, restaurants and other cultural and meeting places; the availability of spaces, including gardens, squares and corners to enable people-watching and other activities such as cultural animation programmes; patterns of mixed land ownership so that self-improvement and small-scale investment in property is possible; the presence of an active street life and active street frontages.

However, the essential pre-requisite for a cultural quarter is the presence of cultural activity. This is axiomatic: cultural quarters cannot exist without cultural activity. Of special significance is the presence of venues. These should be as varied as possible, preferably at the small and medium scale where the objective is to encourage a more active street life. As well as performance venues, there should also be rehearsal and practice spaces. A mixed economy in venues helps generate self-sustaining growth, so that as well as publicly provided theatres and galleries, there should also be private galleries and performance venues. The most successful of the cultural quarters very often have quite deliberately set out to develop a "network" of such venues, and in some cases these have been "planted" as strategic elements in the wider development of an area. Table 5.1 is a fairly straightforward listing of the types and range of cultural activity (deemed necessary success factors in a cultural quarter). Headings under which the comparisons are made focus mainly on the presence or otherwise of cultural activity, and include:

Successful cultural quarters will almost certainly have a strong evening economy (see Part III). Very often, there is a close correlation between cultural quarters and at least part of a city's evening economy. Indeed, much of the attraction of cultural quarters is that it is possible to merge the day into the night, and formal cultural activities with less formal pursuits such as meetings friends for a meal or a drink. It will always be important to achieve a balance of activities across the day and in the evenings.

Wherever possible, cultural quarters should include cultural production (making objects, goods, products and providing services) as well as cultural consumption (people going to shows, visiting venues and galleries). There should be a large representation of small-scale business activity, a high proportion of small and medium enterprises (SMEs) inter-trading and sub-contracting. A successful creative industries cluster will include a good proportion of exporting firms as well as those trading locally. Over time, a network of suppliers and sub-contractors will build up as firms inter-trade with each other. New businesses will set up to produce entirely new products, or more likely to provide products and services locally which hitherto have required to be imported.

A successful creative industries cluster will therefore comprise a *Production-Distribution-Consumption value chain* (see Part I) but this will be underpinned

Table 5.1 Indicators of Good Cultural Activity

1) Cultural Venues at a variety of scales, including small and medium;

2) Festivals and events;

3) Availability of workspaces for artists and low-cost cultural producers;

4) Small-firm economic development in the cultural sectors;

5) Managed workspaces for office and studio users;

6) Location of arts development agencies and companies;

7) Arts and media training and education;

8) Art in the Environment;

9) Community arts development initiatives;

10) Complementary day-time uses;

11) Complementary evening uses;

12) Stable arts funding.

Source: Compiled by John Montgomery.

by technology and specialist infrastructure and also the presence of the creative arts and creative and skilled individuals. Moreover – and although this will vary with the characteristics of each creative industry cluster and the city itself – the creative industries stimulate derived consumption in tourism, catering, retail and leisure. The diagram (Fig. 5.1) is a typical cultural industries cluster. It shows how the production – distribution – consumption-value chain is underpinned by the preserve of the creative arts, technology and specialist infrastructure; it also show how the cultural industries stimulate derived consumption in tourism, food, retail and leisure.

However, it is not possible to conjure up new businesses – especially in knowledge and skill intensive activities such as the creative, design and cultural industries – out of thin air. There must be a ready supply or a potential supply of skilled, educated and creative people willing to set up in businesses for themselves. Quite often, a large percentage of current university graduates intend or would wish to set up their own business. These graduates are the best prospect for business creation in the creative industries. It is no surprise, then, that many cultural quarters have strong, sometimes formal links, with Universities and other education providers.

Most cultural quarters tend to operate at the modern, design and media end of the cultural spectrum. That is to say they are all places of innovation and creativity and, often as not, contemporary in terms of design awareness and appreciation. In the more successful quarters this design ethos is carried through into architecture

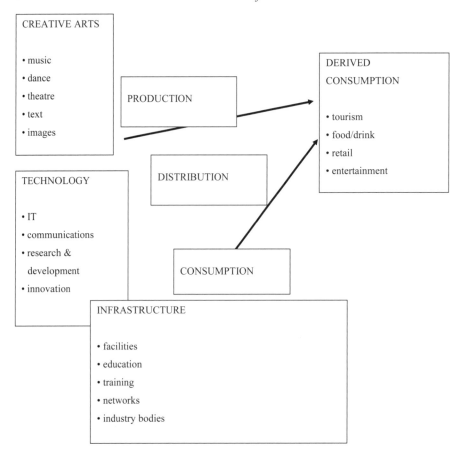

Figure 5.1   An Ideal-Type Creative Industry Quarter
Source: John Montgomery.

(modern but contextual in that it sits within a street pattern), interior design (zinc, blonde wood, brushed steel, white walls), and even the lighting of important streets and spaces (ambient, architectural and signature lighting as well as functional). All of these reinforce a place's identity as modern and innovative. It is important not to go too far and retain a balance between the old and the new, particularly with favourite meeting places and traditional pubs.

Based on the above discussion, Table 5.2 is a summary the elements one would expect to find in a successful cultural quarter. These are presented, as earlier, under three sub-headings: Activity, Form and Meaning. It is important to stress that a good cultural quarter would contain a unique mixture of these elements. Thus a place which has good Activity but an inappropriate Urban Form will not be a cultural quarter in

Table 5.2 Cultural Quarters: Necessary Conditions and Success Factors

Activity

Diversity of primary and secondary land uses;

Extent and variety of cultural venues;

Presence of an evening economy, including café culture;

Strength of small-firm economy, including creative businesses;

Access to education providers;

Presence of festivals and events;

Availability of workspaces for artists and low-cost cultural producers;

Small-firm economic development in the cultural sectors;

Managed workspaces for office and studio users;

Location of arts development agencies and companies;

Arts and media training and education;

Complementary day-time and evening uses

Built form

Fine grain urban morphology;

Variety and adaptability of building stock;

Permeability of streetscape;

Legibility;

Amount and quality of public space;

Active street frontages;

People attractors.

Meaning

Important meeting and gathering spaces;

Sense of history and progress;

Area identity and imagery;

Knowledgeability;

Environmental signifiers.

Source: John Montgomery.

the sense of being a good place which attracts everyday users and visitors, but rather a place (most likely) of cultural production removed from the arena of consumption. This means that cultural quarters and indeed the wider notion of city creative economies cannot be considered in isolation from the geography and characteristics of urban places. Similarly, a cultural quarter without Meaning, *inter alia*, will not be much of a place. Nor will it tend to be contemporary, *avant garde*, or particularly innovative. Culture after all *is* meaning. More than this, a cultural quarter which produces no new meaning – in the from of new work, ideas and concepts – is all the more likely to be a pastiche of other places in other times, or perhaps of itself in an earlier life. A good cultural quarter, then, will be authentic, but also innovative and changing.

This last is perhaps the most telling point. For to remain successful, a good place, a city economy, even an individual enterprise will need to maintain what it is good at but also to be flexible, highly adaptive and embrace change, new ideas, new ways of doing things and new work. Failure to do so will mean that the cultural quarter will disappear entirely, or become simply a collection of publicly-funded venues and facilities, or else an emblem of former culture – "heritage". Some cultural quarters will, no doubt, deserve to ossify or disappear altogether, to be taken over by other competing uses (offices, apartments) or to become part of the heritage industry. Others might well continue to develop and grow into the future, although success too can have its dangers where low value uses are driven out of successful places. This brings us to a conundrum, in that at least a proportion of the activity found in cultural quarters might well require some governmental support in order to survive *in situ*. The issue is one of stimulating new work, new activity and innovation whilst balancing a broader mix of activities, built forms and meanings. Let us consider some historical examples.

Paris

The Left Bank of Paris was the first recognizable cultural quarter in the modern sense. Following the rapid growth of Impressionism and post-Impressionism, by the 1880s the idea of the bohemian was well-established, and indeed had become socially acceptable. From around 1900, artists began to live in studio-houses or "ateliers", usually characterized by two-storey units with double-height ceilings and windows. Picasso moved to Paris in 1905, and there he would live in such an atelier, as did Matisse, Braque, Gris and Leger. The composers Debussy, Ravel and Poulenc were also in Paris at the time, later joined by Stravinsky. In the 1920s many American and English writers would live in Paris, including James Joyce, Pound, Eliot, Ernest Hemmingway and Gertrude Stein. They were joined by the art collector Peggy Guggenhiem, probably the most important collector of the twentieth century, who would have close relationships with Marcel Duchamp, Ernst, Miro and the young writer Samuel Becket.[15] By 1928 F. Scott Fitzgerald, who lived in the less fashionable

---

15 Gill, A., *Peggy Guggenheim: The Life of an Art Addict* (London: Harper Collins, 2001).

Figure 5.2   Courtyard Art, Le Marais
Source: John Montgomery.

but more select Right Bank, would complain that Paris had become "suffocating". In the 1930s the writer Henry Miller would move to Paris to write *Tropic of Cancer*, with his lover Anais Nin.[16] As we have seen, many of these artists would leave for the United States as the threat from Germany mounted. To all intents and purposes, Paris would lose its ascendancy as a world centre for the production of art, although there would be later revivals in film and modern jazz (largely imported from America).

More recently, the eastern parts of central Paris – including the *Marais* and the *Bastille* – have revived over the past thirty years. The *Ordre du Temple* (Order of the Temple) cleared the marshlands in the northeast of the old city to form Philippe Auguste's enclosure. From the fourteenth century onwards, the aristocracy built large residences in the area, a trend which was accelerated by the creation of the Place Royale (which would become the *Place des Voges*) by Henri IV in 1605. The departure of the royal court to Versailles led to a decline in the district. In the mid 19th century, Baron Haussman's urban redevelopment only marginally affected the Marais through new alignment rules and constructions, lending irregular width to many of the neighbourhood's streets. Towards the end of the nineteenth century and in the first half of the twentieth century, the area surrounding the *Rue des Rosiers* became home to many Jews from Eastern Europe, further specializing local labour in the clothing industry.

In 1969, the Marais was designated as the first protected sector (*secteur sauvegardé*), with the area being designated as a home to many museums, art galleries and historic sites, as well as shops serving local populations. This protection measure led to certain comical results, such as a "bakery" selling shoes. It is now one of the city's most fashionable areas. The area combines cafés, restaurants, clubs and galleries, cultural centres and a mixed resident population. Incentives have been introduced to preserve courtyards and allow their active use, particularly by the arts and speciality retailing (Fig. 5.2). The area is also much visited by tourists, and contains many low-priced hotels and hostels.

The cultural centre named after Georges Pompidou, was built in the old Beaubourg area adjoining both the Bastille and the Marais. At the time of the architectural competition, the surrounding area was in serious decline, both of the built form and economic activity. The neighbouring *Les Halles*, which had housed Paris's principal food market for generations, was in the process of demolition, to be replaced by a large commercial development and major public transport interchange. The design competition brief called for a million square foot cultural centre, to consist of four major specialist activities: a museum of modern art, a reference library, a centre for industrial design and a centre for music and acoustic research. Areas for office administration, book shops, restaurants, cinemas, children's activities and car parking were also to be included. Following the competition in 1971, the building was designed and built in six years. Over the years the building sparked a lively

---

16　*The Diary of Anais Nin*, Volume 1, 1931-34 (New York: Harvest), edited by Gunther Stuhlman.

debate about its strange architecture, with air ducts, heating shafts, and stairwells all stuck onto the outside to gain more space inside. It now looks rather dated: a post-modern edifice in the home of post-modernism.

SoHo

By the 1940s, the centre of gravity for modernism was no longer Paris but New York. Following on from the sudden impact of Abstract Impressionism in the 1940s and 1950s (as discussed in Part II), New York artists began to cluster in and around Tenth Street, Greenwich Village and an area south of Houston Street in Lower Manhattan. A later grouping of artists including John Cage, Merce Cunningham, Robert Ranschenberg and Susan Sontag – referred to as "The Fluxists" – began to operate from studio lofts, from which they would exhibit as well as produce work. The group would not survive long, but it did much to establish SoHo (South of Houston) as a place where artists lived and worked. For one thing, space was cheap in SoHo as many light industrial businesses were closing down or relocating.

The Fluxists would be followed in the late 1960s by Pop Art and the post-modernists, by which time SoHo as an arts precinct was well-established. In her account of artists' studios in New York, Sharon Zukin[17] reveals that by the early 1960s, however, New York City Council intended to have what was then known as the "West Village" area designated as a "blighted area" which could then be re-developed as project housing. Resistance to this proposal was led by the artists themselves, and also homeowners of West Village. The area was saved from this fate – a beneficial outcome which Zukin appears to regard as a middle-class conspiracy – and more buildings in SoHo began to be converted to lofts. Some of these lofts were used as performance venues, and by the early 1970s a festival of "Loft Jazz" had been established, led by Ornette Coleman and Sam Rivers. This would last until the late 1970s, by which time more and more of the lofts were residential apartments. Zukin[18] gives the example of a building in Greenwich Village with a highly mixed pattern of usage:

> the ground floor is half residential and half a rehearsal space for a theatre company; the second floor is half residential and half a dental equipment business; the third floor is split between two mixed-use lofts, one in which a nurse and an architect live and which the architect uses for his office, and one occupied by a stockbroker and a woman who runs a plant business in the loft; the fourth floor is entirely residential; on the fifth floor, half is a doctor's home, and the other half is a living and working loft for a graphic artist and a fine artist; the sixth floor is half residential . . . and half is for both living and running a catering business; on the seventh floor, half was sold by an architect to a doctor for a residence, and half is used by two men who live there and run a mail-order business; the eighth floor is divided into a living loft for a young widow with children and a living loft

---

17 Zukin, S., *Loft-Living* (New Brunswick: Rutgers University Press, 1989) (First published 1982).

18 Ibid., pp. 120–121.

for a city planner with work space for her husband, who is a potter; the ninth floor has two living lofts.

The difficulty which would emerge is that young professionals were prepared – indeed eager – to pay higher rents to occupy such large, convenient and newly fashionable spaces. Indeed, if they could they would buy-up entire floors, even whole buildings. In this way, economic pressure in the form of higher rents would directly affect the artists, while landlords and then developers would see the prospect of improved rental income and also capital growth. Although some buildings were retained as co-operatives or held by philanthropists, and despite the efforts of organizations such as the Lower Manhattan Loft Tenants to restrict rent increases, by the late 1970s the lofts had become prime city-centre real estate. Some of the artists themselves became building-owners and developers, individually or in partnership. In chapters 7 and 8 of her important book,[19] Zukin charts how what began as an experimental area for artists ended up becoming some of the most expensive residential property in New York. This she sees as akin to the gentrification of working-class neighbourhoods, but also contributing to a de-industrialization of inner city space. This pattern, as Zukin suggested it would, has been repeated in cities across America, Canada, Europe, the UK – loft living in Wapping, Manchester, Newcastle, Gateshead, Leith – and in Australia, Flinders Lane in Melbourne, Surry Hills in Sydney, New Farm in Brisbane. Zukin sees this as a pre-determined programme for "the reconquest of the downtown for high-class users and high-rent users" so that the city may be "re-valorized".[20] Again, this is too deterministic a theorization for me, and leads Zukin to conclude that art, through a process of "cultural appropriation" is some sort of Trojan Horse for developers and "middle class elites", in which "the State" is complicit. Stripped of its ideological undertones, however, the story of Loft Living in New York in the 1960s-1980s is simply another example of people finding new uses for redundant space, by their work (and image) creating value in that space, followed by increases in market rents and property prices. This should come as no great surprise, for it has always happened in cities. The only difference this time around is that art and creativity are now much more formally linked with economic development, wealth creation and urban regeneration.

South Bank, London

The architecture critic Ian Nairn considered the South Bank to "be the key to London"[21] but in his eyes this role was never fully realized. Although partly laid out as a set of boulevards in the late 18th and early 19th centuries, by the 1960s the area had become a "frightful muddle". The area now known as South Bank is in

---

19 Ibid., pp. 126–172.
20 Ibid., 1989, p. 175.
21 Nairn, I., *Nairn's London* (London: Penguin, 1988, edition with Peter Glasson), p. 90.

the geographical centre of London, running from Westminster Bridge to Blackfriars Bridge, south of the River Thames. For centuries it was largely neglected as a low-lying marshland, prone to flooding. In the eighteenth and nineteenth centuries, the area of Lambeth urbanized and the entertainment world burgeoned. Away from the rigid theatrical duopoly of the north bank, the cheap land of Lambeth enabled individual impresarios to build and develop their own performance venues, creating all-year, all-weather venues. Taverns converted to music halls and fringe "Penny Gaffs" became common. Without artistic restrictions or censorship (unlike the north bank), the theatres of the Marsh were permissive and, in the days before modern film and radio, many were closed down for being "disorderly houses". One such house of bawdy drunkenness was the Royal Victoria Hall, later known as the "Old Vic" where John Gielgud, Laurence Olivier and Alec Guinness would later lead the renaissance of English theatre from the 1930s.

Industry had come to the area in the eighteenth century, utilizing the fresh water supply and river access for the manufacturing and transit goods. In the nineteenth century, the population of the area grew rapidly. The construction of new factories, more bridges and the railway terminus at Waterloo brought in large numbers of people, most of them crammed into little houses alongside the factories and wharves. People worked in coal wharves, timber yards, potteries, dye works, lime kilns, blacking factories and printing houses, transforming Lambeth into a centre of industry. The rows of housing built to accommodate this industrial workforce are still standing today, as are former warehouses and other memorials, like the South Bank Lion (minus his reproductive organs), created by one riverside industry (Coade Stone Manufactory) to advertise another (Red Lion Brewery).

The loss of industries and the area's general decline as a location for manufacturing brought a sudden drop in population. In 1900 the population was 50,000 but by the mid-1970s this figure was less than 4000. Main sources of employment had been lost or relocated, such as the dockyards, shipping and the newspaper industry. This was made all the worse by planning policies of population dispersal during the 1950s and 1960s. During the Second World War the area suffered bomb damage, and a significant amount of housing was demolished, never to be replaced.

In one sense, this was fortuitous. South Bank was chosen as the main site for the 1951 Festival of Britain (Fig. 5.3), a modern version of the Great Exhibition of 1851.

The bombed-out riverside was cleared and built upon, becoming the site of a national celebration. The Royal Festival Hall remained as the only permanent legacy, though the National Film Theatre was born from the popularity of the Télekinema. In subsequent decades, the Festival establishments were joined by other arts venues, such as the Hayward Gallery and the Royal National Theatre, as a replacement to the Old Vic. Built on the site of the Red Lion Brewery, the Royal Festival Hall was designed in a Modernist style by the London County Council Architect's Department. Nairn refers to this as "an unsuspected tragedy",[22] and the building itself as being

---

22 Ibid., p. 99.

Figure 5.3   South Bank during the Festival of Britain, 1951
Source: The National Archives (25/64/25), with permission.

"acoustically perfect but musically dead". In 1965 a redevelopment scheme was completed that now defines much of the outward appearance: the Portland Stone exterior was re-cased; the river frontage was pushed thirty yards forward; and a new riverside entrance was created. Nairn saw this as yet another muddle and a "smoothing over ... that won't do any good". In 2001 a £60 million programme was commenced to renovate and upgrade the facilities, qualities and capabilities of the Concert Hall.

During all of this time, the main cultural buildings were being designed and developed with scant regard for the local environment, the public realm or – for that matter – each other. Meanwhile, a number of more or less commercial redevelopment schemes progressed. These consisted mostly of building, or encouraging to be built, large-scale projects: County Hall and the Shell International Centre among them. In 1973, proposals were announced by the development companies Heron Corporation and Commercial Properties Ltd to build a hotel complex on the land immediately behind the National Theatre. The complex was to be 380ft high with 600 bedrooms, several restaurants, swimming pool, conference facilities, galleries and adjacent flats. Made out of aluminium and tinted glass, it would have been visible from St. James Park and Trafalgar Square. It was known locally as the "Green Giant". The proposed skyscraper development in 1977 threatened to demolish the Oxo Tower Wharf and seal the river off from the interior completely.

Happily, unfavourable market conditions slowed down the development at that moment but more significantly, the vast majority of the community were opposed to the scheme and preferred the construction of affordable housing. In 1977, the Coin Street Action Group had been set up and set about drawing up plans for housing, a new riverside park and walkway, managed workshops, shops and leisure facilities. Seven years of campaigning, including two year-long public inquiries, followed. After the second inquiry planning permission was granted for both the office and the community schemes, and this made some sense as half of the area was owned by the office developers and half by the Greater London Council (GLC). The GLC had originally supported the office developers but after a change of political control in 1981 it supported the community scheme. In 1984 the developers sold their land to the GLC which, in turn, sold the whole site to newly-created Coin Street Community Builders. The Coin Street sites now belonged to the local groups but the financial situation became precarious as the main backer, the GLC, had been abolished.

In August 1984 the first proposals for the area were announced and financially supported by the London boroughs of Lambeth and Southwark. In addition private investment would be sought to finance light industry and shops. The first development, the Mulberry Housing Co-operative, was completed in 1988. A new riverside park was created, opening up views of the Thames, St. Paul's Cathedral and the City. Coin Street Community Builders have since overseen the demolition of old buildings, completion of the South Bank riverside walkway, creation of Bernie Spain Gardens and Gabriel's Wharf market, refurbishment of Oxo Tower Wharf for mixed uses including shops, restaurants, retail design studios and flats, and building of 220

Figure 5.4   Oxo Wharf
Source: John Montgomery.

affordable homes for four fully-mutual Housing Co-operatives.[23] Oxo Wharf had been acquired in the 1920s by a Meat Extract Company, which built great cranes on the riverside frontage to haul meat from Thames barges directly into their factory. In the 1930s, the company also built a tower that carried the illuminated name of their most famous product. Designed to circumvent strict laws about exterior advertising, the letters that spelt out "OXO" were in fact stained glass windows. The building has now been refurbished, by Coin Street Community Builders, as a paved mall area, retail units, exhibition space, restaurants and housing. The Oxo Tower was 1997 Building of the Year Award for Urban Regeneration (Fig. 5.4)

Further improvements would follow in the early 1990s, led by the South Bank Partnership. This group grew weary of the over-blown architecture competitions which promised much but delivered very little in recasting the area as a useable place. The competition of 1993, for example, was won by the Richard Rogers Partnership, and proposed the covering over of the entire area beneath a plastic dome. The scheme was never progressed, but Rogers would later build his dome on Greenwich Peninsula. In some frustration, the South Bank Partnership (then the South Bank Employers' Group) commissioned two Urban Design Strategies, which have formed the basis of many projects and proposals that have produced, amongst others: the improvements to the "spine route", the South Bank Banners; the rebuilding of the Riverside Walk, the creation of Sutton Walk, Gateway to South Bank and the RV1 Riverside Bus. Projects that would follow, such as the London Eye, drew the attention of the world in the mid 1990s.

In 2000, the Tate Gallery's modern art collection was moved to Tate Modern in Bankside, while the existing gallery, now Tate Britain, retained its collection of work by British artists. Tate Modern is a reuse of the former Bankside Coal-fired Power Station, and has helped trigger a round of investment in the adjacent area of Borough Market. In 2003, the art collector Charles Saatchi opened his own modern art gallery close to the Tate Modern, at County Hall. Finally, connections across the river Thames have been improved by the construction of new pedestrian bridges, and the development of a new underground station at Bankside.

This example is notable because the success of new measures adopted since the 1980s is due to their operating at a much different scale to the lumpy modernism of the immediate post-war period. Some critics have argued that the transformation of the area is more image than substance,[24] although this seems harsh. Much of the credit should go to the South Bank Partnership and Coin Street Community Builders who have set about improving the public realm, bringing residents back into the area, shops and markets and small galleries and design workshops, cafés and restaurants. Even so, the area remains too large to work as an urban place, linking the Festival Hall in the west to Tate Modern in

---

23 Tuckett, I., *There is Another Way*, in Montgomery, J. and Thornley, A., *Radical Planning Initiatives for the 1990s* (Aldershot: Gower, 1990).

24 Newman, P. and Smith, I., "Cultural Production, Place and Politics on the South Bank of the Thames", *International Journal of Urban and Regional Research*, 24(1), 2000, 9–24.

the east. The urban design strategy, has therefore set about using memorable buildings, public spaces and nodes of good mixed activity to create a series of more or less connected places.

Pittsburgh Triangle

The 1970s and 1980s was a difficult time of economic restructuring for Pittsburgh, which witnessed the collapse of its old industries. A group of civic and business leaders banded together to transform a derelict area of downtown, that was once considered the theatre district of Pittsburgh, into an arts district once again. Pittsburgh's Downtown Cultural District – the "Golden Triangle" is a fourteen-square block area bordered by the Allegheny River on the north, Tenth Street on the east, Stanwix Street on the west, and Liberty Avenue on the south. A non-profit organization, the Allegheny Conference on Community Development, was established to effect a programme of ambitious projects of urban renewal. This included programmes to reduce air and water pollution, the creation of an urban park at the "Point" of the three rivers, and measures to energize the city's cultural life. Writing on what has become his home city, Richard Florida[25] argues that Pittsburgh's Urban Redevelopment Authority and other local agencies made many mistakes, notably the redevelopment of mixed use districts for big-box retail malls, acres of car parking and two large sports stadia that are unused most of the time. Plans for an "urban mega-mall" in the late 1990s, thankfully, came to nothing.

Due to its location at a major river junction – the Ohio, Allegheny and Monongahela rivers, Pittsburgh became a major colonial trading centre in the 17th and 18th centuries. In the industrial age of the 19th century, Pittsburgh became a major centre for the iron and steel industries, owing to nearby coal and iron ore deposits. It was here that the young Andrew Carnegie, aged 30, would found his first company in 1865, one that would grow to become the largest iron and steel-works in the USA. As well as iron and steel, and the Pennsylvania Railroad Company, Pittsburgh became a centre for aluminium smelting, engineering and electrical engineering. As late as the 1950s, Pittsburgh was a renowned centre of R&D in these industries, home of US Steel, Alcoa, Gulf Oil and Westinghouse. Pittsburgh was the industrial giant of the world, producing steel, iron, aluminium and glass and became known as a "smoky city". However, as these industries began to decline from as early as the 1960s, it became clear that Pittsburgh's economy was just not diverse enough, and lacking in entrepreneurship.[26] By the 1980s Pittsburgh had suffered a significant downturn: industry declined, corporations downsized and relocated or were acquired, downtown storefronts were vacant and the streets were virtually vacant at night.

The *Pittsburgh Cultural Trust* was formed in 1984 as both an arts agency and a real estate and economic development agency. The Trust oversaw the development

---

25 Florida, R., 2002, *op. cit.*, p. 308.
26 Florida, R., 2002, *op. cit.*, pp. 301–307.

of four major theatres in downtown Pittsburgh: the Benedum Centre for the Performing Arts, the Byham Theatre, the O'Reilly Theatre and the Harris Theatre, all located in the 14-block downtown. The Trust's first project was the restoration of the former Stanley Theatre into the Benedum Centre for Performing Arts, completed in 1987. Other organizations include: Artist and Cities – a not-for-profit real estate development and resource organization, "working to foster community and economic growth by partnering with neighbourhoods" and other groups to reclaim under-utilized buildings as affordable living and working space for artists and their families, bringing new residents and workers into city neighbourhoods; and Manchester Craftsmen's Guild – a multi-discipline, minority-directed, arts education and presenting organization that employs the visual and performing arts to educate and inspire inner-city youth.

In 1989 a plan was commissioned by the Pittsburgh Cultural Trust and the City's Urban Redevelopment Authority, with assistance from the Alleghney Conference on Community Development and the City Planning department to define the vision for the Cultural District, and the steps required to make the vision a reality. The plan was built on the foundations of the District's major performance facilities – Pittsburgh Symphony Heinz Hall, the Benedum Centre for the Performing Arts, and the Byham Theatre – and key projects already underway at that time, including the streetscape improvements, Byham Theatre renovations, conceptual design of the O'Reilly Theatre and restorations to buildings in the historic section of the Cultural District.

During the 1990s many projects progressed and these include: the Stanley Theatre and the Fulton Theatres were restored, and the O'Reilley Theatre was opened; a façade restoration programme was commenced; the Mellon Foundation committed $7 million to the Trust for use in land acquisition within the Cultural District; the City committed $3.4 for street improvements and streetscaping; a comprehensive lighting programme was commissioned and Agnes R. Katz Plaza, the central open space of the Cultural District was redesigned. Wood Street Galleries opened and shared office space provided serving small arts organizations and artists; a property, formerly used as a sex shop was razed to the ground in order to use the land for the long-term installation of public sculptures; and Allegheny Riverfront Park was redesigned.

In 2001 the Mellon Financial Corporation Foundation awarded a $25,000 grant to the Mattress Factory, a contemporary art museum and research and development lab for artists. More recently a system of colourful banners, serving partly as public art and to tell you when you are entering the Cultural District have been suspended from historic street lights to unify and enhance the Cultural District and raise awareness of the arts organizations and galleries that make their homes there. Other Cultural District attractions include: the Three Rivers Arts Festival Gallery, Watercolours Gallery, Associated Artists of Pittsburgh, Pittsburgh Opera and the American Institute of Architects Gallery.

The Pittsburgh example is certainly interesting, but curiously old-fashioned. The planning orthodoxy of developing large-scale projects is the opposite of more sophisticated planning methods which encourage "gradual money", a much finer mix and grain and more organic change. Most of the arts projects themselves are larger scale and "institutional" with the exception of the Mattress Factory and some programmes carried out by the Trust. The whole initiative was driven not by local artists but by big business and local government. If any arts-led urban regeneration strategy could be said to be "led by a patrician elite", then this is it. Yet, with its valuable landholdings the Trust found itself in a unique position to secure long-neglected cultural projects. This is a lesson that was applied later in Dublin, as we shall see.

Interestingly, Richard Florida points out that the city's demographics are skewed towards the very old and the very young. He refers to this as the "missing middle", a dearth of entrepreneurs, intellectuals and creatives in their 30s and 40s who have left the city for New York or LA. By failing to meet the aspirations of such people, Pittsburgh is in danger of losing its biggest asset in the coming industrial age – its creative class. For such people are not attracted to or enamoured by large shed-like developments and over-sanitized public spaces. They are more interested in emerging cultural forms, design and the small-scale elements of vital entrepreneurialism, and for these one needs to be in a dynamic city. Much the same relationship can be seen in Australia, between Adelaide and its more dynamic neighbours Melbourne and Sydney. Whilst cities such as Adelaide are seen as good places to bring up families, they find it hard to retain the very people who will be the creators and entrepreneurs of the future.

3. PLANNED CULTURAL AND CREATIVE INDUSTRY QUARTERS[27]

Temple Bar, Dublin

Temple Bar is a 35 hectare (later extended to 50 hectares) urban quarter, sandwiched between O'Connell Bridge to the east, Dame Street to the south and the River Liffey to the north, in central Dublin. The area was largely developed and built in the 17th and 18th centuries, and still retains the street pattern and tight urban grain from that time. There are many layers of building here, which tell a tale of trade and commerce, Georgian elegance and a gradual slide into poverty and decline.

Temple Bar is in fact one of the oldest parts of Dublin, dating back to 1259 when an Augustinian Monastery was built there. In the 17th century a William Temple, secretary to the Earl of Essex and a Provost of Trinity College, built his home there giving the area its name. A bar was the name for a walkway by the river. The area as we see it today dates largely from the 18th century when cargo was loaded and unloaded on ships docking at the Quays on the south side of the Liffey. The network of narrow streets became a hive of buying and selling, with merchants, craftsmen, artisans and shipping companies plying their trades. There were also a large number of Bagnios or brothels. Later, printers, publishers and instrument makers moved into the area,

---

27 This section is a re-working of Montgomery, J., *Cultural Quarters as Mechanisms for Urban Regeneration: Case Studies from the UK, Ireland and Australia, Planning Practice and Research*, 19, 1, March 2004.

Figure 5.5   Temple Bar Gallery and Studios, Dublin, 1990
Source: John Montgomery.

bookbinders, stationers and stockbrokers. With the building of a new Custom House in the 19th Century, the old Essex Quay at Temple Bar fell into disuse, and the area became a centre for the clothing trade – tailors, drapers, cap makers, furriers, woollen merchants. In 1816, a metal toll bridge was erected – the Ha'penny Bridge – to enable Dubliners to cross the Liffey to visit the music hall in Crow Street.

Although Temple Bar is only a few yards from O'Connell Bridge, just around the corner from Trinity College and Dublin Castle, and a stone's throw away from Dublin's main shopping area at Grafton Street, the late 20th century had all but passed the area by. Temple Bar, despite its strategic location more or less in the centre of Dublin, had become something of a backwater. This was just as well. The future of Temple Bar was under doubt for many years, not least because the state bus company (CIE) proposed to redevelop most of it as a new transportation centre, linking bus and rail. CIE began to buy up property in 1981, paving the way for demolition and redevelopment. Paradoxically, the fall in property and rental values which resulted triggered off a process of revitalization. Activities which could afford only low rents on short licences – or no rent at all – moved into the area. These included artists' studios, galleries (Fig. 5.5), recording and rehearsal studios, pubs and cafés and restaurants, second hand and young designer clothes shops, books and record stores, as well as a number of centres for a range of "third sector" organizations. They added an exciting mix of ingredients to those remaining existing businesses who had not yet been bought out or evicted by the CIE – the printers, cutlery shops and seedy hotels. During the mid 1980s, networks of small and medium sized enterprises became established, feeding off each other and larger cultural players such as the Project Arts Centre and the Olympia Theatre. A rare example of planning blight breathing life into an urban area through low-rent arts activities.

By 1990, Temple Bar had many disused industrial buildings, gap sites, problems of poor east/west permeability, a residue of entrepreneurial activity, and many buildings which were simply falling down. Paradoxically, Temple Bar also had a reputation as a place of discovery, vitality and a wide range of social and economic exchange. It was frequently referred to as "Dublin's Left Bank", on account of its relatively high density, a mixture of architectural styles, close proximity to the quay, narrow streets and a lively atmosphere deriving mainly from youth culture – recording studios, video companies, artists studios, theatres and pubs, cafés and restaurants. It was important that this alternative culture should not be lost by wholesale redevelopment of the area or by adopting a property value-led approach to urban renewal. There were many lessons to be learned from British cities where property value-led redevelopment has pushed up rents and effectively driven out the small shops, artists studios and cultural businesses which created the buzz and made localized areas – Covent Garden being the prime example – attractive to developers in the first place. Much needed to be done in Temple Bar, not least to prevent the building stock falling into greater disrepair. But great care had to be taken not to destroy the sense of place that had already been created by the mix of activities that were based there. Businesses and arts organizations in the area organized themselves to form the Temple Bar Development Council as early as 1989, and began to lobby for the area to be regenerated as a cultural quarter.

The strategy adopted to achieve this was, accordingly, a combination of culturally-led urban renewal, physical renewal and urban husbandry, and local enterprise development, particularly in connection with the cultural industries and the evening economy. An early strategic development framework for the area was prepared in 1990–91.[28] This recommended the adoption of a stewardship ethos and management approach to knitting back together the urban area, centred on the development of 12 cultural projects. These included a Film House, sculpture gallery, photography gallery, music venues and the old Olympia Theatre. Provision of business grants and loans would be made to help young cultural and other entrepreneurs set up in business; this was accompanied by a survey of existing businesses in the area and a major training initiative in business skills and the various cultural industries, but also in catering and venue operation. The strategy also recommended the promotion and stimulation of an evening economy; a major initiative to improve permeability and

---

28 Urban Cultures Ltd, *Creating Dublin's Cultural Quarter*, unpublished consultancy report for Temple Bar Properties Ltd, Dublin, 1991.

pedestrian flow through the area, involving the creation of two new public spaces, outdoor venues, niche gardens, corners to sit and watch the world go by, culminating in the design of two new public squares; and a major programme of public art and cultural animation, designed to reclaim and give meaning to the area's public realm. Overall, the approach to property management and upgrading based on balancing the need to improve the area's environment with the need to retain existing activity, backed by the introduction of vertical zoning linked to the provision of grants and tax relief status. It was considered very important that the design of the new buildings should be by young Irish architects, with the accent on modern design within the context of the historic street pattern. Last, but not least was the recommendation for a major marketing and information campaign using good modern design.

This strategy, in the form of a flexible framework plan[29] was largely implemented by Temple Bar Properties Limited (TBPL), a state-owned development company established in 1991. Temple Bar Properties engaged in acquiring properties, renewing them and negotiating rents with occupiers and by undertaking development schemes on its own volition or as joint ventures with private owners and developers. To do this, it was granted an initial £4m from the EC and leave to borrow £25 million privately but with a state guarantee. Monies generated from rental income are ploughed back into the property renewal programme and environmental action, and used to cross-subsidize cultural projects. In the final analysis, a total of public funding for Temple Bar was some IR£40.6 million, the bulk of which (£37 million) was spent on the Cultural Development Programme 1991–2001. A further £60 million has been borrowed and repaid through TBPL's commercial programme. Over 1991–2001, the private sector is estimated to have invested over £100 million in the area.

Over its first 7 years of existence, Temple Bar Properties, amongst other things, commissioned a high-profile architectural framework and urban design competition; devised an economic development strategy to encourage and support entrepreneurship and the cultural industries; created two new urban squares (Fig. 5.6) and an east-west route through the area; adopted mixed use zoning to achieve diversity and to stimulate the evening economy, urban culture and street life; and initiated a major area marketing and information campaign. In 1992 there were twenty-seven restaurants, one hundred shops, half a dozen arts buildings (some of them falling down), sixteen public houses, two hotels, two hundred residents, 70 cultural industry businesses and 80 other businesses in Temple Bar. By 1996, when most of TBPL's own development schemes had been completed, there were five hotels, two hundred shops, forty restaurants, twelve cultural centres and a resident population of 2,000 people. During the construction phase, some 5,000 yearly FTE equivalent jobs had been created in the building industry (most of sub-contracted to Dublin companies). By the end of 1996, there were an estimated 2,000 people employed in Temple Bar, an increase of 300%.

---

29 Temple Bar Properties Ltd, *Development Programme for Temple Bar* (Dublin: 1992).

Figure 5.6   Meeting House Square, Dublin
Source: John Montgomery.

Figure 5.7   Temple Bar: Urban Form
Source: J. Rocques, 1756.

The final major commercial development to be undertaken by Temple Bar Properties was the Old City, designed to create a significant retail and residential cluster in the area between Parliament Street and Fishamble Street in the western end of Temple Bar. Situated around a new pedestrian street, Cow's Lane, the development consists of 191 apartments, 24 retail units, a crèche and landscaped gardens. Temple

Bar Properties Ltd as a property development company was effectively wound up in 2001. By that time, Temple Bar was home to some 3000 residents, some 450 businesses employing close on 2,500 people, and 12 high quality cultural venues. The whole area had become a showcase for urban design, architecture, design and style.

Success, however, brings its own problems. By the mid 1990s, Temple Bar had developed a reputation as the "Stag Night" capital of Europe. Research commissioned by Temple Bar Properties at that time revealed that these visitors – largely groups of young women and men from England – were beginning to cause other visitors to stay away. This problem was addressed by a coordinated management response by landlords and hoteliers in the area, essentially by refusing accommodation to large same-sex groups. By the 2001, Temple Bar was coming under criticism for being too trendy, too popular, too facile. Pete McCarthy's travelogue McCarthy's Bar, for example, contains the following complaint on the "ruthless redevelopment and marketing of Temple Bar".

> Continental café culture has arrived, a forced planting of non-indigenous chrome counters, almond-flavoured latte, and seared yellow-fin tuna in balsamic lemongrass and rhubarb jus. Japanese-besuited media ponces sit in windows sipping bottles of overpriced cooking lager, imported from Mexico, and other top brewing spots, to the banks of the Liffey. Plain, unadorned, authentic pubs, previously unchanged for decades, now reek of new wood and paint, as they're gutted and refurbished to conform to the notion of Irishness demanded by the stag nights from Northampton and conference delegates from Frankfurt who fill the streets, interchangeable inter smug fat smiles and Manchester United replica shirts.[30]

McCarthy overstates his case. Yet it is true that progress and success in Temple Bar have brought many more visitors, not all of whom are well-behaved. But the same can be found in any large city these days. As for tuna in balsamic lemongrass, it is just possible that the greater choice available in Temple Bar is welcomed by Dubliners too, and is a marked improvement on what was previously available. Perhaps McCarthy thinks that good food is only for those who holiday in France and Tuscany!

There is also the temptation to assume that the redevelopment of Temple Bar was all plain-sailing, a more or less straightforward instalments of commercial property development. This view rather conveniently over-looks the fact that the area's other future could have been as a glorified bus depot. Moreover, it is not readily understood that the recession of the early 1990s and the high interest rates of that time, almost led to Temple Bar Properties going into liquidation before it had made much of an impact. The later boom in Ireland's economy certainly played a large part in the success of Temple Bar, but in the early days there was no boom, just risk .

Temple Bar Properties today retains responsibility for managing various matters across the area. A Green Plan is in preparation, including a waste management plan for the area, additional street cleaning and the ongoing maintenance and security

---

30 McCarthy, P., *McCarthy's Bar: A Journey of Discovery in Ireland* (Ireland: A Lir Book, 2000).

Figure 5.8 Butcher Works, Sheffield CIQ
Source: John Montgomery.

of Meeting House Square and Temple Bar Square. TBPL continue to programme outdoor cultural events and markets, all of which are free of charge to the public. A traders' group (TASQ) has been formed to coordinate marketing of the area and to provide additional street cleaning. TBPL is also responsible for managing three writer's studios and an International Visiting Artists' Apartment. Cultural writers acknowledge the importance of Temple Bar as an example of using creativity and design to re-establish an area's economy and sense of place. Florida, for example, writing in 2002, refers to Temple Bar as a "clever and far-reaching strategy of levering authentic cultural assets to attract people and spur economic revitalization".[31]

Sheffield Cultural Industries Quarter

The Sheffield Cultural Industries Quarter was once a thriving industrial and workshop centre, but had become characterized by vacant and derelict buildings and gap sites by the early 1980s (Fig. 5.8). The area of the Sheffield Cultural Industries Quarter is defined in Sheffield City Council's CIQ *Area Action Plan*[32] as extending to some thirty hectares and located just to the south east of the city's administrative, retail and commercial core. The area is roughly triangular in shape, and is bounded by Arundel Gate and Eyre Street to the north, St Mary's Road to the west, Suffolk Road to the south and Sheaf Square and Howard Street to the east. Sheffield Hallam University

---

31 Florida, *op. cit.*, p. 302.
32 Sheffield City Council, SCIQ Action Plan, Sheffield 2000.

occupies much of the area to the immediate north, with parts of its estate within the CIQ itself, including a new Business Studies School, the Northern Media College and the proposed School of Cultural Studies at Porter Brook. The CIQ is within a 10-minute walk of Sheffield City Centre, the main-line Midland Station is a few hundred yards away, and access to the trunk and motorway networks is good.

For a period of some twenty years, the CIQ has been undergoing a transformation. By the mid 1980s, the CIQ had become a classic *zone of transition*: a marginal area of the city centre which was once a thriving industrial and workshop centre. Slowly at first, but with a marked quickening in the pace of development from the mid 1990s, the CIQ is now recognized as a centre for a wide range of cultural production. This includes fine arts, photography, film making, music recording, graphic and product design. Important initiatives within this spectrum include the Yorkshire Arts Space Studios, the Audio Visual Enterprise Centre, the Leadmill night club, Red Tape Studios, the Sheffield Science Park, The Site Photography Gallery, the Workstation managed workspace, and the Showroom Cinema complex. The Quarter is also home to Yorkshire Art Space Society, the Untitled Photographic (now the Site) Gallery, and a cluster of some 300 small businesses related to film, music and TV, design and computers. Important links have been established between the Cultural Industries Quarter and the adjacent Science Park, particularly with regard to the development of new technology in film, photography and recording, while there are now proposals to develop a Culture Campus in the area which would house Sheffield Hallam University's fine art, media studies and design departments.

It should be recognized that Sheffield is a city with a long tradition of cultural production, particularly in Fine Arts, Music, Film and Video. In the early 1980s the City Council started to develop a cultural industry policy, aimed at supporting these activities and assist the economic regeneration of a former car showroom. Two resultant building-based projects – The Workstation and The Showroom are – seen as central to the development of the CIQ. The buildings are owned by Sheffield City Council and were developed by a specially-formed registered charity, Sheffield Media & Exhibition Centre Limited (SMEC). The Charity set up a development subsidiary, Paternoster Limited, who took a 125 year lease on the building. Paternoster Limited run the Workstation purely as a commercial enterprise, charged with operating the building for the benefit of its tenants, and covenants profits to the parent charity (SMEC) for the benefit of the Showroom Cinema operation. The Showroom also receives revenue grant support from Sheffield Arts Department, the British Film Institute and Yorkshire and Humberside Arts. The area designation and the many of the projects within it have been championed by the former Sheffield City Council Department of Employment and Economic Development, and latterly by the Cultural Quarter Team within the Chief Executive's Department. Over seventy organizations now occupy units in the building ranging from the Northern Media School, graphic designers The Designers Republic, the Community Media Association, the Yorkshire Screen Commission, and various film production companies such as Picture Palace North and Dream Factory. Typical of the sector, tenant companies are small to medium size, employing from 2 to 6 staff members, although certain companies employ 25 and upwards.

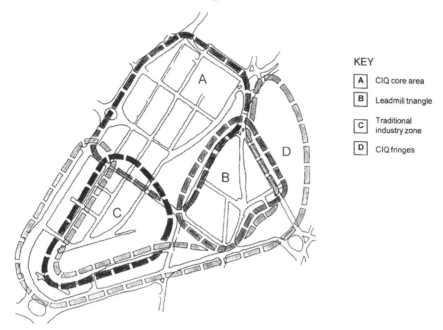

KEY

A   CIQ core area

B   Leadmill triangle

C   Traditional
     industry zone

D   CIQ fringes

Figure 5.9   Sheffield CIQ: Development Strategy
Source: Urban Cultures Ltd and EDAW.

The majority of the strategic cultural developments have been delivered by a series of bespoke development companies, who also have charitable status, including Sheffield Media and Exhibition Centre Ltd, Music Heritage Ltd, Sheffield Independent Film Ltd and Yorkshire Arts Space, and often combining public monies with bank finance. More recently, private sector investment has increased significantly in the area with schemes including Truro Works (student accommodation), the Leadmill Garage (proposed leisure and entertainment complex) and Butcher Works/Fletcher Works (proposed managed workspace and silverware gallery). These building-based projects have been fundamental to the overall development of the CIQ.

By 1997, despite the impressive growth of new organizations, facilities and venues, the CIQ lacked a strong sense of place. There were very few shops in the area, and few bars other than some traditional pubs catering for students of Hallam University. An important strand of both the 1998 CIQ Vision and Development Strategy and the Action Plan for the CIQ was to encourage secondary mixed-use, particularly along ground floor frontages. This was to include small shops, alternative retail, cafés, bars and restaurants. *The Sheffield CIQ Strategic Vision and Development Study* of 1998[33] represents the current thinking on the next phase of development within the CIQ (Figure 5.9). It incorporates the results of consultation,

33 EDAW and Urban Cultures Ltd, 1997, *op. cit.*

research and discussions with the local and wider communities of public and private interests. It should also be read in tandem with Sheffield City Council's Area Action Plan for the CIQ, which provides more detailed planning and urban design guidance, and details of individual sites for development.

In early 1999 the CIQ Agency was established to promote and implement an agreed Development Strategy for the CIQ over a five year period. The Agency's mission is to further develop the CIQ, building on the successes and, importantly, the broad character and nature of the CIQ as a cultural production centre and as an urban place. The aim is to create a thriving cultural production zone with large numbers of small and medium enterprises, a centre for excellence in knowledge creation and creativity, a visitor destination and a largely mixed use area with various complimentary activities throughout the area generating pedestrian flow throughout the day and into the evening, including residences. The Agency is comprised of a non-executive board with members being drawn from local businesses, Sheffield Hallam University, the Science Park and Sheffield City Council. The board is supported by a small, full-time management team. The Agency's five year strategy (to 2004) set the following targets: 50 active exporting firms in the cultural industries and an overall doubling of the businesses base within the area; an additional 350,000 sq ft of workspace for cultural industries; 4,200 jobs (3,000 direct, 1,200 indirect), of which 2,500 will be net additional jobs; 50 new retail, catering and entertainment outlets provided by private investment; 500 additional permanent residents; completion of a new urban culture campus for Sheffield Hallam University; the completion of a number of cultural projects, including a Photography Gallery, Fine Art Gallery and Centre for Performing Arts; continuation of a two-pronged training and education strategy aimed both at enterprise development and community access to new technologies and the cultural industries; considerable upgrading of the urban public realm to provide a more pedestrian-friendly environment, including established access points and routeways and two new urban squares.

Since 1998, substantial private sector investment has been attracted into the area in the form of bars, night-clubs, restaurants and student apartments. A major visitor attraction, the National Centre for Popular Music, opened in 1999, although this has since closed. Despite the Centre's difficulties, the SCIQ as a whole continues to grow. A new 1000 capacity bar and live music venue opened in the summer of 2000, Red Tape Studios is launching a new Internet School, Modal's National Music Convention has been attracted to the Quarter, as has the International Documentary Film Festival. Yorkshire Artspace has developed a new building, Radio Sheffield are opening a new headquarters in the SCIQ, the old Roberts and Belk cutlery factory is being developed as a managed workspace with ground floor café bar, and the former Leadmill Bus Garage is being redeveloped for six café bars, offices and apartments.

This area of the city centre was previously almost totally derelict. Success can be judged by the many new start-up cultural businesses, the establishment of the quarter as a vibrant business environment, the upgrading of the physical environment, and more recent business relocations. Estimates by the CIQ Agency (2002) reveal that the CIQ is home to some 270 businesses and organizations, including film, TV,

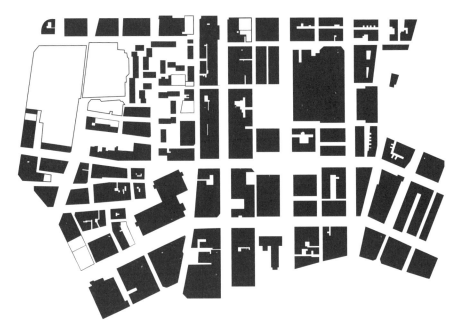

Figure 5.10   Manchester Northern Quarter (MNQ): Urban Form
Source: John Montgomery.

radio, science and technology, new media, training and education, live performance, music, arts, crafts, metalworking and a range of support producer and consumer services. Additionally, new build, private development is now providing millions of pounds worth of residential, student and business accommodation. The Sheffield CIQ is probably the most developed cultural industry "cluster" outside of London. It is uncannily similar to Porter's classic conception of an industry cluster.

Manchester Northern Quarter

Manchester's Northern Quarter (Figure 5.10) lies just to the north and east of the main shopping area around Market Street and the former Arndale Centre. For many years its major streets – notably Oldham Street – were the most fashionable of all shopping streets in the city. Tib Street was once renowned for its choice of pet shops; Smithfield market was once the largest fish and poultry market outside of London. The area began to take shape in the late eighteenth century at which time Stevenson Square was laid out as a mirror to the fashionable St Anne's Square to the west. Oldham Street developed initially as a mix of private dwelling houses and small businesses, but by the late nineteenth century had become a fashionable destination offering shopping and tea rooms which were popular with ladies. By the early twentieth century Oldham Street had two large department stores (Affleck and Browns and Lomas's) as well as a Marks and Spencer's penny bazaar and a Woolworth's. There was also a range of popular pubs and eating places, including a Yates's Teetotal Tavern.

As with many other city centre district's, the area began to lose vitality and meaning from the late 1940s onwards. Initially, two processes were at work: first, the onset of decline in the textiles industry meant that parts of the area and – equally important – Ancoats to the east, began to lose economic activity, businesses and jobs. This had a knock-on effect on the economy of Oldham Street and environs. Second, the wholesale slum clearance of the northern quadrant of the area and much of Ancoats and other adjacent areas effectively removed the resident population that had sustained many businesses in the area. As if this were not bad enough, Smithfield Market was relocated to the outskirt of Manchester in the 1970s, at about which time the Arndale Centre was built. The effect was to tear the remaining life out of what had been one of the most vibrant quarters within the city. Many businesses closed or moved away, and few people remained living locally.

By the late 1980s, the area had few businesses left, mainly fashion wholesalers, some specialist shops (prams, pets and pianos) and a few drinking and transvestite clubs. Manchester City Council became concerned that the area was not regenerating as other parts of the city were at that time, notably Castlefield and the Whitworth Street Corridor. This was despite the fact that the area had been granted Commercial Improvement Area status, allowing landlords and shopkeepers to apply for shopfront improvement grants. By 1993, 27% of the floorspace in the area was vacant, many gap sites had appeared and a large proportion of the building stock was in serious disrepair. By 1991 only 345 people were living in the area. Yet during the late 1980s, a number of new businesses moved into Oldham Street in particular, including the Afflecks Palace (fashion emporium), the Dry Bar, PJ's Jazz Club and others, while some of the other clubs and venues had remained in the area, including Band On The Wall. These businesses formed the Eastside Association in the early 1990s to lobby for improvements in the area. In late 1993 a development strategy for the area was commissioned jointly by the Eastside Association and Manchester City Council.[34]

There then followed a detailed process of consultation and debate over the area's future, culminating with an agreed development strategy in 1994, published in full in 1995. The main thrust of the report's recommendations were to retain the existing rag trade but also to grow new businesses in creative activities, alternative shopping and the evening economy. In addition, a major programme of residential conversion of upper floors was advocated. In analysing property ownership in the area, the consultants advised that the implementation vehicle for the area should be an alliance of landowners, developers and the City Council with a much better resourced Eastside Association (renamed the Northern Quarter Association) having a prominent role in crafting development schemes for the area. A system of sticks

---

34 Urbanistics and Urban Cultures Ltd, *Area Regeneration Strategy for Manchester's Northern Quarter*, unpublished consultancy report for Manchester City Council, 1994.

and carrots was put in place to help convince developers and property owners to engage with the overall area master plan; these included a series of small and large grants, and sophisticated application of planning controls up to and including detailed design briefs for key sites and properties. The problem, as the consultants had diagnosed, was that the whole area suffered from market failure; the trick was to encourage people to start investing again.

One problem with this approach is that although various new venues have been proposed within this area over the years, such new venues as have been built have tended to locate in adjacent areas such as Ancoats or Piccadilly Gardens. A number of small privately-owned clubs and bars – Dry Bar, Café Pop – remain and operate as regular small-scale venues, but the lack of venues arguably undermines MNQ's status as a cultural quarter. That said, a small events programme is organized by the Northern Quarter Association, and this includes the Northern Quarter Street Festival, an annual one-day open-air free event.

Rather the MNQ development strategy is aimed at encouraging business start-ups and growth in the creative industries, largely as market-based enterprises.[35] In 2000, the Cultural Industries Development Service (CIDS) was formed to help develop sustainable cultural and creative enterprises in Manchester's metropolitan core, including the MNQ and Ancoats. CIDS is a demand led agency (that is it responds to requests from bona fide would-be creative businesses). CIDS' services include: an information and referral service, a student and graduate placement service, business start-up and expansion grants, industry marketing grants, network development, and professional development programmes. CIDS is supported by Manchester City Council, Manchester TEC, Salford, Tameside and Trafford Councils, North West Arts Board and various HE/FE Institutions.

Manchester Metropolitan University Institute for Popular Culture have been closely involved in the ongoing development of the MNQ, have published various papers on the area,[36] and host the MNQ web-site. This is seen as having been instrumental in putting the MNQ on the map.

The overall development of the area is expected to include workspace provision, particularly on upper floors, both for refurbishments and new builds. In this way, the provision of workspaces is left to the market, but encouraged by planning guidance and development briefs for key sites. An example is the Smithfield site which Manchester City Council are encouraging to be redeveloped for a mixture of commercial, retail and leisure uses in new and renovated buildings.

The area strategy has been in place for several years, but only can it be said to have been a success since 1999. Indeed, many of the larger projects – such as the redevelopment of Smithfield market – were slow in getting underway. Even so, many new schemes have been successfully completed, including several mixed-

---

35 Blanchard, S., *The Northern Quarter Network: A Case Study of Internet-Based Business Support*, Manchester Institute for Popular Culture, 1999.

36 For example, see M. Banks, *Cultural Industries and the City*, Manchester Institute for Popular Culture, 2000.

use retail and residential schemes along Oldham Street and individual four and five storey buildings throughout the area. By 2002, the Northern Quarter was home to over 550 businesses and organizations, although a good proportion of these were already trading in the area before 1995. It's a place for shopping, music, food and drink, entertainment, fashion, living and working. The mix includes 100 clothing and fashion outlets; 70 cafés, pubs, bars, restaurants and clubs; 50 voluntary organizations; 40 arts, crafts and jewellery shops; 20 vinyl, tape and CD shops; 10 hairdressers/barbers; 7 newsagents; and another 200 + unique specialist shops, services and suppliers.

Unlike other cultural quarters, market failure in the MNQ was able to be addressed by changing the area planning policies in such a way as to encourage private investment. A large number of shops, a few bars and a surviving rag trade pre-dated the MNQ's new identity as a cultural quarter. In this sense, the aim was to develop more mixed use and alongside the overall stimulation of a creative industries economy. The area planning guidance for the MNQ strongly encourages mixed use, evening economy uses in appropriate locations and residential apartments. The MNQ is an example where public intervention and monies have tended to be focused on building improvements (via grants), environmental works (including public art) and in improving transport, parking and access. Comparatively little additional money has been found for new venues or events. Rather, the tack has been to encourage enterprise development of the creative industries, to help bring properties into active use and to invest in area marketing. Today, the MNQ is as much a fashionable residential neighbourhood as a cultural industries or night-life quarter, and that is no bad thing.

Hindley Street, Adelaide

Hindley Street – or the West End as it is also referred to – is Adelaide's naughty, often seedy and sometimes dangerous night-time area, although it is also a shopping street during the day. For much of the 1990s, the area tended to be dominated by strip clubs, tattoo parlours, "pokies" (game machine arcades), 24-hour drinking bars and other, even less savoury, elements. The *West End Crime Prevention Report, May 1998* confirmed that people generally had negative perceptions of Hindley Street. Crime statistics revealed a split between day time crime (shoplifting) and crime at night (some assaults, intimidation, rowdy behaviour, public disorder, drug dealing). The report signalled a commitment by the City Council to upgrade the West End environment, and to achieve a greater and more gentle mix of land uses. This was all the more pressing following the opening of the South Australia University City West Campus in 1997 – including the Faculties of Art, Architecture and Design – and concerns that students felt intimidated walking along Hindley Street. The University building itself resembles a fortress, not to say a high security prison.

In 1999 Adelaide City Council, launched its West End Arts-led Urban Renewal Program, supported by Arts SA and the State Government. The aim was to work

Figure 5.11   Underdale School of Art, Adelaide
Source: John Montgomery.

with artists and arts organizations to develop arts and creative industry projects and programmes within the area, thereby providing the West End and Hindley Street with a more diverse identity and character. Early projects included a relocation of the Adelaide Festival Office to a shopfront on Hindley Street, Shop@rt – a programme of exhibitions in vacant shop windows, an arts market, and the FestWest street festival. There is now an annual event – West End Open House – where all of the venues, a number of shops, restaurants and offices hold open exhibitions along the length of Hindley Street and throughout the West End. Existing arts organizations in the area have become involved in urban design schemes for the area, notably the Lion Arts Centre and the Jam Factory Contemporary Craft and Design Gallery (an impressive contemporary arts and design gallery in any terms). In the late 1990s, some 10 arts organizations have moved into offices along Hindley Street, including FEAST, Aus Music, the Community Arts Network and, in May 2000, Arts SA the Government Arts Department. Projects completed since 2001 include a new $30m (about £12m) Centre for Performing and Visual Arts (CPVA) on Light Square, an arts café on Hindley Street, a relocation of the Adelaide Symphony Orchestra and the SA Underdale School of Art (Fig. 5.11). In addition, a tenancy plan was implemented to effect a reduction in the numbers of Tattoo Parlours, Motor Cycle related shops (most of which are run by Hells Angels) and Pinball Parlours. Meantime, a number of streets were being enhanced (new floors, lighting, shop front improvements). A number of apartment blocks have been or are in the process of being refurbished.

The effect of all of this was that by 2003/4 Hindley Street – along with the Riverbank Precinct and the North Terrace upgrade – had been transformed from a seedy, dark and sometimes frightening place to one that many more people are happy to use. The management approach for the area also seeks to improve the quality of the night-time economy offer as part of Adelaide's strategic programme for the evening economy.

The importance of the West End as an Arts Precinct is as a centre for the arts and creative activities which are locating within the area. If this momentum is to be maintained, then creative businesses will need more places from which to design and make, places to sell from, access to wider markets (nationally and globally) and packages of assistance to help them survive and grow. Accordingly, attention in 2001 turned to the development of one or more business incubator spaces for arts, design and media businesses. Sadly, this initiative was shelved by the incoming Labor government in 2002, a government which, despite its claims to be pro-creativity and a supporter of the arts does not appear to understand the creative industries as a wealth-creating sector. Interest, rather, is focused on major transport infrastructure projects, the wine industry and mining. At a time when Australia's economy as a whole has been growing, the lowest growth level achieved has been in South Australia. In 2004, the state recorded the largest decline in small businesses in Australia, as enterprising people leave for Melbourne and Sydney. Back in the West End, several of the newer private galleries and design studios have closed.

Wood Green Cultural Industries Quarter

The Wood Green Cultural Industries Quarter is located less than four hundred yards to the west of Wood Green town centre, with a core area of 14.07 acres (5.7 Ha). The area is zoned in the London Borough of Haringey Unitary Development Plan (UDP) as a Cultural Quarter but is given over mainly to light industrial and warehousing use. The Quarter is loosely defined to the north by Wood Green Common and to the west by the utilities land and the main line rail corridor. To the south is the gas works site, while the eastern edge is formed by Mayes Road with connections to Shopping City and Wood Green High Street. The UDP designation (CIQ and ACE) (Arts, Culture and Entertainment), makes it clear that there should be no exclusion of other uses consistent with the policies in the UDP. Although fairly compact, the area contains a surprising mix of building styles, ranging from four and five storey turn-of-the-century and 1930s "flatted factories" to 1970s two-storey sheds and glass boxes. This partly mirrors the area's changing economic base, from a largely manufacturing district to one which is almost equally characterized by warehousing and service depots.

Whilst the area is at a walkable scale (one can walk easily from one edge to another in under ten minutes), it presently suffers from a sense of severance from the surrounding areas – and in particular Wood Green town centre. This is due partly to the heavy traffic flows on Mayes Road, a dearth of established pedestrian routes and crossings, and the poor location of the existing crossing on Mayes Road in relation to the rear entrance of Shopping City. The Quarter's urban form is characterized by the contrast of the scale of the Chocolate Factory and other former warehouses with the openness of the surrounding urban fabric. Large flat areas of service yard and hardstanding produce a loose "weave" linking street edge to building edge. The upshot is that the Quarter fails to project a sense of place or identity. The dominant impression is of a largely negative urban environment – vacancy, redundancy, inaccessibility and lack of security.

By early 1998, the Wood Green Cultural Quarter was essentially comprised of four main elements, all of them on the Wood Green Industrial Estate. Quicksilver Place houses the University of Middlesex School of Fine Art. This contains studios and workshops/gallery space, plus staff offices and administration rooms. The Place caters for approximately 250 students. Mountview Theatre School (Conservatoire for the Performing Arts) who lease four premises: Units 1 and 2 Clarendon Road, a large rehearsal room for musical theatre productions; and a two-storey main building (the Ralph Richardson Memorial Studios), a suite of 14 studios where acting is taught, staff have their offices and there is a small cafeteria. Mountview have space in the Chocolate Factory (see below) which is used as three rehearsal studios, three singing studios and the Sir John Mills Scenery Construction Workshop. Mountview have also leased space in an adjacent building – Parma House – for dance studios, the Sir Cameron Mackintosh Studios (opened 1996).

The Chocolate Factory, former confectionery-making industrial premises on Clarendon Road which, since the mid 1990s have been refurbished and converted

Figure 5.12 The Chocolate Factory, Wood Green
Source: John Montgomery.

for use as an arts and cultural industries managed workspace or enterprise centre (Fig. 5.12). The original intention was for the Chocolate Factory to be converted to provide 250 artists' and design studios. The aim is to provide business, studio space and training rooms for micro and small businesses in the cultural, arts and media industries. The Chocolate Factory is now the base for over 100 small creative businesses, many of them recent start-ups, in fine arts, crafts, textile design, film-making, music recording, furniture design, photography, sculpture and ceramics. Rents are set at just under £5 psf, including service charge. This works because the landlord is prepared to forego market rents, but also because of public sector funding through the Government's Single Regeneration Budget (SRB) programme. Converted spaces are fitted out to a minimum standard.

Both Quicksilver Place and Mountview Theatre School have been established at Wood Green for several years. Between them they have in the region of 500 students, plus staff. Quicksilver Place occupies a double height mirrored building, designed by architect Terry Farrell in his early years, while, as we have seen, Mountview's activities range over four sites within the Quarter. Throughout the rest of the area – the Wood Green Industrial Estate – there are another 60 or so businesses, mainly small and medium enterprises ranging from 5 to (at most) 30 employees. Some 35 of these are in the "rag trade" or clothing manufacture, warehousing and distribution. Some of these supply middle market lines (mainly ladies clothing) to the High Street chains, others are CMT (cut, make and trim) sub-contractors, while others can fairly accurately be described as sweat shops. If this area ever worked as an industrial district (where firms inter-trade with each other), there is very little evidence that this is the case today. A number of companies have ceased manufacturing altogether, and have their designs assembled in Morocco or Romania. Some businesses have recently vacated premises in the area, usually because of a relocation, but also because of business closures. The overall sense is that some of these businesses are doing reasonably well, while many others are struggling to hang on.

In addition, to the small cultural enterprises based at the Chocolate Factory, the area also contains an independent publisher and book distributor (the largest gay and lesbian distributor in Europe, employing 26 staff) and an independent commercial recording studio, Livingston Studios, where artists such as Kula Shaker and Placebo record. There is one small breakfast café and one public house. Meanwhile, several of the cultural organizations based in the Quarter began to consider proposals to increase their activity, presence and investment in the area. These included, for example, the opening of a New Deal Learning and Accreditation Centre in music, drama and media, supported by CoNEL, the College of North East London, and Middlesex University; the opening of a Comedy Café ; a new 100 seat studio theatre, set design workshop and TV studio for Mountview Theatre School; five new digital recording studios to be managed by Haringey Arts Council under a franchise agreement with Red Tape Studios (Sheffield); a Digital Photography Centre on one floor, and; a hot desk suite (2 large rooms) let at £50 per desk per month.

Impressive progress has been made in generating new activity and refurbishing a small number of existing buildings in the Quarter. While none of this would have been possible without an injection of grant funding from SRB, the quality of what has been achieved derives in the main from an unusual alliance between a private landlord, the Borough Council and the "third" sector in the shape of Haringey Arts Council (HAC). HAC's involvement has ensured that the overall Cultural Industries Quarter project retains both a cultural and community development ethos, as well as aiming to promote enterprise and wealth creation. It is perhaps still too early to judge whether Wood Green will become as successful a cultural quarter as Temple Bar or the Sheffield CIQ. At the very least, however, Wood Green CIQ will remain a centre for education in the arts and cultural industries, and a place for individual artists and small creative businesses to set up and grow. In 2004 it was announced that Wood Green is to be one of London's chosen cultural hubs.[37] It will be interesting to see how this progresses.

Recent European Examples

The Cable Factory in Helsinki is an interesting example, the largest single cultural complex in Helsinki. The occupiers of the Cable Factory include around 100 Finnish artists and musicians, architects, dancers and designers . It is the everyday workplace for more than 700 professionals. The building was built between 1939–1944, for the Finnish Cable Factory Ltd for the manufacture of telephone and electrical cables, including sea cables. The company itself would later merge to form the Nokia Corporation at the end of 1960's. At the end of 1980s Nokia no longer needed the whole factory building and began renting it out. Several artists settled in quickly in the high and light interiors of the factory. There also are galleries, three museums and dance theatres.

The Culture Park Westergasfabriek in Amsterdam is self-styled as a place of cultural production, notable for new work on fashion, new media, theatre and film. It is intended to provide an "inspiring environment" where new ideas can grow. The Westergasfabriek was constructed in 1883 by the British Imperial Continental Gas Association (ICGA). At the time it was the biggest coal gas factory in Amsterdam. The gas was used principally for public lighting during the first decades. The buildings were constructed between 1885 and 1903. After the discovery of natural gas at Slochteren in the north of the country in the 1960s gas production was terminated. Parts of the buildings were demolished, amongst which the gas factory itself and the water-tower. Until the beginning of the nineties the energy works used the premises for storage and repairs and as a garage for commercial vehicles. In 1989 the remaining buildings, by official recognition as industrial monuments, were saved from demolition. After 1990 the buildings were used temporarily for creative and cultural activities, and this proved very successful. A mix emerged of

---

37 London Development Agency, 2004.

art and daily life, of permanent and temporary hiring out for all sorts of events, such as festivals, commercials, fashion shows, operas and circuses. As a result of all these activities the Westergasfabriek became known culturally in Amsterdam and abroad. This idea of a park, culture and activity were the basis for drawing up the development project for the Westergasfabriek in 1996. It become clear that hosting cultural activities would be the key to the successful redevelopment of the complex. Its characteristic buildings and unique surroundings have proven enormously successful. Of the key buildings, the Gashouder is used for concerts and exhibitions, the Transformationhuis is a series of studios and workspaces and the Machingebouw a café and gallery space. There is also a large area of reclaimed parkland and outdoor performance areas.

Meanwhile, an initiative for a "popcluster" in Tilburg developed in the early 1990s.[38] This was led by local music organizations, the Tilburg Arts Foundation, and supporters in city government, and resulted in the identification in 1997 of the "VMK" as a cultural quarter. The proposal received national and European Union funding. The emphasis for the VMK as a cultural and creative quarter was to blend both cultural production and consumption. Early plans included the conversion of an old school into an arts and creative enterprise incubator, and for a collaboration with Eindhoven (the home city of electronics firm Philips). The VMK is home to a growing number of small cultural enterprises, café-bars and restaurants and converted residential spaces. There are plans for additional incubator spaces, a youth centre focused on social and creative enterprise, and "Rock Academy". Another key project with EU funding is a proposed Multimedia Centre – providing combined accommodation and services for multimedia, including incubation for start-ups and graduates, and access and support in ICT for creative enterprises and "weak users" of new media. An existing cultural facility (Scryption museum for written communication) will be relocated into the Multimedia Centre facility. The Tilburg cultural cluster is particularly interesting, as perhaps the first Dutch example of the role of the arts and culture in urban regeneration.

Evaluation

Appendix B has been devised as a cultural policy and programme matrix, allowing an easier comparison of the relative successes and failures of the cultural quarters researched, and discussed above. Headings under which the comparisons are made are drawn from Table 5.2 (p. 309), and focus mainly on the presence or otherwise of cultural activity. The analysis reveals that in terms of cultural venues, the development and maintenance of these has been most ambitious and consistent in Temple Bar, with some successes also in Sheffield and Adelaide. The weakest performer is Manchester MNQ, where no new venues, open to the public for viewings, screening or performances, have been established. As far as festivals and events are concerned,

---

38 Mommas, H., "Cultural clusters and the Post-industrial City: Towards a Remapping of Urban Cultural Policy", *Urban Studies*, 41 (3), 2004.

Temple Bar offers a varied year-long programme of indoor and outdoor activities. The Northern Quarter Festival in Manchester operates for only three weeks of the year. The Festival and Fringe Festival in Adelaide are very successful, but are organized on a city-wide basis. Sheffield Cultural Industries Quarters has a poor programme of cultural animation.

Regarding workspace for artists, the most impressive achievements have been in the Sheffield Cultural Industries Quarter (recording studios, artists' studios, film companies centre) which has deliberately focused to date on cultural production more than on venues. With the Jam Factory, Adelaide also has an impressive work-based, though largely training, resource for cultural producers, in this case ceramicists, glass-blowers and furniture makers. With the exception of Temple Bar Gallery and Studios, the approach in Dublin has favoured cultural venues over workspaces, while Manchester MNQ has largely failed to make any low cost spaces available for artists and crafts workers. In Manchester there has also been very little public sector involvement in developing managed workspaces for micro and small studio and office-based businesses. This contrasts markedly with the approach in Sheffield, with the development of the Workstation and other developments. Adelaide needs to provide more workspaces for young cultural producers. Of the quarters, only in Sheffield and Manchester is there an active programme of arts and cultural industry business development, and in the case of MNQ this is effectively the cultural programme for the area. As far as the location of key art agencies and organizations is concerned, only in Adelaide has there been a deliberate policy of relocating publicly funded organizations into the cultural precinct. In some ways, a de facto policy has operated in Temple Bar with many of the new venues (the Irish Film Centre for example) doubling up as premises for the industry sub-sector development agencies. Sheffield CIQ is hoping to attract more such agencies, following the example of BBC Radio Sheffield. In Manchester no specific initiative of a comparable nature exists.

What most if not all the cultural quarters have in common is the presence either within the quarter, or very close to it, of a major arts education and/or training institution, whether it's the Northern Media School in Sheffield, the Visual and Performing Arts Centre in Adelaide. Temple Bar is adjacent to Trinity College, and the Manchester Institute for Popular Culture has an office in the MNQ. In the cases of Sheffield and Adelaide this outcome was quite deliberate, and both are seeking to strengthen the links between formal education and enterprise development.

All the quarters researched have a public art policy, and a programme for securing new work, although not always by direct commission. Although to some extent a subjective judgement, the public art programmes in Adelaide and Dublin are the most impressive. However, the extent to which the various cultural quarters actively promote community arts development is also patchy. As in other matters, the approach in Temple Bar is to build a responsibility for community development into the overall remit for several of the cultural venues, particularly in the case of the Ark. Sheffield CIQ takes a more direct approach to this issue, with a cross-programme emphasis on access and participation.

As far as complementary day and evening activities are concerned, policy in Temple Bar from the outset was to encourage as fine-grained a mix of uses as possible, and especially including fashion and other alternative shops, cafés, restaurants and galleries. This has included maintaining low rent levels for certain types of uses. The early aspiration to become a "24-hour city" was toned down, and new residential developments in the Old City are sited away from bars and pubs in particular. One of the problems in Sheffield CIQ is a lack of street life, largely because of a lack of good active street frontages; this problem was addressed by the CIQ Vision and Development Study, and also by the CIQ Action Plan, and reasonable progress is being made. The problem in Hindley Street in Adelaide is that the night-time uses are arguably too energetic, and may be driving out good day-time uses. Manchester's MNQ has arguably more complementary activities –both day and night – than cultural activity per se. In Manchester MNQ, the aspiration to develop an evening economy and greater mixed use remains largely just that, an aspiration. With only a few exceptions, most of the new property investment in the area in the past five years has been for mainstream offices.

With regard to stable and sustainable arts funding, the most powerful example is Temple Bar where the Irish Arts Council played a prominent role in devising and funding the overall cultural development programme. Such a level of commitment is currently not evident in Adelaide, and has been largely lacking from MNQ. In Sheffield CIQ, major projects have come forward either sequentially or on a case-by-case basis, so that each project is subject to an independent feasibility process and has its own funding package, usually comprised of arts board funding, city council inputs, lottery funding and European monies. In Adelaide, a concern must be that so many of the new arts venues and relocating organizations are housed in properties leased from private landlords, there being no complete guarantee that they will not have to move on when rent reviews fall due.

The most successful cultural quarter in terms of image and identity is Temple Bar which has an international reputation, pursued (and still does) an imaginative marketing campaign and cultural programme (events, festivals), and which very deliberately appointed young, modern architects to work on new signature buildings. Sheffield too has embraced modern design, but not to the same degree, while to date the SCIQ marketing has not been especially penetrating. Manchester MNQ has also encouraged modern design, or rather on the edges of MNQ, notably the new Urbis Museum. The MNQ retains its reputation as one of the cool areas in town in which to hang out, but is largely unknown outside of Manchester. The West End of Adelaide is something of a paradox in this regard. Although increasingly fashionable, the area is still viewed by the City Planners as a "heritage precinct" to be retained, since many of the buildings are over 100 years old. Good new architecture can be found, but this is mainly in relation to conversion work (the exception to this general rule is the Embassy Hotel which has recently been voted one of the world's best hotels). This is perhaps understandable, but Adelaide as a whole remains a city which seems unwilling or afraid to encourage greater innovation in building design. Meanwhile, the marketing of the West End is modest stuff, aimed mainly at locals as opposed to inter-state and overseas visitors.

All of this reveals that although there are many similarities between the cultural quarters in terms of their overall cultural and regeneration aims, there are also many differences between them particularly as regards how the cultural programmes (arguably the most important!) have been set up and implemented. Partly these differences reflect different cultures or ways of working, and partly the set of circumstances in each place before and during the development of the quarter. It is therefore difficult to argue, as some may be tempted, that all cultural quarters are essentially the same and these days formulaic to boot. They are certainly a response to urban decline and economic restructuring undoubtedly, and also an attempt to promote new economic activity in post-industrial cities. But beyond this, it is unwise to draw too many conclusions, or set down too many prescriptions. Good cultural quarters will only succeed if they offer a distinctive and varied cultural programme.

The overall conclusion is that all of these examples have been strategic in nature. Whether directly intervening in the property market, or opting to self-build particular strategic projects; whether directing the property market through development briefs and planning permissions, or employing a property leasing plan – all have had a vision and a strategic goal to become a cultural quarter. The type of cultural quarter may have varied (mostly consumption led in Temple Bar, production led in Sheffield, fairly institutional in Adelaide, design and fashion led in Manchester) but all four places explored the relationships between regeneration, creativity and the cultural economy. All four places have succeeded beyond initial expectations. Yet, all too face the problems of success, notably in the guise of land value colonization and gentrification. Whilst each place has a distinct identity and image, nevertheless some common themes emerge. These revolve around the importance of securing a good mix of activity, set within an urban environment or built form which provides a good "fit", and the importance of conveying an image of place. Cultural quarters must contain within them a wide mix of cultural activities and venues. Yet, unless they also succeed as urban places they will not in the end be a readily identifiable entity.

4. A TYPOLOGY FOR DEVELOPING CREATIVE QUARTERS

The above discussion of planned urban cultural quarters and creative industry clusters raises some wider questions as to the validity and applicability of cultural quarters being designated in other towns and cities. The first question is whether arts-led urban regeneration works. The evidence of these four areas is compelling, even if we allow for other factors such as spectacular economic growth (in Ireland from about 1995), or a general property market recovery as in the case of Manchester. The Sheffield and Adelaide examples show that success can be achieved against a backdrop of market failure and fear of crime. The bottom line is that culturally-led urban regeneration works in inner urban areas, depending on the skill of policy-makers.

Second, is it possible to plan a cultural quarter? Again, the answer to this must be yes, particularly given the strategic planning that went into Temple Bar, MNQ and SCIQ, and indeed the VMK in Tilburg. In all of these cases, the objective was to deliver some key cultural projects, but also to address property market failure and attract private sector investment. The balance varies from quarter to quarter. The most market-oriented example, MNQ, is probably the least successful culturally. The most interventionist initiative was Temple Bar, yet curiously also seems the most organic and natural. This is because great care was taken in the design of policy, to include both market and not-for-profit oriented organizations. Both the SCIQ and Hindley Street have some way to go in achieving greater diversity, although private sector investment is now at unprecedented levels. The bottom line is that it is possible to plan a cultural quarter, but resources will also need to be committed to a cultural programme, low-cost studio and business space and public realm improvements.

A third question revolves around the familiar dilemma over policy intent and outcomes. Those writing from a Marxist perspective tend to read outcomes as flowing more or less directly from either intervention or the logic of a capitalist property market. There is little room for fudge or error or things turning out unexpectedly. Nothing can ever truly succeed unless capitalism itself is replaced – although with what no-one seems to know – which means that urban regeneration or the creation of cultural quarters can never be deemed a success either. On the other hand, those free-marketeers who argue that there should be no intervention and no planning of development would need to do without cultural quarters such as those found in Dublin, Adelaide, Sheffield and Manchester. As is often the case, life is messy and more complicated than theory.

Fourthly, and this is a familiar cry, some would argue that whether intended or not, all that cultural quarters will do is add to or fall victim to the cycle of so-called gentrification. The author has set down his views on this elsewhere,[39] but will do so here again. Self-improvement of buildings and urban areas is a positive force, it reclaims lost places, refurbishes decaying buildings, creates value and wealth. It might eventually create so much wealth that low value uses are in danger of being pushed-out, but this is not always a problem if the activities relocated are (say) car body repair shops or tattoo parlours. Even where gentrification is a problem, the majority living in such places are usually content to remain living there, whether it's Islington or Leith or Spitalfields or St Kilda. Maybe they move on and cash in. In a cultural quarter, the danger posed by gentrification is that the artists and creative businesses may be forced to move on and so the living cultural element of the place becomes damaged, and may even die. This must be guarded against, strategically, in advance. It is a question of ring-fencing certain properties (possibly some organizations) and ensuring that they will never be driven out by rising land

---

39 Montgomery, J., "The Story of Temple Bar: Creating Dublin's Cultural Quarter", *Planning Practice and Research*, 10, 2, pp. 135–172, 1995.

values. This has been achieved to a good degree in Temple Bar, and also in Sheffield. Gentrification remains a real concern in MNQ and the West End of Adelaide. But this is not a necessary given outcome, rather a contingent one.

Fifth, there is the issue of authenticity. "I used to love Temple Bar before it became too commercial" or "Hindley Street was more real when there were bike gangs, strip joints and drug dealing on the streets". This is plainly an important consideration, but one in which polarities are too readily adopted. The Marxist academics might argue that capitalism by its nature destroys authenticity, so that one supposes it would be better if we were all still living in caves and mud huts. The traditionalists favour heritage as their brand of authenticity, even if this means replica architecture and street lamps. A meal for liberals might be authentic if it is colcannon, or maybe a Chinese or a curry, but not if it is modern cuisine; it is OK to drink Guinness but not bottled lager – who says? Perhaps we all have our own views of authenticity (personally I hate most heritage museums, preferring modern art galleries) and the related issue of tourism. One of the, for some, irritating things about pluralism is that people don't always like what others think is good for them. (Stuart Hall arguing that modern jazz is culturally superior to 1960s popular music springs to mind!).

Finally, it must be stressed that not every urban area can or should be a cultural quarter – this is not some trick to be pulled out of a hat. Cultural quarters only work where there are venues, workplaces for cultural producers and working artists. It is more likely that small cities and larger towns can only really support one such place. Every town or city will have its retail areas, a market, a civic quarter, office locations. All that is being argued here, is that an area set aside or at least recognized as a cultural place is at least worth consideration.

There is little doubt in this writer's mind that cultural activity, urban characteristics of place and a little style add greatly to the urban and economic mix. One question for policy makers might well be how to go about all of this? In keeping with my practice for earlier parts of this book, I offer a summarized guide to what policy makers should do, or at least consider, if the opportunity to develop a cultural or creative industries quarter should present itself locally.

The first step is to make sure there is a strong enough representation locally of the creative industries to make the effort worthwhile. The essential point is to develop these industries as a dynamic economic sector, along the lines discussed towards the end of Part I. Only once this is in train will it be worth developing the characteristics of an urban quarter which supports the development of the creative industries. Such a place will provide a range of activity, street life, urban culture, some forms of entertainment, residences and cultural venues. The overall aim should be mixture and diversity, nooks and crannies, concentrating in particular on small scale venues, workspaces and complementary activities. Although such places should be interesting places of themselves, it is probably advisable to resist the full-blown development of cultural tourism. It is likely that it will be necessary for local agency intervention to secure premises and property, to address issues of permeability and urban design and to put the area on the map in its early days. Early action will need to be pro-active to kick-start the process. At this point the task is to devise a series of programmes dealing with such matters as workspaces, venues, urban planning, the evening economy, animation and so on. From experience, the broad programme areas will most likely include most of the following.

Programme 1: Developing a Range of Cultural Venues

This would involve investing in the upgrading of existing premises and the development of bespoke buildings to achieve a range of small and medium scale cultural venues. Direct property intervention would involve the making available of premises to a selection of arts organizations already active in the area to either improve current venues or to help establish new venues/facilities in the area. This might be backed by rent controls and/or grants to safeguard such activities from future rises in land values and rents, and indeed it may be necessary to establish either a trust or number of individual trusts for specific buildings. Each new or improved venue would need to be subject to a feasibility study to ensure viability and in particular to address the question of ongoing revenue costs and support.

Selective inward relocation of existing arts organizations from other parts of the city, who are looking for a new home and might be attracted to a cultural quarter, given the right package of support and investment, is another possibility. Often, arts companies come to outgrow their current premises and may therefore require new space, or perhaps a studio/rehearsal space, storage, workshops, and offices, or some combination of these. In some instances, it might be appropriate to have shared space in which, for example, dance, music and theatre or even puppet theatre (Fig. 5.7) might be combined. There might also be Selective Inward Investment of commercial venue operators, particularly in music. This would need to be pursued with some care, and the sort of operators we have in mind are The Mean Fiddler, Ronnie Scott's or local small and medium scale entrepreneurs. In most cases, all that will be required is an approach backed by an area development prospectus; in some case incentives may need to be offered – development grants or rent holidays or some other property mechanism.

Possible projects might include, for example, the conversion, purchase, upgrading and re-positioning of a particular street as an arts street, containing a number of small gallery space, arts retail outlets and bars and cafés. The opening of a new gallery space is another possibility – preferably in tandem with a local artists' group – in a prominent location with a ground floor entrance. An interesting idea is to make available, at low rent, a space for a Print Workshop, as was done in Belfast. Print Workshops are important though often overlooked parts of the arts economy production chain. Or perhaps the setting up of, again at low rent, a space for the popular music bands to perform in, rehearse in and. operate from. This might include a recording studio, café/club area, rehearsal studio, small venue, and perhaps a screen-printing workshop and design room. This approach was

Figure 5.13   Belfast Circus Space
Source: John Montgomery.

followed in Sheffield CIQ. Providing a building for a Community Circus School is another interesting possibility (Fig. 5.13). Such organizations have peculiar and specific space requirements – fairly large volumes, high ceiling heights. This approach was followed in Belfast, Hoxton in east London, Melbourne and Fremantle in West Australia. There may be scope to develop an arts film house within the area, as in the Sheffield CIQ and in Temple Bar, but such venues are difficult to operate viably. More widely, small-scale improvement grants to private galleries, cyber cafés and other cultural venue enterprises are usually beneficial. In the longer term, it is important to establish some mechanism to protect priority projects from rising rents and property values, to secure their long-term stability.

Programme 2: Space for Artistic Production

The aim here would be to open up a number of currently unused and underused properties in strategic locations, and especially on the upper floors, to new active uses and in particular artists studios and craft and design workshops. This would provide accommodation for which there will most likely be an unmet demand in the city, and especially from students studying at and graduating from the local Art College. In the process, empty premises would be brought into productive use. Those newly working in the area will generate greater demand for local services and more demand for café culture. Such activities can be accommodated relatively cheaply because the internal spaces can be fitted out to a basic specification or left for the individual occupant to fit themselves. Space provided needs to be low cost but of a reasonable standard, with water, heating and light, and perhaps some live/work accommodation. It would be prudent to establish likely levels of demand for such spaces. The main requirement is for large spaces with high ceilings and reasonably good natural light. Decent-sized studios would tend to range from 300 sq ft (30 sq m) upwards. With circulation space and (say) a complex of 15 studios, this implies a building with a minimum floor area of some 5,000 to 7,500 sq ft (500–750 sq m). This approach was used in Temple Bar, Sheffield SCIQ and Wood Green (Figure 5.12). A more ambitious approach would be to speculate in the development of loft-style live-work spaces for artists. This approach was used in Huddersfield as part of the development of the media centre. Loft style live work spaces could be accommodated in any old warehouse or flatted factory building. Loft apartments tend to be anything from 500 sq ft to 1500 sq ft (effectively an entire floor).

Project development costs would include officer time and possibly consultants fees initially, followed by scheme by scheme capital costs and professional fees and/or officer time. It is important to stress that there is likely to be ongoing need for rent subsidy, in the form of low rents. All of this involves finding the right buildings, refurbishing them to a modest standard, fitting out where necessary, and then letting/managing the buildings or establishing a management regime and trust for each building.

Programme 3: Economic Development of the Creative Industries

The aim here is to stimulate the economic development of the cultural and media businesses sector, and thereby entrepreneurial activity, micro and SME firm formation and company development, job creation and wealth creation. This means recognising that many creative and cultural sectors are sources of added value and are often commercial activities in their own right. As such, they require similar types of enterprise assistance as other, perceived as more mainstream, sectors of the economy. Potential projects might include the establishment of a Media and Creative Industries Development Initiative, including the provision of tailored Business Skills Development for the creative industries, preferably in tandem with established local economic development agencies. This approach was followed in North Kensington, Sheffield and Manchester, and is now being adopted across London. A Cultural and Media Industries Investment Fund for equipment, start-up capital and training courses could also be considered. This approach was followed in Sheffield CIQ. Another suggestion is the development of a Film Commission, to encourage new film-makers and independent producers, and possibly the setting up of a location bureau and a film production fund. This approach was adopted in Sheffield, and also in Derry. Before committing to any such project a review of the creative and media industries in the city, should be undertaken to establish likely levels of demand.

Programme 4: Creative Industry Business Incubators

An important initiative will be the development of one or more managed workspaces for media and creative businesses, at least one for start-up businesses, and one other for more established businesses seeking to expand and/or consolidate. The important point to stress at is that creative industry business incubators are primarily places of work or, in the jargon, cultural production. They are organized on the premise that those taking space in the building will be earning a living from their activities, that they will be selling goods and services into a market place, whether local or global, as part of the "new economy" and the continuing growth of the creative and cultural industries. Most such businesses will be one or two person, recent or new start-ups and in need of a range of support services to help them survive the first difficult three years of trading. Services of such a nature might include business planning, business advice, joint marketing consortia, shared meeting spaces and office administration, shared technical services such as computers or photo-copying and so on. A pleasant reception area often doubling as a gallery, is also advantageous. Over time, it is often the case that businesses located in an incubator or managed workspace will buy and sell goods and services from each other – they will network and inter-trade. To help with this, and to provide an element of income stability, some "anchor tenants" such as an established design firm or perhaps an arts administration company might be introduced at an early stage. Ideally, all the individual tenants should have to worry about is running

Figure 5.14 Custard factory, Birmingham
Source: www.custardfactory.com.

their businesses and paying the (all-inclusive) rent. This approach was followed in Sheffield CIQ, in Brighton and in North Kensington. To be viable, a creative industries managed workspace needs to be in the region of 2–3000 square metres. Other examples of good practice are the Chocolate Factory in Wood Green, the Workstation in Sheffield and the Custard Factory in Birmingham (Fig. 5.14).

Programme 5: Public Art and the Public Realm

The aim here would be to establish a system of connected public spaces and pedestrian routeways, connecting the area, improving the area's permeability and legibility; and providing spaces for a range of stationary activities – sitting, watching, viewing, listening, tasting, as well as promenading. This would be consistent with any urban design strategy for the area. This is important for it sends signals about the area's emerging character as a place of experimentation and cultural development. Potential projects are of two broad types, the first of which involves the creation of a public space network (urban public spaces as opposed to parks and green space) to be used for promenading and stationary activities such as people watching, and for performances. The design of these spaces to be undertaken by combined teams of urban designers and artists, including design of street furniture, lighting rigs and signage. Such matters are not incidental where a cultural quarter is a place for consuming the arts. A detailed public realm design study would be an immediate

Figure 5.15 Public Art, Temple Bar, Dublin, *The Wounded King* **by Ronan Halpin and Paki Smith**

Source: photo by John Montgomery.

priority. This would be followed by detailed works on spaces, new squares, pocket parks, and pavement widths . It would also be important to identify one or two early public realm demonstration projects. This approach was followed in Temple Bar and Sheffield SCIQ. In the longer term, it may be worth the fixed term appointment of a Public Art Development Officer who would devise and implement a public art installation programme and series of related events (openings, sculpture trails) via a policy of direct commissioning; establish, with the local city council, a percent for art policy for the area; administer an immediate action project of small scale public art works in the area over the first 18 months (Fig. 5.15). This approach was adopted in Manchester MNQ and Temple Bar.

Programme 6. Cultural Animation

The aim would be to generate interest and enthusiasm in and for the area, to raise its profile locally, regionally and nationally, and to attract new business relocations and visitors. This can be achieved by programming a regular but varied event of festivals, events, concerts and other urban happenings, as well as by a strong marketing campaign. This at its simplest involves establishing a Cultural Animation Agency to programme events in the area, and perhaps adjoining areas, parks and squares. This approach has been adopted in Temple Bar, Sheffield CIQ, Adelaide's West End, in Newcastle NSW and in Melbourne. All that is required for this is a small team, an office and a budget, although it will be important to compile a list or schedule of venues and spaces. This is another early action project. The point is to achieve an immediate start-up as a relatively low-cost means of signalling intent. Also a bit of joy. The priority is to get a first year programme in place quickly. Then attention can turn to the longer term events strategy, and especially the proposed seasonal festivals. Initial costs are in setting up the agency, which could be sub-contracted to a commercial or semi-commercial organization.

Programme 7: Café Culture, the Evening Economy and Street Life

The aim would be to generate a more dynamic and varied street life in an area, and to allow for greater pedestrian flows and more variety in usage across different times of the day and night. This will involve agreeing and implementing a strategy for developing, diversifying and managing the evening and night-time economies, and, in particular, to offer a greater mix of activity and avoid the dominance of youth and drinking culture. It is essential to encourage café culture as part of an area's cultural mix, but also to provide places for people to meet. Problems of regulation may need to be overcome in relation to highways, liquor licensing and local planning policies. It is important to stress that evening economy uses such as restaurants, cafés and some venues work well in creative quarters as long as these are compatible with day-time uses and residential buildings. Night clubs and late-nite bars are less good neighbours and should be the exception rather than the rule. To be on the safe side, the preparation of an evening economy and café culture development strategy is advisable. This will involve rehearsing the arguments for encouraging the evening economy, reviewing the current regulatory regimes (planning; liquor and entertainment licensing); and holding a series of presentations/discussions with, for example, licensing committees. This approach was followed in Manchester MNQ. Once a policy position has been agreed (and indeed, if possible, as it is being devised), the strategic and quite deliberate siting of a few new café bars as stimulators of street life. This approach was followed in Cardiff and Temple

Bar. Along the way, it might be necessary to introduce a programme of pavement widening as part of the urban design programme, possibly backed by a Street Life Investment Fund: a series of grants and loans for frontages, opening up visibility, lighting, awnings, glass extensions and similar. Depending on the area's existing characteristics, a major investment in improved street lighting and action to design out urban fear may be required.

Programme 8: Place-marketing and Imaging

The aim would be to generate an image and Unique Selling Point for an area through media representation, promotional campaigns and the style and quality of promotional material. This can then be used to market activities and events within the quarter, across the city, and in marketing to the rest of the country and further afield. The format, content and imagery used should be modern and signal the area's street cred. It is important not only to inform, but also to present a new image of place via contemporary images, graphic design, post-cards, posters, flyers. This will involve identifying a core message an image of the area to be conveyed to potential visitors, investors and relocation agencies, based on the area's cultural USP; area branding via image style and tone of publicity material; the regular production of an area guide to What's On, experimenting with a variety of formats; and ongoing media advertisement and PR campaign (feature placement etc) to generate interest in visiting the area where this is deemed necessary (Fig. 5.16).

Programme 9: Community Development via Culture

The aim here would be to promote wider community development within the area and across the city as a whole by running programmes of in-reach and outreach. These might take the form of a series of cultural workshops – both in the area and in other neighbourhoods – designed to improve knowledge, impart craft skills and to generate more confidence for individuals. This is not always necessary, but may help build support for the quarter's development . Potential projects might include a series of training workshops and adult education classes in creative and cultural fields, in partnership with existing providers, and in particular any local Community Arts Forum; as well as outreach activities, this might include an area lecture and master class series. The establishment of an arts community development resource centre, acting as a base for various arts and community development initiatives, might also be considered. Effectively, this would be a managed workspace with suites of small offices and shared meeting rooms and service facilities. The premises would be made available rent free or at low rents. It might also be beneficial to resource a number of community arts organizations – on a project basis – to provide specific services. There might be six to ten such projects in any one year. The groups would need to raise core funding for their general activities, and this is a potential role for other funding organizations. A series of annual bursaries and competitions

Figure 5.16 Area Branding, Temple Bar, Dublin (1993)

Source: Temple Bar Properties Ltd.

to allow wider take up of opportunities by successful participants on the various projects – in this way, young people, having developed an interest (say) in visual arts or design, could then move onto the next stage of development rather than becoming frustrated or disillusioned.

In this way it is hoped that a general indication of how to establish a creative or cultural quarter has been provided, together with some indication of the types of programmes that might be pursued. In doing so, it is important to remain wary of over-hyping the likely benefits of the quarter, as these may seem slow to emerge at first. It is crucial to work from base/grain of existing activity in the arts and in enterprise development, backed as appropriate by selective relocations and inward investment. Small and medium scale developments are preferable to large projects, that is a process of adding gradual money to help an area develop rather than over-powering it with flagships projects to too grand a scale. It will be important too to vest a number of properties for arts use – to overcome problems at a future, and not-too-distant date. One should also recognize that several existing arts organizations may require long-term commitment (revenue funding) to maintain their activities and especially of they are taking on a building. Artists need money to survive as much as anyone else. Most, if not all, building projects will require detailed feasibility studies to be undertaken to establish costs, income and overall viability. Some form of area implementation vehicle, probably on a time-limited basis, will be essential if good progress is to be made. Any such body should open an area office as a matter of urgency, and might also convert a shopfront to provide an information and exhibition space. Much more besides will emerge as the complicated process of ongoing development, management and profile-raising proceeds. But, by following these basic steps, a good start can be made.

5. DYNAMIC CREATIVE MILIEUX IN THE FIFTH WAVE

For this author at least, the term "urban cultural quarter", especially those that incorporate a creative industries cluster, refers to a high energy, artistic and creative milieu, integrated into the new economy, highly developed technologically and offering the type of working, living and entertainment environment which appeals to creative entrepreneurs, artists and city enthusiasts. This type of place should not be confused with the disastrous monolithic culturally institutionalized precincts such as the south banks of London, Melbourne, Frankfurt and Hong Kong. Rather, they are these days to be found in Dublin, Sheffield, Glasgow, SoHo, Tilburg, and places like Hackney (London), Fitzroy (Melbourne) and Surry Hills (Sydney). The essential point is that as well as being consumed, cultural products must be being made in the *locale*. By doing so, parts of cities – quarters – will provide locations for rapid development of business clusters.

If the creative industries are as I have argued a key growth sector of the fifth wave, then it follows that successful cities in the future will most likely contain a highly dynamic quarter of creative industries. And while high-tech R&D is often drawn to campus-style environments, creative entrepreneurs derive interest, excitement and influences from more urbanized environments. Table 5.3 is a representation of cities as dynamic creative economies, plotting levels of growth, along a scale of low to high, against the extent to which a city is either traditional or modern in its cultural outlook. The more dynamic cities will tend to achieve stronger economic growth and be more innovative, they will have a strong sense of place, be open to modernity but at ease with tradition. They will also achieve a balance between liberalization and measures to deal with crime and anti-social behaviour. Some of these cities are already emerging as economic leaders:

Table 5.3 Cities as Dynamic Creative Economies

Economy:	Dynamic Growth –v– Slow Growth
Creativity:	Innovation –v– Creative Stagnation
Culture:	Tradition –v– Modernity
Place:	Place Identity –v– Placelessness
Morality:	Liberalization –v– Regulation

The cities that will be most successful in the new economy, the Fifth Wave, will be those that have already invested in their capacity for creative enterprise and in business start-ups. This approach has already proved successful in Dublin, Sheffield and Manchester as we have seen. The strategy of developing 10 creative industry clusters in London, in addition to the West End should be watched closely. Thriving cities in the US such as Austin, Portland, Seattle, Boston, Philadelphia or San Francisco, have managed to combine a creative economy with high-tech industries. Bangalore and Mumbai are also cities to watch, as is Toronto. Many of the cities of Europe, with the exception of Barcelona, Berlin, Milan, Copenhagen, Helsinki and Stockholm, are currently lagging in the creative economy. Sydney and Melbourne, possibly Brisbane, have a great opportunity to develop a dynamic creative economy but, with the exception of Brisbane, little convincing policy work on the creative industries has been developed. Adelaide, sadly, is moving in the wrong policy direction, preferring to view the arts as a social good rather than part of the city's future economic development. Perth struggles because of its geographical isolation, and the fact that young artists and designers, often as not, leave for Sydney, Melbourne, London or LA. This trend, however, could be reversed as the example of Dublin demonstrates. Creative entrepreneurs will always be drawn to London or New York, but why would they move to Kansas City or Detroit, Portsmouth or Aberdeen?

They have been moving to – or perhaps remaining in following graduation – Sheffield and Manchester, Dublin and Melbourne, as we have seen. But this has been no accident; it was a deliberate act of policy to create the conditions most conducive to the creative economy. Cities which cannot create similar conditions for their own artists and designers will rapidly fall behind as the brightest and the most enterprising leave town for pastures green. This fate is befalling Adelaide, has threatened Liverpool for a long time (since the 1960s) and seems likely to engulf Pittsburgh once more. Behind them, the creative entrepreneurs and artists leave cities which are on the way to regressing into dull country towns, an ageing population who tend mainly to attend arts events only if they are free, a cohort of young children who will also leave town when the time comes, and a class of middle-ranking civil servants. As such towns (no longer cities) become even duller, so too will the pressure on young people to leave increase. Whole cities might become dormitory towns and retirement homes.

This danger relates to a further point: the lack of balance between the old cultural forms and the new. The Temple Bar experiment deliberately set about developing Irish expertise in modern cultural forms: architecture, visual art, music, fashion and design. It did so against a back-drop of tradition, much of it positive but a proportion of which is nostalgic and cloying. The Irish turned away from a vision of more cobbled streets and Molly Malone statues to embrace modernity. So, too, have Manchester and Sheffield. After many years of looking to cultural forms and identities of the past, London is now a centre for modern culture. The US and Australia are more modern countries than the UK, by and large, but they both have strong conservative streaks, in the sense that at times they fear modernity and artistic development. The point is that as well as respecting and looking after the past, cities will need to embrace the modern. The successful city of the fifth wave will be traditional and modern simultaneously.

Finally, Richard Florida is right to stress the importance of tolerance in dynamic creative economies. This should certainly relate to tolerance of new ideas, risk-taking and unconventional forms of dress. For, as we have seen in Part II of this book, part of the "spark" which produces new technologies and art is the tension between the generations – the essential need to develop beyond what one's parents' generation were doing. This is an intrinsic part of the human condition. But whether tolerance extends as far as to mean that anything goes is much less certain. Drugs, prostitution, gambling, drunkenness, rowdy behaviour, homosexuality, as we saw in Part III, have always been part of city life, and most likely always will be. Some of these are less problematic than others – homosexuality is certainly no longer a taboo except in Islamic and African countries. Prostitution is still a crime in most places, but is quite often tactfully ignored. In Australia, brothels have been licensed and are legitimate businesses in Victoria and New South Wales, but they are still illegal in South Australia. The control of drug abuse is a difficult issue with some calling for a de-criminalization of certain drugs; but others pointing out that most crime against the person is drug-related. Meanwhile, smoking has been banned from the pubs in Dublin, the beach at Bondi and even from the street in New York. And, as we have seen, experiments with the relaxation of liquor licensing – judging from the English experience – have apparently been counter-productive. So it seems the question of tolerance and public morality is, messy though it seems, one of balance. Thus, while it is tempting to argue that the successful cities of the Fifth Wave will be highly tolerant and liberal on social issues, this is not wholly convincing. The reading of the history of liquor licensing in England at least suggest that if all forms of behaviour are tolerated as equally valid, then the general standard of manners and decency declines. This state of affairs has been given credence by what Marxists refer to as "tolerance of otherness" so that no absolute principles or codes of behaviour are deemed possible in post-modern, multi-cultural societies. Rather, morality is seen as needing to be contextualized, and therefore is relative. In 2004, this scenario was the backdrop for artists being murdered in Holland, plays being withdrawn in Birmingham and writers being forced into hiding.

Tolerance should not extend to the intolerant, nor indeed to the criminal and the anti-social. For if it does, then the rise in crime, urban fear and the general coarsening of everyday life will produce an opposite effect to that of creative cities attracting creative and enterprising people. This would be a flight of the (largely) white middle classes from the inner cities. This has occurred in recent history in Birmingham, Liverpool, Detroit and parts of New York. It could just as easily happen again. This realization led Peter Hall,[40] in his conclusion, to identify the future problems that cities must address as being the impact of the car on the environment, relative poverty, the breakdown of the family, poor educational achievement, bullying, drug use and crime. Interestingly, most such problems continue to grow in the UK and in Europe, but not in New York and other American cities where zero-tolerance policies on crime and anti-social behaviour have been introduced. So, in the successful city of the fifth wave it seems, eccentricities and fashions will need to be tolerated, but anti-social behaviour will not.

And so the successful cities of the fifth wave, the next thirty years, will be economically dynamic, with a strong technological base, artistic and highly design-literate, innovative, modern without losing sight of tradition and heritage, be good urban places, be relatively dense and have active street-scapes, and they will be tolerant of creatives and young people, but not of crime and anti-social behaviour. It is likely, too, that many of them will have one or more recognizable creative milieu or quarter. Along the way, problems will be encountered and hopefully overcome, as they have been in Dublin, Sheffield and Manchester. Accusations of "gentrification", "trendy nonsense", "not real jobs", "boys' games" will be made, as they were in the 1980s and 1990s. Much of this will be levelled by the disillusioned left, forced to concede that communism and socialism are unworkable, but still retaining their hostility to enterprise. Some opposition will come from the old right-wing left (the trade unions and traditionalists) who still find it hard to believe that economic development is about more than the factory floor.

In any event, the writing is already on the wall, and the examples of the success of cultural quarters are growing. Moreover, the creative industries are precisely the sorts of economic areas in which black and Asian young people, certainly in Britain, are interested in pursuing. Rather than waiters, shop-keepers, restaurateurs

---

40 Hall, P., *op. cit.*, 1998, p. 983.

or even local government officers, they wish to follow careers in film, TV, the music industry, design and fashion. As in North Kensington,[41] a mainly West Indian part of London, the best way to promote confidence and self-sufficiency amongst ethnic minorities is to provide meaningful job and business opportunities for the brightest and the best. But I digress. The real question is what the city leaders should be doing now to secure prosperity in the future.

41 Urban Cultures Ltd, *North Kensington Media Industries Strategy*, unpublished consultancy report for North Kensington City Challenge, 1996.

Cities of the Fifth Wave

A CONCLUSION

In this concluding chapter I propose to consider further the characteristics of successful cities in the fifth wave of capitalist economic development. This involves an assessment of likely successful cities in the coming period, and those who will lag behind. The future of cities and city-regions, as in previous waves, will be bound up in new forms of wealth creation, new artistic creativity, innovation, new development and city extensions, and in how conducive the everyday life of cities remains or becomes.

It is important too, to consider the likely aims and methods of city planning in the coming half century, as it will be these, linked to economic and cultural development, that will determine the future form of cities, and therefore to some extent their success as centres of the new economy and as living environments. This essentially revolves around the question of what city structure and places will be like, say, in fifty years' time. Possible scenarios include the 100-mile city of Deyan Sudjic,[1] the split-personality of Los Angeles as a city of opportunity and great wealth but also divided by economic class and race;[2] the "infinite city" of northern Italy;[3] or perhaps the old cities will be abandoned in favour of new "edge cities" as argued by Garreau.[4] Another option is the compact city as favoured in Europe, but how compact is compact – what are the limits to density in the 21st century? Will the Americans and Australians build more, ever-higher skyscrapers? Will cities like Singapore, Kuala Lumpur and Beijing continue to raze large swathes of the old city to put up modernist blocks in their place? Will the English embark upon a new wave of garden cities? How will all of this play out in the city regions during the fifth wave? Will the cities get better, or worse?

Attempting to answer this final question – whether cities will get better or worse – takes us into the realms of crime, educational standards, air quality and the degree to which different ethnic and religious groups co-exist peacefully in the same place or in different parts of the same city. These are all important policy considerations in the future management of cities, and they shall need to be addressed sooner rather than later.

---

1   Sudjic, D., *The 100 Mile City* (London: Andre Deutsch, 1992).

2   Davis, M., *City of Quartz: Excavating the Future in Los Angeles* (London: Verso, 1990).

3   Pasqui, G., "The Perspective of the Infinite City", *Planning, Theory and Practice*, 5, 3, September 2004, pp. 381–389.

4   Garreau, J., *Edge City* (New York: 1991).

Before considering these further, we need summarize the arguments put forward in this book.

Summary Argument

The death of the city has been predicted at various points during the last 150 years. Lewis Mumford, for example, argued[5] that the "Megalopolis" would eventually strangle itself. Most cities in the developed world had certainly reached a hiatus by the mid-1980s, the early signs of which were evident from the mid 1970s. In the United States, great cities such as Detroit, Chicago, and Boston appeared to be in terminal decline; in the UK the great northern cities of Manchester, Liverpool, Sheffield, and Newcastle were in apparent free-fall – Birmingham and the West Midlands (the workshop of the Empire), too.

But something happened - exemplified by the Barcelona of the 1980s - to bring life and economic dynamism back to the city, and to varying degrees other cities have followed suit: Manchester and Glasgow, Rotterdam and Antwerp, Boston and Chicago, and Melbourne. All have become centrally concerned with urban regeneration, urban revitalization, urban renaissance … Perhaps for the first time since the early 19th century the prime concern of urban policy-makers is to build cities which combine economic dynamism with cultural vitality, creative innovation, and place-making according to the principles of urban design. Many of the skills and knowledge we require to do this come from a reinterpretation of the past, particularly in the built form and the development of an entrepreneurial culture. Yet these must always be considered against the new modes of production, new technologies, and changing demographic patterns.

The basic proposition of this book is that it is essential to retain in balance a creative and dynamic economy, an innovative cultural life, and a "good fit" of the built form to activity. These conditions will be found in any study of successful cities at a given point in time but especially following the development of capitalism. Historically, some cities have been successful and flexible enough to adjust to changing economic conditions; others have not been.

Cities are first and foremost economic entities. Although many medieval cities were originally built as defensible spaces, seats of government, or holy places, from as early as the tenth century, patterns of trade across Europe were emerging (to a notable extent explaining the locations and development of many of today's cities). The essential dynamic – trade – underpinned the development of mercantile capitalism in Europe from around 1400, which, in turn, transformed into early and then full industrial capitalism from the mid-1700s onwards. By the 1930s industrial capitalism was already entering a long period of decline, so that the era of so-called "flexible specialization" can probably be dated from the 1950s. It seems likely that this relationship between cities and trade will last as long as capitalism itself.

5	Mumford, L., *The Culture of Cities* (New York: Harcourt, Brace, 1938).

Cities achieve growth primarily through a process of exporting goods and services in order to earn surpluses with which to purchase imports.[6] As the economy develops, more and more exports generate greater surpluses, during which time the division of labour among local producers becomes more complex. Various supply chains develop, so that a network of businesses provide inputs to the final export product. Some of the producer service businesses might themselves become exporters in their own right. The outcome is a dynamic network of local businesses, a good proportion of which must export, others of which are producer input suppliers. Over time a strong and/or growing city economy develops the skills and the capacity to replace or substitute imports and make these products locally. By this means, a city economy can then import other goods with its export surpluses, and in the meantime the newly replaced imports may become another successful export product. During this time the city economy continues to export its existing goods and services, while the local division of labour becomes more diversified and complex. The wealth that is created is then re-invested in productive capacity, raw materials, or stock; and a good proportion of it is also spent by local citizens on consumer goods and services. The growth of local consumer spending in periods of rapid economic growth is closely followed by, and in turn creates, increasing demand for new products. Cities where these processes are self-generating and dynamic enjoy periods of "explosive growth".[7]

Competitive success tends to concentrate in particular industries and groups of inter-connected industries.[8] A "cluster" is a grouping of industries linked together through customer, supplier and other relationships which enhance competitive advantage. These clusters are characterized by the presence of internationally competitive firms, which also continuously upgrade and innovate. Such clusters develop around a core of propulsive companies, often applying cutting-edge technology either to make new products or to improve production processes. Networks of supplier businesses and chains of production form, and these are now less horizontally integrated than under industrial capitalism. This in itself encourages new business formations and thus feeds entrepreneurial activity, generated by a steady supply of individuals with the prerequisite skills and attributes. Such clusters or complexes are very often centres of great invention and innovation. At present, the city economies that are growing rapidly are most likely to be those with clusters of technologically-advanced flexibly specialized industries – places such as Seattle or Austin, Texas or Silicon Valley; Bristol and the M11 Corridor in England; the Third Italy; Helsinki; Dublin; and Boston. Such cities and city-regions will also have more established Fordist industries, such as aircraft production or car-making, yet their economies will no longer be dominated by them. By contrast, stagnating and declining cities will tend to have very few flexibly-specialized industry sectors, and will often be dominated by large branch-plant businesses (albeit with more localized supply chains) and a higher proportion of service businesses serving predominantly local consumer demand.

---

6   Jacobs, J., *The Economy of Cities* (New York: Vintage, 1969).
7   Ibid.
8   Porter, M., *The Competitive Advantage of Nations* (New York: Free Press, 1990).

Cities that are dynamic economically will also tend to be more interesting culturally. Over time, this has been demonstrated in Venice and Florence, Paris and London, Vienna and Berlin, New York and San Francisco, and lately in Dublin, Barcelona, and Melbourne. At the very least, cities would be dull and uninteresting and lacking in innovation without culture. Culture can be understood as a general process of intellectual, spiritual and aesthetic development, as in the development of western culture and art; as a particular way of life, whether of a people, a period or a group, covering such matters as language, and customs, local festivals, national holidays, regional cuisines, sports, and religious practices; or as works and practices of intellectual and especially artistic activity.

It is also true that artistic and cultural creation occur within an economic and social framework, and it matters a great deal whether the cities in which artists live and work are in decline or are growing; are using technology to create new work and wealth, or not. But by the same token, a society that is wealthy will not necessarily produce great art. Wealth, particularly the old forms of money, is not necessarily a guarantee of artistic and creative innovation – quite often the reverse. So although a link between economic development and culture does exist, it is impossible to "read-off" or predict.

As far as the arts themselves are concerned, it is important to understand that breakthroughs in new art are the outcome of creative genius, the psychology of the individual in question, the creative environment in which they live (or move to) and the need for each generation to develop work that breaks with that of the previous generation. This explains the development of various "movements" in the various art forms, for example Impressionism, Cubism and Action Painting. These movements occur in particular places at particular points in time, overwhelmingly in cities – "the creative milieux". A handful of original innovators will be joined by others as each artistic movement develops, until that is the next paradigm shift in art. Modernity, although relating to science and technology, is largely a process of developing new art. A distinction can also be drawn between formative creativity and applied creativity, where the latter extends and applies new art of itself or to other products and processes – design, for example.

The built form should give identity to a city but also provide a good "fit" for its unique blend of activities, including its business sector and creative economy. Certainly, all cities must have mixed use, higher density areas within which myriad small businesses can develop and prosper, and from which they can take on the world if need be. Without built environments of this type, creative enterprise will not prosper. A city's micro-environment consists of the pattern of streets and buildings, the relationship between building heights and street widths, building edges and spaces, adaptable usage of the built stock, legibility and permeability and the public realm. This is the area of study of urban designers, who in recent years have been rediscovering the old skills of city building or place-making.[9] This implies designing

---

    9   Montgomery, J., "Making a City: Urbanity, Vitality and Urban Design", *Journal of Urban Design*, 3,1, pp. 93–116, 1998.

neighbourhoods and districts around walkable scales, that is the 400m radius or the 100 acre place.

That mixed use is the new planning orthodoxy is by now evident, although as recently as the early 1990s, this could not be said. This acceptance by town planners, and adoption by developers and investors, happily coincided with demographic changes, changes in employment and the "lifestyle" generations, and not forgetting the falling demand for office accommodation, so that even prime space in city CBDs started to become places of residence and more mixed. Paradoxically, this phenomenon is bringing added pressure to bear on lower value uses in so-called "zones of transition", with many activities being driven out by new wealthier residents. This is not to argue that every district or neighbourhood in the city should be redeveloped for mixed use to higher densities. Nor does it imply that all uses can be mixed successfully everywhere, all of the time. It would be a mistake to re-zone all areas for higher density mixed use. In future, we shall be working within an idiom of place typologies: what places are like or should be like, set within a wider strategic framework or spatial plan.

The past 15 years have been critical in shaping the economic urban geography of the next 50 years – although this is as yet by no means self-evident. The next few years will be crucial: if your city hasn't made its move, it's almost too late to start. Within cities, the primary conflict is not between competing existing businesses, nor between labour and capital as economic classes as the Marxists would have us believe. Rather, the important conflict is between established interests or old money, and new forms of work and wealth creation. Where established interests predominate – as in the guilds of medieval London or the Scottish burghs or in current-day Adelaide – to the detriment of the new, then only economic stagnation can follow. Where new activities come to predominate, economic growth will result. In circumstances where new growth is a possibility, the role of city and state governments is not to defend old against the new, or simply to remain neutral, but it is to actively promote new forms of economic growth. Governments need, therefore, to keep opportunities for economic and technological development open, not closed. This can only be achieved if new work is allowed to grow – even if this is against the established interests of old money.

This point can be transferred to artistic and creative forms, too. If your city spends most of its time subsidizing old art but largely ignoring new work, or is trying to replicate old architecture, then it is likely that your economy is dominated by old money and established interests. If your city embraces new art forms, living artists and designers, new technology, and new architecture, then the chances are that it is succeeding in generating new work too. The key figures in all of this are visionary political leaders and the creative entrepreneurs, the former creating the conditions for the latter to invest, work and prosper.

The main objective for successful city and city-region economies must be to achieve growth in new industries and in micro and small businesses. This need not run counter to environmental sustainability (except in its fundamentalist form where it is more of an ideology than anything practical). Measures dealing with energy conservation, renewable sources, solar heating, and water catchment are to be welcomed; so too the move towards green buildings. But it is only wealthy economies and countries that can afford to be environmentally sustainable.

So, and finally, a city-state or metropolitan region needs to be creating wealth – to provide jobs, income, spending, tax income – but also to pay for environmental husbandry. Much the same relationship exists between wealth creation and "social inclusion", pensions, and also public sector spending on health and education. These things can only be afforded if wealth is created. The only prudent option is therefore to diversify the economy as far as possible, and continue doing so. This in turn means helping city economies to grow, innovate and create. In the process, by a combination of strategic spatial planning and place-making at the local level, the cities can be made better too.

Fifth Wave Cities

The ascendant city economies of the fifth wave will be those that compete successfully in the new industries. Like Manchester and Glasgow, Birmingham and Detroit, London and Paris, Los Angeles and San Francisco, Seattle and Bristol, Philadelphia and London (Hertfordshire) in previous waves, the cities of the new economy will long be associated with a particular episode of growth, and particular industries. Some of these are already evident: Seattle and Portland for software and processors, southern California for computer design and the Internet, London and New York for design, Los Angeles for digitalized films, London for television production, Philadelphia for pharmaceuticals, Helsinki and Stockholm for mobile communications, Bangalore for computers and software. The successful cities of the next 50 years will be those which achieve highly dynamic economies centred on the new digital industries, the knowledge economy generally and the creative industries. Cities that manage to combine some representation of some of these industries with high levels of artistic creativity and design will also flourish. These will be the successful cities of the fifth wave, plus any others that find a creative niche.

In the conclusion to Part IV, I argued that cities can be assessed against a schema made up of the propensity to achieve dynamic growth, balanced against the need to maintain traditional cultural and urban forms, but also to remain open to modernity. Crudely this can be characterized as dynamic growth, artistic creativity, entrepreneurship, balancing the old and the new, manners and personal freedom, the need for both high and low density neighbourhoods. I referred to this as the "Traditional-Modern City".

- *High Growth Modern*: the combination of a dynamic economy with modern cultural forms.
- *High Growth Traditional*: the combination of a dynamic economy with traditional cultural forms.

Figure 0.5   Cities: Winners and Losers

Source: John Montgomery.

- *Low Growth Modern*: the combination of low growth modernity and placelessness.
- *Low Growth Traditional*: the combination of low growth with old cultural forms.

The important point is whether or not economic growth is present, and how this inter-plays with the culture and form of a city. It is likely that in real life, most cities will combine some elements of high and low growth, tradition and modernity, place and placelessness, certainly across city regions such as Milan or Greater London or southern California. The cities that have most to fear are those with low levels of new wealth creation and either a placeless form or identity, or too much emphasis on the past.

Closely related to this is the issue of innovation and creativity as opposed to creative thrombosis. Cities that are already creative and innovative in this regard are New York, Seattle, Los Angeles, Boston, London, Tokyo, Manchester, Dublin, Milan, Austin and San Francisco, Helsinki and Raleigh-Durham in North Carolina (Figure 0.5).

Cities that will join the grouping due to investments in new technology, R&D and the creative industries will include Bangalore (India's Silicon Valley), Shanghai and Shenzhen in China, Barcelona, Mumbai (home of Bollywood), Toronto and possibly Brisbane.

By contrast, cities with low levels of dynamic creativity will experience relative decline. These include places such as Birmingham, Vienna, Paris, Madrid, Rome, Dresden, New Orleans and Detroit. Some of these will continue to be seats of government, while others will remain attractive as places to retire to or bring up children. Others will need to take action now to avoid lagging behind. Many other cities, especially in Europe, will find themselves more reliant on older cultural forms and their attractiveness to tourists. Others will remain associated with primary goods such as particular food-stuffs (Dijon, Modena) or wines (Lyon, Beaune). Cities which seem likely to struggle to gain a share of the new economy include Moscow, Belfast, Detroit, Adelaide, Athens and Beunos Aires.

There is a simple enough correlation between innovation and economic dynamism. Not so, necessarily, between the traditional and the modern. Cities that innovate and therefore grow will also tend to embrace modernity in the arts, fashion and architecture. This is true, for example, of New York and Tokyo and these days London. Yet it is also the case that the new economy tends to thrive in places that are more interesting (that is the traditional mixed-use city) or else offer, by way of climate, environment or "life-style", a better living environment. Cities which offer this and engage with modernity and innovate will be successful. This probably now includes Manchester, Dublin, Melbourne, Barcelona and Antwerp, will no doubt soon encompass Berlin, and might in future extend to currently unfashionable places such as Toronto, and indeed the fast-growing cities of the Baltic States. Cities will also continue to exert an influence over their own city regions, so that successful economic entities of the future will be cities plus countryside. Again, this is already true of San Francisco and Seattle, London and Milan. It could also happen in Brisbane and Lisbon. Meanwhile, cities that have good urban form and are interesting culturally have greater opportunities to become part of the new economy than those that do not: Edinburgh, Prague, St Petersburg and Budapest.

In this way, successful cities will need to be creative milieux, and such creativity must be applied dynamically. For this to happen, cities will need a repository of advanced technological, artistic and craft skills, or they will need to import and/or educate to provide these. Unless new businesses are more or less continually created and opportunities to pursue creative careers are provided, this will result only in the city becoming a net exporter of skills and entrepreneurs as the brightest and the best leave for greener pastures. In addition to this, creative entrepreneurs will only remain in cities that are themselves artistic, have a healthy arts scene and access to good food and ambient restaurants, bars and clubs. Without an appealing café culture and evening economy, cities will be lacking one of the factors for competitive advantage. This, in turn, will depend to a large extent on the attractiveness, conviviality and sophistication of the city as a physical entity, that is to say its built form, scale, architecture, walkability and the interest of its streets and squares. The question of the city as a built form is therefore not incidental, and "place identity" and urban design will continue to play an important – perhaps heightened – role. In keeping with the idiom of cities as places of design, developing new architecture will be essential, as in Barcelona or Prague or Berlin or Dublin. This should not be a return to "high-modernism" and the wholesale redevelopment of cities, for it is also essential to maintain traditional street-scapes, building types and heights. Architects cannot be trusted to re-design cities, but they should be welcomed to design new buildings.

Urban Planning in the Fifth Wave

Place Types

If history is to guide us, it is almost a given that successful city economies will continue to develop as city-regions. Growth can be accommodated in a number of ways: by increasing densities, allowing development to spread into the urban periphery, by planning new satellites or by rural transports of some forms of city work. This will be a matter for detailed consideration within individual cities, but it seems likely that this will involve a combination of higher densities in inner areas, more mixed use, the redevelopment of former inner industrial areas, nodal settlements on public transport corridors, lower density residential areas, new towns and expansions to existing villages and towns, and all of this accompanied by growth boundaries and more prescriptive strategic spatial planning. This implies that a place-typology of sorts might be helpful.[10]

- city centres or CBD
- zones of transition
- older residential areas, close to city centres
- older inner commercial and industrial areas
- largely residential suburbs
- suburban commercial and industrial areas
- market and country towns and coastal resorts
- rural areas and villages
- sensitive landscapes
- new settlements

- *City centres*   These will continue to accommodate the city's higher end uses (office and retail), but they will also become increasingly mixed both as residential areas and entertainment districts. One of the main policy issues in the coming years will be reconciling potential conflicts between domesticity and night-life, as more

---

10 I have borrowed and emended this categorization from *The Urban Environment and Planning*, Spatial Planning Department, Ministry of Environment and Energy, Copenhagen, Denmark, 1995.

entertainment uses are allowed. Another will involve debating the three-dimensional shape of CBDs, and in particular the issue of tall buildings and their impact on the micro-climate. A third issue will be the treatment of the public realm; a fourth the removal of car dominance over city streets.

•   *Zones of Transition*   These will continue to be those places surrounding the CBD where development pressure for the expansion of the CBD is most keenly felt. This is true of East Darling Harbour in Sydney, for example, or Spitalfields in London. Such places already contain good economic activity – in Sydney's case a working port, in Spitalfields' a thriving market and mixed use area. Nevertheless, the land values in such newly central locations makes the temptation to redevelop for office use almost irresistible. Governments often find themselves in the position of wishing to cash in on their own land holdings, raise large amounts in property taxes, or achieve "development gain" by allowing over-development. Governments who behave in this way are rightly condemned for short-termism. That said, it will be for politicians and local people to decide whether and in what ways such places should be redeveloped. These will be the most contentious planning battlegrounds of the next 20 years, and especially as the next up-wave property boom kicks in.

•   *Older Residential Areas*   Being close to urban centres, these will remain popular places to live for the wealthy, young professionals, artists and the urban poor, although not always in the same neighbourhood. This is true of Maida Vale in London, Fitzroy in Melbourne, the Marais in Paris, Surry Hills in Sydney, and the west end of Glasgow. Such places tend to be developed to reasonably high densities, and so the scope for new development will tend to be restricted to appropriate infill development. Rather than abrupt changes to the built form, such places will experience change as their social mix alters. In some cases, the new rich will hang on to a newly valuable part of the city; in others the comings and goings of migrants will be accommodated. Most will gentrify to a degree.

•   *Older Inner Commercial and Industrial Areas* are similar to zones of transition because they exist in a relative state of flux. In their case, this comes not from the development pressure exerted by an expanding CBD, but rather by the decline of old industries and activities. This process will continue, with such areas re-emerging as mixed residential, artistic and small business locations. The examples are already with us: the Sheffield CIQ, Ancoats and Castlefield in Manchester, Newtown in Sydney, Clerkenwell and Shoreditch in London, Fortitude Valley in Brisbane. There will be more, and these will include Northside in Belfast, Sunniside in Sunderland, Digbeth in Birmingham and Wood Green in London. In these places it is not the old industries of the industrial age that are declining (this has already happened) but service industries that can be more cheaply and effectively located elsewhere. This includes activities such as car repair workshops, garage showrooms and even local government depots and buildings.

- *Outer Residential Suburbs* will remain broadly as they are, good places for families, children and schools. There will be some intensification of the built form as some very large gardens are broken up into housing plots. This is already happening in Adelaide, in the suburbs of Unley and Brighton; so too in Bristol. But there are limits as to how far this should be allowed to go. The example of controversial proposals to triple densities in outer Melbourne suburbs is compelling. Such places will need to develop their existing shopping streets and district parades into strong nodes of retailing, quiet evening economy activities and offices for small businesses. The more successful such places will also be well-connected by good public transport.

- *Suburban Commercial and Industrial Suburbs* are those which have tended to grow up on the edges of cities, dating from the 1930s, 1950s and 1960s. In London, examples are places such as Wembley or Alperton where the growth of the electrical and electronic industries was accommodated, and where London's film studios congregated. Similar places can be found in almost every city, certainly on the edges of Barcelona as we have seen or in Western Sydney. In many cities such places have become the subject of disastrous new development in the form of the out-of-town shopping mall, the retail warehouse park, the multi-plex cinema, the "leisure centre". The future of such places will be amongst the most difficult of urban problems to resolve. Those that have not already succumbed to big box retailing will probably be re-planned as new mixed use and residential neighbourhoods.

- *Market and Country Towns and Coastal Resorts* are combined here as a category for ease of presentation, and yet this covers a range of different place-types. In the UK, during the 1980s and early 1990s, the fastest population growth was experienced in such free-standing towns within "easy" reach of London in particular. This includes places like Stroud in Gloustershire, Salisbury (in fact a cathedral city), Bedford, Banbury and Brighton. Such places – with the exception of Stroud – are attractive to live in their own right, whether as part of a retreat to the country, the style of places such as Tunbridge Wells or the combination of the sea-side and alternative arts as found in Brighton. University towns such as Oxford and Cambridge, Warwick and even Reading are prized as good places to live, but not Derby or Coventry or Hull. Some resorts too – Margate in Kent, Blackpool, Skegness – have become deeply unfashionable. In Australia, the dominant cultural romanticism is not the escape to the country, as in England, but rather "sea-change", baby-boomers getting away from the city, retiring or moving to the coast to become ageing beach-bums and surfers. The Australian coast is now littered with new developments promising the sea-change lifestyle. In America too, many people will tend to tell you that good places to live are New England (pleasant towns but cold winters), Portland as we have seen, Charlestown, Philadelphia and southern California outside LA, Denver, parts of Texas, and even the South now that air-conditioning has been invented. The task for such places, in town planning terms, is to accommodate growth sensibly by grafting new areas onto the old, well-planned in terms of social facilities, neighbourhood centres and access to good public transport – the exact opposite of what occurred on the outskirts of Reading in the 1980s.

• *Rural Areas and Villages* have for long been the poor relations of urban, economic and social policy. This has led to the curious phenomenon where wealthy outsiders buy up village and rural properties, either to live in or as second homes, whilst simultaneously village shops (competition from out-of-town superstores), post offices, pubs (drink-driving laws) and village halls are closed down one by one. This is certainly the case in the UK, and in Australia too there is pressure mounting for clearer government policies towards "regional Australia", that is the countryside. In the near future governments will need to take a more strategic approach not only to built development in the countryside, but also to economic development of new industries, assistance for some existing industries that need to restructure, export drives and the retention of key public facilities such as village halls and post offices.

• *Sensitive Landscapes* are simply those places that hold deep cultural attachments – the Vale of White Horse, the White Cliffs of Dover, Ayer's Rock, the Great Barrier Reef – are important landscape elements, or are either water collection areas, habitats for wildlife or even bush-fire reserves. Such places should be protected from development, with only limited exceptions.

• *New Settlements* will become more and more necessary as, in the UK and Australia and many European cities, the opportunities to build on "brown land", intensify existing urban neighbourhoods and graft new places onto old towns are used up. Rather than the ill-considered sprawl of malls and undistinguished housing estates of the 1980s, such places will be planned from first principles, using many of the theories and devices discussed in Part IV of this book. In part, this will be a return – pre-modernism – to the laying out of cities in the 19th century, plus elements borrowed from the garden cities (clean air, recreation space, a mixture of work, home and play) and the City Beautiful (avenues, street patterns, some buildings set in dramatic landscapes). Such new places will become imperative in the south of England at least; and in Australia if population growth becomes a priority. In the US, some of this has already been happening since the 1980s. The model of the "Edge Cities" is not one to replicate, neither the dismal non-planning of the Gold Coast in Queensland.

This notion of place "characterization" allows us to see what types of place we are dealing with, and to establish patterns or norms to work towards. It would then be appropriate to devise strategies for such places, depending on circumstances and the problems to be addressed. In some cases, the need will be for physical and cultural *Renewal*, in others *Improvement* or *Preservation* of the built stock, in others a *Management* approach to complex issues, and in some cases entirely new *Development*. For example, an inner urban area with a decayed built form will present the opportunity for renewal, or perhaps some combination of this with new development on vacant sites. Areas where the problem is largely to do with disrepair of the built stock – in older areas, but also now in the inter-war and post war estates and suburbs - the response will be improvement. In some places, the need will be to maintain the existing character of places through refurbishment of heritage buildings and areas. The upshot of all of this, is that cities and their regions will continue to plan, manage and develop a range of different place types, and these too should be as diverse as possible within an overall spatial framework. Not everyone is able to or wants to live in apartments in the CBD or in new developments around railway stations; demand for housing units in city suburbs will remain; so too the movement away from cities for reasons of retirement, bringing up children or "lifestyle". There can be no simple, single solution to these matters. Having said that, it will be important to restrict urban sprawl, to achieve areas of more as opposed to less density and activity, and to refit tired outer as well as inner urban suburbs, providing them with more economically sustainable local neighbourhood and district centres. Each place within the city should be identifiable and have character.

Property Booms

There will of course continue to be property booms, and it is likely that these will follow much the same patterns as in previous waves. That is, there will be a long-boom as economic development takes off, followed by a slump as the wave peaks somewhere around 2030. Another boom will probably occur as returns on stocks and shares fall, following a stock market collapse sometime in the 2040s, that is the property boom of the down-swing will occur in the 2050s or thereabouts. As I write this, it does seem somewhat deterministic in the sense that one is predicting a series of booms and crashes in the property market, based on a model of long-wave cyclical development of the capitalist economy. Nevertheless, the evidence exists, at least in the past during previous booms. The great upturns in city building caused by rapid increases in wealth creation occurred in the 1790s, 1850s and 1860s, 1900s, and in the late 1950s. These tend to be followed, some 12 years later, by a further boom in housing construction as wealth trickles down and sparks wider property ownership. This occurred in the 1960s, the early 20th century, the 1870s and around 1800–1810. Major property crashes occurred in the late 1820s when Nash's plans for London were abandoned, during the 1880s, the early 1930s, and late 1980s. All of these followed a collapse in the value of stocks and shares at the halfway point in the downswing, that is as growth moves from slow to negative. In each case this was followed by a recovery in the value of property as investors switched from stocks and shares to real estate. This occurred in the late 1990s, the mid 1930s and the 1890s. Periods of frantic and ultimately ill-advised speculation in property occur in the period between the collapse of stocks and shares and the following property crash, that is to say in the late 1980s, late 1920s, and the early 1890s. These were the speculative bubbles that burst.

It would therefore not be too surprising, to the author at least, if there were to follow over the next 50 years something along the following lines. There has already been a property boom associated with the end of the downswing, that is to say from the late 1990s to around mid 2003. This will be followed by a period of low growth generally, although specific areas and developments may prove exceptions to the trend. Later, there will be a property boom associated with the generation of new wealth from the new industries. Growth in property values will occur from about 2010, and by 2015 the boom will be obvious. This should be a prolonged period of growth, peaking as the upswing reaches the top of the cycle. On past evidence, a property crash is likely to occur around the time of the peak of the up-wave, roughly some time in the late 2020s. This may well be followed by a period of some 12–15 years of sluggish growth in the property market, and allowing for inflation returns from property will be negative during this period. A stock market collapse may occur in the 2040s or early 2050s, and again judging from previous cycles, it seems probable that this will be followed by a loosening of monetary policy and a reduction in real interest rates. This in itself would help spark a wave of feverish investment in property. At some point such a boom would end with a property crash similar to that of the early 1990s. The property market would then remain depressed for the better part of a decade. By the late 2050s, the downswing should be levelling out and investors will return to the stock market in the expectation of gains. These will be fitful to begin with, and so a boom in property will occur for a period. This in part would involve property values recovering some of the losses of the preceding crash. By 2060, the next long wave – the sixth – will be underway. This does seem somewhat prescriptive, admittedly. Yet, if wrong and these booms and crashes in the property market do not occur, then no real harm is done. But if right, then we might benefit, as city planners, from having an inkling about when the next crests of development pressure in cities and city-regions will occur.

Strategic Spatial Planning

Urban trends as we have understood them for most of the post-war period have tended towards greater decentralization and suburbanization – low rise residences, car commuting, car usage, edge development of shopping malls, new commercial and industrial zones, and so on. This broadly corresponded with the rise to prominence of the modernist city, the need to rationalize land uses and their use of space, and experiments in urban planning. As with the previous age of planning legislation, during the late 19th century, policy makers were responding to conditions which had their roots in an earlier time of rapid economic growth and urbanization. Thus, from the 1950s, decentralization of activities from the cities was not only market-led (the new housing areas, malls, business parks of the motor age) but also planning led, since planning orthodoxy of the time came to view cities as the harbringers of social ill. Many of the outlying estates of the 1950s and 1960s in cities such as Glasgow, Barcelona and Paris were led, not by the market, but by the state. Such places, together with the modernist high-rises which proved unsuitable living environments for poorer families, are the great planning disasters of the 20th Century.

They produced large outer areas where connections to the dynamics of economic growth and wealth creation were largely missing.

Meanwhile, the new middle class suburbs proved very successful as living environments, although travel to work patterns became more complex, main routes back to the city became increasingly congested and the daily commute took longer. With the rise of car ownership, property developers saw their chance to provide free-standing malls, leisure complexes and business parks surrounded by seas of car parking. This represented the peak of the modernist city, at a time when the economic dynamic of capitalism was moving from Fordism and into its post-Fordist phase. The planning disasters of the 1980s were thus market driven, as they sought to anticipate demands for greater car usage.

However, the most recent economic and social trends described in this book point to an altogether different set of locational and place-type preferences. This has been evident from the early 1990s, and in some places the 1980s. Many businesses today need less rather than more space, small businesses networks work best on face-to-face contact; and people generally are more aware of choices, are more sophisticated and place greater emphasis on quality in their everyday environment. These trends are already producing a re-centring of older city districts – whether parts of the CBD, older residential neighbourhoods or old industrial districts. The new urban lifestyles appeal to urban elites, but other people too – the retired, the wealthy, young people and young couples, at least until the kids come along. In the UK and Australia, this is leading us towards the development of new urban districts – certainly on "brown-field land" and in urban regeneration areas, but also for many peripheral locations. Such places tend to be near public transport exchanges, are fairly compact and walkable and are built to relatively high densities (low and medium rise). Much of urban policy across Europe is now being directed to renewing or otherwise regenerating older urban districts. This can in my view be seen as the emergence of the post-Fordist city of flexible specialization, where the cities are having to adapt to a greater plurality of demands and preferences. This trend will carry on for some time, and indeed should become more complex as the overall levels of wealth increase and the consumer becomes more sophisticated. It is for this reason I believe that consumption patterns generally will become even more complex, and that people will develop an even greater interest in design and works of art. This will certainly hold for the middle classes which will continue to grow in number unless they are taxed out of existence by leftist governments. Opportunities for self-improvement amongst the "working classes" will be at their greatest level to date, provided they are prepared to attain education, skills, cultural capital and indeed to work as opposed to remaining on welfare. This has always been the only successful means by which class mobility can be improved.

There is still the danger that a large proportion of the population will be content with following the lives of "celebrities", eating junk food, watching films, TV and DVDs on their home entertainment systems, binge drinking, and generally lacking manners and social graces. Thus the illnesses which afflict the "poor" will be obesity, diabetes and heart disease, not from smoking but from bad diets, over-eating and a lack of exercise. The concomitant danger is one of a general coarsening of public social life and cultural values, added to which there will be growing problems of crime, anti-social behaviour and racial conflict.

Accordingly, there will always be those who opt to live away from the city to escape the masses, or else for reasons of a better overall quality of life, more space, better schools, less hustle or simply to retire. This means that there will always, in turn, be pressure to decentralize from the cities as my old colleague, the late Mike Breheny, pointed out.[11] Those who work will tend to retain contacts with the city they previously lived in; even retirees will return occasionally to visit friends, go to the theatre, see an exhibition, go shopping. Some of these ties might well weaken over time, but then perhaps the children will have grown up and themselves moved back to the city. The city's influence does not stop at the built edge, or even the orbital motorway, but extends in numerous ways across the emerging city regions. For one thing, this means that more and more people will be travelling from home to the city, albeit sporadically in many cases, than ever before. Modern communication makes a greater geographical distribution of people across a city region (or beyond it) possible, yet the old-fashioned technologies of rail and road transport remain essential when, rather than bits or bytes of information, people need to transport themselves. All of this will translate into more demand for accommodation in rural and coastal areas, and in market, resort and University towns.

More formal development pressures will be exerted too. For the property industry, as well as responding to demands for new space, also is tempted to speculate in anticipation of future needs. Should there be any more shopping centres, and if so, where? How can we best accommodate another million people in South East England? Should Sydney build a new CBD along the lines of Canary Wharf, La Defense or Battery Park City? Where should new residences be located in Dublin? Should they all be apartments, or should we be building houses with gardens too? What should we do with the old film studios on the edge of Prague? What about the old Hertfordshire airfield that was once a motor-racing circuit? What do we do with the old docks now that a bigger port has been constructed further down-stream? Do we really still need a green-belt around Stevenage or Portland? How big should Melbourne become? Is our airport good enough? Should we be protecting arable land? Should we protect more natural habitats? Plant more forests? Should we build any more skyscrapers? If we decide to build new towns, even a new city or two, where should these be located? Will the birth-rate keep declining in western societies, or has it bottomed out? If we are all living longer, will there be more people in New York in the next 20 years or fewer?

These are all difficult questions, some more so than others. But they are all issues of a strategic importance in the future planning of existing cities, extensions to them, the growth or otherwise of satellite towns, the building over of the

---

11 Breheny, M., "Centrists, Decentrists and Compromisers: Views on the Future of Urban Form", in M. Jenks, E. Burton and K. Williams (eds), *The Compact City: A Sustainable Urbna Form?* (London: Spon, 1996).

countryside, the impact on the environment and the need or otherwise to build new settlements. These issues will gain in importance and urgency in the next ten years or so as the building boom of the fifth wave gets underway. The sooner they are faced up to, the better. This will involve a return to spatial planning at the city-region level as exemplified by Copenhagen's "Finger Plan" of the 1940s, updated in the late 1980s. This is about how and where and when new development should occur, and how it can best be distributed geographically. The idea is not to centrally plan the economy, for this would be doomed to failure, but rather to anticipate market trends and demands, and direct these towards a beneficial, perhaps even optimal, spatial structure. Thus, while cities need to understand the different types of place and how these work, they also need to understand regional geography too.

Renaissance or Enlightenment?

It has become the orthodoxy – indeed fashionable – for policy towards cities to be framed as a latter-day "Renaissance". This is true of the UK, where the policy pronouncements on the "urban renaissance" have often bordered on the pretentious and the embarrassing, led by the pompous-sounding "Office of the Deputy Prime Minister". Policy towards cities has certainly improved from the 1970s, but this trajectory can be traced back to the mid 1980s when it was known simply as urban regeneration. In truth, not much has changed as the bulk of regeneration programmes in the UK are still channelled through the Single Regeneration Budget and, of course, the European Regional Structural and Social Funds. Even the marked improvement in new architecture is a continuation of what had gone before, since the Lottery Fund to pay for such excellence was set up in the early 1990s. Meanwhile, the return to compact, traditional cities has been a feature of European city planning since at least the early 1990s, in some cases the mid 1980s. That said, it is also the case that the USA and Australia both lack coherent policies on city development, preferring to delegate responsibility for urban policy to the State Governments. Certainly in Australia's case this is something of an oversight, especially now that Sydney and possibly Melbourne have reached the limits to sensible growth, while on current trends Australia accepts 1 million new migrants every ten years, enough for two or three small European cities. At present this growth is not planned in any way, let alone spatially.

The word "renaissance" is certainly apt in so far as, as I have argued, new life was breathed into the cities from the early 1980s. This coincided with the second half of the downswing of the fourth Kondratieff Wave. As we have seen, each of these waves is a re-birth of capitalism itself, brought about by the impact of new technologies on consumer markets and production processes. "Renaissance" too in the sense that urban design is a re-application of traditional forms of city building, that is to say those before modernism, as opposed to a return to the antiquity of Rome and Athens. In any event, it is certainly the case that the cities have already been reinvigorated by a combination of new industries, the knowledge economy, increased sophistication and urbanity and a re-design of city streets and squares. A reasonable assumption is that this will continue for a few more years at least. But at some point, the upswing of the fifth wave will produce an even greater episode of wealth creation, as did the waves before it. And as also happened in previous waves, great pressure for the cities to grow even further will be felt as more people are drawn to the centres of wealth creation.

Yet, by the same token, people very often have a love-hate relationship with cities, or at least some of them – some people and some cities. Peter Hall argues that the outstanding problems faced by cities[12] are traffic congestion and damage to the environment, a growing welfare-dependent underclass of single parent families with poor educational attainment, and urban crime. Jones also points to pollution and too rapid urbanization in China, for example. He draws attention to the tensions caused by waves of large-scale immigration by differing ethnic and religious groups.[13] Fear of crime, poor schools, a sense of unease, the simplistic doctrine of multiculturalism, political correctness, the perceived attack on indigenous ways of life, falling educational standards, drugs, street violence, public drunkenness ... so that it is tempting at least for the middle classes to flee the larger cities in favour of the market town, the countryside or the beach. Nearly 250,000 leave London each year in this way, a phenomenon now referred to as "white flight"; in Sydney the arrival of new migrants each year is balanced almost exactly by Australians leaving for the country and the Gold Coast.

This means that even the best town planning in history will prove to be unsuccessful for so long as the cities are dogged by high levels of crime, ideologically-driven governance and a lowering of standards in the public services, especially education. While many of our towns and cities have improved considerably as built environments, the problem is the people who, by their own standards of behaviour, drive others away. It is true that compared to the 1970s and 1980s – and indeed to London in the present time – New York and other American cities are paragons of safety and sociability. This has been brought about by zero tolerance of anti-social behaviour and petty crime, school bullying and street gangs, drug pushing and illegal street prostitution. The generation that brought multi-culturalism, hippies, free love, black militantism, the civil rights movement, the wilder extremes of feminism and more ... has quite possibly come to a point where its basic assumptions about humanism are being challenged, not least by that generation itself. If true, then there is a possibility that the fifth wave will not be an era of over-liberalization, ill-considered blanket tolerance, moral relativism and the intellectual dead-end of post-modernism; but rather may come to be associated with a move towards more mannered and respectful – in terms simply of respecting other people - forms of public social life. This will not be easy.

---

12 Hall, P., *Cities in Civilization* (London: 1998), chapter 30.
13 Jones, E., *Metropolis: The World's Great Cities* (Oxford University Press, 1990), Chapter 9.

The Enlightenment of the early and mid 18th century was a secular movement based on rational and humane views of mankind. As such, it was a reaction to theological obscurantism and religious intolerance. It was notable for the works of Voltaire, Hume and Smith, the towering genius that was Sir Isaac Newton, the astonishing Henry Cavendish, and the notable development of historical research by Gibbon and Montenesquieu who would also write a major treatise on manners. Its towering achievement was the American Constitution, although it would also help set the conditions for the Terror in France. The academic John Carroll has argued that the major flaw with humanism and Western culture generally is that it rejects cheerfulness and gratitude for all that is beautiful, and degenerates instead into narcissism and rancour – the cult of the "I".[14] He asserts that there are eternal laws, both moral and metaphysical, and that at its deepest level …"the human conscience is born understanding them". Because of this "the great markers of the central way of …our culture survive, and are there for each new generation to read, if it will". A new Enlightenment would achieve this, but this time it need not be exclusively secular, for under enlightened self-interest religious and secular beliefs can exist side-by-side as long as each respects the others' rights to believe whatever they believe. The problem arises where fundamentalists try to gain ascendancy over others.

The building blocks for such an Enlightenment are already with us. These are:

1.   Economics – the ascendancy of capitalism and free trade as a dynamic system for producing, distributing and consuming goods and services, and for wealth creation. There is no prospect of an alternative economic system coming into being in the next 200 years at least, probably much longer. Capitalism will continue to create wealth, alongside new cultural forms. Everyone gets wealthier as a consequence, certainly in material goods, although the entrepreneurs, the already rich and the new rich will continue to accumulate more wealth than the average person. This is not a question of "the rich getting richer and the poor getting poorer" as the left argues, but simply the outcome of a system which values risk and investment. The "poor" will have greater opportunities than ever before to increase their own wealth and that of their families. They will in any event continue to become wealthier. Countries such as Britain and Australia should trade globally, provide low-tax business environments, have highly skilled and well-educated workforces, remove barriers to employment, reform the public services, tackle crime head-on in the cities, extend choice into the health, pensions and education sectors.

2.   Politics – liberal democracy is, as Churchill is reputed to have said, far from perfect but it is better than any other system of governance. With the collapse of communism and the end of "cradle to grave" socialism, the option would appear to be the corrupt dictatorships of Africa or the regressive feudalism of most of the Middle East. The dangers to western democracy come from within: the widespread disdain

---

14 Carroll, J., *The Wreck of Western Culture* (Melbourne: Scribe, 2004).

for professional politicians and the main political parties, falling voting rates and the prospect of extremist groups seeking to overthrow western society. By 2050, between a third and half of the people living in Europe will be non-European, and at present these show little sign of assimilating with the host cultures or indeed respecting western democracy. The dangers of the coming period will be heightened religious and racial conflict caused by too rapid an influx of migrants and the rise of Islamic militantism. This is already happening in the race riots of Birmingham, Sydney and Antwerp. There are serious questions over whether the demands of radical Islam are reconcilable with Western civilization, market economies and democracy.

3.   *Culture* – the convergence of cultural products with new technologies means that to a large degree the Fifth Wave will see an ever-closer relationship between culture and economics, as well as with traditions, the high arts and local identities. Societies will need to retain their historical cultural identities, but also be open to the new. This will include learning from other cultural traditions as in the past: the Renaissance was in part a rediscovery of antiquity, Debussy was greatly influenced by Japanese art and Indonesian music, early jazz was a fusion of African rthymns, French classical music and Scottish and Irish sets, modern jazz borrowed much from Debussy, Ravel and "Les Six". Nash was influenced by Adam, so too the American architects of the late 19th century, Scott was inspired by the German Romantic Poets, Philip Glass and the Minimalists by eastern music, Handel by the *opera seria* of the Italian courts, Bertholt Brecht by the Beggars Opera, Hollywood by the German, French and Russian film-makers of the early 20th century. This "borrowing" of ideas and motifs from previous generations and ages has always been a feature of art, music and literature. This will no doubt continue and new movements will emerge, possibly combining traditional forms with a revisiting of modernism. This is already true of interior design, for example, or the digital landscape movement. This is an opening up of culture rather than the dead-hand of post-modernism and its rejection of progress. In turn this implies a return to genuine forms of historical research and criticism, based on much better knowledge and a respect for the past. There may be no absolute certainties any more, but there are known facts that can be learned and built upon. Every so often, prior assumptions will be challenged by new evidence, and this is entirely consistent with logical positivism. As Camille Paglia puts it, "If there were no facts, buildings would fall down, there would be no internet, no medical advances and no technology…The fashionable post-modernist posturing that "there are no facts" has got to stop".[15]

4.   *Ethics* – that is to say, the set of values that govern the life and workings of a society. The enlightened self-interest of David Hume is located within a broader philosophical approach which includes the works of John Locke, Thomas Hobbes, Bertrand Russell and Karl Popper. This involves a rejection of metaphysical speculation (Hegel, Marx) and is therefore to this extent compatible with Foucault's

---

15 Paglia, C., *Sex, Art and American Culture* (New York: Penguin, 1992), p. 231.

dismissal of totalizing systems of thought. This, however, is not to agree with the post-modernist Marxists that the rejection of a single explanatory theory leads inevitably to the rejection of all theory and all value systems. That way lies the ruin of moral relativism and a regression to the lowest common denominator. Just because everything cannot be deemed to be wrong in every case does not mean that it is right either. Thus while the taking of life might at least be understandable in certain circumstances – in self-defence, in times of war, possibly in ending suffering, for the most part murder and manslaughter are crimes even allowing for extenuating circumstances. Rape is also wrong, but so too are false accusations of rape or sexual harassment. Insider dealing and wilful tax evasion are wrong, so too is welfare fraud. Of course, precise definitions of right and wrong vary between cultures. Acts such as adultery and homosexuality are punishable by death in Islamic countries, but not in the western democracies. Spitting and chewing gum in public are crimes in Singapore, vandalism is punishable by caning and drug trafficking by the death penalty. Corruption in Nigeria goes largely unpunished; indeed, is a way of life. Clearly, some laws and customs are the products of particular places at particular times. This has always been the case, although we might hope that international cooperation will help codify crime and punishment to a greater extent. But not if this is marked by a collapse into moral relativism and the fetishization of "human rights" or what the philosopher Roger Scruton calls "the social entropy (that) is the root cause of our 'post-modern' condition".[16] All of this implies that enlightened self-interest is the best and most realistic course, together with respect for others and the rule of law, plus a sense of compassion. This is really about the values of a society and standards of behaviour, and the ethically practical.

5.   *Epistemology* – that is, the theory of knowledge, developed initially by Aristotle as the "know why" of scientific analysis.[17] This argues that scientific truths are, at least within the paradigms of the day and often across paradigms, universal, largely invariable and exist independent of context. An example would be Newtonian physics and its assimilation into Einstein's conception of the universe. Epistemology relates closely to *ethics* in that fundamental laws about what is right and wrong are forms of universal truth. It also fits with the rejection of totalizing meta-theories in that scientific truths must be tested empirically, and in relation to systems of logic. This is certainly more difficult to apply to the everyday workings of societies, as opposed to experiments in laboratories and research centres. Yet it is not impossible either, certainly in relation to economics or even political science. Incumbent on researchers and academics would be the obligation to demonstrate factual conclusions rather than simply falling back on ideological totems and mantras. In this way, the study of culture, society and economics will hopefully extract itself from the quicksands of

---

16 Scruton, R., "Conserving the Past", in Bartlett and Scruton, *Town and Country* (London: Vintage, 1999), p. 327.

17 Flyvbjerg, B., "Phroentic Planning and Research: Theoretical and Methodological Reflections", *Planning Theory and Practice*, Vol. 5, No. 3, September 2004, pp. 283–306.

post-modernism, multi-culturalism as an ideology, the everything is equally valid, anything goes society. The only way to do this is by applying reason and objectivity. This stands in marked contrast to what Popper[18] referred to the "pseudo-sciences" of Marxism and psychoanalysis, as these never specify in advance the conditions under which they can be tested and/or refuted. Rather, an elaborate game of shifting the goal-posts is followed, where rather than admit they are wrong, Marxists simply move on to another construct, each more complicated and linguistically contorted than its predecessor. Now that the cracks have appeared in post-modernism and multi-culturalism, the latest vogue is the obtuse and largely incomprehensible meanderings of Lacan. What this has to do with cities, planning, wealth creation or anything else remains a mystery. A return to empirical research and verification linked to more grounded theories is long overdue. In turn, this implies that planning education – all other kinds too – should put learning back at the centre. This means learning historical facts, skills and methods as opposed to endless interpretation and contextualism. There would have been no Renaissance in Florence had Brunelleschi and Donatello not studied the architectural principles and methods of ancient Rome. In the arts and humanities, therefore, the need in my view is for historical study, learning and illumination. Again, as Paglia puts it: "The distant past holds the key to the present and the future. It is up to each person to seek knowledge…"[19] Or, as John Carroll has argued the modern university might once again become a place for the advancement of knowledge and the teaching of ways of thinking.

6.   *Morality* – is the way in which we deal with ethical problems on a day-to-day level and over the life-span of societies. As Oliver Thomson has pointed out,[20] this tends to fluctuate over time as codes of behaviour are relaxed in one generation, only to be reintroduced for a later one. Punishment too – its severity – varies in tandem with social attitudes to crime, anti-social behaviour and indeed to the form of punishment itself. In Britain, for example, slavery was abolished in the late 18th century, although it remains widespread in Africa and the Middle East, female flogging was abolished in 1820, the pillory in 1837, public hanging in 1864, army flogging in 1868, prison treadmills in 1895, the death penalty in 1964. This has tended to occur as the middle classes have grown and have become dismayed and unsettled by cruelty sanctioned and carried out by the state. Certainly very few people in western societies would consider adultery or homosexuality sins punishable by death. Yet there is a rising concern, not only that crime is escalating out of control, but that everyday standards of decency are also in decline. Bad language in public and on television is the least of it, general rudeness appears to be endemic, certainly in England. Anti-social noise, shouting and swearing in the street, drunkenness and violent behaviour, inappropriate clothing in social settings, all of these are symptoms of moral change. There appears to be a growing "obscenification" of everyday life.

18 Popper, K., "The Logic of Scientific Discovery" (London: Hutchison, 1959).
19 Paglia, *op. cit.*, 1992, p. 169.
20 Thomson, O., *A History of Sin* (Edinburgh: Canongate, 1982).

It seems the challenge will be to combine tolerance of different ways of living, tastes and preferences with an over-arching respect for others, minimum standards of public behaviour and at least some recognition that societies have, or should have, shared core values. At its simplest this might mean a revival of saying "please" and "thank you", observing the everyday courtesies of urban life.[21] As Don Watson has observed, the place to start is with the language itself.[22] But even this may require a change to how people are taught to behave in schools. At its simplest, morality is some inner restraint within society, and unless this and the rule of law are in broad terms upheld on an everyday basis by citizens, then the alternative suggested may be the police state. Those free thinkers and free lovers who hark back to the 1960s, and who find it fashionable to denounce western nations as police states, might ponder what happened to their predecessors in France during the Terror and in the Soviet Union under the perfect system of communism. Whatever the modern embodiment of fundamental decencies may be, observed through manners and everyday conduct, we need to consider these soon and urgently. Otherwise, extremes of bad and anti-social behaviour will push us, as individuals living in a society, ever further apart.

I see the first three of these as more or less given, the fourth – ethics – within reach, but I am much less certain about morality and the basic ground-rules of living in human societies. This is not simply because of ideological opposition from the left who have most to gain from moral relativity and politicized and heavily unionized public services, it is also likely that the majority of people are simply uninterested in such questions, except perhaps in relation to crime and punishment. For improvements in the conduct of everyday life in any society can only be brought about by agreement, that is government by consent. Where governments try to impose upon or alter behaviour by regulation and dictat, only resentment and a disengagement from politics will follow. As Plato observed, trying to govern by an ever-increasing panoply of rules and regulations is like fighting the Hydra: for every head one cuts off, another two grow in its place. Even so, there are beginning to be signs of improvements in everyday morality, for example in the question of appropriate clothing for women in the workplace and at social functions.

What is being described, of course, is a society based on shared principles, acknowledged truths, respect and tolerance, decency, manners and a set of core values. This is not too dissimilar to the Athens of ancient Greece, although with some improvements (female voting, abolition of slavery). Nor indeed is it, therefore, divorced from the renaissance that, after all, combined a rediscovery of classicism (conceptual and technical knowledge) with new ways of doing things. This would be a combination of principles, objectivity, proportion, scale, reason and manners, as argued by Lord Kames. This would not run counter to personal freedoms, liberal

---

21   Truss, L., *Talk to the Hand: The Utter Bloody Rudeness of Everyday Life* (London: Profile Books, 2005).

22   Watson, D., *Death Sentence: The Decay of Public Language* (Sydney: Random House, 2003).

democracy or wealth creation, or religious faith, but would provide a framework within which these would sit. However, this can only be achieved in an economic system where increases in the levels of wealth are achieved.

All of this implies an at first sight odd mix of policy attitudes: liberal on economics – and therefore supporting wealth creation in market economies; a reliance on parliamentary democracy and the rule of law; interventionist in urban planning, spatial planning and local place-making through urban design; interventionist too in the sense of helping to grow particular economic sectors; progressive and modern in the arts and culture, whilst learning from the past; and fairly conservative when it comes to manners, public social life, everyday decency and civility. The essential point is that free markets deliver not just prosperity and wealth, but also economic and cultural dynamism. This includes great experiments in city building and urban planning.

And so we return to where we started. What is the future for cities in the fifth wave? I have set out my views on this earlier in this final chapter, and have gone so far as to propose a typology of places for the coming two generations of urban planning. I have also drawn attention to the need for strategic spatial planning in relation to the distribution of population and economic activity across city regions. For as the next Wave gains momentum, we shall once again need to consider how best to either expand and/or intensify existing settlements and/or build entire new towns and cities. Similar choices were faced by the great city builders of the past – Edinburgh New Town in the 1770s, Nash's London, Hausemann's Paris, Cerda's Eixample for Barcelona, the expansion of Amsterdam and Copenhagen, the layout of Manhattan, the grid design of central Melbourne. Later, in the 1930s, 1950s and 1960s the wrong decisions were made, and we have been living with some of the consequences ever since. Even so, the cities have recovered from the premature announcement of their death. The future holds a new wave of city building. We can do better this time.

Appendix A :
City Night-time Policy Frameworks

POLICY AREA	AMSTERDAM	PARIS	BERLIN	NEW YORK	MANCHESTER
1. Overall Policy	Concentration of city centre evening activities in the Leidesplein and the Rembrandtplein.	Paris is a city of 2.2 million, and as such has café and other evening activities distributed around the inner areas.	Berlin is a city of 3.3 million.	New York city has a population of 7 million.	Manchester has a population of around 875,000, but is a regional centre for some 3-4 million in Greater Manchester, Lancashire and Cheshire.
	Premises including 'brown cafés' (pubs), grand cafés, smoking coffee shops (cannabis) and coffee shops, are able to stay open until 4am at weekends, 1am at other times.	The Bastille area has developed as the largest concentration of evening entertainment in recent years. The area combines cafés, restaurants, clubs and galleries, cultural centres and a mixed resident population. The area is also much visited by tourists.	The city has two main concentrations of evening economy activity. Charlottenburg in the West and Mitte in the East.	The most lively areas of night-time activity are also residential neighbourhoods, notably Greenwich Village, SoHo, NoHo and Little Italy, all of which are in Manhattan Borough.	The development of the city's cultural and evening economies has been the policy of Manchester City Council since 1992.
	There are some 1500 cafés throughout the inner city.		Berlin's culture has been one of unprominent, tucked-away drinking establishments. These include small cafés, small bars which become clubs at night, temporary illegal bars, larger fashionable bars.	Planning policies are prepared by the Department of City Planning and administered by the City Planning Commission.	There are now over 500 licensed premises in Manchester city centre, an effective doubling since 1992. During this time the resident population of Manchester has grown also doubled to around 12,000.
	Cafés and bars are allowed in the two designated 'zones of concentration', although there is no policy to increase their numbers.	The relevant area-specific regulatory plan supports mixed-use, but there are no specific polices on this, nor any system of use classes.	In the Mitte area there are 7-800 licensed premises; the area's population is 320,000.	Local consultation and deliberation is effectively maintained by local Community Boards.	Between 100,000 and 150,000 people regularly visit Manchester City Centre on Fridays and Saturdays.
	Outside these zones, no new bars or restaurants are permitted.		Planning policy is to develop all centres for mixed use, a polycentric urban structure based on residence and mixed-use character.	The Local Community Board for Greenwich Village does not wish to see any further increase in bars and restaurants generally, but is less opposed to 'white-clothed' restaurants.	Particular concentrations of evening economy activity are found in Peter Street, Castlefield, Canal Street (gay), China Town, Oldham Street and the Whitworth Street Corridor.

POLICY AREA	AMSTERDAM	PARIS	BERLIN	NEW YORK	MANCHESTER
2. Numbers and Location of Licensed Premises	*Policy aim is to maintain the balance of uses, but increasing the amount of non-entertainment uses in the central areas.*	*No specific planning policies are pursued, other than maintaining a balance between residential and non-residential uses.*	*Policy is aimed at concentrating entertainment uses on the main streets subject to them not causing a nuisance.*	*This is difficult to enforce as there is no difference in use class between bars, restaurants or shops.*	*The impact of entertainment issues is considered to be an issue for Manchester City Centre, but these have not yet reached saturation point.*
	Within the zones of concentration no further hot food takeaways, bars, restaurants or discos are allowed, although some limited changes between types is permitted.	*The Code de la Sante Publique states that licensed venues cannot be within 75 metres of each other.*		*The State Liquor Authority does not grant new alcohol licences for premises within 500 ft of each other.*	*Policy remains to encourage both A3 land uses (pubs, cafes, restaurants) and new residences in mixed-use areas.*
	Policy overall is to contain and control night-time uses within the concentration zones, and not allow any further increase in entertainment uses.	*Each arrondissement has a quota of how many licensed premises can be in operation. No extra premises above this number are permitted.*			*The City Council operates a very strict policy on Entertainments Licensing, licences needing to be renewed every 3-6 months. Breach of conditions – on matters such as the training of door staff, the closure of windows and doors after 11pm, the prohibition of external loud speakers, acoustic double glazing, double door sound vestibules – may lead to licences being withdrawn.*
		These quotas are periodically challenged (or circumnavigated) with the interests of tourism and economic development offered as reasons for relaxation.			

POLICY AREA	AMSTERDAM	PARIS	BERLIN	NEW YORK	MANCHESTER
3. Liquor Licensing	Controlled by the Department of Inner City Government, via licences for liquor, food and entertainment. There are 30 types of licence with detailed differentiation between them on opening hours and other arrangements. For most licensed premises, closing hours are 1am during weekdays and 4am at weekends. Night shops are also licensed. Licences for new discos are not permitted anywhere, capacity having been determined by the numbers of existing outlets and safe fire egress. Regular checks are made on all licensed premises, both planned and unannounced.	Regulated by the Prefecture de Police. All venues selling alcohol must close by 2am, and all customers must have left the premises. Venues are allowed to open again at 4am. Special dispensations can be granted to remain open between 2am and 4am, subject to noise levels, previous complaints and record of responsible management.	Administered by local municipality Economic Department. Licensed premises include bars, pubs, cafes, restaurants, clubs and fast-food outlets. There are no distinctions between types of licensed premises, although the playing of live music requires a special licence. Applications are dealt with on their merits. Fixed closing times are between 5am and 6am.	Types of licence are more varied, and include: Liquor Licences with closing times defined as 4am to 8am Mondays to Saturdays and 4am to mid-day on Sundays. Food Establishment Permits from the Department of Health. Cabaret Licences for dancing. Place of Assembly Permits (fire and safety) for venues with a capacity over 75. Sidewalk Café Licences from the Department of Consumer Affair's on the payment of 'security fees' of around $40,000. Sidewalk cafés are allowed to remain open until midnight Monday to Thursday, until 1am Friday and Saturday, and midnight on Sundays. Licencees are held strictly accountable for the maintenance of good order, for the conduct of their patrons and for noise.	Liquor Licensing will also be the responsibility of the City Council from January 2005. Manchester's aim over the past 12 years has bee to encourage a more relaxed and civilised drinking culture, and café society. The '24 Hour City Concept' is still supported but a new emphasis is on making the city centre more family-friendly, including in the early evenings.

POLICY AREA	AMSTERDAM	PARIS	BERLIN	NEW YORK	MANCHESTER
4. Categorisation of Land Uses	Precise categories of land use are employed to distinguish between night-time economy outlets. The categories are: I Fast food II Night clubs/discos III Grand cafes and bars ; IV Restaurants, cafes and bars serving food. A special category exists for cafes which are part of theatres, museums and hotels.	None.	None, although cafes, pubs and restaurants have been identified as having reached 'saturation level'.	None.	A3 uses include restaurants, bars, cafes, clubs and hot-food takeaways. There is concern across the UK, not only in Manchester, that these categories are too broad in that planning permission for a restaurant or a café can easily 'convert' to a fast food outlet or a pub, without any need for further approval. This situation may be addressed by reported new class orders currently being considered by the UK government.

POLICY AREA	AMSTERDAM	PARIS	BERLIN	NEW YORK	MANCHESTER
5. Responsible Management	*Local grouping of bar owners meet to discuss overall issues, but main concern is improvements to the public realm.*	*Monitored by the Police as part of the general liquor licensing regime.*	*No particular initiatives exist.*	*Holders of a Cabaret Licence are under a duty to ensure customers do not cause excessive noise or litter, or behave in a manner that would disturb the peace or compromise public safety.* *They must also have indoor waiting areas, and not employ door staff with a criminal record during the previous 5 years.*	*In recent years operators of several bars – notably in Peter Street – have pooled resources to buy-in extra police.*

POLICY AREA	AMSTERDAM	PARIS	BERLIN	NEW YORK	MANCHESTER
6. Noise Control	Decibel levels are specified in all licences. Complaints are investigated by enforcement offices and the police. Decibel limiters may be fitted to sound equipment.	Paris-wide campaign of leaflets.	City Council and local municipal polices on noise control are strong, the aim being to minimise disturbance to residents. Noise restrictions are set for each licensed premise individually. Higher fines for non-compliance are imposed during prescribed 'quiet periods' which vary according to the type of entertainment cluster: 8pm to 10pm, 6am to 7am, 10pm to 6am, and all day on Sundays and bank holidays. Complaints must be dealt with by the Police within 14 days, and fines ranging from £200-£30,000 can be levied. Landlords and staff are responsible for music levels, and for noisy customers on the street outside their premises. Music is generally forbidden in outside spaces such as beer gardens and pavement tables and chairs.	All businesses are prohibited from operating sound systems for advertising purposes outside of their buildings. For residential areas levels of noise from a commercial establishment must not exceed 45 dB inside the dwelling.	Manchester has adopted many innovative policy measures to reduce noise and disturbance. These are administered through conditions attached to new licences, renewals and planning consents. Measures imposed include: Acoustic glazing; Acoustically treated ventilation; Acoustic insulation; Acoustic lobbies at entrances; Sound Limiters on amplification equipment; Prohibition of external playing of amplified music; Restrictions on the hours of operation of outdoor drinking areas; Establishment of maximum noise levels; Restrictions on hours of opening in sensitive locations; Acoustic insulation of new residential units; Separate entrances for apartment blocks above licensed premises.

POLICY AREA	AMSTERDAM	PARIS	BERLIN	NEW YORK	MANCHESTER
7. Environmental Services	Refuse collection is undertaken by the City Council at fixed hours in the early morning.	Housing Improvement initiative funded by the State. Subsidies made available to private landlords for renovation works.	The main issue is refuse collection which is controlled by the City Council. In areas with a concentration of evening economy uses, collections are made more frequently, in some streets daily.	Sidewalks in front of any building in New York are the required to be maintained by the owner. This includes sweeping and cleaning of gutters. Businesses are also required to keep backyards, courtyards, alleyways and air shafts clean at all times. Refuse disposal is organised by commercial establishments themselves, usually by contracting licensed private operators.	Outdoor seating is encouraged but is only permitted outside licensed premises up to 11pm, 10:30pm on Sundays. Street cleansing times have been rescheduled to occur in early morning.

POLICY AREA	AMSTERDAM	PARIS	BERLIN	NEW YORK	MANCHESTER
8. Transport	Trams and metros run until about midnight when night buses take over. Night buses run hourly during the week and half-hourly at weekends (9 routes). There are a limited number of taxi ranks.	The Metro runs until 0:50 hours. Night buses run from 01:30am until 05:30. Taxis are readily available.	The S-Bahn, trams and Metro all end at midnight, when the night bus service commences. Advertising campaigns promote the frequency and safety of public transport at night. However, with its polycentric structure, many people elect to remain in their local centre. There are 6,400 taxis in Berlin.	The New York subway operates 24 hours a day. Taxis are also plentiful.	Manchester's tram system runs until around mid-night, at which time night bus services commence.

POLICY AREA	AMSTERDAM	PARIS	BERLIN	NEW YORK	MANCHESTER
9. Crime and anti-social behaviour	*Additional police are deployed in 'stress area' at closing times.* *Extra surveillance between 10pm and 7am, including police checks for weapons.*	*Monitoring of all incidents used in deliberating on applications for extended hours, or the closure of a venue.* *Drunkenness in a public place is an arrestable offence.*	*This is not viewed as a problem in Berlin.* *The highest crime frequencies are for shoplifting, pick-pocketing, drug dealing and mugging.*	*New York has 1 police officer for every 161 citizens. This compares, for example with 1 per 290 people in London.* *Since 1994 there has been a dramatic decrease in reported crimes in New York City. This is attributed to the 'zero tolerance policy' and also the increase in the numbers of police officers.* *In 2000 the numbers of reported crimes in New York City was 288,000, compared to 1,052,000 in London.*	*Manchester has adopted a policy of high-profile policing and targeted action on crime 'hot-spots'.* *This is backed by referral schemes for alcohol abuse, awards for well-managed premises, leaflet campaigns on safe drinking, advice and assistance for licensed premises.* *There has also been a clampdown on problem licensed premises through policing and licensing controls.*

POLICY AREA	AMSTERDAM	PARIS	BERLIN	NEW YORK	MANCHESTER
10. Urination	On weekends, mobile plastic pissoirs are provided at night to reduce urination in the streets.	None.	Public toilets are provided and maintained by the private sector, and financed by advertising revenue.	No specific programme.	'Super-toilets' have been installed in Stevensons Square and Piccadilly Gardens.

POLICY AREA	AMSTERDAM	PARIS	BERLIN	NEW YORK	MANCHESTER
11. Other					A bye-law was introduced in 2000 to prevent drinking in the street. This does not apply to pavement chairs and tables.

POLICY AREA	AMSTERDAM	PARIS	BERLIN	NEW YORK	MANCHESTER
12. Comment	Highly concerned about saturation levels and the impact on residential amenity. Restrictions on locations and numbers of licensed premises.	Laissez-faire planning system, so regulation is via the issuing and monitoring of liquor licences, up to pre-determined limits.	Polycentric city approach appears to work well, despite the broad categories which operate under the planning system.	Control exercised through system of liquor and other forms of licensing.	Growth-oriented policy on the evening economy, being somewhat temporised as more residents move into the city centre, and in an effort to attract families in the early evenings.
	Dutch liberalism has reached its limits?	Evidence of licences being traded to get around these limits, and a concern that the system is restricting tourist-related business growth.	Noise pollution taken very seriously.	Major crackdown on crime has been beneficial.	Noise controls far-reaching and effective.
			Do what you like but don't make noise!	The 'City That Never Sleeps' is more regulated than it appears.	Good example of coordinated policies on planning, policing and liquor licensing.
		Paris a bit old-fashioned?			The British way of 'muddling through' is working.

Appendix B:
Cultural Quarters Evaluation Matrix – Cultural Activity

INDICATOR	TEMPLE BAR, DUBLIN	SHEFFIELD CIQ	MANCHESTER MNQ	HINDLEY STREET, ADELAIDE
1. Variety of Cultural Venues, including Small and Medium Scale	12 small and medium scale venues. Half of these were developed from pre-existing venues or arts organisations, the remainder being entirely new projects. Venues include: The Ark, Project Arts Centre, Irish Film Centre, Photography Gallery, Design Yard, Olympia Theatre, Art House. The costs of the Cultural Development Programme over 1991–2001 – and including development of the venues – was IR£37 million.	Showroom Cinema Complex (four screens) and Site Gallery (photography) are the main alternative venues in the area. The Showroom is Britain's largest regional independent cinema, and opened in March '95. The Leadmill is the city's leading alternative music venue. The SCIQ is also adjacent to the redeveloped City Art Gallery and the Winter Gardens of the 'Heart of the City' Project', a major lottery millennium project. The National Centre for Popular Music (NCPM) is now defunct. The building is currently (2002) used as club and conference venue.	The Band on the Wall music venue predated the area regeneration. Various new venues have been proposed within this area, although in the event these have tended to locate in adjacent areas such as Ancoats or indeed the Urbis museum of the modern city. A number of small privately-owned clubs and bars – Dry Bar, Café Pop – operate as regular small-scale venues.	The Jam Factory is a centre for the production, exhibition and sale of Contemporary Crafts and Design. The Lion Arts Centre is a performance venue for music, theatre, film. Adelaide Symphony Orchestra has recently moved to a new rehearsal and concert hall along Hindley Street itself.

INDICATOR	TEMPLE BAR, DUBLIN	SHEFFIELD CIQ	MANCHESTER MNQ	HINDLEY STREET, ADELAIDE
2. Cultural Animation – Events and Festivals	Year-round programme of festivals and events, managed by Temple Bar Properties Ltd. This is one of four roles retained by TBPL following completion of the physical development phases. Includes seasons of open air film screenings at Meeting House Square.	A sporadic events programme, with activities occurring mainly in the summer months, organised by CIQ Development Agency. The SCIQ also hosts a number of industry-based festivals and conferences, for example the Sheffield International Documentary Film Festival. This event is the only festival in Britain covering this genre and is now in its 15th year. Lovebytes, is a digital arts festival of film, video, graphics and animation. An ongoing exhibition programme of local, national and international artists work is also run in The Workstation through the Exhibit Programme.	Events programme organised by the Northern Quarter Association, includes the Northern Quarter Street Festival, an annual one-day open –air free event.	Important location for the biennial Adelaide Arts Festival and the Fringe. Adelaide Festival has offices on Hindley Street itself.

INDICATOR	TEMPLE BAR, DUBLIN	SHEFFIELD CIQ	MANCHESTER MNQ	HINDLEY STREET, ADELAIDE
3. Space for Production – Artists' Studios	Temple Bar Gallery and Studios provides studio space for 30 artists. The ongoing Cultural Programme includes managing three Writers' Studios and an International Visiting Artists' Apartment.	Yorkshire Arts Society Studios first moved into the area in the mid 1980s. A successful arts lottery application resulted in a new building at Brown Street, which contains gallery and workshop spaces and studios for 20–30 artists.	The Craft Centre on the site of the former Smithfield Market provides studio space and market stalls for 40 or so individual craft workers.	The Jam Factory provides studio and workshop accommodation for over 30 artists and designers, in a combination of individual, open and training studios. Proposals are being developed by Craftsouth, the development agency for contemporary crafts and design in South Australia, for a cultural business incubator within the area, focusing on design, music and arts businesses.

INDICATOR	TEMPLE BAR, DUBLIN	SHEFFIELD CIQ	MANCHESTER MNQ	HINDLEY STREET, ADELAIDE
4. Small Firm Economic Development	No specific economic development strategy for the cultural industries, other than through the various building-based projects, for example Design Yard. Temple Bar Properties Ltd used its powers as a landlord to offer lower rents to arts and other organisations taking retail or office or studio space.	Sheffield is a city with a long tradition of cultural production, particularly in Fine Arts, Music, Film and Video. In the early 1980s the City Council started to develop a cultural industry policy, aimed at supporting these activities. Various programmes have operated over a period of some 15 years. Current economic development support is provided by Action for Business and Culture Ltd, and includes help with business plans, start-up grants and sector-specific advice. There are now over 150 cultural and creative organisations located within the CIQ, the majority of them micro and small enterprises working in music, design, film and technology.	The MNQ development strategy is aimed at encouraging business start-ups and growth in the creative industries, largely as market-based enterprises. This is backed by an area planning policy which encourages mixed use and especially arts-related business activity. In 2000, the Cultural Industries Development Service (CIDS) was formed to help develop sustainable cultural and creative enterprises in Manchester's metropolitan core, including the MNQ and Ancoats. CIDS is a demand-led agency (that is it responds to requests from bona fide would-be creative businesses). CIDS' services include: an information and referral service, a student and graduate placement service, business start-up and expansion grants, industry marketing grants, network development, and professional development programmes. CIDS is supported by Manchester City Council, Manchester TEC, Salford, Tameside and Trafford Councils, North West Arts Board and various HE/FE Insitutions.	There are no specific enterprise support or development programmes for the arts and cultural industries, although the Adelaide Metropolitan Area Consultative Committee and Arts SA support the development of business incubators for creative businesses.

INDICATOR	TEMPLE BAR, DUBLIN	SHEFFIELD CIQ	MANCHESTER MNQ	HINDLEY STREET, ADELAIDE
5. Managed Workspace Provision	None. Early initiatives included the Temple Bar Independent Producers Workspace, but this has been discontinued	A number of these have been developed since the late 1980s, including the Audio Visual Enterprise Centre (AVEC) and The Workstation, some 70,000 square feet of Managed Workspace for cultural and media industries. Over seventy organisations now occupy units in the building ranging from the Northern Media School, graphic designers The Designers Republic, the Community Media Association, the Yorkshire Screen Commission, and various film production companies such as Picture Palace North and Dream Factory. Typical of the sector, tenant companies are small to medium size, employing from 2 to 6 staff members, although certain companies employ 25 and upwards. A small number of managed workspaces have also been developed by the private sector, and there are plans for more workspaces under the auspices of The Workstation management.	Floorspace within the former Corn Exchange predates the area regeneration initiative. The overall development of the area is expected to include workspace provision, particularly on upper floors, both for refurbishments and new builds. In this way, the provision of workspaces is left to the market, but encouraged by planning guidance and development briefs for key sites. An example is the Smithfield site which Manchester City Council are encouraging to be redeveloped for a mixture of commercial, retail and leisure uses in new and renovated buildings.	A Design and Creative Industries Business Incubator (Design Works) is currently the subject of a feasibility study. A number of PR, design and commercial art companies have moved into refurbished properties in the area over the past two years. There are also a number of private studio and gallery complexes, notably also a number of small galleries Red Dog Gallery and Gray Hawk Design.

INDICATOR	TEMPLE BAR, DUBLIN	SHEFFIELD CIQ	MANCHESTER MNQ	HINDLEY STREET, ADELAIDE
6. Presence of Arts Development Agencies and Companies	These are largely accommodated within the new venues, for example the Irish Film Commission and Film Archive, Design Yard and others.	BBC Radio Sheffield have moved into new premises within the Quarter. The area is is also home to Yorkshire Screen, Red Tape Studios, YASS, Sheffield Independent Film Producers and others.	Mostly micro and small businesses rather than arts development agencies or organisations.	Offices opened in the past two-three years by Arts SA (arts policy and funding body for South Australia), as well as the Adelaide Festival Office. In the past 18 months, some 10 arts organisations have moved into offices along Hindley Street, including FEAST, Aus Music, the Community Arts Network and Aus Dance.

INDICATOR	TEMPLE BAR, DUBLIN	SHEFFIELD CIQ	MANCHESTER MNQ	HINDLEY STREET, ADELAIDE
7. Arts and Media Education and Training (vocational)	No specific arts education provision, although Trinity College borders the area to the east. The Gaeity Theatre School is located within Temple Bar, at Meeting House Square.	Sheffield Hallam University is located within the CIQ, and is a major partner in the area regeneration initiative. The Northern Media School occupies two floors of the Workstation. Proposals have been mooted to relocate Sheffield Hallam School of Art and Design to form a new 'culture campus' within the Quarter.	Manchester Metropolitan University Institute for Popular Culture have been closely involved in the ongoing development of the MNQ, have published various papers on the area, and host the MNQ web-site.	Projects most recently completed or developed include a new A$30m Centre for Performing and Visual Arts (CPVA) on Light Square, combining the fine art, design and performing arts departments of the University of South Australia.

INDICATOR	TEMPLE BAR, DUBLIN	SHEFFIELD CIQ	MANCHESTER MNQ	HINDLEY STREET, ADELAIDE
8. Public Art Programmes	Public art was an important early initiative within the development of Temple Bar as a cultural quarter, 1991-95. Temporary installation pieces continue to be commissioned, especially in Temple Bar Square and Meeting House Square.	A Public Art Policy is included within the CIQ Action Plan, supplementary planning guidance for the area, published in 1999. Relatively few stand-alone works have been commissioned, but any developments authorised are expected to be of a high design quality and include art.	This is seen as having been instrumental in putting the MNQ on the map. Various site-specific works have been commissioned, and a public art residency established.	In 1999 Adelaide City Council launched its West End Arts-led Urban Renewal Program. The aim was to work with artists and arts organisations to develop arts and creative industry projects and programmes within the area, thereby providing the West End and Hindley Street with a more diverse identity and character. Early projects included a relocation of the Adelaide Festival Office to a shopfront on Hindley Street and Shop@rt – a programme of exhibitions in vacant shop windows.

INDICATOR	TEMPLE BAR, DUBLIN	SHEFFIELD CIQ	MANCHESTER MNQ	HINDLEY STREET, ADELAIDE
9. Arts Funding Regime	Ongoing arts funding is the general responsibility of the Irish Arts Council and Dublin Corporation. Temple Bar Properties Limited have tended to contribute in kind via property development and rent assistance. Each venue and/or project development initiative was subject to detailed feasibility study.	Responsibility of Yorkshire Arts Board and Sheffield City Council. A number of organisations in the SCIQ are core revenue and project funded from these sources.	The responsibility of North West Arts Board and Manchester City Council. No specific commitment is made to organisations based in the MNQ.	Individual client organisations are funded by Arts SA. There is no overall West End cultural development or arts programme as such.

INDICATOR	TEMPLE BAR, DUBLIN	SHEFFIELD CIQ	MANCHESTER MNQ	HINDLEY STREET, ADELAIDE
10. Community Arts Development Initiatives	No specific programme, although this role is built-in to the business plan remit of most of the venues, notably The Ark.	Considerable stress is placed on social inclusion, certainly amongst the publicly-funded arts organisations and the various training providers. This includes out-reach and in-reach programmes and various access and entry-level training courses.	A number of funded arts organisations have community arts development remits. These are funded on their merits as part of the overall arts funding regime for Manchester as a whole.	No specific programme.

INDICATOR	TEMPLE BAR, DUBLIN	SHEFFIELD CIQ	MANCHESTER MNQ	HINDLEY STREET, ADELAIDE
11. Area Marketing and Audience Development	Marketing and area-branding has been very important to the area's redevelopment from the beginning. Innovative and quirky promotional materials and a good web-site raised the profile of Temple Bar as a fashionable and artistic place. This role is being maintained by Temple Bar Properties Ltd. A traders' group, TASCQ, was formed in 1999, and contributes towards an annual fund of IR£200,000 for additional street cleaning, free events and free information.	In the early years, marketing was not given a high priority, with the focus concentrating on building and facilities-based projects. Following the publication of the SCIQ Vision and Development Strategy in 1998, a new CIQ Agency was established with responsibility – amongst other roles – for area marketing and branding. A good web-site now exists: www.ciq.org.uk. A new CIQ logo is currently (2002) being finalised.	Area marketing is carried out by the Northside Association who also publish a regular area newsletter Arts audience development across Manchester is the responsibility of Arts About Manchester.	As the West End Arts Precinct is becoming more established, more joint marketing – for example the Open House Night – is being devised. As yet, there is no overall area marketing for the arts or other activities.

INDICATOR	TEMPLE BAR, DUBLIN	SHEFFIELD CIQ	MANCHESTER MNQ	HINDLEY STREET, ADELAIDE
12. Presence of Complementary Day and Night-time activities (specialist retail, fashion, cafes, restaurants)	The development strategy for Temple Bar stressed the importance of mixed use, including a sizeable residential community (now some 2000 people). Complementary day-time activities include independent and non-mainstream retailers, for example in fashion and jewellery and book and music stores. Regular events include the Temple Bar Food Market which takes place on Saturdays in Meeting House Square. Night-time activities include bars, restaurants, cafes and hotels, but not night-clubs. Again, this was part of a deliberate policy for the area, with the aim of creating continental-style café culture and a more active public social life. Although this strategy has undoubtedly succeeded, the area gained a reputation as the Stag Night Capital of Europe in the mid 1990s, and this issue was addressed by a management approach and cooperation between hoteliers and restaurateurs. With the development of more residential apartments, policy makers have been careful to control the location of late-night and noisy activities, particularly in the new residential area at Old Town.	By 1997, despite the impressive growth of new organisations, facilities and venues, the CIQ lacked a strong sense of place. There were very few shops in the area, and few bars other than some traditional pubs catering for students of Hallam University. An important strand of both the 1998 CIQ Vision and Development Strategy and the Action Plan for the CIQ was to encourage secondary mixed-use, particularly along ground floor frontages. This was to include small shops, alternative retail, cafes, bars and restaurants. A number of new bars and café-bars have opened in the area since 1999, two new restaurants and a few new shops, but this aspect of the area's character is still developing.	The area planning guidance for the MNQ strongly encourages mixed use, evening economy uses in appropriate locations and residential apartments. Unlike other cultural quarters, market failure in the MNQ was able to be addressed by changing the area planning policies in such a way as to encourage private investment. A large number of shops, a few bars and a surviving rag trade pre-dated the MNQ's new identity as a cultural quarter. In this sense, the aim was to develop more mixed use and alongside the overall stimulation of a creative industries economy.	Hindley Street – or the West End as it is also referred to – is still perceived to be Adelaide's naughty, often seedy and sometimes dangerous night-time area, although it is also a shopping street during the day. The area tended, until recently, to be dominated by strip clubs, tattoo parlours, 'pokies' (game machine arcades), 24 hour drinking bars and other, even less savoury, elements. The West End Crime Prevention Report, May 1998 confirmed that people generally have negative perceptions of Hindley Street. Crime statistics reveal a split between day time crime (shoplifting) and crime at night (some assaults, intimidation, rowdy behaviour, public disorder, drug dealing). The report also signalled a commitment by the City Council to upgrade the West End environment, and to achieve a greater and more gentle mix of land uses. This was all the more pressing pending the opening of the University of South Australia City West Campus in 1997 - including the Faculties of Art, Architecture and Design - and concerns that students felt intimidated walking along Hindley Street. The presence of so many design and arts students was seen as a significant opportunity for the growth of new creative businesses, and also for smaller scale leisure and retail.

INDICATOR	TEMPLE BAR, DUBLIN	SHEFFIELD CIQ	MANCHESTER MNQ	HINDLEY STREET, ADELAIDE
13. Ongoing Cultural Programme	The ongoing Cultural Development Programme remains the responsibility of Temple Bar Properties Ltd, backed with core funding by the Irish Arts Council.	This is developed by individual organisations, partnerships amongst organisations and via the CIQ Agency and the Cultural Business Network. Funding support tends to come from mainstream local authority or Regional Arts Board sources for particular organisations and projects. The Workstation and The Showroom are seen as central to the further development of the CIQ. The buildings are owned by Sheffield City Council and were developed by a specially-formed registered charity, Sheffield Media & Exhibition Centre Limited (SMEC). The Charity set up a development subsidiary, Paternoster Limited, who took a 125 year lease on the building. Paternoster Limited run the Workstation purely as a commercial enterprise, charged with operating the building for the benefit of its tenants, and covenants profits to the parent charity (SMEC) for the benefit of the Showroom Cinema operation. The Showroom also receives revenue grant support from Sheffield Arts Department, the British Film Institute and Yorkshire and Humberside Arts. The CIQA's role is one of management and brokerage, aimed at maximising the potential of the CIQ and helping to create conditions for the growth of the creative industries.	Coordinated by the Northern Quarter Association, via a network of individual small-scale venues concentrating mainly on music and fashion. No specific commitment to a Northern Quarter cultural programme per se.	This is somewhat loosely organised at present, comprising a combination of some direct investment in new buildings and facilities, help for landlords to refurbish properties and find arts-related tenants, some programming of events and overall support of key arts organisations located within the area. Management of the area overall id the responsibility of a Precinct Manager employed by Adelaide City Council. There is also a Precinct Committee and Association made up of businesses based in the area.

INDICATOR	TEMPLE BAR, DUBLIN	SHEFFIELD CIQ	MANCHESTER MNQ	HINDLEY STREET, ADELAIDE
Comment	An example of arts-led urban regeneration where the focus was on venue development and capacity building amongst existing and emerging arts organisations. Backed by very good marketing and a very substantial events programme, Temple Bar is probably the most successful initiative if its type anywhere. The accent on urban design and the creation of a more permeable urban form, was also innovative.	These building-based projects have been fundamental to the overall development of the CIQ. This area of the city centre was previously almost totally derelict. Success can be judged by the many new start-up cultural businesses, the establishment of the quarter as a vibrant business environment, the upgrading of the physical environment, and more recent business relocations. Additionally, new build, private development is now providing millions of pounds worth of residential, student and business accommodation.	The MNQ is an example where public intervention and monies have tended to be focused on building improvements (via grants), environmental works (including public art) and in improving transport, parking and access. Comparatively little additional money has been found for new venues or events. Rather, the tack has been to encourage enterprise development of the creative industries, to help bring properties into active use and to invest in area marketing.	This is an example of area branding allied to a Precinct Management Strategy and the deliberate relocation of arts organisations into the area, to build on the pre-existing strengths of the West End as a location for cultural producers and businesses (as opposed to mainstream cultural venues, most of which are located elsewhere at North Terrace).

Bibliography

Abrams, M.M., *The Mirror and the Lamp: Romantic Theory and the Critical Tradition* (London & New York: 1953).

Abu-Lughod, J., *New York, Chicago, Los Angeles: America's Global Cities* (Minneapolis: University of Minnesota Press, 1999).

Abu-Lughod, J., *From Urban Village to East Village: The Battle for New York's Lower East Side* (Oxford: Blackwell, 1994).

Ackroyd, P., *All the Time in the World*, in *The Collection* (London: Vintage, 2002).

Ackroyd, P., *London: The Biography* (London: Chatto and Windus, 2000).

Ackroyd, P., *Dickens* (London: 1990).

Ackroyd, P., *T.S. Eliot* (London: 1984).

Adams, R., "Melbourne: Back from the Edge", in Charlesworth, E. (ed.), *City Edge: Case Studies in Contemporary Urbanism* (London: Architectural Press, 2005), chapter 3.

Adams, S., *The Impressionists* (Philadelphia: Running Press, 1990).

Alexander, C., *A Timeless Way of Building* (New York: Oxford University Press, 1979).

Andersson, A., "Creativity and Regional Development", *Regional Studies Association*, 1985.

Appleyard, D., "Styles and Methods of Structuring a City", *Environment & Behaviour*, 2, 1970, pp. 100–116.

Arnold, M., *Culture and Anarchy* (Cambridge University Press, 1960).

Ashton, D., *The New York School* (New York: Viking, 1972).

Bacon, R. and Eltis, W., *Britain's Economic Problem: Too Few Producers* (London: Macmillan, 1976).

Banks, M. *Cultural Industries and the City*, Manchester Institute for Popular Culture, 2000.

Baudrillard, J., *Simulations* (New York: Semiotext(e), 1983).

Bauldie, J., "Wanted Man" (London:1992).

Beauregard, R., *The Resilience of US Cities: Decline and Resurgence in the 20th Century*, Paper presented to the Leverhulme International Symposium *The Resurgent City*, London School of Economics, April 2004.

Beckman, R., *The Downwave* (London: Pan Books, 1983).

Bentley, I. *et al.*, *Responsive Environments: A Manual for Designers* (London: Architectural Press, 1982).

Berendt, J.E., *The Jazz Book* (London: Paladin, 1964), chapter 1.

Berry, B.J.L., *Long-Wave Rhythms in Economic Development and Political Behavior* (Baltimore: Johns Hopkins University Press, 1991).

Bianchini, F., "The Crisis of Urban Public Life in Britain", *Planning Practice & Research*, 5 (3), 1990, pp. 4–8 and pp. 17–18.

Bianchini, F., "Urban Cultural Policies in Western Europe", *Urban Networks in Europe* (no date).

Bianchini, F., Montgomery, J., Fisher, M. and Worpole, K., *City Centres, City Cultures* (Manchester: Centre for Local Economic Development Strategies, 1988).

Blanchard, S., *The Northern Quarter Network: A Case Study of Internet-Based Business Support* (Manchester Institute for Popular Culture, 1999).

Bolton, R., *A Brief History of Painting* (London: Robinson, 2004).

Bourdieu, P., *The Field of Cultural Production* (Columbia University Press, 1993).

Bourdieu, P., *Distinction: A Social Critique of the Judgment of Taste* (Cambridge, Mass.: MIT Press, 1984).

Braudel, F., *Civilisation and Capitalism from the Fifteenth Century to the Eighteenth Century: Volume III Perspective of the World* (New York: Harper and Row, 1984).

Breheny, M., "Centrists, Decentrists and Compromisers: Views on the Future of Urban Form", in M. Jenks, E. Burton and K. Williams (eds), *The Compact City: A Sustainable Urban Form?* (London: Spon, 1996).

Breheny, M., Hart, D. and Howells, J., *Health and Wealth: The Development of the Pharmaceutical Industry in the South East* (Stevenage: South East Economic Development Strategy, 1993).

Briggs, A., *Victorian Cities* (London: Odhams Press, 1963).

British American Arts Association, *The Arts and the Changing City* (London: 1989).

Buchanan, P., "What City? A Plea for Place in the Public Realm", *Architectural Review*, 1101, November 1988, pp. 31–41.

Building Design (1994) "Safety in the Eye of the Beholder", January 1994.

Burke, P., *The Italian Renaissance: Culture and Society in Italy* (Cambridge University Press, 1987).

Burke, T., *English Nightlife: From Norman Conquest to Present Blackout*, 1941 (Ayer, 1972).

Burrows, D., *Handel* (London: 1994).

Busquets, J., "Barcelona Revisitied: Transforming the City Within the City", in Charlesworth (ed.), *City Edge: Case Studies in Contemporary Urbansism* (London: Architectural Press, 2005).

Butterworthy, N., *Haydn* (London: 1978).

Calthorpe, P., "The Region", in P. Katz (ed.) *The New Urbanism* (New York: McGraw Hill, 1994).

Calthorpe, P. and Fulton, W., *The Regional City* (California: Island Press, 2000).

Calvino, I., *Invisible Cities* (London: Vintage, 1997).

Cameron, K.N., *Shelley: The Golden Years* (London: 1974).

Campagni, R., "The Concept of Innovative Milieu and its Relevance for Public Policy in Europe's Lagging Regions", *Papers in Regional Science*, 74 (4), 1995, 317–340.

Canter, D., *The Psychology of Place* (London: Architectural Press, 1977).

Carmoda, M., Heath, T., Oc, T. and Tiesdell, S., *Public Places: Urban Spaces* (London: Architectural Press, 2003).

Carpenter, H., *W.H. Auden: A Biography* (London: 1981).

Carroll, J., *The Wreck of Western Culture* (Melbourne: Scribe, 2004).

Castells, M., *The Power of Identity: The Information Age: Economy, Society and Culture* (Oxford: Blackwell, 1997).

Chatterton, P. and Hollands, R., *Urban Nightscapes, Youth Cultures, Pleasure Spaces and Corporate Power* (London: Routledge, 2003).

Chatwin, B., *The Songlines* (London: Jonathan Cape, 1987).

Christensen, D., *A Tale of Two Cities – Copenhagen*, Paper presented to the conference: *The European City – Sustaining Urban Quality*, Copenhagen, 24–28 April 1995.

Civic Trust, *Creating the Living Town Centre* (London: Civic Trust, 1989).

Coleman, A., *Utopia on Trail* (London: Hilary Shipman, 1985).

Comedia, "The Position of Culture", Appendix to the London World City Report, available from the London Planning Advisory Committee, 1991.

Comedia, *Out of Hours: A Study of the Economic and Social Life of Town Centres* (London: The Gulbenkian Foundation, 1991).

Comedia, *Film, Video and Television: The Audio-visual Economy in the North-west*, December 1988.

Conlin, M., "Job Security, No. Tall Latte, Yes", *Business Week*, April 2 2001, pp. 62–63.

Cook, R., *Zoning for Downtown Urban Design* (New York: Lexington Books, 1980).

Coppelstone, T., *Modern Art* (New York: Exeter Books, 1985).

Cosgrove, D. and Daniels, S. (eds), *The Iconography of Landscape* (Cambridge, 1993).

Crace, J., *Arcadia* (London: Jonathan Cape, 1992).

Cullen, G., *Townscape* (London: Architectural Press, 1961).

Davis, M., *City of Quartz: Excavating the Future in Los Angeles* (London: Verso, 1990).

Dawley, T., *Bach His Life and Times* (London: 1985).

de Castella, T., "Salford's Cultural Catalyst", *Regeneration and Renewal*, 10 November 2000.

Dearborn, M.V., *Peggy Guggenhein: Mistress of Modernisn* (London: Virago, 2005).

Demos, *Northern Soul: Culture, Creativity and Quality of Place in Newcastle and Gateshead* (London: RICS Books, 2003).

Department of Culture, Media and Sport (DCMS), *Creative Industries Economic Estimates*, Statistical Bulletin, July 2003.

Dong, S., *Shanghai: The Rise and Fall of a Decadent City* (New York: Harper Collins, 2001).

Dovery, K., *Fluid City: Transforming Melbourne's Urban Waterfront* (Sydney: University of New South Wales Press, 2005).

Driver, P., *Manchester Pieces* (London: Picador, 1996).

Dublin Corporation, *Temple Bar Area Action Plan*, 1990.

Echenique, M. and Saint, A. (eds), *Cities for the New Millenium* (London: Spon, 2001).

The Economist (2000), "The Geography of Cool", April 15 2000, p. 91.

EDAW and Urban Cultures Ltd., *Sheffield Cultural Industries Quarter: Strategic Vision and Development Study*, available Sheffield CIQ Agency, Sheffield, 1997.

Edwards, J.M.B., "Creativity: Social Aspects", in Sills, D.L., *International Encyclopedia of the Social Sciences*, 3 (New York: Macmillan, 1967), pp. 442–57.

Eliot, T.S., *Notes Towards the Definition of Culture* (London: Faber & Faber, 1948).

Ellmann, R., *James Joyce* (London: 2nd edition, 1982).

Engels, F., *The Condition of the Working Class in England* (Oxford: Blackwell, 1958).

Engericht, D., *Towards an Eco-City* (Sydney: Envirobook, 1992).

English Heritage, *Conservation Bulletin: Characterisation*, Issue 47, Winter 2004–2005.

European Commission, *Green Paper on the Urban Environment* (Brussels, 1990).

Evans, G., *Cultural Planning: An Urban Renaissance* (London: Routledge, 2001).

Evening Economy and the Urban Renaissance, HC 396–1. Twelfth Report of the House of Commons ODPM: Housing, Planning, Local Government and the Regions Committee. HMSO, July 2003.

Farrall, A., "The Nature of the City, its Resurgence and Planners", *Planning, Theory and Practice*, 5, 3, September 2004, pp. 389–392.

Fitzgerald, M., *The Genesis of Artistic Creativity: Asperger's Syndrome and the Arts* (London: Jessica Kingsley, 2005).

Flannery, T., *The Birth of Melbourne* (Melbourne: Text Publishing, 2002).

Florida, R., "Smart Move, Sydney", *The Sydney Morning Herald*, April 23–24, 2005, Spectrum, pp. 23–24.

Florida, R., *The Flight of the Creative Class* (New York: HarperCollins, 2005).

Florida, R., *The Rise of the Creative Class: And How It's Transforming Work, Leisure, Community and Everyday Life* (New York: Perseus Books Group, 2002).

Flyvbjerg, B., "Phroentic Planning and Research: Theoretical and Methodological Reflections", *Planning Theory and Practice*, vol. 5, No. 3, September 2004, pp. 283–306.

Fukuyama, F., *End of History and the Last Man* (New York: Free Press, 1992).

Gardner, H., *Art, Mind and Brain: A Cognitive Approach to Creativity* (New York: Basic Books, 1982).

Garnham, N., "Concepts of Culture-Public Policy and the Cultural Industries", in *The State of the Art or the Art of the State* (London: Greater London Council, 1985).

Garreau, J., *Edge City: Life on the New Frontier* (New York: Anchor/Doubleday, 1991).

Gay, P., *Weimer Culture* (New York: Harper and Row, 1968).

Geddes, P., *Cities in Evolution* (London: Williams & Norgate, 1915).

Gehl, J., *Life Between Buildings* (Copenhagen: Arkitekens Forlag, 1996).

Gehl, J., *Creating a Human Quality in the City*, unpublished paper (1995).

Gehl, J., "A Changing Street Life in a Changing Society", *Places* (Fall 1989, pp. 8–17).

Gehl, J. and Gemzoe, L., *New City Spaces* (Copenhagen: Danish Architectural Press, 2000).

Gehl, J. and Gemzoe, L., *Public Spaces – Public Life* (Copenhagen: The Danish Architectural Press, 1996).

Gerkens, K., *Strategies and Tools for Shrinking Cities – the Example of Leipzig*, paper presented to the International Cities and Towns Conference.

Gill, A., *Peggy Guggenheim: The Life of an Art Addict* (London: Harper Collins, 2001).

Girouard, M., *The English Town* (Newhaven: Yale University Press, 1990).

Glaser, E., "Are Cities Dying?", *Journal of Economic Perspectives*, 12, 1998, pp. 139–160.

Golledge, R., *Learning About Urban Environments*, in Carlstein, Parkes and Thrift (eds), *Timing Space and Spacing Time* (London: Edward Arnold, 1977).

Gordon, D., *Greening the Cities: Ecologically Sound Approaches to Urban Space* (Montreal, 1990).

Gordon, I., "The Resurgent City: What, Where, How and For Whom", *Planning Theory and Practice*, 5, 3, September 2004, pp. 371–379.

Grant, R., *History, Tradition and Modernity*, in Barnett, A. and Scruton, R. (eds), *Town and Country* (London: Vintage, 1999).

Greater London Authority, *Creativity: London's Core Businesses*, 2002.

Greater London Council, *The State of the Art or the Art of the State? Strategies for the Cultural Industries in London*, 1985.

Greater London Council, *The London Industrial Strategy*, London, 1985.

Greed, C., "Design and Designers Revisited", in *Introducing Urban Design*, Greed, C. and Roberts, M. (Harlow: Longman, 1998).

Greenhalgh, L., *Greening the Cities in Town and Country*, A. Barnett and R. Scruton (eds) (London: Vintage, 1999).

Griffiths, P., *Stravinsky* (London: 1992).

Griffiths, R., "The Politics of Cultural Policy in Urban Renewal Strategies", *Policy and Politics*, 21 (1), 1993, pp. 39–46.

Grosskurth, P., *Byron: The Flawed Angel* (London: 1997).

Hadfield, P., "Invited to Binge?", *Town and Country Planning*, 73 (7) 2004.

Hajer, M. and Reijndorp, *In Search of the New Public Domain* (Rotterdam: MAI Publishers, 2001).

Hall, P., *Cities of Tomorrow* (Oxford: Blackwell, 1988).

Hall, P., *Cities in Civilisation* (London: Weidenfield and Nicholson, 1998).

Hall, P., Breheny, M., McQuaid, R. and Hart, D., *Western Sunrise: The Genesis and Growth of Britain's Major High Tech Corrector* (London: Allen & Unwin, 1987).

Handy, C., *The Age of Unreason* (London: Century Business, 1990).

Hart, D., Breheny, M., Doak, J., Montgomery, J. and Strike, J., *Bright Green: an Industrial Strategy for Hertfordshire* (Hertfordshire County Council, 1994).

Harvey, D., *The Condition of Post-Modernity: An Enquiry into the Origins of Cultural Change* (Oxford: Blackwell, 1989).

Hawking, S., *A Brief History of Time* (London: Bantam Press, 1988).

Heartfield, J., *Great Expectations: The Creative Industries in the New Economy* (London: Design Agenda, 2000).

Hebdige, D., *Hiding the Light* (London: Comedia, 1988).

Heikkila, E.J., "What is the Nature of the 21st Century City?", *Planning Theory and Practice*, 5, No. 3, September 2004, pp. 379–387.

Herman, A., *The Scottish Enlightenment* (Fourth Estate, Levilon).

Hillman, J., "A New Look for London", Royal Fine Art Commission (London: HMSO, 1988).

Hoskins, W.G., *The Making of the English Landscape*, revised edition with notes by Christopher Taylor (London, 1988).

Horstmann, J.J., Mayne, D. and Schuster, J.M.D., *Arts and the Changing City: Case Studies* (London: British American Arts Association, 1988).

Howkins, J., *The Creative Economy: how people make money from ideas* (New York: Penguin, 2001), 116.

Howkins, J., "The Creative Economy", *Business Week*, 28 August 2000.

Hughes, R., *Barcelona* (London: Harvill, 1992).

Hutton, T.A., "The New Economy of the Inner City", *Cities*, 21 (2), 2004, 89–108.

Ignasi de Solà-Marales, *Fin De Siecle Architecture in Barcelona* (Barcelona: Gustavo Gili, 1992).

Jacobs, A., *Great Streets* (Cambridge, Mass.: MIT Press, 1994).

Jacobs, J., *Cities and the Wealth of Nations* (New York: Random House, 1984).

Jacobs, J., *The Economy of Cities* (London: Jonathon Cape, 1969).

Jacobs, J., *The Death and Life of Great American Cities* (New York: Vintage, 1961).

Jameson, F., "Post-modernism, or the cultural logic of late capitalism", *New Left Review*, 146, 1984.

Jencks, C., *Modern Movements in Architecture*, Second Edition (London: Penguin Books, 1985), chapter 3.

Jones Lang Lasalle, *Rising Urban Stars* (World Winning Cities Program, 2003).

Jones, E., *Metropolis: The World's Great Cities* (Oxford University Press, 1990).

Kames, Lord, *Historical Law Tracts* (Edinburgh, 1759).

Kennedy, M., *Portrait of Manchester* (Manchester: Robert Hale, 1970).

Koestler, A., *The Act of Creation* (London: Hutchinson, 1964).

Kondratieff, N.D., *The Long Wave Cycle* (New York: Richardson and Snyder, 1984).

Kostof, S., *The City Assembled* (London: Thames and Hudson, 1992), p. 92.

Kratke, S., "City of talents? Berlin's Regional economy, Socio-Spatial Fabric and Urban Governance", *International Journal of Urban and Regional Research*, 2004.

Krier, L., "Charter of the European City", paper presented to the conference, *The European City – Sustaining Urban Quality*, Copenhagen, 24–28 April 1995.

Krietzman, L., *The 24 Hour Society* (London: Profile Books, 1999).

Kuhn, T.S., *The Structure of Scientific Revolutions* (Chicago: University of Chicago Press, 1962).

Kunstler, J., *The Geography of Nowhere: The Rise and Decline of America's Man-Made Landscape* (New York: Touchstone, 1994).

Kuznets, S., "Schumpeter's Business Cycles", *American Economic Review*, 30, 1940, 250–71.

Landry, C., *The Creative City* (London: Earthscan Publications, 2000).

Langdon, P., *A Better Place to Live* (Amhurst: University of Massachussetts Press, 1994).

Larson, E., *The Devil in the White City* (London: Bantam Books, 2004).

Leavis, F.R., *Mass Civilisation and Minority Culture* (Cambridge University Press, 1930).

Lee, L., *Cider With Rosie* (London, 1959).

Lehnert, G., *A History of Fashion in the 20th Century* (Cologne: Koremann, 2000).

Lewis, J., *Art, Culture and Enterprise* (London: Routledge, 1990).

Lewis, M., *Melbourne: The City's History and Development* (City of Melbourne, 1995).

Linklater, A., *Measuring America* (London: Harper Collins, 2003).

Lockhart, T.G., *Memoirs of the Life of Sir Walter Scott* (Edinburgh, 1839).

Lofland, L., "The Morality of Urban Public Life", *Places*, Fall, 1989.

Lomborg, B., *The Skeptical Environmentalist* (Cambridge University Press, 1998).

London Labour Market Study 1992, available from the London Planning Advisory Committee.

London World City, London Planning Advisory Committee, 1992.

Lopez, R.S., "The Trade of Medieval Europe", in Postan, M. and Rich, E.E. (eds), *The Cambridge Economic History of Europe, 2: Trade and Industry in the Middle Ages* (Cambridge University Press, 1952), pp. 257–354.

Lowenthal, L., *Literature, Popular Culture and Society* (Palo Alto, CA: Pacific Books, 1961).

Lynch, K., *A Theory of Good City Form* (Cambridge, Mass.: MIT Press, 1981).

Lynch, K. *What Time is this Place?* (Cambridge, Mass.: MIT Press, 1972).

Lynch, K., *The Image of the City* (Cambridge, Mass.: MIT Press, 1961).

Lyotard, J-F., *The Post-modern Condition: A Report on Knowledge* (Manchester: Manchester University Press, 1984).

Madanipour, A., *Design of Urban Space* (Chichester: John Wiley and Sons, 1996).

Manetti, A., *The Life of Brunelleschi*, edited by Howard Saalman and translated by Catherine Enggass (Pennyslvania State University Press, 1970).

Marek, G.R., *Beethoven: Biography of a Genius* (London: 1969).

Marshall, T., *Transforming Barcelona* (London: Routledge, 2004).

McCarthy, D., *Pop Art* (London: Tate Galley Publishing, 2000).

McCarthy, J., "Making Spaces for Creativity: Designing 'Cultural Quarters'", paper presented to the 41st IsoCaRP Congress, 2005.

McCarthy, P., *McCarthy's Bar* (London: Hodder & Stoughton Ltd, 2000).

McGuigan, J., *Cultural Populism* (London: Routledge, 1992).

McKay, E.N., *Schubert: A Biography* (London: 1996).

Melbourne City Council, *Grids and Greenery* (Melbourne, 1987).

Melbourne, *City of Grids and Greenery: Case Studies* (Melbourne, 1998).

Mommas, H., "Cultural Clusters and the Post-industrial City: Towards a Remapping of Urban Cultural Policy", *Urban Studies*, 41 (3), 2004.

Montgomery, J., "A Theory of Urban Sociability", paper commissioned by the Department for Victorian Communities, Melbourne, February 2006.

Montgomery, J. "Beware the Creative Class: Creativity and Wealth Creation Revisited", *Local Economy*, Vol. 20, No. 4, November 2005, pp. 337–343.

Montgomery, J. "Cities of the Fifth Wave: The Rise of the Traditional-Modern City", *Town and Country Planning*, June 2005.

Montgomery, J., "City Dynamics: How Cities Work", *Town and Country Planning*, January 2005.

Montgomery, J., "Dublin, Sheffield, Manchester and Adelaide: Cultural Quarters as Urban Regeneration", in Charlesworth, E. (ed.) *City Edge: Case Studies in Contemporary Urbanism* (London: Architectural Press, 2005).

Montgomery, J., "Born to Binge? – the Rise of Night-time Disorder", *Town and Country Planning*, March 2004, pp. 82–83.

Montgomery, J., "Cultural Quarters as Mechanisms for Urban Regeneration: Case Studies from the UK, Ireland and Australia", *Planning Practice and Research*, 19, 1, March 2004.

Montgomery, J., "Cultural Quarters as Urban Regeneration: Conceptualizing Cultural Quarters", *Planning Practice and Research*, 18, 4, November 2003.

Montgomery, J., "Making a City", *Journal of Urban Design*, 3, 1, 1998, pp. 93–116.

Montgomery, J., "Cafe Culture and the City: The Role of Pavement Cafes in Urban Public Social Life", *Journal of Urban Design*, 2, 1, 1997, pp. 83–102.

Montgomery, J., "Developing the Media Industries", *Local Economy*, Vol. 11, No. 2, August 1996, pp. 158–167.

Montgomery, J., "Animation: A Plea for Activity in Urban Places", *Urban Design Quarterly*, 53, January 1995, pp. 15–17.

Montgomery, J., "The Story of Temple Bar: Creating Dublin's Cultural Quarter", *Planning Practice & Research*, Vol. 10, No. 2, 1995, pp. 135–172.

Montgomery, J., "Planning for the Night-time Economy of Cities", *Regenerating Cities* 7, December 1994, pp. 32–39.

Montgomery, J., "The Evening Economy of Cities", *Town and Country Planning*, 63 (11), 1994.

Montgomery, J. "Dressed To Kill off Urban Culture", *Planning* 989, 9 October 1992.

Montgomery, J., "Cities and the Art of Cultural Planning", *Planning Practice and Research*, Vol. 5, No. 3, 1990.

Montgomery, J. and Thornley, A., *Radical Planning Initiatives for the 1990s* (Aldershot: Gower, 1990).

Morris, H., "Obstacles remain to continental culture", *Planning*, 8 August 2003, p. 11.

Motion, A., *Keats* (London: 1997).

Mulgan, G. and Worpole, K., *Saturday Night or Sunday Morning* (London: Comedia, 1986).

Mumford, L., *The Highway and the City* (London: Secker & Warking, 1964).

Mumford, L., *The Culture of Cities* (New York: Harcourt, Brace, 1938).

Murray, R., "Benetton Britain", *Marxism Today*, July, 1985.

Myerscough, J., *The Economic Importance of the Arts in Britain* (London: Policy Studies Institute, 1988).

Nairn, I., *Nairn's London*, Revisited by Peter Gasson (London: Penguin, 1988).

Nairn, I., *Counter Attack Against Subtopia* (London: Architectural Press, 1957).

Newman, P. and Smith, I., "Cultural Production, Place and Politics on the South Bank of the Thames", *International Journal of Urban and Regional Research*, 24(1), 2000, 9–24.

Nichols, R., *Debussy* (London: 1973).

Nin, A., *The Diary of Anais Nin*, Volume 1, 1931–34 (New York: Harvest), edited by Gunther Stuhlman.

Nolapot, P., *Reflection on the Disposition of Creative Milieu and its Implications for Cultural Clustering Strategies*, paper presented to the 41st IsoCaRP Congress, 2005.

Norman, P., *Shout!* (London: 1981).

Oosterman, J., "Welcome to the Pleasure Dome: Play and Entertainment in Urban Public Space", *Built Environment*, 18 (2) 1992.

Oskam, A.W., *A Tale of Two Cities – Amsterdam*, paper to The European City – Sustaining Urban Quality Conference, Copenhagen 24–28 April 1995.

Paglia, C., *Sex, Art and American Culture* (New York: Penguin,1992).

Paglia, C., "Junk Bonds and Corporate Raiders: Academe in the Hour of the Wolf", in Paglia, *Sex Art and American Culture* (New York: Penguin, 1992).

Pasqui, G., "The Perspective of the Infinite City", *Planning, Theory and Practice*, 5, 3, September 2004, pp. 381–389.

Paumier, C., *Designing the Successful Downtown* (Washington: Urban Land Institute, 1988).

Peat Marwick McLintock, "The Nottigham Crime Audit", published by the Home Office, London, 1989.

Peck, J., "Struggling with the Creative Class", *International Journal of Urban and Regional Research*, 29.4, December 2005.

Pegrum, R., *The Bush Capital* (Sydney: Hale and Iremonger, 1983).

Perine, J., *Brownfield Redevelopment in Bushwick, Brooklyn, New York*, paper presented to the International Cities and Towns Conference, Yepoon, Queensland, Australia, June 2005.

Philips, M., *London: Time Machine* in *Whose Cities?*, Fisher, M. and Owen, U. (eds) (London: Penguin, 1991).

Pirenne, H., "Les Periodes de l'Histoire Sociale du Capitalisme", *Bulletin de l'Academie Royale Belgique*, 5, 1914, 258–99.

Pool, P., *Impressionism* (London: Thames & Hudson, 1967).

Porter, M., *The Competitive Advantage of Nations* (London: Collier Macmillan, 1990).

Portman Group, *The Keeping The Peace Report (A Guide to the Prevention of Alcohol-related Disorder)* (London: 2000).

Priem, R., *Dutch Masters* (Melbourne: National Gallery of Victoria, 2005), p. xxxi.

Punter, J., "Participation in the Design of Urban Space", *Landscape Design*, 200, 1991, pp. 24–27.

Punter, J., "The Privatisation of the Public Realm", *Planning Practice and Research*, Vol. 5, No. 3, 1990, p. 9.

Quinlan, T., *Quinlan's Film Directors* (London: B.T. Batsford Ltd, 1999).

Raban, J., *Soft City* (London, Hamish Hamilton, 1974).

Raine, K., *William Blake* (London: Thames & Hudson, 1970).

Redfield, R. and Singer, M., "The Cultural Role of Cities", 1954, in Sennet, R., *Classic Essays on the Culture of Cities* (New York: Meredith, 1969).

Rees, G. and Lambert, J., *The Cities in Crisis* (London: Edward Arnold, 1985).

Reform of Licensing, Home Office White paper, HMSO, 2001.

Relph, E., *The Modern Urban Landscape* (Baltimore: Johns Hopkins University Press, 1987).

Relph, E., *Place and Placelessness* (London: Pion, 1976).

Robbins Landen, H.C., *Mozart and Vienna* (London: 1991).

Robbs, G., *Balzac* (London: 1994).

Rosenberg, B. and Manning White, D. (eds), *Mass Culture: The Popular Arts in America* (New York: Macmillan, 1957).

Russell, P., *Study of the Temple Bar Cultural Development Programme*, Working Paper No. 21, Department of Regional and Urban Planning, University College Dublin, 2000.

Sabel, C., *Work and Politics* (Cambridge University Press, 1982).

Santagata, W., "Cultural Districts, Property Rights and Sustainable Economic Growth", *International Journal of Urban and Regional Research*, 26 (1), 2002, 9–23.

Sargeant, H., *Shanghai: Collision Point of Cultures* (New York: Crown, 1990).

Sassen, S., *Cities in a World Economy* (Pine Forge Press, 1994).

Saunders, P., *Social Theory and the Urban Question* (London: Hutchison, 1981).

Schama, S., *The Embarrassment of Riches: An Interpretation of Dutch Culture in the Golden Age* (New York: Vintage, 1997).

Schatz, T., *The Genius of the Systems: Hollywood Filmmaking in the Studio Era* (New York: Pantheon, 1989).

Schumpeter, J., *Business Cycles* (New York: McGraw & Hill, 1939; Philadelphia: Porcupine Press, reprinted 1982).

Schuster, M., "The Role of Street Festivals in the Cultural Animation of the City: the examples of Boston First Night and La Merce in Barcelona", paper presented to the First National Conference on the Evening Economy of Cities, Manchester, 1993.

Scott, A.J., *The Cultural Economy of Cities* (London: Sage, 2000).

Scottish Arts Council, *A Charter for the Arts in Scotland* (Edinburgh: 1996).

Scruton, R., "Conserving the Past", in Bartlett and Scruton, *Town and Country* (London: Vintage, 1999).

Seigel, J.E., *Bohemian Paris: Culture, Politics and the Boundaries of Bourgeois Life 1830–1930*, new edition (Baltimore: Johns Hopkins University Press, 1999).

Sennett, R., *The Conscience of the Eye: The Design and Social Life of Cities* (London: Faber & Faber, 1990).

Sennett, R., *The Fall of Public Man* (London: Faber & Faber, 1977).

Sheffield City Council, SCIQ Area Action Plan, Sheffield, 1998.

Sheffield City Council, *The Cultural Industries* (Sheffield City Council, 1988).

Sherman, B., *Cities Fit to Live In* (London: Channel 4 Books, 1988).

Shopfront Security Campaign, *The Shopfront Security Report*, available from the British Retail Consortium, London, 1994.

Smith, A., *The Wealth of Nations*, 1776, version published by Penguin Classics (London: 1986).

Smith, "Aesthetic Curiosity: The Root of Invention", *New York Times*, 24 August 1975.

Smith, N. and Williams, P. (eds), *Gentrifcation of the City* (Boston: Alllen & Unwin, 1986).

Snow, C.P., *The Two Cultures* (Cambridge University Press, 1964).

Spencer, C. and Dixon, J., "Mapping the Development of Feelings About the City", *Transactions of the Institute of British Geographers*, 8, 1983, pp. 373–383.

Storey, J., *An Introductory Guide to Cultural Theory and Popular Culture* (Hemel Hempstead: Harvester Wheatsheaf, 1993).

Sudjic, D., *The 100 Mile City* (London: Andre Deutsch, 1992).

Sydney Morning Herald, "Perth: A City on the Edge", 9 August 2005, Insight p. 9.

Sydney Morning Herald, "The Beat Goes On", 7 September 2005, p. 11.

Taine, H., *Philosephie de l'Art*, as translated by Peter Hall, *Cities in Civilization* (1998), pp. 15–16.

Talen, E. and Ellis, C., "Cities of Art: Exploring the Possibility of an Aesthetic Dimension in Planning", *Planning Theory and Practice*, Vol. 5, No. 1, pp. 11–32, March 2004.

Tallis, M. and Tallis, J., *The Silent Showmen* (Adelaide: Wakefield Press, 1999).

Taruskin, R., *The Oxford History of Western Music* (Oxford University Press, 2005).

Taylor, L., "Private View", *The Listener*, 24 November 1988.

Temple Bar Properties Ltd, *Development Programme for Temple Bar* (Dublin: 1992).

Temple Bar Properties Ltd, *"Temple Bar Lives", A Record of the Architectural Framework* (Dublin: Temple Bar Properties Ltd, 1991).

Thakara, J., *Design After Modernism* (London: Thames & Hudson, 1988).

Thomson, O., *A History of Sin* (Edinburgh: Cannongate Press, 1993).

Törnqvist, G., *Creativity and the Renewal of Regional Life* (quoted in Hall, 1998, *op. cit.*, 1983).

Truss, L., *Talk to the Hand: The Utter Bloody Rudeness of Everyday Life* (London: Profile Books, 2005).

Tuckett, I., *There is a Better Way*, in Montgomery, J. and Thornley, A. (eds), *Radical Planning Initiatives for the 1990s* (Aldershot: Gower, 1990).

Unglow, J., *The Lunar Men: The Friends Who Made the Future* (London: Faber and Faber, 2002).

Urban Cultures Ltd, "A Theory of Urban Sociability", paper commissioned by the Department for Victorian Communities, Melbourne, March 2006.

Urban Cultures Ltd, "Creative Industry Business Incubators: A Review of Good Practice", unpublished consultancy report prepared for the Committee for Melbourne, November 2005.

Urban Cultures Ltd, "A Strategy to Tackle All Night Disorder (STAND)", unpublished consultancy report prepared for Colchester Borough Council and Colchester Safer Cities, October 2003.

Urban Cultures Ltd, "Sunderland Statement on Licensed Premises", unpublished consultancy report prepared for Sunderland City Council, 2002.

Urban Cultures Ltd and David Lock Associates, "Sunniside Area Regeneration Strategy", unpublished consultancy report prepared for Sunderland City Council, 2001.

Urban Cultures Ltd and Colin Buchanan and Partners, "Sunderland Evening Economy Study", unpublished consultancy report prepared for Sunderland City Council, 2000.

Urban Cultures Ltd, "A Strategy for the Development of the Broadcast Media and Related Industries in West London", unpublished consultancy report prepared for the West London Training and Enterprise Council, 1996.

Urban Cultures Ltd, "North Kensington Media Industries Strategy", unpublished consultancy report for North Kensington City Challenge, 1996.

Urban Cultures Ltd, "John Lyall Architects and Bruce McLean Art Square: A New Public Realm for Barnsley", unpublished consultancy study prepared for the Metroplitan Borough of Barnsley, 1994.

Urban Cultures Ltd, "Developing the Evening Economy of Bristol City Centre", unpublished consultancy report prepared for Bristol City Council, December 1994.

Urban Cultures Ltd, "The Merchant City: A Strategy for Culturally-led Urban Renewal and Urban Vitality", unpublished consultancy report prepared for Glasgow Devlopment Agency, Glasgow City Council and the Scottish Arts Council, 1994.

Urban Cultures Ltd, "Prospects and Planning Requirements of London's Creative Industries", London Planning Advisory Committee, 1994.

Urban Cultures Ltd and ppartnerships, *Manchester First: An Arts and Cultural Strategy* (Manchester City Council, 2 volumes, 1992).

Urban Cultures Ltd, "Creating Dublin's Cultural Quarter", unpublished consultancy report prepared for the Irish Government (1991).

Urban Task Force, *Towards An Urban Renaissance* (London: HMSO, 1999).

Urbanistics and Urban Cultures Ltd, "Area Regeneration Strategy for Manchester's Northern Quarter", unpublished consultancy report for Manchester City Council, 1994.

Wakeman, F., *Policing Shanghai* (Berkeley: University of California Press, 1997).

Walker, P., *Zola* (London: 1985).

Walmsley, D.C., *Urban Living: The Individual in the City* (London: Longman, 1988).

Wansborough, M. and Mageean, A., "The Role of Urban Design in Cultural Regeneration", *Journal of Urban Design*, Vol. 5, No. 2, 2000, 181–197.

Watson, D., *Death Sentence: The Decay of Public Language* (Sydney: Random House, 2003).

Wechsler, H.J., *The Lives of Famous French Painters* (New York: Pocket Books, 1952).

Weightman, G., *Bright Lights, Big City* (London: Collins and Brown, 1992).

White, H.C. and White, C.A., *Canvases and Careers: Institutional Changes in the French Painting World* (New York: John Wiley, 1965).

Whitehead, G., *Civilising the City: A History of Melbourne's Public Gardens* (Melbourne: State Library of Victoria, 1997).

Whitt, J.A., "Mozart in the metropolis: the arts coalition and the urban growth machine", *Urban Affairs Quarterly*, Vol. 23, No. 1, 1987, pp. 15–36.

Williams, R., *Keywords* (London: Fontana, 1975).

Williams, W., "Cultural Industries and Local Revitalization", chapter 9 of his book *Consumer Services and Economic Development* (London: Routledge, 1997).

Worpole, K., *Towns for People* (Buckingham: Open University Press, 1992).

Wright, P., *A Journey Through The Ruins* (London: Flamingo, 1992).

Wright, P., *On Living in an Old Country* (London: Verso, 1985).

Wynne, D., *The Culture Industry: The Arts in Urban Regeneration* (Aldershot: Avebury, 1992).

Youngson, A.J., *The Making of Classical Edinburgh* (Edinburgh, 1966).

Zukin, S., *Loft Living: Culture and Capital in Urban Change* (New Brunswick: Rutgers University Press, 1982; reprinted 1989).

Index